Afterlives of the Plantation

BLACK LIVES IN THE DIASPORA: PAST / PRESENT / FUTURE

BLACK LIVES IN THE DIASPORA: PAST / PRESENT / FUTURE

Editorial Board
Howard University
Clarence Lusane, Rubin Patterson, Nikki Taylor, Amy Yeboah Quarkume
Columbia University
Farah Jasmine Griffin, Frank Guridy, Josef Sorett

Black Lives in the Diaspora: Past / Present / Future is a book series that focuses on Black lives in a global diasporic context. Published in partnership with Howard University's College of Arts and Sciences and Columbia University's African American and African Diaspora Studies Department, it builds on Columbia University Press's publishing programs in history, sociology, religion, philosophy, and literature as well as African American and African Diaspora studies. The series showcases scholarship and writing that enriches our understanding of Black experiences in the past, present, and future with the goal of reaching beyond the academy to intervene in urgent national and international conversations about the experiences of people of African descent. The series anchors an exchange across two global educational institutions, both located in historical capitals of Black life and culture.

Lauren Coyle Rosen and Hannibal Lokumbe, *Hannibal Lokumbe: Spiritual Soundscapes of Music, Life, and Liberation*

Laura E. Helton, *Scattered and Fugitive Things: How Black Collectors Created Archives and Remade History*

Sarah Phillips Casteel, *Black Lives Under Nazism: Making History Visible in Literature and Art*

Aïssatou Mbodj-Pouye, *An Address in Paris: Emplacement, Bureaucracy, and Belonging in Hostels for West African Migrants*

Vivaldi Jean-Marie, *An Ethos of Blackness: Rastafari Cosmology, Culture, and Consciousness*

Imani D. Owens, *Turn the World Upside Down: Empire and Unruly Forms of Black Folk Culture in the U.S. and Caribbean*

Gladys L. Mitchell-Walthour, *The Politics of Survival: Black Women Social Welfare Beneficiaries in Brazil and the United States*

James V. Koch and Omari S. Swinton, *Vital and Valuable: The Relevance of HBCUs to American Life and Education*

For a complete list of books in the series, please see the Columbia University Press website.

Afterlives of the Plantation

Plotting Agrarian Futures in the Global Black South

Jarvis C. McInnis

Columbia University Press

New York

Columbia University Press
Publishers Since 1893
New York   Chichester, West Sussex
cup.columbia.edu

Copyright © 2025 Jarvis C. McInnis
All rights reserved

Library of Congress Cataloging-in-Publication Data
Names: McInnis, Jarvis C., author.
Title: Afterlives of the plantation : plotting agrarian futures in the global Black South / Jarvis C. McInnis.
Other titles: Plotting agrarian futures in the global Black South
Description: New York : Columbia University Press, [2025] | Series: Black lives in the diaspora : past / present / future | Includes bibliographical references and index.
Identifiers: LCCN 2024048142 (print) | LCCN 2024048143 (ebook) | ISBN 9780231215749 (hardback) | ISBN 9780231215756 (trade paperback) | ISBN 9780231560955 (ebook)
Subjects: LCSH: African Americans—Southern States—Intellectual life. | African Americans—Education—Southern States. | African Americans—Agriculture—Southern States. | African Americans—History—1877-1964. | Washington, Booker T., 1856-1915—Influence. | Tuskegee Institute—Influence. | Plantations—Southern States. | Southern States—Social conditions. | United States—Relations—Caribbean Area. | Caribbean Area—Relations—United States.
Classification: LCC E185.92 .M45 2025 (print) | LCC E185.92 (ebook) | DDC 338.1089/96072—dc23/eng/20241207
LC record available at https://lccn.loc.gov/2024048142
LC ebook record available at https://lccn.loc.gov/2024048143

Printed and bound by CPI Group (UK) Ltd, Croydon, CR0 4YY

Cover design: Noah Arlow
Cover image: Frances Benjamin Johnston, *Students Taking Care of Flowers in Beds Near Green Houses, Tuskegee Normal and Industrial Institute, Alabama*, Frances Benjamin Johnston Collection (Library of Congress). Map: Jamaica, Panama Canal, and Central and South America (New York: Great White Fleet, United Fruit Company Steamship Service, 1912).

GPSR Authorized Representative: Easy Access System Europe, Mustamäe tee 50, 10621 Tallinn, Estonia, gpsr.requests@easproject.com

For my parents

Contents

Acknowledgments   ix

Introduction: Regenerating Black
Life in Plantation Ruins   1

Plot I

1. An Experiment in Black World Making:
Cultivating Intellectuals of the Land in
the Alabama Countryside   45

2. Performing the Tuskegee New Negro:
The Racial and Gendered Aesthetics of the
Repurposed Plantation   81

Plot II

3. Strategic Translations: Race, Nation,
and the Affordances of Booker T. Washington and
Tuskegee in Cuba   141

viii CONTENTS

4. Joining Hands Across the Sea: Agricultural Education, Black Economic (Inter)Nationalism, and Haitian–African American Relations 177

Plot III

5. Becoming New Negroes: Student Aspirations, Hemispheric Migration, and the Otherwise Uses of Tuskegee 223

6. At the Crossroads of Diaspora and Empire: Harvesting a Plot Logic in Claude McKay's Jamaica 257

7. Aestheticizing Labor, Performing Diaspora: Zora Neale Hurston and the Scene of the Work Camp 296

8. Of Ships and Plantations: Marcus Garvey and the UNIA's Vision of a Pan-African Agro-industrial Empire 338

Epilogue: Gathering and Assessing Our Harvests; or, Lessons from Our Experiment Plots 369

......

Notes 377

Bibliography 421

Index 441

Acknowledgments

The completion of this book is an answered prayer, and it would not have been possible without the love, support, and labor of a host of people and communities who sustained me intellectually, emotionally, and spiritually. The seeds of many of the inquiries at the heart of this project were planted on the hallowed grounds of my alma mater, Tougaloo College, a historically Black institution that—as a former cotton plantation turned school for formerly enslaved peoples and their descendants—exemplifies Black people's brilliance, ingenuity, and resilience in the *afterlife of the plantation*. I am grateful to my undergraduate professors Candice Love Jackson, Barbara Crockett Dease, Jacqueline Wheelock, Elise Morse-Gagne, Loye Ashton, Miranda Freeman, and Kathy Castilla for their mentorship, teaching, and commitment to my intellectual development. I am especially indebted to Drs. Jackson and Dease for setting me on this path and their continued guidance and sacrifice. They not only set the bar high but also ensured I had the tools to clear it.

At Columbia University, where I earned my doctorate in English and comparative literature, I was blessed to be taught and mentored by Farah Jasmine Griffin, Brent Hayes Edwards, and Robert "Bob" O'Meally, a dream team that guided me with rigor and generosity. They have believed in this project from the very outset, supported my career at every turn, and exemplify the kind of scholar and mentor I aspire to be. Brent's meticulous attention to detail taught me how to analyze more astutely and define my key concepts with precision. Bob is a terrific listener, reader, and thought partner who sustained me with hilarious stories and steadfast encouragement. And I am eternally grateful for Farah's ever-wise council and friendship. Her course, Mapping the Black South, helped me find my way back home to the South, both intellectually and spiritually, and gave me permission to see it with new and more critical and loving eyes. For their mentorship, teaching, and support, I am grateful to Daphne Brooks, Saidiya Hartman, Tina Campt, Marcellus Blount, David Scott, Josef Sorett, Frances Negrón-Muntaner, Jenny Davidson, Thadious Davis, Marlon Ross, Kenrick Ian Grandison, and Deborah McDowell, who reminded me at a critical stage that "all that you need is already within you."

This book has been written across numerous cities and institutions. I am fortunate to be a part of a rich intellectual community at Duke University, where colleagues have offered their time and resources to help me bring this project to completion. I could not have wished for a better place to write and nurture this book. Thank you to my wonderfully supportive colleagues and staff in Duke's English Department. I am especially grateful to Tsitsi Ella Jaji and Priscilla Wald for their tireless mentorship and encouragement, from reading and providing crucial feedback on chapter drafts to joining me on long walks to work through conceptual challenges, questions, and ideas. I am also grateful to Taylor Black, Tom Ferraro, Ranjana Khanna, Nathaniel Mackey, Chris Ouma, Akhil Sharma, Charlotte Sussman, and Aarthi Vadde for their support, advice, and camaraderie. Thank you to Joseph Winters, J. Kameron Carter, Norbert Wilson, Wylin Wilson, Gustavo Silva, and Sherilynn Black for their friendship and helpful insights over meals, between classes and committee meetings, and over text exchanges. The wisdom and mentorship of Mark Anthony Neal, Thavolia Glymph, Valerie Ashby, Gary Bennett, Abbas Benmamoun, and Rick and CT Powell have likewise been invaluable.

I have presented parts of this project at various Duke workshops and seminars. My sincere thanks to the organizers of the Americanist Speakers Series and the Franklin Humanities Institute and all those who attended and provided valuable feedback. For their collegiality and community, thank you to the WRAP Black faculty writing group. Our retreats in the mountains and on the beaches of North Carolina afforded me the time and space to make significant progress on the project at critical junctures, as well as much needed nourishment and respite. A special thanks to my wonderful students in my Zora Neale Hurston, Black Mobilities, and Contemporary Black South courses, the Black Mobilities and the Archive Migration Lab, and my research assistant, Karen Little. For their early support of this project, I would also like to thank my friends, colleagues, and students at the University of Notre Dame, especially Steve Fallon, Leonardo Francalanci, Z'étoile Imma, Laura Knoppers, Jesse Lander, Sara Marcus, Barry McCrea, Azareen Van Der Vliet Oloomi, Richard Pierce, Dianne Pinderhughes, Jason Ruiz, Roy Scranton, and Laura Walls.

ACKNOWLEDGMENTS xi

I have benefited from the scholarly generosity of numerous colleagues and collaborators over the years. For offering their time, feedback, and intellectual insights, I am grateful to Frank Guridy, Chantalle Verna, Laurent Dubois, and Grace Johnson, who read portions of chapters or had extended conversations with me about them at critical junctures. I am especially grateful for the eyes, ears, and insight of Robin D. G. Kelley and Faith Smith, whose meticulous feedback has made this a much better manuscript. In New Southern studies and Global South studies, my sincerest thanks to Erich Nunn, Anne Garland Mahler, Amy Clukey, Amy King, Jeremy Wells, Gina Caison, Jon Smith, Judson "Jay" Watson, Matt Dischinger, David Davis, Katherine McKee, Leigh Anne Duck, and Adam Gussow for their steadfast support of and critical engagement with my work. A special thank you to Anna Arabindan-Kesson and Clare Corbould, with whom I co-organized the Global Plantation symposium. Our discussions during planning meetings and the exciting contributions of our presenters helped refine my thinking about the plantation in significant ways.

Completing this book would not have been possible without the support of numerous research fellowships, grants, and mentorship programs. I am ever grateful to Cynthia Neale Spence, Donna Akiba Sullivan Harper, and Ada Jackson of the UNCF/Mellon Mays Undergraduate Fellowship, where I began my scholarly journey. Thank you to Sean X. Goudie, Priscilla Wald, and my fabulous cohort at the First Book Institute at Pennsylvania State University for helping me to reconceptualize the project as a book at an early stage. Through Kerry Haney and his team at the Summer Institute on Tenure and Professional Advancement, I gained a fantastic mentor in Erica R. Edwards, whose brilliance, savvy, and generosity have been a constant source of guidance, inspiration, and support. Thanks also to Duke's Office of Faculty Advancement and the Reckoning with Race in the U.S. South grant, which has provided much-needed research funding and travel support.

My time as a postdoctoral research associate in the Department of African American Studies at Princeton University was invaluable. Conversations with Tera Hunter helped me clarify my book's intervention (and title!), and Imani Perry's, Eddie Glaude's, and Simon Gikandi's excitement about and feedback on the project was most affirming at a time when I was still figuring out its contours. My deepest gratitude to Thadious Davis, Simon Gikandi, and Carter Mathes, whose meticulous feedback at my manuscript workshop helped me to reconceptualize the book at a critical stage. I am also grateful to Courtney Bryan (Dr. Maestra!), Tao Leigh Goffe, Desmond Jagmohan, and Britt Rusert—my fellow postdocs at Princeton—for their camaraderie and critical engagement with my work, as well as the department's delightful and expert staff, April Peters and Dionne Worthy.

I was most fortunate to be awarded my dream research fellowship in the Scholars-in-Residence program at the Schomburg Center for Research in Black Culture, which gave me the much-needed time to complete some of the archival and conceptual heavy lifting for chapters 3 and 4. The brilliant scholars in my cohort and the director, Brent Hayes Edwards, read significant portions of the manuscript, and it is much better for their prodding, questioning, and critiques. Shout out my fellow cohort member Laura Helton for her thoughtful and affirming engagement, and I am especially grateful for the support of my wonderful research assistant, Naomi Bland.

As I often tell my students, librarians and archivists are a researcher's most valuable resource. This has certainly been the case for me. Thank you to the numerous librarians and archivists who have supported this project, including the fabulous team at the Schomburg Center for Research on Black Culture, which is second to none; Cheryl Ferguson, Dana Chandler, and their team at the Tuskegee University Archives, who tracked down many an archival source for me and showed me immense kindness over the years; and countless other librarians and archivists at Columbia University, Princeton University, the University of Notre Dame, Duke University, the National Library of Jamaica, the Beinecke Library, the University of Florida, Gainesville, the Library of Congress, and the University of the West Indies.

For the opportunity to share and workshop portions of this book as it progressed, I am grateful to the Modernist Studies Association; Donald Pease and the Summer Institute on American Studies at Dartmouth College; Yael Lipschutz, Cameron Shaw, and the California African American Museum; the National Humanities Center; Gregg Mittman, Monica White, and the Plantationocene Sawyer Seminar at the University of Wisconsin, Madison; and Melanie Price and Marco Robinson at the Ruth J. Simmons Center for Race and Justice at Prairie View A&M University. I am also grateful to numerous colleagues and students at Arizona State University; Cornell University; Gettysburg College; Harvard University; Mercer University; Millsaps College; New York University; Rice University; Stanford University; University of Chicago; University of Illinois, Urbana-Champagne; University of North Carolina; Chapel Hill; and the University of Virginia. Portions of material from chapters 1, 2, and the epilogue are forthcoming in *Occasion* journal and the exhibition catalogue for *World Without End: The George Washington Carver Project* at the California African American Museum.

ACKNOWLEDGMENTS

At Columbia University Press, a huge thank you to my editor, Philip Leventhal, for finding such careful and generous anonymous readers and providing vital feedback and expert guidance and insights throughout the process. The press's wonderful team of designers and production and copy editors, especially Michael Haskell and Emily Elizabeth Simon, have my gratitude. A tremendous thanks to the anonymous readers: this book is much better for their critical questions and suggestions. To my agent, Kevin O'Connor, thank you for your expert guidance through the long and arduous process of obtaining a book contract and helping me to find the right press home. I am also grateful to several editors who have supported this project over the years: Gisela Fosado and Walter Biggins for their interest in the book from its earliest stages; Lucas Church for encouraging me to tell a "big story"; and my exceptional developmental editor, Pamela Haag, for helping me to rein it in! When I needed a French-to-English translator, it was my greatest honor that Dr. Barbara Crockett Dease readily agreed to assist me, more than a decade after serving as my undergraduate professor and Mellon-Mays advisor at Tougaloo. I wish she could have been here to see this book to publication. I hope it makes her proud. I am also grateful to Kathryn Litherland for so ably assisting me with most of the Spanish-to-English translations.

This book would not be possible without the support of numerous communities of friends, colleagues, coconspirators, and mentors. At Columbia, I was blessed to be part of a brilliant and dynamic group of graduate student colleagues and friends who continue to be sources of wisdom and inspiration for me, including Courtney Bryan, Imani Owens, Robin Hancock, Mariel Rodney, Autumn Womack, Alex Alston, Emily Hainze, and Erica Richardson. A huge shout out and thank you to the inimitable Sharon Harris and Shawn Mendoza for embracing me as a part of the Institute for Research in African American Studies (IRAAS) family. Being in community with the "Columbia Homies"— Matthew Morrison, J. T. Roane, and Nijah Cunningham—has been nothing short of a blessing. Their brilliance, care, levity, collegiality, and generosity have sustained me during the best and hardest moments (especially our group chat!), from the time we met in graduate school through the completion of this manuscript. Thank you for grounding me and always reminding me *why* we do this work. My comrades, Randi Gill-Sadler, Adom Getachew, Justin Hosbey, Regina Bradley, Kaneesha Parsard, Robert Bland, and Charisse Burden-Stelly, have all been an important part of my intellectual community at various moments, sustaining me with their brilliance and humor alike. Tia Madkins, Rufus Burnett, and Koritha Mitchell, thank you for being my lifelines during our time together in South Bend. To my mentors, William "Bill" Keyes and Sherle Boone, I am ever grateful for your encouragement and inspired by your example.

I am fortunate to have found a wonderfully supportive community of friends in Durham, North Carolina, who have embraced me with open arms. To my "Durham Crew"—Sherilynn Black, Tiffany Elder, Samario King, Allison Mathews, Amanu Nwaomah, Gustavo Silva, and Erikka Taylor—thank you for your friendship and care. From our road trips to our celebration dinners to our nights out on the town, you all have sustained me. Thank you for celebrating so many victories with me, no matter how small, and for reminding me that that we must work as well as play! Shout out to Marcus Hawley, Quincey Farmer, Anissa Gainey, Marcel Mercer, and Cecily Mitchell for helping me maintain my sanity with bike rides, hikes, game nights, and personal training sessions. Thank you to Matt Kreiner for always listening with such care. I'm grateful to my Monument of Faith Church family for supporting me with food, community, spiritual nourishment, and calls and check-ins if I disappear for too long (shout out to Ms. Bea Laney!). A special thank-you to Bishop Clarence Laney, who is not only my pastor but my brother and friend, who prays for me, checks on me, and encourages me to be all God has called me to be—fully and unapologetically. My sincerest gratitude to Javier Wallace, Ronald Williams II, William Sturkey, Youssef Carter, Nikki Lane, Diante Harris, Tolu Harris, and Xavier Pickett for being such an integral part of my community, joining me for coworking sessions, commiserating over the joys and difficulties of the writing process, and sharing tips, resources, and professional connections. I am especially grateful to my friend and collaborator, Iyun Ashani Harrison, for countless coworking sessions, shared meals, long walks, and being a helpful sounding board as I navigated some of the most demanding parts of this journey.

A huge shout-out and thank-you to my chosen siblings—Brittany Coleman, Elijah Heyward, DeMarcus Pegues, Evan Pitts, Bianca Salazar, Imani Uzuri, Katy Webb, and Renaldo Williams—for their love, community, and care. Thank you for always picking up the phone when I call, checking on me when I disappear, and for your prayers, sage wisdom, encouraging text messages, and tireless faith that I could indeed bring this project to completion. Your friendships have sustained me, so thank you for helping me to make it through this process whole. Julius Fleming Jr., what can I say? You have been my most important interlocutor and coconspirator since our days at Tougaloo. You have seen this manuscript in all its iterations, read nearly every word of it (sometimes more than once!), and believed in it from the very first. Thank you for countless writing retreats, from New Orleans to Belize; daily coworking sessions, even when I didn't feel like writing; reassuring words when self-doubt crept in; and for always reminding me that if we work hard, we can play hard too! Most importantly, thank you for always celebrating my successes as if they were your own and for being committed to a friendship and brotherhood that we were told wasn't possible in academia. Malcolm J. Merriweather, you have been nothing short of blessing to me—a source of light, inspiration, and care. Thank you for delicious meals, fun trips when I've needed respite, encouraging calls, texts, prayers, and care packages and an always listening and sympathetic ear. Your brilliance, tenacity, and courageous spirit inspire and sustain me.

I am blessed to stand on the shoulders of a rich family and community of loved ones and supporters in Mississippi—countless aunts, uncles, cousins, and church and community members and mentors—who have championed, invested in, and sacrificed for me from the time I was a little boy. A special shout out to my aunts Sherri Enge, Audrey Beard, Shelia Floyd, and Erica Joyce; cousins Jor'Dan Beard and LaNisha McInnis; and my church sister, Kay Redmond, for feeding me, checking on me, cousins' game nights, and making time to see me during my visits home. I am supremely grateful for my grandmother, Mrs. Minnie Mae Smith, who makes sure to know my teaching schedule every semester, routinely checks the weather wherever I live to ensure I'm keeping safe and well, asks about my plants, and tries to always have a hot meal waiting for me during my visits home. I am blessed to have an incredible friend, confidant, and champion in my big sister, Harriet M. Harris, who never ceases to remind me (and others) of how proud she is of her "little brother," and I am grateful to my nephews and niece, KJ, Camden, and Kayleigh, who keep me youthful, grounded, and thoroughly entertained.

Finally, to my parents, Pamela and Harry McInnis. Words are insufficient for capturing the depths of my love, admiration, and appreciation for you. You have been my most ardent supporters and prayer warriors, and your tireless encouragement and sacrifice have sustained me. Thank you for loving me without condition, believing in me without qualification, and for teaching me how to pray. This book is dedicated to you.

Afterlives of the Plantation

Introduction

Regenerating Black Life in Plantation Ruins

Black modernity in the Americas is, first and foremost, agricultural. Beginning in the sixteenth century, enslaved Africans were forcefully transplanted to the Americas to labor on plantations and cultivate agricultural staples for global consumption. After emancipation, formerly enslaved peoples across the Western Hemisphere continued to grapple with the plantation and its afterlives through new forms of labor exploitation and incarceration, such as sharecropping, tenant farming, debt peonage, and corporate plantation agriculture. Indeed, the plantation system in its various forms was the catalyst for racial-capitalist modernity. Yet Afro-descendants also attempted to do something different with the plantation: drawing out its "otherwise" uses—materially, culturally, economically, ontologically, and even ethically and spiritually—to sustain and advance Black life.[1] As the formerly enslaved stood on the precipice of a precarious and uncertain freedom, they must have wondered: What else can grow on the site of such unspeakable violence beyond cotton, sugar, rice, tobacco, indigo, and other cash crops whose overproduction depleted the earth and Black being alike? Can such a contaminated and degraded space ever generate "freedom dreams" and otherwise futures, or will it always bear traces of its former purpose and haunt Black life with past horrors?[2] How Black people went about resolving this existential and apocalyptic dilemma is, at its core, the story I tell in *Afterlives of the Plantation: Plotting Agrarian Futures in the Global Black South.*

In the U.S. South, one approach to the problems of (un)freedom was to repurpose the plantation into autonomous communities and educational institutions for the formerly enslaved. One of the most notable examples, of course, is the Tuskegee Institute, which was established on a former cotton plantation in rural Macon County, Alabama. In his acclaimed autobiography *Up from Slavery* (1901), the African American educator, orator, and political leader Booker T. Washington describes Tuskegee's founding atop plantation ruins: "About three months after the opening of the school . . . there came into the market for sale an old and abandoned plantation which was situated about a mile from the town of Tuskegee. The mansion house—or 'big house,' . . . which had been occupied by the owners during slavery, had been burned. After making a careful examination of this place, it seemed to be just the location that we wanted in order to make our work effective and permanent."[3] Washington's recollection here captures the myriad paradoxes that inspire this book: the persistence and regeneration of Black life amid the ruins of enslavement and plantation capitalism.[4] It examines how formerly enslaved peoples and their descendants navigated the afterlife of the plantation in the U.S. South, the Caribbean, and Latin America by repurposing plantation geographies, logics, and cultural practices toward different and more life-sustaining ends. To be sure, these efforts were motivated by diverse and sometimes even contradictory aims; therefore, throughout this book, I grapple with the limits and possibilities of such a fraught but often necessary project.

As an agricultural and industrial school built on the ruins of a former cotton plantation, Tuskegee Institute is the paradigmatic afterlife of the plantation and is central to this project. Its transformation by 1900 from an "old, worn-out plantation," as Washington described it, to a "modern farm" and school captures the essence of Black rural, agricultural modernity in this period.[5] Though unquestionably conservative, by the time of Washington's death in 1915 Tuskegee had become a locus of Black diasporic activity in the heart of the rural Jim Crow South. It was committed to a vision of modern Black subjectivity and self-determination that inspired a host of freedom dreams throughout the Black world. Following his now-infamous Atlanta Exposition Address in 1895, in which Washington accepted social segregation in exchange for interracial economic and commercial relations, he gained international recognition as a leader of the Black race in the United States and weighed in on the affairs of the broader diaspora. Though he was staunchly opposed to African American immigration to Africa, he supported the first Pan-African Congress in London in 1900 and corresponded with Black political leaders, students, and parents across the diaspora, including Cuba, Haiti, Jamaica, Central and South America, and South Africa, among other locales. He reasoned that because many Afro-Caribbean peoples in particular shared with African Americans a common heritage in agriculture, they, too, would benefit from agricultural and industrial education as taught at Tuskegee. So beginning in 1898, Washington actively recruited Afro-Caribbean students to the institute, initiating a Black transnational student migration network to the heart of the Alabama Black Belt. Tuskegee thus came to represent a potential solution to a "Negro problem" that was increasingly global and connected the challenges that southern African Americans faced under Jim Crow to the challenges created by colonialism and imperialism in the Caribbean, Latin America, and Africa.

On April 17–19, 1912, Tuskegee hosted the International Conference on the Negro (ICON), convening 125 missionary, educational, and government officials representing twenty-one foreign countries. The ICON was "the first time in the history of the race," Washington claimed, that "Negroes from every part of the world, where there is any large population of African descent, met together . . . in a three days' conference in the interest of their common welfare."[6] News of the conference circulated throughout the Black world and was prominently featured in the inaugural issue of the *African Times and Orient Review*, a militant anticolonial journal founded and edited by the London-based intellectual Dusé Mohamed Ali. It was almost certainly through this publication that a young Jamaican printer and labor activist named Marcus Garvey, who began working as an editorial assistant for the journal in 1913, was introduced to the global scope of Washington's work at Tuskegee. Likewise, a young peasant poet named Claude McKay was inspired to emigrate from Jamaica to study agronomy at Tuskegee after conferring with Mr. W. H. Plant, one of the colony's numerous ICON delegates, who also gave lectures on Tuskegee upon his return to the island. Indeed, as Washington later reflected, the ICON "scatter[ed] to the ends of the earth the seeds of an educational movement in which . . . the hope of my race in America and elsewhere finally rests."[7]

What drew such a diverse set of Black leaders to the ICON? And though it influenced Garvey and McKay, two of the most important theorists of early twentieth-century Black internationalism, why is the ICON—and by extension Tuskegee and the U.S. South—so rarely included in accounts of diaspora in Black studies? What if we were to situate the ICON amid other early twentieth-century efforts to interrogate the race problem globally, such as the Pan-African Congress of 1900, the Universal Races Congress of 1911, and the Universal Negro Improvement Association's first international conference in 1920?[8] What have we overlooked by consistently routing Black studies through the urban Global North? What new epistemologies might emerge by thinking and theorizing with, through, and from the rural, agricultural regions of the Americas as well?

Afterlives of the Plantation: Plotting Agrarian Futures in the Global Black South uses Washington and Tuskegee to interrogate Black modernity and diasporic relation in and from the "Global Black South."[9] Scholarship in African Diaspora literary and cultural studies tends to privilege intercontinental networks among Europe, Africa, and the Americas as well as migration to the urban centers of the industrial Global North. However, I propose the Global Black South as a heuristic for reorienting the geography of Black transnational and diaspora studies toward Black south–south relations and to reclaim the cultural practices and political knowledges produced therein from the putative waste bin of modernity. In *Afterlives of the Plantation*, I specifically center the hemispheric ties among Black diasporic communities in the U.S. South, the Caribbean, and Latin America because they share a similar origin in plantation slavery. Furthermore, in this region the material and ideological legacies of the plantation as a modern colonial technology of spatialization, labor organization, and subject formation persisted well into the twentieth century as the organizing principle of Black social and political life. The plantation was unequivocally an oppressive regime of power, insidious violence, and domination against enslaved African peoples. But even under slavery, forms of life persisted that contributed to Black modernity, and it is those practices and strategies of "Black aliveness" that I attend to here.[10]

"Afterlives of the plantation in the Global Black South" is a spatial-temporal paradigm that captures how Black people across the Western Hemisphere grappled with plantation geographies, logics, and epistemologies in slavery's aftermath. A distinct component of what the literary historian and cultural theorist Saidiya Hartman has called the "afterlife of slavery," my framework refers specifically to how the geographic, ecological, political-economic, and cultural logics of "plantation modernity" continued to shape Black life after emancipation.[11] For example, still in the throes of the Haitian Revolution (1791–1804), Toussaint L'Ouverture reinstated coffee and sugar plantations to ensure the founding Haitian nation-state's economic survival. In the late nineteenth century, as the colonial plantation gave way to the corporate plantation, Afro-Caribbean laborers from across the hemisphere became the economic backbone of the burgeoning banana trade and fruit industry and continued to buttress the global sugar industry. And in the United States, African Americans worked as sharecroppers and tenant farmers on large cotton, tobacco, and sugar plantations well into the mid–twentieth century. Hartman's notion of the "afterlife of slavery" rightly emphasizes how the juridical and ontological violence of the "peculiar institution" continue to haunt the present and constrain Black futures through "skewed life chances, limited access to health and education, premature death, incarceration, and impoverishment."[12] However, my conception is more attuned to how Black people exploited the plantation's "affordances" to create alternative

INTRODUCTION 5

futures, particularly through farming and agriculture, that could sustain Black life rather than perpetuate Black subjection.[13] *Afterlives of the Plantation* thus emphasizes practices of Black self-determination and world making and is informed by the provocative query of the Black geographer and cultural theorist Katherine McKittrick: "What if the plantation offered us something else?" "What if we acknowledged that the plantation is, as Toni Morrison writes, a space that everybody runs from but nobody stops talking about, and thus that it is a persistent albeit ugly blueprint of our present spatial organization that holds in it a new future?"[14] In short, this book is situated between the discourses on afterlives and futures in Black studies and their respective hauntological and anticipatory connotations.

Throughout *Afterlives of the Plantation*, I trace and examine how a range of African American and Afro-Caribbean artists, intellectuals, and political leaders—Booker T. Washington, George Washington Carver, and Margaret Murray Washington of Tuskegee, Alabama; Rafael Serra y Montalvo of Cuba; Jean Price-Mars of Haiti; Claude McKay of Jamaica; Zora Neale Hurston of Florida; and Marcus Garvey of Jamaica, among many others—grappled with the paradox of the plantation as a site of "social death," on one hand, and the genesis of modern forms of life, on the other, as well as how these figures articulated alternative futures *within and against* its legacies.[15] In so doing, I make a critical intervention in African American studies, where the plantation is understandably almost exclusively regarded as an oppressive regime of power and domination and a metonym for the chain, whip, bit, and other technologies of torture that disciplined and exploited Black people.

In Caribbean studies, by contrast, scholars have proposed a more nuanced rendering of the plantation as the genesis of Black modern life and culture, and in New Southern studies the plantation has been reconceptualized as the link that tethers the U.S. South to the Global South.[16] With these more expansive conceptions of the plantation in tow, this book interrogates and revises traditional notions of Black modernity predicated on urbanity, northward migration, and Western conceptions of cosmopolitanism. I explore how agricultural and industrial education at Tuskegee and labor migration to the hemisphere's agro-industrial enterprises such as the Panama Canal Zone and United Fruit Company (UFCO) plantations produced alternative networks of cultural, intellectual, and political exchange and cosmopolitan mobility that preceded and were coterminous with the Harlem Renaissance and the New Negro Movement of the 1920s and 1930s.

In examining the plantation and its afterlives as a crucible of Black modernity, *Afterlives of the Plantation* reconstructs Tuskegee's significance as a model for resolving one of the fundamental predicaments of "New World" Blackness:

the problem of labor and freedom. The greatest challenge of emancipation throughout the Global Black South was the transformation of a mass of formerly enslaved people into autonomous and self-determined subjects. By the turn of the twentieth century, Black intellectual and political leaders as well as students, parents, and laypersons across the world began to adapt Washington's vision of an agrarian and industrial future as a strategy for racial uplift, self-determination, and even nation building. Whereas Washington's southern reformism is commonly reduced to a foil for W. E. B. Du Bois's northern radicalism, this book delineates an alternative cultural and intellectual genealogy that foregrounds the contributions and affordances of a historically Black educational institution in the rural U.S. South at the helm of Black transnational and diaspora studies.[17]

Through Washington's recruitment of southern African American and Caribbean students and convenings such as the ICON, the rural U.S. South became a *destination* for Black people, not simply a point of departure for African Americans fleeing Jim Crow violence and oppression. Whereas southern port cities such as New Orleans, Mobile, and Charleston have a long history of international traffic, where sailors and riverboat men frequented seedy bars and red-light districts, Tuskegee is landlocked and located in the heart of the Black Belt. It was neither an urban commercial center and racial contact zone like New Orleans nor a major train depot like Atlanta. Reconstructing Tuskegee's place as a diasporic hub thus broadens our understanding of the Great Migration and the geography of the New Negro Movement to include the south–south migrations among the rural plantation regions of the hemisphere as well.[18]

Booker T. Washington is, to put it mildly, a polarizing figure in Black studies. However, Washington and the Tuskegee project were neither as tyrannical as some have made them out to be nor as revolutionary as they could have been. In recent decades, African Diaspora studies has understandably been consumed with narratives of Black radicalism and resistance, but such a singular focus has rendered less explicitly radical discourses, figures, and projects unpopular and seemingly unworthy of study. With a few exceptions, scholars have tended to overlook the nuances of Washington's work at Tuskegee and its diasporic offshoots, further obscuring how Black cultural and intellectual production from the U.S. South contributed to Black modernity and transnational engagement in the late nineteenth to early twentieth centuries. Furthermore, while there is often a metonymic relationship between Washington and Tuskegee, it is crucial to remember that they are not reducible to each other. So although I paint a more nuanced portrait of Washington by grappling with the myriad contradictions and shortcomings of his political vision, my focus on Tuskegee exceeds

INTRODUCTION 7

Washington the man to consider the contributions of the institute's all-Black faculty, staff, and students as well as its symbolic value throughout the Global Black South. Where possible, I show how the institute shaped Black modernity in ways that exceeded Washington's efforts to micromanage its meaning and image. By assembling a hemispheric diasporic archive, I tell a lesser known and more nuanced story about the ways that the cultural and intellectual contributions of a rural southern Black educational institution circulated among and influenced other Black diasporic peoples also wrestling with the plantation's various and sundry afterlives. Crucially, I examine the ways global Black southerners did not simply embrace Tuskegee's project wholesale but strategically translated, critiqued, and adapted its methods and reputation to accommodate their own visions of modernity, progress, and self-determination.

Ultimately, this book illuminates how the cultural practices, political knowledges, and intellectual networks of the Global Black South contributed to articulations of Black modern subjectivity and diasporic relation in the early twentieth century and beyond. Redrawing the map renders visible some of the ways Black people engaged in countergeographic and placemaking practices that disrupt hegemonic geographic knowledges and provides a critical framework for reconceptualizing Black people's relationship to rural life and agriculture as modes of self-determination in slavery's aftermath. While recent scholarly attention to Black geographies, Black ecologies, the Black outdoors, and the plantationocene rightly emphasize the plantation as a technology of racial-capitalist and ecological extraction and degradation that drove the coterminous domination of both people and the earth, I redirect our attention to the ways Afro-descendants engaged in practices and strategies of reuse, regeneration, and repair, repurposing the plantation to support education, economic self-help, political cooperation, and aesthetic innovation, with the ultimate aim of sustaining and propagating Black life.

MAPPING THE TERRITORY: THE GEOGRAPHY OF THE GLOBAL BLACK SOUTH

The modern plantation was first developed in the Mediterranean region in the fifteenth century and later exported to the Americas as a genocidal and ecocidal technology of settler colonialism and enslavement, racial-capitalist accumulation, and nation-state formation. The plantation ultimately became a system of forced-labor organization for producing large-scale agricultural commodities—sugar, cotton, tobacco, rice, coffee, and indigo—for sale on the global market. It was made possible and maintained by the widespread dehumanization, displacement, and enslavement of Indigenous populations and West and Central Africans. Indeed, it is "one of the bellies of the world" that paradoxically digested and gave birth to new forms of Black life and being.[19]

The plantation did not simply disappear after emancipation but rather continued its reign of terror and exploitation. In the United States, it metamorphosed into sharecropping, tenant farming, debt peonage, the crop-lien system, and prisons. Planters in the Caribbean and Latin America imported indentured laborers from China and India to work their colonial sugar estates. U.S.-owned corporations such as UFCO colonized tens of thousands of acres of land in the Caribbean and Central America to establish corporate fruit plantations, and British-owned syndicates such as the Delta and Pine Land Company established the world's largest cotton plantation in the Mississippi Delta.[20] As the West continued to carve up and cannibalize the globe, the plantation remained one of its choice colonial and imperial tools from Africa and Australia to China and India. The plantation persists in many guises and forms today—as a physical, geographic space; in the logics and values that shape modern subjectivity, such as liberal individualism, property ownership, and racial-sexual identity formation; and as a system of labor organization, commodity production, and capital accumulation.

By situating the U.S. South and the Caribbean within a comparative, hemispheric context, I show how the plantation emerges as a figural and literal organizing principle for tracing Global Black South relations. I focus on the U.S. South and the Caribbean in particular because of their geographic proximity, overlapping histories of plantation slavery, and sustained artistic, intellectual, economic, and political ties. I use the designation *global* to acknowledge the pioneering work of scholars in the field of New Southern studies, who have theorized how the plantation connects the U.S. South to a broader context.[21] In their introduction to *Look Away! The U.S. South in New World Studies* (2004), the literary critics Jon Smith and Deborah Cohn observe, "The plantation—more than anything else—ties the South both to the rest of the United States and to the rest of the world."[22] They extend the Global South—a geopolitical designation that first emerged in economics and development theory to refer to the most impoverished and underdeveloped countries of the world, formerly known as the Third World—to include the former plantation regions of the southern United States based on similar histories and patterns of underdevelopment.[23] My hemispheric frame also extends the Caribbean archipelago—an important geographic formation in Caribbean studies—to mainland North,

INTRODUCTION

Central, and South America to elucidate the "marginal migrations" and south-to-south exchanges that often go underexamined in diaspora studies.[24]

Up to the mid–nineteenth century, the plantation regions of the Americas were deeply connected through the transatlantic trade in flesh and commodities. South Carolina, for instance, was established by planters and enslaved peoples from Barbados, and as early as the 1840s southern U.S. planters plotted to annex parts of the Caribbean and Latin America to expand their plantation empire.[25] Social scientists and historians have studied this region as a geopolitical and cultural contact zone since the early twentieth century at least, and it has figured prominently in American cultural studies since the transnational turn of the 1990s. It has been variously called the "American Mediterranean," the "circum-Caribbean," the "hemispheric Americas," and the "plantation Americas." In African Diaspora studies, it overlaps with Paul Gilroy's groundbreaking conceptualization of the Black Atlantic, and in Global South studies it approximates Caroline Levander and Walter Mignolo's formulation of the "Hemispheric South."[26] I insist on the designation "Global Black South" instead of, say, "Black Atlantic," to capture the rich, dynamic ways Black life is lived in the various "souths" of the world and to illuminate how an otherwise degraded geopolitical coordinate—"the sign 'South'"—does not connote backwardness or antimodernity but is in fact a space of Black vitality and world making.[27] Indeed, as Marlon Ross observes, "It's at the bottom, where the risk of burning and being burned is, that the African Diaspora brews its most potent mixture."[28]

This book foregrounds the cultural and intellectual contributions of Black peoples in the U.S. South precisely because their contributions are often ignored in Black transnational and diaspora studies. It is the transnational and late nineteenth- to early twentieth-century companion to what might be called "New Black South studies," an emerging field that examines contemporary southern African American identity and culture in the wake of the sociopolitical and cultural shifts following the Civil Rights Movement and the rise of hip-hop.[29] I elaborate on the literary scholar Thadious Davis's conceptualization of a "southscape" as thinking at the intersection of "space, race, and society" in the U.S. South, with an especial focus on the region's ties to the broader hemisphere.[30] I also follow the trajectory of the pioneering *Callaloo* journal, established in 1976 as "A *Black South* Journal of Arts and Letters" (meaning the U.S. South) but had by the 1980s expanded its scope to encompass the "*south and south of the south*," as the writer and literary scholar Melvin Dixon put it, to become a premier "Journal of *African Diaspora* Arts and Letters."[31] Though U.S. Blackness is often considered hegemonic within the field, as Gilroy famously argued, such critiques rarely refer to the U.S. South, a region regarded as backward, provincial, and the prime locus of anti-Black violence and oppression. Centering the U.S. South, however, illuminates how the logic of underdevelopment that organizes Global South studies can also be present in Global North geographies and how the conditions of Black life in, say, Mississippi or Florida resemble those in the Caribbean and Latin America, given their similar histories of slavery and the plantation.[32] Such an approach calls attention to how southern African Americans navigated racial-capitalist underdevelopment within one of the most developed countries in the world and how they exchanged strategies and ideas about racial progress and modernity with their Afro-Caribbean and Latin American counterparts. Although this book focuses primarily on diasporic ties within the plantation regions of the Western Hemisphere, the Global Black South is meant to be a capacious geographic configuration, and my hope is that it will function as a framework for exploring a host of Black south–south relations: the knowledges, cultural practices, liberatory strategies, (mis)translations, asymmetrical power relations, and solidarities forged between and among Black peoples in the various "souths" of the world.

In his essay "Closed Place, Open Word" (1997), the Martinican theorist Édouard Glissant proposed that the spread of the "Plantation system" created a "rhythm of economic production" and a "style of life" that linked the U.S. South to the Caribbean and parts of Latin America.[33] Glissant's title captures a fundamental paradox of the plantation as a transnational structure and organizing principle of the Global Black South. Essentially, there is no singular plantation. On the one hand, as "closed place[s]," individual plantations were quasi-self-contained units that bore similarities to the feudal societies of medieval Europe. Everyday conditions could thus vary widely from one plantation to the next, even within the same colony or (nation-)state. A Jamaican sugarcane plantation would have operated differently from a Haitian coffee plantation, a Mississippi cotton plantation, or a South Carolina rice plantation. On the other hand, as an "open word," the individual plantation spread throughout the Western Hemisphere (and globally), producing a "system" governed by similar "structural principles" and logics.

Despite local differences, these plantation regions shared important structural and ideological similarities and produced similar conditions that persisted well into the twentieth century. The Jamaican economist George Beckford and the New World scholars at the University of the West Indies at Mona established that the plantation economy was the source of perpetual poverty, dispossession, and underdevelopment in the "Third World." For most "Third World" peoples, the United States represents Global North imperial domination—that is, European colonialism in a different guise. However, Beckford maintains that Black

INTRODUCTION

people in the U.S. South were dispossessed from causes similar to the "causes of poverty in the Third World" and should be considered "Third World people" as well.[34] Likewise, the African American communist Harry Haywood maintained in the late 1940s that the Black Belt of the U.S. South was "a kind of 'internal colony' of American imperialism, made to function mainly as the raw material appendage of the latter" and that the "character of the oppression" of African Americans "in no sense differs from that of colonial peoples."[35]

Indeed, the rise of Jim Crow in the U.S. South overlapped with European colonialism and the rise of U.S. imperialism throughout the Caribbean and Latin America. So when the United States began its imperial encroachment on the Western Hemisphere, U.S. officials often used the racial logics of Jim Crow and the subjugation of African Americans as the basis of their imperialist policies. In their administration of the Panama Canal Zone, for instance, U.S. government officials explicitly drew on racist notions about African Americans in the U.S. South to establish policies for governing Afro-Caribbean migrant laborers.[36] As the U.S. journalist Harry Franck remarked, "Panama is below the Mason-Dixon line."[37] A similar exportation of Jim Crow racism occurred in Cuba, Puerto Rico, the Dominican Republic, Haiti, and elsewhere. This period also saw the rise and spread of UFCO's infamous hemispheric fruit and tourism industries, which connected port cities in the southern United States—Mobile, Alabama; Galveston, Texas; Charleston, South Carolina; and especially New Orleans, Louisiana—to ports in Havana, Cuba; Kingston and Port Antonio, Jamaica; Bocas del Toro, Panama; and Port-au-Prince, Haiti, so that the corporate plantation further tied the region together.

Ironically, these material and economic networks, rooted in Western colonialism and imperialism and in corporate plantation agriculture, also enabled Black diasporic affiliation through student and labor migration, print-culture circulation, and political activism. "Empire," the literary scholar Michelle Ann Stephens argues, "provided the material conditions for Black solidarities to emerge across nation, language, gender, and even class."[38] In the case of Booker T. Washington and Tuskegee, the historian Manning Marable maintains that these political-economic conditions "created the intellectual groundings for conservative Black nationalism throughout the Black diaspora," wherein "Washington's narrowly conservative, upwardly mobile ethos" influenced the rise of a Black "ghetto bourgeoisie" that promoted "a method of training which allowed the Black man or woman to participate within the colonialist's civil and political society."[39]

Afterlives of the Plantation examines how Washington and Tuskegee's faculty, staff, and students proposed the educational strategies initially devised for southern African Americans as a blueprint for diasporic uplift and political-economic development for the Black world and how Afro-Caribbean intellectuals and statesmen such as Rafael Serra y Montalvo and Jean Price-Mars translated that blueprint into their own visions of Afro-Cuban and Haitian modernity, respectively, while decrying U.S. imperialism. I track Afro-Caribbean student migration to Tuskegee alongside African American and Afro-Caribbean labor migration to the centers of agro-industrial capitalism, such as the Panama Canal zone, UFCO's Caribbean and Latin American corporate plantations, and southern Florida's lumber and sawmill camps. I interrogate Zora Neale Hurston's theories of Black diasporic performance based on southern African American and Afro-Bahaman migrant laborers in the Everglades; Claude McKay's transplantation to the United States to study agronomy at Tuskegee by way of a UFCO steamship; and Marcus Garvey's vision of a Black agro-industrial empire based in part on Washington's self-help philosophy and UFCO's fruit and tourism empire. These figures illuminate the Global Black South as a dynamic geography of contradictions in which Black people wrestled with the material grounds, racial logics, and epistemological tools of plantation modernity while they made the leap from slavery to a circumscribed freedom, from property to colonial and citizen-subjects.

PLANTATION MODERNITIES AND FUTURES

Within the discourse on Black modernity, the Global Black South is typically regarded as the underside of modernity, a "scene of subjection" or zone of "social death."[40] According to the Guyanese historian and political activist Walter Rodney, "The West Indies and the American South share the dubious distinction of being the breeding ground of world racialism."[41] Until relatively recently, scholarship in African American studies has tended to prioritize migration *away* from the U.S. South and the Caribbean to the urban centers of the industrial Global North, designating cosmopolitan mobility as the telltale signifier of modern subjectivity.[42] But what exactly do we mean by describing certain people and geographies as "modern," while designating others as "folk," "primitive," or "backward"? The enslaved and their descendants who remained in the hemisphere's rural, plantation regions did not occupy an alternative temporality. They, too, were modern, not least because the exploitation of their knowledges and labor enabled and fueled the racial-capitalist development of the modern world. Picking cotton or operating a sugar mill was no less modern than writing a novel, the quintessential modern literary form that emerged and developed precisely because of enslaved labor on "New World" plantations.[43] Accordingly, this book mines Global Black South cultural and intellectual production for articulations of modern subjectivity, diasporic practice, and cosmopolitan mobility that revise, open up, and challenge traditional geographic biases and temporal frameworks of modernity.

Though the plantation has often been described as a feudal socioeconomic system, scholars have long argued that because it arose conterminously with the market economy, it is inherently a modern institution, "bound up with the discovery of new lands and the expansion of commerce, with the steamship, the railway and other new means of transportation," and with "the growth of colonies and cities, and of a world market."[44] As Sylvia Wynter observes, "The plantation system was the new idea, the new institution in which the first mass labor force totally at the disposal of capitalism was to be 'seasoned' and transformed into a purely productive unit, producer of surplus value."[45] For C. L. R. James, not only was the plantation system modern, but West Indian "Negroes" also lived an essentially "modern life" precisely because they produced sugar for sale on the global market and consumed imported food and clothing.[46] Elaborating on James's conception of how the plantation transformed enslaved peoples into modern subjects, the anthropologist David Scott contends that "the slave plantation might be characterized as establishing the relations and the material and epistemic apparatuses through which *new subjects were constituted*: new desires instilled, new aptitudes molded, new dispositions acquired." The enslaved were "conscripts of modernity" but modern nonetheless.[47]

The Global Black South is thus a crucible of Black modernity; its violence and arrested development are not antithetical to the modern condition but rather constitutive and indicative of it. The epistemological conceits of Western modernity—notions of progress, reason, rationality, equality, and especially freedom—were possible only through the invention and subsequent exploitation of "the Negro." Of course, I am not invested in recuperating the plantation but rather in demonstrating how its history of violence has shaped scholarly tendencies to align certain peoples, spaces, and cultural practices with progress and liberation while rejecting others as inherently carceral and backward. I illuminate the Global Black South as a geography of Black social life, instead of solely a zone of social death, by examining the cultural practices and political strategies that emerged to survive, subvert, counter, and uproot the plantation's attempted stranglehold on Black futures.

I am especially compelled by Glissant's conception of Black modernity as the persistence of humanity in the face of the brutalizing conditions that the plantation engendered: "Within this universe of domination and oppression, of silent or professed dehumanization, forms of humanity stubbornly persisted," he contends. "In this outmoded spot . . . the tendencies of our modernity begin to be detectable."[48] I thus interrogate the plantation's "contradictions" as a geography that is at once local and global, barren and fecund, static and fungible, feudal and modern.[49] I attend to the many ways Black artists, intellectuals, and political leaders drew on the plantation to imagine new futures, however fraught that project might have been. Black people not only stubbornly persisted but also created, innovated, and regenerated their subjectivities even within a context that was explicitly established to exploit and extinguish Black life and had no regard for Black futures beyond the Black body's potential as a unit of labor.

For politically marginalized peoples, the aesthetic is an especially critical mode for forging alternative socialities and imagining more liberatory futures. Accordingly, I mine Black diasporic literature, broadly conceived, for strategies and articulations of modernity, agrarian futures, social life, and diasporic relation within and against the plantation's afterlife. I show how McKay's Jamaican poetry, fiction, and short stories, for instance, reimagine Jamaican peasants as intellectuals of the land and cosmopolitans from below and how Hurston's fiction and folk concerts depict the southern work camp—an offshoot of the plantation—as a locus of diasporic relation between southern African American and Afro-Caribbean migrant laborers. In doing so, I remap the geography of the Harlem Renaissance and New Negro Movement as also necessarily southern and hemispheric. In Alain Locke's edited volume *The New Negro* (1925), the urtext of the Harlem Renaissance, for instance, essays not only highlight Harlem but also Washington, DC; Tuskegee, Alabama; Hampton, Virginia; Durham, North Carolina (dubbed the "capital of the Black middle class"); and the "Tropics" as sites of New Negro activity. Three of the five essays from the book's section entitled "The New Scene" focus on cultural and intellectual contributions from the U.S. South and the Caribbean, and the volume's southern and Caribbean-born contributors are numerous. Global Black South peoples and cultures were thus integral to the conception of the New Negro Movement, even as the volume was predicated on migration from the region to Harlem and other global northern metropoles. This is not to say that what occurred in Harlem and Paris was not unique but to acknowledge that the forms of aesthetic innovation and political imagination that characterized them were derived from and shaped by the Global Black South also. Through this remapping, *Afterlives of the Plantation* contributes to what the historian Davarian L. Baldwin calls a " 'renaissance' in New Negro studies" by expanding its temporal, geographic, and conceptual scope.[50]

INTRODUCTION

Scholars of early African American literary and cultural studies have long argued for a more capacious approach to the "literary" to include not only novels, poetry, and plays but a range of nonfiction genres also.[51] *Afterlives of the Plantation* similarly brings together a dynamic archive of literary texts and genres—autobiography, poetry, essays, newspaper articles, fiction, conference proceedings, school catalogs, scientific bulletins, folk concerts, ethnographies, letters, speeches, and lectures—that place African American and Caribbean artists in dialogue with statesmen, club women, political organizers, scientists, journalists, students, and teachers. In doing so, I insist on the importance of print culture, broadly conceived, for producing new subjectivities in the face of colonial and imperial domination well before Harlem's emergence as a Black mecca. To capture the dynamism of Global Black South modernity, I also analyze how these artists and intellectuals experimented with music and sound recordings, dance and performance, photography and film. Examining the aesthetic practices that Black people harvested from plantation ruins in their efforts to imagine new futures elucidates the Global Black South as a fundamentally modern geography of "Black aliveness," irreducible to slavery, colonial and imperial underdevelopment, or racial violence.

BOOKER T. WASHINGTON AND THE TUSKEGEE INSTITUTE: AN AMBIVALENT LEGACY

In the almost century and a half since Tuskegee's founding in 1881, Booker T. Washington has variously been depicted as a formerly enslaved person working against insurmountable odds to construct an educational institution for other formerly enslaved people and their descendants in the midst of racist retrenchment and retribution; a cunning, tricksterlike political strategist who publicly accommodated white supremacy while covertly working to dismantle it through personal financial contributions to civil rights campaigns; a race champion and proto-pan-Africanist; and a conservative political boss who controlled Black politics, media, and philanthropic contributions to Black institutions from his armchair on his southern plantation.[52] Likewise, Tuskegee has been regarded as either a servant- and manual-labor-training school or a petit bourgeois institution that produced a Black middle-class elite who aspired to manage and discipline the Black masses.

Afterlives of the Plantation is part of a recent critical reassessment of Washington and Tuskegee. Historically, there has been ample emphasis on how

Washington and Tuskegee constrained Black politics and education. From his contemporaries W. E. B. Du Bois and Ida B. Wells-Barnett to the historians C. Vann Woodward, Donald Spivey, and James D. Anderson, activists and scholars have routinely underscored the pedagogical and political limitations of the Tuskegee model of education and racial uplift.[53] I take my cue instead from scholars such as Manning Marable, Frank Guridy, Robert J. Norrell, Michael Bieze, Marybeth Gasman, Desmond Jagmohan, and especially Houston A. Baker Jr. in his early work on Washington and Tuskegee, who offer a more nuanced approach that grapples with Washington's personal ideological idiosyncrasies and limitations, the social and structural conditions that constrained him, and, most importantly, what the Tuskegee project produced and enabled for the Black world. I thus read Tuskegee expansively as a physical, geographic space in rural Alabama, an aesthetic and ontological project, an educational and political model, and an imagined and symbolic geography for the African Diaspora.

The ambivalence toward Washington and Tuskegee in contemporary Black studies is perhaps best illustrated in the work of the literary critic and cultural theorist Houston Baker. In his now-classic study *Modernism and the Harlem Renaissance* (1987), Baker designates Washington's Atlanta Exposition Address (1895) as the "commencement of Afro-American modernism" because it was the first time that "an agreed upon . . . direction was set for a mass of black citizens who had struggled through the thirty years since emancipation." Baker contends that "Washington is 'modern' . . . because he earnestly projected the flourishing of a southern, black Eden at Tuskegee—a New World garden to nurture hands, heads, and hearts of a younger generation of agrarian black folk in the 'country districts.'"[54] By contrast, in his monograph *Turning South Again: Re-thinking Modernism/Re-reading Booker T.*, published a little more than a decade later in 2001 and considered a foundational text of New Southern studies, Baker drastically revises his position on Washington's and Tuskegee's "modernism," viewing them as complicit in Black subjection. Washington's "retrofitting" of an old plantation, Baker argues, is "a terrible augury against black modernism," another node on the plantation-to-prison pipeline. For Baker, the Tuskegee model was essentially on par with sharecropping, debt peonage, and other carceral practices that represented "plantation black abjection."[55] As might be surmised from my description of *Afterlives of the Plantation* thus far, I find Baker's initial assessment of Washington's and Tuskegee's "modernism" more generative than his later one.

Baker reconsidered his position on Washington after reading Louis R. Harlan's definitive two-volume biography, which, according to the historian Robert J. Norrell, largely depicted Washington unfavorably. In his own revisionist biography *Up from History: The Life of Booker T. Washington* (2009), Norrell attributes Harlan's critical portrayal to the fact that he was C. Vann Woodward's student and thus "recycled his mentor's" bias against Washington. Harlan sided with Washington's critics, Norrell argues, and "chose not to show the mounting white hysteria about Washington's role in politics." By contrast, Norrell paints a more sympathetic portrait of Washington by detailing the immense constraints under which he labored amid "intensifying opposition to black education" and persistent threats against his life. Ultimately, Norrell considers much of Washington scholarship anachronistic for "applying 1960s expectations of protest to a man who had lived two generations earlier."[56]

Regardless of such ambivalence in contemporary scholarship, Washington and Tuskegee had a profound impact on the Black diaspora from the working classes to the political and intellectual elite. What would it mean, then, to take their contributions to Black modernity and futurity more seriously? Answering such a question requires a different and more capacious orientation to Washington and Tuskegee by exploring how they circulated as symbols of and strategies for Black self-determination throughout the Black world. I, too, am critical of Washington's political accommodationism and the hegemony he exacted over Black politics, but I also take issue with efforts to flatten Tuskegee into a symbol of southern African Americans' lack of cultural and intellectual sophistication, acquiescence to Jim Crow, or antimodernity. I detect in that reasoning not only political and intellectual critique but regional and class bias as well. As Robin D. G. Kelley has argued, "Too often our standards for evaluating social movements pivot around whether or not they 'succeeded' in realizing their visions rather than on the merits or power of the visions themselves."[57] The failures and limits of the Tuskegee project have been so thoroughly examined that it is practically synonymous with political accommodation and backwardness, but we have given less attention to what it enabled for Black modernity. Recalling Gary Wilder's important observation that to "read generously is not to suspend critical evaluation," I read Tuskegee both generously *and* critically to ascertain the dynamism of the future they envisioned—what they understood themselves to be doing—while critiquing their imaginative constraints also.[58]

To better understand Tuskegee's modernity, we must recognize rural, agricultural life as a viable future for Black people, especially at the turn of the twentieth century. This was by no means merely an accommodation to the U.S. South's racist labor economy, as many have argued. To associate the rural with backwardness is reductive and runs contrary to the Tuskegee faculty and students' understanding of themselves as New Negroes and to rural Black people's genuine affinity for farming and agriculture in the United States, the

Caribbean, and Latin America. For many, Tuskegee is a cautionary tale about the folly of attempting to use "the master's tools [to] dismantle the master's house," as Audre Lorde famously put it. But, in reality, across the Americas farming was the dominant skillset to which newly emancipated peoples and their descendants had greatest access, and most postplantation societies were agricultural; in this context, Tuskegee's legibility as a viable model and method of progress is clear.

In her study of Black liberatory agriculture in the United States, Monica White contends that some forms of resistance are "not disruptive but rather constructive," wherein "the aggrieved actively build alternatives to existing political and economic relationships." White astutely inquires, "Is it possible to conceptualize these ways of building self-sufficiency and self-reliance as resistance in their own right?"[59] By taking seriously Tuskegee's transformation from a plantation to a world-renowned school, I answer White's query in the affirmative. In fact, Washington himself insisted that whereas slavery was "a great evil, which was to be destroyed," his postemancipation work was to be that "of construction rather than a work of destruction," and agriculture was his chief method for doing so.[60]

In relation to Tuskegee, I am less interested in what "the white architects of black education" intended by funding industrial education to discipline formerly enslaved peoples and colonial subjects into an agricultural and industrial labor force than in what Black artists, intellectuals, politicians, organizers, students, and parents did with these limited resources and degraded spaces—reimagining and transforming them into strategies of self-determination, racial uplift, and literary and aesthetic innovation.[61] I highlight how diverse populations customized and strategically translated the Tuskegee project—in some cases in ways that Washington himself may have disavowed or even outright rejected. Above and beyond what Washington intended, Tuskegee's symbolic value and methods inspired a range of approaches to Black diasporic uplift in response to the new realities of Jim Crow, colonialism, and imperialism.

One of the chief criticisms of Washington's leadership is the stranglehold he exacted over Black politics through the "Tuskegee Machine." Rather than reinscribing his social and political dominance, however, this book begins by putting him in conversation with his contemporaries and counterparts, such as Margaret Murray Washington (his third wife) and George Washington Carver at Tuskegee; other Black agrarian reformers in the United States, such as T. Thomas Fortune; as well as Rafael Serra y Montalvo and Jean Price-Mars in Cuba and Haiti, respectively. However much these figures embraced aspects of Washington's educational philosophy, their legacies are not reducible to his alone, and their archives paint a richer portrait of Tuskegee and the Global Black South as geographies of cultural and intellectual exchange.

In the latter part of the book, I explore Tuskegee's "students" and the dynamism of their respective aesthetic and political projects. I define "students" broadly to encompass those who were educated at Tuskegee and its diasporic offshoots, such as Claude McKay and Zora Neale Hurston, respectively, as well as those who were informally educated in its curriculum, such as Marcus Garvey. Whereas McKay emigrated from Jamaica to study agronomy at Tuskegee and become an agricultural instructor, Hurston attended an industrial school in Eatonville, Florida, founded by Tuskegee graduates and modeled on its curriculum and was thus essentially a Tuskegee student once removed. Garvey, in contrast, was never educated in Tuskegee's curriculum in any formal way. But, of course, education is not reducible to formal schooling alone. I thus propose Garvey as a self-taught and self-proclaimed student of Washington's sociopolitical and economic thought who immersed himself in Tuskegee's curriculum through its print culture. Like the students of all educational institutions, Tuskegee's students held their own social and political aspirations and views on race, gender, class, education, labor, and global affairs. While Tuskegee promoted racial uplift and envisioned the southern New Negro as a bourgeois independent farmer, artisan, and homemaker, as I explore in chapter 2, the lives and work of the students I examine here moved within and against the school's articulated mission. Both McKay and Hurston, for instance, rejected the notion of "racial uplift" and the civilizing mission and regarded the rural and urban working classes not as subjects to be managed (Washington's view) but as intellectuals of the land and arbiters of culture, respectively.

Each of these students was a theorist and practitioner of diaspora whose works reflect the dynamism of the Global Black South as a contact zone and hub of Black cultural and intellectual production. McKay's Jamaican poetry and fiction depict Caribbean labor migrants as "peasant cosmopolitans," whose travels within the international circuits of labor and commerce accorded them a worldliness and sophistication typically associated with the Western bourgeois cosmopolitan subject. Hurston used her theories of Black vernacular expression derived from her anthropological fieldwork in southern Florida's work camps to illuminate the similarities and differences between southern African American and Afro-Caribbean folk cultures and to stage diasporic ties in her folk concerts, fiction, and lectures. Garvey's Universal Negro Improvement Association (UNIA) largely comprised agricultural laborers in the U.S. South, the Caribbean, and Central America who envisioned land ownership and the production and consumption of healthy foods and cash crops such as cotton and sugar as crucial to facilitating Black economic cooperation and self-determination on a global scale. Far from Washington acolytes, these students exploited the affordances of Tuskegee to craft aesthetic and political futures all their own.[62]

THE REPURPOSED PLANTATION

It has been argued that Washington aimed to rehabilitate slavery and retrofit the plantation, but in actuality he sought to construct something at Tuskegee that served an entirely different purpose.[63] As McKittrick argues, space and place are "alterable" precisely because geography is socially produced: "Social practices create landscapes and contribute to how we organize, build, and imagine our surroundings." Crucially, this means that the "interrogations and remappings [of hegemonic geographies] provided by black diaspora populations can incite new, or different, and perhaps more just, geographic stories."[64] Rather than *rehabilitating* or *retrofitting* (terms that connote "restoring" or only slightly "adjusting" the original structure), Washington deployed a material, aesthetic, and rhetorical strategy I term "the repurposed plantation," wherein he, along with Tuskegee's faculty and students, reterritorialized a former cotton plantation into a modern farm and transnational educational institution aimed at ensuring Black vitality through agriculture, industry, and economic self-help. Tuskegee was thus an experiment in altering the plantation by investing it with new and, ultimately, more just meanings.

Repurposing plantation geographies and other sites of subjection toward new and more liberatory ends was a strategy of Black world making across the Global Black South. Following the Civil War, many plantations in the U.S. South were confiscated from treasonous Confederate planters and fell into ruin and disrepair from want of Black laborers. These abandoned landscapes were the sites of some of the earliest experiments in transforming formerly enslaved people into free laborers, landowners, and quasi-citizens. They included the Port Royal experiment in South Carolina and Special Field Order No. 15, commonly known as "40 acres and a mule," which decreed that land from Charleston, South Carolina, to the St. John's River in Florida was to be "set apart for the settlement of the negroes." Some formerly enslaved peoples also reclaimed plantation lands, such as the grandfather of the civil rights activist Ella Baker, who purchased 250 acres of the old plantation where he had been enslaved in North Carolina, "which he then parceled out in small tracts to other family members, constructing an enclave of kinship," and even "mortgaged his own land to provide for

INTRODUCTION

local people in need."[65] As with Tuskegee, plantations were also repurposed into educational institutions such as Hampton Institute (later Hampton University) in Virginia, Tougaloo College in Mississippi, and Alta Vista Agriculture and Mechanical College of Texas for Colored Youth (later Prairie View A&M University), among many others. Beyond the United States, in the early 1930s the Negro Progress Convention of British Guiana, a Black self-help organization, acquired five hundred acres of an old coffee, cocoa, and fruit planation to establish an industrial school based on Tuskegee, and in 1948 the University College of the West Indies (present-day University of the West Indies) was established on two adjoining former sugar estates in Mona, Jamaica.

Washington's vision of an agrarian future to resolve the problem of free labor has long been misunderstood as a desire to keep southern African Americans bound to plantations and other forms of menial labor. Yet this strategy was instead part of a longer (though perhaps no less fraught) diasporic tradition of repurposing plantation logics and geographies. In *The Black Jacobins* (1963), C. L. R. James grapples with the decision made by the Haitian revolutionary leader Toussaint L'Ouverture to repurpose the plantation by practically forcing Haiti's new freedwomen and men back to work on the very estates from which they had just emancipated themselves as a way to support the republic's economy. Toussaint's vision of an agrarian future for Haiti vis-à-vis the plantation system was based on the imperative of "the prosperity of agriculture," distinguishing postemancipation plantation labor from its antecedent by paying the "workers" in kind. Instead of breaking up colonial plantations, he "confined the blacks to the plantations under rigid penalties," giving "them their keep and a fourth of the produce." As James describes, Toussaint faced an unenviable conundrum: "He was battling with the colossal task of transforming a slave population, after years of licence, into a community of free labourers, and he was doing it in the only way he could see."[66]

On one hand, Toussaint's strategy was successful, for "in a year and a half he had restored cultivation to two-thirds of what it had been in the most flourishing days of the old régime."[67] On the other hand, the freedmen understandably viewed plantation labor in any form as equivalent to enslavement. As the historian Laurent Dubois notes, "Ex-slaves strongly believed that the land should be theirs; land ownership would give freedom its full and true meaning."[68] Putting a finer point on the fundamental incongruency between revolutionary leaders and the newly freed masses, the Haitian sociologist Jean Casimir calls the freedmen's desire for small plots of land where they could practice subsistence farming the "counter-plantation," a system of "joint collective ownership [that] helped to avoid the colonial land tenure system and its harmful consequences."[69]

This competition between state-controlled plantation labor and autonomous subsistence farming remained one of the central challenges of nineteenth- and twentieth-century Haiti. "Subsistence production resulted in economic decay and every variety of political disorder," James writes. "Yet it has preserved the national independence."[70]

For Toussaint, the plantation was the economic foundation of the Western Hemisphere and inextricable with Enlightenment and liberal-humanist traditions. And it was precisely his inability to imagine a future outside of the plantation order that precipitated his project's failure. "Toussaint's failure was the failure of enlightenment," James writes, "not of darkness."[71] His intimacy with French civilization and Enlightenment thought as well as his "condition" as a "conscript of modernity" foreclosed alternative future possibilities for him. Toussaint "could not choose *not* to be modern," contends David Scott. "He was its conscript. He was a man who had come up in a world that had been coercively reorganized by the material and epistemic violence of a modern regime of power and forcibly inserted into a global order in a state of subordination and dependence." Washington was similarly conscripted into and "constrained" by modernity, and as Scott says of Toussaint, "obliged . . . to seek his freedom in the very technologies, conceptual languages, and institutional formations in which modernity's rationality . . . sought his enslavement": the plantation order.[72]

Unlike Toussaint, Washington did *not* advocate returning Black laborers to plantations; rather, he implored Black people to acquire land and regarded agricultural and industrial education as a "newer kind of education," more practical and useful than older models that encouraged people to abandon the "soil," "farm," "kitchen," and "country."[73] At the same time, he was no revolutionary hero like Toussaint, willing to take up arms to protect Black people's freedom. Having lived through the brutality of the Civil War and the precarity of its aftermath, Washington chose a form of racial reconciliation that required Black self-sufficiency and political accommodation over armed resistance. In this way, Washington and Toussaint are quite distinct. Nevertheless, I position Washington, Tuskegee, and the U.S. South alongside Toussaint and Haiti to show how the idea of an agrarian future based on repurposing plantation logics and geographies was part of a longer Global Black South tradition. The repurposed plantation was a battle over both the future of Black life and the future of the plantation itself, attempting to redirect it from its original purpose as a technology of Black subjection. Whereas Toussaint transformed a colonial plantation society into a nation-state and the first Black republic, Washington established Tuskegee as a site for regenerating Black being—from the Old Negro of slavery to a southern New Negro—where the plantation turned modern school and farm could indeed produce new and more just futures. Despite the shortcomings of their respective visions, their attempts at repurposing the plantation—to see if this modern political-economic form could yield more liberatory possibilities—are no less important than more explicitly radical strategies of Black world making.

PLOTTING AGRARIAN FUTURES: ECO-ONTOLOGY, THE EXPERIMENT PLOT, AND TRANS-PLANTATION

In her foundational work on the plantation as a critical geography for Black identity formation in the so-called New World, Sylvia Wynter establishes a bipartite schema of the colonial plantation and the slave garden plot, or provision ground. Most often associated with the experience of slavery in the Caribbean, especially Jamaica, "the plot" refers to the small parcel of land that white planters allotted to the enslaved to feed themselves and their families and is akin to Casimir's notion of the "counter-plantation" in postemancipation Haiti. In Wynter's New World schema, the trans-plantation "of a human race into a stranger soil," as Jean Price-Mars put it, generated multiple transformations or metamorphoses: "The multi-tribal African was converted into a 'negro' and a social, cultural human being was metamorphosed into a commodity"; their labor became "labor power"; and through the establishment of plantations, "the earth" and "nature became land," reduced to their productivity and property relations.[74]

On the plot where enslaved Africans produced for their subsistence instead of for the plantation and its global capitalist imperatives, however, they retained something of their African peasant identity. Enslaved peoples therefore developed "a dual and ambivalent relationship with the new land," Wynter argues. This contradiction and tension between the plot and the plantation lie at the heart of the New World Black experience. The plot was crucial to the "rerooting of the uprooted," Wynter argues, through the retention of traditional African knowledges, cultural and religious practices, and relations to the land. The "ideology of the provision ground, and the culture based on it, rehumanized the object/property created by the plantation ideology."[75] Similarly, Casimir contends that through "joint collective ownership," the "counter-plantation" in Haiti broke "the economic stranglehold of the planters on land and people" and evolved into "a unique societal plan, combined resources, a family organization, a language, a religion and symbolic systems [that became] a palpable utopia."[76]

The plot and the counter-plantation, both of them counterhegemonic Black geographies, provide an alternative lens to reexamine Tuskegee and the repurposed plantation as an experiment in Black world making.

Tuskegee exemplifies this historical tension between the plot and the plantation within Black modernity. Its commitment to Black vitality through self-help and communal uplift represented a "plot logic," even as its adherence to civilizationist, paternalistic, and pro-capitalist discourses perpetuated aspects of the plantation's ideological hegemony. Slave garden plots were similarly paradoxical spaces. They unintentionally benefited the planter class because they fueled Black people to continue laboring for the market economy; even Maroons, the paragons of Black resistance to slavery, forged treaties with colonial governments by which they agreed to return Black fugitives from slavery to plantations in order to maintain their own precarious freedom. A "plot logic" is thus inherently and always entangled with plantation hegemony. Black people's efforts to dismantle, disrupt, and/or *do something otherwise with* the hegemonic plantation are necessarily "plot acts," even as they sometimes reproduce the plantation's more deleterious logics—property ownership, capitalism, and so on—in the process. The plot, then, is not a utopic geography, despite Casimir's description of the counter-plantation as a "palpable utopia." It is always responding to and circumscribed by the violence of the plantation and sometimes inadvertently reinscribing it; however, at its most liberatory it is unequivocally committed to Black life, self-determination, and freedom. Tuskegee exemplifies this struggle as well as the Black diasporic peoples who adapted its model to new ends.

In Wynter's schema, the "novel form [genre]" and the plantation societies of the Caribbean are "twin children of the same parents."[77] The exploitation of Black life on "New World" plantations enabled Britain's Industrial Revolution, which created the socioeconomic conditions for the expansion of the British middle class and the rise of the novel as a new, modern literary genre. "The plot" thus has at least two connotations: the slave garden plot and the novel or story plot. More recently, scholarship in Black geographies and Black ecologies has taken up the plot and the act of plotting to recover a host of cultural knowledges and strategies of resistance that disrupted the plantation's hegemonic hold on Black life.[78] Building on these rich contributions, my conception of the plot retains not only its material, geographic, and ecological connotations but also its significance as a locus of modern Black aesthetic and cultural practices: literature and storytelling; food, music, and dance; spiritual and communal values; and other practices of survival and resistance.

I propose that plotting, much like planting, is an expressly speculative and sacred act of hope and faith that what one sows today will bear fruit at a future time. As a practice rooted in sustaining Black life and imagining better futures, plotting contravenes the logics of commodities speculation and futures markets that reduced Black people to abstract racial-capitalist values and placed them in fungible relations with land, plants, and animals. As we will see in the rich literary and cultural archive assembled here, plotting agrarian futures encompasses regenerating Black being, nourishing and adorning the Black body, beautifying the home, stewarding the landscape, and ensuring Black people's political and economic self-determination. Its most defining feature (again, at its most liberatory) is an "ethic of care," or what the literary scholar and cultural historian Farah Jasmine Griffin describes as "the ways people within communities depend upon one another" and insist that their "most vulnerable members . . . deserve special consideration and attention."[79]

In rereading Tuskegee for its plot logics, ethics, and sensibilities, I linger not only on the ruins of the burned big house but also on the degraded cotton fields surrounding it to consider the ecological dimensions of plotting agrarian futures in the rural, Jim Crow South. The logic and practice of regenerating poor, depleted land and making it productive again were central features of Washington's agenda that most accounts have failed to adequately engage.[80] George Washington Carver, the renowned agricultural scientist who served as director of Tuskegee's Department of Agriculture, conducted numerous experiments to regenerate Tuskegee's worn-out soils after decades of degradation by abusive cotton cultivation. In his recruitment letter to Carver, Washington wrote: "Our students are poor, often starving. They travel miles of torn roads, across years of poverty. We teach them to read and write, but words cannot fill stomachs. They need to learn how to plant and harvest crops."[81]

Washington's and Carver's collective efforts to regenerate both people and the soil illuminate "eco-ontology" as the crux of Tuskegee's plot logics and ethics, whereby planting and harvesting crops were inextricably intertwined with the ontological aims of racial uplift and what Washington described as the journey "from degradation, poverty and waste to full manhood."[82] Eco-ontology is especially concerned with how some of the very people most devastated by the plantation—whose coerced labor, ironically, contributed to the plantation's ecological degradation—imagined and participated in regenerating plantation lands alongside their own transformation from enslaved property to quasi-citizens and self-determined subjects. Indeed, the repurposed plantation is an eco-ontological strategy for the coterminous regeneration of Black being and the earth.

Throughout his oeuvre, Washington frequently lamented how monocropping among poor Black farmers in central Alabama's "plantation districts" put a stranglehold on rural life. Instead of growing both cotton for the market and foodstuff to sustain themselves, Black farmers often "plant[ed] nothing but cotton . . . up to the very door of the cabin" and purchased food from the local commissary, thus ensnaring themselves in perennial cycles of debt and economic dependence.[83] Since cotton still reigned supreme in the U.S. South, Tuskegee aimed to teach farmers how to grow it more efficiently but at the same time also encouraged them to engage in subsistence agriculture to provide food and nourishment for their families. "We cannot quit cotton," Washington insisted, "but we must raise our stock and our meat [too]."[84] By promoting Black farmers' self-sufficiency, Tuskegee mobilized the plot to circumvent the exploitation of the South's plantation economy.

Tuskegee's agricultural experiment plots and robust extension program, which were central to its curriculum, illustrate the school's plot logics and ethics most of all.[85] In fact, rereading Tuskegee through these two endeavors invites its reconsideration as an early model of Black studies. In 1896, the State of Alabama provided funding to establish an agricultural experiment station, also called the "experiment plot," at Tuskegee for developing new scientific agricultural knowledges and techniques. The experiment plot was Carver's laboratory for his research on soil regeneration, crop rotation, chemical and organic fertilizers, organic paints, and crop varieties that were best suited for Alabama's soils, and his findings were disseminated through Tuskegee's agricultural extension program. Through initiatives such as the Tuskegee Negro Conference (sometimes referred to as the Farmers' Conference) and the Jesup Agricultural Wagon, or "Movable School," faculty, staff, and students translated and distributed cutting-edge agricultural knowledge and resources among Black farmers unable to attend Tuskegee or pursue formal education by other routes. Carver also published and circulated the results of his experiments in bulletins that instructed farmers how to grow more nutritious foods and adopt more affordable and ecologically sustainable farming techniques. To encourage crop diversification and help farmers raise their food supplies, the school provided "all kinds of garden seeds" free of charge to conference attendees who could not afford to buy seeds on their own as well as flower seeds to encourage women attendees to "beautify[] their home[s]."[86]

Through its ethic of care, of individual and communal uplift, Tuskegee's experiment plot functioned as a postemancipation iteration of the slave garden plot. It was a locus for teaching formerly enslaved peoples and their descendants how to navigate the social and ecological carnage wrought by the plantation and the new forms of unfreedom it engendered—a geography of rehumanization where they could reclaim their ancestral roots as stewards of the earth using modern, scientific methods. This focus on Tuskegee's investment in democratizing scientific agricultural knowledge and making resources more equitable and readily available for rural and often poor Black people reflects the core tenets of Black studies as a political project committed to sustaining and advancing Black life and culture. This is precisely what we miss when we reduce Tuskegee to the shortcomings of Washington's legacy alone.

Despite the myriad industrial trades offered at Tuskegee, it was agriculture that Washington prioritized in his vision of Black modernity and where Carver made his most significant contributions to science and environmentalism. In Tuskegee's early years, most of its students hailed from the "country districts," and the school reckoned that "eighty-five per cent of the coloured people in the Gulf states" made a living through agriculture. Washington was thus determined "not to educate our students out of sympathy with agricultural life" and insisted that "our pathway must be up through the soil."[87] Washington was not anomalous in his belief in farming and agriculture as the foundation for Black progress. Even as Tuskegee's students, faculty, and admirers across the Global Black South adapted and translated the Tuskegee model toward various ends, agriculture remained central to Black freedom struggles well into the twentieth century: from individual and communal land ownership to institution building, nation-state formation, and pan-Africanist visions of a Black "transnation."[88] Ultimately, "plotting agrarian futures" captures how agriculture was constitutive to the dynamic, multipronged set of strategies Black people pursued to ensure racial progress and self-determination in slavery's wake.

By foregrounding agriculture, I also pursue a more capacious conception of Black modernity that at once encapsulates practices of rootedness and place-making as well as movement and migration. On one hand, I argue that the rural Black people who did not migrate to the urban Global North were no less modern than their more mobile counterparts and were often still engaged in transnational networks that circulated plantation commodities, print culture, political ideologies, and other cultural artifacts. As Nanny tells Janie in *Their Eyes Were Watching God* (1937), "Us colored folks is branches without roots," effectively capturing the profound dislocation at the heart of the diasporic condition.[89] Through Tuskegee's conception of the southern New Negro as the bourgeois farmer and homemaker and McKay's depictions of the prosperous Jamaican peasant, for instance, I demonstrate how Global Black South peoples actively embraced farming, land ownership, and other placemaking practices as viable futures in an attempt to "reroot the uprooted." On the other hand, I show how those who did migrate often did so to engage in agricultural labor on corporate plantations or, as in McKay's case, to study agronomy and become an agricultural instructor back home in Jamaica. Hurston viewed migrant agricultural and industrial laborers as arbiters of modern Black culture, while Price-Mars and Garvey viewed farming and agricultural education as modes of racial uplift and self-determination needed to sustain a Black nation-state. Reading the Black diasporic archive for such articulations of agrarian futures challenges the field's overemphasis on Black modernity as necessarily northern, urban, and industrial and thus allows us to texture our narratives with the knowledges and experiences of those who stayed put.

In the exploration of how Black people repurposed the plantation and plotted agrarian futures in slavery's aftermath, the archive is often skewed toward Black men's cultural, intellectual, and political contributions. Indeed, the plantation is a fundamentally heteropatriarchal and paternalistic institution, and as Black people navigated its precarious afterlives, they also negotiated the logics of race, gender, class, and sexuality that it established as the proving ground of liberal subjecthood. Perhaps unsurprisingly, then, Washington and Tuskegee reflected these patriarchal and paternalistic norms, as did many of the artists, intellectuals, and political figures who embraced and adapted the Tuskegee model. However, just as Black women's manual, reproductive, and intellectual labors sustained colonial and antebellum plantations, Black women were equally integral to plotting agrarian futures in the plantation's afterlife. Throughout the Global Black South, Black women actively debated, strategized, and theorized their unique contributions to racial progress. At the Tuskegee Negro Conference in 1915, for instance, the (unfortunately nameless) "wife of a Negro farmer" maintained that it was "us womenfolks" who told "our menfolks" that they "can't eat cotton" and thus encouraged their husbands to raise more food for their families alongside the cash crops they cultivated for sale.[90] Janey Leonard, one of Tuskegee's former female students, embraced the school's southern New Negro philosophy wholesale by becoming a prosperous farmer and acquiring 180 acres of land and a home "as modern and attractively furnished as any city home."[91] And Clara Shepard, an "instructress" of French at Tuskegee and a principal translator of *La revue du monde noir*, a foundational journal of the Négritude Movement, proposed that teaching southern African American students French could inspire them with examples of successful labor organizing among farmers in French-speaking West Africa and thus disrupt the perpetual exploitation of Black farmers in the U.S. South.

Margaret Murray Washington, Booker T.'s third wife, is a particularly noteworthy example of Black women's intellectual contributions to forging agrarian futures. She directed Tuskegee's women's curriculum and was a leading figure in

INTRODUCTION 29

the Black women's club movement. Working alongside figures such as Ida B. Wells-Barnett, Mary Church Terrell, and Mary McCleod Bethune, Margaret Murray helped to shape the contours of early twentieth-century Black womanhood. By organizing initiatives such as the Mothers' Meetings, the Woman's Meeting, and the Tuskegee Women's Club, she addressed issues such as women and girls' relationship to education, labor, and womanhood in a postslavery milieu where gender oppression and the threat of racial-sexual violence were ever present. Margaret Murray served two terms as president of the National Association of Colored Women and in the early 1920s founded the International Council of Women of the Darker Races of the World, further evidence of Tuskegee's internationalism. Significantly, she also inspired "a course of study on conditions of women in foreign lands" at Tuskegee, believed to be one of the first international women's studies courses.[92] Although Black women and girls are not always at the forefront of the diasporic relations I trace here, I mine the seams of the archive to illuminate their crucial role in repurposing the plantation toward new and more liberatory ends.

The image of Tuskegee disseminating vegetable and flower seeds to Negro Conference attendees is an apt metaphor for how its influence spread throughout the Global Black South. In its early years, Tuskegee was primarily a teacher-training school that equipped students to go into the country districts of the U.S. South to uplift Black communities by establishing agricultural and industrial schools modeled on Tuskegee. These "little Tuskegees" eventually spread throughout the U.S. South and inspired similar efforts—some successful, others less so—in Cuba, Haiti, Jamaica, British Guiana (now Guyana), Montserrat, South Africa, Liberia, and elsewhere.[93] As the historian Frank Guridy observes, "In the two decades before the emergence of Harlem as a Black political and cultural capital, one could argue, Tuskegee was the prime epicenter of Afro-diasporic activity in the world."[94]

Diaspora studies scholars have traditionally drawn on numerous botanical and maritime metaphors to theorize the historical and ongoing relations between Africa and its diaspora. *Diaspora*, a Greek term that connotes the dispersal of seeds and people alike, has been variously defined in terms of roots and routes, rhizomes, and, more recently, cultivation.[95] Gilroy's field-defining Black Atlantic framework also proposes "the image of ships in motion" as "the living means by which the points within that Atlantic world were joined."[96] I wish to add to this already rich critical lexicon the concept and practice of *transplantation* to capture the relationship between mobility and stasis, the terrestrial and the oceanic, that organizes Black transnational and diaspora studies. In botany, the term *transplantation* refers to the removal of a plant from one context to another. As a metaphor for diaspora, trans-plantation acknowledges that Black people and plants were similarly and sometimes simultaneously uprooted, replanted, and exploited to sustain and advance global capitalism. Many of the crops that spurred plantation modernity were not indigenous to the Americas but were transplanted to the region from other parts of the world as a part of a broader colonial botanical project. As Elizabeth DeLoughrey, Renée Gosson, and George Handley remind us, "Often the same ships contained flora and fauna as well as human beings for transplantation to colonial botanical gardens and sugar plantations across the Atlantic."[97] In short, my conception of *trans-plantation* elucidates the ways Western modernity facilitated and depended on the forced transportation and colonization of peoples and plants alike; it also indicates how the genocide of plantation slavery and settler colonialism was inextricably tied to the ecocidal practices of monocropping and soil exhaustion.

In addition to capturing the historical processes of dislocation and dispersal that produced the modern world, the term *trans-plantation* also connotes a mode of "relation" and a "practice"—to build on Glissant and Brent Hayes Edwards, respectively—of agricultural cultivation and cultural and intellectual exchange between Black diasporic communities as they negotiated the new demands of emancipation and new forms of unfreedom that emerged after enslavement.[98] I use it to encompass the translation, transformation, and transportation of literary texts and photographs, agricultural commodities, and political knowledges, strategies, and methods between Afro-descended communities.

Critically, sometimes a transplant thrives, and sometimes it withers and dies. It may be customized by the inhabitants of its new ecosystem or cross-pollinate with new flora to create something altogether new. Each of these scenarios proved true for Tuskegee's influence in the Global Black South, where its trans-plantation to other settings produced new ideas and hybrids. Just as the Hampton and Tuskegee models were adapted from colonial education in Hawaii, Black diasporic peoples adapted aspects of the Tuskegee model to meet and address the conditions of their respective countries and eras. Trans-plantation thus encompasses transforming or repurposing Tuskegee from an old, worn-out cotton plantation into an agricultural and industrial school; the linguistic, cultural, and ideological translations that occurred when Afro-Cubans and Haitians read the Spanish and French editions of *Up from Slavery*; African American and Afro-Caribbean students' migrations to Tuskegee; as well as Afro-Caribbean labor migration to the region's corporate plantations.

INTRODUCTION   31

THE ANTINOMIES OF UPLIFT: RACIAL PROGRESS, THE CIVILIZING MISSION, AND TUSKEGEE'S OTHERWISE AFFORDANCES

Even though the Tuskegee model of education appealed to a host of Black diasporic leaders and laypersons as a strategy for racial uplift and self-determination, it paradoxically also appealed to white industrial capitalists, European colonizers, and U.S. imperialists committed to perpetuating Black subjection. Indeed, the Tuskegee model bears out the observation made by the historian of education William H. Watkins that "education can be used both to oppress and to liberate."[99] Much of the scholarship on Tuskegee's internationalism focuses on its origins in colonial education in Hawaii (by way of the Hampton Institute) and Washington's collaborations with European missionaries and colonial powers, especially in Liberia, South Africa, Sudan, and Togo.[100] (Though Africa is often elided in African Diaspora studies, the scholarship on Tuskegee's relationship to Africa is a noteworthy exception and illustrates how the Global Black South can be taken up to explore a range of Black south–south relations that exceed the scope of the present study.) Yet Tuskegee's international influence is far more nuanced than Washington's alleged power brokering for colonial governments or the curriculum's co-optation as a disciplinary technology for the spread of racial capitalism. There was a strain of a conservative Black nationalism—and perhaps even a proto-pan-Africanism—within Washington's uplift program that inspired myriad freedom dreams throughout the diaspora.

Tuskegee's uplift agenda promoted Black self-sufficiency (if not always wholesale self-determination) through land ownership, thrift and economy, scientific agriculture, improved hygiene, a philosophical attunement to the beauty and dignity of labor, and the adoption of bourgeois aesthetic and domestic values. Yet uplift—the belief that the educated African American elite were responsible for the rehabilitation of the race through the moral, cultural, and educational development of the Black masses—was an inherently contradictory and sometimes detrimental racial philosophy, suffused with class paternalism, masculinist chauvinism, and, perhaps most ironically, a form of intraracial civilizationism that "reinforced . . . Afro-diasporic hierarchies" and "reified U.S. models of development in the United States and overseas."[101] Like many of his fellow African American elites who also subscribed to uplift, including W. E. B. Du Bois, Pauline Hopkins, and Alexander Crummell, Washington's uplift philosophy "bore the stamp of evolutionary racial theories positing the civilization of elites against the moral degradation of the masses."[102]

Even among Washington's contemporaries, however, his brand of uplift was uniquely conservative and sometimes trafficked in racist caricatures of the very people for whom he advocated. He liberally used the rhetoric of the "scale of civilization" in his public and private writings and believed "Negroes" were the "weaker race."[103] He also believed that establishing a firm economic foundation through agriculture and industry—securing "the useful before the ornamental"—would yield a more dynamic set of options for future generations.[104] As such, he was both conscript and perpetrator of "Black patience," or what the literary and performance studies scholar Julius B. Fleming Jr. has brilliantly theorized as a project of racial domination that subjected Black people to "coerced performances of waiting" for freedom, equality, and citizenship.[105]

At the same time, what is perhaps so confounding about Washington is that he was also a proponent of race pride, categorically rejected notions of Black people's inherent inferiority, and eventually questioned the scale of civilization and the colonial racial schema that undergirded it in his later writings.[106] In contrast to the racist pseudoscience of the day, he espoused a cultural relativist racial philosophy wherein Black people's status as a "weaker race" was based on differences in "circumstances" and "conditions" rather than on "innate qualities" or "general rules" that predetermined their futures or "fix[ed]" them at the bottom of society "for all times."[107] He asserted that "no race can succeed which is ashamed of itself" and believed that "the Negro boy should study Negro history," just as Japanese and German boys studied their respective histories, and as early as 1909 Tuskegee offered such courses as "The Negro in Africa" and "The Negro in America."[108]

Washington and his fellow elites' commitment to racial uplift at home was tethered to the civilizing mission abroad. Since the antebellum period, argues Kevin Gaines, this class of African Americans held "an avid missionary interest in Africa," believing "African heathenism" was the source of their own degraded social status and that Africa needed to be redeemed.[109] In 1901, Washington sent a delegation of Tuskegee students and one faculty member to Togo, West Africa, to aid the German colonial government in training the native Togolese in modern agricultural methods. He explicitly linked the school's work in Togo to the spread of Tuskegee's "missionary spirit" throughout the Caribbean and Latin America:

> Since beginning this experiment [in Togo], we have received applications from both English and Belgian cotton-raising companies that wish to secure Tuskegee men to introduce cotton-raising in their African possessions. The Porto Rican Government makes an annual appropriation for the purpose of

maintaining eighteen students at Tuskegee in order that they may learn our methods. The Haytian Government has recently arranged to send a number of young men here, mainly with the view of their being trained in farming. Besides, we have students present from the West Indies, Africa, and several South American countries.[110]

Through agricultural and industrial education, Washington crafted a diasporic uplift project that aimed to equip Black people with the tools to ascend the putative civilizational scale. However, he sometimes failed to discriminate between the motives of those with whom he collaborated. He corresponded and partnered equally with both Black and white missionary organizations, colonial powers, and Black diasporic political elites—each group with its own aspirations for Black people. For instance, though Washington believed "rationalized, modern cotton culture would protect the Togolese farmers from what he perceived as the backwardness and forced labor that haunted so many Africans" (admittedly, a view with little to no consideration for the Togolese people's attitudes and desires for their own futures), the German colonial government considered cotton growing in Togo as strictly concerned with capital accumulation and resource extraction, and it had no regard for indigenous growers' well-being.[111]

Nevertheless, rather than intentionally aiding and abetting white supremacists in subjugating Black people, as is often claimed, Washington attempted to work within the constraints of "what was deemed politically possible" under Jim Crow and its colonial and imperial siblings instead of against these structures—choosing assimilation, subversion, and covert civil rights agitation over outright resistance.[112] His chief failures were his excessive circumspection, racial and class paternalism, underestimation of the depths of anti-Blackness, and unwillingness to explicitly challenge white-supremacist ideologies and power structures, while laying the burden and responsibility for the "Negro problem" too heavily on Black people themselves. Still, it is crucial to understand how his nuanced uses of uplift intervened in and ultimately subverted a racial discourse that otherwise left Black people fixed permanently at the bottom of society.

Class tensions between the Black masses and Black elites were an abiding dynamic across the Global Black South. Though Tuskegee's faculty and students democratized agricultural knowledge, for instance, they also articulated condescending attitudes toward the very farmers they sought to uplift. Yet it would be a mistake to reduce uplift to social control alone, for it was often accompanied by a kind of care work—that is, the logics and ethics of the plot—that aimed to garner material resources for the most vulnerable. We cannot overlook the importance of helping impoverished Black communities secure better-quality food, clothing, housing, and education in the face of conditions that approximated the material scarcity of slavery, just as we cannot excuse those instances when the care work of uplift amounted to paternalism and veered dangerously close to social control. Throughout this book, then, I wrestle with and draw out uplift's inherent contradictions, affordances, and limitations.

Through his leadership at Tuskegee, Washington forged a diasporic uplift project that linked the fates of African Americans with the fates of Afro-descendants in the broader diaspora. "Whatever contributes, in any degree to the progress of the American Negro," he insisted, "contributes to the progress of the African Negro, and to the Negro in South America and the West Indies."[113] He served as vice president of the Congo Reform Association, explicitly criticizing "forced labor" in the Belgian Congo, and actively advocated on behalf of Black diasporic peoples in the face of racist, imperialist policies practiced by the U.S. government.[114] In January 1915, he launched a major media campaign to kill the passage of the African Exclusion Bill, which sought to prohibit the immigration of foreign-born Afro-descended peoples into the United States. He sent letters to the editors of the *New York Evening Post* and the *Atlanta Constitution* that also appeared in numerous other major newspapers, vehemently denouncing the bill as an "unjust, unreasonable, and unnecessary" affront on peoples of African descent, "classing them with alien criminals." He reasoned, "The services of the Jamaica Negro were invaluable in building the Panama Canal," and "now that we are celebrating the completion of this great canal," it would be "most unjust and unreasonable" to prohibit their entrance into the country.[115] Through Washington's influence, the bill was decisively defeated. Later that same year, at the onset of the U.S. occupation of Haiti, Washington admonished the U.S. government for its mistreatment of Haitians—perhaps his harshest public critique of white supremacy—and encouraged it to be patient with the Black republic, even as he unfortunately regarded the intervention as "necessary."[116]

Perhaps most importantly, just as Tuskegeeans disseminated seeds to poor Black farmers, Washington spread the "seeds" of an admittedly conservative Black nationalism, or even pan-Africanism, to the Black world. Tuskegee stood as a symbol of a (semi)autonomous Black institution, an example of what Black people could do for themselves, that inspired generations of people throughout the Global Black South. Marable has shown how Washington's "conservative, petit bourgeois nationalism" was embraced by Black South African political leaders such as John Langalibalele Dube, who visited Tuskegee in 1897 and subsequently founded a school in South Africa based on the Tuskegee model and forged his own brand of "conservative African nationalism." Yet while "Washington's pro-capitalist and pro-colonialist attitudes markedly influenced his direct activities in Africa," Marable continues, "far more important was Tuskegee's black nationalist and independent image to young blacks[,] . . . [who] actively struggled for black capitalism and black power." In this way, Marable at once critiques the limits of Washington's "accommodationist rhetoric" while also acknowledging how diasporic peoples were inspired by his "racial pride and black nationalist tendencies."[117]

Frank Guridy's more recent work on Tuskegee's relationship to Cuba has also been crucial for modeling a more nuanced approach to Washington's and Tuskegee's internationalism. Guridy not only examines the "Tuskegee–Cuba connection" from above—as an exchange between African American and Afro-Cuban political and intellectual elites—but also considers how Afro-Cuban students, parents, and laypersons interacted with Washington and Tuskegee and adapted them to fit their own desires for Afro-Cuban modernity.[118] As I show in chapter 3, Afro-Cubans not only sent scores of students to Tuskegee but also established the Instituto Booker T. Washington, a school modeled on Tuskegee, and the Booker T. Washington Society, a social organization for Afro-Cuban youth. Similarly, Garvey, who inspired the largest mass movement of Black people in the twentieth century, initially aimed to establish a "Tuskegee in Jamaica" that would teach farming and industrial development. And even when Garvey's local vision broadened to a global, pan-African one, Washington's emphasis on economic self-help through agriculture remained a core tenet of Garvey's and the UNIA's political-economic thought. Ultimately, in establishing Tuskegee as a crucible of diasporic relation, I attend to both the limits and the possibilities of what Washington envisioned on behalf of Afro-descended peoples as well as to how Afro-descendants exploited Tuskegee's affordances in turn—transplanting and cross-pollinating the seeds of racial progress bred in Tuskegee's eco-ontological laboratories to facilitate progress and self-determination on their own terms.

PREPARING THE GROUND, SELECTING THE SEEDS: A NOTE ON METHOD

In mining the Global Black South for articulations of diasporic relation, I have pursued a method that carefully attends to the nuances and complexities of identity within and between Black diasporic communities. Throughout

Afterlives of the Plantation, I rely mostly on the archives of the cultural, intellectual, and political elite. In some ways, the book is a literary and cultural history from "above." However, when possible, I incorporate the voices, experiences, political activities, and aspirations of Black people from "below" as well, including students, sharecroppers, tenant farmers, peasants, and labor migrants. Yet the latter were not necessarily static identities. We first meet McKay as a "prosperous peasant" in Jamaica, but by the end of this book he will have become a leading artist of the Harlem Renaissance and author of many works of poetry, fiction, and nonfiction. Tuskegee begins as a struggling school operating in a stable and chicken coop on a former cotton plantation, but by the turn of the twentieth century commentators frequently described it as a "city" or "colony" unto itself, and by the 1930s it was a petit bourgeois institution. Similarly, the Haitian elite were not tantamount to the African American elite, and the same holds true for constructions of race and gender. I thus specify and tease apart these differences wherever possible to prevent a simplistic flattening of identities across so many distinct cultural and political histories and geographies.

Accordingly, the Global Black South is not only concerned with how Black people responded to external forces such as white supremacy and its colonial and imperial offshoots but also especially attuned to the intra-racial politics of class, gender, language, ethnicity, region, and nationality. One of the challenges of juxtaposing the Global North and Global South is how to account for the asymmetries of power between diasporic communities. The U.S. South shares history with the Caribbean, but by the turn of the twentieth century the United States was well on its way to becoming a global imperial power. African Americans, though treated as second-class citizens at best, somewhat benefited from their access to the titans of American industrial capitalism who funded Black education; yet it was precisely because federal and state governments failed to adequately fund Black education that Washington and his contemporaries had to pursue philanthropic support that ultimately circumscribed their efforts. So even as African Americans lived in the crucible of global capitalism, racial inequality in the United States created conditions that were tantamount to those in the colonial and developing world.

Finally, even as I foreground Tuskegee and the U.S. South, the Global Black South is first and foremost a network of exchange *among* diasporic communities, a multidirectional flow of peoples, commodities, and ideas. My method reflects the call-and-response structure that characterizes so much of Black diasporic culture, tracing how Global Black South peoples spoke to, forged solidarities with, and critiqued each other. On one hand, I examine how Tuskegee and the cultural and intellectual production of southern African Americans

INTRODUCTION   37

influenced Global Black South relations. On the other, I draw on insights from
Caribbean studies to reconsider the temporal and epistemological grounds of
Black modernity in general and in the U.S. South in particular. I am especially
attentive to the literary genres, cultural modes, and political strategies these figures used to imagine and facilitate diasporic relations in more symbiotic and
egalitarian ways. Hurston, for instance, has been roundly criticized for her chau-
vinistic political commentary in her Caribbean ethnography *Tell My Horse*
(1938). I argue, however, that through performance, in particular her folk concerts and numerous essays and lectures on Black cultural expression, she arrived
at a conception of diaspora that is more respectful of ideological, political, and
cultural differences among diasporic communities.

Through a practice of exchange I have termed "Black economic (inter)nation-
alism," I attend to how global Black southerners repeatedly envisioned economic
cooperative schemes to link up Black agro-industrial and commercial interests
across national borders. For instance, the African American businessman
Major R. R. Wright established the Haitian Coffee and Products Trading Company to purchase Haitian coffee, the country's leading export, and hired African
American salespeople to distribute it to U.S. buyers. In doing so, Wright hoped to
buttress the Haitian economy while lowering African Americans' unemployment.
Garveyites likewise proposed establishing farms and plantations, schools, steamships, factories, and grocery stores to connect diasporic communities and ensure
their economic autonomy and protection against racial-capitalist exploitation.

PLOTTING THE COORDINATES

Afterlives of the Plantation spans the period from the end of Reconstruction in
the United States to the beginning of World War II. It opens with Tuskegee's
founding in 1881 and concludes in the early 1940s as the New Negro Movement
came to a decisive end. Loosely organized around the tension between the plot
and the plantation, each chapter depicts how Black artists, intellectuals, organizers, and students plotted Black life in the plantation's wake, grappling with
the paradoxical and precarious conditions left by the cotton plantation in the
U.S. South, the sugar industry in Cuba, Jamaica, and Haiti, and the banana and
fruit industries across the broader Caribbean and Central America. Drawing on
George Washington Carver's use of Tuskegee's experiment plot to test new solutions for Black agrarian futures and on Wynter's association between the slave
garden plot and the novel plot, the book is divided into three "plots," or sections.

Plot I explores the antinomies of Black modernity and agrarian futures in the Jim Crow South as conceived at Tuskegee under Washington's leadership (1881–1915). Plots II and III explore Tuskegee's transplantations to and strategic translations in Cuba, Haiti, Puerto Rico, Jamaica, and British Guiana as well as the new roots and shoots propagated by its African American and Caribbean students, who became the luminaries of the New Negro Movement of the 1920s and 1930s. Across all three plots, I examine how Global Black South peoples took the seeds of the Tuskegee project and cross-fertilized them with their own visions of progress and modernity to sprout new political and aesthetic projects committed to advancing and sustaining Black life.

Plot I, chapters 1 and 2, draws on Washington's, Carver's, and Margaret Murray's work at Tuskegee to examine the repurposed plantation as both an eco-ontological and aesthetic strategy for Black modernity. I show how their efforts to regenerate the worn-out soils of the Bowen plantation into an agricultural and industrial school and modern farm (chapter 1) were tied to the aesthetic and gendered curation of the southern, Tuskegee-trained New Negro by resignifying the meaning of Blackness in music, sound, and visual culture in slavery's aftermath (chapter 2). Through my analysis of the experiment plot and the extension program, I argue that Tuskegee emerges as both a model and cautionary tale for contemporary Black studies: exemplifying at once an ethic of care by using institutional resources to democratize knowledge in support of Black communities as well as the pitfalls of racial and class paternalism.

Plot II, chapters 3 and 4, demonstrates how Washington attempted to enfold Cuba and Haiti into his vision of an agrarian future, on one hand, and how Afro-Cuban and Haitian intellectuals, political officials, and youth adapted these ideas, on the other. In 1898, following the Spanish-American War, Washington launched a campaign to recruit Black Cuban and Puerto Rican students to Tuskegee. The subsequent translation and circulation of *Up from Slavery* into "Cuban-Spanish" sparked robust commentary on and appropriation of Washington and Tuskegee among Afro-Cubans. Chapter 3 explores how although Washington sought to transplant the Tuskegee Idea to Cuba based on an agricultural heritage similar to that of the U.S. South, prominent Afro-Cuban political and educational leaders such as Rafael Serra y Montalvo "strategically translated" select elements of the Tuskegee Idea to Cuba to meet the sociopolitical conditions in its new "soil." I thus show how Afro-Cubans weighed an educational and sociopolitical philosophy conceived under the "racial order" of the Jim Crow South against Cuban conceptions of racial fraternity and democracy as the specter of U.S. imperial occupation and annexation threatened to displace their own visions of Afro-Cuban modernity.

INTRODUCTION   39

In 1904, the Haitian medical doctor and statesman Jean Price-Mars spent two weeks at Tuskegee to assess the effectiveness of Washington's educational model. Over the next three decades, Price-Mars (who would become the foremost Haitian intellectual of the twentieth century) promoted the Tuskegee model of agricultural education for the Haitian masses. In chapter 4, I trace the numerous entanglements of Tuskegee and Haiti in the early twentieth century to detail how agricultural education and development were often at the center of debates about Haiti's self-determination and political-economic future. In some instances, agriculture was conceived as a strategy for racial uplift and solidarity between Haitians and African Americans, such as proposals to send Haitian students to Tuskegee and efforts to facilitate Black economic (inter)nationalism through buying and selling agricultural commodities. However, I also acknowledge the contradictory and violent uses of agrarian futures in Haiti: as a tool of imperial domination during the U.S. occupation and as a tool for the Haitian elite's extraction of the cultural, intellectual, and economic resources of the Haitian peasantry, the backbone of the country's agricultural economy.

Plot III, chapters 5–8, shifts from Washington and his counterparts to consider the experiences of Tuskegee's southern African American and Caribbean students as they navigated the intersections of diaspora and empire and adapted the Tuskegee project toward new and different ends. In doing so, plot III demonstrates how Tuskegee helped to set the stage for and actively contributed to the New Negro Movement of the 1920s and 1930s in unexpected and often contradictory ways. Indeed, the experimental impulse that undergirded Tuskegee's experiment plot is inextricably tied to the literary and political experiments of these architects of Black modernism.

Using correspondence from Washington's and Tuskegee's various archives, chapter 5 amplifies the voices of students and parents from the United States, Cuba, Puerto Rico, Jamaica, Haiti, British Guiana, and elsewhere to show how Tuskegee became a node of diaspora in the rural, Jim Crow South. Through its students, whose experiences have received comparatively less attention in the scholarship, I examine the many and divergent "uses of Tuskegee" for a new generation of Black diasporic subjects who often spoke in different languages and accents. I show how through trans-plantation and its linguistic-ideological counterpart, strategic translation, students cross-fertilized the Tuskegee Idea with a variety of contemporaneous cultural attitudes and discourses on race, labor, diaspora, empire, gender, and aesthetics to articulate their own visions of New Negro subjectivity. Finally, by examining several of the most important publications and ur-texts of the Harlem Renaissance and New Negro Movement, I demonstrate how Washington, Tuskegee, and the Global Black South remained relevant to the cultural and political debates of the 1920s and 1930s alongside Harlem, Paris, and other more well-known global northern locales.

In the summer of 1912, Claude McKay departed Port Antonio, Jamaica, aboard an UFCO steamship, bound for Tuskegee, Alabama. W. H. Plant, a member of Jamaica's delegation to the ICON earlier that year, had encouraged him to attend Tuskegee to become an agricultural instructor. Though McKay ultimately departed Tuskegee a few months after his arrival, I argue in chapter 6 that the conditions surrounding his initial transnational migration—traveling aboard an UFCO steamship to study agronomy in the U.S. South on the heels of the ICON—exemplifies how the plantation system and agricultural labor continued to animate Black diasporic movement throughout the hemisphere in slavery's aftermath. By examining McKay's Jamaican writings within the context of these various networks of hemispheric migration and Black internationalism, I show how his conception of agrarian futures championed both ambitious peasant farmers rooted in the Jamaican countryside and labor migrants who uprooted themselves to work on UFCO's corporate plantations and the Panama Canal. Holding together these two ostensibly disparate visions of agrarian futures is McKay's philosophical commitment to a "plot logic" that insisted on peasants' right to self-determination. Finally, I show how McKay's "plot logic" was the unifying thread linking his advocacy for the peasantry in his Jamaican writings with his ideological return to and defense of Tuskegee as a model of racial self-help and economic cooperation in his late thought.

Born in Macon County, Alabama, home of the Tuskegee Institute, and educated at an industrial school founded by a Tuskegee graduate, Zora Neale Hurston was a Tuskegee student once removed. In chapter 7, I examine Hurston as both a performance and diaspora theorist who documented and grappled with the afterlife of the plantation on two primary fronts: first, through her depictions of Black laborers as arbiters and progenitors of culture to disrupt the minstrel tradition and Western aesthetic hegemony in American theater and performance and, second, by capturing an undertheorized diasporic labor-migration network from the Gulf- and mid-Atlantic U.S. South and the Caribbean to Central and South Florida that revises northern-centric narratives of the Great Migration and the New Negro Movement. Hurston's characters and interlocutors work in agricultural and industrial jobs where they are subjected to plantation styles of management, but she uses performance to disrupt the plantation's geographic and cultural stronghold on Black life. Just as Tuskegee transformed the plantation into a site of Black eco-ontological regeneration, Hurston transformed the work camp, another afterlife of the plantation, into a

INTRODUCTION

scene of Black performance and diasporic relationality to evince the dynamism and complexity of Black folk expression throughout the hemisphere.

In January 1925, Marcus Garvey and the UNIA launched their second steamship line. The main vessel, the S.S. *Booker T. Washington*, made its first and only voyage from New York to Central America, the Caribbean, and parts of the U.S. South, hoping to facilitate economic cooperation through corporate plantation agriculture and tourism. Chapter 8 explores how Garvey coupled his experience as a former timekeeper on an UFCO banana plantation and his ideological affinity for Washington's economic self-help philosophies to imagine a Black agro-industrial empire. Just as Washington repurposed an abandoned cotton plantation into an industrial school, Garvey and the UNIA recast the plantation as a productive space where the political economy of corporate plantation agriculture could facilitate Black economic (inter)nationalism. Although it is well known that the UNIA promoted creating Black-owned industries such as steamship lines, scholars have paid less attention to the organization's agricultural pursuits, such as one of the UNIA's earliest goals to establish a farm and institute in Jamaica modeled on Tuskegee. In the *Negro World* and UNIA Convention proceedings, members consistently promoted agricultural education and development as integral to racial progress, and a significant number of Garveyites worked in agriculture, especially in the rural U.S. South, the Caribbean, and Central America. This chapter thus recovers the ways farming and agriculture were inextricably entangled with the ship and the factory in the UNIA's vision of pan-African solidarity and diasporic citizenship.

TENDING, GATHERING, AND ASSESSING THE HARVEST

Afterlives of the Plantation concludes by gathering the harvest from our various experiment plots and reflecting on what thinking with and through the Global Black South can illuminate for Black studies as the field confronts some of the most challenging issues of our day. Examining how Afro-descended peoples, once conscripted into plantation modernity, adapted its geographies, logics, and technologies into visions and practices of freedom and world making has much to teach us about repurposing modern political-economic forms and negotiating with power under oppressive and seemingly impossible conditions. Indeed, the plantation and the violence it wrought persist in the present, materially, ideologically, and economically: from the environmental toxicity of agribusiness to the historical erasures and revisionism of the plantation tourism and wedding industries, the systemic anti-Blackness of the prison-industrial complex, and the dismantling of affirmative action and diversity, equity, and inclusion initiatives in higher education. If space is indeed alterable and socially produced, then what tools and strategies do we need to dismantle the plantation's stronghold once and for all? Recovering the history of Black people's efforts to reclaim agriculture and repurpose the plantation toward new and more liberatory ends is a fitting place to begin.

Many of the figures explored here understood agriculture as essential to Black progress and survival locally, nationally, and internationally. Agriculture was not backward but rather a mode of subsistence and nourishment, political-economic development, self-determination, and, ultimately, freedom. What lessons do their agricultural knowledges hold for our current ecological crisis, plagued by food deserts, water insecurity, rising sea levels, disappearing shorelines in coastal and island communities, and other environmental injustices that plantation capitalism set in motion? How can we mine these historical models of plotting agrarian futures for otherwise ways of caring for Black people and other vulnerable populations in the face of state neglect? And, finally, what do repair and justice look like in the wake of such irreparable harm? The lessons and potential answers, I am convinced, are right there in the archives and soils of the Global Black South, if only we are willing to redraw the map and wrestle with the possibilities and contradictions that such a geographic and necessarily "southern" reorientation requires.

PLOT I

I

An Experiment in Black World Making

Cultivating Intellectuals of the Land in the Alabama Countryside

The founding of Tuskegee Normal and Industrial Institute illuminates the plantation as a palimpsest of racial, geographic, and ecological violence, where the removal of Native peoples was intertwined with the expansion of African slavery and abusive monocrop agriculture. Both the institute and the town where it was founded were erected on lands that once belonged to the Creek Nation and bear the name of the Creek chief Taskigi, who also led the Creek town of the same name. The white town of Tuskegee was established in 1833 by General Thomas S. Woodward, a white settler, as "a speculative endeavor a couple of miles north of 'Indian Tuskegee.'"[1] In the spring of 1836, "armed conflict" broke out between the Creeks, on the one hand, and white land speculators and settler colonialists, on the other, during the Second Creek War. The federal government intervened, and by early September the first wave of Creek removal began. In February 1837, "whites raided the remaining Creek communities, burning and plundering Creek landholdings. The Creeks fled the county and were escorted by the army to Mobile and from there" to Indian Territory in present-day Oklahoma.[2] Over the next three decades, the town of Tuskegee and surrounding Macon County were transformed into a plantation society. By 1850, more than 50 percent of Macon County's population of 26,898 people were enslaved (15,612), and "Alabama led the nation in cotton production."[3] In 1881, when Booker T. Washington purchased the former Bowen plantation to establish the Tuskegee Institute, the property had been a part of Creek territory less than half a century earlier, a sobering reminder of the inextricable link between the forced removal of and expropriation of lands from Indigenous peoples and the spread of the domestic slave trade and coerced migration of enslaved Black people from the Upper South to the Lower South.

The Tuskegee Institute was founded at the behest of Lewis Adams, a formerly enslaved tinsmith and community leader, and George W. Campbell, a former slave owner. Adams had helped to secure the Black vote in Macon County for W. F. Foster's state Senate reelection and in return requested a school for African Americans. Foster agreed, and once the legislation was passed, Campbell joined Adams on the school's board of commissioners and sent the request to Hampton Institute for a teacher to lead the new school. Booker T. Washington, a recent Hampton graduate, answered the call. Upon arriving in Tuskegee, Washington immediately set about scouting land to establish the school. He received a loan from James F. B. Marshall, the treasurer at Hampton, and purchased the hundred-acre property for $500 from Colonel William Banks Bowen, a Confederate veteran, white Republican, lawyer, and postmaster. The Bowen property had once been a cotton plantation but was abandoned after a portion of it was burned during the Civil War. Washington used the remaining outbuildings as classrooms, and it was upon these plantation ruins that he and his faculty constructed a modern campus as an experiment in Black world making in the New South.

Tuskegee is located in the hilly regions of Macon County, on the edge but not technically a part of the ten counties that make up Alabama's traditional Black Belt, where "the great plantations" were located.[4] The Black Belt, which spans from "eastern, south-central Alabama into northwestern Mississippi," became the locus of the South's cotton kingdom in the nineteenth century.[5] As Washington describes in *Up from Slavery*, "The term ['Black Belt'] was first used to designate a part of the country which was distinguished by" its "thick, dark, and naturally rich soil[, which] was, of course, the part of the South where the slaves were most profitable, and consequently they were taken there in the largest numbers." Following the Civil War, "the term . . . [was] used wholly in a political sense . . . to designate the counties where the black people outnumber the white."[6]

Despite its proximity to the Black Belt, Tuskegee was located in the "bottoms," writes the landscape architect Kenrick Ian Grandison. As a geological designation, *bottomland* typically refers to very fertile land located near a river. After slavery, as some African Americans became landowners, they usually could purchase only the poorest-quality land, so over time and particularly in African American vernacular *bottom* took on a socioeconomic meaning, signaling both the poor quality of the land and Black people's marginalization to the bottom of society.[7] In some instances, Washington and other founders of early Black educational institutions were strategic in selecting these "waste places"— where the soil was either inherently inferior or had been depleted and eroded by years of abusive cotton cultivation during slavery—precisely because they were undesirable to and had been abandoned by white people and were geographically distant from town. By the racial logics of the era, these waste places were perfectly suited for Black people, who were also regarded as the waste of plantation modernity. But for Washington and other Black leaders, waste places afforded some freedom from white surveillance.

When Marshall inquired about the quality of Tuskegee's land, Washington replied, "[It] is a hilly country and it is hard to find a level place in a tract." Despite its rough and infertile quality, however, Washington consistently emphasized in his communications with Marshall, "The land is deeded to the trustees not to be held as state property, hence the state has no control over the land."[8] Indeed, the possibility of Black autonomy was more crucial than good land quality. Washington also strategically referred to Tuskegee's campus as "the Farm" to signal at once the site's distance from slavery while retaining the metonymy between Black people and agricultural labor to prevent the ire of the surrounding white community in response to establishing an all-Black school in their midst.[9]

From Tuskegee's inception, agriculture was constitutive to its practice of autonomy and self-determination. Upon the purchase of the farm, one of Washington's first priorities was to begin clearing the land to produce a crop the following year. After "school hours" each day, he "call[ed] for volunteers to take their axes and go into the woods to assist in clearing up the grounds. The students were most anxious to give their service in this way, and very soon a large acreage was put into condition for cultivation."[10] This practice of communal agricultural labor was common throughout the Global Black South, variously referred to as "going through together" in the United States and as the *coumbite* in Haiti. In Jamaica, peasants often sang what Claude McKay calls "jamma songs" as they helped each other clear and plant their land.[11] Navigating the imperatives of the U.S. South's plantation economy alongside the alternatives offered by the plot, students and faculty cultivated both cotton for sale and fruits and vegetables for their own nourishment. In this way, Tuskegee became a self-sustaining community.

In 1896, Washington recruited George Washington Carver, then a recent graduate of the Iowa Agricultural College and Model Farm, to join Tuskegee's faculty. As director of the Department of Agriculture, Carver played a crucial role in Tuskegee's mission to teach students not only how to "read and write" but also how to "plant and harvest crops" and bring themselves "from degradation, poverty and waste to full manhood."[12] Born into slavery in 1865 near Diamond Grove, Missouri, Carver found himself "in a strange land and among a strange people" when he relocated to Tuskegee. He recalled finding "devastated forests, ruined estates, and a thoroughly discouraged people, many just eking out a miserable sort of existence from the furrowed and guttered hillsides in neglected valleys called farms." He quickly determined that "the first and prime essential was to build up the soil and demonstrate to the people that a good living can be made on the farm."[13]

Carver explicitly connected the uplift of southern farmers with ecological regeneration, insisting on "the mutual relationship of the animal, mineral and vegetable kingdoms, and how utterly impossible it is for one to exist in a highly organized state without the other." The "virgin fertility of our southern soils and the vast amount of cheap and unskilled labor that has been put on them, have been a curse rather than a blessing to agriculture," he lamented, exhausting the soil and destroying the forests. To address this ecological dilemma and realizing that most small farmers could not afford commercial fertilizers, he experimented with environmentally friendly fertilizers that farmers could easily find around them, such as "decayed leaves, dead animals, decayed night soil, [and] animal manures that have washed from hillsides."[14]

Carver's insistence on using animal and plant waste to regenerate waste places is a powerful metaphor for how Black people—deemed the waste of modernity—regenerated themselves by simultaneously regenerating the land around them. Although Carver's research program was vast, he also dedicated considerable energy to rebuilding Tuskegee's depleted lands after decades of degradation by abusive cotton cultivation and to disseminating the results to poor Black farmers so that they, too, could rebuild their poor-quality soil. By linking agricultural cultivation to the regeneration of Black life and being, Washington and Carver partook in an eco-ontological experiment of repurposing the plantation toward new and more life-sustaining ends. They thus intervened in a racial and ecocapitalist system of valuation wherein people, land, and crops were deemed fungible and thus mutually exchangeable. In contrast to the conflation of Black people with the soil, as represented in the designation "the Black Belt," Washington and Carver proposed the mutual regeneration of Black health and soil health.

In this chapter, I argue that the agricultural and ecological components of Tuskegee's uplift agenda are the hallmark of its contribution to Black modernity. Repurposing and regenerating the plantation marked an attempt to make meaning of the slave past for the postemancipation present and to transform southern African American farmers into intellectuals of the land who could apply modern agricultural science to the cultivation of their fields. Importantly, Washington and Carver's approach to plotting agrarian futures shared ideological affinities with other agrarian reform and education efforts in the New (U.S.)

South and the broader Global Black South. Though Tuskegee was singular in its success and influence, its promotion of agriculture reflected the zeitgeist of the era on both sides of the color line. Contextualizing Tuskegee in this way makes clear that it was neither backward nor provincial but expressly modern and scientific, practical and conservative, and arguably subversive at times.

Finally, this chapter argues that though care work for rural and often impoverished Black communities was a crucial component of Tuskegee's social mission, this component is often overlooked or downplayed in contemporary scholarship. Of course, scholars are right to critique faculty and students' paternalism toward rural Black people; however, Tuskegeeans' efforts to disseminate and democratize up-to-date agricultural knowledge and techniques to sustain and propagate Black life were rooted as much in the communal ethics of the plot as in the class and intra-racial paternalism of uplift. By grappling with the tensions between care and paternalism at the heart of the school's uplift agenda, this chapter establishes Tuskegee as both a model and a cautionary tale for Black studies: of how to imagine a path for Black liberation that enacts care for the most vulnerable while not reinscribing the deleterious racial-sexual hierarchies endemic to plantation modernity.

THE REPURPOSED PLANTATION: MAKING MEANING OF THE SLAVE PAST

In transforming the charred ruins of the Bowen plantation, Washington deployed "the repurposed plantation" as a material and rhetorical strategy of reterritorialization and aesthetic innovation and as an overall political and philosophical approach to negotiating the slave past. In his monograph *The Future of the American Negro* (1899), Washington articulated the significance of the antebellum plantation for Black modernity and futurity. Confronted with the immense challenge of transforming a mass of formerly enslaved people and their descendants into skilled workers within an increasingly volatile and precarious socioeconomic milieu, Washington reimagined the plantation past as a training ground for citizenship and "in a limited sense, an industrial school":

> On these plantations there were scores of young coloured men and women who were constantly being trained, not alone as common farmers, but as carpenters, blacksmiths, wheelwrights, plasterers, brick masons, engineers, bridge-builders, cooks, dressmakers, housekeepers, etc. I would be the last to apologise for the

curse of slavery; but I am simply stating facts. This training was crude and was given for selfish purposes, and did not answer the highest ends, because there was the absence of brain training in connection with that of the hand. Nevertheless, this business contact with the Southern white man, and the industrial training received on these plantations, put the Negro at the close of the war into possession of all the common and skilled labour in the South.[15]

Instead of condemning plantation slavery as the violently coercive and extractive institution it unquestionably was, Washington, a formerly enslaved person, curiously reimagined it as a quasi-industrial school and the originary scene of Black modernity. This analogy between slavery and industrial education, which appears most famously in *Up from Slavery*, has rightfully frustrated readers since its publication. Yet when contextualized within a postbellum slave-narrative tradition, Washington's sanitization of slavery seems less idiosyncratic. Whereas Frederick Douglass, Harriet Jacobs, and many other antebellum fugitive-slave narrators were unequivocal in their accounts of the "peculiar institution" as an inhumane system of oppression, postbellum slave narrators, the literary critic William Andrews contends, no longer had to denounce slavery because it "no longer carried the same social or moral import." "The large majority of postbellum ex-slave autobiographers," including Douglass in his postbellum autobiographies, viewed slavery "in an increasingly pragmatic perspective" and took "pride in having endured [it] without having lost their sense of worth or purpose and without having given in to the despair that the antebellum narrator pictures as the lot of so many who languished in slavery."[16] Similarly, rather than reprise slavery's brutalities, Washington sought to salvage the agricultural and vocational "training" received on antebellum plantations to resolve postemancipation problems of labor and freedom. As an exponent of Jeffersonian democracy and conscript of modernity, he believed that free labor and property ownership were the foundations of liberal individualism. Whereas slavery had reduced Black people to mere beasts of burden, appropriate training would transform the newly emancipated masses and their descendants into a propertied class of yeoman farmers, artisans, and small-business owners.[17]

In the original 1938 edition of *The Black Jacobins*, C. L. R. James described slavery with the same derision as antebellum slave narrators such as Frederick Douglass and Harriet Jacobs. However, in his appendix to the 1963 edition, published at the dawn of West Indian emancipation, James observes: "The large-scale agriculture of the sugar plantation . . . was a modern system" wherein enslaved Africans "live[d] together in a social relation" as a "proletariat." The sugarcane they reaped was transported to factories and then exported abroad for sale on the global market, and their food and clothing were imported, too; thus, the "Negroes . . . lived a life that was in its essence a modern life."[18] David Scott describes this shift in James's thought about plantation slavery thus: "It is not that slavery is no longer recognized as the system of coercion that it was. . . . Rather, James is concerned with the new conditions of life and work constituted by the slave plantation, its socializing as well as its individualizing disciplines."[19] To be clear, I am not excusing Washington's euphemistic account of slavery, but in reading it alongside James's accounts of the Haitian Revolution and its aftermath, it becomes evident that Washington's effort to exploit slavery's and the plantation's affordances was not anomalous and was part of a broader Global Black South strategy of making meaning of the slave past for the postemancipation and postcolonial present.

Through a strategy that is counterintuitive for contemporary readers, Washington imbued the plantation with the rudiments of Black progress and futurity. The repurposed plantation reflects Washington's efforts to adapt and redeploy the individualizing logics of liberal humanism—property ownership, global capitalist production and consumption, and free labor—toward the new ends of securing a measure of freedom, autonomy, and citizenship in the wake of emancipation. Throughout his writings, Washington celebrated Tuskegee as paradigmatic of this revisionary logic. By 1900, he would proudly tout that Tuskegee had flourished into "an industrial and educational village. Instead of the old, worn-out plantation that was there fifteen years ago, there is a modern farm of seven hundred acres cultivated by student labor."[20] By delineating Tuskegee's transformation in this way, Washington articulated a theory of Black modernity based on adapting and repurposing the material, industrial, and geographic legacies of the slave past; in doing so, he captured the paradox of the antebellum plantation as an institution that at once subjugated and generated Black modern life and culture.

For Washington, the repurposed plantation was a practical response to the racial retrenchment and backlash that followed the end of Reconstruction in 1877, when, he wrote, "the Negro had lost practically all political control in the South."[21] As he looked out across Macon County, he encountered a bleak sociopolitical landscape where Black people were primarily tenants on large plantations, and the few Black landowners occupied "thin," "light soil and cheap lands in the northern half of the county."[22] Virtually none of Macon County's African American residents owned land in the county's Black Belt region, which continued to belong to the plantation system, and in many ways the Black people who lived there did too. Washington and many of his contemporaries determined that "the race could no longer look to political agitation and the opportunity of holding office as a means of gaining a reputation or winning success." Though "the Negro in the South was surrounded by many difficulties," they reasoned, "there was practically no line drawn, and little discrimination in the world of commerce, banking, storekeeping, manufacturing, and skilled trades, and in agriculture; and in this lay his great opportunity."[23] Hence, Washington's decision to establish Tuskegee as an agricultural and industrial school and his promotion of economic self-help as the cornerstone of racial progress.

Given the acceleration of racial retrenchment in Macon County and the persistence of the plantation regime, Washington's turn away from politics was seemingly practical. As early as 1867, formerly enslaved people in Macon County exercised their enfranchisement rights by voting to ratify a new state constitution. By 1901, however, the constitutional convention disfranchised virtually all the state's Black voters. And though Tuskegee was eventually funded by northern industrialists, its success depended on placating local white leaders, some of whom had been slave owners. In this way, Tuskegee's leadership had to negotiate with white benefactors, north and south, who supported a certain brand of education for Black people while actively restricting their political enfranchisement and citizenship rights.

In response to these precarious conditions, Washington came to believe "the great body of the Negro population must live in the future as they have done in the past, by the cultivation of the soil" and the pursuit of "agriculture with intelligence and diligence."[24] With the aid of Tuskegee's faculty and staff, many of whom had ironically received classical educations, he cultivated a vision for Black agrarian futures that promoted land and home ownership, crop diversification, soil regeneration, subsistence farming, improved seed selection, and avoidance of the crop-lien system and cotton monoculture.

On one hand, Washington's repurposing was a decidedly conservative mode of reform, perhaps unsurprising given his conservative political outlook. However, the term *conservative* also shares etymological roots with *conserve* and is thus linked to the practice of conservation in environmentalism and sustainability. An eco-ontological analysis, then, allows us to see how repurposing and regenerating the land through improved agricultural practices represented a proto-conservationist tendency in Black culture. Encouraging Black farmers to circumvent the plantation system through landownership and self-sufficiency was a politics of survival through subversion that sought to secure for poor and often exploited Black people such essentials as good housing and healthy, nourishing food. Furthermore, Grandison observes that because Tuskegee's buildings and roads were constructed in "intimate response to the natural folds of the land," the construction of the campus may be the closest thing to "socially sustainable development" in the nineteenth century.[25] Though conservative, pragmatic, and utilitarian, Tuskegee's agrarian future reflected a genuine commitment to sustaining and propagating Black life through an ethic of care for the most vulnerable and the earth.

At the same time, it also reflected the "evolutionary racial theories" that undergirded uplift ideology, such as its civilizing mission and class biases.[26] What began as a poor, underresourced institution established by Adams and Washington became by the end of Washington's life one of the most well-resourced Black educational institutions in the country. By 1912, the school reportedly had an endowment of $1.4 million (approximately $45.3 million today), and as early as 1904 Washington's publishers, Doubleday, Page, "had given permission to eighteen translators" for *Up from Slavery*, helping to cement his status as an international celebrity and icon.[27] Despite Washington's and Tuskegee's humble beginnings, the school became a breeding ground for the Black middle class and a decidedly bourgeois institution.[28] Washington and his racial uplift philosophy were neither anticolonial nor anticapitalist nor even politically radical. Instead of critiquing capitalism, Washington sought to train Black people to participate in it more effectively, and he held a distinctly paternalistic attitude toward the Black masses. At best, he sought to endow poor, rural, working-class Black people with the knowledge and skills to be self-sufficient in the face of persistent exploitation. At worst, he attempted to train a Black managerial class to oversee the masses, promoting self-sufficiency as long as it accorded with his vision for the race and stopped short of their full self-determination. A true commitment to self-determination would have meant a far less hegemonic and moralist approach to racial uplift. Like Toussaint L'Ouverture, Washington's failure lay in his inability to fully excise the epistemological conceits of Western modernity as he attempted to make meaning of the slave past and to reenvision Black people's place within the racial order of things.

WASHINGTON AND HIS CIRCLE: CRITICISMS, ALTERNATIVES, AND OTHERWISE AGRARIAN FUTURES

In the U.S. South alone, there were numerous other initiatives for African Americans that, like Tuskegee, prioritized land acquisition, agriculture, and education, some of which were much more radical and revolutionary. The promise of "forty acres and a mule," efforts at cooperative farming, the establishment of all-Black towns, and populism are just some of the grassroots and electoral strategies that rural Black peoples pursued following emancipation.[29] In the broader Global Black South, Haitian freedwomen and men established the counter-plantation system, and formerly enslaved peoples in the British West Indies established free villages on former plantation estates.[30]

T. Thomas Fortune, one of the most prominent Black radical thinkers and civil rights activists of the late nineteenth century, espoused perhaps the most revolutionary counterpoint to Washington's agrarian future in the United States. Fortune, born into slavery in Marianna, Florida, in 1856, was a militant journalist and editor of Black periodicals such as the *New York Freeman*, *New York Age*, and the UNIA's *Negro World*. Finding racial violence and injustice intolerable in Florida, Fortune moved to New York City in 1881, the same year that Washington established Tuskegee. Though he no longer resided in the U.S. South, he remained steadfast in his interest in the region's fate, using his pen to denounce disenfranchisement and other juridical assaults on Black life and citizenship. In 1887, Fortune organized the Afro-American League, a political organization for "'Afro-American agitators' who would sound the 'death knell of the shuffling, cringing creature in black who for two centuries and a half had given the right of way to white men.'"[31]

Despite their opposing political ideologies, Fortune and Washington forged an unlikely and complicated friendship and "literary alliance" that spanned several decades.[32] Fortune was a staunch supporter of Tuskegee and worked as Washington's ghostwriter and "literary mentor" for many of his early twentieth-century publications, including *Up from Slavery*. As Elizabeth McHenry has brilliantly shown, Fortune was largely responsible for Washington's success as an author. He overlooked his political differences with Washington because he regarded him as "a fellow Southerner of his own generation who, to some extent, shared his experience, and whose leadership was in keeping with his own vision of the practical questions at stake in the future of the Black South." In Fortune's estimation, the northern Black educated elite were too removed from the experiences of Black southerners. The race needed what he called a "single figure head" to fill the void left by Frederick Douglass's death, and Fortune determined that "the leader ought to originate from and be situated 'in the South.'" In his work with Washington, Fortune depicted the Black U.S. South "as a place associated with the richness of black thought and wisdom rather than characterized by violence, inferiority, poverty, or lack of opportunity," and he envisioned Tuskegee as a literary and geographic center for African American writing.[33] Over time, however, what began as a friendship between equals devolved as Washington's star rose and Fortune succumbed to alcoholism and accrued debts. Moreover, the two men had a "bitter argument" in the spring of

1904 when Fortune divulged information about Washington's "secret challenges to the Alabama constitution['s]" disenfranchisement of Black voters. Fortune also wrote an editorial rightly castigating Washington for referring to African Americans as a "child race," though it is unclear if the editorial was ever published.[34]

Fortune's most radical reimaginings of Black agrarian futures in the South are found in his writings from the 1880s (before his partnership with Washington), where he proposed that the lands of the South should belong to those who worked it. In his important though understudied volume *Black and White: Land, Labor, and Politics in the South*, published in 1884, just three years after Tuskegee's founding, Fortune called for interracial coalition building among Black and white workers in the South and the end of monopoly ownership of land. He criticized the country's failure to redistribute land fairly after the Civil War, leaving "the unrepentant rebel a far more valuable species of property": "The United States took the slave and left the thing which gave birth to *chattel slavery* and which is now fast giving birth to *industrial slavery*" through individual and monopoly ownership of land.[35]

Fortune regarded land monopoly in all forms, whether by individuals, corporations, or syndicates, as a "transgression of the common right of man" that ran "contrary to the intentions of Providence."[36] It was the chief source of inequality, he argued in *Black and White*, "desolat[ing] fertile acres turned over to vast ranches and into bonanza farms of a thousand acres, where not one family finds a habitation, where muscle and brain are supplanted by machinery, and the small farmer is swallowed up and turned into a tenant or slave." Land, like air and water, was the "common right" and "common property of the people," Fortune insisted, and should be "regarded *only* as *property* as *long as it was cultivated.*" Everyone should have "an opportunity to cultivate as much land as they could wherever they found any not already under cultivation by some one else."[37]

The agrarian future Fortune initially envisioned was far more radical than the one Washington proposed, which ultimately aimed to use agricultural and industrial education to help Black people better navigate the vicissitudes of racial-capitalist exploitation. Fortune's proto-socialist vision of land and labor politics aimed to uproot the system entirely. Yet he also understood that such "views are contrary to the established order of things." Therefore, since land ownership was the basis of wealth accumulation, and wealth in turn "defines man's position in the social scale," he encouraged readers "to adjust ourselves to the order of things which governs us if we do not govern them" and "to let every colored man get as much land as he can and let him keep as much of it as he can."[38] In this way, his vision of agrarian reform ultimately converged with

Washington's, understanding autonomy through property ownership as the most practical solution to fighting Black labor exploitation.

In Tuskegee's early years, numerous other prominent Black intellectual and political leaders supported Washington and the idea of industrial education for the Black masses, including Frederick Douglass, Anna Julia Cooper, and Mary McLeod Bethune. Cooper and Fortune, in particular, espoused views that prefigured many of Washington's justifications for industrial education and in terms that have almost exclusively become associated with the Tuskegee leader. A fellow southerner from Raleigh, North Carolina, Anna Julia Cooper was a prominent educator, activist, and club woman. In *A Voice from the South, by a Black Woman of the South* (1892), a collection of essays that placed southern Black women at the center of the "Negro problem," Cooper proposed a land-resettlement scheme similar to the repurposed plantation. She wrote, "Let some colored capitalists buy up a few of those immense estates in the South, divide them into single farms with neat, cheery, well-ventilated, healthsome cottages" for poor Black tenants "toiling . . . in the one-room log hut, like their own cheerless mules." Cooper also commended Washington's work at Tuskegee and engaged in a similar rhetorical revision of slavery into an industrial school. During enslavement, she argued, "we had master mechanics" with "ingenuity of brain and hand," but the post-slavery moment saw "skilled labor" going to white foreigners, an observation Washington also made three years later in the Atlanta Exposition Address of 1895. Though Cooper understood why freedwomen and men pursued classical education to evince racial "manhood," she also believed that "labor must be the solid foundation stone" for Black progress and that industrial education was the best means to accomplish it: "The youth must be taught to use his trigonometry in surveying his own and his neighbor's farm," Cooper contended, and "to employ his geology and chemistry in finding out the nature of the soil."[39] Likewise, Fortune argued that although he did "not inveigh against higher education . . . the sort of education that colored people of the South stand most in need of is *elementary and industrial*." His reasoning, like Cooper's and Washington's, was practical: "To educate him [the Negro] for a lawyer when there are no clients, for medicine when the patients, although numerous, are too poor to give him a living income, to fill his head with Latin and Greek as a teacher when the people he is to teach are to be instructed in the ABC's—such education is a waste of time and a senseless expenditure of money."[40]

Though many Black women educators also supported industrial education—such as Mary McLeod Bethune with her establishment of the Daytona Normal and Industrial School for Negro Girls in Florida in 1904—their views on race, education, labor, and especially gender were not necessarily Washingtonian, nor were they reducible to the Tuskegee model. As the historian Brittney C. Cooper reminds us, women such as Fannie Barrier Williams and Mary Church Terrell disrupt the "overdrawn Washington–Du Bois binary" and invite us to reckon with the shortcomings of such masculinist master narratives in the first place. Though Williams was an "ardent Bookerite," Cooper maintains, she was also "a strong defender of training Black women in communities to be intellectuals and social theorists[,] . . . a critical dissention from" Washington's views on educating Black women and girls.[41] Although Anna Julia Cooper supported Washington and industrial education, her own work as an educator prioritized classical education at the M Street School in Washington, DC, which sent students to some of the top universities in the country. Both Bethune and Nannie Helen Burroughs, who founded the National Training School for Women and Girls in 1909, established curricula that trained Black girls in both industrial and classical instruction alike.[42] Like the Afro-Caribbean artists and intellectuals whom I take up in plots II and III, this generation of Black women educators exploited the affordances of industrial education and grew to embrace more liberal educational and social reform over time.

Of course, there was also ample outright disagreement with Washington and Tuskegee. Though W. E. B. Du Bois initially praised the Atlanta Exposition Address as "a word fitly spoken," his subsequent takedown of Washington in *The Souls of Black Folk* in 1903 has become the most renowned critique of Washington's accommodationist political philosophy. "Mr. Washington represents in Negro thought the old attitude of adjustment and submission" to racial oppression, Du Bois asserted. His "programme naturally takes an economic cast, becoming a gospel of Work and Money to such an extent as apparently almost completely to overshadow the higher aims of life . . . and practically accepts the alleged inferiority of the Negro races."[43] Much later, in a letter marked "personal and confidential," Washington retorted that Du Bois was "puffed up with insane vanity and jealousy . . . depriv[ing] him . . . of common sense. He misrepresents my position on most occasions. He knows perfectly well I am not seeking to confine the Negro race to industrial education nor make them hewers of wood and drawers of water."[44] Among the African American educated elite, other dissenters included William Monroe Trotter, who was arrested for inciting a riot in protest of Washington at a convention in Boston, and Ida B. Wells-Barnett, the renowned journalist and antilynching activist, who vehemently rejected Washington's educational philosophy and retreat from politics. A southern New Negro woman and journalist who was also born into slavery, Wells-Barnett was unsparing in her castigation of Washington. She was especially critical of the consequences of Tuskegee's hegemony over Black education, which had led many philanthropists to support only Tuskegee and other industrial schools, while leaving Black higher-education institutions "struggl[ing] to maintain existence." When the New Orleans Board of Education "cut the curriculum" for Black children "down to the fifth grade," its members cited Washington's educational philosophy as their inspiration, Wells-Barnett argued. Though Washington disavowed the board's decision, Wells-Barnett contended that his absolutist rhetoric was to blame. While she did not object to industrial education wholesale, she insisted that "industrial education will not stand him [the Negro] in place of political, civil, and intellectual liberty." "If Mr. Washington can not use his great abilities and influence to speak in defense of and demand for the rights withheld when discussing the Negro question, for fear of injury to his school by those who are intolerant of Negro manhood," Wells-Barnett emphatically concluded, "then he should be just as unwilling to injure his race for the benefit of his school."[45]

Equally if not more important than dissent coming from the Black (southern) intellectual elite, however, was how the masses of rural Black people, the subjects of Washington's uplift agenda, perceived him and his work at Tuskegee. During his lifetime, Washington was an international celebrity, and many working-class Black people regarded him as such. His public appearances drew thousands of people, and his image even adorned the walls of Black people's homes, but his views were not uncritically embraced. Upon seeing Washington speak in Mound Bayou, Mississippi, an all-Black town founded on Jefferson Davis's former plantation, Chalmers Archer Jr., a tenant farmer turned landowner in Holmes County, Mississippi, recalled: "I agreed with most of what Booker T. had to say that day, but disagreed with his philosophy of casting down one's bucket wherever one was," he reflected. "This smacked of the white man's idea that Black people should be satisfied with what they had, rather than make any attempt to better themselves. Booker T. Washington had long been known to hobnob with influential whites, even, it is said, to ride in the whites only section of the segregated trains, but thought other Blacks should not. Thus, statements like 'cast down your bucket where you are' were not favorably received by many. However, his school was first-rate and he was impressive overall."[46]

Washington and Tuskegee had an uneven reputation within Alabama's Macon County. The sociologist Charles Johnson observed in his study of Black plantation laborers in Macon County in the 1930s that "Washington was remembered and liked by some of the older individuals . . . [as] a great man with a personality which took them in, which understood them, and which they could understand."[47] Mrs. Mary Simpson, who owned 160 acres of land and earned a Merit Farmer's Certificate from the Tuskegee Negro Farmers'

Conference, recalled that she "always" tried to follow Washington's advice: "I would never take up all my credit at the store. I would take eggs, chickens and other things to town to sell for what I needed in exchange. . . . I plant cover crops. All my hilly lands are terraced and my tenant houses are sealed. I have two tenants, one on each place."[48] However, Johnson also detected a "cultural and social distance" between Tuskegee and Macon County's Black residents. One resident accused Tuskegee of colorism and class bias, noting, "That school ain't got no race pride."[49] Ned Cobb, a Black tenant farmer who grew up going "to them big . . . commencement days at Tuskegee," where he saw and heard Washington speak, acknowledged that Washington was "a big man" who had "authority," "courage," and "influence," but Cobb also thought that Washington "didn't feel for and didn't respect his race of people enough to go to rock bottom with em. He leaned too much to the white people that controlled the money—lookin out for what was his worth" and "pullin" for himself. The "veil was over the nigger's eyes," Cobb concluded, but Washington "didn't try to pull that veil away like he shoulda done."[50]

Such criticisms are an important reminder that Washington was not uncritically embraced by the rural, working-class Black people for whom he advocated, and the Tuskegee model was not the only option available to them. In the years leading up to and immediately following Washington's ascension to race leadership, African Americans in the rural U.S. South deployed a dynamic range of strategies to resist the setbacks caused by white southerners' calls for Redemption and the acceleration of anti-Black violence. These efforts, some of which accorded with Washington's rhetoric but some of which did not, included labor organizing, boycotts, and strikes; the establishment of mutual-aid societies and political organizations to advocate for better working conditions and to contest rampant disfranchisement; biracial coalition building with white populists (despite the populist movement's fastidious commitment to racial segregation and Black disfranchisement); property acquisition and the establishment of all-Black towns; migration to the urban South, North, and West, prefiguring the Great Migration of the twentieth century; and even immigration to Liberia. Far from a lumpen proletariat or the simplistic caricatures Washington sometimes used to illustrate his speeches and writings, waiting to be uplifted and molded by Tuskegee's faculty and student emissaries, rural Black people in the U.S. South were active in creating a dynamic political and associational life that was committed to attaining the promises of freedom and citizenship.

As the gains of Reconstruction were routinely, systematically, and violently stripped away, southern African Americans faced increased political and legal repression and racial violence, including vagrancy laws, land dispossession, debt peonage, the convict-lease system, disenfranchisement, and lynching. "By the mid-1880s across the rural South," writes the historian Steven Hahn, "landlords had gained first lien on the growing crop for rent and advances, creditors were demanding that debtors waive protection against property seizures, hunting and foraging rights had been dramatically curtailed, and sharecroppers had been relegated to the status of wage laborers, with no claims to the crops that they had cultivated."[51] Yet even as the door to Black electoral politics closed, southern African Americans sought alternative avenues to political mobilization, persistent in their pursuit of better living and working conditions, fair pay, free labor, and, ultimately, self-determination.

During the 1880s and 1890s across the U.S. South, Black agricultural workers established and joined the ranks of mutual-aid societies and political organizations such as the Colored Farmers' Alliance (CFA), the Colored State Agricultural Wheel, the Knights of Labor, and the Cooperative Workers of America. Many of these organizations included both men and women in their ranks and took on issues such as wages, rents, work conditions, and even "matters of social welfare, politics, and civil rights." In South Carolina, for instance, members of a Cooperative Workers of America lodge met clandestinely to discuss establishing a cooperative store, and in Louisiana a "Knights' local of nearly four hundred members leased a plantation to work as a cooperative."[52] Robert Lloyd Smith, who founded the Farmers' Improvement Society in Texas in 1890, shared a commitment to racial uplift along the lines of the CFA and Tuskegee, "advocat[ing] a 'politicized agenda,' specifically, to abolish the credit system. By raising foodstuffs at home and purchasing cooperatively, Smith believed black farmers could circumvent the Texas lien law."[53]

By 1890, the CFA, which originated in Texas in 1886, had a foothold in every southern state and claimed to have a membership of around one million Black farmers, including three hundred thousand women (though this number is likely inflated).[54] It began "as a strictly 'non-partisan' mutual benefit association focused inwardly on economic cooperation and education," and many of its stated objectives mirrored the principles and aims of Tuskegee: finding homes for Black families, pursuing agricultural education for Black children, becoming "better farmers and laborers," being "less wasteful in their methods of living," being "more obedient to the civil law," and "withdraw[ing] . . . from political partisanship."[55] The CFA would eventually abandon its antipolitics position and "develop into one of the most radical organizations of the era . . . [by] launch[ing] boycotts and strikes and then help[ing] to found the People's Party to directly challenge Democratic authority."[56] At the annual convention in

Ocala, Florida, in 1890, the CFA superintendent R. M. Humphrey decried monopoly ownership of land in terms that recall Fortune's arguments in *Black and White*: "Land is not property ... [and] holds no allegiance but to the man who lives on it. ... The land belongs to the sovereign people."[57]

What should be abundantly clear by now is that there was a broad ecosystem of farmers, educators, and reformers engaged in plotting agrarian futures. Although many rural Black people saw the wisdom and practicality of agricultural and industrial education, it was not the only or most viable strategy available to them. Moreover, many of the ideas that have become associated with Washington and Tuskegee, such as economic self-help through education, thrift, and agriculture, were not his alone but were part of the zeitgeist of the era. Tuskegee achieved such prominence because of Washington's unique ability to fundraise among white northern industrialists, who viewed African American education as a way of training more efficient workers for the ongoing project of racial-capitalist exploitation, and because of his willingness to accept social segregation and disavow political agitation—at least publicly—in exchange for educational and economic advancement. Washington's program was practical, but many of his contemporaries, from the educated elite to tenant farmers, were rightfully concerned that he conceded too much ground politically and that his promotion of industrial education foreclosed Black people's access to other modes of education and political futures.

TUSKEGEE'S AGRARIAN FUTURE: THE EXPERIMENT PLOT AND AGRICULTURAL EXTENSION PROGRAM

Scholars, then and now, have tended to describe Tuskegee's curriculum as fundamentally backward, but this was not the case, especially its agricultural curriculum, which was the cornerstone of its vision of Black modernity. This attitude toward Tuskegee is likely a response to Washington's accommodationist political philosophy and, I would argue, biases against rurality, agriculture, and the South among scholars and laypersons alike. Tuskegee's approach to improving Black rural life through scientific agriculture was, in fact, consistent with the aims of the broader rural reform movement of the late nineteenth century. As the historian Charles Postel has shown, rural reform through "science-based education" was a part of the zeitgeist of the late nineteenth century for Black and white Americans alike. Farm reformers, "like many other Gilded Age Americans, ... subscribed to the notion of progress through education," a commitment they shared "with urban reformers as well as with prosperous and politically conservative farmers." "Between 1860 and 1890 the number of farms in the United States nearly tripled," Postel maintains, and "land under the plow rose from 407 million to 828 million acres." Widespread federal support for agricultural and mechanical education through the first and second Morrill Acts of 1862 and 1890, respectively—which set aside federal lands for establishing land-grant colleges—suggests that farming was considered a viable and desirable profession and that making rural life more efficient and attractive was an important objective throughout the country on both sides of the color line. Rural reformers such as the all-white Farmers' Alliance and its Black counterpart, the CFA, promoted and embraced business acumen, scientific and technological innovation, and especially education "as a means to renovate, improve, and modernize rural life," states Postel, their objectives consistent with "New South and other mainly urban and elite constituencies of reform."[58]

In reevaluating Tuskegee's contributions to Black modernity, it is crucial to consider the institute on its own terms and, given the centrality of agriculture, to make a closer inspection of the dynamic and robust set of strategies school leaders innovated to improve Black rural life. In a Sunday Evening Talk in the Tuskegee campus chapel in 1903, Washington detailed his agrarian philosophy before the student body. Most successful people and races first "planted themselves in the soil in agriculture," he maintained. Even if they eventually pursued other forms of business and industry, agriculture was their "foundation." In the South, students had the "advantages" of "cheap land" that, within "fifty or one hundred years," would appreciate by "twenty or thirty times." The "pure air" of the farm and "pure water" of its springs would fortify students' "bodily strength" and develop their minds, he argued. Whereas the factory worker "becomes a part of the factory, a machine," "one cannot live upon the farm without thinking, without planning." Farming is a necessarily intellectual enterprise, Washington insisted, and Tuskegee students must therefore become intellectuals of the land.

Aware that many students were likely disinterested in farm life and skeptical of his message, Washington assured them that he did not wish to "limit" their "ambitions" or "aspirations"; rather, he wanted them to become "producers" and not only "consumers" and thus be "counted among the useful peoples of the earth." He concluded his address with a dramatic appeal for students' adoption of his agrarian philosophy for their sakes and for the sake of the race: "I beseech you, young men, young women, to become the owners of a farm, of at least a portion of land, and lay the foundation for future success. . . . Go to school, get any kind of education that any other people have secured but have something back of you. People in poverty, living upon other people's land and in other people's houses are not in very good position" to make demands.[59] Ultimately, Washington articulated an agrarian philosophy that promoted land ownership and farming as the keys to better health, future wealth, and autonomy.

In addition to the institute's formal agricultural curriculum, which is explored further in chapter 2, Tuskegee built an elaborate infrastructure for supporting Black farmers in the countryside that was both ecologically sustainable and financially affordable. On February 23, 1892, Washington convened the first Tuskegee Negro Conference, drawing nearly four hundred women and men, mostly farmers and mechanics but also a few teachers and ministers, to campus to share best practices and teach the newest trends in agricultural science.[60] Attendance doubled at the conference in 1893, with representatives from "almost every section of Alabama and the South," and by 1898 attendance grew to more than two thousand people.[61] Through George Washington Carver's connection to U.S. secretary of agriculture James Wilson, his mentor and former teacher, the institute procured and disseminated garden seeds to attendees who otherwise could not afford them. The seeds were provided free of charge to encourage farmers to grow their own food and diversify their crops. For women attendees, the school provided flower seeds "for beautifying their home surroundings," reflecting how Tuskegeeans conceived of the aesthetics of eco-ontological regeneration as a specifically gendered enterprise.[62] Carver also prepared and disseminated the Farmer's Calendar, "which gave the months in which the various standard vegetables should be planted and what crops should be used in rotation." [63] Conference attendees adopted a "declaration of principles" that included a commitment "to abolish and do away with the mortgage system," "to raise our food supplies . . . at home rather than to go in debt for them at the store," and "to urge upon all Negroes the necessity of owning homes and farms, and . . . to beautify and improve them."[64] These values and principles could have been taken directly from the CFA's stated objectives and reflected the bourgeois respectability politics that the uplift movement shared with white Progressive Era reformers. The school also prepared a guide for establishing local farmers' conferences, further disseminating Tuskegee's model of rural Black associational life throughout the South.

In 1897, the State of Alabama passed legislation allocating $1,500 to establish an Agricultural Experiment Station on campus. The station, also known as the "experiment plot," was managed by George Washington Carver. Washington insisted that the Experiment Station "should not be used for scientific experiments of interest only to experts, but should deal with the fundamental problems with which the Negro farmers of Alabama were daily confronted."[65] The results of Carver's experiments were thus published in bulletins that were then distributed among farmers throughout Alabama and the broader U.S. South. In 1904, the school initiated the six-week "Short Course in Agriculture" for farmers who resided nearby. The course was eventually reduced to two weeks, and, though it was tuition free, the school offered attendees wage work to help "offset the travel and food expenses farmers necessarily incurred by being away from their farms."[66] In these ways, Tuskegee's leadership seemed particularly sensitive to the socioeconomic challenges confronting poor farmers and used institutional resources to counter or at least reduce them, indicating its commitment to a plot logic and ethic of care. Following the success of the first short course, a writer in the *Tuskegee Student* observed, "Tuskegee Institute is primarily a school for the masses of our people . . . both old and young and in all degrees of development."[67]

In addition to bringing farmers to campus, Tuskegee's faculty and students took modern agricultural education into the countryside through its extension program. In 1901, Carver helped to establish the Bureau for Nature Study and Hints and Suggestions to Farmers, "mark[ing] the first attempt to institutionalize extension work within the institute's agricultural department. Carver also asked northern philanthropists to donate 'small traveling libraries,' especially 'books on nature study and agriculture.' "[68] Shortly after arriving at Tuskegee, Carver and a student took a wagon and mule equipped with "a few tools, seed packets . . . and boxed demonstration plants" and went into the country districts to show farmers how to can fruits, make butter, and other skills.[69] Shortly thereafter, Washington acquired funding for the design and construction of a more elaborate vehicle, and in May 1906 George Bridgeforth, Carver's assistant, operated the Jesup Agricultural Wagon for the first time. The Jesup Wagon "was a peripatetic farmers' school" that "took a concentrated essence of Tuskegee's agricultural department to the farmers who could not or would not come to Tuskegee."[70] It was "outfitted with a large number of seeds, fertilizers and tools sufficient to carry out practical demonstrations with the farmers and homemakers."[71] It eventually included a demonstration plot as well, another iteration of the slave garden plot and its attendant ethics of sustaining and propagating Black life within and against the plantation regime.

Thomas M. Campbell, a graduate of Tuskegee's Agricultural Department, was hired to run the Jesup Wagon and was eventually employed by the U.S. Department of Agriculture, becoming the first Black cooperative-extension agent in the country.[72] For Campbell, the goal of the Jesup Wagon was to "place before the people concrete illustrations, and to prove to the farmer that he can do better work, make more produce on a smaller number of acres of land and

[with] less expense," especially through "deep cultivation and thorough preparation of the soil."[73] Washington "described it as 'A Farmer's College on Wheels which educated the farmer in the field, while the Institute is teaching his children—a kindergarten method of making thrifty land owners out of hand-to-mouth Negro tenants.' "[74] In 1908, the institute also hosted four-day summer schools throughout Macon County for farmers who could not travel to campus for the short course and officially established an Extension Department in 1910.[75]

Through its Printing Office, Tuskegee routinely disseminated knowledge among Black farmers, essentially cultivating a rural reading public. The Extension Department distributed printed bulletins, circulars, farmers leaflets, and pamphlets issued by the school's numerous departments, especially Carver's Experiment Station. Between 1898 and 1943, Carver and the Experiment Station staff issued forty-four bulletins that were distributed freely to "individuals, schools, and local farmers' conferences." Given poor farmers' uneven literacies, the bulletins were intentionally "elementary and simple in character." From 1905 to 1913, the Extension Department also published the *Messenger*, a newspaper for Alabama farmers, and from 1914 to 1918 the school established the *Negro Farmer* (later the *Negro Farmer and Messenger*) "in the 'interest of Negro landowners, tenant farmers and those who employ Negro labor.'" It was edited by Isaac Fisher, a dynamic Tuskegee graduate who went on to produce an early Black film titled *When True Love Wins* in 1915. The *Negro Farmer* was essentially "a Dictionary of agricultural knowledge as well as a practical guide to farming" and claimed a circulation of two million Black farmers. It included a regular column entitled "The 'Big Words' and Events Explained: Farmers' Dictionary," which defined technical terms such as *compost, mulch, germinate*, and *insecticides* and explained world events.[76] The paper also included photographs and poetry by writers such as Alice M. Dunbar-Nelson that celebrated rural, agricultural life. In "To the Negro Farmers of the United States," which graced the cover of the April 11, 1914, issue, Dunbar-Nelson extolled Black farmers as God's "favored ones, who's [*sic*] backs bend o'er the soil" performing "a service sweet" to "foil / The bare-fanged wolves of hunger in the moil / Of Life's activities." In an editorial note, Dunbar-Nelson maintained, "The poet must sing to and for the toiler. Too long poesy and labor have been divorced. They must re-wed . . . [to] send and carry some helpful messages of beauty from the temples of poetry, literature, painting, sculpture, music, and science to those who work with their hands."[77] Dunbar-Nelson's depiction of farmers reflects her class paternalism and condescension, but its inclusion in the *Negro Farmer* shows how Tuskegeans viewed beauty, art, and literature as entirely compatible with plotting Black agrarian futures, as discussed in chapter 2. Such publications also illuminate how Black southern farmers, largely believed to be illiterate, actively participated in a reading public not unlike that of more well-known Black periodicals such as the NAACP's *Crisis* magazine. For instance, Chalmers Archer Jr., the Mississippi tenant farmer who criticized Washington's directive to "cast down your bucket," "por[ed] over such publications as the *Farm Journal* and the *Progressive Farmer*" as well as "government publications" and followed Carver's work "closely, faithfully employing whatever procedures Dr. Carver suggested."[78]

Tuskegee's extension program eventually included as many as forty different activities, such as boys' and girls' clubs, mothers' clubs, conferences, fairs, various demonstrations, and agricultural parades with food, decorated floats, and prizes.[79] Beginning in 1909, Washington encouraged families and especially women in the Tuskegee community to grow chrysanthemums to beautify their otherwise barren back and front yards. Thereafter, Tuskegee hosted the Annual Chrysanthemum Show each fall, where families could exhibit their flowers, and the school's bandmaster furnished an orchestra for the event. The school established a committee to award prizes for the best potted and cut chrysanthemums and distributed a pamphlet entitled *The History and Culture of the Chrysanthemum*.[80] Such gatherings reflect how Tuskegee's extension program helped facilitate leisure, pleasure, beauty, and fun despite the socioeconomic realities of living under Jim Crow. By 1923, such initiatives as the Moveable School included not only farming equipment but also "a moving picture projector," "kodaks," and "playground apparatus for recreational games."[81] Given that many rural people experienced an "empty and depressing loneliness," observed Thomas Campbell, this new and improved Moveable School was outfitted with "athletic equipment" "to teach this isolated people organized play," such as "volley ball, dodge ball, tug-o-war, . . . foot races, potato races, jumping, hurdling, and many other simple games."[82]

Critically, the school also attempted to relieve farmers' financial burdens. The Tuskegee Savings Department provided "black-controlled banking services" to help local farmers circumnavigate predatory loan activities, "purchased their garden vegetables, loaned stud animals to help improve their livestock, and even purchased land with the intent of selling it cheaply to black farmers."[83] In 1914, the school purchased a tract of land to establish Baldwin Farms, an experimental "colony," for graduates of the Agricultural Department. As in Anna Julia Cooper's land-reform scheme, the goal was to help graduates purchase property, acquire homes, and establish a farm "clear of debt" where they could apply the methods they learned at the school firsthand.[84] By helping graduates establish their own farms, the school prevented them from wasting "years of monotonous drudgery as a mere farm or plantation labourer" and thus becoming ensnared in the predatory sharecropping and tenant-farming systems.[85]

Tuskegee's agricultural initiatives were numerous and dynamic, and though they were suffused by uplift ideology, they were also guided by the logics of the plot. Indeed, agriculture was the domain of some of the school's most important innovations and interventions in sustaining and propagating Black life, especially through Carver's research on the experiment plot and the myriad efforts to disseminate up-to-date knowledge and techniques to rural farmers through its various extension initiatives. With these efforts, Tuskegee promoted Black self-sufficiency as a way of circumventing the plantation economy's ongoing exploitation. The school was not backward but rather decidedly rural, modern, and arguably subversive in its attempt to undermine plantation subjection. It promoted an ethical and, as we will see, ecologically sustainable vision for enhancing Black life in the heart of the rural Jim Crow South.

REGENERATING "WORN-OUT" SOILS ON THE AGRICULTURAL EXPERIMENT PLOT

George Washington Carver's research on the school's experiment plot and the knowledge derived from it were the cornerstone of Tuskegee's repurposing of the plantation through eco-ontological regeneration. As a graduate of the Iowa Agricultural College, Carver would have been trained in the most up-to-date agricultural techniques and methods. For Carver, agriculture was neither backward nor simplistic. He maintained that it "is all too erroneous and false to say or think that it requires little or no intelligence to be a farmer. On the contrary it requires the highest intelligence."[86] Accordingly, he sought to aid Black farmers in becoming intellectuals of the land. Tuskegee's experiment plot was Carver's laboratory for studying soil regeneration and sustainable and affordable cultivation methods for poor Black farmers striving to eke out a living on Macon County's worn-out soils. To that end, he designated a section of the Marshall Farm, located on Tuskegee's campus, for agricultural experiments, noting, "The soil selected is excellently adapted for experimental purposes, having formed part of an old field which has been planted by the wasteful methods of the tenant system, year after year, for a long period."[87] If Washington saw that tenant farming kept Black southerners subjected to the labor and economic exploitation of the postslavery plantation system, Carver also saw that it continued the vicious cycle of soil exhaustion.

Washington and Carver collectively set out to regenerate Black life by regenerating the soil, but despite the compatibility of their agrarian philosophies, their relationship was often strained. Carver expressed frustration with Washington's micromanaging of the Agricultural Department and the lack of resources to do his own work effectively. He routinely complained of the difficulties of balancing his teaching, research, and administrative responsibilities to the department, the campus farm, and the experiment plot. From Washington's vantage, Carver was a "fine instructor" and lecturer with a "strong forte" in "inspiring and instructing young men" in classes, and he possessed a "very unusual ability in the direction of original research"; however, when Carver attempted to "put his teaching into practice on the farm," Washington maintained, "there he is weak."[88] In 1904, Carver even entertained an offer to leave Tuskegee to teach agriculture in Puerto Rico.[89] One wonders if Carver would have been more successful on the farm if he were not so overburdened by campus responsibilities. Despite their personal differences, Carver's regeneration of Tuskegee's degraded land was the terrestrial and ecological arm of Washington's broader repurposed plantation philosophy, and together they developed an eco-ontological strategy for improving Black rural life and being.

As director of the Agricultural Department, Carver aimed to demonstrate to local farmers "that with [the] right methods their acres can be made to yield unfailing profit, and that they can win in the fight against the deadly mortgage system," as Washington put it.[90] From the experiment plot, Carver developed an agricultural philosophy that reflected a profound belief in the interdependence of Black health and soil health through economically and ecologically sustainable cultivation methods. "Wherever the soil is wasted the people are wasted," he maintained. "A poor soil produces only a poor people—poor economically, poor spiritually and intellectually, poor physically."[91] Like his African ancestors, he sought God in the natural world and frequently used scripture in his lectures. The earth was sacred, as were the people who stewarded it.

During slavery, provision gardens were geographies of "crop experimentation, seed exchanges, and dietary practices," where enslaved peoples maintained "African foodways" in the New World, notes the environmental historian Judith Carney.[92] Accordingly, Carver used Tuskegee's experiment plot to instruct Black farmers on how to prepare the ground, select the best seeds, grow nutritious and affordable foods, and rotate crops to restore nutrition to the soil. Carver's agricultural experimentation situates him squarely within the genealogy of African Americans who practiced what the literary scholar Britt Rusert calls "fugitive science," a coinage that captures the myriad ways African Americans in the nineteenth and early twentieth centuries used empiricism, science, and technology to refute the anti-Black protocols of racial science and to insist on Black freedom. In reading Carver within this legacy, however, I depart from Rusert's view of Tuskegee as an "experimental plantation" complicit with the infamous Tuskegee Syphilis Experiments. Given "racial uplift's relationship to eugenics and reproductive surveillance," Rusert is right to caution "us against understanding African American engagements with science as wholly emancipatory, or as something unfreighted by the complications posed by class and gender."[93] However, although Carver's bulletins were sometimes shot through with the moralizing rhetoric of uplift, his research on the experiment plot was undoubtedly rooted in fugitivity, fusing scientific experimentation with ethical stewardship of the earth, notions of beauty and pleasure, and the nourishment and regeneration of otherwise exploited Black people.

Tuskegee imparted the value of agricultural experimentation and study to both its students and the Black farmers who participated in its various extension services. The *Negro Farmer*, for instance, instructed readers to "study your own farm" to learn the character of the soil and what grows best there. Despite farmers' initial "strong prejudice against deep plowing," Tuskegee's extension agents eventually "persuaded" a few of them to try it on a "small scale as an experiment." One farmer who "got results the first year" "bought 500 acres of land, gave each of his four sons 100 acres, and kept 100 acres for himself," and through the Annual Chrysanthemum Show, Black women learned to experiment with creating new flower varieties.[94] " 'Disbudding' and 'transplanting,' and other terms of the trade are in the common vocabulary of most of the women and children of Macon County," noted the *Southern Letter*, "while some few have brought the culture of the flower to the point of grafting and breeding and naming new varieties."[95] Through the experiment plot and extension program, Tuskegee helped to transform everyday farmers into lay-fugitive scientists— facilitating a mode of Black study in the countryside.

Carver's commitment to ecologically sustainable agriculture exemplified Tuskegee's plot logics because it included a sense of social responsibility and an ethic of care as he translated and disseminated his scientific knowledge to local farmers. As already described, he published articles and bulletins on how to make farm life more productive and sustainable (figures 1.1–1.3). His bulletins encouraged improved plowing, watering, and fertilization methods, and they used photographs, charts, graphs, and hand-drawn diagrams to illustrate his findings.

Carver meticulously documented the cultivation practices and results of his experiments and insisted that his "chief aim was to keep every operation within reach of the poorest tenant farmer occupying the poorest possible soil."[96] To this end, his bulletins emphasized "basic principles" and were written in "nontechnical language... so that every farmer can master the problems of 'when, with what, and how shall I fertilize my crops in such a manner as to produce the maximum yield and do it with the least financial expense and the least injury to the soil.' "[97] Bulletins were especially concerned with ensuring Black self-sufficiency and helping farmers become intellectuals of the land. As the environmental historian and Carver biographer Mark Hersey argues, a hallmark of Carver's agricultural philosophy, what distinguished him from many of his contemporaries, was his desire "to inculcate a mode of thinking" that emphasized the ecological relationships among organisms "rather than a set of agricultural methods among the African American tenants of the region." Carver strove to convince farmers that "plants were real, living things, and that sunshine, air, food, and drink, were as necessary for their lives as for that of the animal." Once they realized this, he insisted, farming could be "at once intellectual, enjoyable, and practical."[98]

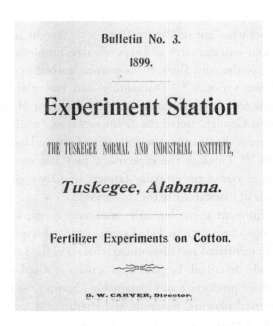

FIGURE 1.1. Cover page of Tuskegee Experiment Station Bulletin No. 3: *Fertilizer Experiments on Cotton* (1899).

Sources: National Agricultural Library, https://www.nal.usda.gov/exhibits/ipd/carver/exhibits/show/bulletins/carver; Tuskegee University Archives, https://archive.tuskegee.edu/repository/digital-collection/george-washington-carver/the-bulletins/.

AN EXPERIMENT IN BLACK WORLD MAKING   71

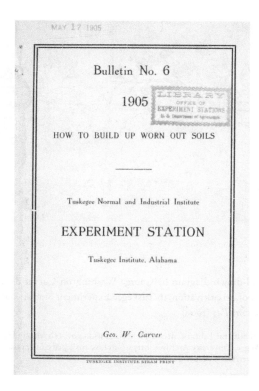

FIGURE 1.2. Cover page of Tuskegee Experiment Station Bulletin No. 6: *How to Build Up Worn Out Soils* (1905).

Sources: National Agricultural Library, https://www.nal.usda.gov/exhibits/ipd/carver/exhibits/show /bulletins/carver; Tuskegee University Archives, https://archive.tuskegee.edu/repository/digital-collection /george-washington-carver/the-bulletins/.

In *How to Build Up Worn Out Soils* (1905), Carver detailed how he conducted a range of experiments to improve soils over an eight-year period, beginning in 1897. He routinely selected the poorest-quality land for his experiments because many Black farmers were working land of a similar poor quality. Notably, Carver prioritized sustainable regeneration practices by using natural resources that would otherwise go to waste, such as "fill[ing] the ditches with pine tops, hay, bark, old cotton stalks, leaves, . . . [and] rubbish of any kind that would decay and ultimately make soil." Over several years, he successfully brought this rundown land back to life, "br[inging] to the surface much latent fertility that had sunken below the depth." By 1902, "the character of the land was noticeably changed," Carver observed. "Instead of the thin grey sandy soil, it began to look dark, rich and mellow."[99] And by 1905, he concluded that with such regenerative

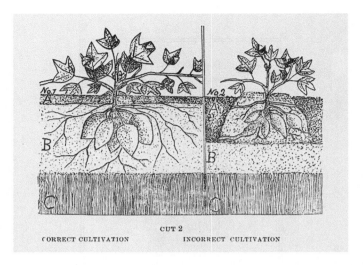

FIGURE 1.3. Hand-drawn diagram by George Washington Carver demonstrating proper soil tillage for sweet potato cultivation, in Tuskegee Experiment Station Bulletin No. 14: *How To Make Cotton Growing Pay* (1908).

Sources: National Agricultural Library, https://www.nal.usda.gov/exhibits/ipd/carver/exhibits/show/bulletins/carver; Tuskegee University Archives, https://archive.tuskegee.edu/repository/digital-collection/george-washington-carver/the-bulletins/.

practices, even "our poorest sandy soils can be economically made to produce a full 500 pound bale of lint [cotton] to the acre."[100]

Like most nineteenth-century agricultural scientists, Carver was trained to believe in the utility of commercial fertilizers, but he turned away from them because they were financially out of reach for most Black farmers. (It was not until later in his career that he would express concern about their potential harm to humans and the environment.)[101] In place of chemical fertilizers, he encouraged compost manuring and conserving what would otherwise be considered detritus. "We are allowing to go to waste an almost unlimited supply of the very kind of fertilizer the majority of our soils are most deficient in," he lamented, such as swamp muck and leaves on the forest floor. "Many thousands of dollars are being spent every year in the South for fertilizers that profit the user very little, while Nature's choicest fertilizer is going to waste." He therefore implored farmers to use "every spare moment" to collect leaves and swamp muck to nourish their soils and bring their farms back to life.[102]

Using waste to regenerate poor, denuded land was akin to Tuskegee's efforts to uplift exploited, dispossessed Black farmers—regarded as the waste of plantation modernity—by encouraging crop rotation, subsistence farming, and land ownership. Carver's desire to "produce the maximum yield [for poor farmers] and [to] do it with the least financial expense and the least injury to the soil" was a counter-plantation logic because he was not motivated solely by market imperatives or the avarice of global capitalist accumulation. In fact, many of his bulletins instructed farmers on how to grow foodstuff to feed their families (and not just cotton), with the aim of becoming more physically healthy and economically independent. They included recipes developed by Tuskegee students to give farmers examples of how to prepare these native and more affordable crops for maximum nutrition and flavor, and the recipes prioritized fruits and vegetables that farmers could either grow or forage from the woods around their homes.[103] For Carver, rural Black women played a crucial role in racial progress in the countryside and were much more than mere appendages of their husbands. His bulletins targeted Black housewives, and he believed it "is just as important for the housewife to know how to use . . . farm products wholesomely and economically as it is to produce them." He hoped "that every housewife and all those in charge of the preparation of foods would see to it that some kind of green, leafy vegetable is served everyday" to ensure "greater vitality, clearer thinking and . . . a greater determination to be a worthwhile somebody in life."[104]

Although king cotton is now all but synonymous with plantation slavery, it reigned supreme in the southern economy well into the twentieth century and persisted even as a mode of Black economic autonomy. Carver thus experimented with cotton varieties to ascertain which ones grew best in the region's soils and could resist diseases and the "ravages of the boll weevil."[105] In a bulletin in 1915, he announced that he had discovered "a new and prolific variety of cotton" through crossbreeding several existing varieties.[106] Carver's new cotton variety is thus a metaphor for the logic of eco-ontological regeneration undergirding Tuskegee's New Negro project, wherein transforming a commodity associated with Black subjection into a new and more prolific and economically viable variety was inextricably linked to the regeneration of rural Black southern life and being.

THE UNDERSIDE OF UPLIFT: ON THE ENTANGLEMENTS OF CARE AND PATERNALISM

As we have seen, Tuskegee's plot logics and ethics resided in its commitment to using institutional resources to address the needs of the most vulnerable. The school claimed to be dedicated to building *with* poor, rural Black people (and not solely *for* them) by giving them a space to express their needs, hardships, and desires for their own self-determination. The Tuskegee Negro Conferences, for instance, were structured to prioritize attendees' testimonials in order "to find out from the people themselves, the facts as to their conditions," "their ideas as to the remedies for the present evils," and "information as to how the young men and women now being educated can best use their education in helping the masses."[107] Furthermore, an account of the conference of 1915 is particularly revealing about the gendered dimensions of these gatherings and how Black women participated in agricultural life—not only in the domestic sphere but on the farm as well. A woman identified only as "the wife of a Negro farmer" shared before the audience: "'Our men folks is foun' out dat they can't eat cotton.' As the outburst of laughter that greeted this remark died down, Mr. Washington said in his incisive way: 'What do you mean?' The woman replied: 'I mean dat we womenfolks been tellin' our menfolks all de time dat they should raise mo to eat.'" By encouraging her husband to grow both food for the table and cotton for the market, this nameless farmer's wife articulated her ideological attunement to the logics of the plot. She proceeded to display the family's canned fruits and share their successes in raising and selling turkeys, chickens, eggs, and hogs. They had ample food to last them throughout the year, she informed listeners: "We can eat chicken every day if we want it." Following her testimony, Washington emphasized "that all this had been done on 178 acres of the poorest land in Macon County," a testament to the possibilities of eco-ontological regeneration even on worn-out soils.[108]

Tuskegee's care work for Black farmers is further evinced by Washington's advocacy for the expansion of the extension system so that more farmers would have access to the kind of scientific agricultural knowledge Tuskegee provided. Following the passage of the Smith-Lever Act of 1914, which established a national cooperative-extension system, Washington campaigned to ensure that African Americans received their rightful share of federal funds. When "a committee of white [Alabama] farmers" proposed that white agricultural colleges receive 70 percent of the funds and that Tuskegee and the State Agricultural and Mechanical College for Negroes (now Alabama A&M University) receive only 30 percent, Washington wrote to Secretary of Agriculture David Franklin Houston to intervene. This disproportionate allocation of funds would be an "injustice," Washington maintained, because it was "impossible" to "do any effective and practical work for the colored farmers except as it is done through and by colored people themselves."[109] Shortly thereafter, as southern states urged farmers to grow less cotton, Washington expressed great concern that

Black tenants, who "had been trained to grow nothing but cotton and do not know how to grow anything else," would be negatively affected. He thus proposed that the Smith-Lever Fund be used to place a Black demonstration agent in every county to train Black tenants on how to "produce a good food crop."[110]

Perhaps this argument was simply a rhetorical strategy to ensure equal resources for Black farmers and the expansion of the extension system. However, the idea that Black farmers did not know how to produce a good food crop also indicates Washington's paternalism: his simultaneous underestimation of the masses and overestimation of the Tuskegee project. Even if Black tenants were unfamiliar with the science behind crop rotation and seed selection or the economics of debt, they surely would have known how to grow food to feed their families, especially since many enslaved people supplemented their meager rations with crops from their provision gardens. (This was so even in the U.S. South, where provision gardens were less systematic than in the British Caribbean.) In fact, it would not be too farfetched to imagine that these tenants were possessed of their own plot logics and ethics well before their interactions with Tuskegee's extension program. Washington's underestimation of rural Black people's knowledges reflects the entanglements of care and paternalism that characterized the underside of uplift.

In an account of the Moveable School, the Tuskegee graduate and extension agent Thomas M. Campbell described Washington as a beneficent leader who invited poor farmers to campus to listen to and "talk over their problems" and "creat[ed] a desire among these untrained people to learn how to grow better crops."[111] Despite Washington's seeming altruism, however, he also policed how farmers expressed their discontentment and disillusionment at the Negro Conferences. He "confined" discussions only "to matters which the people had in their power to remedy" and determined that "other organizations could better discuss outrages perpetrated upon the race" and its political rights.[112] In line with his accommodationist political philosophy, Washington primarily used the conferences to highlight the school's successes with racial and regional reconciliation. Furthermore, the way Campbell referred to Black farmers as "these untrained people" and, in another instance, "these simple people" bespeaks his own elitism and how Tuskegee's extension agents, guided by the missionary zeal and class paternalism inherent within uplift ideology, also condescended to the very rural people they served and sought to help.[113]

At the same time, the Tuskegee agents' attempts at care work (albeit steeped in class bias) were also met with significant surveillance by white planters. As the historian Karen J. Ferguson observes, the extension "service's benefactors and local whites prevented the agents from delivering to farm tenants an undiluted message of self-determination." Once the agents placated white landowners and assured them they posed no threat to their bottom line—growing as much cotton as possible—many Black tenants were understandably suspicious of the agents, perceiving them to be in cahoots with the white landowners who routinely cheated and dispossessed them. Tenants might have viewed Tuskegee's extension agents as simply encouraging them to work harder to benefit the planters, and one wonders if tenants perceived the agents' condescension. Though not formally educated, they could surely detect class prejudice.[114]

To be fair, Tuskegee's agrarian reformers' willingness to placate Alabama's planter elite does not necessarily mean they were in cahoots with white supremacy; rather, they were trying to navigate an impossible system between local white planters and the national extension service on one hand and the interests of Black tenants on the other.[115] Moreover, the security of the campus and its students and faculty was contingent on its not being viewed as disrupting the white-supremacist status quo. Though Washington often touted Tuskegee as a Black oasis, anti-Black violence and discrimination were ever imminent. For instance, in 1902 George Washington Carver was nearly lynched upon accompanying Frances Benjamin Johnston, the renowned white woman photographer, to the Mt. Meigs School, one of the "little Tuskegees" near campus.[116] The potential threat of racial violence was even built into the campus design and landscape as the school intentionally placed the young women's dorms and the more ornate buildings in the interior of campus to protect female students from sexual violence and to ensure that its modern infrastructure did not draw the ire and envy of the surrounding white community and thus invite violence against Black life and property.[117]

In short, Tuskegee's extension program was unequivocally dedicated to improving the lives of poor, rural African Americans, but the missionary zeal that undergirded it was tied ideologically to the civilizing mission. This is especially evident when we consider the ways uplifting Alabama's rural masses at home was considered part and parcel of the expansion of Tuskegee's civilizing agenda abroad. In 1900, Washington sent a delegation of Tuskegee students and one faculty member to Togo, West Africa, to establish an experimental farm and aid the German colonial government in training Togolese "natives" in modern agricultural methods. He wrote of "spreading the Tuskegee spirit" in Togo, intimating how he conceived of agriculture and farming as technologies of civilization and of the plantation as a pedagogical geography. "Wherever these natives were given work on the plantations, and employed their muscles as well as their brains, a change for the better was soon apparent," Washington observed. "It is usually true that when a native is kept employed in one place, he will begin to build a home, consisting of a number of huts; he will clear a farm or plantation, and stock it with cattle, sheep, pigs and fowls. He will plant vegetables, corn, cassava, yams, etc. This happened among the Africans who were employed on the plantations cultivated by our graduates."[118]

This cotton-growing experiment in Togo was an outgrowth of Tuskegee's social, educational, and ecological experimentation in Alabama. However, it did not serve the same purpose for the German colonial government under which it was established. Just as Tuskegee's agents had to navigate white plantation owners in Alabama in order to educate tenant farmers, they had to navigate in Togo the fine line between racial uplift as pan-African solidarity and aiding and abetting colonial exploitation. Because "Tuskegee's commercial schemes in Togo worked exclusively with German colonial interests, rather than with independent black Africans," Marable argues, they were uncritically "pro-capitalist and pro-colonialist."[119] However, as Sven Beckert has shown, Tuskegee's aims for the native Togolese did not necessarily align with the German colonial government, either.[120] For Washington and the Tuskegee experts, introducing cotton growing to Togo was part of a diasporic uplift project akin to Washington's agrarian future in the U.S. South. "When the African Negro succeeds," Washington wrote, "it helps the American Negro. When the African Negro fails, it hurts the reputation and the standing of the Negro in every other part of the world."[121] For the German colonial government, however, cotton growing in Togo was strictly meant for capital accumulation and resource extraction, with little concern for the futures of the indigenous rural growers. Germans sought to institute cotton monoculture, but Washington and the Tuskegee experts rejected this idea. Racial uplift depended on the Togolese becoming more efficient farmers through agricultural science, which included growing for both the market and subsistence. Thus, Washington advised German colonial officials: "I should very much hope that your Company will not make the same mistake that has been made in the South among our people, that is, teach them to raise nothing but cotton. I find that they make much better progress financially and otherwise where they are taught to raise something to eat at the same time they are raising cotton."[122] The Germans ultimately ignored Washington and the Tuskegee experts' efforts to facilitate an agrarian future for the Togolese like that of their southern African American counterparts. The Germans instead schemed to control Togolese laborers by ensuring their complete dependence on the colonial government.[123]

Although the Tuskegee agents' work in Togo was more nuanced than is often considered, their failure to acknowledge the legitimacy and value of African agricultural knowledges was an egregious oversight. The Togolese did not have to be taught subsistence farming because they already practiced a less labor-intensive form of intercropping, whereby cotton was mixed with corn and yams. [124] This failure raises a separate problem underlying Washington's notion of diasporic uplift, specifically his view of Africans as peoples who needed to be civilized (similar to his view of poor, rural African Americans) instead of regarding them as cultural and intellectual collaborators and working *with* them to see how Tuskegee's methods could complement their indigenous agricultural knowledges and practices.

The Togo experiment represented the limitations of Tuskegee's agrarian future for the broader diaspora. In the United States, however, Washington's vision not only had "considerable practical merit," but was quite plausible in a period when Black landownership was on the rise and most African Americans lived in the South and worked as either farmers or domestic servants. [125] As Ferguson argues, and as Washington knew all too well, "Black self-determination in the countryside depended on land ownership," and the period between 1890 and 1915 was one of the most economically progressive periods since Reconstruction. Beginning in 1890, Ferguson points out, Black landownership in the South steadily increased, peaking in 1910, when Black farmers made up 16.5 percent of all southern farm owners. [126] On one hand, Tuskegee helped to make significant strides in that direction. For instance, as late as 1900 close to 95 percent of Black farmers in Macon County were tenants who worked for white landlords, and no more than 157 owned their farms. By 1912, however, when Tuskegee's extension program was well underway, the number of Black landowners rose to 503, evidence of the school's positive influence, according to Washington. [127]

Nevertheless, the barriers to ownership were numerous, especially in Macon County, where a significant proportion of land was "held . . . in the form of big plantations and worked by tenants." [128] So while Black landowners benefited from Tuskegee's extension efforts, Black tenant farmers, the bulk of Macon County's Black residents, had little agency over how they used the land they rented. In December 1914, Washington acknowledged that many Black tenants were still not permitted to grow anything other than cotton. [129] Carver, too, admitted that in applying his advice, renters had a more "complex problem to solve" because they "must co-operate with the landlord" for permission and resources. [130] While Tuskegee's efforts to "mak[e] thrifty land owners out of hand-to-mouth Negro tenants," as Washington put it, [131] were well intentioned and arguably subversive, they were ultimately thwarted by social, economic, and ecological forces so entrenched—the plantation and crop-lien systems, disfranchisement, the boll weevil, racial violence, and the codification and intensification of Jim Crow—that it would have been impossible to overturn them through self-help strategies alone. Hence, many Black sharecroppers' and tenant farmers' ultimate decision to escape these constrictive conditions through migration, first to the urban South and eventually to the urban, industrial North.

In an era characterized by increasingly new modes of systemic anti-Black violence and political repression, regarded as the nadir of African American history, Tuskegee's strategies of liberatory agriculture through eco-ontological regeneration faced considerable challenges. The repurposed plantation was decidedly practical and conservative, especially in relation to other Black land-reform efforts, such as Fortune's rejection of individual property ownership and the CFA's eventual decision to pursue agrarian reform through and alongside electoral politics. Tuskegee also practiced an intra-racial paternalism that condescended to the very people whom it claimed to advocate for and uplift. And yet rather than resituating Tuskegee on a success-versus-failure binary, this chapter has redirected our attention to the vision of Black vitality and world making that Washington, Carver, and other faculty and staff imagined on Tuskegee's experiment plot in the plantation's precarious afterlife. Indeed, the thing about experiments is that they often fail and must be tweaked and repeated many times before they are successful. By reevaluating Tuskegee from this vantage, we can arrive at a more nuanced understanding of its contributions to Black modernity.

To be sure, the repurposed plantation bore the stamp of uplift ideology and its racial, class, and gender biases and hierarchies. Yet we cannot lose sight of the ways it also reflected the logics and ethics of the plot—enacting an ethic of care that attempted to help Black farmers become intellectuals of the land. Given that Tuskegee's very grounds had been expropriated from the Creek Nation only fifty years before its founding and were then transformed into a plantation society that prolonged African American enslavement and dehumanization, the project of reinvesting the land with new meanings, uses, and possibilities for sustaining Black life was indeed an important counter to the plantation's logics of anti-Black deracination. Through the experiment plot and the resources and programming derived from it, Tuskegee made its most significant contribution to Black agrarian futures and, arguably, to Black studies. Carver's research, buttressed by the institute's robust extension program, reclaimed and regenerated the land from the ravages of plantation agriculture and empowered Black farmers with the tools, resources, and know-how to feed their families and circumvent debt. This democratization and dissemination of knowledge and resources to people who otherwise could not afford formal education capture the communal and subversive ethics of the slave garden plot and the spirit of Black studies as a political enterprise committed to sustaining and propagating Black life and culture.

2
Performing the Tuskegee New Negro

The Racial and Gendered Aesthetics of the Repurposed Plantation

"No race can prosper till it learns that there is as much dignity in tilling a field as in writing a poem," declared Booker T. Washington in the Atlanta Exposition Address of 1895.[1] This chapter lingers in the space between the tilled field and the poem, the line of crops and the line of verse, to take seriously Washington's equation of agricultural labor and aesthetics. If the repurposed plantation was a material, geographic, and ecological strategy for regenerating Tuskegee's degraded lands and African Americans' relationship to agriculture in slavery's aftermath, as argued in chapter 1, it was also an explicitly aesthetic project that aimed to redress racial-sexual representation in media and popular culture. Because Washington fashioned himself as too serious and driven to enjoy fiction and other amusements, his aesthetic contributions and those of Tuskegee's faculty and students have often been overlooked. Although Tuskegee has often been regarded as a servant-training school that prepared Black students to accommodate themselves to the South's racist and segregated labor economy, it was, on the contrary, a modern educational institution with defined aesthetic conventions and ideals.

As an international orator at a time when "public speaking was the chief form of public entertainment," Washington was a leading Black performer, to say nothing of *Up from Slavery*'s tremendous influence on American letters.[2] At Tuskegee, he exhibited a "devotion to design detail" that ranged from initiating and judging students' flower-arranging competitions in the dining hall to collaborating with faculty about the design, layout, and style of the campus grounds and architecture.[3] Tuskegee's faculty, staff, and students understood themselves as southern New Negroes: modern, educated subjects who gave special care to dress and style and who comported themselves in accordance with bourgeois conceptions of proper racial and gender conduct. They participated in numerous literary societies, and the *Tuskegee Student* newspaper regularly reprinted poetry and ran columns such as "Book and Magazine Table" and "About Books and Authors." [4] In 1905, some of the most popular books in Tuskegee's Carnegie Library included John Milton's *Paradise Lost*, John Bunyan's *Pilgrim's Progress*, Homer's *Iliad* and *Odyssey*, Charles Dickens's *David Copperfield,* and Sir Walter Scott's *Ivanhoe*. Students were especially fond of Charles Chesnutt's novels *The Marrow of Tradition* and *The House Behind the Cedars* for their ability to capture the specificity of students' lived experiences and cultural traditions as Black southerners, and Tuskegee's young women found great historical value in Harriet Beecher Stowe's *Uncle Tom's Cabin*. Apparently, students were so fond of reading that they sometimes forgot to return their books to the library, and the school had to keep multiple copies of the most popular texts on hand.[5] Washington and Tuskegee's faculty held strong convictions about the school's music performance culture, especially the singing and preservation of "plantation melodies," and embraced photography and film to document and project the school's successes to the world. As early as 1900, faculty and students even performed canonical theatrical works, such as William Shakespeare's *Othello*.

In rereading Tuskegee for its plot logics and ethics, this chapter argues that Washington's repurposing of a former site of enslavement into a modern campus required an eye and appreciation for aesthetics. Though antebellum plantations were often quite beautiful, their beauty belied the terror of human bondage and ecological exploitation. Slave garden plots, however, were the "botanical gardens of the dispossessed" where the enslaved cultivated beauty and created a folk culture through music, dance, storytelling, and the coaxing of plants from the ground to nourish and heal Black bodies ravaged by the plantation system.[6] Tuskegee similarly used art and performance to exemplify the beauty and vitality of Black life and culture. I use the term *repurpose* in this chapter with both its primary meaning and the etymology of its root word, *purpose*, in mind: to design and to propose.[7] In doing so, I capture how the intentional *design* and regeneration of Tuskegee's landscape, as discussed in chapter 1, were part and parcel of the careful aesthetic curation of Black subjectivity. Furthermore, through the school's dynamic performance culture, I show how Tuskegeeans *proposed* the southern New Negro as the exemplar of Black progress and futurity uniquely equipped to meet the challenges of the new century.

Washington and his staff aimed to "reconstruct the image" of Black people by repurposing the phonic and visual legacies of the plantation against the continued hegemony of racial stereotypes derived from slavery and minstrelsy.[8] Through oratory, singing, and new media technologies such as sound recording, photography, and cinema, the Tuskegee-trained New Negro resignified the sounds and sights of the modern, emancipated Black body at a moment when Black people were largely regarded as a sociopolitical problem for the nation-state. Washington and his staff thus staged the southern New Negro as one who was no longer embittered by the slave past and could therefore master and repurpose it—materially, rhetorically, and aesthetically—for the postemancipation future.

Although Tuskegeeans did not explicitly proscribe the "criteria of Black art," as would the subsequent generation of New Negroes, Washington's writings and the school's performance culture reveal an aesthetic preference for merging quotidian forms derived from southern Black vernacular culture and the slave past (the plantation, plantation melodies, and agricultural labor) with Victorian notions of beauty, morality, domesticity, and the dignity of labor.[9] In effect, Tuskegee's aesthetic vision grafted New England ideals onto Black southern life and culture, the industrial North onto the rural South, in hopes that "pretensions to middle-class respectability" would culminate in a gradual and non-threatening enfranchisement.[10]

In his oratory and especially in his support for preserving and innovating the plantation melodies, Washington celebrated Black sonic practices that balanced naturalness and simplicity with training, technique, and virtuosity. He preferred expertise devoid of excess, acumen without affectation, mastery cloaked in modesty. Tuskegee's visual archive similarly attempted to reconcile agricultural and industrial labor with Victorian sartorial aesthetics because the school was especially keen to prove that agriculture was compatible with the new, postemancipation desires of Black southerners. By juxtaposing Tuskegee's photographic archive alongside the writings of Mrs. Margaret Murray Washington, who served as lady principal and director of the Women's Department, I also show how Tuskegeeans used sartorial aesthetics and self-fashioning to regender the Black body in freedom and to reclaim domesticity for a people who had relatively recently been denied both.

Booker T. Washington's aesthetic philosophy was materialist, pragmatic, and utilitarian. Rather than "mere abstract public speaking," he explained in *Up from Slavery*, he preferred "to do something to make the world better and then to be able to speak to the world about that thing." And "the actual sight of a first-class house that a Negro has built," he insisted, "is ten times more potent than pages of discussion about a house that he ought to build, or perhaps could build."[11] According to the literary scholar William Andrews, "by claiming a radical distinction between action and speech and by disclaiming language as anything more than a referential medium, Washington denie[d] the performative dimension of representation."[12] I argue, however, that repurposing, as the strategy of world making that unifies Washington's political and aesthetic philosophies, is, in fact, a highly performative, imaginative, aspirational, and even speculative act. Much like plotting, repurposing envisions things that are not (yet) as though they are, can be, or will be. Ironically, though Washington famously professed to enjoy biography and newspapers over fiction, preferring to read about "a real man or a real thing," repurposing is precisely the praxis that links his work to the domain of fiction and the imagination, wherein he marshalled aesthetics *to propose* and speculate on new futures.[13] For instance, upon sending his editor, Walter Hines Page, a collection of photographs, drawings, and "a water color representation" of school grounds, Washington was careful to include the following caveat: "With respect to the colored drawing of the grounds . . . you will note that there are several buildings *which are not here now but we were drawing on our imagination* only to the extent that they are buildings which we expect to erect as soon as we can get the money for them. . . . The luxuriant foliage which you see displayed on the colored drawing is supposed to represent Tuskegee in the summer time when everything is then at its best."[14]

By drawing on his imagination and depicting the campus as he hoped it could be rather than how it was at the time, Washington was engaged in a proto-speculative and Afro-futurist endeavor long before such concepts existed as Black studies praxes. Alongside *designing* the landscape to imagine its transformation, Tuskegeans used aesthetics to *propose* new possibilities for Black being. Photographs of Tuskegee campus life depict faculty and students dressed in ornate suits, ties, hats, dresses, and blouses even as they perform agricultural and industrial labor. Despite Washington's preference for "a real man or a real thing," Tuskegeans routinely used artifice and performance to clean up and dress up, repurposing the "raw material" of slavery and the plantation to propose new possibilities for Black being: the southern, Tuskegee New Negro.[15]

In what follows, I examine Tuskegee's vast discursive, sonic, and visual archives to demonstrate how the logic and practice of repurposing the plantation landscape through eco-ontological regeneration animated the school's broader aesthetic vision for the southern, Tuskegee New Negro. In the first half of this chapter, I explore how Washington's oratory and the Tuskegee Institute Singers' performances of plantation melodies moved within and against the ludic tones of minstrelsy to imagine new indexical possibilities for modern Black sound on the turn-of-the-century stage. In contrast to Houston Baker's reading of Washington as a trickster figure who "mastered" the tones and types of the minstrel mask to transform Tuskegee into a "flourishing" "southern, black Eden" in the rural south, I argue that Washington's caricaturing of the Black masses in his speeches exposes the limits of mastering violent aesthetic and political-economic forms and falls short of a wholesale repurposing because it threatens to reproduce subjection.[16] By contrast, Washington's support for the Tuskegee Institute Singers, who continuously distinguished their sound from that of minstrel performers, represents a more effective regeneration of the sounds of slavery toward new and more liberatory ends.

The second half shifts to how Washington and his staff used visual culture to intervene in a turn-of-the-century scopic regime that reduced the Black body to the scripts of slavery and minstrelsy. Through photography, Washington crafted an "aesthetics of work" at Tuskegee that resignified the laboring Black body as proficient and autonomous and evinced to white and Black audiences alike how Tuskegee was training students for a bourgeois middle-class future in the Global Black South, equipping them with the tools and knowledge to resolve the postemancipation dilemma between labor and freedom. Tuskegee's visual archive also illuminates the distinctly gendered dimensions of its conception of the southern New Negro. Whereas slavery "ungendered" the Black body—forcing enslaved women to perform field labor alongside their male counterparts and enslaved men to perform domestic tasks usually assigned to enslaved women—Tuskegee established a strict gendered code of conduct, dress, and labor to contest the racial-sexual abuses of the plantation past. Before subsequent generations (rightly) challenged traditional gender norms and pursued cosmopolitan mobility, Tuskegeeans regarded the ability to "stay put," erect homes, and embrace the forms of femininity and masculinity denied them under slavery as constitutive of their eco-ontological regeneration and ability to plot agrarian futures rooted in autonomy and self-determination.

SOUNDING THE NEW NEGRO ON THE
TURN-OF-THE-CENTURY STAGE

Booker T. Washington was hardly alone or unusual in his effort to generate a Black aesthetic tradition from plantation ruins. A host of turn-of-the-century Black artists and performers—Harry T. Burleigh, Charles Chesnutt, Samuel Coleridge-Taylor, Paul Laurence Dunbar, Henry O. Tanner, Aida Overton Walker, and Bert Williams, among others—were also variously engaged in adapting and reforming plantation aesthetics in literature, music, and performance. In the years immediately following emancipation, white and Black composers compiled and rearranged enslaved people's folk songs, many of them created on southern plantations, into Western art music. Ironically, these Negro spirituals were often mobilized to fundraise for Black educational institutions, such as Fisk University and Tuskegee, and to evince African Americans' propensity for Western conceptions of "high culture." Similarly, by the 1890s Black performers dominated blackface minstrelsy, capitalizing on white nostalgia for the "happy darky" stereotypes of the antebellum South. Despite their debased caricatures of Blackness, however, minstrelsy and vaudeville provided Black performers with the financial means to develop a more dynamic Black theater.[17] Thus, at the same time that slavery, the plantation, and minstrelsy signified a shameful past, they also equipped these artists and race leaders with the rudiments of a distinctly African American cultural tradition that set the stage for the Harlem Renaissance and the New Negro Movement of the 1920s and 1930s.

As an internationally acclaimed orator, Washington was in effect a performer who actively shaped and was shaped by the soundscape of turn-of-the-century Black performance culture. He toured the United States, giving speeches on the Negro problem, education, and business to help raise money for Tuskegee and Black education more generally. "An audience brought out his latent powers of persuasion," writes his biographer, Louis Harlan. "On the platform he lost a little of his formalism and dignity, scored points by humorous anecdote and inverted metaphor, played one part of his audience against another like a choir director, and evoked in each segment of his audience in turn the emotions of pride, hope, nostalgia, amusement, and mutual esteem."[18]

Alongside minstrelsy and vaudeville, the lecture circuit was an important site of nineteenth- and early twentieth-century performance and entertainment. In the antebellum period, Black orators such as Frederick Douglass and Sojourner Truth mounted the lecture stage to denounce the atrocities of slavery and to advocate for abolition and gender equality. Through oratorical performance, Washington inherited the mantle of Black leadership when he delivered the Atlanta Exposition Address in 1895. Houston Baker designates Washington's Atlanta Address as the "commencement of Afro-American modernism," for it was the first time when Black citizens "found an overriding pattern of *national* leadership or an approved plan of action that could guarantee at least the industrial education of a considerable sector of the black populace."[19]

Ironically, Washington's performance of Black modernity required him to don and appropriate the "minstrel mask," for "the mastery of the minstrel mask by blacks," Baker argues, was the "primary move in Afro-American discursive modernism."[20] Washington thus slipped into the "phonic legacies" of minstrelsy, peppering his speeches and essays with folksy anecdotes rendered in Black southern dialect to ingratiate himself with and seemingly garner the sympathies of white listeners and readers. He recalls in *Up from Slavery*: "One morning, when I told an old coloured man who lived near, and who sometimes helped me, that our school had grown so large that it would be necessary for us to use the hen-house for school purposes, and that I wanted him to help me give it a thorough cleaning out the next day, he replied, in the most earnest manner: 'What you mean, boss? You sholy ain't gwine clean out de hen-house in de *day*-time?' "[21]

Washington's use of such minstrel conventions contradicts the aims of his broader uplift project, which sought to counter debased caricatures of Black people. However, Baker suggests that Washington, as a trickster figure, is not only in on the joke but redeploys it with aplomb because the minstrel mask "constituted the *form* that any Afro-American who desired to be articulate—to speak at all—had to master during the age of Booker T. Washington."[22] Indeed, this mastery of the political and aesthetic forms of modernity was a crucial strategy that African Americans used to prove their fitness for inclusion and citizenship. Yet Washington's detractors, then and now, have rightfully taken issue with such sonic blackening up. Ida B. Wells-Barnett, for instance, contended that such antics had the degrading effect of suggesting "that the Negroes of the black belt [*sic*] as a rule were hog thieves until the coming of Tuskegee."[23] For the historian Kevin Gaines, Washington and his contemporaries' donning of the minstrel mask was consistent with an uplift ideology that held up "culturally backward, or morally suspect" African Americans as evidence of the educated African Americans' "own class superiority."[24] The rural, country folk were essentially used as a foil to the bourgeois Tuskegee-trained New Negro.[25]

Baker's conception of the "mastery of form" *seemingly* reflects the logic of the repurposed plantation; however, there is a nuanced and significant distinction between them, at least as it relates to Washington's sonic blackening up. Mastering and redeploying the tones and types of minstrelsy, however strategically, ultimately risks perpetuating its debased caricatures of Black people. Repurposing, in contrast, insists on the wholesale transformation of the original form toward new and more life-sustaining ends. Though Washington's intention was to advance the cause of uplift, this sonic blackening up still adhered too closely to the original, degraded form and demonstrates the potential limits of the "mastery of form" as a strategy of Black resistance.

Listening to Washington's and Tuskegee's broader sonic archive, however, reveals that he also generated new indexical possibilities for Black sound that contradicted those of minstrelsy. Through oratory and especially his support for preserving and innovating the plantation melodies at Tuskegee, Washington articulated a loose set of criteria for New Negro sonic aesthetics that masked intense training, technique, and virtuosity under the cloak of naturalness and the everyday. These sounds were no doubt imbricated (and in tension) with the ludic tones of minstrelsy and vaudeville, but Washington ultimately believed that Black art should be rendered "in the language which the masses of people spoke ... [and] which they could understand."[26] This practical positionality that reconciled the most modern training with naturalness and simplicity was the crux of his aesthetic philosophy.

In *Up from Slavery*, Washington recalls his student days at Hampton, where he studied the mechanics of oratory and elocution and received "private lessons in the matter of breathing, emphasis, and articulation." Yet he also acknowledges that even the best technique cannot "take the place of *soul* in an address." *Soul* here refers to the seemingly organic and improvisatory performance style often associated with Black vernacular culture. It is the ability "to forget all about the rules for the proper use of the English language, and all about rhetoric and that sort of thing, and ... to make the audience forget all about these things, too."[27] Washington knew all too well, though, the rhetorical and literal dangers of disregarding "the proper use of the English language" for Black people on the turn-of-the-century stage and how it could be used to reinforce stereotypes about their alleged intellectual inferiority. Even an orator of Washington's stature was not immune to such crude associations. In a review of the Atlanta Exposition Address, James Creelman, a reporter for the *New York World*, at once revealed the importance of the occasion and the precariousness of the Black stage performer:

> The eyes of the thousands present looked straight at the Negro orator. A strange thing was to happen. A black man was to speak for his people.... There was a remarkable figure; tall, bony, straight as a Sioux chief, high forehead, straight nose, heavy jaws, and strong, determined mouth, with big white teeth, piercing eyes, and a commanding manner. The sinews stood out on his bronzed neck, and his muscular right arm swung high in the air, with a lead-pencil grasped in the clinched brown fist. His big feet were planted squarely, with the heels together and the toes turned out. His voice rang out clear and true, and he paused impressively as he made each point. Within ten minutes the multitude was in an uproar of enthusiasm.... It was as if the orator had bewitched them.[28]

Creelman's account of this momentous occasion in southern and African American history blurs the lines between antebellum and postbellum stages. His objectification and scrutiny of Washington's body resembles nineteenth-century performances of Black subjection, especially the auction block, where slave traders engaged in the detailed anatomization of the enslaved Black body, inspecting teeth, groping muscles, and tasting sweat. This slippage between the lecture platform and the auction block demonstrates the easy diminution of performances of Black self-fashioning and Washington's colossal challenge: despite his notoriety and accomplishments, he could easily be reduced once again to the status of a slave, at least rhetorically.

In his review of *Up from Slavery* in 1901, William Dean Howells, regarded as the dean of American letters, hailed Washington as an "Afro-American of unsurpassed usefulness, and an exemplary citizen," while also writing that the "ancestral Cakewalk seems to intimate itself for a moment in Mr. Washington's dedication of his autobiography to his 'wife, *Mrs*. Margaret James Washington,' and his 'brother, *Mr*. John H. Washington.'"[29] Originally, the cakewalk was an embodied practice of resistance whereby enslaved peoples parodied their owners' affected dance and sartorial stylings. After emancipation, it became an international dance craze featured in minstrel and vaudeville performances. Howells quickly disavowed the cakewalk as not at all characteristic of the author, but the fact remains that he reduced Washington's simple gesture to bestow respect on his wife and brother by using an honorific before their names to a form of racial caricature. That Howells could not imagine Washington's gesture of respect outside of minstrelsy demonstrates how the Black body in freedom continued to bear the marks of enslavement for white readers and the challenge Washington and his generation of artists confronted on the stage and page.

Creelman and Howells tethered Washington to the auction block and the minstrel stage, respectively, but Washington's voice in the lone extant recording of his speech (recorded about ten years after the original Atlanta Address, most likely for his personal archive) departs dramatically from these geographies of Black subjection and positions him firmly on the postbellum lecture platform. It is the sound of uplift. In the recording, Washington speaks with a quick, clipped Victorian diction. He rolls his Rs and enunciates every syllable with the utmost precision, likely a result of his elocution training at Hampton and despite his own emphasis on naturalness and the importance of disregarding proper English grammar. Paradoxically, he sounds more like a New Englander, the touchstone for his moral and aesthetic philosophies, than a southerner or a formerly enslaved person.

Washington's pivot toward Victorian bourgeois sound to announce Black southern modernity elucidates the aesthetics of his uplift philosophy more generally. In writing his two-volume study *The Story of the Negro* (1909), a sketched history of the race from its origins in Africa to the present day, Washington adapted and distilled into an aesthetic principle the sounds of the rural, country folk who surrounded Tuskegee.[30] At the Tuskegee Negro Conferences, attendees often shared their success stories in farming, acquiring land, and purchasing homes. "In this way," Washington wrote in 1910, "there grew up out of our conference a sort of oral literature which led us to take a wholesome pride in the progress that colored people were making. . . . In writing 'The Story of the Negro' I have tried to do on a larger scale just what the stories of the Negro conference have done—to supply a kind of literature that will inspire the masses of my own people with hope, ambition, and confidence."[31]

T. Thomas Fortune, Washington's ghostwriter and sometimes friend, admonished Washington for a writing style in his early publications that adhered too closely to public speaking. " 'You have ideas to burn,' Fortune told him, 'but your style of expression is more oratorical than literary, and in the written word the oratorical must be used most sparingly.' "[32] However, in *The Story of the Negro* Washington (and presumably his other ghostwriters) intentionally developed an oral-literary style derived from the sounds of the folk masses that aimed to give expression to "what was stirring in the minds of the Negro people during that long period when there was no one to voice their thoughts or tell their story."[33] Elevating and regenerating vernacular practices through intense training and contemporary methods, while retaining their ordinary and quotidian essence, reflect the logic of the repurposed plantation as both a political and aesthetic philosophy. Washington's oratorical mastery did not excuse his caricaturing of rural Black southern dialect, but his innovation of modern Black sound was on much firmer ground when he used the orality of Black farmers to develop a writing style that was both accessible to and in service of the masses of Black people.

THE SOUNDSCAPE OF THE TUSKEGEE INSTITUTE

By the turn of the twentieth century, Tuskegee had developed a rich performance culture that included oratory, singing, band and instrumental music, and theater. Students participated in weekly "rhetoricals" where they performed orations on themes related to their respective trades and industries, such as "Choosing and Preparing the Land," "The Crops," and "Constructing the Farm House."[34] This practical use of oratory—what Washington called "dovetailing" or "correlation," a pedagogical innovation that aimed to close the gap between the academic and industrial curricula—reflects Washington's insistence on naturalness and practicality in Black southern performance.[35] Tuskegee's students and faculty also introduced performance practices that exceeded and sometimes clashed with Washington's more utilitarian approach. In 1898, the renowned Shakespearean Charles Winter Wood joined Tuskegee's faculty to teach grammar and elocution. "Wood introduced Shakespeare and other classics to the Tuskegee students and faculty" and founded the Tuskegee Players, one of the earliest drama clubs in a southern Black school.[36] In 1900, they staged a production of *Othello,* described in the campus newspaper as "the first pretentious effort to give private theatricals at Tuskegee."[37] The institute's soundscape included European classical music, and Black vernacular music and performance practices such as ragtime and dancing were especially popular among students during mealtime and other recreational activities.[38]

Nevertheless, what Washington called "plantation melodies" remained the centerpiece of his sonic aesthetic philosophy and Tuskegee's influence on modern Black sound. Plantation melodies referred to spirituals and work songs composed during slavery and those penned by Black composers after emancipation. "Wherever companies of Negroes were working together, in the cotton fields and tobacco factories, on the levees and steamboats, on sugar plantations, and chiefly in the fervor of religious gatherings, these melodies sprang into life," Washington wrote in 1905. He described the plantation melodies as "wild and weird" music possessed of "pathos and beauty," "foster[ing] race pride," and as the "only distinctively American music" besides that of Native Americans. These songs were "the most precious records of slave-life," he maintained, providing rare insight into "how slavery looked to the masses of the people," and therefore needed to be preserved.[39]

Washington wrote about plantation melodies at length in *The Story of the Negro* and elsewhere and supported the early careers of some of the foremost Black composers, including Samuel Coleridge-Taylor, Harry T. Burleigh, and James Weldon Johnson.[40] Their efforts to adapt plantation melodies were "especially gratifying" for Washington at a time "when the Negro song is in too many minds associated with 'rag' music and the more reprehensible 'coon' song." With harmonies that could make an "abiding impression upon persons of the highest culture," these repurposed plantation melodies were a more dignified brand of New Negro music consistent with Washington's pragmatism and bourgeois values.[41]

Washington enjoyed a long-term friendship and business partnership with Harry T. Burleigh, who accompanied him on summer fundraising tours for nearly fifteen years. During this time, they corresponded about plantation melodies and potential music instructors for Tuskegee, and Washington enlisted

Burleigh's assistance in writing a preface for Coleridge-Taylor's *Twenty-Four Negro Melodies*, a collection of spirituals from the United States, Africa, and the Caribbean.[42] Although the plantation songs are derived from Africa, Washington informed readers in the preface, they are particular to the New World Black experience of enslavement and oppression. "According to the testimony of African students at Tuskegee," he continued, nodding to the school's diasporic student population, "there are in the native African melodies strains that reveal the close relationship between the Negro music of America and Africa, but the imagery and sentiments to which the plantation songs give expression are the outcome of the conditions in America which the transported children of Africa lived." Consistent with his repurposing of the plantation past, Washington lauded Coleridge-Taylor's ability to "preserv[e]" Black folk songs' "distinctive traits and individuality" while "giving them an art form fully imbued with their essential spirit."[43]

In a letter to W. C. Buckner, manager of the Original Dixie Jubilee Concert Company and the Columbia Tennessean Jubilee Singers, Washington expounded on the historic value of these songs. "The plantation hymns, that is the songs that were and are still sung in the churches, are the only documents we have for studying and understanding the inner life of the Negro during the long period before he had the opportunity or ability to express himself in a literary form," he explained. "They helped to lighten their [enslaved people's] labors; and to relieve their minds from the feelings of sorrow and despair that would have left them embittered, if they had not found expression and relief in this way." They were crucial to Black people's survival during slavery, and he encouraged Buckner to "study the words as well as the music for . . . in these words [are] many flashes of imagination; many picturesque and exceedingly condensed expressions, which show genuine literary quality."[44]

Given the historical importance of these songs, Washington established Tuskegee as a locus for their collection, performance, study, and preservation—thus cultivating a living sonic archive. "I am convinced that we cannot do a better service for our cause in the line of music than to make a thorough study of the older and newer plantation songs and let Tuskegee be a place where those songs are kept alive," he informed Charles G. Harris, one of the school's early instructors of vocal music.[45] In the summer of 1884, upon witnessing the success of the Fisk Jubilee Singers and a similar group at Hampton, Tuskegee assembled a quartet to travel throughout the U.S. North singing "the 'plantation songs' as they hear their parents sing them in Alabama, without any polish," in hopes of raising $4,000 for the completion of Alabama Hall.[46] Washington constantly instructed Tuskegee's music directors to collect new songs from different parts of the South, including "the peculiar songs that are sung in Louisiana while the people are boiling syrup; also some of the rice plantation songs of South Carolina as well as of the Mississippi bottom songs. A few of the Mississippi steamboat songs will do well. I think, by making a constant effort among the new students, we can get hold of many new songs of this character."[47] Under the leadership of Mrs. Jennie C. Lee, the directress of music, members of the 250-member choir traveled throughout "the different country districts of Alabama ... for the purpose of hearing these folk songs sung in their original state by the old people in their cabins, in their churches and camp meetings."[48] In doing so, Tuskegee students and faculty functioned as lay ethnomusicologists, mapping the geography of Black southern vernacular music.

At least two of Tuskegee's early music directors, Robert H. Hamilton and Nathaniel Clark Smith, published collections of their own arrangements of Black folk songs.[49] Nevertheless, Washington, ever the micromanager, was often at odds with them about "the quality and tone" of the music and voiced considerable frustration that they underemphasized the plantation songs in the school's "public singing" and playing.[50] In correspondence with Charles G. Harris, another music director, Washington complained that "there is almost no plantation singing in the chapel except when I make a personal request for it." He later clarified that while he did not "mean of course that all the singing is to be those of the plantation songs ... I want at least ½ or ⅓ of the singing by the school or choir to be of that character, and then I want to cultivate the singing of such Southern songs as the Old Kentucky Home, Swanee River, etc., more than we have in the past."[51] It may seem curious that Washington directed Harris to include the two Stephen Foster Wallace standards in the school's repertoire considering that they were popular minstrel songs that reference "darkies" and romanticized the "old plantation." However, the fact is that "Old Kentucky Home" was originally composed as an antislavery song inspired by Harriet Beecher Stowe's novel *Uncle Tom's Cabin* (1852). In his autobiography *My Bondage and My Freedom* (1855), Frederick Douglass observed that despite the degrading uses of such "Ethiopian songs" as "Old Kentucky Home," these songs "awaken the sympathies for the slave, in which antislavery principles take root, grow, and flourish."[52] Though "Old Kentucky Home" was later appropriated as a minstrel ditty, it is likely the song's original antislavery sentiment that Washington sought to capture by encouraging its performance at Tuskegee.[53]

Not all Black educational institutions shared Washington's sentimental attitude toward the value of plantation melodies, however. When in 1909 President Wilbur Thirkield of Howard University "made a number of eloquent appeals" urging the "singing of plantation melodies as an important part of the

University's musical repertoire," numerous students objected on the grounds that it was not "becoming [of] this Institution devoted to the higher aims and ideals of the race to emphasize these melodies as a part of the mission," as the Howard mathematics professor Kelly Miller informed Washington. Students especially objected to Thirkield's request that they sing these songs to "entertain guests" because the songs "were a vestige of slavery." Less than fifty years after emancipation, Howard's students were particularly sensitive to practices that could reinforce the history of bondage. Furthermore, Howard was in a somewhat urban setting, and its students did not necessarily come from the South, so they may have been further removed from slavery than their peers at Tuskegee, who were largely southern in origin. "Our student body comes largely from the North and West," Miller reminded Washington, "where these melodies are not generally appreciated because probably, their spirit and meaning is [sic] not fully understood."[54]

It is unclear if Tuskegee's students ever objected to singing plantation melodies, but a letter to William Henry Baldwin Jr., a white northern philanthropist and Tuskegee trustee, in May 1904 suggests that Washington's insistence on the melodies may have been influenced by pressures from donors and other supporters. Following a report stating that Tuskegee's students sang "classical music to the exclusion of plantation singing" during a visit by a group of white northern philanthropists, Washington assured Baldwin that "four-fifths of the singing was purely plantation. It is wholly untrue that our students refuse to sing or dislike to sing the plantation songs; that question is never raised here. They sing the plantation songs just as willingly as they do any other class of songs."[55] That Washington was so emphatic that Tuskegee's students proudly embraced the plantation melodies elucidates the paradox of these songs: for many African Americans, they were sacred records of enslaved people's interiority, whereas for white donors they were often romantic and pastoral portraits of the slave past akin to minstrelsy and the plantation literary tradition and thus represented Black people's contentment with their inferior social position.

Whatever the truth of Tuskegee's students' attitudes toward plantation melodies, Tuskegee's music faculty did not always embrace Washington's overbearing directives to make this style the centerpiece of the school's music curriculum. Though some of Tuskegee's music directors performed and published their own arrangements of plantation melodies, they desired the flexibility to teach and perform European classical music as well. In correspondence with Nathaniel Clark Smith, Tuskegee's bandmaster from 1907 to 1913, Washington complained that Smith was "losing a great opportunity by not making more of the plantation melodies in connection with the band music" while on tour. "It is always a safe policy to do the thing which one can do better than anybody else," he reasoned, for "if you attempt to play the high classical music to imitate Sousa and other great band leaders, you will find that people will compare your music with theirs to your disadvantage."[56] Washington made a valid point about Smith's ability to "make a distinct and unique reputation" for himself by mastering the plantation melodies, a distinctly African American genre, but Washington's reticence about the Tuskegee band's performance of "high classical music" and other genres also seemed to be couched in fear of outside criticism and uncertainties about Smith's abilities. In response, Smith informed Washington emphatically that he wished to be "permitted to use his own judgement" regarding music selection and requested that Washington "not embarrass me any more with letters of this kind." Smith had been working on "Negro music" for "many years," he reminded the Tuskegee principal, and found it "embarrassing to have authorities dictate to one about his own structure, as to the merits good or bad, when they know absolutely nothing about it."[57] This little drama over plantation melodies demonstrates how Tuskegee's faculty and students challenged Washington's authoritative leadership style and suggests they may not have necessarily shared his aesthetic vision for modern Black sound.

As detailed earlier, African American singers and composers in the early twentieth century navigated a performance landscape dominated by minstrelsy and its attendant taste for racial caricature. This was no doubt on the mind of Will Marion Cook, another leading African American composer, when he approached Washington about organizing "a company of nine—eight singers and a pianist—who shall be known as, 'Tuskegee's Real Negro Singers'" in 1901. "There [sic] aim shall be to demonstrate just how much the Negro has done to cultivate the plantation melodies," a goal that certainly would have piqued Washington's interest. Using compositions by Coleridge-Taylor, Burleigh, and himself, Cook sought to prove "that there is an abundance of musical material in the themes of the Southern Negro capable of thorough development and may form a basis for the growth of a music which shall be called truly American; further—the compositions . . . may be taken to show that the Negro himself is to play some part in the development of this music (a fact not hitherto conceded)." The company's proposed appellation, "Tuskegee's Real Negro Singers," points indirectly to popular entertainment forms such as the sideshow and blackface minstrelsy that promoted a culture of racial caricature and spectacle that distorted the Black voice and body. And although "the Negro voice" was thought to be possessed of an inherent "tenderness and sweetness," technological innovations such as sound recording separated voice from body and made it increasingly difficult to assign a racial identity to recorded sound.[58] So Black entertainers often branded themselves with appellations such as *real, genuine, authentic,* and *Negro* to distinguish their art from that of white competitors and to allay anxieties about their possible (in)authenticity.

Washington's own staff experienced precisely these difficulties in the field. During a fundraising tour in New York, a frustrated Isaac Fisher, the Tuskegee Singers' chaperone and future editor of the *Negro Farmer* (see chapter 1), complained to Washington that their efforts to raise money for the institution had been thwarted by "one trifling young colored man" who with "the accompaniment of his guitar began singing 'Negro Minstrel' songs. I think I have never been so handicapped before as I am here," Fisher despaired. "Every colored man is regarded as a beat, because of the great numbers of fakes who have been here and are yet here." The Tuskegee Singers confounded northern audiences, who were not only accustomed to Black minstrels but also preferred them: "We are told to our faces often that though our quartette is one of the best that has ever been heard up here, they would like us better if we would 'play the Nigger— their words—more' " (figure 2.1).[59]

As at least two audience members explained to Fisher, "You are the most gentlemenly [*sic*] set of colored young men I have ever met—just as nice as you can be, but you look and act so cultured and refined that we don't dare ask you to play the ignorant Darkey, as some do who come up here." Fisher worked hard to keep the Singers' spirits up and their performances "above the level of the Negro Minstrels," but he noted that they often became discouraged when they received $12 for their "worthy cause" of fundraising for Tuskegee, "while *one* Negro, representing in every particular, the minstrel type, working for himself alone should receive for acting the fool and servile Negro the handsome sum of $40."[60]

Other audiences and venues denied the Singers for fear that they would perform minstrelsy and thus "act[] the fool." "The Presbyterian minister refused me after consulting with his advisers," Fisher wrote to Washington, "because he was inclined to the idea that we were minstrels."[61] Such concerns elucidate the era's anxieties over "the real" as well as the fungibility of Blackness on the early twentieth-century stage. Just as Creelman, the reporter, read Washington's body as both slave and free subject, conflating the antebellum auction block with the postbellum lecture platform, for the Presbyterian minister and northern audiences more generally Blackness produced a fluid relationship between the striving New Negro quartet and the minstrel performer. Yet Fisher's frustration suggests that the Tuskegee Singers sought to counter the phonic legacies of the minstrel mask, not simply to master it. "When I have about three persons ask for the Plantation Songs and about four score ask that we dance and sing songs which tell of Negroes stealing chickens," Fisher informed Washington emphatically, "I

FIGURE 2.1. The Tuskegee Institute Singers, c. 1900.

Source: Max Bennett Thrasher, *Tuskegee: Its Story and Its Work* (Boston: Small, Maynard, 1900), between pp. 138 and 139.

make no pretensions to try to please."[62] One wonders if Fisher was aware that his rejection of such minstrel antics was an implicit critique of Washington, too.

The Tuskegee Singers toured throughout the North, Midwest, and West, performing in schools, churches, and music halls. Their shows, which received rave reviews, consisted of plantation melodies, folk songs, dialect readings, as well as some instrumental numbers. "The quintet sang the plaintive melodies with rare sympathy, the voices blending beautifully," stated a review from a performance in Los Angeles in 1915.[63] Another reviewer championed them as "the finest singing organization sent out by a colored institution since the days of the Fisk Jubilee singers."[64] Charles Winter Wood, "the famous elocutionist" and Shakespearean, accompanied the Singers on tour, performing dialect readings of Paul Laurence Dunbar's poetry and character sketches to wide acclaim.[65] Essentially, these musical and oratorical performances were the soundtrack to the repurposed plantation.

Between 1914 and 1916, the Singers traveled to Camden, New Jersey, on three separate occasions to record with the Victor Talking Machine Company, becoming the first group "to record choral versions of spirituals."[66] They performed such standards as "Steal Away," "Swing Low, Sweet Chariot," and "Go Down Moses." Each song is rendered without instrumental accompaniment.

The voices—a lead, tenor 1, baritone, and bass—dip and slide between notes in barbershop-style harmonies.[67] Their records were used in Victor's exhibit at the Panama-Pacific International Exposition in 1915.[68] Through sound recording, the Tuskegee Singers participated in the modernization and dissemination of plantation melodies, repurposing and regenerating these sounds for a new era.

Although the Singers played an important role in preserving and innovating these songs, their primary responsibilities were to raise funds and promote Tuskegee's educational model, as Washington reminded Wood in their correspondence.[69] In the *Chicago Defender*, reviewer Eloise Bibb Thompson assured readers that the student performers were continuing their industrial training while on tour and would resume their study of "brickmaking, harnessing, broom and mattress making, carpentry and shoemaking" upon their return to campus.[70] Since the Singers were not pursuing performance careers, they were still expected to adhere to Washington's dignity-of-labor philosophy, and their performances of modern Black sound annealed to his conception of the agricultural and industrial worker as the model New Negro.

By the 1920s, the Singers more directly integrated industrial and agricultural education into their performances. Under the leadership of Robert R. Moton, Washington's successor, they demonstrated the various crafts and trades taught at Tuskegee on stage, including a performance before a "huge crowd" at Carnegie Hall and, curiously, a radio audience in 1925.[71] The show, *Songs and Scenes from Dixie*, included a variety of spirituals and folk songs performed by the Hampton Institute Glee Club and the Tuskegee Quintette, a film screening, an agricultural demonstration, and an industrial tableaux, accompanied by a performance of "Go Down Moses." A curious hodgepodge of music and choreographed labor of brickmaking, plastering, frame-cottage construction, and blacksmithing, the Singers' performances mobilized music and embodied labor to disseminate the school's mission to train head, hand, and heart.[72]

Even as the Singers engaged new technologies such as radio and sound recording to innovate and preserve Black folk music, associations with minstrelsy continued to haunt them. Following a performance broadcast on the radio in 1923, listeners sent messages by telegraph praising the quartette while simultaneously tethering their performance of New Negro subjectivity to the ludic sounds of minstrelsy: Mrs. M. E. Wakenfield of Brownwood, Texas, remarked, "The male quartet was great. We always enjoy those old songs. Were the singers real Negroes? If they were not they were good imitators."[73] Despite the Singers' efforts to disrupt continuities between the minstrel and the New Negro, listeners insisted on mishearing them within minstrelsy's economy of racial artifice and spectacle. No doubt aware of how entrenched such prejudices were to the soundscape of the American racial imagination, Tuskegee took a multipronged approach by combatting racial subjection on the visual front as well.

VISUALIZING PROGRESS IN TUSKEGEE'S PHOTOGRAPHIC ARCHIVE

Despite Washington's oratorical mastery and fastidious commitment to preserving plantation melodies, his aesthetic and political philosophies privileged material evidence of progress over discourse. He insisted, "It is *the visible, the tangible*, that goes a long ways in softening prejudices."[74] In U.S. media and popular culture, the Black body was ensnared in a scopic regime where it was reduced either to the ludic excesses of minstrelsy or to the degradation of slavery. With these governing significations, Washington and his contemporaries were faced with the immense challenge of resignifying Blackness within the American cultural imagination. A staunch proponent of visual culture's evidentiary capacity, Tuskegeeans embraced photography and early cinema to visualize racial progress and uplift and to project them to the world. Tuskegee's vast photographic archive indicates how Washington used visual culture to articulate a quotidian theory of beauty and racial progress. Institutional publications were often illustrated with images of Tuskegee campus life, from its impressive modern buildings to students working at their various trades. Through images of skilled Black workers and middle-class homes, Washington proposed the southern, Tuskegee New Negro as the exemplar of modern Black subjectivity.

In *Photography on the Color Line* (2004), the visual culture scholar Shawn Michelle Smith establishes W. E. B. Du Bois as an early theorist of Black visual culture.[75] By depicting Black middle-class respectability in his Georgia Negro photographs—displayed as part of the American Negro Exhibit at the Paris Exposition of 1900—Du Bois constructed a "counter-archive" to combat scientific racism and eugenics. Though Smith's study focuses primarily on Du Bois, Booker T. Washington also participated in the production of this visual counternarrative. He was instrumental in organizing the exhibit and was largely responsible for securing funding for it through his close ties to President William McKinley. The top center of the exhibit featured a portrait of a young Washington dressed in a suit coat, white dress shirt, and bowtie, effectively announcing his position as the foremost leader of the race. To depict African American progress, the exhibit also featured images from several Black educational institutions, including Tuskegee.

Whereas the image of the Black body at the turn of the twentieth century was ever haunted by the specters of slavery and minstrelsy, Washington and Du Bois deployed photographs to reconstitute the very meaning of Blackness in visual culture. Unsurprisingly, their respective visual archives reflect their distinct philosophies of Black progress. Whereas Du Bois's Georgia Negro photographs depict the "talented tenth," or the Black educated elite, Washington's images depict Tuskegee faculty and students engaged in agriculture and various trades. According to a contemporaneous account of the American Negro Exhibit, Tuskegee submitted "a very fine collection of work turned out at the school, consisting of wood-turning, joining, painting, graining, forging, harness-making, etc."[76] Instead of depicting Black bodies captured in exploitative labor relations, Tuskegee's images depict them laboring for themselves. In effect, Washington used visual culture to transform the meaning of labor for the postemancipation era, representing the repurposed plantation in visual form.

Following the Civil War, newly emancipated African Americans were confronted with the problem of free labor. Black leaders such as Frederick Douglass and Washington viewed labor and economic development as strategies for building wealth, accruing property, and preparing African Americans for citizenship. Yet labor was still used as a mode of discipline and social control for the newly emancipated Black masses. Sharecropping, the crop-lien system, debt peonage, Black codes, and many other legal and extralegal technologies of power exploited Black people by controlling their labor. Black people were both integral to the southern labor economy and expendable—fungible—should they dare to pursue social equality and their full citizenship rights. In response to such a fraught sociopolitical landscape, Washington attempted to resignify the meaning of labor for Black modernity. He observed, "As a slave the Negro was worked; as a freeman he must learn to work. There is a vast difference between working and being worked. Being worked means degradation; working means civilisation."[77] This rhetorical maneuver that rebranded labor as dignified and self-proprietorial for the postemancipation Black subject was integral to Tuskegee's portrayal of the southern New Negro in visual culture.

According to Henry Louis Gates Jr., the New Negro was essentially a battle over racial representation, where African American artists and intellectuals used visual culture to challenge anti-Black propaganda in mainstream media.[78] In response to the proliferation of racist caricatures in popular culture that depicted Black people as lazy and idle, Washington used photographs to depict the beauty and dignity of the laboring Black body. The art historian Michael Bieze has attributed Washington's visual aesthetics to the Arts and Crafts movement of the late nineteenth century, especially to "John Ruskin's aesthetic philosophy, which united the worker, beauty, and morality."[79] Washington's aesthetics also privileged nature and the pastoral and georgic modes. The images that illustrate his books and magazine articles portray the southern New Negro as the simple farmer cloaked in Victorian sartorial flair, the skilled tradesman, the fastidious homemaker scrupulously managing and beautifying the domestic sphere, and the autonomous industrial worker operating modern machinery. By depicting Tuskegee students and faculty performing agricultural and industrial labor while dressed in their most professional attire, Washington produced what I have termed an "aesthetics of work" that used Victorian ideals to resignify the fraught relationship between Blackness and labor.

Throughout his career, Washington employed several leading Black photographers, including C. M. Battey, A. P. Bedou, Peter Jones, and Addison Scurlock. He also collaborated with Frances Benjamin Johnston, a prominent white woman photographer who famously photographed the Hampton Institute for the American Negro Exhibit at the Paris Exposition of 1900.[80] In 1905, Washington requested funding to establish a photography department at Tuskegee to "train students who would go out and establish galleries in different parts of the South." As he wrote to George Eastman, he believed that although there was prejudice in photography, the fact that a number of "colored men in the South" were already succeeding in the field was a promising sign that Tuskegee's students "would have almost as good opportunity to succeed as a white man."[81] Washington understood all too well, of course, that the prejudice in photography was not limited to employment but also included how Black people were depicted in popular media and print culture. He therefore sought to provide what he considered more respectable images of the race to combat the less favorable ones. For instance, Tuskegee contributed several photographs to Sir Harry Johnston's *The Negro in the New World* (1909), an anthropological account of Black life in the Americas. In a review of the book, Washington took especial issue with the photographs Johnston selected: "It appears to me that in some instances much more representative types could have been given," he wrote. "For example, the picture of the Kru man from the Kru Coast, Liberia, as representing the typical Negro will, I am afraid, be misleading to the average reader, in that the type here shown does not represent that to which the present Negro race is tending, but rather that away from which it is tending."[82] Washington's disapproval of the Negro "type" pictured in Harry Johnston's study reflects the influence of social Darwinism on his thought. It is also mired in a logic that elevated African Americans as the "type" to which "the present Negro race is tending" over native Africans. This condescending, civilizationist rhetoric was commonplace among the African American elite who subscribed to uplift ideology and its promotion of African redemption.[83] Nevertheless, Washington's critique demonstrates his preoccupation with visual culture's capcity to (mis)represent Black progress.

Alongside photographs, Tuskegee produced its own moving pictures as early as 1910 to aid in its scholarship fundraising efforts, helping to shape what Allyson Nadia Field has called "uplift cinema."[84] Isaac Fisher, the Tuskegee graduate turned chaperone for the Singers, became an early Black filmmaker. Perhaps given his frustration that the Singers were constantly mistaken for traveling minstrels, Fisher produced a Black romance film in 1915 entitled *When True Love Wins*. It was shown to an audience of "nearly four thousand people packed into the Champion Theatre" in Birmingham, and its reception, observed the *Tuskegee Student*, "indicate[s] that our people have come to parting of the ways with moving pictures which ridiculed the race and will hereafter demand the class of pictures in which the race is represented as men and women possessing the qualities of intelligence culture and refinement."[85] Fisher's film was also likely a response to D. W. Griffiths's *The Birth of a Nation*, released earlier that year, which Washington personally campaigned to censor. He categorically refused to allow Tuskegee's images to be shown with the horrendous film, despite requests to do so: "Such an exhibit would be an indirect endorsement," Washington wrote. "We consider The Birth of a Nation a thoroughly harmful and vicious play, and want to do everything possible to prevent its being exhibited."[86]

In 1902, Washington commissioned Frances Benjamin Johnston to photograph Tuskegee campus life and "some of the small Alabama Black schools that represented 'little Tuskegees.'"[87] In the fall of that year, Johnston visited Tuskegee and made more than six hundred photographs, which were used for exhibitions and to illustrate many of Washington's early twentieth-century publications.[88] Critics of Johnston's photographs of the Hampton Institute for the American Negro Exhibit have described them as "hauntingly beautiful," acknowledging their effort to enfold Black Americans into national identity, but also reading their "codified construction" and "stiffness" as indicative of Black subjection and objectification.[89] Shawn Michelle Smith writes, "Hampton students never meet the camera with curious, approving, or challenging eyes; instead, they are depicted as the objects of a scrutinizing gaze, one that has been invited to evaluate their 'progress and present conditions.'" Johnston "pose[s] Hampton students as the willing objects of an outside investigation, the test subjects of an external study." Ultimately, Smith reads Johnston's images as "assimilationist," ensnaring Hampton's students in what bell hooks calls the "white supremacist gaze."[90] Laura Wexler similarly suggests that "from Johnston, the Hampton administration got the averted gaze it sought, and from Hampton's leaders, New South businessmen and northern industrialists got the assurance they sought that black militance could be diverted." Although Johnston could have made different choices in how she depicted Hampton students, giving us access to their sociality, her photographs were ultimately consistent with the school's accommodationist values. "The Hampton that we see is a Hampton she envisioned," Wexler concludes.[91]

In her reading of Johnston's Tuskegee images, Smith finds the same disciplinary qualities she ascribes to the Hampton photographs: they "aim to exemplify the Tuskegee program of character building through discipline and manual labor," and they "replicate her [Johnston's] signature style; they are perfectly balanced, formal photographs of students at work in classrooms and outdoors, performing the tasks of various trades." Hardly any of the images show students returning "Johnston's gaze with a curious glance or stare," leading Smith to wonder if "the downward looking poses might also suggest the objectification of African American students who play their roles for the white lady photographer and other white patrons."[92]

I wish to read against the logic of discipline and objectification in Johnston's Tuskegee photographs and the school's larger visual archive, however, and propose that we view these classroom scenes through the logics and ethics of the plot—as depictions of training, striving, and (Black) study instead. In Washington's writings, *training* is not simply a euphemism for plantation discipline. Much like training to be a musician, vocalist, or dancer in the performing arts, educating students in agriculture and the industrial arts required repeated practice, rehearsal, and study. Whereas *discipline* was associated with "being worked" and "degradation" and thus the exploitation of slavery and sharecropping, *training* connoted the cultivation of southern New Negro identity by resignifying labor as a self-proprietorial enterprise. Although this mode of training surely reflected the civilizational aims of uplift, we cannot lose sight of the fact that Tuskegee was also preparing and educating students for the new demands of citizenship and survival in a milieu where Black people's failure to adhere to Jim Crow could easily result in incarceration or death. To be clear, I am not arguing that discipline is not at work here, for all forms of education require discipline in some way. However, creating a wedge between training and discipline makes space for a more capacious and dynamic interpretive logic for Tuskegee's visual archive that acknowledges the ethic of care that motivated such an approach. At the same time, I do not wish to overdetermine the white-supremacist gaze and its influence at Tuskegee and instead propose that the concept of "training" also captures faculty and students' intentional performances of beauty, dignity, and grace. The concept is akin to Imani Perry's notion of "black formalism," used to describe the rich cultural rituals that Black communities developed, such as teaching Black school children the "Negro national anthem," as "an articulation and expression of grace and identity that existed in refuge from the violence of white supremacy."[93]

Like Washington, Tuskegee's administrators and students would certainly have had their own ideas about aesthetics and self-fashioning in visual culture. So to view these images only through the lens of subjection misses their inherent performativity and the dynamism of Black self-fashioning and self-determination at Tuskegee. What if Johnston staged the photographs in collaboration with Tuskegee's administrators, faculty, and students? How might the industrial and scientific settings and props or the faculty and student actors' sartorial and kinesthetic choices indicate their agency and performance of New Negro subjectivity? Skeptical of photography's evidentiary capacity, Wexler argues, "Photography has always been an enforcer, with the power to make certain things invisible just as surely as it has made other things appear."[94] However, as Autumn Womack has recently reminded us, despite "photography's dual frequency of freedom and repression, in its promise to index life and living" it was also "a fertile ground for staging new racial formulas."[95] By lingering in photography's visual ambivalence, then, I propose greater agency for these subjects as they fashioned themselves as southern, Tuskegee-trained New Negroes.

Johnston's images capture Tuskegee students fixed in a perennial state of building and working, seemingly recalling plantation discipline. Crucially, however, although many of the images depict stillness, there is a lack of uniformity that contrasts significantly with many of the Hampton images. Tuskegee faculty and students are pictured working assiduously, but they are often working at different tasks, which disrupts the perceived disciplinary quality, and the variation in clothing and posture suggests further individuation and movement. Field, too, observes that Johnston's Tuskegee photographs are "far more dynamic" than the Hampton photographs. "Students are shown at work, casually captured rather than carefully posed." Many of the "exterior shots . . . are more chaotic and frenetic, less crisp in line and orderly. . . . The tension between the stillness of the human subjects and the compositional busyness of the environment" stands in contrast to "the tidy world [Johnston] created for the Paris Exposition." Despite this observation, however, Field frequently reduces Tuskegee's "aesthetics of uplift" to accommodation, arguing that "though Washington disapproved of the prevalent belief in scientifically determined racial inequity, his rhetoric skirts the issue of eugenics but does not directly challenge it" in the way that Du Bois did in the Georgia Negro photographs and later in the " 'antiracist propaganda' of the *Crisis*."[96] Not only does this view uphold Du Bois as the standard for turn-of-the-century Black visual culture practices, but it also misses how Washington and Tuskegee's faculty and staff actively resignified labor for Black modernity. Moreover, and perhaps most importantly, Black people were not always resisting or responding to white supremacy. Instead, they also created anew, independent of the white gaze. Such acts were not "skirting" or accommodating to white-supremacist violence but rather refused to center it. In short, Tuskegee's visual archive was used both to resist and challenge racism *and* to project the school's own vision of Black modern subjectivity to the world.

Whereas the visual iconography of slavery and sharecropping depicted the Black body in exploitative labor arrangements, Johnston portrayed Tuskegee students working with steam engines, sewing machines, printing presses, and scientific instruments to demonstrate not only their willingness to work but also their mastery of science and industrial technology. Depicting Black people's aptitude with examples of industry was key in Washington's effort to aestheticize and resignify work as beautiful, pleasurable, and self-proprietorial. He observed:

> If this [industrial] training has any value for the Negro, as it has for the white man, it consists in teaching the Negro how rather not to work, but how to make the forces of nature—air, water, horse-power, steam, and electric power—work for him, how to lift labour up out of toil and drudgery into that which is dignified and beautiful. . . . Let him who doubts this contrast the Negro in the South toiling through a field of oats with an old-fashioned reaper with the white man on a modern farm in the West, sitting upon a modern "harvester," behind two spirited horses, with an umbrella over him, using a machine that cuts and binds oats at the same time,—doing four times as much work as the black man with one half the labour.[97]

By juxtaposing the unskilled Black laborer in the South with the technologically efficient white laborer in the West, Washington insisted that a facility with machinery is a hallmark of the modern worker. And whereas plantation labor exclusively extracted and exploited Black labor power, modern machinery could help to preserve Black energy and thus reclaim Black life.

Washington used a similar rhetorical strategy of juxtaposing old and new forms of labor in the layout of his periodical publications. In his article

"Twenty-Five Years of Tuskegee" published in 1906, he juxtaposed images of the "Old Negro" against the Tuskegee-trained New Negro. In one pairing, an image of "an unskilled laborer" (figure 2.2) is contrasted with that of "a skilled student in the Tuskegee shoe shop" (figure 2.3).[98]

Pictured from left to right, the images are in a before-and-after format. The image of the unskilled laborer is that of a scraggly and unshaven, middle-aged man wearing a ragged shirt with holes in one sleeve and what appears to be a makeshift hat, perhaps to protect his head from the brutal Alabama sun. On the opposite page, a Tuskegee student is pictured operating a machine in the school's shoe shop. He is clean-shaven and sports a newsboy cap and work apron to protect his white shirt, though the shirt appears to be slightly soiled from working in the shop. Unlike the unskilled laborer, who looks directly into the camera, the student is too preoccupied with work to notice the photographer's presence. Rather, his gaze is fixed on the machine. Whereas the unskilled laborer is captioned as being "as shiftless and improvident as he is good-natured; his physical and mental powers wasted for lack of *training*," the caption accompanying the skilled student worker enthusiastically proclaims, "Thorough *training* will make him a valuable and productive member of the community" (emphasis added). Such pairings, common in Tuskegee's visual archive, at once illuminate the class bias at the heart of uplift and challenge critiques of Tuskegee by scholars such as the southern historian C. Vann Woodward, who lampooned the institute for insisting on outmoded forms of labor while the South was rapidly industrializing.[99] The images accompanying Washington's various publications tell a different story, albeit a distinctly classist one. Instead of viewing Tuskegee as an antebellum plantation, these images aestheticize students' technical proficiency in the "higher forms" of work and visualize the otherwise futures that were possible on the grounds of the repurposed plantation.

Charles Pierce, head of Tuskegee's Electrical Engineering Department, also used images to convey the school's industrial proficiency. In his article "How Electricity Is Taught at Tuskegee," published in the *Technical World* in 1904, Pierce described how the school used science, technology, and architecture to present itself as a modern industrial center, illuminating minds and buildings alike. Pierce was fluent in his trade's argot: "The first dynamo used by the school was a 50-K. W. monocyclic alternator furnishing 43 amperes at 1,040 volts," he informed readers. Pierce then delineated the school's equipment, the backgrounds of the students enrolled in the department, and the curriculum. Students learned both theory and practice in order to "raise the workman above that of the plain, practical man by giving him theoretical knowledge of his work." Importantly, Pierce noted that the Academic Department "is one of the largest consumers of electrical

FIGURE 2.2. "An Unskilled Laborer." Washington's representation of the "Old Negro."

Source: Booker T. Washington, "Twenty-Five Years of Tuskegee," *World's Work* 11 (1906): 7436.

A SKILLED STUDENT IN THE TUSKEGEE SHOE SHOP
Thorough training will make him a valuable and productive member of the community

FIGURE 2.3. "A Skilled Student in the Tuskegee Shoe Shop." Washington's representation of the Tuskegee-trained New Negro.

Source: Washington, "Twenty-Five Years of Tuskegee," 7437.

power" on campus—indicating its centrality within the curriculum—and that "the division supplies lights to several places off the school grounds," including the home of Colonel Charles Thompson, a local white congressman.[100]

The images accompanying Pierce's article mostly depict campus buildings to illustrate the beauty of its architecture as well as the kinds of buildings students wired and for which they maintained the electricity. The most striking image, however, depicts the "students at work" moving the 150-kilowatt alternator into the dynamo room (figure 2.4). Despite the caption, the students are not working at all. They treat the alternator as a prop: leaning on it, sitting next to it, and propping their legs up on it. They look directly into the camera. One student, sporting a newsboy cap and full suit, rests his hand on his waist as he returns the

FIGURE 2.4. Tuskegee faculty member Charles Pierce and electrical engineering students.

Source: Charles Pierce, "How Electricity Is Taught at Tuskegee," *Technical World* 1, no. 4 (June 1904): 429.

photographer's gaze. Pierce, also in a full suit and hat, stands proudly on the opposite side of the alternator, with his left arm akimbo, his right hand touching the machine, and his right leg propped up slightly higher than his left. His stance and gaze exude authority, the same authority we perceive in the article itself. The student who sits in front of the machine, with his left leg crossed over his right, hands clasped tightly on his knees, his back straight as he looks confidently into the camera, is perhaps the most striking. His pose and attire look more appropriate for a parlor in a middle-class home than for a site of labor and instruction. These students' performances of self—their bodily comportment, sartorial choices, and overall self-fashioning—at once exemplify and exceed Washington's rhetoric of the dignity and beauty of labor.

If Pierce used photographs to project a vision of Tuskegee as a center of technical-scientific enlightenment and industry for Black and white southerners alike, Tuskegee's leadership also marshaled photography to defend the school's reputation against its growing number of critics. Two volumes of institutional literature, *Working with the Hands* (1904) and *Tuskegee and Its People* (1906), used Johnston's photographs to this end. By the early 1900s, Washington and his program for Black education faced considerable criticism regarding the limits of industrial education for African Americans. Like Du Bois, Ida B. Wells-Barnett rejected Washington's attempted repurposing of labor. "This gospel of work is no new one for the Negro," she wrote. "It is the South's old slavery practice in new dress. It was the only education the South gave the Negro[;] for two and half centuries she had absolute control of his body and soul. The Negro knows that now, as then, the South is strongly opposed to his learning anything else but how to work."[101]

Working with the Hands and *Tuskegee and Its People* were published in response to such sharp criticisms. In his extended introduction to the subscription edition of *Working*, Washington insisted that the "value of labour with the hands" is just as important for the farmer, craftsman, or domestic as it is "for those whose occupations are more in the direction of mental work alone." He emphasized that "industrial work" and "academic training" are mutually constitutive at Tuskegee, whose "policy" was "to make an industry pay its way if possible, but at the same time not to sacrifice the training to mere economic gain," no doubt in response to Du Bois's and Wells-Barnett's accusations that he simply promoted a "gospel of Work and Money."[102] Likewise, in the preface to *Tuskegee and Its People*, Emmet J. Scott, the volume's official editor, refuted the "mistaken idea" that "Tuskegee Institute is a 'servant training school,' or an employment agency," and in its general introduction, Washington challenged the misconception that "industrial education means class education, that it should be offered to the Negro because he is a Negro, and that the Negro should be confined to this sort of education." Schools such as Hampton and Tuskegee promoted industrial education not "because colored people are to receive it," he argued, "but because the ripest educational thought of the world approves it; because the undeveloped material resources of the South make it peculiarly important for both races; and because it should be given in a large measure to any race, regardless of color, which is in the same stage of development as the Negro."[103] Critically, in both *Working with the Hands* and *Tuskegee and Its People*, Washington and Scott used images to illustrate the dynamism of the school's curriculum and prove its compatibility with the material and class aspirations of the New Negro.

Working with the Hands, though advertised as a sequel to *Up from Slavery*, was less of an autobiography of Washington than an institutional autobiography of Tuskegee, detailing the school's curriculum and educational philosophy. The first edition was published in May 1904, and a "special subscription edition" was released just a few months later, circa July 1904.[104] Both editions incorporate numerous photographs depicting Tuskegee's students and faculty engaged in the various agricultural and industrial trades taught there. Unlike Pierce's depiction of Tuskegee as a locus of Black industrial modernity, the images in *Working with the Hands* attempt to recast Tuskegee as a distinctly literary space while also depicting the complexity of its vision of Black agrarian futures. Both editions open with a portrait of Washington sitting at his desk, performing the bourgeois Victorian (figure 2.5).

His arm rests gently on the desk "in the manner of the literate man of purpose." Papers are strewn indiscriminately but still relatively neatly across his desk; a small bouquet of flowers sits to his left, and an inkwell in front of him. He looks directly into the camera, returning Johnston's gaze. "By the turn of the century," writes Smith, "posing a man at his desk with pen in hand, suspended over paper, was a classic way of suggesting his intellect, power, and importance."[105] The first edition of *Working* is bookended by an image of Tuskegee students "typesetting" in the printing office. Tuskegee owned a printing press, taught the printing trade as early as 1885, and published numerous periodicals detailing the institute's work. The *Tuskegee Student* observed in May 1904, "An

MR. WASHINGTON IN HIS OFFICE AT TUSKEGEE

FIGURE 2.5. "Mr. Washington in His Office at Tuskegee."

Source: Booker T. Washington, *Working with the Hands: Being a Sequel to "Up from Slavery" Covering the Author's Experiences in Industrial Training at Tuskegee*, special subscription ed. (New York: Doubleday, Page, July 1904), frontispiece. Photograph by Frances Benjamin Johnston.

effort is being made by the institution to secure every pamphlet and book of every description written by a Negro, the purpose being to make Tuskegee a center of information for Negro literature."[106] Despite Washington's seemingly cavalier attitude toward books in his speeches and writings, the images that frame the first edition "highlight the production of texts," as Smith points out.[107]

Although Washington was not behind the camera, he played an important role in choosing photographs and advising publishers about layout.[108] When publishers requested roughly twelve cuts for the subscription edition of *Working with the Hands*, Washington instructed his personal assistant and secretary, Emmett J. Scott, to "take the matter up with a good deal of care" and select "cuts" that better illustrate "the higher forms of work being done at Tuskegee," such as classes in "outdoor geometry" and "physiology."[109] Washington thus instrumentalized these photographs to contradict his critics.

In the first edition, the first image following Washington's portrait is that of a farmer pushing a team of eight oxen and "breaking up new ground" (figure 2.6). In the subscription edition, however, Washington's portrait is almost immediately followed by an image of Porter Hall, the "first building erected on

BREAKING UP NEW GROUND WITH AN EIGHT-OX TEAM

FIGURE 2.6. "Breaking Up New Ground with an Eight-Ox Team."

Source: Booker T. Washington, *Working with the Hands: Being a Sequel to "Up from Slavery" Covering the Author's Experiences in Industrial Training at Tuskegee* (Toronto: William Briggs, May 1904), between pp. 16 and 17. Photograph by Frances Benjamin Johnston.

school grounds" (figure 2.7), and then by the image of the farmer and oxen. It seems Scott decided to emphasize both "higher forms of work" and the school's impressive architectural design. Porter Hall, with its mansard roof, is framed by a water tower to the right, as tall as the building itself, and is surrounded by immaculate landscaping with well-manicured plants, trees, and bushes. This image tells a different origin story than the one Washington crafts in *Up from Slavery*, where he delineates the school's humble beginnings on a burned and abandoned plantation and how its first classes were held in a chicken coop.

The subscription edition's closing image is equally compelling. Following the photograph of students typesetting on the school's printing press is a two-page spread of what Bieze describes as an "idealistic bird's-eye view" lithograph of the Tuskegee campus (figure 2.8).[110] It appears to be a little city and is almost certainly a speculative, aspirational depiction, perhaps the one Washington sent to his editor to show Tuskegee "at its best," as discussed earlier. This imaginative, idealistic view of Tuskegee exemplifies how Washington and his staff used visual culture as a mode of Black world making. It is a plantation palimpsest—a strategic writing over the degraded landscape, building and constructing anew to efface its history of violence.

FIRST BUILDING ERECTED ON SCHOOL GROUNDS

FIGURE 2.7. "First Building Erected on School Grounds": Porter Hall.

Source: Washington, *Working with the Hands*, subscription ed., between pp. 12 and 13. Photograph by Frances Benjamin Johnston.

FIGURE 2.8. "Birds-eye View of Grounds and Buildings of Tuskegee Normal and Industrial Institute, Tuskegee, Alabama" (1904).

Source: Washington, *Working with the Hands*, subscription ed., between pp. 244 and 245.

"LAYING OUT THE GROUNDS ARTISTICALLY": BEAUTY, EMPIRICISM, AND AGRICULTURE

Tuskegeeans' efforts to "train" students into New Negroes were inextricably linked to the retraining of the ground to make it productive again, as detailed in chapter 1. Although *Working with the Hands* is devoted to the full spectrum of Tuskegee's curriculum, Washington's text emphasized Black farm life above all. Early in *Working*, he describes a visit to the Alabama countryside, where the "few textbooks" he saw in rural people's "cabins were full of pictures and reading matter relating to city life.... pictures of great office buildings, ships, street-cars, warehouses, but not a single picture of a farm scene, a spreading apple-tree, a field of grass or corn, a flock of sheep, or a herd of cows."[111] *Working with the Hands* was his effort to remedy this absence and produce a textbook of sorts with visual evidence of the beauty and dignity of the rural Black experience.

In both editions, the photographs depicting farming and agriculture illuminate how Tuskegee envisioned Black agrarian futures. As discussed, in the first edition the image following Washington's framing portrait is that of a farmer with an eight-oxen team. Next are two images of students cutting

FIGURE 2.9. "Cutting Sugar-cane on the School's Farm": students at work.

Source: Washington, *Working with the Hands*, subscription ed., between pp. 26 and 27. Photograph by Frances Benjamin Johnston.

sugarcane on the campus farm using machetes, after the fashion of their enslaved ancestors, and grinding it in the mill (figure 2.9). At first glance, these images are unremarkable and fit squarely within the era's scopic conventions: viewers would have expected to see Black bodies in sugarcane fields or bended over rows of cotton. However, a closer look reveals an important incongruency. One of the figures, just right of center, presumably the instructor, is dressed differently from the rest. He is working just as assiduously, with eyes cast down at the cane stalks, but, curiously, he is wearing a full suit and hat, a reminder that Tuskegee's visual archive is at once fact and fiction, evidence and aspirational *performance* of the southern New Negro as middle-class subject. The second image (figure 2.10) depicts students "grinding sugar-cane at the school's sugar mill" to produce syrup for campus consumption. Their facility with machinery reiterates Washington's insistence on industrial technology to redefine the fraught relationship between Blackness and labor.

FIGURE 2.10. "Grinding Sugar-cane at the School's Sugar-mill": students at work.

Source: Washington, *Working with the Hands*, 1st ed., between pp. 32 and 33. Photograph by Frances Benjamin Johnston.

In both editions, Johnston's photographs illustrate how Tuskegeeans appropriated the pastoral and georgic modes, sartorial self-fashioning, and scientific experimentation to present agriculture as beautiful, self-proprietorial, and fundamentally modern. Instead of caricaturing rural Black people and trafficking in the sounds of minstrelsy, Washington celebrated the rural farmer as "a real man and not an artificial one—one who can keep me in close touch with the real things. From a simple, honest cultivator of the soil . . . I have secured more useful illustrations for addresses . . . than from hours of reading books."[112] As a "real man" of "action," the farmer epitomizes Washington's conception of the southern New Negro.[113] In fact, Washington even stylized himself as a simple farmer. In the chapter entitled "Pleasure and Profit of Work in the Soil," he wrote, "There springs up a feeling of kinship between the man and his plants, as he tends and watches the growth of each individual fruition from day to day."[114]

For Washington, the landscape is the canvas, and the farmer is the consummate artist. Yet the three images that illustrate the chapter contradict his rhetoric about the bucolic simplicity of farm life. In the first image (figure 2.11), Washington stands in a horse pen gently petting a horse and her foal against an expansive rural Alabama landscape. In the second, he is surrounded by a herd of hogs in a hog pen and feeding them from a metal bucket (figure 2.12). And in the

Courtesy of The Outlook Company

WHEN AT TUSKEGEE I FIND A WAY BY RISING EARLY IN THE MORNING TO SPEND HALF AN HOUR IN MY GARDEN OR WITH THE LIVE STOCK

FIGURE 2.11. "When at Tuskegee I Find a Way by Rising Early in the Morning to Spend Half an Hour in My Garden or with the Live Stock." Booker T. Washington petting a horse and her foal.

Source: Washington, *Working with the Hands*, 1st ed. and subscription ed., between pp. 154 and 155. Photograph by Frances Benjamin Johnston.

third image (figure 2.13), he is pictured kneeling in the dirt, gathering plants and teaching a child (presumably his son) "something about real country life."

The viewer cannot help but notice an incongruency between the images and the caption "*real* country life": though engaged in farmwork, Washington is bedecked in a full suit, vest, and tie, all topped by a homburg hat. The child, too, is dressed in his Sunday best, much more formally than a simple plant gatherer, as the caption suggests. There doesn't appear to be any dirt on either of them. Washington's depiction of farm life is a curious amalgam of the rural peasant farmer and bourgeois Victorianism. This tension between working with the hands and middle-class aspirations is a central characteristic of his southern New Negro aesthetic. And despite his description of the farmer as a "real man" without artifice, very little is at all "real" about these images. Washington's performance of the quotidian before Johnston's camera is, in effect, fictional and aspirational.

FIGURE 2.12. "Hogs as Object Lessons." Booker T. Washington feeding a herd of pigs.

Source: Washington, *Working with the Hands*, 1st ed. and subscription ed., between pp. 156 and 157. Photograph by Frances Benjamin Johnston.

If we read Washington's pastoral images alongside the portrait of him at his desk, his vision of the southern New Negro comes into clearer focus. Washington sought to combine the putative simplicity of agricultural work with the aesthetic sophistication of bourgeois domesticity. The Tuskegee-trained New Negro was a modern Black worker who was as comfortable in the fields as in the middle-class home. "For the young farmer to be contented," Washington wrote, "he must be able to look forward to owning the land that he cultivates, and from which he may later derive not only all the necessities of life, but some of the comforts and conveniences." For the southern New Negro, beauty and art lie in properly landscaping and furnishing the modern farmhouse with "bathtubs, carpets, rugs, pictures, books, magazines, a daily paper, and a telephone." The home, as an extension of the tilled field, becomes the canvas for this artist-worker to convey a middle-class sensibility. Perhaps most surprising is Washington's intimation that this New Negro farmer should have time to engage in such leisurely activities as "study and investigation, and a little time each year for travel and recreation, and for attending lectures and concerts," given that

TEACH THE CHILD SOMETHING ABOUT REAL COUNTRY LIFE

FIGURE 2.13. "Teach the Child Something about Real Country Life." Booker T. Washington kneeling in the dirt teaching (presumably) his son about plants.

Source: Washington, *Working with the Hands*, 1st ed. and subscription ed., between pp. 160 and 161. Photograph by Frances Benjamin Johnston.

FIGURE 2.14. "Cultivating a Patch of Cassava on the Agricultural Experiment Plot": Tuskegee students doing "field work."

Source: Washington, *Working with the Hands*, 1st ed. and subscription ed., between pp. 164 and 165. Photograph by Frances Benjamin Johnston.

Washington otherwise portrayed himself as the tireless worker who cared little for games or fiction and had to be all but forced to take a vacation.[115] In *Working with the Hands*, Washington seems to somewhat soften his stance on leisure and consumerism to quell the growing criticism among his contemporaries that "hand-training" was a form of "class-training."[116]

In addition to using the pastoral mode to fashion himself as a "gentleman farmer," equally at home in the field and in the concert hall, Washington depicted agricultural education at Tuskegee as explicitly empirical.[117] In "The Experimental Farm" chapter of *Working with the Hands*, the text and accompanying images elucidate Carver's experiments in crop rotation and soil analysis as well as the school's efforts to disseminate his research findings to poor Black farmers. Both editions include an image of students and faculty "cultivating a patch of cassava on the agricultural experiment plot" (figure 2.14). Stylistically, the image is similar to the Hampton photographs. A group of eight male students hold hoes as if they are frozen in place. However, its staged, performative quality is indicated by their dress—or costuming. Most are dressed, uncharacteristically for farmers, in vests, dress shirts, dress slacks, and hats. The students look down at the ground, failing to return Johnston's gaze. The white fence running along the edge of the photo suggests enclosure, order, and containment. Yet the use of "experiment plot" in the caption suggests these students are not planting and hoeing haphazardly but are engaged in training and (Black) study, using scientific experimentation to enhance the institute's commitment to the plot as a site of Black survival and self-determination. As Washington reminded readers, agriculture is both an art and a science. So just as the New Negro farmer must "lay out the grounds artistically," he must also allow "science [to] shed light upon his art."[118]

The caption's reference to cassava, a root vegetable native to South America, elucidates Tuskegee's experiment plot as a geography of global agriculture as well. On it, Carver grew "ten varieties of corn, ... vetch, clovers, cassava, sugar beet, *Cuban sugar cane*, eight kinds of millet, the Persian and Arabian beans, and many other food and forage plants."[119] In 1899, Bishop Henry McNeal Turner, a prominent African American politician, emigrationist, and leader of the African Methodist Episcopal, or AME, church, sent Washington grape seed that he acquired in South Africa to see if Carver could get them to grow in the United States. "It makes a large beautiful grape that has the flavor of honey," Turner informed him. In response, Carver agreed to "plant them at once [likely on the experiment plot] and give them the best care." [120] The image of Carver in rural Alabama growing South American cassava, South African grapes, and Cuban sugarcane, perhaps conveyed to campus by one of the school's many Afro-Cuban students, reminds us that Tuskegee was in fact a global institution, both botanically and demographically.

The experiment plot also illuminates the speculative aspect of Tuskegee, where Carver hypothesized and tested different methods for plotting and sustaining Black agrarian futures for small farmers (see chapter 1). In *Working with the Hands*, the second image illustrating "The Experimental Farm" chapter shows how Carver speculated on Black futures using visual aesthetics in particular. Instead of a photograph, the image is a hand-drawn diagram made by Carver, illustrating for readers how to design and plant a forty-acre farm and use crop rotation to improve soil productivity over a span of seven years (figure 2.15). Just as Washington sought to regenerate the relationship between Blackness and labor in photographs, Carver's diagram visualized the regeneration of former plantation lands.

Furthermore, that Carver's template could be scaled up or down, "perfectly applicable" to a farm "of any size, even down to a garden patch," is an apt metaphor for how the Tuskegee model circulated throughout the Global Black South: it operated at multiple scales, influencing at once individual students and political leaders, the educational and political-economic aspirations of entire nation-states, and even Garvey's vision of pan-African solidarity.[121]

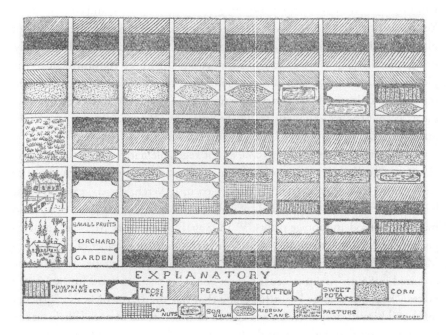

FIGURE 2.15. George Washington Carver's hand-drawn diagram for how to lay out a forty-acre farm.

Source: Washington, *Working with the Hands*, 1st ed. and subscription ed., 167.

Tuskegee's reclamation of agriculture through science is especially evident in two of the additional images in the subscription edition. If the images of students hoeing the ground and cutting and milling sugarcane recall agricultural labor of the old order, then the images of students conducting experiments in agricultural laboratories in the later edition counters or at least balances that depiction of manual labor (figure 2.16).

In the first image, students are depicted using beakers, test tubes, glass pipettes, and numerous other scientific instruments. They are dressed in suit coats and ties. Carver, pictured in the righthand corner, supervises one student, but most of them work unsupervised. The students' eyes are fixed on the task at hand, engaged in deep study and analysis. A pestle and mortar are displayed prominently in the foreground of the photograph, and scores of beakers and other containers are positioned on shelves throughout the laboratory. In another image captioned "chemical laboratory," printed later in the volume, "Soil Analysis" is written in beautiful cursive script on the chalkboard behind Carver (figure 2.17).

FIGURE 2.16. Eco-ontology at work: George Washington Carver (right foreground) observing Tuskegee students conduct experiments in an agricultural laboratory.

Source: Washington, *Working with the Hands*, subscription ed., between pp. 46 and 47. Photograph by Frances Benjamin Johnston.

Carver observes a student as he pours a solution into a glass using a filtration system, perhaps to mix the soil with water or other solvents to then separate particles from miscible molecules. Another student seems to be performing the same process using a funnel and a cylinder in the back left corner of the laboratory. The students weigh, measure, analyze, experiment, and study. This photo is not meant to depict mere manual-labor training but brain training as well.

Taken together, the agricultural images in *Working with the Hands* illuminate how Tuskegee used photographs to portray the full scope of Black agrarian futures through eco-ontological regeneration. Though the images of students pushing plows and cutting and milling sugarcane are perhaps initially reminiscent of slavery and sharecropping, the figure cutting cane in a suit, pastoral images of Washington as a gentleman farmer, and images of students working on the experiment plot and in agricultural and chemical laboratories rebrand Black farm life as compatible with science and middle-class aspirations and

FIGURE 2.17. Eco-ontology at work: George Washington Carver (*center*) teaching Tuskegee students about soil analysis in a chemical laboratory.

Source: Washington, *Working with the Hands*, subscription ed., between pp. 94 and 95. Photograph by Frances Benjamin Johnston.

establish the Tuskegee-trained New Negro as the exemplar of Black modern subjectivity.

REGENDERING THE SOUTHERN NEW NEGRO AND RE-ESTABLISHING THE HOME

Notably, in the "Soil Analysis" image (figure 2.17), both female and male students are portrayed conducting experiments in Carver's lab, a testament to his advocacy for enrolling women and girls into the school's Agricultural Department. The young women appear to be working independently of their male counterparts, suggesting their proficiency and equal treatment in a department that had only begun admitting female students a few years earlier.[122] In this way, Tuskegee's visual archive provides crucial insight into the gendered dimensions of the school's conception of the southern New Negro. Perhaps unsurprisingly,

Tuskegee's gender ideals reflected the heteronormative, patriarchal values that characterized racial uplift ideology. This was especially evident in the leadership structure, dress code, curriculum, and even the landscape and campus design. Booker T. Washington served as principal, while his third wife, Margaret Murray Washington, who insisted on being called "Mrs. Booker T. Washington," was designated "lady principal" and oversaw the Women's Department. Together, the Washingtons represented the pinnacle of southern New Negro manhood and womanhood to which students, faculty, and the entire race were to aspire. Their respective gender ideologies and performances were crucial to the institute's aesthetics, reflected most explicitly in their promotion of placemaking through homeownership and domesticity. Just as the farmhouse was the domain of Tuskegee's conception of the artist-worker through landscape design and the acquisition of middle-class décor, training students in "proper" gender conduct and ideals was deemed a crucial component of its vision of eco-ontological regeneration for the southern, Tuskegee-trained New Negro.

Although there has been some attention to how Booker T. Washington shaped New Negro manhood at the turn of the twentieth century, much less has been said of how Mrs. Washington shaped New Negro womanhood at Tuskegee and through her leadership in the Black women's club movement.[123] Though Mrs. Washington would never attain her husband's celebrity, she was a leading race woman in her own right. Born of mixed-race parentage in Macon, Mississippi, in either 1861 or 1865, Margaret attended Fisk University, where she earned a liberal arts education. She joined Tuskegee's faculty in 1889 as an instructor of English literature and was promoted to the position of lady principal in 1890. She and Booker wed in 1892. Mrs. Washington was an active and leading member of the Black women's club movement, a robust national network of educated middle-class Black women reformers dedicated to racial uplift. They were especially concerned with education for Black women and children as well as with more explicitly political issues, such as lynching, prison reform, and women's suffrage. In 1895, Mrs. Washington helped establish the Tuskegee Women's Club, a branch of the National Association of Colored Women (NACW); founded the Alabama Federation of Colored Women's Clubs and the Southern Federation of Colored Women's Clubs in 1898 and 1899, respectively; and from 1912 to 1916 served two terms as president of the NACW. Around 1922, she founded the International Council of Women of the Darker Races of the World and established what was essentially an international women's studies course at Tuskegee. The Black women's club movement included an impressive roster of activists, educators, and reformers, such as Ida B. Wells-Barnett, Anna Julia Cooper, Fannie Barrier Williams, Nannie Helen Burroughs, and Mary McLeod Bethune.

These powerhouse Black women were Mrs. Washington's contemporaries, with whom she forged a vision of New Negro womanhood at the turn of the twentieth century.[124]

In August 1895, just weeks before her husband delivered the Atlanta Exposition Address, Mrs. Washington delivered an address entitled "The New Negro Woman" before the First National Conference of Colored Women in Boston. She claimed sisterhood with and paternalistic responsibility for "the masses of negro women" and espoused an agenda for New Negro womanhood rooted in the domestic sphere. "The two words, home and woman, are so closely connected that I could not, even if I desired, separate one from the other," she declared.[125] Under her leadership, Tuskegee's women's curriculum reflected a vision for New Negro womanhood that was synonymous with home and hearth, imparting the cult of domesticity that shaped the Victorian gender norms at the heart of racial uplift ideology and the Black women's club movement alike. As Kevin Gaines argues, though club women such as Wells-Barnett and Cooper "challenged expectations of women's subordination within marriage," they "agreed with the importance of home, family, and marriage among blacks, and for American civilization."[126]

Tuskegee's vision of New Negro womanhood and manhood was based on a distinctly gendered division of labor. Industries for Girls, later the Department of Women's Industries, taught "mattress making, plain sewing, dressmaking and millinery, cooking, laundry work, and general housekeeping."[127] Conversely, the Department for Boys, later the Department of Mechanical Industries, taught trades such as carpentry, steam engineering, electrical engineering, brick masonry, printing, and mechanical drawing. In the Academic Department, young women and men took classes together, and as the leadership's ideas about women's and girls' education and labor evolved, young women were encouraged to enroll in the Agricultural Department. Other trades that enrolled both young women and men included typesetting, tailoring, caring for the sick, market gardening, poultry raising, beekeeping, horticulture, and floriculture.[128]

Tuskegee paid considerable attention to training students' bodies to comport with its gender norms and ideals. "It is of the greatest importance that girls be properly clothed," stated the 1901–1902 *Tuskegee Annual Catalogue*, "not only for the preservation of their health but also to aid in teaching them economy and correct ideas of dressing." Young women were required to wear "a braided navy blue, sailor, uniform dress and a plain sailor hat," accessorized with a "red tie and turnover" during the week and a "white ribbon" on Sundays.[129] There is no comparable justification given for the young men's attire, only that they must wear a dark-blue coat, pants, and military cap. Alongside dress, the school inculcated gender ideals through "physical training." Young women were taught gymnastics "to counteract the evils resulting from habitually incorrect positions, to improve the general carriage, bring about healthy respiration and circulation and to tone up the whole body." Young men, in contrast, were instructed in military training to cultivate "habits of order, neatness and unquestioned obedience." Military drills were considered "good physical training" that promoted "a manly bearing."[130] While it is unclear what constituted the "evils" of "habitually incorrect positions" among young women or "a manly bearing" among young men, Tuskegee was adamant about training students' bodies to adhere to strict gender expectations.[131] Thus, students' bodily comportment was routinely scrutinized. As one observer noted, "If a girl does not carry herself erect" when students file out of the daily chapel services, "or if any detail of her dress or general bearing is not absolutely satisfactory, the hand of the teacher stops her and she has to fall out of line and stand there in the eyes of all, embarrassed and humiliated." Likewise, "the deportment and dress" of male students was expected to be "perfect," too. "Untidy hair, unbrushed clothes, dirt, unblacked shoes, a button off or even a button of a coat left unfastened, and out of the line the unhappy culprit comes."[132]

Tuskegee's gender ideals were even built into the landscape and campus design. As mentioned, the girls' dormitories were strategically placed in the interior of campus as added protection from the threat of racial-sexual violence in a milieu that viewed Black education as an affront to the racial order (thus easily the object of white vigilantism) and Black women as the always-already sexually available objects of white male power and desire. The boys' dormitories, along with the less ornate industrial buildings, were placed on the outside of campus, likely as a buffer of protection for girls and women and to resist drawing attention to the institute's more pretentious buildings and bourgeois aspirations.[133] This gendering of protection is further reflected in the disciplinary code printed in the annual catalog, wherein "male students, when permitted to leave the grounds," were required to "wear the regulation cap," whereas "no young woman is permitted to leave the grounds of the Institute unless accompanied by a lady teacher."[134] Albeit heteronormative, patriarchal, and restrictive, such were the realities of ensuring the safety of Black students, especially Black girls and women, in the Jim Crow South.

Ironically, as much as Tuskegee promoted traditional gender norms, much of Booker T. Washington's performance of New Negro manhood and the school's insistence on cleanliness and domesticity reflected the values of the white northern schoolmarms he had encountered at Hampton. Although masculinity was traditionally aligned with outdoor labor and femininity with indoor pursuits,

Marlon Ross brilliantly argues that Washington routinely recounted how he achieved "civilization" by mastering indoor, domestic activities such as sweeping and cleaning that were usually performed by Black women under the supervision of "white ladies." In fact, it is the "infamous sweeping incident" in *Up from Slavery*, Ross reminds us, "that initiates Washington's transition from boyhood to manhood." Washington's performance of New Negro manhood was thus suffused by what Ross terms "sissy housekeeping." This was no doubt a fraught strategy considering that enslaved Black men were "compelled to perform the menial work usually assigned to women in U.S. society" and that Black male identity continued to be "cemented to domestic service" during Jim Crow.[135] Washington's "sissy" gender performance was thus in tension with many members of the African American elite who viewed reestablishing "proper" gender norms and asserting "racial manhood" as a primary goal of racial uplift.

Based on Tuskegee's curriculum, it is unclear if Washington required Tuskegee's male students to perform such tasks as sweeping, though they were certainly expected to practice cleanliness and good hygiene. The domestic sphere—cooking, cleaning, and so on—was primarily the domain of young women students. However, when Washington oversaw a cohort of Native American male students at Hampton—wherein he performed his achievement of liberal subjecthood and civilization by imitating "the white colonial posture toward native peoples," as Lisa Lowe puts it—he insisted that they make their beds properly; thus, it stands to reason that Tuskegee's male students would have been responsible for similar personal domestic tasks.[136]

Ultimately, Washington's manhood was affirmed through his heterosexuality: he was married three times and fathered as many children. However, the same cannot be said of George Washington Carver, who remained unmarried his entire life and whose effeminate bodily comportment, high-pitched voice, and interest in conventionally feminine pursuits (such as painting and laundering) were often read as queer and "sissified" behavior among his Tuskegee colleagues. In one institutional publication issued in 1916, Carver is described as "an old bachelor of pure African descent, without a drop of white blood, who in himself refutes two popular fallacies: the one that bachelors cannot be skilled in domestic affairs, and the other, that pure-blooded Africans cannot achieve intellectual distinction."[137] On one hand, this touting of Carver's racial and gendered exceptionality challenges the myth of Africans' inherent intellectual inferiority and subtly celebrates his adroitness in the domestic sphere as transgressing gender norms. On the other hand, according to Ross, Carver's "effeminacy became both a subject of concern for Washington and a target of his [Carver's] academic rivals" at Tuskegee and led to "rampant rumors" of his homosexuality.[138] Nevertheless, as two of Tuskegee's most prominent Black male figures, Washington and Carver projected versions of New Negro manhood that integrated domesticity. This is not to say that either figure was in fact queer or held same-gender desires but rather to illuminate the contradictions of Tuskegee's New Negro aesthetics and gender performances. Despite the curriculum's efforts to train male students to cultivate a "manly bearing," one wonders how the examples of Washington and especially Carver may have created space for much more fluid performances of Black masculinity on campus that would never make it into institutional literature.

Beyond Washington's and Carver's respective "sissy" pursuits, it is within Tuskegee's women's curriculum that we see its most significant contributions to ideas about gender, labor, and education. In many institutional publications, at least one chapter, often penned by Mrs. Washington, was dedicated to the education of girls and women, who composed about one-third of the student population in 1900.[139] Mrs. Washington's writings suggest that there was a fundamental tension over educational objectives for Black girls and women. While poor, rural parents viewed traditionally feminine occupations such as sewing as worthy pursuits for their daughters, white philanthropists and social reformers such as Susan B. Anthony donated money to help "plant" the "new industry" of broom making precisely because it gave "girls other means of livelihood besides sewing, housework, and cooking." Accordingly, Tuskegee developed a curriculum that gave "special attention to the training of girls in all that pertains to dress, health, physical culture, and general housekeeping."[140]

"Girl life at Tuskegee is strenuous," wrote Mrs. Washington. The Women's Department consisted primarily of traditional domestic trades such as millinery, dressmaking, laundering, and sewing, but a few girls also studied typesetting and tailoring in the Boys' Trades Building: the "girl tailors" were admitted as "equals of the young men," Mrs. Washington noted, and proved to be just as "capable workers" and of "equal aptitude." In the broom-making division, girls learned to operate machinery, just as their male counterparts did in the Department of Mechanical Industries. Alongside their chosen trades and academic work, all girls were required to take housekeeping and cooking twice a week, so that "no girl is graduated from the school without the finishing touch of the little home." Beyond schoolwork, Tuskegee's young women participated in lectures, girls' clubs, and "circle entertainments"; took gymnastics, sewing, or swimming; and sat on the campus green, listening to "band concert[s] on the lawn" and wearing "the blue skirts and white waists of the season."[141]

While Tuskegee's conception of New Negro womanhood prioritized the domestic sphere, the Washingtons also revised these bourgeois ideals by introducing "out-of-door industries" into the women's curriculum—courses in dairying, poultry raising, horticulture, floriculture and landscape gardening, market gardening, and livestock raising. "All through the period of slavery," Booker T. Washington wrote in *Working with the Hands*, "the idea prevailed that women, not slaves, should do as little work as possible with their hands.... When the coloured girl became free, she naturally craved the same education in which she had seen the white woman specializing."[142] Tuskegee's women students—many of whom were no more than one or two generations removed from slavery—naturally equated manual work with what the literary theorist Hortense Spillers has famously termed the "ungendering" of Black women's bodies during slavery.[143] "In the awful days gone by," Mrs. Washington observed in her address in 1895, "the word 'home,' the word 'woman' was a mockery, so far as we are concerned; in fact, there was no home, there was no manhood. All were chattel, bought, used, and sold at the master's will."[144] Tuskegee's women were at first understandably "very timid," Booker T. Washington observed, and "felt ashamed to have any one see them at work in the garden or orchard" because such outdoor activities conjured the violent ungendering and objectification of Black women's bodies that their foremothers had endured during slavery.[145] As Mrs. Washington's address makes clear, New Negro womanhood at the fin de siècle was largely conceived in heteronormative terms as a process of regendering Black women's bodies and reestablishing the family unit. By creating outdoor industries for women, Tuskegee was somewhat ahead of its time because before women fought to work outside of the home, they first had to be persuaded to work outdoors.

There were ample employment opportunities for women's outdoor work, Washington maintained, because the South had a mild climate and was primarily agricultural. And since most of Tuskegee's women students were "the daughters of colored farmers, living on small plantations," the institute sought to train them how to properly establish gardens to help their families benefit from such a "profitable" industry when they returned to their home communities.[146] So successful was the school at enrolling young women in the Agricultural Department that by 1904, Mrs. Washington would observe, "gardening and greenhouse work are becoming so attractive . . . that there are constant applications for transfers from the sewing divisions to this outside work."[147]

Tuskegee's outdoor curriculum gave women a central role in the Washingtons' conception of the artist-worker. The garden and greenhouse were especially important, allowing women to raise food for the table and the market and to cultivate plants and flowers to beautify the home. "A sense of the beautiful is

GIRLS GARDENING.

FIGURE 2.18. "Girls Gardening." A group of Tuskegee's young women students cultivating vegetables.

Source: Washington, *Tuskegee and Its People*, between pp. 344 and 345. Photograph by Frances Benjamin Johnston.

cultivated and given expression in floriculture," Washington wrote in *Working with the Hands*, allowing "more of nature's beauty" to "pervade the home and its surroundings."[148] Images of the women's outdoor industries, used to illustrate Tuskegee's various publications, depict the feminine dimensions of Washington's aesthetics of work (see, for example, figures 2.18 and 2.19).

In photographs of young women students tilling a field of crops and tending to a flower garden, none of the young women look directly into the camera, for they are seemingly too absorbed in their work to notice the photographer's presence. Though pictured in the garden with hoes in hand amid rows of dirt, crops, and flowers, their clothing is more appropriate for indoor work. In one image, the young women wear white or light-colored dresses without a trace of dirt on them. Instead of the headscarf that enslaved women often wore to protect their hair from dirt and the harsh southern sun, these women wear stylish hats, perhaps crafted in the institute's millinery division, or simply pin their hair back in neat plats or braids away from their faces. Once again, these images of the agricultural worker cloaked in middle-class attire underscore the paradox of

FIGURE 2.19. "Outdoor Work for Girls": a class in floriculture.

Source: Washington, *Working with the Hands*, 1st ed. and subscription ed., between pp. 108 and 109. Photograph by Frances Benjamin Johnston.

Tuskegee's southern New Negro aesthetic as both fact and fiction, empirical evidence and aspirational performance.

Though Washington emphasized women's outdoor industries as a social and curricular innovation, Mrs. Washington observed that dressmaking and millinery were the most highly sought-after trades in the Women's Department. Students in the Dressmaking Division spent their day "filling orders for tailor-made dresses in silk and cloth, measuring, drafting, cutting, and fitting." She continued: "The girl in the millinery work, shaping forms, trimming hats, blending colors, drawing designs, studying textiles and fabrics for analysis in her theory classes ... completes hat after hat ... and then comes her own creation, a pattern hat, undersized of course, but a real dress hat and a thing of beauty." Combining theory and practice, these student-artists wove "many a fanciful thought ... in with the reed and raffia of the Indian baskets, African purses, belts, and pineneedle work-baskets."[149] By designing and crafting dresses, hats, and other accessories, Tuskegee's New Negro women were interested not only in beautifying the landscape but also in "cultivating beauty" for themselves, as Farah Jasmine Griffin observes of Black women's dressmaking and sewing practices and as indicated by the students' refined costumes in figures 2.18 and 2.19.[150] I say "costumes" deliberately here because theirs was not the typical dress for women in Tuskegee's Agricultural Department, who usually wore "an overall gingham apron and sunbonnet of the same material."[151] The women being photographed were actively performing New Negro womanhood before Johnston's camera through their sartorial choices, hybridizing Victorian aesthetics with agricultural and industrial labor.

Mrs. Washington also led several initiatives extending the institute's conception of New Negro womanhood to rural Black women and children in surrounding towns and communities. Although numerous women were present at the inaugural Tuskegee Negro Conference in 1892, Mrs. Washington quickly realized that "they had little actual place in it."[152] In response, she established the Woman's Meeting in the town of Tuskegee, which used the extension program to export the bourgeois domestic values of Tuskegee's curriculum and the Black women's club movement into the countryside. The Woman's Meeting grew from six attendees to nearly three hundred by 1904. They met for two hours every Saturday, discussing topics such as food preparation and diet, beautifying and cleaning the home, encouraging "morals among young girls" to "resist men who attempt to rob them of their honour and virtue," and "teaching boys and men to respect women." There was especial emphasis on self-presentation, such as clothing choices, encouraging rural Black women to stop going barefoot as they had in the days of slavery and to braid their hair instead of wrapping it with handkerchiefs. Woman's Meeting attendees were instructed to develop more self-respect by staying away from "street corners, depots, and . . . excursions" and to cultivate "race pride" as they would their "crops," an eco-ontological dictum if there ever were one, albeit couched in the explicitly classist and moralist rhetoric of uplift.[153] Importantly, Mrs. Washington's extension efforts also included prison reform for Black youth, especially Black boys routinely exploited by the convict-lease system and housed in adult prisons with hardcore criminals. Through her leadership in the Alabama Federation of Colored Women's Clubs, the organization founded two reform schools for wayward Black youth: the Mt. Meigs Reformatory for Juvenile Negro Law-Breakers and later the Mt. Meigs Rescue Home for Girls.[154]

Alongside Tuskegee's proscriptions for New Negro womanhood and manhood, its domestic vision promoted land acquisition and homeownership as the pinnacle of achievement for Black eco-ontological regeneration. At the Tuskegee Negro Conference, attendees pledged to jettison "the habit of living in one-room houses" and to own and beautify homes and farms, and attendees at the Woman's Meeting made similar pledges.[155] In Washington's periodical publications, he frequently juxtaposed images of slave cabins or sharecroppers' shacks with middle-class homes to illustrate racial progress. For instance, his article "Negro

Homes," published in *Century Magazine* in 1908, opened with an image of a quaint, one-room slave cabin (figure 2.20) that contrasts starkly with the images of lavish and stately residences of the Black professional class that illustrate the rest of the article (figure 2.21).[156]

Washington endeavored to make southern farm life more attractive in part because he was suspicious of cities, a popular sentiment among Progressive Era reformers. He strongly discouraged the earliest waves of the Great Migration and even encouraged Black businessmen to move to the South, where the masses of African Americans still lived. Undoubtedly, migration and mobility were part of the fugitive spirit that characterized modern Black subjectivity, but they were modes of Black subjection also. The transatlantic and domestic slave trades, for instance, depended on the coerced movement of immobilized, captive African people, tearing families and communities asunder. Thus, following emancipation, Black home life, much like Black gender, became an important battleground for regenerating Black being and forging a new relationship to the nation-state. While racist terrorists waged an unremitting campaign against Black domestic life through lynchings, land dispossession, and sexual assaults against Black women and men, African Americans sought to (re)constitute the Black home to evince their humanity and readiness for citizenship. As Washington observed, "The Negro has had to learn the meaning of home since he learned the meaning of freedom. All work which has to do with his uplifting must begin with his home and its surroundings."[157] In contrast to fugitive mobility, the Washingtons imagined freedom in terms of local, grassroots practices of placemaking such as farming, domesticity, and community building to counter the rootlessness and coerced migrations of the diasporic condition.

While movement, migration, and the "routes" of transnationalism are often the predominant paradigms of modernity in contemporary Black studies, the historian and visual culture theorist Tina Campt proposes homemaking and "staying put" as equally significant expressions of Black modern subjectivity. Within this context, domesticity is not immobilizing or carceral but linked instead to a concept Campt calls "homeostasis," the "active and effortful balancing of multiple flows that produce motion even in stillness." In the context of the immobilizations of slavery and Jim Crow, the Washingtons proposed domesticity and placemaking as forms of upward socioeconomic mobility. The reconstitution of the Black home and Washington's efforts to make Black domestic life legible through visual culture perform the politics of refusal and disruption that Campt associates with stasis: "the very normativity they enact was itself a refusal to recognize an ideology that refused them."[158]

NEGRO HOMES
BY BOOKER T. WASHINGTON

THE first Negro home that I remember was a log-cabin about fourteen by sixteen feet square. It had a small, narrow door, which hung on rusty, worn-out hinges. The windows were mere openings in the wall, protected by a rickety shutter, which sometimes was closed in winter, but which usually hung dejectedly on uncertain hinges against the walls of the house.

Such a thing as a glass window was unknown to this house. There was no floor, or, rather, there was a floor, but it was nothing more than the naked earth. There was only one room, which served as kitchen, parlor, and bedroom for a family of five, which consisted of my mother, my elder brother, my sister, myself, and the cat. In this cabin we all ate and slept, my mother being the cook on the place. My own bed was a heap of rags on the floor in the corner of the room next to the fireplace. It was not until after the emancipation that I enjoyed for the first time in my life the luxury of sleeping in a bed. It was at times, I suppose, somewhat crowded in those narrow quarters, though I do not now remember having suffered on that account, especially as the cabin was always pretty thoroughly ventilated, particularly in winter, through the wide openings between the logs in the walls.

I mention these facts here because the little slaves' cabin in which I lived as a child, and which is associated with all my earliest memories, is typical of the places in which the great mass of the Negro people lived a little more than forty years ago; and there are thousands of Negro men and women living to-day in comfortable and well-kept homes who will recognize what I have written as a good description of the homes in which they were born and reared.

Probably there is no single object that so accurately represents and typifies the mental and moral condition of the larger proportion of the members of my race fifty years ago as this same little slave cabin. For the same reason it may be said that the best evidence of the progress which the race has made since emancipation is the character and quality of the homes which they are building for themselves to-day.

In spite of difficulties and discouragements, this progress has been considerable. Starting at the close of the war with almost nothing in the way of property, and with no traditions and with little training to fit them for freedom, Negro farmers alone had acquired by 1890 nearly as much land as is contained in the European states of Holland and Belgium combined. Meanwhile there has been a marked improvement in the character of the Negro farmer's home. The old, one-roomed log-cabins are slowly but steadily disappearing. Year by year the number of neat and comfortable farmers' cottages has increased. From my home in Tuskegee I can drive in some directions for a distance of five or six miles and not see a single one-roomed cabin, though I can see thousands of acres of

---

FIGURE 2.20. Title page of Booker T. Washington's "Negro Homes" article.

Source: Booker T. Washington, "Negro Homes," *Century Magazine*, May 1908.

FIGURE 2.21. Images from Booker T. Washington's "Negro Homes" article.

Source: Washington, "Negro Homes."

By lingering in the interstice between "tilling a field and writing a poem," Tuskegee's eco-ontological experiment in Black world making emerges as not only a material and geographic strategy but a deeply aesthetic and performative one as well. Through the school's dynamic sonic and visual performance culture, Tuskegeeans resignified the racial indexicality of modern Black sound and the laboring Black body, redesigned the plantation landscape, reclaimed and redefined Black gender and domesticity, and ultimately staged the southern New Negro as uniquely positioned to meet the challenges of the new century. In response to a "Negro problem" of epic proportions, Washington and Tuskegee's faculty and staff devised this elaborate set of strategies to ameliorate Black life on virtually every possible front and, in doing so, forged a vision of the southern, Tuskegee-trained New Negro as one who could seamlessly integrate modern scientific agriculture and industry with the accoutrements and values of the bourgeois Victorian. Here was the exemplar of Black progress and proficiency in the heart of the rural, Jim Crow South.

While plot I has focused primarily on Tuskegee within a domestic context, plots II and III will trace how this vision of an agrarian, repurposed plantation future influenced Black artists, intellectuals, and political leaders throughout the Global Black South. Tuskegee's literary and performance culture—especially Washington's oratory and autobiography as well as the school's photographic archive and annual catalogs—helped to circulate and project its vision of Black modernity to the broader diaspora as a viable strategy for navigating the plantation's protean afterlives. Although the story of Tuskegee's transplantation to Africa, especially Togo, has been rightly criticized for Washington's failure to engage indigenous African knowledges and peoples, plot II follows Tuskegee to Cuba and Haiti to elucidate a more symbiotic praxis of diasporic exchange. Afro-Cuban and Haitian elites strategically translated Washington and the Tuskegee project across a range of linguistic, cultural, and political contexts—selectively embracing some aspects of them but vehemently rejecting others—as they navigated the vagaries of their respective internal, domestic challenges alongside the ongoing international threats of European colonialism and U.S. imperialism.

PLOT II

3

Strategic Translations

Race, Nation, and the Affordances of
Booker T. Washington and Tuskegee in Cuba

At Hampton Institute's commencement exercises in 1875, two students, Robert J. Whiting and a young Booker T. Washington, engaged in an "animated debate" on the "annexation of Cuba." Whiting maintained that annexation would result in "the emancipation of the Cuban blacks, the doing away of the slave trade, the increase of the colored vote, and the new market for products." Washington's counterargument—described variously by contemporaneous reviewers as "excellent and logical," "terse and vigorous," and "lawyer-like"—insisted that "Spain has a right to Cuba by discovery and colonization" and that Cuba would be an added burden to the United States, which was already dealing with the aftermath of slavery and civil war.[1]

Though Afro-Cubans were still enslaved in 1875, as Washington himself had been only a decade earlier, his argument, or at least the press's coverage of it, expressed no sense of racial solidarity based on a shared experience of bondage. Rather, Washington starkly distinguished Afro-Cubans from African Americans. On one hand, Washington's position was anti-interventionist in that he did not view Cuba as a "new market for products" or celebrate the potential acquisition of territory. On the other hand, he failed to critique Spanish imperialism or slavery. Ever the pragmatic nationalist, Washington insisted on ameliorating issues at home in the United States before engaging in a conflict abroad. It is impossible to know whether the young Washington was in earnest in his isolationist attitude toward Cuba or if he was simply an effective debater. Nevertheless, almost a quarter of a century later, as the Spanish-American War drew to a close, Washington would articulate a vastly different attitude toward U.S. intervention on the island, positioning himself and the Tuskegee Institute at the nexus of U.S. empire and Black diasporic uplift.

In August 1898, just three years after his now-infamous Atlanta Exposition Address—where he first encouraged Black and white southerners to embrace a segregated system where they could be "as separate as the fingers" socially, "yet one as the hand in all things essential to mutual progress"—Washington launched a newspaper campaign to solicit financial support for educating Cuban and eventually Puerto Rican students at Tuskegee. He proposed "to bring a number of the most promising negro young men and women to this institution to receive training, that they may return to Cuba, and start in the interest of the people industrial training on the island. Tuskegee is so near Cuba that it is conveniently located for this work."[2] Previously, at the outset of the Spanish-American War, Washington had advocated sending southern African Americans to Cuba because they were more accustomed to the climate than the white man and had successfully sent a group of five Tuskegee nurses to the frontlines.[3] Educating Cuban students at Tuskegee presented yet another opportunity for African Americans to prove their usefulness to the U.S. nation-state.

This chapter interrogates Washington's diasporic imagination by detailing how he enfolded Afro-Cubans and, to a lesser degree, Afro–Puerto Ricans within his vision of agrarian futures in the Global Black South. In his speeches and writings about the Spanish-American War, Washington championed African Americans' heroism as evidence of their worthiness for full civil rights, on one hand, and promoted his school as uniquely positioned to help uplift Black Cubans and Puerto Ricans, on the other. Perceiving Cuba and Puerto Rico as primarily agricultural societies, much like the U.S. South, Washington proposed to transplant his agrarian, repurposed plantation future by training Afro-Cuban and Afro–Puerto Rican youth in industrial and agricultural methods. The southern New Negro thus became the basis for articulating a diasporic uplift project that radiated out from Tuskegee and the rural U.S. South. Although Washington forged ties with both Cuba and Puerto Rico alike, the nature of Tuskegee's relationship with each island was distinct. Therefore, this chapter focuses primarily on Tuskegee's transplantation to Cuba, and chapter 5 examines Tuskegee's relationship with Puerto Rico.

Washington's efforts to export the Tuskegee model to Cuba were enthusiastically supported by several Afro-Cuban leaders. Juan Gualberto Gómez, an Afro-Cuban revolutionary leader in the Spanish-American War, aided in facilitating what Frank Guridy has called the "Tuskegee–Cuba connection," whereby Afro-Cuban students made the journey to rural Alabama to take up agricultural and industrial training. Many of these students and their parents were first introduced to Washington and Tuskegee through *De esclavo á catedrático* (From slave to professor, 1902), the "Cuban-Spanish" translation of *Up from Slavery.*[4] Subsequently, hundreds of Afro-Cuban and Afro–Puerto Rican students and parents wrote to Washington in Spanish, requesting copies of the Tuskegee annual catalog in their own language and admission to the school (see also chapter 5).

Taking seriously Brent Hayes Edwards's claim that "the cultures of black internationalism can be seen only in translation,"[5] I show how Afro-Cubans grappled with the relevance of the Tuskegee project to their own lives and (re)interpreted the literary and visual economies of Washington and Tuskegee to address the unique conditions of race, nation, and empire they confronted in the early years of the Cuban republic. Though Washington attempted to enfold Afro-Cubans into his primarily agrarian vision of Black futures, Afro-Cubans pursued other affordances of Tuskegee—namely, its industrial curriculum, strategy for facilitating interracial cooperation and securing philanthropic support for Black education, and depiction of middle-class subjectivity. Tuskegee's transplantation to Cuba's experiment plot and subsequent cross-fertilization with Afro-Cuban cultural and political aspirations thus produced a new variety.

The life and work of Rafael Serra y Montalvo is one of the most salient examples of this hybridization of Tuskegee and Cuba. An Afro-Cuban cigar worker turned journalist, translator, editor, educator, politician, and nationalist, Serra would have encountered Washington during his twenty-year exile in the United States after Cuba's Ten Years' War (1868–1878). The 1907 edition of Serra's book *Para blancos y negros: Ensayos políticos, sociales y económicos* (For blacks and whites: Political, social, and economic essays) imagined a biracial democratic future for the burgeoning Cuban republic and drew on Washington and the Tuskegee project to achieve that end. Serra reproduced images of Washington's family and Tuskegee campus buildings, reprinted a Spanish translation of the school's course catalog, and, most importantly, published an essay criticizing the Cuban elite for their mistranslation of Washington's bootstrap political philosophy as a rationalization for ignoring Cuba's poor Black and recently emancipated populations. Critically, though, Serra did not embrace the Tuskegee project wholesale and was staunchly opposed to U.S. annexation of and African American immigration to Cuba. Rather, he incorporated aspects of the Tuskegee model to ameliorate the racial and class fractures that he believed impeded Cuban sovereignty. Both Serra and Washington performed what I call "strategic translation," whereby a member of one diasporic community engages the ideas and strategies of a different diasporic group, while each member remains committed to their respective nationalist projects at home.

I close this chapter by analyzing how Washington and Tuskegee circulated in early twentieth-century Cuban periodicals and inspired at least two Afro-Cuban social, political, and educational organizations: the Instituto Booker T. Washington and the Booker T. Washington Society. Through these efforts, Afro-Cubans strategically translated Washington and the southern, Tuskegee New Negro to fit their own conceptions of modern Afro-Cuban identity. Even as the architects of the new republic touted racial democracy, Afro-Cubans were well aware of how race influenced and often circumscribed their daily realities. Thus, they laid claim to the nation-state while contesting the ongoing delimitations imposed on them. Washington and Tuskegee appealed to Afro-Cubans as a model for reconciling race and nation as well as the power and possibility of Black institution building in the aftermath of war and as the specter of U.S. imperial occupation and annexation loomed. Yet, like Serra, Afro-Cubans did not embrace Washington's educational philosophy wholesale and were critical of what they viewed as Tuskegee's passiveness in the face of racial oppression. Ultimately, these strategic translations capture both the alliances and frictions that necessarily emerged among Global Black South communities as they negotiated distinct yet overlapping social, cultural, and political values and aspirations in the plantation's afterlife.

BOOKER T. WASHINGTON AND "CUBAN EDUCATION"

In an address entitled "Cuban Education" delivered before the Chicago Peace Jubilee in 1898, Booker T. Washington touted African American soldiers' bravery during the Spanish-American War as evidence of their loyalty to the U.S. nation-state. He skillfully constructed an image of the Black soldier as the consummate patriot and champion of the oppressed. When "the safety and honor of the republic" was "threatened by a foreign foe," the Black soldier "chose the better part" despite "his own wrongs ... [and] discrimin[ation] ... in his own country."[6] Like many of his African American contemporaries, Washington mobilized the Spanish-American War as the mechanism by which African Americans could improve their relationship to the United States by aiding their transition from formerly enslaved subjects to war heroes, patriots, and citizens.

Following Reconstruction, national attitudes toward African Americans shifted from sympathy to pathology, regarding them as obstacles to the reunification of the republic. Much of Washington's project was committed to recuperating the image of African Americans as a national asset instead of a national problem. Whereas the Civil War had divided the nation, pitting brother against brother, the Spanish-American War could potentially unify it by shifting ire away from Black Americans as a threat to national unity and instead toward Spain as a foreign foe. This American nationalist logic echoed Washington's "cast down your buckets" mantra, first articulated in the Atlanta Exposition Address, where he encouraged white southerners to forge commercial and economic ties with Black southerners instead of new European immigrants.

In "Cuban Education," after celebrating the recent U.S. victory over Spain, Washington turned his attention to the "one other victory for Americans to win": the "blotting out of racial prejudices," which was as "important as any that has occupied our army and navy." He observed, "We can celebrate the era of peace in no more effectual way than by a firm resolve on the part of Northern men and Southern men, black men and white men, that the trenches that we together dug around Santiago shall be the eternal burial place of all that which separates us in our business and civil relations."[7] This effort to bury American "racial prejudices" in the trenches of Santiago is a figurative expression with material implications, indicating Washington's utilitarian and quasi-imperial attitude toward Cuba. Historically, American colonies were the dumping grounds for Europe's deviants and criminals; thus, dumping U.S. racial prejudice into Cuba would enact a similar imperial violence. I suppose one could argue that Washington proposed to *bury* American racial prejudice in Cuba, not simply to transplant it. However, the waste of plantation modernity has tended to be radioactive and, even when buried, has seeped through the soils of history to infect present conditions. As it happened, the United States would indeed export its legacy of interracial tensions to Cuba, both unburied and thoroughly imperial.

The "Cuban education" Washington promoted in the address was less about educating and improving the lives of Afro-Cubans per se than about educating white Americans about African Americans' loyalty to the nation-state during an international conflict and issuing "not a threat but a warning" to the "white race" that "the only solution of the 'Negro Problem' which will remove all menace to the tranquility and interest of the country is a universal recognition of the Negro's civil rights."[8] Ever the educator, Washington held up the Spanish-American War as an object lesson on the possibilities and "danger" of interracial conflict. Thus, his relationship to Cuba was primarily functional and utilitarian. Nevertheless, if Washington has been criticized for dissembling and masking his civil rights activism beneath accommodationist rhetoric, his "Cuban Education" speech is one instance when he seemingly advocated more forcefully for Black civil rights; in fact, he faced considerable backlash for the speech in the white southern press and ultimately issued a corrective to reassure white southerners that he only meant eliminating racial prejudice in "business and civil relations" and had not changed his position on his "separate as the fingers" social philosophy.[9]

Alongside reconstructing the image of African Americans as citizens, patriots, and unifying agents, Washington also exploited the specter and recent memory of the Civil War to suggest that something like the Cuban backlash against Spain was not inconceivable in the United States if racial inequality persisted: "God has been teaching the Spanish nation a terrible lesson ... that for every one of her subjects that she has left in ignorance, poverty and crime, the price must be paid; ... [either] with the very heart of the nation, [or] ... with the proudest and bluest blood of her sons and with treasure that is beyond computation. From this spectacle I pray God that America will learn a lesson in respect to the 8 million Negroes in the South."[10] Significantly, Washington did not critique Spanish colonialism and imperialism in his Chicago speech. He was no anti-imperialist and held no sustained critique of colonialism either. Rather, he accepted as a fact of modern life that European countries, the United States, and other powerful nations would attempt to colonize less powerful ones and spread the "light of civilization." He directed his critique instead to colonial powers' exploitation of the peoples they colonized. God punished Spain not because it had colonized Cuba in the first place but because it had failed to lift its subjects out of "ignorance, poverty, and crime." Colonialism and imperialism were inevitable, Washington intimated, so Black people's best option was to use industrial education to achieve "civilization." Indeed, in response to a proposition that African Americans immigrate to Cuba, Washington responded, "But even if the Negro should go off to some other part of the world, and prosper, what reason have we to believe that the white man would stay away from him? If he went away to some inhospitable part of the world and failed the white man would possibly leave him alone, for a time, but just so sure as he was successful the white man would follow him and then we would have another race problem."[11] While Washington accurately ascertained the insatiability of white people's desire for possession, conquest, and accumulation, his error was in overestimating white investment in the civilizing mission while underestimating their investment in white supremacy and the inherent depravity of the civilizing mission. Thus, Washington's cautionary tale for the United States about the consequences of ongoing unequal treatment of its Black citizenry failed to heed one of the most significant lessons of the Civil War and plantation modernity in general: that white supremacy will go to any lengths to sustain itself, even if that means sacrificing white life and capital to do so.

If his "Cuban Education" speech was invested in Cuba only insofar as it improved conditions for Black Americans in the United States, Washington would soon forge more material relations with Afro-Cubans by actively recruiting Cuban students to Tuskegee. Extending his domestic racial uplift program to the Caribbean territories newly acquired by the United States would solidify Tuskegee's newfound prominence and secure his own position as the chief representative of his race domestically and possibly internationally. As early as August 1898, Washington launched a newspaper campaign, "Industrial Education for Cuban Negroes," to bring Cuban students to Tuskegee and train them in industrial methods. He reasoned:

> I believe all will agree that it is our duty to follow the work of destruction in Cuba with that of construction. One-half of the population in Cuba is composed of mulattoes or negroes. All who have visited Cuba agree that they need to put them on their feet the strength that they can get by thorough intellectual, religious, and industrial training, such as is given at Hampton and Tuskegee. . . . It will do for them what it is doing for our people in the South.
>
> If the funds can be secured, it is the plan of the Tuskegee Normal and Industrial Institute . . . to bring a number of the most promising negro young men and women to this institution to receive training, that they may return to Cuba. . . . Tuskegee is so near Cuba that it is conveniently located for this work.[12]

Whereas his "Cuban Education" address painted Afro-Cubans as "the oppressed from a distant isle," his newspaper campaign cited Afro-Cubans' geographic proximity and shared racial background as justification for facilitating a hemispheric migration network. Unlike Martin Delany, one of the most prominent Black hemispheric thinkers of the nineteenth century, often touted as a father of Black nationalism, Washington was not a proponent of African American immigration to the Caribbean or Africa. Rather, he proposed bringing Cubans to the U.S. South—rural Alabama no less—to prepare them for what Saidiya Hartman calls the "burdened individuality of freedom" and citizenship.[13] Though this period is commonly referred to as the nadir of African American history when anti-Black violence was at an all-time high, driving African Americans away from the South in droves, Washington's international recruitment efforts established the region as a destination rather than a point of departure, connecting this rural pocket in the Alabama Black Belt to the broader Global Black South and transforming Tuskegee into a culturally diverse and cosmopolitan hub.

148   PLOT II

Not everyone supported Washington's proposal to educate Afro-Cubans and Afro–Puerto Ricans in the U.S. South, however. Shortly following the publication of Washington's appeal, T. Edward Owens of the Young Men's Institute in Asheville, North Carolina, penned an impassioned plea against the proposition on account of "caste prejudice" in the South. Though Owens agreed that it was important to educate the students, he insisted it was "not necessary to bring them to the South," "where negro men, educated or uneducated, are considered as inferiors, and negro women as toys and playthings" acutely vulnerable to both racial and sexual violence. Owens perceived so "little, if any, caste prejudice" in Cuba and Puerto Rico that he worried that introducing Cuban and Puerto Rican students to the hostile racial climate of the U.S. South would make them "feel that they were less." He instead proposed "establish[ing] schools in their own land, but, for the love of humanity, do not bring them to this country."[14]

Indeed, racial discrimination and anti-Blackness obtained in both the postemancipation U.S. South and postindependence Cuba; however, as the historian of Cuba Aline Helg has argued, violence against Black people in Cuba "was not institutionalized" as it was in the United States. Moreover, in the U.S. South Jim Crow segregation, lynching, and mob violence were compounded by disfranchisement, whereas "Cuba was the only nation in the Western Hemisphere with a substantial population of African descent and universal male suffrage." Ultimately, at the turn of the century "Afro-Cubans enjoyed broader freedom than did southern African Americans."[15]

Despite Owens's vehement objection, Washington proceeded with his hemispheric recruitment effort. In "Signs of Progress Among the Negroes" (1900), he elaborated on the importance of industrial education for Black Cubans and Puerto Ricans. Asserting himself as both an agent of U.S. imperialism and a diasporic race leader, he linked Afro-Latine futures with those of southern African Americans:

> In addition to the problem of educating eight million negroes in our Southern States and ingrafting them into American citizenship, we now have the additional responsibility . . . of educating and elevating about eight hundred thousand others of African descent in Cuba and Porto Rico. . . . The experience that we have passed through in the Southern States during the last thirty years in the education of my race, whose history and needs are not very different from the history and needs of the Cubans and Porto Ricans, will prove most valuable in elevating the blacks of the West Indian Islands.[16]

Like the American South, Cuba and Puerto Rico were former plantation societies that had just cast off the yoke of slavery. Thus, their Black populations were at a similar stage in the march toward "civilization," Washington reasoned, as that of southern African Americans, who had been emancipated only about a quarter century earlier. In effect, he situated the repurposed plantation within a hemispheric context, plotting the Global Black South along educational, commercial, and economic lines. Washington's effort to transplant industrial education to Cuba and Puerto Rico was part of a broader project of establishing the southern, Tuskegee New Negro as the model for modern Black subjectivity globally. Though he often acknowledged differences between diasporic groups, he remained convinced that industrial education would elevate the entire race since all its members were confronting the legacies of slavery, colonialism, and imperialism. However, he often failed to account for empire and the asymmetries of power between diasporic groups. For instance, recently emancipated southern African Americans, although impoverished and largely abandoned by state and federal governments after Reconstruction, were still part of the United States and sometimes benefited from its wealth and emergent status as an imperial power.

Washington further justified transplanting the Tuskegee model to Cuba and Puerto Rico by underscoring their shared agrarian backgrounds. "The negroes on these islands are largely an agricultural people," he wrote in "Signs of Progress," "and for this reason, in addition to a higher degree of mental and religious training, they need the same agricultural, mechanical, and domestic training that is fast helping the negroes in our Southern States."[17] Indeed, the rural countryside attracted many Cubans after the Spanish-American War owing to the revived sugar industry.[18] According to Cuba's 1899 census, most Afro-Cubans were concentrated in the major sugar-producing provinces of Matanzas and Santa Clara, and "the vast majority labored in agriculture, especially as sugar workers."[19] As an "agricultural people"—that is, people formerly enslaved on the islands' sugar and tobacco plantations and those who returned to the countryside following the war—Afro-Cubans experienced a similar "style of life" as southern African Americans and therefore "need[ed] the same... training," Washington reasoned.[20] Repurposing agriculture, a legacy of the plantation, into a mode of self-determination was thus the organizing principle of his diasporic uplift project for the Global Black South. Contrary to Washington's efforts to "ingraft" Afro-Cubans into his conception of an agrarian future, however, most Cuban students who attended Tuskegee were not from rural areas. They were artisans and tradespeople who resided in urban centers such as Havana and

Matanzas.[21] Thus, even though Washington managed to build a little "black village" in rural Alabama, most Cuban students who attended Tuskegee were city dwellers with little use for or interest in Washington's vision of the bourgeois New Negro farmer. Nevertheless, Afro-Cubans' agrarian backgrounds remained central to Washington's hemispheric imagination.

To recall, in *Working with the Hands* (1904) Washington noted that Tuskegee's faculty and students grew "Cuban sugar cane" on the experiment plot. The process of transplanting Cuban cane to Tuskegee invites further consideration of how the institute engaged the afterlife of the plantation in the Global Black South by facilitating the transnational circulation of peoples, plants, and agricultural knowledges. Washington could have received the Cuban cane from the many Cuban students who attended the school, from the Tuskegee agents who traveled to southern Florida and Havana to recruit Cuban students, or from his longtime friend and colleague John Stephens Durham. A native of Philadelphia, Durham was an African American lawyer and diplomat who served as U.S. consul to Haiti following Frederick Douglass. He then worked for the Spanish Treaty Claims Commission in Cuba before managing the U.S.-owned Francisco Sugar Company in the island's Camaguey province. In 1896, prior to Washington's recruitment campaign, Durham was scheduled to deliver a series of lectures on Cuba before the Tuskegee student body.[22] In their correspondence, which spanned nearly two decades, Durham and Washington discussed the possibility of investing in sugarcane production in Liberia and introducing "modern machinery and methods" to help resolve the country's industrial problems, and they communicated often about the vagaries of plantation management in Cuba and Haiti.[23] As indicated by his correspondence with Durham, Washington continued to experiment with growing plantation commodities and with agriculture more generally as part of a viable commercial and economic program for the Black diaspora. He sought to translate agricultural and industrial training into modes of Black self-determination, encouraging Black people to learn a trade and to grow food for subsistence and cash crops such as sugarcane and cotton for sale on the global market.

In "Signs of Progress," Washington fashioned himself as an agent of both U.S. empire and diasporic uplift, asserting, "*We* now have the responsibility" of educating peoples of "African descent in Cuba and Porto Rico." Throughout the article, he depicted Tuskegee as an autonomous, self-sufficient "black village of about twelve hundred people" and a "colony" spreading its light to the formerly enslaved millions throughout the U.S. South and now possibly Cuba and Puerto Rico in the Caribbean.[24] The educational model Washington inherited from Samuel Armstrong, his beloved mentor and the founder of Hampton

Institute, was indeed a civilizing tool for Black and Native Americans based on Armstrong's missionary experience in Hawaii in the 1830s. Yet to read Washington as an "imperialist educator over the country districts," as Jeremy Wells has described him, misses how Tuskegee's mission was also guided by the logics and ethics of the plot.[25] Just as Washington repurposed the antebellum plantation, he also attempted to adapt the colonial logics undergirding industrial education into a strategy for diasporic uplift.

In "Signs of Progress," then, Tuskegee was depicted not only as a plantation turned industrial school but also as a symbol of Black nationalism and economic self-help that could be exported to other parts of the Global Black South with similar histories of slavery and the plantation. Though Washington emphasized interracial cooperation in commercial matters throughout the article, he did not mention the school's white northern philanthropic donor base. Rather, he underscored that students made the bricks and constructed the buildings and that the school's printing office did "a large part of the printing for the white and colored people" in the region.[26] By depicting Tuskegee as a self-sustaining "black village" and "colony," Washington sought to prove to both its supporters and detractors alike Black people's capacity for self-government and self-determination. Industrial education in Washington's hands is transformed from a technology of colonial subjection into a strategy for Black world making.

Like his appropriation of the Spanish-American War, "Signs of Progress" primarily articulated a utilitarian attitude toward educating Cuban and Puerto Rican students. The success of his program in Cuba and Puerto Rico would buttress Tuskegee's legitimacy in the United States. At the conclusion of the essay, however, Washington took up conditions on the ground in Cuba and Puerto Rico more explicitly. If Owens was concerned about Cuban and Puerto Rican students' encounter with Jim Crow when they migrated to the U.S. South, Washington expressed concern about whether the United States would extend the color line farther south as a part of its imperial administration of the islands. He observed, "Certainly it will place this country in an awkward position to have gone to war to free a people from Spanish cruelty, and then as soon as it gets them within its power to treat a large proportion of the population worse than did even Spain herself, simply on account of color."[27] Like Owens, Washington held the view that anti-Black racism in Cuba and Puerto Rico was less pronounced than in the United States, a condition that would ease the goals of spreading racial uplift. Whereas African Americans had been "cowed and unmanned" by the stultifying conditions of racial terrorism and oppression, he maintained, Afro-Cubans experienced considerably more freedom in "civil, political, military and business matters."[28] A master of indirection, Washington raised doubts about U.S. foreign-policy decisions toward Cuba and Puerto Rico, acknowledging the contradiction of fighting to free a people from a cruel and oppressive colonial power only to replace it with a new form of imperial violence—Jim Crow. This subtle skepticism and oblique criticism somewhat echo the warning in "Cuban Education" about the possibility of Black revolt in the United States and represents how he strategically translated Black Cubans and Puerto Ricans to improve conditions for African Americans at home.

Despite Owens's objections and Washington's own misgivings, Washington initiated a student migration network from Cuba and Puerto Rico to Tuskegee that lasted until the 1920s. In chapter 5, I elaborate on how Tuskegee's Cuban and Puerto Rican students, alongside their African American, Haitian, Jamaican, and Central and South American counterparts, navigated the politics of race, language, class, translation, and empire as they journeyed to the Alabama Black Belt. Here, however, I focus on how Afro-Cubans on the island responded to Washington's call, strategically translating and transposing it for their own articulations of Afro-Cuban modernity and desires for the postemancipation future.

RAFAEL SERRA Y MONTALVO AND TUSKEGEE'S LITERARY AND VISUAL AFFORDANCES

More than a decade before Washington initiated the Tuskegee–Cuba connection, thousands of Cubans sought asylum in the United States during the Ten Years' War (1868–1878), the colony's first effort to secure its independence from Spain. As tobacco was one of Cuba's main cash crops, many Cuban exiles migrated to Florida and New York and worked in the cigar industry. Rafael Serra y Montalvo, an Afro-Cuban intellectual, journalist, politician, and advocate for Cuban education and independence, was a prominent member of this expatriate community in the United States. Though born to a formerly enslaved family in Matanzas, Cuba, he was a *tabaquero*, or tobacco worker, by trade as well as an educator and community leader. In 1877, he cofounded a " 'society for mutual aid and instruction' " in Matanzas for Black and mixed-race (or what was then called "mulatto") children and adult artisans.[29] Following persecution by the Spanish colonial administration and its policies, Serra fled to Key West, Florida, in 1880, briefly working in the cigar industry, and then moved to New

York City, where he spent most of his time while in exile. His profession as a cigar maker elucidates how the plantation and its co-conspirator—the factory—facilitated Black hemispheric migration even in freedom.

In New York, Serra continued his commitment to education and activism. He befriended the Cuban national hero José Martí and was an active member of Martí's radical organization, the Partido Revolucionario Cubano, and a contributor to the organization's organ, *Patria*. Serra founded La Liga, an organization that educated exiled Cubans and Puerto Ricans, many of whom worked in Florida's and New York's cigar factories. He also befriended Afro–Puerto Rican bibliophile and archivist Arturo "Arthur" Schomburg, a luminary of the Harlem Renaissance and the New Negro Movement of the 1920s and 1930s. Serra is perhaps best known for his newspaper *El Nuevo Criollo*, or *The New Creole*, which he founded shortly after returning to Cuba and ran from 1904 to 1906. It was "devoted to the dismantling of myths of racial equality and ideologies of racial discrimination in Cuba."[30] The concept of the "Nuevo Criollo" was akin to that of the New Negro in the United States. Much like Tuskegee, then, Cuba's Nuevo Criollo captures the ways formerly enslaved peoples throughout the Global Black South announced themselves as new subjects well before the 1920s and 1930s and thus how the idea of the New Negro exceeded Harlem and its renaissance, both geographically and temporally. Moving among Cuba, Florida, and New York, Serra was a hemispheric intellectual who translated (African) American print culture for his Cuban and Puerto Rican readers, constantly negotiating the nuances of language, race, nation, empire, and diaspora.[31]

After a twenty-year exile in the United States, with brief stints in Jamaica and Panama, Serra returned to Cuba in April 1899.[32] He soon published *Para blancos y negros: Ensayos politicos, sociales y económicos* (1907), a volume of political essays and journalism written mostly in the decade following the Spanish-American War. The essays focus on the challenges and possibilities of Cuban independence, both on the island and in relation to the threat of U.S. imperialism. Alongside his own writings, Serra included translations into Spanish of news items about U.S. racial politics and gave special attention to the work of "the illustrious Booker T. Washington" and Tuskegee Institute. Though Serra celebrated African Americans' accomplishments, his commitments were first and foremost to Cuban independence and securing resources for Afro-Cubans in the new republic. *Para blancos y negros* thus illustrates how he engaged in a strategic translation practice that at once upheld African American achievements as a model for Afro-Cuban modernity, decried annexation, and cautioned against African Americans' potential encroachment and displacement of Afro-Cubans under U.S. annexation.

Serra likely encountered Washington during one of the Tuskegee principal's fundraising tours in New York in the 1890s. They may have also met through the National Negro Business League, an organization Washington founded in 1900 to promote the interests of Black business owners and for which he served as president until his death in 1915. *Para blancos y negros* features translations of the proceedings from the league's conference in 1905, and according to Schomburg, Serra and General Evaristo Estenoz, leader of the Partido Independiente de Color (PIC), a prominent Afro-Cuban political party, attended one of the conferences "to study conditions with the view of submitting the result of their observations to their compatriots in Cuba and improving matters at home."[33] *Para blancos y negros* frequently cites Washington's work at Tuskegee as a model for racial uplift in Cuba and features several photographs of Tuskegee's campus buildings and a family portrait of Washington, Margaret Murray, and their children. Serra was influenced by Washington's ideas and methods as well as by Tuskegee's literary and visual aesthetics, but he was measured in his promotion of Washington's project and vehemently objected to U.S. annexation and what he perceived as the possibility of African Americans' trans-plantation to the island and displacement of Afro-Cubans.

Serra engaged with the Tuskegee project strategically and selectively, adapting it to his own vision of Cuban modernity. His essay "Promesa cumplida: Booker T. Washington, interpretado por la preocupación cubana" (Promise fulfilled: Booker T. Washington, interpreted through the Cuban concern) is his most explicit engagement with Washington and Tuskegee in *Para blancos y negros* (figure 3.1). It opens with epigraphs by Washington and José Martí, indicating both men's influence on Serra's thought. Martí's canonical essay "Nuestra America" (1891) imagined an alternative geography of the Americas that encompassed Latin America and the Caribbean and excluded the United States because of its nascent imperialism. However, Serra's inclusion of Washington alongside Martí placed Tuskegee and the U.S. South within this hemispheric geography. Notably, both Martí and Frederick Douglass died in 1895, the same year that Washington delivered his Atlanta Exposition Address and ascended as a race leader in the United States. With this framing, Serra replaced Douglass with Washington and invited readers to consider Washington, alongside Martí, as a diasporic and hemispheric thinker. In fact, Martí once referred to Serra as "un [Booker] Washington en cierne"—"a blossoming [Booker] Washington."[34]

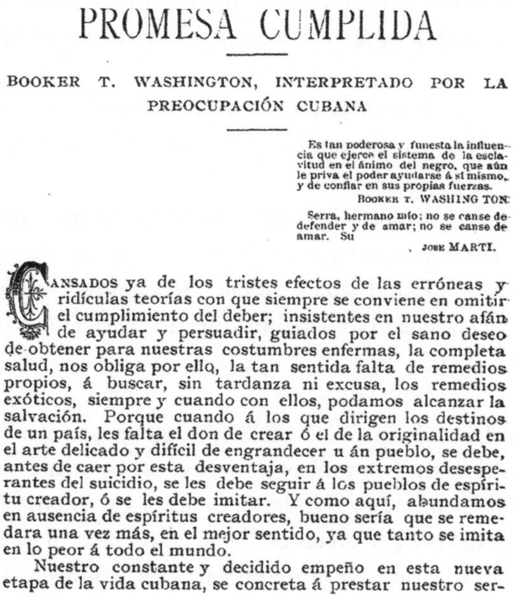

STRATEGIC TRANSLATIONS

PROMESA CUMPLIDA

BOOKER T. WASHINGTON, INTERPRETADO POR LA
PREOCUPACIÓN CUBANA

> Es tan poderosa y funesta la influen-
> cia que ejerce el sistema de la escla-
> vitud en el ánimo del negro, que aún
> le priva el poder ayudarse á sí mismo,
> y de confiar en sus propias fuerzas.
>
> BOOKER T. WASHINGTON.
>
> Serra, hermano mío; no se canse de
> defender y de amar; no se canse de
> amar. Su
>
> JOSÉ MARTÍ.

CANSADOS ya de los tristes efectos de las erróneas y ridículas teorías con que siempre se conviene en omitir el cumplimiento del deber; insistentes en nuestro afán de ayudar y persuadir, guiados por el sano deseo de obtener para nuestras costumbres enfermas, la completa salud, nos obliga por ello, la tan sentida falta de remedios propios, á buscar, sin tardanza ni excusa, los remedios exóticos, siempre y cuando con ellos, podamos alcanzar la salvación. Porque cuando á los que dirigen los destinos de un país, les falta el don de crear ó el de la originalidad en el arte delicado y difícil de engrandecer u án pueblo, se debe, antes de caer por esta desventaja, en los extremos desesperantes del suicidio, se les debe seguir á los pueblos de espíritu creador, ó se les debe imitar. Y como aquí, abundamos en ausencia de espíritus creadores, bueno sería que se remedara una vez más, en el mejor sentido, ya que tanto se imita en lo peor á todo el mundo.

Nuestro constante y decidido empeño en esta nueva etapa de la vida cubana, se concreta á prestar nuestro ser-

FIGURE 3.1. Rafael Serra, "Promesa cumplida" (Promise fulfilled), about the importance of Washington's work for Cuba. It includes epigraphs from Washington and José Martí.

Source: Rafael Serra, *Para blancos y negros: Ensayos políticos, sociales y económicos* (Havana, Cuba: El Printa "El Score" Aguila 117, 1907), 141.

Serra's "interpretation" of Washington "through the Cuban concern" demonstrates the significance of translation for Global Black South intellectual exchange. In what is essentially a review of *Up from Slavery*, "Promise Fulfilled" critiqued the Cuban elite for their "erroneous" and "malicious" misreading or mistranslation of Washington's project for the island's recently emancipated Black masses. After reading this "useful and lovely work, we are left," Serra complained, "in the same position we were in before we read it." Given Serra's own investment in racial democracy in Cuba following slavery and colonialism, Washington's persona as an "illustrious champion of regeneration" and an intermediary who could heal U.S. racial and sectional tensions was particularly important to him. In 1879, prior to his exile, Serra played a leading role in establishing Sociedad la Armonía in Matanzas, a mutual-aid society that provided, among other services, education for both Black and white children alike and night classes for working adults.[35] Therefore, he likely viewed Tuskegee as a model for racial reconciliation in Cuba as well.

156 PLOT II

Serra especially criticized the Cuban elite for misinterpreting Washington's Black self-help philosophy to justify divesting from Afro-Cuban uplift:

> From this colossal work, with its lofty humanitarian principles and great teachings for the world in general and for us in particular, Cuba has deduced the following:
> "If the black man wants to be worth something, he must raise himself up on his own." "He should not get involved in politics, as they suppose, says Booker T. Washington, and dedicate himself to learning a trade, because that is the reason that the great Industrial Institute has been founded in Tuskegee, Alabama."[36]

Here, Serra elucidates the paradox of Washington's project: it was malleable enough to be used both as a tool of colonization by white supremacists and imperialists and as a mode of self-determination by colonized peoples. Ultimately, Serra rebutted the Cuban elites' "violent and inaccurate manner of interpreting" Washington, citing Washington's acknowledgment that the effects of slavery had been so detrimental to Black people that Black self-help efforts still required interracial economic support. Serra's interpretation of Washington reveals what he viewed as most valuable about the Tuskegee project—namely, Washington's ability to secure white philanthropic support for Black education and racial uplift. Through Washington's example in the U.S. South, Serra insisted that interracial cooperation—in particular white philanthropic support—was necessary for the advancement of Afro-Cubans and the Cuban republic alike.[37]

As Serra challenged the Cuban elite's "malicious" misinterpretation of Washington's Black self-help philosophy for Afro-Cubans, he grappled with and sought to explain Washington's public position that southern African Americans should disengage from politics. Most Black southerners were Republicans, and, given the backlash against the Republican Party in the South following emancipation, Serra reasoned that Black southerners' political participation would open them up to "the most impious form of revenge. And it is because of this, and nothing else, that Washington opposes—with good reason—the involvement of Blacks in politics, at least in the South."[38] Yet Serra did not advocate the same policy for Afro-Cubans, likely because Black Cuban men already had the franchise. Furthermore, he refuted the elites' "misguided interpretation" of Washington's uplift project that "blacks must dedicate themselves only to agriculture and other mechanical trades" and thus that "blacks in Cuba should follow that lesson," too. In doing so, he quoted Washington's Carnegie

Music Hall address in 1897, in which he observed that "our brothers, the blacks of Cuba ... have two very major advantages over we the American blacks. The first is that here we are generally employed as servants, and there, in general, the majority of blacks are artisans and tradesmen. The second is that blacks were an important factor in that country's glorious war for independence. All this means an advancement over us, for their greatness and dignity."[39] By highlighting Washington's distinction between the two groups and acknowledgment of Afro-Cubans' important political role, Serra argued that relegating Afro-Cubans to industrial and agricultural education alone would be inconsistent with Washington's own view of Cuba's more progressive racial politics. Indeed, in "Signs of Progress," where Washington wrote explicitly about Afro-Cuban and Afro–Puerto Rican futures, he cautioned that his emphasis on industrial education "does not mean that the negro is to be excluded from the higher interests of life, but it does mean that in proportion as the negro gets the foundation— the useful before the ornamental—in the same proportion will he accelerate his progress in acquiring those elements which do not pertain so directly to the utilitarian."[40] As a skilled linguistic and cultural translator, Serra drew on such qualifications in Washington's writings to rebut what he regarded as the elite's willful misreading and attempted misapplication of Washington's sociopolitical philosophy.

Serra's selective and strategic translation practice is especially evident in his engagement with Tuskegee's visual archive and architecture. *Para blancos y negros* features three images of Tuskegee campus buildings—the Huntington Memorial Academic building (contemporaneously described elsewhere as the school's "most pretentious building"), the Carnegie Library, and Science (Thrasher) Hall—each of which was funded by U.S. northern industrial philanthropists (figures 3.2–3.4).[41] In "Promise Fulfilled," Serra described Tuskegee's campus, with its "57 beautiful and salubrious buildings," as being the result of interracial cooperation: though "founded by the very helpful effort of the greatest of blacks," Serra remarked, "there is nary a single stone that is not owed directly to the foresight, to the good morals, and to the constant and real philanthropy of white Americans."[42] Serra thus used photographs of Tuskegee's built environment to insist on the necessity of interracial collaboration for (re)constructing the Cuban republic.

Because Washington viewed racial uplift as inseparable from training the masses to build, he often touted that much of Tuskegee's campus was constructed by student labor. Yet Serra did not include images of Tuskegee students at work, although such images are featured in *De esclavo á catedrático*, the "Cuban-Spanish" translation of *Up from Slavery* that popularized Washington

FIGURE 3.2. Tuskegee's Collis P. Huntington Memorial building in Rafael Serra's *Para blancos y negros*.

Source: Serra, *Para blancos y negros*, 161.

FIGURE 3.3. Tuskegee's Carnegie Library building in Rafael Serra's *Para blancos y negros*.

Source: Serra, *Para blancos y negros*, 185.

and Tuskegee throughout the island. Perhaps such images would have undermined Serra's critique of the Cuban elite's efforts to pigeonhole Afro-Cubans in agriculture and mechanical trades. The only Tuskegee image featuring people in Serra's volume is of Washington and his family (figure 3.5), perhaps to reinforce the importance of heteronormative domesticity for the fledgling republic and reconstituting Afro-Cuban home life after slavery. Indeed, as the historian José I. Fusté notes, Serra was "radically prescient" on "white supremacy and U.S.

FIGURE 3.4. Tuskegee's Thrasher Hall in Rafael Serra's *Para blancos y negros*.

Source: Serra, *Para blancos y negros*, 186.

FIGURE 3.5. Booker T. and Margaret Murray Washington pictured with their children, Portia, Booker T. Jr., and Ernest, in Rafael Serra's *Para blancos y negros*.

Source: Serra, *Para blancos y negros*, 145.

neocolonialism," but "his ideas about racial and national belonging were steeped in an uncritically embraced economic liberalism and a hetero-patriarchal vision of nationhood."[43]

In "Los que ayudan á los negros" (Those who help the blacks), another short feature on Tuskegee in *Para blancos y negros*, Serra again emphasized notable "protectors" such as John Rockefeller and Andrew Carnegie, whose philanthropic contributions supported Washington's work and represented the possibilities of interracial cooperation and racial fraternity in a similar postslavery society. For many critics, white northern industrialists' philanthropic support for Tuskegee has come to connote Washington's divided values and commitments and has cast doubt on the integrity of the Tuskegee project. Thus, Serra's unequivocal support for this model of uplift seems naive at best and highly questionable at worst to anyone wary of collusion with industrial capitalism and the ways it has undermined Black freedom struggles. However, it is crucial to remember that Serra remained vigilantly critical of U.S. economic imperialism and thus was likely operating from a Martían racial schema, whereby Black and white Cubans could work together for the republic's regeneration (a schema that has since been roundly criticized for its inherent anti-Blackness).

Following "Promise Fulfilled," Serra reprinted "La escuela de Tuskegee" (The Tuskegee School), a promotional article for the institute originally published in his newspaper, *El Nuevo Criollo*. The article is preceded and framed by the portrait of Booker T. and Margaret Murray Washington and their children, Portia, Booker T. Jr., and Ernest, and a photograph of the Huntington Academic building on Tuskegee's campus. The article was written and translated from English into Spanish by Alfredo Pérez y Encinosa, one of Tuskegee's first Afro-Cuban students. It provided a general overview of the school for its Cuban readers and celebrated Tuskegee's built environment as a symbol of Black nationalism and self-determination. "The Tuskegee School represents the intellectual epitome of the black race," Pérez wrote. "If the example of Tuskegee were imitated in all countries where blacks live, the so-called 'race problem' would be resolved satisfactorily," he insisted, promoting the school's utility for global Black uplift. Pérez proudly touted the campus's "one hundred twelve buildings ranging from large to small, of which forty are splendid brick buildings, and all but four having been built by the students themselves, who are taught at the same time under the direction of competent instructors in the most practical and modern methods applicable to agriculture and to the building trades."[44]

Whereas Serra emphasized Tuskegee as a model of interracial cooperation for Black uplift, Pérez's article cited it as an example of what Black people could do for themselves. Although funded by white northern industrialists, each of the featured buildings was designed by the famous African American architect Robert R. Taylor, an alumnus of the Massachusetts Institute of Technology who led Tuskegee's architecture program and trained several of the Cuban students enrolled there. In fact, most of the male students from Cuba who successfully graduated from Tuskegee took up architecture as their trade of choice, including Luís Delfín Valdés, who designed the headquarters for the Club Atenas, a preeminent Afro-Cuban social and political organization, which opened in 1929 and still stands today.[45] Pérez's promotional article alongside Serra's essays and reproduction of Tuskegee photographs suggest that Tuskegee became legible for Afro-Cubans through its architecture and material and economic successes. No longer a plantation, its buildings represented Black self-determination, industriousness, and modernity. "There is no building of importance on the school's grounds that could not serve to grace any city," Pérez contended.[46] In addition to interracial cooperation and racial fraternity, then, Afro-Cubans saw in Tuskegee a blueprint for the material, educational, and ideological infrastructure of the new Cuban republic.

DIASPORIC FRACTURES: U.S. IMPERIALISM AND THE LIMITS OF TRANS-PLANTATION

If Washington cited Cuba's geographic proximity to Alabama as justification for educating Afro-Cuban youth, then Serra viewed that same proximity as a threat to Cuban sovereignty. The essays and photographs celebrating Tuskegee in *Para blancos y negros* were immediately followed by essays opposing Cuba's annexation to the United States. In stark contrast to Serra's essays on Tuskegee, his commentary on annexation represents African Americans as potential agents of U.S. imperialism and further illuminates how his strategic translation praxis encompassed disagreement, refusal, and critique.[47]

Following the articles praising Washington and Tuskegee, Serra published a translation of "The American Blacks," a "history of the American Negro" detailing their achievements in the arts, education, labor, politics, and wealth and property accumulation from 1863 to 1894 and written by the prominent African American lawyer Dr. R. O. C. Benjamin. Serra's editorial commentary, which bookends the article, sheds light on his views on annexation and the threat of African American immigration to Cuba. Even as he celebrated African Americans' material and economic achievements in the thirty years following emancipation, he portrayed their success strategically and cautiously. For Serra, if Cuba were annexed to the United States, racial violence and oppression in the U.S. South would push African Americans to relocate to Cuba. He thus translated Benjamin's article to make "the American black" legible to Cubans as both a model of self-determination in the aftermath of slavery and colonialism and a potential threat to Afro-Cuban uplift. Serra worried that if the United States were to annex Cuba, African Americans, with their "complete aptitude for self-governance," would exploit "the fertility of our soil" in a "climate favorable to

[them]," perhaps suggesting his suspicion that African Americans' visions of agrarian futures could be displaced onto Cuba as a settler-colonial project.[48] Washington, of course, would not have promoted African American migration to Cuba; in fact, he was staunchly opposed to migration in any form: from the U.S. South to the U.S. North and certainly to anywhere outside of the United States.

Yet Serra maintained that "American blacks have still more advantages thanks to their civilization and their wealth" in order to disabuse Cuban supporters of annexation of the "assumption that in an annexed Cuba American blacks would experience the same pitiful condition that—to the disgrace of humanity—they experience in some parts of the United States." Instead, like the "despised" and "disinherited classes" from Spain who, once settled in Cuba, "were invested with an excess of authority" over the "American-born," African Americans would enjoy disproportionate authority should they emigrate.[49] According to the historian Nancy Raquel Mirabal, however, "There is very little to indicate that African Americans transcended their racialized conditions simply through the act of emigration, especially if they were moving to an island under U.S. control."[50] Indeed, Serra did not account for racial difference in his association between African Americans and the disinherited classes in Spain, who migrated to Cuba and reinvented themselves as a ruling class. Rather, he identified nationality as the cause of Spanish immigrants' domination over native-born Cubans and thus deduced that African Americans would acquire and enjoy similar privileges under U.S. annexation of the island.

Nevertheless, it seems Serra's concern was at least somewhat warranted given how colonial governments construct racial hierarchies, sometimes within the same racial group. In the administration of the Panama Canal Zone, for instance, the United States developed a segregated remuneration system, paying white Americans in gold and Caribbean and Indigenous workers in silver. The relatively few African Americans who worked in the Canal Zone posed a problem for this system because they were racial "others" but still American citizens. So the United States devised "special" contracts that granted African American workers some privileges.[51] Such were the contradictions of race and nationality under empire; hence, Serra's wariness of annexation was not altogether groundless.

Serra's conflicted attitudes toward African Americans is further demonstrated by the placement of "The American Blacks" in his volume. Its anti-annexationist commentary is followed by images of Tuskegee's Carnegie Library and Thrasher Hall, indicating Serra's admiration for Washington's project of interracial economic and philanthropic cooperation. Next came Serra's essay

"La anexión," where he elaborated on his vehement objection to annexation and suspicion of "the unfortunate black American" as a potential agent of U.S. empire. He argued trenchantly that "Cuba excites Yankee greed" because its "exuberant vegetation" would become "the premier tobacco and sugar market" worldwide and because of its geopolitical advantages for the United States.[52] Serra's keen geopolitical insights illuminate how the afterlife of the plantation informed U.S. imperial designs on Cuban agriculture. Indeed, in the early twentieth century, U.S. companies controlled much of the sugar industry in Cuba, Puerto Rico, and the Dominican Republic.[53] Cuba was also highly coveted by the United States because its geographic location would increase U.S. economic and military domination over the hemisphere.

In "La anexión," following his critique of general "Yankee" designs on Cuba, Serra returned his attention to "American blacks." "Tired of fighting in the [U.S.] South," where they are "cruelly lynched," and "starve[d] from hunger in the North" because they cannot find employment, African Americans would "not hesitate" to immigrate to Cuba, he reasoned, where they would be given "more assurances in order to stimulate patriotism" and prove their loyalty.[54] Formerly exiled in the United States, Serra was doubtless familiar with Black American emigrationist desires and debates that had circulated since the nineteenth century. Some proposed immigrating "back" to Africa, but others, such as Martin Delany, promoted immigration to locales with large Black populations in the Western Hemisphere, such as Haiti, Cuba, and parts of Central America. Following the Spanish-American War, African Americans and white Americans alike continued to imagine Cuba as a potential resolution to the race problem. To underscore his point, Serra cited an article from 1906 in which the author ultimately promoted "moving the bulk of the black population from the [U.S.] South" onto Cuban soil "to resolve our problem." This pro-emigration sentiment was popular in the African American press as well.[55] If this plan were carried out, Serra feared, Black Americans would become agents of U.S. empire who would act as colonial administrators over Afro-Cubans to prove their "blind obedience to the proud gods of Yankee paganism." Given their material success "in the South—in spite of the enormous hostility with which they are treated," they would surely be able to do the same in Cuba, "where the entire job market would be for them."[56]

John S. Durham, Washington's longtime friend, epitomized Serra's dual concern about U.S. domination of Cuba's sugar market and African American emigration. To recall, Durham worked as an assistant attorney for the Spanish Treaty Claims Commission in Cuba and then managed the Francisco Sugar Company in Camaguey province, where he earned $9,000 a year. In 1898, he spoke at the Hampton Negro Conference on "the business outlook for the Negro" and showed "by personal experience in the sugar business" the equal opportunities for white and Black men in the West Indies "if [they are] equipped with equal intelligence and business ability."[57] Although Durham was effectively an agent of U.S. corporate plantation imperialism, his correspondence with Washington suggests that he was aware of how his position affected the foundering republic's challenges. Writing to Washington in 1906 and discussing the work of plantation management, Durham noted: "Cuba is still in the experimental stage of self-government and we who represent heavy investments of capital bear the brunt of government mistakes."[58] Nevertheless, Durham's and other African Americans' successes in Cuba would have buttressed Serra's contention that Black American uplift in the context of annexation would necessarily come at the expense of Afro-Cubans. "The American sort would have to consider themselves masters," Serra wrote in "La anexión," "encouraged by the hypocritical compliments of their white neighbors. . . . The difference in language, the educational superiority of American blacks, and many other circumstances, would always make the condition of the unhappy Cuban black worse."[59]

Much like Washington's approach to Afro-Cubans, Serra's strategic translations of Washington and Tuskegee's literary and visual culture demonstrate how he at once forged diasporic ties with African Americans while remaining fundamentally committed to Cuban independence and to securing resources for Afro-Cubans. For both men, racial solidarity was qualified and refracted by an unwavering commitment to their respective national identities and nation-building projects at home. This was a hallmark of diasporic affiliation in the Global Black South.

TRANSPLANTING BOOKER T. WASHINGTON TO HAVANA: PRINT CULTURE AND AFRO-CUBAN SOCIAL ORGANIZATIONS

In the preface to *De esclavo á catedrático* (1902), the widely circulated "Cuban-Spanish" translation of *Up from Slavery*, Washington included a personal note to Afro-Cuban youth: "If you can appreciate my efforts for the teaching and welfare of the race to which you belong, I will consider myself paid in full for the time employed in writing the present work. The only thing that I want with all of my soul is to fix in the spirit of the youth, the idea that work, of whatever kind, is never dishonorable, while idleness degrades and debases."[60] Here,

Washington sought to imbue Afro-Cuban youth with a southern New Negro sensibility that similarly foregrounded the "dignity of labor." In contrast to his "Cuban Education" address, where he referred to Cubans as the "oppressed from a distant isle," this note expressed a sense of shared racial heritage and belonging and demonstrates how he exported his vision for Tuskegee to the broader Global Black South.

In the first three decades of the twentieth century, Washington's call to Afro-Cuban youth elicited an array of responses on the island. Just as Serra grappled with Washington and Tuskegee in the pages of *Para blancos y negros* and *Nuevo Criollo* to encourage support for Black education, other Afro-Cuban intellectuals, professionals, parents, and youth embraced and upheld Washington as a symbolic figure, integrating him into the country's pantheon of Black diasporic race leaders and its long history of Black social organizations. Besides *De esclavo a catedrático* and Serra's publications, several other Cuban periodicals covered Washington's and Tuskegee's domestic and international activities.[61] *La lucha: A Cuban-American Paper with the News of the World* was published in Havana in both Spanish and English and began covering Washington and his political activities in the United States around 1903. It was a liberal newspaper edited by Antonio San Miguel, a white Spaniard who immigrated to Cuba in the mid–nineteenth century. *La lucha* (The struggle) was one of the most popular periodicals in Havana, so its articles about Washington and Tuskegee would have reached a broad readership and expanded their popularity.

La lucha's coverage included topics such as U.S. race relations, especially the "Negro Problem," debates about Black education and lynching, the National Negro Business League, and President Theodore Roosevelt's visit to Tuskegee in 1905. In July 1910, the "Nuevos libros," or new books, section advertised the recent arrival of *Saliendo de la esclavitud* (Leaving slavery, 1905), a second Spanish translation of *Up from Slavery*, at La Moderna Poesia, one of Havana's leading bookstores, suggesting the autobiography remained popular among Cuban readers.[62] *La lucha* also covered various efforts to export the Tuskegee project to the broader African diaspora, including the Danish West Indies, South Africa, Liberia, and Togo, West Africa, where it was conducting a cotton-growing experiment. In April 1911, San Miguel published Washington's invitation to "los elementos de color de Cuba" to the ICON, to be held at Tuskegee in 1912.[63]

Afro-Cubans also strategically translated Washington and the Tuskegee project to establish Afro-Cuban social and political organizations on the island, including a Tuskegee-inspired school in Havana. In November 1905, Emilio Céspedes Casado, a prominent Afro-Cuban professional, wrote to Washington to inform him of the establishment of the Instituto Booker T. Washington and request a photograph of Washington to place in the main entrance to inspire Afro-Cuban students.[64] On February 26, 1906, *La lucha* announced the Instituto Booker T. Washington's inception in a brief article describing its aims and mission: "This institute has been founded in order to popularize elementary and higher primary education, and knowledge of the social sciences among workers, paying special attention to individuals of the race of color and trying, at the same time, to establish the greatest currents of harmony between the different components of the popular classes. Teaching will be completely practical."[65] There is scant information on the institute's daily activities, and there is no annual catalog, but an ad in Serra's *Nuevo Criollo* that ran throughout 1905 and 1906 described it as an "institute of elementary and higher education" offering "special Baccalaureate classes" and courses in music, bookkeeping, typing, line and natural drawing, languages, and preparation for teaching (figure 3.6). Significantly, the advertised curriculum did not focus on agricultural education and thus did not strictly align with Washington's vision of Black agrarian futures for Afro-Cubans. The course offerings were seemingly more consistent with training a Black professional class.

On April 21, 1906, Emilio Céspedes Casado delivered a lecture in the institute's *biblioteca*, or library, that elucidated how the building served as an educational institution and a space for Afro-Cuban social and political organizing. Entitled "La cuestion social Cubana," or "The Cuban Social Question," this was the keynote address for a conference on racial politics.[66] The image of Afro-Cubans

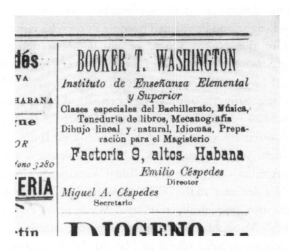

FIGURE 3.6. Ad for the Instituto Booker T. Washington in Rafael Serra's *Nuevo Criollo*.

Source: *Nuevo Criollo*, 1905 and 1906.

working out racial politics and identity in the early years of the republic in a building named in honor of a southern African American race leader epitomizes the ways Washington and Tuskegee provided the infrastructure, form, or blueprint for diasporic uplift, while Afro-Cubans provided the content based on their unique social and political context.

Casado's speech focused on racial uplift and Afro-Cubans' place within the new republic. Critically, he prefaced the address with "Dos palabras á los negros" (two words to the blacks), though he immediately qualified his use of *negros*. While the word *negros* was somewhat dissonant ("disuena algo") owing to custom, he acknowledged, he also found it to be the more "natural," "logical," and "appropriate" way to refer to "those whose skin is darkly pigmented and who have thick lips and hair that is more or less curly." Still, openly acknowledging "this fact infuse[d]" no small fear in him: Cuban newspapers were often reluctant to use the term *negros* and were prone to euphemisms, "as if we were sad to call each thing by its name and each action by its corresponding verb." Casado defied this "deceit and coquetry" by dedicating his speech to Black people of all shades: "los morenos, morenitos, mooros, moritos, etiopes, chinos de la tierra, chinitos, achinados, pardos, parditos, pardos achinados, zambos, mestizos, mulatos, mulaticos, mulaticos de pelo, mulatos franceses, cuarterones etc. etc."[67] This list of colloquialisms for Afro-descended peoples encapsulates the dynamism of Blackness in Cuba and much of Latin America at this time. These societies had very elaborate ways of distinguishing peoples of African descent based on skin color, ethnicity, hair texture, class, and so on (some of which were rooted in anti-Blackness). In Casado's racial taxonomy, it seems, anyone with African ancestry was now considered a "*negro*," collapsing these historical distinctions and categories to create a collective Black identity. Whereas in the Caribbean and especially in Latin America, notions of Black racial identity are historically more capacious than in the United States, with its "one-drop rule," Casado proclaimed a Black racial identity that was, in fact, more akin to the U.S. bipartite racial schema. Importantly, however, this was not simply the importation of a U.S. racial schema into Cuba; rather, it was Afro-Cubans working out the terms of Blackness on their own, arguably an early articulation of Afro-Latinidad.

Even as the Instituto Booker T. Washington's leadership sought to establish "harmony between the different components of the popular classes," Casado recognized that Afro-Cubans often bore the brunt of the class problem; therefore, he encouraged organizing around racial identity as well. Despite critics who disapproved of racial organizing, the "conversation" was not meant to "abrogate" the representation of any other race or class, he maintained, but to aid the institute's mission of "contributing to the popular education" of the working classes and especially of the "black race."[68] Casado's disclaimer regarding racial identity exemplifies the political and philosophical challenges Afro-Cubans confronted in a country that touted itself as a racial democracy and regarded political organizing around racial identity as inherently divisive. For instance, José Martí, a chief theorist of race and Cuban nationalism in the new republic, advanced a "construction of nationhood [that] left little room for racial identities," argues the historian Alejandro de la Fuente. "Martí's discourse assumed the existence of different races but stressed that national identity should be placed above race."[69] Although Cuba had a rich history of Black social organizations—composed of religious, cultural, and mutual-aid societies—that dated back to the *cabildos de nación* of the colonial period, following independence, many white and Afro-Cubans alike viewed political organizing around racial identity as controversial.[70]

Nevertheless, Casado essentially acted as a racial philosopher in his address, briefly sketching the history of Black racial oppression in Cuba, explicating how race was at the center of the current Cuban social question, and outlining possible solutions. By his account, Afro-Cubans had been well on their way to finding their place in the nation before the "odious Intervention" by the United States, which "introduced its barbarism and its selfishness into Cuba and its civilization." Furthermore, he accused "the detritus of colonialism and the supporters of Americanization today [of] conspir[ing] against the rights of poor blacks." These conditions could be ameliorated only by educating the popular and working classes (apparently referring to Afro-Cubans) and equipping them with skills to improve their social and economic condition. He placed especial emphasis on educating and elevating Afro-Cuban women, insisting that "each woman is worthy of our protection and care."[71] Casado thus shared many of the racial and class values and biases of the uplift movement in the United States, especially as articulated at Tuskegee.[72]

Through the Instituto Booker T. Washington, Afro-Cubans enfolded Washington into their long history of Black social organizations. "Several clubs designated well-known public figures as their honorary presidents," such as Juan Gualberto Gómez, while "other societies were named after these leaders." In doing so, members gained access to patronage, educational opportunities, and the political establishment. For instance, "the Juan Gualberto Gómez Center constantly requested all sorts of favors from [Gómez], including public jobs and scholarships for members and their families."[73] Afro-Cuban students enrolled at the Instituto Booker T. Washington may have made similar appeals to their namesake, potentially viewing their enrollment as a route to Tuskegee and access to his influence. In a letter dated January 14, 1912, for instance,

Bernardo C. Calderón of Havana informed Washington that he had studied at the Instituto Booker T. Washington for a year and hoped to transfer to Tuskegee. Calderón, who claimed to be one of the institute's most assiduous and punctual students, was working as a bank mechanic ("mecanico de banco") but had formerly worked as a mechanic's assistant at an automobile factory in Havana. He requested a copy of the Tuskegee catalog and was curious to know if Tuskegee had mechanical lathes as he hoped to study mechanics and, with theory and practice, become a good turner and adjuster in the future, at the least.[74] Calderón's letter intimates that just as Washington folded Afro-Cubans into his vision of Black diasporic uplift through agriculture and industry, Afro-Cubans incorporated him and Tuskegee into their own sociopolitical structures also.

In 1915, a group of Afro-Cuban youth began publication of *Labor nueva*, or *New Labor*, a weekly illustrated magazine. The historian Melina Pappademos observes that *Labor nueva* reflected "elements common to early republican black periodicals." It displayed "refinement and intellectual prowess, promoted bourgeois-liberal and patriarchal values, and demonstrated participation in the island's 'modern' political culture."[75] It explained in its first issue that its mission was "to strengthen the bonds of fraternity between all the elements that constitute Cuban society," stimulate "the colored race to elevate its moral, intellectual, and economic standing," and "champion" Afro-Cuban culture. With these goals in mind, the editorial staff advocated interracial solidarity to cultivate "a greater sense of shared identity among all Cubans, as a measure of our national salvation." Like Casado's address at the Instituto Booker T. Washington, the editors diligently articulated their affinity for and solidarity with white Cubans, so that the publication would not be perceived as "exclusionary." In doing so, they seemingly embraced what would be regarded in the United States as white paternalism but in Cuba was understood as "racial fraternity": "We hope that in its columns the loftiest of Cuban thinkers of the white race will present their points of view regarding the orientation and current situation of Cuba's colored people; that they will illuminate our race through their advice; that they will encourage our race through their cooperation and encouragement, trusting as we do that their words will not echo in a vacuum and that their generous effort will bear fruit in abundance, like ripe seed in fertile soil."[76]

Labor nueva's editors' willingness to establish goodwill between Black and white Cubans by embracing white paternalism in this way is perhaps why Washington and Tuskegee were both palatable and legible to editors as models for racial uplift. Whereas in the United States Washington came to be castigated for political accommodation, in Cuba his efforts to work with white southerners was consistent with some Afro-Cubans' vision of racial democracy, even as they would have rejected his compromise on racial segregation. It is entirely possible, of course, that *Labor nueva*'s editors were careful about how they crafted their commitment to racial uplift because of the massacre of Afro-Cubans four years earlier. From May to June 1912, the Cuban government murdered more than two thousand Afro-Cubans in an overzealous and disproportionate backlash against the PIC's armed but nonviolent protest against the Morúa Amendment of 1910, which outlawed race-based political parties.[77] *Labor nueva*'s editors were no doubt aware of the potential consequences of race-based organizing that did not explicitly profess their commitment to "the success of Cuban solidarity and culture."[78]

Like *La lucha*, *Labor nueva*'s editors kept an eye on Washington and Tuskegee and frequently reported on the activities of the Booker T. Washington Society (BTWS), a scientific and recreational society ("sociedad científica y de recreo") and "cultural institution" established by Afro-Cuban youth that "had purely intellectual ends."[79] BTWS members promoted "high social culture" but insisted their "purpose" was not an "exclusivist one" but to "popularize," and they shared *Labor nueva*'s commitment to forging solidarity and racial fraternity with white Cubans.[80] The BTWS proclaimed to be the "greatest moral and intellectual monument" to educated Afro-Cuban youth, and its members vehemently distanced themselves from older generations, declaring they were "no longer" "morally enslaved," did not "hold patriotism as an obligation," and rejected the notion that freedom was simply a "favor" "granted" by the "kindhearted masters of our great-grandparents."[81]

The emergence of BTWS was part of a larger movement among Afro-Cuban youth who were disillusioned with and critical of the old Black societies as "colonial, atavistic, and out of touch with the needs of 'modern' and 'civilized' blacks," writes de la Fuente. "They labeled [these old societies as] 'African cabildos' and 'dens of iniquity' whose only function was to organize dances."[82] The BTWS was at the forefront of this effort among Afro-Cuban youth to "break the old molds" of the Afro-Cuban societies, as Abelardo Vasconcelos declared in "Clarinada" (Clarion call) in *Labor nueva*'s October 1916 issue. "No old-fashioned, corrupt persons will be admitted into its bosom, nor will it admit vote-traffickers. It will be, in short, the '*plus non ultra*' of social and moral achievement." The society aimed to "set an example that demonstrates to those other organizations that they are nothing short of useless." With the grandiosity and hubris that often accompanies youth, Vasconcelos declared that the BTWS "opens the gate to the road" of moral and intellectual achievement.[83]

It is striking that the BTWS understood itself primarily as an intellectual organization, given Washington's insistence on educating the hand, head, and heart and Tuskegee's commitment to rural and working-class Black people. It is also ironic that the organization named itself after Washington at the same time that detractors in the United States increasingly came to view him as an antiquated proponent of an "Old Negro" ideology. The BTWS's appropriation of Washington is thus instructive of the utility of strategic translation between diasporic communities. Members were inspired by Washington and Tuskegee but did not seek to mimic them precisely. Washington was legible to Afro-Cuban youth as a New Negro, perhaps even as a Nuevo Criollo, but not as a proponent of industrial and agricultural education. Just as Serra selectively translated Washington's ideas, rejecting political accommodation while embracing interracial cooperation, BTWS members embraced the class component of racial uplift but not its emphasis on trades and agriculture.

With this emphasis on intellectualism, the BTWS came to espouse elitism and to distance itself from the very class of Afro-Cubans that Tuskegee was established to train, educate, and uplift—the working masses, or what Cubans referred to as the "popular classes." In response to Vasconcelos's "Clarion Call," G. Bécquer Altuna, another reader of *Labor nueva*, accused him of sowing "seeds of discord [semillas de discordias]" and cautioned BTWS members to be more generous to their predecessors and less arrogant. Vasconcelos had created "divisions between imbeciles and educated persons, between intellectuals and non-intellectuals," Altuna alleged, and he reminded Vasconcelos that "it is easier to demolish than to construct." "If a portion of those men who today you call vote-traffickers, decrepit elders, licentious . . . were not to have taken up the job of conquering, of raising up edifices that have become worm-eaten over the years, I say: others would have done so. But let us maintain some respect for those persons. Let us not treat those who do not think like us as imbeciles."[84]

As Altuna's criticism underscores, the "new" is almost always entangled with the old and is in fact made possible by it. In the African American context, the New Negro Movement of the 1920s was made possible by the Washington-era New Negro from the turn of the century. As the Harlem Renaissance writer George S. Schuyler observed, "None of these things like the Negro renaissance just comes up full blown out of the ground. It's a result of forces that have been at work for some time, and . . . we don't realize the contributing factors to it."[85] Likewise, Altuna cautioned BTWS members against drawing such a hard line between themselves and their predecessors. He admonished them for "carry[ing] exclusivism as their flag" and "uphold[ing] only intellectuals as their trophies," for they needed the very "ignorant persons" they castigated to be successful in their work. "It is necessary that you have ignorant persons to teach, so that you can be the new Nazarenes."[86]

Together, the Instituto Booker T. Washington and the Booker T. Washington Society illuminate the paradox of Tuskegee's racial and class politics. The institute reflected Tuskegee's mission to uplift the poorest and most vulnerable students, who by the turn of the century were often still only a generation or two out of slavery. The BTWS, however, reflected the ways that as Tuskegee established itself, it became a training ground for the cultivation of a Black middle class, or "ghetto bourgeoisie," as Manning Marable would have it.[87] As for Tuskegee and many other Black bourgeois institutions (then and now), the anti-racist aims of these early Afro-Cuban social and political organizations were entangled with class prejudice as well.

THE LIMITS OF STRATEGIC TRANSLATION: NEGOTIATING ANTI-BLACK RACISM IN THE U.S. SOUTH AND CUBA

Though Washington advertised the ICON in *La lucha*, there is little to no evidence to suggest that Afro-Cubans were in attendance—possibly because the ICON took place in April 1912, just weeks before the race war against the PIC that resulted in the massacre of more than two thousand Afro-Cubans (May–June 1912). In October 1912, Washington published "Race Friction in Cuba—and Elsewhere," where he linked the PIC's protest and the murderous backlash against it to racial uprisings throughout the diaspora—namely, the Jamaican Maroons' resistance to slavery and the Haitian Revolution. Curiously, instead of describing the heinous attack as the massacre that it was, he offered no moral critique of state and vigilante violence against Afro-Cubans. Instead, he used it as an opportunity to query why "there has been no negro rebellion in the United States." "The American negro has had much more reason for a resort to physical violence" than Afro-Cubans, he argued, because there was no legalized racial discrimination in Cuba, and "lynchings, which have done more than anything else to embitter the negro in this country [the United States], are practically unknown in Cuba." Washington then advanced an economic argument depicting the massacre as an Afro-Cuban uprising that threatened national and business interests. "If we had today in the South the same kind of racial bitterness and unrest as now exists in Cuba," he continued, "investments would not be safe, and the whole material progress and development of the South would halt."[88]

Washington's critique of the PIC seemingly turned a deaf ear to more nuanced commentary by his contemporaries in Cuba and the United States alike. The Afro-Cuban politician Juan Gualberto Gómez, Washington's friend, was also critical of the PIC's tactics but condemned white Cubans for their indiscriminate and disproportionate display of violence against their Black compatriots. Most significantly, about three months before the publication of Washington's article, Arturo Schomburg published a piece in *Crisis* magazine arguing that Afro-Cubans' political rights were being strategically dismantled by white Cubans who contested their political mobilization along racial lines, specifically the establishment and subsequent popularity of the PIC. Afro-Cuban leaders "are hunted by spies, threatened with imprisonment and misrepresented in the press whenever they attempt to assert their rights," Schomburg informed readers.[89] Schomburg's account explicitly explained the crisis as a matter of anti-Black racism, not as an instance of Black rebellion.

As in his "Cuban Education" address, Washington instrumentalized the Cuba situation for African American interests. He treated Cuba as a prop to highlight African Americans' putative docility and how the African American elite functioned as "sentinels" who oversaw the Black masses, squelching potential violent revolt seen in Cuba, Haiti, and Jamaica. He concluded "Race Friction in Cuba" by turning to the importance of education for preventing war. "The past forty-eight years has not only demonstrated the value to the South and the whole country of negro schoolhouses, but it has also proclaimed the wisdom and the patriotism of those who, for the first time in the history of the world so far as I know, have made the school the medium for the solution of a great and perplexing social problem."[90] Washington again mobilized Cuba to make the case for the importance of his work at Tuskegee—in this case by distancing African Americans from Afro-Cubans.

A more generous interpretation of Washington's intentions would be that he was trying to quell fear among white Americans that what happened in Cuba could happen in the U.S. South and to prevent the possible backlash that such a fear could inspire. On an already deteriorating racial landscape where lynching was on the rise and racial segregation was becoming more codified nationwide, Washington may have feared that the Afro-Cuban uprising would lead to more preemptive anti-Black violence in the United States (much like white slaveholders' response to the Haitian Revolution a century earlier). He thus appealed to two of white America's most prized and fiercely guarded interests—the security of the U.S. nation-state and private property—to downplay African Americans' propensity for violent revolt and at the same time to elevate Black education and the Black middle class as means of keeping the Black masses in check. If white Americans had little moral motivation to protect Black life, then perhaps the prospect of another civil war would persuade them.

174 PLOT II

Whatever Washington's motivations, his article was ultimately a problematic portrayal of what is now widely regarded as a massacre of Afro-Cubans. His "Cuban Education" speech had been a relatively innocuous instrumentalization of Cuba and the Spanish-American War to celebrate African American heroism and advocate for their civil rights, but "Race Friction in Cuba—and Elsewhere" exposed the limits of strategic translation if used carelessly because it cited anti-Black violence against Afro-Cubans solely to elevate African Americans as more "civilized"—lending credence to Serra's concerns about African Americans' potential displacement of Afro-Cubans under U.S. annexation.

We see a similar breakdown of strategic translation in the pages of *Labor nueva*. As in *La lucha*, *Labor nueva*'s editors kept an eye on U.S. race relations and used Tuskegee as a lens through which to view African American life and culture. Though its editors supported the BTWS, contributors were critical of the society's namesake and condemned his social philosophy. In a June 1916 issue, editors republished an article from *El mundo*, another important Havana-based newspaper, entitled, "En el Sur," or "In the South." The article reported on a racial incident involving family members of Washington's successor at Tuskegee, Robert Moton, whose wife and brother were expelled from a train in Troy, Alabama, on account of white passengers' discomfort with their presence in the Pullman car. The article was written by the Washington, DC, correspondent and columnist Victor Muñoz, who went by the penname "Attaché." Following the incident, the U.S. press censured Moton for his wife's and brother's failure to observe southern social conventions and criticized him for "rebel[ling] against the white people who protect the institution he directs," perhaps a veiled threat to the Tuskegee campus and student body.[91] In response, Moton released a statement reassuring the white South that he had advised his wife and brother against taking the Pullman car and that as a native southerner he always respected the "traditions of this region."[92]

Attaché's commentary on the Moton incident demonstrates the breakdown of strategic translation among Afro-Cubans. His commentary failed to understand the specificity of white racial violence in the U.S. South and how carefully Moton, the leader of an institution charged with ensuring the protection and safety of thousands of students, faculty, and staff, had to navigate it. Attaché lamented the treatment of Black Americans in the U.S. South but also betrayed his own class bias as a member of the Afro-Cuban elite. Though he criticized lynchings as "barbarous," he took greater issue with the fact that this act of discrimination could happen against the African American elite. In particular, Attaché was confused that white southerners, who were "generous and hospitable," could have such disdain for Black Americans that they could so mistreat people of the Motons' stature. He noted that the Motons were justified in not wanting to leave the Pullman car and go to the "colored car" not only because they had paid for their seats in the car but also because "one imagines that one would not want to travel together with such unfortunate persons who, due to the ignorance in which they have been immersed, are more like animals than men." In a footnote, Attaché added that these "hatreds" would end when the Black American, "weary of so much ignominy, resolves to defend his dignity as a civilized man using the weapons that the circumstances demand."[93]

Labor nueva's editors were much more explicit about this position in Lino Dóu's response to Attaché's commentary. A veteran of the Spanish-American War and regular contributor to *Labor nueva*, Lino Dóu inveighed against Moton's "attitude" as "more harmful, lamentable, and disconsolate than the act committed by the white Americans. That the most distinguished educational center for black Americans would recommend such passiveness reveals that black Americans do not deserve freedom, and that it should be considered a great misfortune that Booker T. Washington became a professor when there is no question that he never stopped being a slave."[94]

Attaché's and Dóu's commentary on the Moton incident departed significantly from Afro-Cubans' tendency to tout Washington and Tuskegee as models for racial uplift. Dóu's condemnation is much more consistent with Washington's detractors in the United States, who had long been critical of his accommodationist rhetoric. For Dóu, Tuskegee's passive approach to racial conflict was tantamount to "denigrating servility." This comports with the contemporaneous belief that whereas Afro-Cubans played a key role in Cuba's liberation from Spain, African Americans were much more passive in the struggle for their freedom in the United States. Thus, for Dóu, African Americans did "not deserve freedom" because they were unwilling to fight for it. Elevating Afro-Cubans' willingness to take up arms over Tuskegee's submission to Jim Crow, Dóu cited Afro-Cuban revolutionary hero Antonio Maceo as a model for African Americans to follow instead of Washington or Moton: "Our great Maceo so affirmed and practiced: 'Freedom is not asked for; it is conquered with the edge of the machete.'"[95] By declaring the necessity of armed resistance, Dóu effectively inverted Washington's criticism of Afro-Cubans in the "Race Friction" article, but he also replicated Washington's misapplication of strategic translation by criticizing African Americans in order to champion Afro-Cubans.

Ultimately, both groups mistranslated each other in these instances, but such misunderstandings are productive. Strategic translation is not simply a praxis of slight adaptation or paraphrase; rather, refusal, critique, disagreement, and misunderstanding are crucial to its efficacy. Making space for such incongruency and tension and viewing them as essential to diasporic practice prevent the flattening of diasporic identities under the banner of racial solidarity or the hierarchies that can emerge between diasporic communities with asymmetrical access to power and capital. Attending to the afterlife of the plantation in the Global Black South calls for a symbiotic, call-and-response structure, whereby the story of the Tuskegee–Cuba connection is as much about how Afro-Cubans responded to and adapted Washington and Tuskegee as about what Washington envisioned as he ingrafted Afro-Cubans and Afro–Puerto Ricans into his conception of Black agrarian futures and the southern New Negro. Crucially, when we consider Afro-Cuban perspectives, repurposing the plantation and eco-ontological regeneration, the cornerstones of Tuskegee's approach to Black modernity, fall to the wayside. Instead, Afro-Cubans celebrated Tuskegee as a symbol of Black middle-class aspirations and as a model for reconciling interracial tensions, securing philanthropic support for Black education, and interrogating the contours of Afro-Cuban racial identity. Rather than promoting agricultural and industrial education or divestment from political agitation, Afro-Cubans exploited the affordances of Tuskegee, taking what was useful and rejecting what was not.

Afro-Cubans' strategic translations of Tuskegee recall Carver's research on soil regeneration on Tuskegee's experiment plots. Just as each plot yielded distinct results based on the different organic materials applied or crops put into rotation, Washington's and Tuskegee's trans-plantation to Cuba yielded distinct and dynamic responses from Afro-Cubans intent on navigating the fraught relationships among race, labor, education, and empire as well as the meaning of freedom and citizenship on their own terms. As we will see in the following chapter, Tuskegee's trans-plantation to Haiti was also governed by strategic translations of Washington's educational philosophy at the intersection of diaspora and empire. However, given Haiti's distinct social, political, and cultural history and the nearly twenty-year occupation of the country by the United States, this trans-plantation would produce an altogether different "crop yield" than Cuba's: one that essentially restaged the standoff between the plot and the plantation at the heart of Global Black South modernity.

4

Joining Hands Across the Sea

Agricultural Education, Black Economic (Inter)Nationalism, and Haitian–African American Relations

In 1904, Jean Price-Mars, a young Haitian medical doctor and nascent statesman, set sail for the United States as head of the Haitian delegation to the Louisiana Purchase Exposition in St. Louis, Missouri. As he made the journey from Haiti to the United States, he may have reflected on the numerous ties linking the first two independent, postcolonial nation-states in the Americas. Both Haiti and the United States had originated as colonial plantation societies, and both struggled to loosen the grip of this legacy on their respective futures. In the eighteenth century, Haitian soldiers fought in the American Revolutionary War in Savannah, Georgia, aiding the thirteen North American colonies in securing their independence from Great Britain. The very exposition to which Price-Mars was traveling was held in honor of the Louisiana Purchase of 1803, which virtually doubled the country's size overnight and was made possible by Haiti's own war of independence from France. The Haitian Revolution (1791–1804) also led to the decline of cotton production in Haiti, which cleared the way for the United States to build an unprecedented cotton kingdom driven by slavery that propelled U.S. global economic supremacy in the twentieth century.[1] Haiti was tied inextricably, both directly and indirectly, to U.S. independence, geographic expansion, and political-economic growth. The irony that the United States did not recognize Haiti's independence until 1862 and contributed to its political and economic isolation in the Western Hemisphere certainly would not have been lost on Price-Mars and his fellow delegates as they prepared to represent the Black republic on the world stage and on the precipice of the U.S. American century.

During his stay in the United States, Price-Mars wrote to Booker T. Washington, requesting to observe Tuskegee firsthand. The two had initially met in Paris in 1903, when Washington was on a lecture tour. In Washington's article "On the Paris Boulevards," published during his first visit to Paris in 1899, he reflected on his desire to visit the tomb of the "great hero" Toussaint L'Ouverture as well as on his initial encounters with Haitians in the city: "There are a good many well educated and cultured Haytians [*sic*] in Paris" who "take high rank in scholarship. It is greatly to be regretted, however," he lamented, "that some of these do not take advantage of the excellent training which is given here in the colleges of physical sciences, agriculture, mechanics and domestic sciences. They would then be in a position to return home and assist in developing the agricultural and mineral resources of their native land."[2] Price-Mars was precisely the kind of "well educated and cultured" Haitian whom Washington referenced in his reflections. In 1899, Price-Mars earned a scholarship from the Haitian government to complete his medical education in Paris and while there took courses in sociology and anthropology and served as secretary of the Haitian Legation in the city.[3]

Characteristically, in "On the Paris Boulevards" Washington diagnosed Haiti's challenges based on his own uplift philosophy: "Hayti will never be what it should until a large number of the natives receive that education which will fit them to develop agriculture, public roads, start manufactories, build bridges, railroads, and thus keep in the island the large amount of money which is now sent outside for productions which these people themselves can supply."[4] One wonders what emboldened Washington to speak on Haitian conditions so authoritatively, considering that he had never visited the country. Nevertheless, in his Parisian sojourn of 1903 he must have left a lasting impression on the young Price-Mars and the other legation secretaries, Massillon Coicou and A. Cambuy. In a letter published in the *Tuskegee Student*, they commended Washington for his devotion to "morally elevating the black race" and insisting "that no race is indelibly inferior; but that men are different only by reason of their intelligence, the nobility of their character, and the consciousness of their dignity. . . . [B]y a rational system of education," they continued, Washington undertook "to modify the soul of your race by awakening in it a sense of the magnitude of its duties, and the grandure [*sic*] of its moral responsibility."[5]

One year later Price-Mars wrote to Washington again, this time requesting to see his little black "colony" in Alabama firsthand. When his letter arrived at Tuskegee, Washington was away on travel. Emmett J. Scott, Washington's secretary, responded and invited Price-Mars to visit campus after September 10, when Washington would be back in town and the school would be in "full operation." Price-Mars enthusiastically accepted Scott's invitation, asking him to "please excuse my bad english [*sic*]. It is only four weeks ago that I learn your language and I kan [*sic*] not write or speak as I would do it."[6] The image of Price-Mars, the soon-to-be preeminent Haitian intellectual and statesman, wrestling with English grammar and syntax as he arranged to visit the U.S. South is a poignant reminder of the great and urgent lengths to which Black diasporic intellectuals went in the early twentieth century to exchange ideas about securing and maintaining freedom and self-determination in slavery's aftermath.

Furthermore, that Price-Mars wrote this response to Washington from the Douglass Hotel in St. Louis—the self-proclaimed "largest Negro hotel in the West"—symbolizes the passing of the mantle of race leadership from Frederick Douglass (who had served as U.S. minister and general consul to Haiti in 1889–1891 and had died just months before the Atlanta Exposition Address in 1895) to Washington, from the nineteenth century to the twentieth century, and from the U.S. North to the rural U.S. South. While the broader diaspora was certainly aware of racial violence and oppression in the Jim Crow South, for a moment at least Washington's educational experiment at Tuskegee represented the promise and possibility of Black economic and material advancement. The U.S. South was no longer just a region where the enslaved millions of the United States labored in chains but a place where Black modernity and citizenship were being worked out, in part, through agricultural and industrial educational pursuits. Indeed, Tuskegee was becoming an intellectual and cultural hub within the Black diasporic imagination.

Price-Mars visited Tuskegee for a fortnight in mid-September 1904, "confront[ing] all the ignominies of color prejudice" as he traveled throughout the U.S. South. "Once, in the course of my trip to the Black Belt," he recalled in "Le préjugé des races" (The prejudice of races, 1919), "I was almost penned up in a compartment for beasts; I was often ejected from restaurants; refused lodging at hotels; insulted in cars." This was no doubt a strange and harrowing experience for someone who hailed from a Black country, had studied in Paris's leading universities, and had served as a diplomat in both France and Germany. Yet he "cheerfully bore these awful insults" to "better and more closely analyze all the variations of complex data of the problem of the races," and he ultimately concluded that he "saw things that spoke well for the future."[7]

Tuskegee's emphasis on agriculture must have made quite an impression on Price-Mars because he returned to Haiti committed to integrating agricultural and industrial training into the country's education system and continuously cited Tuskegee, Washington, and George Washington Carver throughout his writings over the next several decades.[8] Like the U.S. South, Haiti was a primarily agricultural country with a significant rural population (more than 90 percent). Price-Mars thus surmised that Tuskegee's strategy for uplifting rural southern African Americans was potentially viable for Haitians, too.

In the years after Price-Mars and Washington's meeting in Paris, Washington initiated a campaign to recruit Haitian students to Tuskegee. With the aid of the U.S. minister to Haiti, William F. Powell, Washington helped establish an education migration network between the first Black republic and Alabama. In the fall of 1903, the *Tuskegee Student* announced that "quite a little colony of students have come to us from Haiti," some of whom paid their own way, while others received scholarships from the Haitian government, specifically requesting the education of "industrial and scientific leaders" and the training of young men in farming.[9] These students were expected to return to Haiti to teach and apply the modern agricultural methods acquired at Tuskegee.

Price-Mars's visit to Tuskegee and Washington's recruitment of Haitian students were part of an ongoing effort among early twentieth-century Haitian and African American intellectuals to introduce industrial and especially agricultural instruction into Haiti's education system. For much of the nineteenth century, Haiti's education system was primarily classical, patterned after the French system. At the behest of Toussaint L'Ouverture, the Haitian government employed French instructors in Haitian schools and, as constitutionally mandated, provided scholarships for study in France, thereby "fuel[ing] a Francophile outlook among most Haitian statesmen and intellectuals."[10] By the late nineteenth and early twentieth centuries, however, a small contingency of influential Haitians, including Price-Mars, grew critical of the country's mimicry of French civilization and, given Washington's growing prominence in the United States, were persuaded that the Tuskegee and Hampton models could be viable in Haiti with its rural agricultural majority.

In what follows, I argue that the numerous entanglements of Tuskegee and Haiti in the early twentieth century elucidate an important albeit understudied Global Black South cultural and intellectual network that further illuminates the centrality of agriculture to debates about Black diasporic progress and futurity. As shown in chapter 3, Washington first attempted to export his vision of Black agrarian futures to Cuba and Puerto Rico, but Haiti was perhaps most compatible with and somewhat receptive to such a project. A century earlier, as Haiti made the transition from a French colonial plantation society into an independent Black republic (the originary repurposed plantation, perhaps), Toussaint was convinced that "the ultimate guarantee of freedom was the prosperity of agriculture."[11] Agriculture, industry, and the mechanic arts were even enshrined in Haiti's Constitution of 1805 and thus sewn into the very fabric of

Haitian modernity.[12] Agriculture was to be "honored and protected," the Constitution stated, and "every Citizen must possess a mechanic art." Thus, the Haitian elite's interest in Tuskegee represented the continuation of a century-long investment in agriculture and industry for the nation's political-economic development rather than a wholly new direction.[13] Washington, like Toussaint and his successors, was charged with drawing out the affordances of the plantation for the sake of Black modernity. In turn, Price-Mars and his fellow Haitian elites embraced the Tuskegee model as a means of transforming, training, and uplifting the peasant masses into what the elites regarded as productive and efficient laborers.[14]

In this chapter, I focus on three distinct historical flashpoints: the preoccupation period (1901–1914), the U.S. occupation (1915–1934), and the immediate postoccupation period (circa 1934–1940). In each of these moments, I show how Haitian and African American relations were driven by a belief that educational reform along agricultural and industrial lines, especially according to the Tuskegee model, could enhance Haiti's economic development. Significantly, I also show how Black diasporic leaders' advocacy for agricultural education was often tied to forging economic cooperation between Haitians and African Americans through agriculture and commerce. I argue that these practices of Black economic (inter)nationalism, though important examples of Global Black South exchange, also represented how strategies of liberation can, at times, still be entangled with plantation logics and practices.

As the preeminent Haitian intellectual of the twentieth century who was a staunch supporter of agricultural education for the Haitian peasantry, Jean Price-Mars was a crucial link between Tuskegee and Haiti. Price-Mars served as Haiti's director general of education and through his work as a medical doctor and lay ethnologist became an authority on Haitian folklore and Vodou as well as a spiritual father of the Négritude Movement. As such, this chapter also attends to his specific vision of Haitian agrarian futures. Throughout Price-Mars's writings and speeches, his continuous engagement with Washington's rhetorical, literary, and ideological contributions elucidates how and why Tuskegee became legible as a viable strategy for Haitian modernity. Several other Haitian intellectuals and statesmen, such as Fleury Fèquiére and Antenor Firmin, championed the Tuskegee model as well. Together with Price-Mars, these men strategically translated aspects of *Up from Slavery* and even the Atlanta Exposition Address to uplift the peasantry, reform the Haitian economy, and forge a distinctly Haitian cultural nationalism in the face of U.S. imperialism. In short, I argue that Price-Mars and his fellow Haitian elites viewed Washington's educational philosophy as a solution to a problem that had plagued the republic since emancipation: the problem of free labor and agriculture in a postslavery and putatively postcolonial society built on plantation ruins.

Finally, in examining agriculture's centrality to early twentieth-century Haitian–African American relations, this chapter also interrogates the contradictory and sometimes exploitative nature of these agrarian futures. In most instances, agriculture was conceived as a strategy for Haiti's self-determination. Through education, the peasantry, seen as the "economic backbone of the nation," would become better stewards of the land and more efficient producers. Furthermore, diversifying exports by moving away from a singular focus on coffee would increase the country's agricultural output and make it less susceptible to economic woes stemming from global market fluctuations and competition. However, agricultural education was also used as a tool of U.S. imperial domination as well as of the Haitian elite's extraction of the peasantry's cultural, intellectual, and economic resources—aiding the Haitian "state" (the urban political elite) while effectively exploiting the nation (the rural peasantry), as the Haitian anthropologist and theorist Michel-Rolph Trouillot has so astutely described Haiti's primary political and class division.[15]

The story of Haitian–African American relations that I tell here is primarily that of the educated and political elite. Because the Haitian peasantry was largely illiterate, it was the elite who had the means to forge transnational linkages with African Americans through literary translation and print cultural exchange. Indeed, Haitian conceptions of agrarian futures were not monolithic and had been plagued by internal class fractures at work since the country's inception. Like Jean Casimir's notion of the "counter-plantation" and Sylvia Wynter's "plot–plantation paradigm," Trouillot's "state against nation" dichotomy captures the tensions between a (mostly urban) governing elite that "was firmly attached to the plantation system" and a peasantry, or nation, that only "wanted land and food" and "dreamed simply of larger garden plots."[16] This tension between export agriculture and subsistence agriculture, the plantation and the plot, was at the center of Haiti's postplantation dilemma. As C. L. R. James puts it, "Subsistence production resulted in economic decay and every variety of political disorder. Yet it has preserved the national independence."[17] Indeed, what was often missing in the Haitian and African American elite's discourse about agrarian futures was any real consideration of the peasantry's attitudes toward agricultural cultivation, land use, migration, and their own self-determination more generally, thus betraying yet again the class chauvinism embedded in racial uplift ideology.

CENTENNIAL AMBIVALENCES: HAITI IN THE AFRICAN AMERICAN PRESS, 1901–1914

For such a small country, Haiti has loomed large for African Americans. As Washington observed, many an enslaved African American, though "ignorant of everything but his master and the plantation, had received tidings of the Haytian struggle for liberty."[18] The lore surrounding the first and only successful slave revolt influenced both attempted and successful revolts in the United States by Denmark Vesey and Nat Turner, respectively, and caused considerable fear among white slave owners throughout the Global Black South. By the start of the twentieth century, however, one hundred years of internecine violence and political coups in Haiti (caused in part by its political marginalization and economic exploitation by other world powers) left African Americans more ambivalent than hopeful about the future of the first Black republic, so they turned their attention toward strategies for building up the Haitian nation-state as an example to the world of Black people's capacity for self-determination.

In the years leading up to and immediately following Price-Mars's visit to the United States in 1904, the question of Haiti and its future was frequently discussed in the African American press. Across a host of newspapers, journals, and magazines, U.S. Black intellectuals vigorously debated (what they perceived as) Haiti's precarious future in its centennial year. For some commentators, Haiti represented an opportunity to resurrect the emigration debates of the mid–nineteenth century, whereby African American agriculturists could own land free from the threat of racial violence and dispossession; for others, Haiti was an opportunity to reflect on the limits and possibilities of segregation in the U.S. South. What they all shared was a desire for Black self-determination through material and economic means, and, as the first Black republic, Haiti carried the immense burden of being the global proving ground for Black sovereignty and self-determination.

In the United States, emigration was still deemed a viable solution to the "Negro problem," and, like Cuba, Haiti was envisioned as a possible destination for African American refugees. In his article "Hayti as a Refuge" (April 1901), William F. Powell, U.S. minister to Haiti from 1897 to 1905, encouraged African American agriculturists to immigrate to Haiti. Writing from Port-au-Prince, Powell extolled the virtues of Haiti in purely agricultural, climatic, and ecological terms, mimicking the rhetoric of colonial travelogues and foreshadowing that of U.S. agro-imperialism and the emerging tourist industry. Haiti's climate was "delightful" and "healthful," Powell assured readers, and the soil fertility "wonderful." Corn was easily cultivated, and sugarcane and coffee needed to be planted only once in ten and five years, respectively. There was an "immense" opportunity for cultivating bananas, oranges, lemons, lime, pineapples, and coconuts that "would yield large results and quick returns." Yet currently "all of this cultivation . . . is done with the crudest of farming utensils," he observed. "I do not think that there are a dozen plows on the island, or any labor-saving farming utensils that would alleviate the labor of the agriculturist." With "no manufacturers," Haiti provided "a wide field for this class of enterprise, especially cotton mills, as the principal articles of clothing of all classes are of this material." He continued: "What Hayti needs is a class of agriculturists who will take the initiative to cultivate the soil on a different principle than has been done heretofore and introduce therein such farming utensils as are common on any farm or plantation, in the states [sic]." Instead of immigration to Africa, with its "pernicious" climate, Powell encouraged immigration to "an island peopled by our race, with a progressive and independent government of its own and near to our shores." Those "who emigrate," he insisted, "have to be people who are willing to work" and "bring with them improved farming utensils and such labor-saving machines."[19]

Powell's agrarian future betrays the elitism and quasi-imperialism that undergirded racial uplift. This preferred class of emigrant was likely the bourgeois Tuskegee New Negro, who was trained in modern agricultural and industrial methods. Indeed, the very next year Powell helped to secure funding from the Haitian government to "send twenty young men to Tuskegee to be trained," inaugurating a student migration network between Haiti and rural Alabama.[20] Although this kind of educational exchange—training Haitian students to educate the Haitian peasantry—could have been a productive instance of Global Black South solidarity, Powell's invitation for African American emigrants to invest in Haitian agriculture and industry also recalls Rafael Serra y Montalvo's fears of African American imperialism in an annexed Cuba.

In early 1904, the *Voice of the Negro*, an African American periodical based in Atlanta, published a forum titled "The Dominican and Haitian Republics and Their Revolutionary Drawbacks." It covered the countries' political revolutions, Haitian sovereignty, U.S. imperialism, and the possibility of annexation to the United States. The range of opinions expressed represents African Americans' ambivalences toward Haiti: on one hand, its revolution evoked pride that a race of formerly enslaved people could overthrow one of the most powerful militaries in the world and establish a modern republic. On the other hand, Haiti's political turmoil raised doubts about the possibility of a thriving and autonomous Black nation-state. Calling for "a halt . . . to the reign of anarchy which now exists in the island," the editors of the *Voice* observed, "The United States

Negro's interest in affairs down there in the Negro Republic is perfectly natural. We want order down there for our own sakes. We are struggling in this country to be recognized as a class who ought to be allowed to participate in affairs of the Government. If the confusion continues in Haiti and San Domingo where Negroes have full control of their government, this very condition of things will further prejudice the world against our cause."[21]

Overall, the sentiments expressed in the forum articles range from sympathetic and cautiously optimistic to downright offensive and misguided. Most commentators expressed little consideration for the numerous and unique challenges Haiti confronted in its first century of existence that contributed to its perpetual economic dependence and political turmoil. Rather, their attitudes reflect how U.S. Americans used Haiti as a point of comparison for African Americans' political futures. For some, Haiti was a cautionary tale about the threat of Black self-government in the Black Belt, given its comparable Black majority. As one *New York Times* commentator reasoned, "The two races in the South must live and work out their own salvation together, at the peril of both. We cannot contemplate such a separation of the races as would reduce the black belt [*sic*] of the South to the state of the black Republic of Haiti, where, in the absence of the whites, the blacks are reverting to mere African savagery."[22]

In the *Voice*, John Stephens Durham's article "The Hidden Wealth of Hayti" provided perhaps the most balanced portrait in the series, doubtless owing to his firsthand experience on the island. To recall, Durham was good friends with Washington and was named U.S. consul to Haiti in 1891 following Frederick Douglass's resignation. He continued working in the Caribbean throughout the early twentieth century, managing large sugar plantations in Haiti, the Dominican Republic, and Cuba and even owning a sugar plantation. Around 1901, Durham offered to help Washington recruit Haitian students to Tuskegee and frequently conferred with him about his plan to "organize a sugar company" there.[23] For Durham, Haiti's future was bound up with the peasantry. The "man who will learn the patois of Hayti" and "approach the people with human interest and fellow feeling" will understand "the real wealth of Hayti" out of which its future would emerge, he contended. On one hand, Durham was sympathetic toward Haitian peasants and legitimized their language, Kréyol, anticipating the importance of its reclamation during the Haitian Indigenist Movement two decades later. Countering accusations of Haitians' laziness, Durham argued, "They are not lazy. I know of no other laborer who puts in a harder day, with so little incentive than does the Haytian—when at work." Yet his writing also reflects the elitist, civilizing rhetoric so popular among race leaders at the turn of the century. Durham's sympathy was based on racial uplift ideology and refracted through class paternalism. Though the "Haytian man" is "primitive" and "barbaric," he maintained, he is "surely pregnant with civic possibilities." Durham made especially bewildering and offensive comments about Haitian women, noting they are "generally unattractive in face" but have the admirable qualities of strong work ethic and hospitality to strangers, and they have "preserved the art of the gardener," which has sustained "Port au Prince as the best vegetable market in the West Indies."[24]

Durham's portrait of Haitian women as artist-gardeners resonates with Tuskegee's conception of New Negro womanhood, whereby Black girls and women were encouraged to engage in outdoor work and enroll in the school's Agriculture Department (chapter 2). Like Washington, Durham viewed agricultural cultivation as both an art form and an integral part of Black self-determination. Accordingly, in concluding the article he outlined three areas where Haiti needed to develop in "the new century"—public roads, public schools, and a national system of agriculture—and explicitly yoked the country's future to Tuskegee: "Sugar, coffee and cocoa, cultivated by modern methods and worked with modern machinery, would be the centres around which would be organized the individual work. The art of gardening would be helped by the introduction of the best agricultural implements and the employment of capable, sympathetic, directors, such as Tuskegee could readily furnish, to demonstrate the use of the tools."[25] In short, Durham posited the cultivation of cash crops, originally cultivated during plantation slavery, as the foundation of Haiti's political economy for the "new century" and established Tuskegee as a model for diasporic uplift at the intersection of agriculture and education. Yet, as the historian Brandon Byrd rightly argues, Durham failed to take seriously the peasantry's modes of and attitudes toward agricultural cultivation: they disdained sugar production and prioritized subsistence instead of large-scale agricultural production.[26] Durham's proposal thus elucidates the ongoing tension between plantation and counter-plantation logics at the heart of Black agrarian futures at the turn of the twentieth century.

Later in 1904, the Black bibliophile and archivist Arturo Schomburg published "Is Hayti Decadent?," where he, too, insisted on the necessity of agricultural development for Haiti's future and proposed the Tuskegee model for uplifting the Haitian people and addressing the country's agricultural and industrial dilemma. Like Durham and his fellow forum contributors in the *Voice*, Schomburg contemplated Haiti because it "is of great importance to the young people" and thus the future of the race. In contrast to nineteenth-century depictions of Haiti's military prowess, Schomburg contended, "the Haytians of today . . . could do no better good to their country, than bury the implements of warfare as other nations have done, and commence to lift up the country from the present lamentable condition in which we find her." Schomburg deemed Haiti's once-celebrated military might as the root cause of internal rebellions and revolutions that had plagued the republic since its inception a century earlier. Instead of "the implements of warfare," he maintained, "let them purchase agricultural implements, instill in the minds of the people the economic conditions and principles that a country whose wealth depends entirely on agriculture should be ready to do the things that lie within her powers to increase her material wealth."[27]

To interrogate Haiti's putative decadence, Schomburg examined "the conditions in which the island flourished" during the "French occupation." The article essentially becomes an accounting ledger, detailing the country's agricultural output when "'every plantation laid out with the greatest care and neatness, was so arranged as to bring every part of the soil into use in its proper order of succession.'" He then detailed the decline of Haitian agriculture following independence, noting, for instance, that sugar exports fell from 163,405,220 pounds in 1791 to 652,541 pounds in 1882. Paradoxically, Schomburg's exploration of an agrarian future in Haiti was rooted in the country's plantation past. Though he acknowledged that "this high state of material prosperity was reached under the enforced labor of slaves," he insisted nevertheless that "it shows something of the natural productiveness of the soil" and has implications for the country's future. He inquired: "Is there any essential reason why the same remarkable degree of prosperity cannot under free institutions be reached and maintained, if not even surpassed there, if only the internal peace and domestic tranquility be assured and wise and economical conditions open to all alike be established and kept with vigor?"[28]

Ultimately, Haiti's "decadence" did not lie in its soil, Schomburg argued, but rather in the people's failure to develop agriculture and industry, "the foundation upon which nations have been built." "You may look over and over the field and you will not be able to find anything coming from Hayti that can bear the trade mark 'Made in Hayti,'" he lamented. To bring this agro-industrial future to fruition, he longed to "infuse in Hayti graduates of Booker T. Washington's technical school" to uplift and "increase the wealth of the people and country." Tuskegee, he intimated, provided a strategy for repurposing the meaning of agriculture for Haitian modernity and self-determination, as it was doing in the U.S. South.[29]

Though Schomburg rightly posited agricultural development as an integral part of nation building, the practice of producing cash crops on such a large scale still reeked of a colonial plantation logic and was likely impossible to attain without violence and coercion. Unfortunately, Schomburg seemed to misapprehend the significance of having an expendable labor force to work the island's extremely fertile soil, which is not to suggest that he intended to diminish the extreme brutality and exploitation of slavery; rather, I wish to underscore the limits of his strictly economic and materialist model of Black progress. It threatened to reduce people to statistical abstractions or aggregates and "progress" to mere numbers instead of as a measure of the qualitative experiences of people's lives. Furthermore, as Raphael Dalleo argues, "the modernizing project Schomburg propose[d] ... relie[d] on Eurocentric authors ... whose views of the limits of Caribbean people led to the notion that outsiders must 'infuse' Haiti with modern ideas."[30]

Perhaps most importantly, Schomburg failed to grasp the meaning of the plantation for the Haitian masses. In the immediate postemancipation era, formerly enslaved Haitians and their descendants were in constant tension with the Haitian government over their labor as the leaders of the new republic sought to keep the plantation intact as the engine of the Haitian economy.[31] The Haitian masses, however, opted to work on small collectively owned family farms, where they could grow food for subsistence and cash crops for the market. Through "joint collective ownership," Casimir maintains, the Haitian masses "disobeyed the principles on which the recruitment of labour to sustain the dominant economy were based," broke "the economic stranglehold of the planters on land and people," and forged "a unique societal plan, [of] combined resources, a family organization, a language, a religion and symbolic systems into a palpable utopia." In short, "the system of joint collective ownership" "was the main-stay of the counter-plantation."[32] This contestation over agriculture in Haiti is the local, qualitative history that Schomburg's primarily quantitative analysis failed to account for.

Schomburg was an Afro–Puerto Rican immigrant to the United States who staunchly supported the Cuban and Puerto Rican liberation movements from Spain and was perhaps the most prolific Black archivist of the twentieth century, so his recounting of French wealth under colonial slavery as evidence of Haiti's potential prosperity during freedom is puzzling. However, as Lorgia García Peña has recently argued, Schomburg's later writings on Haiti demonstrate a profound commitment to defending the Black republic against its numerous critics in a milieu characterized by "global anti-Haitianism." In several profiles of Haitian revolutionary leaders, "Schomburg consecrate[d] Haiti as a site of modernity and political advancement, contradicting the narratives of savagery and incivility that dominated public opinion." In doing so, Peña continues, Schomburg challenged narratives of Black inferiority "through the very language and tools of the oppressor."[33] If we use this logic to contextualize "Is

Hayti Decadent?," then we can begin to understand differently Schomburg's emphasis on Haiti's prosperity under the colonial plantation system: not as disregarding the plantation's immense brutalities but rather as reminding readers of the country's past fecundity, *even under such horrendous conditions*, in order to challenge the myth of its inherent decadence for the "young people." With the tools and methods taught at Tuskegee, Schomburg believed, Haiti could be prosperous once again. Schomburg's essay thus reflects the conundrum at the heart of the repurposed plantation and the broader Black liberation struggle: how (and whether) to appropriate the master's colonial tools for Black progress without reproducing their violences.

Washington, too, addressed Haiti in several early twentieth-century publications, routinely criticizing Haitian leaders for their failure to incorporate industrial and agricultural methods into the country's mostly classical education system. In *Working with the Hands*, also published in 1904, Washington addressed the challenges facing "our people in the republic of Hayti, who were freed many years before the emancipation of our race in the Southern States." Like Schomburg, he compared Haiti to the U.S. South since the Civil War and attributed Haiti's political and economic instability to its neglect of agricultural and industrial education. Although "Haytians had distinguished themselves in the study of philosophy and the languages," he acknowledged, "the sad fact remained that Hayti did not prosper." By focusing exclusively on "mental training" in a country where there is "almost no industrial development," the Haitian professional has no clients and therefore "spends much of his time in writing poetry, in discussing subjects in abstract science, or embroiling his country in revolutions." Washington saw a direct correlation among idleness, "mental training," and political rebellion. Alongside "mental training," he contended, "a large proportion of the brightest [Haitian] youths . . . should have been educated as civil, mining, and sanitary engineers, and others as architects and builders; and most important of all, agriculture should have been scientifically developed," reprising the argument of his article "On the Paris Boulevards" from 1899.[34]According to Washington and his contemporaries, industrial and agricultural education could both sustain an educational institution such as Tuskegee and be scaled up to support the political economy of an entire nation-state such as Haiti.

In line with his conception of the southern, Tuskegee New Negro, Washington conceived of Haiti's future in terms of its agricultural productiveness. Despite its prodigious exports, "the people live almost wholly upon the primitive products of undisturbed nature, and the greater part of the harvesters and other workers are women." In dodging "honest productive labour," he wrote, "the people acquire a fatal fondness for wasting valuable hours in discussing politics and conspiring to overthrow the government." Training in scientific agriculture and industrial education, however, could yield productive citizens capable of "upbuilding" the republic.[35] Ironically, though Haitian peasants were not trained in scientific agriculture, they had long practiced the kind of subsistence cultivation Washington encouraged among southern African Americans, so his critique was seemingly aimed primarily at the Haitian elite.

As Powell, Durham, Schomburg, and Washington demonstrate, agricultural labor and cultivation remained central to notions of Black modernity within the Global Black South even after slavery, and Tuskegee became a key site for thinking through the possibilities of a Black agrarian future that was at once modern and self-governing. The problem is that most of their conceptions of agrarian futures in Haiti failed to engage Haitian peasants as self-determining subjects. For instance, if Haiti were to be a "refuge" for African American agriculturalists, as Powell proposed, then what of the rural peasantry who already worked the land? How did they figure into his emigration scheme? Whereas the Tuskegee–Cuba connection was facilitated by both political leaders and laypersons alike, the Tuskegee–Haiti connection was most often a discourse between African American and Haitian elites *about* the urban poor and rural peasantry.

Perhaps unsurprisingly, not all African Americans supported exporting Tuskegee to Haiti. In the pages of the *Chicago Broad Ax*, Rev. Owen M. Waller, M.D., an Oxford-educated Episcopal priest in Washington, DC, and a founding member of the NAACP, vehemently rejected Washington's patronizing attitude toward Haiti. "What does Mr. Washington hope to gain by belittling the struggling, heroic Republic of Haiti?," Waller inquired. "All the lucre of Wall Street and his Wall Street friends will not outweigh in the balances of human admiration the glorious liberties of that beautiful pearl of the Antilles." Waller disparaged Washington's vision of agrarian futures and eco-ontological regeneration by adding that Haiti had been more concerned about "the making of a man" than the "acquisition of the cabbage patch." "Let Mr. Washington sneer at Haiti," Waller continued. "I prefer the vision of Toussaint L'Ouverture defying Napoleon to Mr. Washington, bowing, hat in hand, to an unwashed cracker. 'Certainly, sah! We know our place, we know we are inferior to the white man, we do not expect any form of equality.' "[36] Waller's is a vehement rebuke of Tuskegee's hegemony and how Washington's ability to curry favor with white industrial titans and white global political leaders was perceived to have had the adverse effect of placing a stranglehold on Black political and educational efforts.

Several other Haitian and African American commentators also defended Haiti against such negative depictions. In an article in the *North American*

Review in 1903, Jacques Nicolas Léger, a Haitian lawyer, politician, and diplomat living and working in Washington, DC, refuted offensive statements about Haiti circulating in the U.S. press. In 1907, Léger expanded his essay into a book-length defense of his native land, *Haiti, Her History and Her Detractors.* Several points responded to criticism from the likes of Washington, Durham, Schomburg, William Pickens, and others in the United States, both Black and white: "For the purpose of showing that the Haitians are reverting to barbarism, their detractors affect to praise the prosperity of the island at the time of the French domination," Léger observed. "Instead of finding out from trustworthy sources the exact truth of the matter, they hasten to draw the conclusion that the Haitians are lazy and unworthy of possessing such a rich and beautiful island."[37] As if directly countering Schomburg's account of Haiti's agricultural decline, Léger sympathetically portrayed the revitalization of Haitian agriculture from the "mass of ruins" of the immediate postemancipation period to the present and despite "all the great Powers being ill-disposed toward them." Although sugar exports waned in Haiti after emancipation, he maintained that "one hundred years after taking over a devastated land the Haitians succeeded by their own unaided efforts in exporting" considerably more coffee, cocoa, logwood, and other commodities than during the immediate postemancipation period. When compared to Schomburg's accounting ledger, Léger's catalog is an important reminder that how we interpret numbers and statistics is often subjective. Furthermore, he refuted the charge that Haiti's presumed agricultural "decadence" was due to Black inferiority because even "the supremacy of the white man, was unable to preserve the former prosperity of the British possessions of the West Indies" after emancipation.[38] Indeed, as Léger indicates, plotting agrarian futures without exploited labor means relinquishing some prosperity and productivity for human vitality.

Dr. Henry W. Furniss, U.S. minister to Haiti from 1905 to 1913, agreed that Haiti had been "much maligned by the American press . . . [and had been] a frequent victim of a class which has gone there to exploit it." Like Powell, Furniss sought to make Haiti legible to African Americans through its agricultural fecundity and possible investment opportunities. "Haiti, from a standpoint of natural resources," he wrote, "is a very rich country, and offers great possibilities to emigrants with a little capital. The soil is very rich, and is practically virgin." Furniss depicted President François C. Antoine Simon as "a practical farmer" who, "realizing that Haiti is essentially an agricultural country[,] . . . is using every possible means to stimulate and encourage agriculture." For Furniss and other U.S.-based commentators writing in the years leading up to the U.S. occupation of 1915–1934, Haiti represented the necessity of agricultural development for Black modernity and self-determination and thus had a "great need for schools like those at Tuskegee and Hampton."[39] And as the twentieth century got underway, several prominent Haitian leaders began to espouse a similar view.

When Jean Price-Mars returned to Haiti from his sojourn to the United States in 1904, he published widely and gave several lectures imploring the Haitian elite to reform their primary education system to reflect the Anglo-Saxon, or Tuskegee, method. In an address in 1906, he reflected on his time in the United States, gave listeners a brief overview of African Americans' strides since emancipation, and described Booker T. Washington as "the most powerful American orator" of the day. "One cannot form from a distance," he enthused, "a comprehensive idea of the social scope of Booker T. Washington's work, which is to prepare for all branches of industry skilled workers who, not only will be able to make an honorable living for themselves, but also, by their discipline and training, will be in a position to exercise great influence in the gigantic struggle between Capital and Labor."[40] According to his biographer Jacques C. Antoine, Price-Mars viewed Washington as "the harbinger of the rehabilitation of the Black masses through collective and individual efforts."[41]

Price-Mars published many of these lectures in *La vocation de l'élite* (1919), a volume criticizing the Haitian elite for their defeatist attitude toward the U.S. occupation and "conceiving of themselves as 'colored Frenchmen' as opposed to proud Haitians."[42] To unify the urban elite and the rural masses, Price-Mars argued in the title essay, "the elite must be simultaneously, and pragmatically, industrial, commercial, and agricultural, without being exclusively intellectual."[43] Like Washington, Price-Mars believed that industrial and agricultural education was crucial for Haiti's development, and yet even more than Washington he viewed models of agricultural and classical education as complementary. In "L'education technique," published in October 1912 during his tenure as general inspector of Haitian schools (1912–1915), Price-Mars strategically translated Washington by promoting the convergence of classical and technical education in Haitian primary schools. Tuskegee's ongoing influence on his vision of Haitian modernity is evident in his recommendations to establish in each department "central schools of arts and crafts with agricultural sections suitably equipped with laboratories and experimental gardens." Furthermore, given the success of "normal institutes" in the United States, Price-Mars proposed using "the Anglo-Saxon negro"—that is, African Americans—"to direct these institutions of a higher nature."[44] Much like the proposals made by Durham, Schomburg, and Furniss, Price-Mars's desire to transplant African American teachers to Haiti exemplifies the centrality of agricultural education to Global Black South intellectual exchange well before the artistic turn of the 1920s and 1930s.

Several other prominent Haitian statesmen also promoted the Tuskegee model: Fleury Féquière, who served in Haiti's House of Representatives, and Antenor Firmin, a politician now recognized as a nineteenth-century forefather of anthropology for his radical study *De l'égalité des races humaines* (*The Equality of the Human Races*, 1885), which dispelled myths of Black racial inferiority. Féquière was deeply influenced by *Up from Slavery*, which had been translated into French in 1903 as *L'autobiographie d'un nègre* (The autobiography of a slave).[45] In writing *L'éducation haitienne* (1906), a volume on the history of Haitian education, Féquière dedicated an entire chapter to Washington and his work at Tuskegee, and in the volume's appendix he cited *L'autobiographie d'un nègre* and Theodore Roosevelt's *The Strenuous Life* (1899) as especially influential texts.[46] Like Price-Mars, Féquière supported vocational training for the Haitian masses, and under his leadership Haiti's House of Representatives established the École Elie Dubois, a vocational school for girls in Port-au-Prince.[47] Likewise, Firmin cited *Up from Slavery* throughout his volume *M. Roosevelt, président des États-Unis, et la République d'Haïti* (1905), and Washington inquired about Firmin's *The Equality of the Human Races* in 1902, suggesting their mutual awareness of and interest in each other's work.[48] The two men met in person in Washington, DC, in the summer of 1908 and corresponded at least once thereafter. For Haitians, as for Afro-Cubans, *Up from Slavery* was not only a slave narrative but also a political document detailing African Americans' political subjectivity and economic and material progress.

Haitian intellectuals and statesmen remained interested in Tuskegee well into the next decade. In a newspaper article in July 1911, "Haitiens Need Tuskegee Ideas," for instance, Dr. Jean Jacques, a Haitian official, asserted, "The country needs more practical education" as "the average Haitien [*sic*] aims too high and is too impractical."[49] John S. Durham corresponded with Washington about arranging for the Haitian ministers H. Pauleus Sannon and John Hurst to visit Tuskegee. Sannon had heard Washington give a "practical address" at Howard University and determined to visit the Tuskegee campus in person. He also invited Washington to "make an inspection of conditions" in Haiti, and Washington accepted.[50]

For Haitians and African Americans alike, what Washington was doing on a local level at Tuskegee could be transplanted to Haiti and scaled up into a national system of education if the country's leadership could establish similar schools throughout the countryside. For diplomats such as Powell and Furniss, Haiti also represented an opportunity for African American investors to engage in commercial development along agricultural lines, a project that would continue to inspire economic (inter)nationalism between Haitians and African Americans well into the 1930s, as I explore later in this chapter. Yet while these Haitian and African American intellectuals were conceiving of ways to train Haitian peasants in modern agricultural methods, by 1913 many peasants began migrating away from the Haitian countryside to work on sugar plantations in Cuba because of poor economic conditions at home. Though often depicted as poor and illiterate, rural peasants were taking their futures into their own hands, even if it meant entering the uncertain and volatile currents of hemispheric migration.[51]

Critically, what many of these diasporic leaders failed to fully appreciate is that Haiti's past agricultural glory was not simply the product of fertile land and industriousness but rather also of the coercion and inhumanity of slavery. The wealth generated under the plantation system did not belong to Haitians but to the planters, merchants, bankers, and the French ruling class. Furthermore, the Haitian Revolution left colonial economic infrastructures—plantations, sugar mills, irrigation systems, and so on—in shambles. Even when the country achieved independence, Haiti was politically isolated by the major world powers. Though the war officially concluded in 1804, France did not recognize Haitian independence until 1824 based on an agreement that Haitians would essentially indemnify France for the loss of its wealthiest colony. The Franco-Haitian Agreement kept Haiti in a state of perpetual debt and France in a position of power over Haitian finances until 1947, when the debt was finally cleared. This was the precarious afterlife of the colonial plantation that plagued Haiti throughout the nineteenth and twentieth centuries.

As if that were not enough, at the dawn of the twentieth century Haiti became the unlucky apple of U.S. imperialism's avaricious eye. Between 1896 and 1915, Haiti elected nine presidents: six were overthrown, and three were killed in office. In July 1915, after killing scores of his political opponents and dissidents, President Jean Vilbrun Guillaume-Sam was executed in the streets of Port-au-Prince by a mob of Haitian citizens. As a result, President Woodrow Wilson of the United States sent U.S. marines to restore order in Haiti, citing fears that Germany would take advantage of Haiti's political instability to gain a foothold in the Western Hemisphere during World War I. Although this was a legitimate concern, Wilson also sought to protect U.S. investments in Haiti made several years before the invasion. In 1908, President Antoine Simon of

Haiti signed the McDonald Contract, giving U.S. companies the right to build railroads in Haiti, and "soon after, the United Fruit Company and Citibank took control of most of the production and financial activities in the country."[52] In 1910, the United States took command of the Banque Nationale, and in 1912 the Haitian American Sugar Company was established, representing the corporate plantation's further encroachment on Haiti's economy. In 1914, President Sam "negotiated a deal to grant the United States control over Haiti's Custom Houses and thus over its main source of revenue."[53] In short, the occupation was the culmination of a series of calculated efforts to gain a political and economic foothold in the Black republic. The United States would occupy Haiti for nearly twenty years, claiming to improve its agricultural sector, infrastructure, education system, and finances, while in actuality inflicting a litany of heinous abuses on the Haitian people and undermining the national sovereignty.

IMPERIAL AFFORDANCES: TUSKEGEE AND THE U.S. OCCUPATION OF HAITI, 1915–1934

On October 21, 1915, mere weeks before his death, Booker T. Washington dispatched a statement to the *New York Age*. The United States had just occupied Haiti in July of that year, and Washington was greatly distressed by reports of American soldiers killing Haitians. Unable to sleep, this "dying man on the impulse of a moment" awakened his "stenographer and dictated an article" pleading for a fair course of action in Haiti.[54] Washington was deeply committed to maintaining Haitian sovereignty and encouraged the U.S. government to be patient and reassure Haitians that the primary objective of the United States was "to help the Haitians govern their own country." Washington acknowledged Haiti's alleged culpability in the occupation, criticizing the Haitian elite's corruption and tendency to "ape French civilization," but he also categorically refuted myths of Haitian degeneracy and acknowledged the country's virtues as an independent Black nation-state with "some semblance of a republican form of government." He painted a somewhat sympathetic portrait of the Haitian masses. They are "in a very primitive way, farmers," he wrote, and, though "unlettered," "are an industrious, law abiding, sober people, seeking only to be let alone to earn their living." Then he made one of his most explicit public critiques of the U.S. government and its foreign relations, asserting in no uncertain terms that it was "white men" from the United States and Europe who had exploited and instigated "numerous revolutions" in Haiti and were therefore also responsible for the country's volatile political state.[55]

Washington deemed the Haiti–U.S. treaty that gave the U.S. government significant control over Haitian affairs "harsh and precipitate" and forcefully criticized the U.S. marines' use of excessive violence against the Haitian people. "Shooting civilization into the Haitians on their own soil will be an amazing spectacle," he argued. "Sending marines as diplomats and Mauser bullets as messengers of destruction [will] breed riot and anarchy, and are likely to leave a legacy of age-long hatreds and regrets." Washington reminded the U.S. government that many Haitians harbored "deep-seated prejudice against White Americans" because of anti-Black violence in the United States. He explicitly established racial solidarity with Haitians and voiced his own distrust in white Americans' ability to be fair with Haiti, noting, "It is very difficult for any White man to understand, to put himself in a Black man's place, to understand Black people, to understand, or even undertake to understand, the American Negro, and there are still fewer White men in this country who can go into Haiti and get the sympathy, the co-operation and the confidence of the Haitians, simply and mainly because it is not possible for many White people to even try to understand and work with Black people."[56] This is an uncharacteristically overt critique of American racism for Washington, who spent most of his career advocating for (and often overstating) the possibility of interracial harmony in the U.S. South. Perhaps his impending death inspired him to share his true feelings about the worsening state of American race relations. Whatever the case, he was greatly concerned that the United States had deployed southern politicians and marines to take up posts in Haiti because their Jim Crow prejudices were foreign to Haitians. "Every Haitian would rather be swept from the face of the earth than give up his independence or his country," Washington asserted. "He does not wish the dominance of the white man."[57]

Washington's treatise on the occupation demonstrates how African Americans and Haitians navigated U.S. imperialism to establish racial solidarity through a shared commitment to uplift and self-determination. In the midst of the occupation, for instance, Washington proposed a teacher- and student-exchange program between Haitians and African Americans that would enhance Haiti's public-education system.[58] Like Price-Mars's proposal three years earlier to bring African American instructors to Haiti, this was an example of Global Black South collaboration, despite the power asymmetry between the United States and Haiti. By internationalizing his agricultural and industrial education program as a diasporic uplift project and model for Black self-determination in the U.S. South as well as in Haiti, Washington demonstrated the "practice" of "forging diaspora in the midst of empire."[59]

Despite his many misgivings, however, Washington ultimately upheld the Monroe Doctrine and viewed the occupation as "absolutely necessary," given Haiti's political and economic instability. However, claims that he "celebrated" the occupation "as the only way to civilize" Haitians are somewhat overstated.[60] Many African American elites, including the more radical W. E. B. Du Bois, initially supported the occupation as well, as did some Jamaican and Haitian elites.[61] Washington's qualified support was thus consistent with that of many of his contemporary Black elites across the diaspora, who viewed Haiti's political instability as a challenge to the goals of Black self-determination. As the abuses of the occupation came to light, however, Du Bois, James Weldon Johnson, and numerous other African Americans reversed course and were critical of the exploitative and imperial U.S. practices in Haiti. Washington died in November 1915, so there is no way to know if he, too, would have altered his position. To be sure, Washington was neither anticolonial nor anti-imperial, and he believed in circumventing, subverting, or working within the confines of oppressive structures rather than opposing them explicitly. In this instance, however, his emphasis on Haitians' warranted distrust of the United States because of a long history of anti-Black violence and a foreign "'policy of territorial expansion under the cloak of benevolent aid'" in the Caribbean and Latin America suggests he was far more concerned about Haiti's well-being than celebratory of the U.S. invasion.[62]

Despite Washington's deathbed pleas for patience, the U.S. government would pursue military occupation of Haiti for nearly twenty years. President Woodrow Wilson, a virulent racist, used the oppressive domestic policies and attitudes toward African Americans in the United States as the basis of U.S. foreign policy toward Haitians, just as Washington feared. One of the most insidious policies was a revision of the Haitian Constitution that allowed U.S. companies to own land in Haiti and thus expand their neoplantation empires in the hemisphere. Foreign land ownership had been outlawed in Haiti's Constitution of 1805 to prevent foreign control and preserve national independence. Through enterprises such as the Haitian American Sugar Company, the United States incorporated Haiti into its already expansive Caribbean sugar empire, which included Cuba, the Dominican Republic, and Puerto Rico. It also imposed two presidents on Haiti, Philippe Sudré Dartiguenave and Louis Borno, neither of whom had much of a popular following among Haitians.[63]

The U.S. occupation significantly disrupted rural life in Haiti. Attempts to modernize Haitian agriculture through vocational education and large-scale corporate plantations displaced peasants from their family plots and led thousands of rural Haitians to migrate to work on U.S.-owned sugar plantations in Cuba and the Dominican Republic, where they faced precarious living conditions and anti-Haitian prejudices.[64] In order to build more roads in the country, the United States reintroduced the corvée system, a long-defunct forced-labor system from the French colonial era. Many Haitians were also forced to work on U.S.-owned corporate plantations, and if they refused, they were incarcerated for vagrancy.[65] As Dalleo argues, "The peasant-based subsistence farming on the island was seen as the primary obstacle to modernization, and the occupation attempted to expropriate peasant land in order to consolidate large, plantation-style holdings oriented toward export."[66] Haitians rightfully regarded these policies as a form of slavery, which led to a second Caco rebellion. The Caco, an "organized insurgent group" of peasants from the northern region, revolted against the U.S. marines in a conflict that lasted from 1918 to 1920.[67] Though they were defeated, their insurrection led to a U.S. Senate investigation into the occupation administration's abusive policies.

Throughout the occupation, the Haitian and African American elite continued to promote agricultural education for the rural masses, and Tuskegee remained central to how U.S. and Haitian government officials alike conceived of such reforms. In November 1916, the Haitian periodical *Le moniteur* reported that Rev. Churchstone Lord, a Tuskegee graduate and pastor of an African Methodist Episcopal Church in Port-au-Prince, requested the government's assistance to transplant the Tuskegee model to Haiti and to staff schools with African American instructors.[68] Rev. Lord's support for agricultural education did not equate to support for the occupation, however, which he described as "an iniquitous act." He was especially critical of U.S. marines, accusing them of "evil and intrigue and duplicity and murders and debauchery of the young womanhood of every class in Haiti."[69]

As we've seen, the Tuskegee–Haiti connection was initially conceived and carried out by the Haitian and African American elite and was primarily a diasporic project; however, during the occupation the U.S. government attempted to co-opt the Tuskegee project as part of its imperial scheme. At the behest of the Harding administration, President Louis Borno of Haiti invited Tuskegee's president and Washington's successor, Robert Moton, to visit the country to help establish an educational system based on Tuskegee because "officials in Washington think that by inculcating into the youth [the education] taught at Tuskegee the future of the island will be made more secure."[70] According to the historian Leon D. Pamphile, President Borno was a pawn of the Harding administration, which had taken over Haitian finances, so his invitation to Moton was sullied by U.S. imperial designs. The Harding administration recognized Moton's educational expertise, Pamphile argues, but it also wanted to use Moton's "influence and reputation to dazzle the Haitians while covering up the shortcomings of the american [*sic*] military occupation." Having "'the most prominent Negro in the country'" on their side would certainly decrease criticism, the Harding administration reasoned.[71]

The plan failed, however, because Moton was unable to visit owing to a prior commitment and sent W. T. B. Williams, another Tuskegee administrator, in his place.[72] Williams's reflections on the visit published in the *Southern Workman* were "evenhanded but uncritical of the occupation," argues the historian Millery Polyné. However, Pamphile maintains that Williams "did not blindly comply with the request of the State Department that . . . the Tuskegee model be imposed upon the Haitians . . . [with] no consideration for deep-rooted local and cultural traditions." Rather, Williams's report reflected "objectivity and enlightened respect" for improving the Haitian education system, argues Pamphile, and proposed a "balanced curriculum" of academic and vocational education.[73]

When Williams returned to Tuskegee, he gave an address about his Haitian visit in the institute's chapel. According to reports, he vividly described Haiti's grandeur and fertility as well as the "elegant manners of the inhabitants." He rued that "we colored people in America do not know the Haitians better and that we are not better acquainted with the possibilities which our business men could develop in Haiti."[74] As Williams's comments indicate, Black diasporic leaders typically viewed educational reform as inextricably tethered to economic development. President Borno shared this philosophy as he, too, encouraged African Americans to invest in Haiti along educational and agro-commercial lines. In "Haitian President's Message to the United States," an article "written exclusively for the Afro-American" in 1926 (translated and published in the *Baltimore Afro-American* by Rev. Churchstone Lord), Borno, like Haitian leaders before and after him, invited African Americans to Haiti to aid in the country's agricultural and industrial development and praised Booker T. Washington's "practical genius" in making the American Negro "a productive force." While the professions were "full" in Haiti, he maintained, there was "plenty of room for skilled workers and farmers." Thus, Borno welcomed African Americans as agricultural instructors to Haiti to help restore the country to its past agricultural glory: "I would have no one forget, that during the early Colonial period, Haiti as well as Santo Domingo were the richest of all the French Colonies. . . . It is to be hoped that Haiti will recover this great prosperity of the past."[75]

Like many Haitian and African American leaders, President Borno envisioned agrarian futures in Haiti through the memory of its past productivity under plantation slavery. Ultimately, he hoped the United States would not only supply teachers to train the peasant masses in efficient agricultural production but also facilitate "the organization of a service in agricultural technique, and in professional instruction, and thereby putting into effect in the country districts of the Republic the methods of land cultivation so profitably adopted in the United States; also to constitute a corp[s] of able workers in manual industries."[76]

Ironically, the U.S. mismanagement of the Service Technique du département de l'agriculture et de l'enseignment professionnel, Haiti's agricultural and vocational education program, would become one of the most contentious policies of the occupation. Instead of merging industrial and classical education, as Price-Mars proposed in his early essays and as President Borno at least rhetorically endorsed in his message to African Americans, U.S. officials promoted technical education to the exclusion of classical education, utterly disregarding the educational system that had been in place in Haiti for more than a century. They staffed the schools with ill-equipped U.S. teachers who earned excessively high salaries, did not speak French or Kréyol, and made little attempt to learn either language. Whereas Washington viewed agricultural and industrial education as important for all races, many white Americans mobilized it as a disciplinary technology fit exclusively for the Black and colonial "other" and brought these racist attitudes to their work in Haiti.

It was through the Service Technique that the U.S. government attempted to misappropriate the Tuskegee model in Haiti. Although Tuskegee was by no means the only model of industrial education, it was certainly top of mind for the U.S. government as it devised a plan for Haiti's educational future. It essentially exported the prevailing policy for Black education in the United States, viewing it as a mode of social control rather than social mobility. Pamphile asserts that the occupation's educational program evoked memories of "similar policies toward Blacks" in the U.S. South, based on the "false assumption that Blacks were incapable of being educated in a formal sense," but this was not the viewpoint of African American and Haitian supporters of agricultural education.[77] Price-Mars and other supporters such as Maurice Dartigue, director of rural education (1931–1941) and minister of public instruction (1941–1945), maintained that Haiti was primarily an agricultural country and thus should educate its rural citizenry in advanced, scientific agriculture.[78] For Black diasporic leaders, agricultural education was a mode of social mobility, not an indication of Black people's inferior intellect. And yet their commitment to uplift ideology and its underlying paternalism points to the ways that, much like the tension between training and discipline at Tuskegee, even forms of care work, such as facilitating Black social mobility, can also be suffused by elements of social control.

Across class backgrounds, Haitians held competing views toward agricultural and industrial education specifically and the U.S. occupation more generally.[79] For some of the "Haitian urban elite," this mode of education was "specific to the plight of newly freed" African Americans but "belittled Haitians who were products of self-emancipation."[80] Yet other middle- and upper-class Haitians such as Max Vieux, whose father owned a coffee factory and whose uncle was a businessman and farm owner, embraced the Service Technique precisely because it did not prioritize the liberal arts and would "prepare them to work as agricultural professionals."[81] For the Haitian peasants who disapproved of the U.S. administration of the Service Technique, their disapproval was due to internal class tensions and skepticism of the elite: "Left by themselves for so long without direction from an unconcerned elite, the peasants looked skeptically at proposals to modernize agriculture," Pamphile explains.[82] Their own farming techniques, however crude, at least afforded them some autonomy over their labor and left their cultural and familial traditions intact. Though some elite Haitians viewed agricultural education as a way to uplift the peasantry, the ultimate aim of such an education was to create more efficient laborers to buttress the Haitian economy, regardless of the peasants' attitudes toward education and agriculture or their desires for their own futures. For instance, many peasants wanted their children to be educated to work in clerical, professional, or commercial work in the cities, but the Service Technique aspired to keep peasants "on the farms."[83] Failure to adequately respect and incorporate local attitudes toward education and agricultural cultivation practices would ultimately be the Achilles' heel of attempts at agrarian reform in Haiti. Both African American leaders and many of the Haitian elite, to say nothing of the white U.S. officials, failed to build *with* the Haitian masses in any meaningful way. Guided by class paternalism at best and the avarice of racial capitalism at worst, they sought to build *for* them, instead.

Despite Price-Mars's admiration for Washington and the Tuskegee model, he was staunchly opposed to the U.S. occupation and likely strongly disagreed with Washington's position that it was necessary. Nevertheless, he continued to view agricultural and industrial education as crucial for Haiti's future, and he championed the Service Technique in particular. In October 1929, Price-Mars delivered an address at the agricultural school in Damien on the importance of agricultural training for the Haitian masses. The address was no doubt in response to growing student unrest regarding the Service Technique and the U.S. administration of Haitian education more generally. Price-Mars assured students that he had long been a supporter of improving Haiti's education system through the Tuskegee and Hampton models, or the "Anglo-Saxon manner," and then, critically, he proceeded to interrogate the common refrain that "Haiti *is an essentially agricultural country*."[84]

In doing so, Price-Mars articulated his own conception of eco-ontology and agrarian futures in Haiti, in which he conceived of Haiti's future as tied to both the soil and the peasantry alike. Upon reviewing the quality and productivity of Haiti's soil and climate, he concluded that "there is perhaps some truth" to the claim that it is "an essentially agricultural country." However, he quickly redirected listeners from the question of soil quality to the people themselves: alongside the "aptitudes of the soil, there is the Man, there is the Haitian whose *essential*, specialized occupation is the culture of the earth." His is a radical reformulation of Haitian identity and culture, from the intellectual culture and achievements of its elite to the agricultural practices of its peasantry. In particular, Price-Mars asserted that it is "the plasticity of the human element that characterizes the people and that gives them their commercial value, their ethical value, their specific value in the process of progress." If "the Negro" was once transformed from a slave into a peasant, he reasoned, then he or she can be molded into a more efficient worker as well. The "greatest wealth" of Haiti is "the laborer, the peasant, the Negro," he surmised, for it was the "Negro" laborer who successfully transformed the landscape under slavery. Ultimately, Price-Mars formulated a distinctly Haitian conception of eco-ontology based on both "the natural aptitudes of its soil and the special aptitudes of its people" alike.[85]

In light of this history, Price-Mars inquired how it could be that in an "essentially agricultural" country, no agricultural school had been founded since 1804. He reasoned that "Haitian pedagogy" was concerned primarily with "making selections of great men" who "can by their sole existence and their great culture refute the thesis sustained by others that the Negro is inferior." Haitians therefore prioritized "classical education" from "primary school" up to professional degrees in law and medicine. To counter the postenslavement bias against "manual labor"—this "contradiction . . . at the base of our collective personality"—he implored the students to commit themselves to the "transformation of our rural economy" in ways reminiscent of Carver's ecological regeneration work at

Tuskegee and throughout the U.S. South. "Your action must be addressed to . . . the soil," Price-Mars argued.[86]

One of the primary aims of Price-Mars's investment in agrarian reform was the improvement of the Haitian economy. He therefore instructed students to "increase" the kinds of products cultivated as well as their "quality and quantity" to meet the erratic "demands of the global markets." His vision of agrarian futures was thus fundamentally capitalist, committed to uplifting and "training" the Haitian peasantry to be more efficient workers: "Transform the peasant in replacing the methods that he has been using for thousands of years to establish his domination on the soil," he implored. Throughout the address, he consistently described the peasantry as "plastic" "human matter" that can be "manipulate[d]" "between your hands," thus betraying his paternalistic outlook as a member of the Haitian elite.[87]

To encourage the peasant to remain on the land, Price-Mars further instructed the audience, "Tell him that there is no separation between manual and intellectual culture. The one completes the other" in "perfect harmony." Critically, despite regarding the peasant as manipulable "human matter," Price-Mars beseeched the students not to consider "him" as "incapable" or "inferior." Given "all the causes of destruction" he has overcome, "the morbid promiscuity of slavery, murdering and repeated epidemics, wars of emancipation and liberation, fratricidal and criminal wars, miseries of all sorts . . . he is endowed at least with one superiority: that of resistance and duration. . . . [for] he has increased, his numbers grew in proportion to these miseries." And he possesses "the power of adaptation." Price-Mars concluded his address by imploring students to embrace "the American method" of "*learning by doing*"—the Tuskegee model—and urging them to have "great sympathy" for their work as agricultural instructors as well as for those they would teach, the peasantry.[88]

Ultimately, Price-Mars articulated his own vision for Black eco-ontological regeneration in Haiti by improving the soil while transforming the peasantry. His insistence on the compatibility of "manual and intellectual culture" recalls Washington's efforts to imagine the southern New Negro as both a farmer and a bourgeois Victorian (chapter 2). The sympathy for the peasantry that he encouraged among the students parallels the racial uplift project in the United States, and the emphasis on agricultural and industrial education indicates Tuskegee's specific influence on his thought. Just as Washington envisioned educated African Americans as "sentinels" presiding over the masses, Price-Mars attempted to inculcate within the elite a sense of noblesse oblige toward the Haitian peasantry. In both cases, however, care work and seemingly genuine concern for the most vulnerable were entangled with class paternalism.

Despite Price-Mars's best efforts, Haitian students became increasingly dissatisfied with the U.S. administration of the Service Technique and the Haitian education system. In December 1929, just a few months after Price-Mars gave this speech, students staged a massive strike initially sparked by a change in the scholarship policy but ultimately grounded in a larger dissatisfaction with the U.S. occupation. The strike and the ensuing riots eventually led to a commitment from the United States to begin withdrawing forces from Haiti.[89]

In 1930, largely in response to the student strike, President Herbert Hoover selected Tuskegee's president, Robert R. Moton, to lead a controversial and woefully underfunded commission to investigate the Haitian education system and make recommendations for improvement. The Moton Commission supported an agricultural and industrial education system in Haiti but not without qualification. By the late 1920s and early 1930s, Tuskegee's own curriculum had undergone significant changes and was "far more liberal" than it had been under Washington's leadership, and the Moton Commission report reflected this ideological shift.[90]

The report raised important concerns about the limits of U.S. intervention in Haiti's education system. The occupation had erred in separating the vocational and regular school systems, which, as the historian Magdaline W. Shannon observes, left education "worse off than when it had been exclusively under Haitian control."[91] The report also criticized the government for not providing public education.[92] The Moton Commission enumerated sixteen objections made by Haitian intellectuals to the Service Technique as well as a list of thirteen recommendations to improve it. Of particular note, the report acknowledged Haitians' concern that the Americanization of the Haitian education system would "destroy their cherished ideals of a Latin culture, leaving in its place a type of American civilization wholly materialistic[,] which is revolting to them and would quickly destroy the soul of Haiti."[93] The commission also noted Haitians' charges of racist preconceptions by American administrators of the Service Technique, which diminished their effectiveness. In short, the commission attempted to provide a balanced assessment that was critical of U.S. and Haitian officials alike.

The commission's report emphasized the centrality of agriculture for Haitian identity and culture and delineated its geography, topography, animal life, and vegetation. "Since Haiti is so largely dependent upon the products of her soil," the report maintained, "improved agriculture must be relied upon both for raising the standards of living and for increasing revenues for governmental purposes." In many ways, the report is an eco-ontological analysis of Haiti, acknowledging the importance of the coterminous regeneration of land and people. Improving peasant life, the commission concluded, would require "greater production on the land under cultivation and the reclamation of land now arid and otherwise unsuitable for farming"; "a better system of farming and a higher type of peasant home" with "ordinary conveniences and comforts"; the "security of land titles and a plan for reforestation to provide building material"; and "nutritious food and a well-balanced diet."[94]

Despite the report's attempt at a balanced critique, readers in both countries took issue with it. The U.S. State Department found it embarrassing and "was reluctant to see it published, let alone acted upon."[95] The U.S. government ultimately ignored the commission's recommendations, just as it had ignored Washington's plea to "be patient with Haiti" fifteen years earlier. For their part, Haitians took issue with the report's "suggestion that the government of the United States contribute to the support of education in Haiti, since for them, it raised the possibility that the United States would wish to retain control over the educational system."[96] A commentator in the *New York Liberator*, a Black-led Communist newspaper in the United States, further criticized Hoover's appointment of Moton, declaring "the head of the petty-bourgeois Negro Tuskegee institute [*sic*]. . . . [and] enemy of the Negro masses in the United States is sent to Haiti to help betray the Negro masses there."[97] African Americans, like many Haitians, were divided about the Tuskegee model, so its potential transplantation to Haiti was fraught and contested, demonstrating the challenge of diaspora in the context of empire. Furthermore, the *Liberator* commentator's class-based castigation of Tuskegee suggests that although some early critics took the school to task for producing a class of menial laborers, by the 1930s others came to view it as a place that produced a petit bourgeoisie. Nevertheless, despite the U.S. government's repeated efforts to co-opt Tuskegee as a tool of imperialism in Haiti, both W. T. B. Williams and President Moton resisted by insisting on a balanced set of recommendations that foregrounded Haitian criticisms of the United States and elevated Haitian cultural and educational values.

Notwithstanding the paternalistic tone of his address at the agricultural school in Damien, Price-Mars was ultimately a champion of the peasantry and thought in deeply ethical ways about how to improve their socioeconomic plight. He was no armchair academic who simply prescribed agricultural education from the ivory tower or the urban metropole. Rather, his continued investment in industrial and agricultural education for the rural masses—and his broader vision of

Haitian agrarian futures through eco-ontological regeneration—was derived from his fieldwork and ethnological studies of the Haitian peasantry. In the early years of the occupation, he spent considerable time traveling on horseback throughout the Haitian countryside, addressing peasants' medical needs and studying their customs and beliefs. In addition to his lectures on industrial and agricultural education for the masses, he lectured to the elite on Haitian Vodou, the virtues of the peasant family, and Haitian folklore as the lifeblood of the nation. Price-Mars's time in the Haitian countryside culminated in the publication of his book *Ainsi parla l'oncle* (*So Spoke the Uncle*) in 1928, an ethnological study of Haitian folklore that, importantly, validated Vodou as a legitimate and complex religion. It had a tremendous impact on the Haitian elite, inspiring a reappraisal of Haitian folklore and its African origins as the basis of Haitian national identity. *So Spoke the Uncle* became a foundational text of several cultural-nationalist movements that arose in response to the U.S. occupation, including indigenism, noirism, and the Négritude Movement.[98] Together with the Harlem Renaissance, it inspired a younger generation of Haitian intellectuals to embrace Haitian folklore and led to the publication of *La revue indigène* in 1927, a monthly journal dedicated to promoting Haitian literature and culture and to opposing the U.S. occupation.[99] Price-Mars's educational-reform efforts were thus two-pronged: agricultural and industrial education for the peasanty and a psycho-spiritual *re*education for the elite rooted in Haitian folk culture and its African origins.

Price-Mars was essentially a "cultural mediator," as the literary scholar Imani D. Owens argues, not only translating between the Haitian elite and the peasantry but between Haitians and African Americans as well.[100] In an essay published in 1932, Price-Mars described the Harlem Renaissance as the "rise of black values in the world," recounted the story of African Americans from enslavement to freedom, and acknowledged that abundant and inexpensive agricultural labor (on American and Antillean plantations) linked African American and Afro-Caribbean peoples and histories.[101] He wrote at length about Harlem as an epicenter of Black cultural production through literature and jazz; the importance of Howard and Fisk Universities for the development of the African American elite; and the significance of urbanization and migration to cities such as Philadelphia, Chicago, and New York. By exploring the "rise of black values" in African American culture, Price-Mars attempted to make "our American brothers" legible to the Haitian elite. He blamed Haitian economic and cultural "isolation" on "our boasting of a fictive and absurd superiority" over African Americans and warned that such intra-racial frictions must "disappear" if they "do not wish to cook in the juice of our stupidity and boastfulness." He thus implored his comrades to draw inspiration from the Harlem Renaissance and African American history more generally instead of always looking to France.[102]

Given Price-Mars's investment in agricultural and industrial education in Haiti, it is curious that his overview of African American culture failed to mention Tuskegee. Despite this omission, however, he did circle back to Washington at the conclusion of the article, observing, "I am reminded that in his autobiography, *Up from Slavery*, Booker T. Washington recounts that a boat adrift in the waters of the South Atlantic was making desperate signals to a large ship asking for fresh water. The ship responded stubbornly: 'Cast down your buckets.' "[103] Price-Mars then proceeded to repurpose one of the most (in)famous lines from the Atlanta Exposition Address—Washington's "cast down your bucket" anecdote—which was republished in *Up from Slavery*. In the original speech, Washington implored African Americans to cultivate "friendly relations with the Southern white man" and to "cast down your buckets" among "people of all races by whom we are surrounded. Cast it down," he declared, "in agriculture, mechanics, in commerce, in domestic service, and in the professions."[104] Although Washington was concerned primarily with improving labor and commercial relations between Black and white southerners at a time when European immigrants threatened to displace Black laborers, "cast down your bucket" has commonly been interpreted as a call for African Americans to acquiesce to the injustices of Jim Crow. Washington's vision for Black economic uplift and interracial commercial relations, many would argue, ignored the brutalities and indignities that Black southerners suffered at the hands of white-supremacist violence and oppression. However, the painful legacy of racial violence that his anecdote came to symbolize for many African Americans contrasts starkly with Price-Mars's strategic translation of it to encourage the Haitian elite to take pride in their folklore and the Haitian peasantry: "Now, to all our intellectuals, and all those who live in this country and from this country, and who recognize the rich potential in human values, to all those who do not know that they can find art and beauty in the intangible bronze that is our community, I say, in a symbolic way: 'Cast down your buckets!' "[105]

Just as Rafael Serra y Montalvo appropriated Washington's philanthropic strategy in Cuba, Price-Mars strategically translated the aspect of Washington's social philosophy that acquiesced to segregation in the U.S. South into a more radical call for Haitian cultural nationalism in the context of occupation. Price-Mars insisted that solidarity across class lines is necessary to Haitian progress in the fight against U.S. imperialism. Instead of grafting French aesthetic values onto Haitian culture, Haitians should follow African Americans' example, he argued, by celebrating their own folk culture and thus forging a distinctly Haitian identity. As with the repurposed plantation, Price-Mars excised Washington's (in)famous lines from their problematic context and through strategic translation and ideological paraphrase transplanted them from the U.S. South to Haiti. In doing so, he demonstrated how *Up from Slavery*, Washington's vision of Black modernity in the U.S. South, was taken up as both a literary text and a political document that influenced the articulation of new futures throughout the Global Black South.

In this way, Price-Mars represents a crucial link between the pragmatic and materialist aims of Washington's diasporic uplift project at the turn of the century, on one hand, and the more decided shift toward aesthetics as the chief indicator of Black modernity in the 1920s and 1930s, on the other. Whereas the Tuskegee project under Washington's leadership sought to uplift the masses through agricultural and industrial education and economic self-help, the next generation of Black artists and intellectuals—shaped by the radical psychological, geographic, and sociopolitical disruptions of World War I and the Great Migration—came to question uplift and instead embraced primitivism and folk culture as legitimate alternatives to the civilizational project. As we will see in plot III, the next generation, including Zora Neale Hurston (a Tuskegee student once removed) and Claude McKay (who only briefly attended Tuskegee but championed it in his late writings), questioned and often rejected civilizationist logics and instead celebrated individualism and the putative primitivism of the Black urban and rural masses (a position that was not without its own limitations, of course). Price-Mars's writings reflect both strands of thought, promoting agricultural education for the Haitian masses while challenging elite Haitians to shift their cultural and intellectual allegiances from France and Europe to the Black world and to the Haitian peasantry in particular.

The cultural-nationalist aims of Price-Mars's writings on Haitian Vodou and the Harlem Renaissance were inextricably tied to his educational, economic, and agricultural agenda for the republic. In his essay "The Problem of Work in Haiti" (1931), published in English just one year before the Harlem Renaissance article, he elaborated on how his vision of agrarian futures through education would improve the economic outlook for both the peasantry and the Haitian nation-state alike. On one hand, Price-Mars expressed great sympathy toward the Haitian masses. He recognized the unique gendered labor of Haitian peasant women responsible for conveying crops to the market on their heads, while traveling on poor roads and carrying their infants on their backs; acknowledged farmers' frustrations with poor weather conditions and low pay; and criticized the Haitian state's "preoccupation" with "perfect[ing] the methods of revenue collection without ever concerning themselves about the paying capacity of those taxed," the peasantry. Yet, despite this sympathy, as a member of the intellectual and political elite Price-Mars did not consider the rural masses as self-determining subjects or equals. He did not regard peasants' decisions to migrate to work on sugar plantations in Cuba and the Dominican Republic, for instance, as a practical or necessary survival strategy in the face of national and imperial exploitation but rather as the "simplicity of . . . reasoning" of a rural population "festered by ignorance." Instead, Price-Mars again proposed agricultural education for "the proletariat in order that they might become more apt and more efficient producers and that they might evolve into consumers" by elevating "their standard of living."[106]

Furthermore, to rectify the country's economic woes exacerbated by the Great Depression and the failures of the U.S. occupation, he recommended "intensive and varied production of exportable goods." Growing a variety of tropical fruits, he reasoned, "is a remarkable way to escape from obsession of the monoculture of coffee," "reduce the evil of periodic unemployment peculiar to Haiti" that led to out-migration, and "conquer" markets in the United States, Canada, and Europe.[107] Through agricultural education, diversified exports, and improved trade relations, Price-Mars outlined a strategy for Haiti's political-economic development that was to be mutually beneficial to both the peasant nation and the elite-controlled state. The challenge, of course, was that such large-scale agricultural cultivation, devoid of a thorough uprooting of class paternalism and exploitation, veered too closely to plantation-style labor arrangements and social hierarchies, as evinced by the numerous Haitian–African American partnerships that emerged in the immediate postoccupation period.

POSTOCCUPATION ALLIANCES: FORGING BLACK ECONOMIC (INTER)NATIONALISM

As resistance to the U.S. occupation peaked and talks of U.S. withdrawal accelerated, Haitians and African Americans continued to forge alliances through agricultural and commercial cooperation, what I have termed *Black economic (inter)nationalism*. As we have seen, Haitians and African Americans had imagined and sometimes actively practiced racial solidarity through commercial relations since the mid–nineteenth century, and the 1930s extended this century-long project. Facilitating Black economic (inter)nationalism was a part of the era's zeitgeist, made most famous by Jamaican activist and organizer Marcus Garvey's commercial endeavors through the UNIA and its affiliate organizations (chapter 8). Haitian and African American politicians, intellectuals, and entrepreneurs were also encouraged by the rhetoric of goodwill that characterized Pan-Americanism and President Franklin Delano Roosevelt's Good Neighbor policy. Motivated by this new approach to hemispheric relations that promised economic cooperation instead of military interventionism, they augmented early twentieth-century discourses of racial self-help and solidarity into a diasporic uplift project that "both reflected and challenged U.S. power politics."[108] Haitian leaders such as President Stenio Vincent invited African American commercial development, and, in turn, several African American entrepreneurs cultivated business ventures that were to be mutually beneficial to Haitians and African Americans alike. Significantly, Tuskegee and agriculture continued to play an important role in these efforts at Black transnational connectivity, even as New York and Paris were becoming the new epicenters of diasporic activity and thought.

During a visit to the United States in 1934 to meet with President Roosevelt about "American financial supervision" of Haiti following the occupation, President Vincent also lunched informally with African American leaders at the 135th Street YMCA in Harlem.[109] Despite the "handicap" of his "scant knowledge of English," he urged "a solidarity of interests between the Haitian people and the American Negro," largely along agricultural lines.[110] Like his predecessor Louis Borno, President Vincent encouraged Black "agriculturists" in the United States to cultivate cotton and coffee in Haiti as "the fertile land of Haiti offered unlimited opportunities for the Negroes of America" that had largely gone "unexploited." To inaugurate this effort of "racial solidarity" through agro-commercial cooperation, he invited a delegation of African Americans to visit Haiti "to exchange ideas and viewpoints" with Haitian leaders.[111] Such efforts would not only "rehabilitate his country" but also "ameliorate the bond of understanding between the Haitian and his American brother."[112] President Vincent's visit helped to launch a number of initiatives that aimed to facilitate Haitian–African American cooperation throughout the 1930s, including the Haitian Afro-American Chamber of Commerce, *Goodwill* magazine, and Major R. R. Wright's Haitian Coffee and Products Trading Company.[113] For each of these efforts, agriculture, industry, and thus a confrontation with the plantation's afterlife in the postemancipation Black world (and especially in Haiti) were central to the practice of Black economic (inter)nationalism. As the historian Millery Polyné argues, "Black Pan American entrepreneurs and intellectuals of this era truly saw no alternative to modernization other than Western capitalist development as modeled by advances in the U.S. society."[114]

The Haitian-Afro-American Chamber of Commerce was organized following the Harlem luncheon given in President Vincent's honor. Claude Barnett—a Tuskegee graduate who founded the Associated Black Press, "arguably one of the most important news-gathering organizations of Black life in the Americas from the 1920s to the 1950s"—was instrumental in establishing the chamber and in facilitating Haitian–African American partnerships for more than thirty years.[115] Taking President Vincent's invitation seriously, members visited Haiti later that same year to "study the agricultural, industrial, and commercial possibilities in the Republic for Negroes wishing to make investments there," effectively "cast[ing] in our lot," they proclaimed, "with the policy of Good Neighborliness launched by Franklin Delano Roosevelt." The group set sail from New York City and arrived in Port-au-Prince on August 22, 1934, "one day after the last of the U.S. Marines had departed and the military occupation officially concluded." In an address at the welcome ceremony in honor of the chamber's arrival, Nathan Huggins, a chamber member, regretted that they "were unable to have been present at the grand celebration" of the marines' departure, signaling their commitment to Haitian sovereignty and Black diasporic cooperation outside of the constraints of U.S. imperialism.[116]

Essentially, these Haitian leaders and African American businessmen viewed African Americans as potential investors and a market for Haitian goods. Whereas the Moton Commission as well as Washington and Price-Mars before it had focused primarily on education, the chamber investigated the possibilities for a "commercial alliance" that would encourage African Americans "to aid in agriculture, animal husbandry, in the building of roads and bridges, in the development of business, and in all the fundamental arts of peace." In making its recommendations for postoccupation Haiti, the chamber borrowed a strategy from the postemancipation U.S. South, encouraging "retired teachers in America, black and white," to "go down there and help, during this transition period, in the spirit of the 'Yankee School Marm' who went into the deep South to aid the blacks during Reconstruction." Yet this was not some facile projection of a U.S. racial schema onto Haiti, for chamber members were all too aware of the egregious abuses and inequities Black people faced in the United States. Rather, by helping to "reconstruct" Haiti, it seems, they viewed the country as a possible haven for Black Americans, writing, "Haiti, in the years to come, will be an asylum to harassed Black folk who no longer will be able to endure the slings and arrows of outrageous fortune in America." "More and more socially," they declared, "will we join hands across the sea with you."[117]

The chamber envisioned a broad and multipronged partnership of economic cooperation and an "intellectual entente cordiale" with Haitians. Its members even proposed establishing literary contests that would encourage "amity" among Haitian and African American youth and award African American youth with a trip to Haiti. Here, however, I focus on the agricultural component of the chamber's vision because it "concerned itself principally with plans for aiding Haitian export trade." To this end, "the commission made trips to Laogane to inspect the plantations of President Vincent and Monsieur Geffrard; to Damien to inspect the new Agricultural and Teachers Training School; to Hinche to inspect the Agricultural Experimental Station; to the Artibonite Plain to observe that vast underdeveloped area which awaits settlers from America who with patience, money, and brain, can make that valley blossom like a rose. The Commission also made many side trips to see peasants at their homes and in the fields."[118]

Joshua Cockburn, vice chairman and shipping member of the commission, proposed "group owned shipping links" for "conveying exports and imports" between the two countries.[119] Cockburn had served as captain of the *Yarmouth*, the first ship of Marcus Garvey's and the UNIA's Black Star Line, suggesting that Black economic (inter)nationalism was indeed a part of the era's zeitgeist and was taken up by peoples across a range of political ideologies. In addition to Major R. R. Wright's coffee cooperative, which I discuss later in this chapter, the Haitian-Afro-American Chamber of Commerce endorsed development of the Haitian banana industry so that the country could "enter the fruit market of New York and New Orleans" and "other southern states"; it also promoted increased rice cultivation, tobacco production, and another sugar company to provide competition for Haiti's U.S.-controlled sugar industry.[120]

Although the Haitian and African American leaders who conceived of these diasporic alliances were seemingly sympathetic to peasants' poverty, they rarely asked the peasantry how they envisioned their futures or considered the possible utility of peasant cultivation methods or cultural values. Instead, the chamber's report blamed the peasantry for the country's ecological challenges with deforestation, observing, "In the past timber has been cut indiscriminately by the peasant and used in the manufacture of charcoal. Today it is necessary for lumber to be imported as the mountain sides have been denuded and the only timber that is available is scrub and second growth."[121] Although attention to the unique ecological conditions facing Haitian agricultural development was crucial, the chamber did not mention the *laikou*, *coumbite*, or other peasant familial and agricultural arrangements—all components of the counter-plantation and thus central to the peasant lifeworld. Nor was there an effort to ascertain peasants' attitudes or *affective* relationships to agriculture, the plantation, or the cultivation of global commodities. For instance, while many peasants readily cultivated coffee, they were averse to labor-intensive crops such as sugarcane. Such recognition would have been crucial to more egalitarian agricultural-reform efforts. The Haitian-Afro-American Chamber of Commerce thus represented a diasporic alliance from above, whereby, as Polyné points out, "capitalist ventures became a strategy for achieving racial progress and individual gain within inter-American affairs."[122]

To promote potential commercial alliances, Haitian leaders also turned to print culture. In December 1934, they established *Goodwill* magazine, a bilingual publication, billed as "the first journal with French and English texts" in the history of Haitian journalism.[123] The inaugural issue noted both President Vincent's visit to the United States and the Haitian-Afro-American Chamber of Commerce's goodwill visit to Haiti earlier that year as antecedents to the magazine's founding. *Goodwill* struck a very different tone than some Haitian attitudes toward African Americans and the United States in the period, instead promoting economic cooperation and confraternity with "our American brothers."[124] *Goodwill* was an unabashedly and self-proclaimed propagandist publication. In particular, the magazine "endeavor[ed] to promote a widespread advertisement in favor of *agricultural resources* as well as innumerable possibilities which assure full success to foreign investors and to develop friendly and good neighbor relations beetween [*sic*] Haiti and the United States of America."[125] Although *Goodwill* sought to mutually introduce African Americans and Haitians, it was a mostly one-sided endeavor of Haitians reaching out to African Americans. Editors consistently reminded the "Friends of America" of Haiti's military aid during the American Revolution and of how Haiti's own revolutionary struggle for liberty facilitated the Louisiana Purchase and the expansion of the United States. As one article put it, "Toussaint's statesmanship caused Napoleon to give up his dream of an American Empire and make a bargain of the immense state of Louisiana for a song."[126] Through such ingratiating tactics, *Goodwill* encouraged readers to "co-operate with its people to make it [Haiti] a Paradise for the Negroes of the World."[127]

A fundamentally nationalist publication, *Goodwill* supported President Vincent (and was perhaps his mouthpiece). It was very pro–United States, suspiciously so, publishing numerous articles extolling the virtues and possibilities of President Roosevelt's Good Neighbor policy and his belief that the United States and "the western Hemisphere [*sic*] countries . . . can get along without the rest of the world."[128] Notwithstanding Haitians' criticism of their "attachment" to the United States and "preference for an essentially American *modus vivendi*,"

Ludovic J. Rosemond, the magazine's editor and founder, was insistent about cultivating "a movement of InterAmerican solidarity." To this end, he deployed Washington and Tuskegee as models for how to reconcile with one's former oppressors. Following emancipation, Rosemond wrote of Booker T. Washington that while "the painful impression of his commander's whip" was still "warm and alive" in Washington's mind, "the former slave called out" with "ardor and enthusiasm" "for the support of the powerful people of the time. . . . The work being realized was worthy of being sustained and its happy influence saw the birth of Tuskegee Institute, the Center of Culture and Education, which remains the brilliant homage of the illustrious deceased to the talents and virtues of his race."[129] Washington's willingness to reconcile with white Americans paralleled Haitians' efforts to cooperate with the United States, their former colonizer. Like Rafael Serra y Montalvo in Cuba, Rosemond in Haiti celebrated Washington and Tuskegee as symbols of reconciliation in exchange for economic and philanthropic support.

Goodwill's propaganda campaign sought to generate interest and sympathy for Haiti by depicting it as a Black paradise and diasporic homeland and was linked to its promotion of tourism, another afterlife of the plantation, to boost the Haitian economy. Numerous articles marketed Haiti to (African) American readers as an "Eden of the Western World," and the magazine even billed itself as a "guide for tourists and business people."[130] In a 1936 issue, *Goodwill* published "Let Us Go to Haiti," a poem by Theophile Salnave, a Haitian actor, songwriter, and playwright who would make a name for himself on Haitian radio. The poem is essentially a tourist brochure and a plantation pastoral:

> Yes, let's go to Haiti,
> To hear negro society, talking French fluently.
> Sugar cane is full . . .
>
> She has the best coffee,
> And a first class cotton. Life is easy.
> There is no winter time.
> One dollar change will give you five gourdes to make good time.
> . . . .
> Yes, let us go to Haiti.
> It's where we will find plenty
> Bananas, Rum, Coconut, sugar cane,
> All fruits are eaten fresh and not in can.
> Yes, let us go to Haiti.[131]

Salnave's depiction of Haiti as a tropical paradise of relaxation and pleasure contrasts markedly with the poor living conditions of the peasants who cultivated these agricultural commodities and often migrated away from Haiti for want of economic opportunity. For them, life was in fact not "easy," and they were not a part of "negro society, talking French fluently," because most Haitian peasants spoke Kréyol. Salnave's poem instead recalls the plantation romance tradition in the United States, which obscured laborers and the racial-capitalist conditions that made plantation commodities possible.

Across numerous articles, *Goodwill* reiterated the refrain that "Haiti is principally an agricultural country."[132] In the second issue, editors republished an excerpt from Price-Mars's essay "The Problem of Work in Haiti" (1931), discussed earlier, regarding diversifying the country's agricultural products and selling them to the U.S. market.[133] Tellingly, to prevent offending U.S. readers and, thus, potential buyers and investors, the article was retitled "Haiti's Exportable Articles" and did not include Price-Mars's criticism of the U.S. failure to improve Haiti's coffee industry, nor did it include his sympathetic assessment of the conditions affecting peasant women and farmers. Rather, in the next issue *Goodwill* praised President Vincent's efforts to make Haiti "a leading banana producing country," advertised the Haitian American Sugar Company, and noted that "the production of sisal has also been showing a strong inclination towards progress."[134] For these commercial leaders, "progress" meant agrocommercial development, especially the growing banana and fruit trade driven by corporate plantation imperialism.

A series of articles on Haiti's economic structure published in 1937 meticulously delineates the economic possibilities of Haiti's port cities, describing each city's geographic position, geological attributes, and economic promise. Whereas the Moton Commission noted that "the Haitian Government, heretofore, has discouraged large agricultural enterprises on the ground that the plantation system dispossesses the peasant of the land," this was apparently no longer true in a postoccupation Haiti, which viewed improved large-scale agricultural production as the savior of the country's economy.[135] The agrarian future depicted in these articles emphasized a plantation logic based on increased efficiency and productivity, and the *coumbite*—a communal peasant cultivation practice integral to the counter-plantation—was effectively dismantled. The series' author praised the arrondissement Môle-Saint-Nicolas (spelled "Mole St-Nicolas" in the series) for breaking "from our gardens and *enclos* [enclosures] as well as our system of COUMBITE" and asserted that "when the country becomes covered with multiple PLANTATIONS, it is that city that will provide our defense." Essentially, the author reimagined a Haitian geography where the plantation replaces the *coumbite* and its counter-plantation logics. The author also wrongly insisted that cultivating Haitian plantations can limit "human exportation," or labor migration, thus blaming the peasantry for not "holding out for the future."[136]

Despite the growing influence of the Haitian Indigenist Movement and its effort to promote sympathy and respect for the Haitian peasantry, *Goodwill* ultimately reflected the attitudes of Haiti's political elite. The magazine embraced and reprinted folklore as part of a nationalist project but not because its editors were necessarily committed to collaborating with the peasantry to create a more egalitarian future.[137] Instead, editors marketed Haiti to investors as a place rich with agricultural and industrial resources and opportunities— "labor being cheap and conditions of living surprisingly low"—while obscuring and neglecting to engage in any meaningful way with the very people who performed said "cheap" labor.[138]

One of the most successful Haitian–African American commercial alliances was Major R. R. Wright's Haitian Coffee and Products Trading Company, a cooperative through which African Americans purchased Haitian coffee. The company was based in Philadelphia and was made possible through Wright's role as president of the Citizens & Southern Bank and Trust Company of Philadelphia. Wright was a friend of Booker T. Washington and likely a member of the National Negro Business League. He viewed the initiative as a way to reduce African American unemployment, noting that "the introduction of this coffee has given employment even in the city of Philadelphia to nearly 50 persons, and has elicited nearly 500 inquiries from all parts of this country [the United States] asking for coffee which many of them are taking because . . . the coffee comes from a Negro republic and is being distributed by Negroes. It seems to me that this is evidence that we can co-operate for the solution of our Negro problem."[139] By 1940, the company could proudly tout that "more than 10,000,000 pounds of Haitian Coffee have come into this country since its introduction in 1933." African Americans were "learning to appreciate the high quality of Haitian coffee and to realize that every cup they drink helps reduce unemployment among our people." [140] It is unclear if "our people" refers to African Americans, Haitians, or both, however.

George Schuyler, a luminary of the Harlem Renaissance, proposed elaborating on Wright's coffee-buying scheme. In a series of articles published in the *Pittsburgh Courier*, Schuyler encouraged African Americans to purchase Haitian coffee, sugar, molasses, "cashew nuts," and "tropical fruits." His articles were compiled, translated, and republished in *La relève*, an economic and literary journal published in Haiti and promoted by the Vincent regime. In response to an ongoing crisis in the sale of Haitian coffee, Schuyler asked readers: "What can American Negroes do to help Haiti?" In response, he proposed a broad "project of Black international commerce" wherein African Americans, though not wealthy, could assist Haiti. While acknowledging the significance of Wright's coffee-buying scheme, Schuyler determined that "a greater quantity of Haitian coffee could be sold" in the United States. The Haitian government must recognize the "formidable purchasing power of the Black American," he argued, and "capture the Negro market in this country [the United States]." This "cooperative spirit" could also be extended to molasses and sugar, Schuyler argued, for "American Negroes consume a great quantity of both products." Schuyler's scheme is perhaps the most elaborate articulation of how economic cooperation could be mutually beneficial for Haitians and African Americans. Though critical of what he called the increasing propensity toward "racial chauvinism" in "Black America," he aimed to "test the sincerity of these patriots of race" by encouraging them to "organize their purchasing power" for the mutual "improve[ment of] the economic conditions of Haitians and our Black American group."[141]

On one hand, Wright's and Schuyler's respective cooperative schemes may have aided the Haitian economy. After all, coffee was Haiti's leading export and most important postrevolution crop, and it was among peasants' preferred agricultural commodities to cultivate.[142] Though sugar made colonial Saint Domingue one of the richest colonies in the world, formerly enslaved people viewed sugar cultivation as too labor intensive and thus refused to return to sugar plantations after independence. "They opted instead for cash crops that complemented rather than competed with foodstuffs and that could be cultivated and harvested without injury to provisions," which, ironically, was consistent with Tuskegee's vision of agrarian futures, despite Washington's frequent criticisms of Haiti's alleged failure to develop its agricultural sector.[143] Though coffee was, like sugar, a "colonial commodity," as a tree crop it was not nearly as labor intensive and often grew semiwild in Haiti and near to "home for most peasants."[144] "Peasants gathered the cherries from the half-wild shrubs rather than cultivating them," writes the historian Brenda Gayle Plummer, a practice that "proved most compatible with the subsistence agriculture that characterized their economy" and their views of "family life" and effectively "shield[ed]" them "from the more direct exploitation that plantation agriculture would have entailed." In these ways, coffee was ultimately quite compatible with the logics and ethics of the counter-plantation.[145]

On the other hand, many African Americans did not understand the complexities of Haiti's class and taxation structure.[146] As Brandon Byrd argues, their "perception was based on a middle-class African American model of racial uplift that assumed that Vincent and other Haitian leaders would act in the best interests of the masses."[147] But this was not necessarily the case, despite Price-Mars's sympathetic efforts. "The state relied on the coffee crop not only for operating expenses," argues Plummer, "but as the basis of credit and as a guarantee of the currency."[148] "By 1909, more than 95 percent of government revenues came from multiple taxes collected at the various ports on a single crop—coffee ... [and] it was the peasant who was footing the bill."[149] Furthermore, as Plummer observes, "there was no effective program of crop diversification"—hence, Price-Mars's insistence on ending coffee monoculture.[150] The U.S. occupation only exacerbated these problems, increasing Haiti's "economic dependence by enlarging the role of coffee as an export" from 67 percent to 78 percent (between 1916–1921 and 1932–1933).[151]

The Haitian elite, because of their overreliance on the peasantry as "a source of forced taxation," were often antagonistic toward peasant cultivation methods, such as the *coumbite* and subsistence farming, and desired to reinstitute the plantation and its logics of increased productivity and capital accumulation.[152] And while Haitian leaders were correct in their conviction that peasant cultivation methods were outmoded, very little effort was made to conceive of an agrarian future from the ground up. As indicated by *Goodwill*'s attack on the *coumbite*, President Vincent's ownership of a "model banana farm," and, in fact, much of Haiti's agricultural politics since the revolution, the Haitian elite were desirous of getting rid of peasant cultivation and landholding practices by reinstituting plantations and so invited African American investors to do the same. Notwithstanding Price-Mars's paternalistic sympathy for the peasantry, plotting agrarian futures was, for many elite Haitians, not simply an altruistic commitment to improving the lives of their rural, illiterate compatriots. Rather, it was inextricably tethered to producing more efficient workers—and sometimes exploiting them—to underwrite the Haitian economy.

Jean Price-Mars's visit to Tuskegee in 1904 symbolized an important, if contested, shift within Haitian cultural and intellectual thought and Haitian–African American relations. For many Haitians, embracing the Tuskegee model meant exchanging their French cultural and intellectual heritage for a mode of education rooted in the belief of Black people's inherent intellectual inferiority and enforced by U.S. imperialism. Yet, for others, Tuskegee represented the promise and possibility of Black self-determination through agricultural education, economic self-help, and material development, temporarily shifting the locus of Black diasporic progress to rural Alabama.

This instance of Global Black South exchange was based on both the Haitian and African American elite's conception of Haiti as a primarily agricultural country whose past productivity was evidence of a potentially robust agrarian future. Through agricultural and industrial education and economic (inter)national cooperation, the Haitian and African American elite hoped to uplift the Haitian peasantry, strengthen Haiti's economic and geopolitical standing, and improve African American elites' economic and social standing in the United States. Drawing inspiration from African Americans' material advancement, Price-Mars in particular attempted to reconcile the conflicting elements of Haitian society—its African and French heritages and class fractures—into an agrarian future that he believed would be mutually beneficial to the peasantry and elite alike.

If all things had been fair and equal, perhaps Haiti would have benefited from transplanting elements of the Tuskegee model into its education system. However, there were numerous geopolitical, social, and ideological challenges to such efforts, not least the economic exploitation of Haiti at the hands of France and the United States that kept it mired in a state of perpetual debt. Furthermore, Haiti's class structure reflected a considerable rift between the peasant majority and the governing elite minority, who viewed the peasantry as ignorant and incapable of self-determination. Unlike Price-Mars, who, despite his paternalism, ultimately attempted to cultivate sympathy and respect for the peasantry, many elite Haitians envisioned an agrarian future for the country that produced an educated peasantry only insofar as that education produced more efficient laborers for the state's coffers. Haiti's struggle against the plantation was thus twofold: the *internal* class tensions between the elite and the peasantry and the *external* exploitation by European and U.S. imperialism.

Throughout plot II, I have shown how Cubans, Haitians, and African Americans strategically translated the Tuskegee model and each other's distinct histories to articulate disparate and often competing visions of racial progress and modernity within and against the rise of U.S. empire. Significantly, large-scale agriculture was often at the center of these efforts at diasporic exchange, indicating how Global Black South peoples continued to struggle within and against the plantation well into the twentieth century. As we transition to plot III, we will see how Tuskegee's Caribbean and southern African American students both embraced and challenged Washington's conception of the southern, Tuskegee New Negro and agrarian futures. Indeed, the intellectual and cultural contributions of the Global Black South remained central to Black modernity and diasporic relationality during the New Negro Movement of the 1920s and 1930s, even as the locus shifted to the urban Global North.

PLOT III

PLOT III

5
Becoming New Negroes

Student Aspirations, Hemispheric Migration,
and the Otherwise Uses of Tuskegee

In the summer of 1899, Wesley Warren Jefferson, a recent graduate of Tuskegee's Printing Division and native of Florence, South Carolina, set sail for Montserrat, British West Indies. Jefferson had so excelled at Tuskegee that he was named class salutatorian and was recommended by Washington to lead an industrial school on the small Caribbean island. The school, established on a former sugar plantation much like Tuskegee's origins on an old cotton estate, signals the ways the repurposed plantation functioned as a strategy for plotting Black futures in both the U.S. South and the Caribbean alike. Upon his arrival, Jefferson faced no shortage of challenges. Though he found the people "fairly intelligent," he quickly determined that Montserrat was the "poorest place on earth." Education was "compulsory," and the schools were "very good," "much better than the average American public school," in fact. However, "Negroes . . . are in a condition of slavery," he informed Washington. "There is a good deal of starvation. . . . Many have not clothes with which to cover their bodies. They are willing to work but actually there is nothing to do." In response to the dearth of jobs and resulting poverty and hunger, many people emigrated from the island, while others resorted to stealing to survive. The problem, Jefferson determined, was that "the white man has the monopoly of every thing [*sic*] in the Island, and no money is being spent, so the poor Negro must suffer." Although Jefferson had complete faith in Washington's educational philosophy, he "found that it did not seem applicable to the West Indies since whites would not hire blacks to work." It was a problem "more intricate than the American problem," he concluded. After less than two years, Jefferson returned to the United States in "ill health and disappointed at the extreme poverty and lack of opportunity that seemed to make West Indian advancement impossible." Changing course, he enrolled in Howard University's dental school and launched a successful dental practice in Norfolk, Virginia.[1] Jefferson's frustrated attempt to transplant Tuskegee to Montserrat and subsequent decision to pursue a career that radically departed from his training as a printer usefully illustrate how Tuskegee's students both participated in Global Black South exchange and took advantage of the school's social and political capital to craft futures all their own.

In plots I and II, we saw how Tuskegee repurposed the antebellum plantation into an agrarian future and how the African American, Afro-Cuban, and Haitian cultural, intellectual, and political elite adapted and strategically translated the Tuskegee model into their own visions of Black modernity as they contended with the intensification of Jim Crow violence and disenfranchisement, ongoing European colonial domination, and a burgeoning U.S. imperialism. In plot III, I turn to the lives and work of Tuskegee's southern African American and Afro-Caribbean students to more fully ascertain how Tuskegee shaped and influenced modernity in the Global Black South. After all, Tuskegee was first and foremost an educational institution committed to producing graduates who would carry its mission into the world. Many of the strategies Washington and his contemporaries developed for establishing Black modernity and diasporic relation explored in plots I and II—repurposing the plantation, eco-ontological regeneration, plotting agrarian futures, strategic translation, and trans-plantation—were also utilized by Tuskegee's students, many of whom became architects of the New Negro Movement of the 1920s and 1930s. Crucially, however, this new generation of New Negroes also developed their own theories and practices of Black modern subjectivity and diasporic relation as they responded to the new ways the plantation constrained and shaped Black life.

In *Tuskegee and Its People: Their Ideals and Achievements* (1906), Emmett J. Scott, Washington's executive secretary, compiled and edited short autobiographies of some of Tuskegee's most accomplished U.S.-born graduates to date.[2] By featuring graduates who worked in a range of industries and professions, from education to business and agriculture, Scott hoped to demonstrate the breadth of Tuskegee's curriculum and the dynamic uses of a Tuskegee education to dispel the erroneous notion that "Tuskegee Institute is a 'servant training school' or an employment agency." Modeled on the bildungsroman quality of *Up from Slavery,* each chapter details graduates' "experiences from childhood, the school-life of the writer, and the results achieved in the direction of putting into practise what was learned in school."[3] Many of them born just after emancipation, the authors relate their circuitous journeys from one-room shacks on southern plantations where they slept on beds of cottonseed to learning their respective trades at

Tuskegee to their postgraduate efforts to uplift the Black masses through their respective professions as teachers, farmers, a lawyer, a druggist, and institution builders. *Tuskegee and Its People* essentially details how Tuskegee contributed to a local and regional diaspora within the United States, attracting students to rural Alabama and encouraging their dispersion throughout the country and even to Togo, West Africa, to do their part in uplifting the race.

In the spirit of *Tuskegee and Its People*, plot III tends to the lives and work of Tuskegee's students to demonstrate how the dispersion of this educational experiment throughout the Global Black South gave birth to wholly new and dynamic practices of Black cultural and political futurity. There is no comparable volume that includes the experiences of Tuskegee's non-U.S.-born students, so this chapter pays special attention to correspondence in Booker T. Washington's papers to examine how Tuskegee's Cuban, Puerto Rican, Haitian, Jamaican, and Guianese students and their parents navigated international travel and, in some cases, English-language acquisition once they arrived on campus.[4] Many of Tuskegee's Afro-Caribbean students hailed from urban centers such as Havana, San Juan, Port-au-Prince, and Kingston and thus had to adjust to the unique conditions of the rural Jim Crow South. I also explore how students' unique cultural backgrounds and career aspirations moved within and against Washington's conception of the southern New Negro and how they navigated the thorny intersections of race, class, labor, and empire. Alongside this archive of correspondence, I examine how Tuskegee's literary output—for example, its annual catalogs, Washington's autobiographies, and their Spanish and French translations—was especially important for facilitating this dynamic student migration network within the Global Black South.

I begin this chapter by reconstructing the experiences of Tuskegee's students in the first two decades of the twentieth century, after the school enrolled its first international students and became a diasporic contact zone. Though Tuskegee sought to inculcate students with its vision of agrarian futures, I show how many of the projects and ideologies pursued by students exceeded, critiqued, contradicted, or explicitly departed from the school's articulated mission. Like Serra's and Price-Mars's strategic translations, Tuskegee's students took the ideas they were taught there and cross-bred them with contemporaneous discourses on race, labor, diaspora, empire, gender, and aesthetics to articulate their own views of agrarian futures, New Negro subjectivity, Black self-determination, and diasporic relation.

Although several scholars have acknowledged Washington's and Tuskegee's contributions to the construction of the New Negro in the postbellum, pre-Harlem period, much less work has been done to examine their ongoing influence in the 1920s and 1930s.[5] Yet many of Tuskegee's students and faculty went on to become members of the Black intellectual and cultural elite and luminaries of the New Negro Movement in Harlem and elsewhere in the Black world.[6] I thus conclude this chapter by examining how Tuskegee continued to play a crucial role in shaping Black modernity even as Harlem and Paris became the new hubs of Black diasporic activity, and art became the new battleground for cultivating the New Negro. Though often overlooked, Tuskegee's influence on the New Negro Movement was reflected in several of the era's most important publications and ur-texts of Black literary modernism and diasporic practice: *Opportunity* magazine, the organ of the National Urban League, edited by the sociologist Charles S. Johnson; Alain Locke's *The New Negro* (1925); *La revue du monde noir* (1931), a short-lived, bilingual cultural and political journal published by sisters Jane and Paulette Nardal in Paris; and *Negro: An Anthology* (1934), compiled and edited by the British writer and publisher Nancy Cunard.

Ultimately, this chapter is a chorus of sorts, bringing together a range of southern African American and Afro-Caribbean student voices and experiences—singing in different languages and English accents—to help us hear Tuskegee as a locus of Global Black South exchange, while the remaining chapters in plot III are akin to solo performances by three of Tuskegee's most prominent students of the New Negro Movement: Claude McKay, Zora Neale Hurston, and Marcus Garvey. To recall, I define "students" broadly to encompass those who either studied or were educated in Tuskegee's curriculum directly or indirectly: McKay attended Tuskegee to study agronomy; Hurston attended an industrial school established by Tuskegee graduates and modeled on its curriculum; and Garvey was a self-taught and self-proclaimed student of Washington's sociopolitical and economic thought who immersed himself in Tuskegee's curriculum through reading texts such as *Up from Slavery* and the *Tuskegee Student*. Through this more expansive conception of Tuskegee's students, plot III charts an alternative transnational intellectual and cultural genealogy that demonstrates how Tuskegee set the stage for and actively contributed to the making of the New Negro generation of the 1920s and 1930s in unexpected and often contradictory ways.

NEGOTIATING DIASPORA AND EMPIRE

In the first nearly two decades of Tuskegee's existence, its students hailed primarily from the United States (including Indian Territory), the vast majority from Alabama. Tuskegee's first Afro-Caribbean students arrived following Washington's rise to race leadership, sailing on the waves of U.S. empire and corporate colonialism. Following the Spanish-American War, Afro-Cubans were preoccupied with acquiring education, much like African Americans following the Civil War.[7] Given the limited educational opportunities available to Afro-Cubans and following U.S. military intervention on the island, Washington's program became an appealing and viable option. As noted in chapter 3, Washington actively recruited Afro-Cuban students by sending agents from Tuskegee to cities in the U.S. South with large Cuban populations, such as Key West and Tampa, Florida, and then to San Luis and Havana, Cuba. In 1898, he employed the recent graduate Thomas Austin as a recruitment agent because Austin was one of Tuskegee's "most reliable students," "had considerable contact with the Cubans," and spoke Spanish.[8]

Austin initially had trouble recruiting Cuban students in Florida because they were eager to return to the island and take part in building the new republic. Writing from Tampa in November 1898, he informed Washington: "I am sorry to say that my progress is poor, it is due to the fact that they are more anxious to return to Cuba, than to do anything else. I have explained everything to them and succeeded in getting only one to promise me positively. It seem [sic] as though they fail to realize what an opportunity is offered them. Their sentiments are expressed in the words 'On to Cuba.'"[9] Austin proceeded to publish advertisements in Cuban newspapers, and Washington solicited the support of African American military officers such as Allen Alexander Wesley, who had served as a surgeon in the Spanish-American War and still resided on the island, as well as from Cuban political leaders and government officials, such as Juan Gualberto Gómez, an Afro-Cuban Spanish-American War veteran and prominent member of the Afro-Cuban elite. In a letter to Wesley in November 1898, Washington requested help in "get[ting] hold of eight students, four boys and four girls if possible." This desired gender parity suggests that Tuskegee considered its program as applicable to Afro-Cuban girls as to boys. He also included a statement that Wesley could share with Cuban parents that Tuskegee was "responsible for their [children's] education and careful treatment," an important reminder that Tuskegee was first and foremost an educational institution committed to students' well-being and not just a political machine.[10] When the first cohort of students was secured in 1899, Washington had to reassure Alabama's governor, Joseph Forney Johnston, that "there is not one in the party who under any circumstances could be mistaken for a white," in response to erroneous claims that the school had recruited "five white boys" whose parents were unaware that Tuskegee was "exclusively for the education of colored youths." Educating white Cubans, Johnston reminded him, would defy the Alabama state code prohibiting "coeducation of the races."[11] Their exchange is a sobering reminder of the ways Tuskegee was always-already navigating white surveillance amid the constraints imposed by Jim Crow.

In a studio photograph from around 1900 depicting what was likely the first cohort of Cuban students, there are eight boys and one girl pictured (figure 5.1). I am particularly drawn to the lone girl student. She is almost certainly Celestina Ramírez from Havana, Cuba, the first Afro-Cuban girl to attend Tuskegee. All the boys are dressed in dark suits with white shirts and ties. Celestina wears a dark dress with a belt tied about her waist and a row of buttons on the lefthand side leading up diagonally to a long sleeve covering her entire arm and ruffled at the shoulder and wrist. Like most of the boys, Celestina is dark-skinned and wears her hair pulled back from her face, drawing attention to her round eyes and half-smile. Six of the boys stand in the background, and Celestina appears to be seated one row in front of them. The last two boys, much younger than the rest, are pictured in front of her. Celestina rests her left arm on the left shoulder of the youngest-looking boy, like an older sister or mother who will help care for this child who has entered the circuits of transnational migration and is now so far from home.

FIGURE 5.1. "A Group of Cuban Pupils at Tuskegee."

Source: Thrasher, *Tuskegee*, between pp. 82 and 83.

Like their Cuban counterparts, Puerto Rican students also clamored for educational opportunities following the Spanish-American War. While Cuba secured its independence from Spain, the United States claimed Puerto Rico as a territory. So instead of sending recruitment agents to Puerto Rico, Washington secured students by partnering with U.S. government officials presiding over the island's education system. By 1902, the U.S. commissioner on education for Puerto Rico had received hundreds of letters and "many urgent applications" from students and parents, "willing to do anything, make any sacrifice, to obtain an education in the States."[12] The Legislature of Puerto Rico, with the aid of Martin Grove Brumbaugh, commissioner of education for the colonial government in Puerto Rico in 1900–1901, and his successor, Samuel McCune Lindsay, passed two laws to fund scholarships for Puerto Rican students to attend schools throughout the United States. Selected through competitive exams held in seven cities across the island, twenty-five "poor young men of robust constitution and good conduct" were sent to "smaller colleges and the best preparatory schools" in the United States, and another twenty were sent to "industrial and manual-training" schools, such as Tuskegee, Hampton, and the Carlisle School for Native Americans, in hopes of "preparing [them] for careers as artisans."[13] The students sent to Tuskegee and Hampton were "colored boys" who had graduated eighth grade, although Puerto Rican girls were soon permitted to enroll also. The first cohort was chosen from across the island by the education commissioner and given $250 stipends to pursue "industrial studies" and return to aid in Puerto Rico's industrial development.[14] Students worked with the commissioner to determine their trades before departing the island, and the commissioner had personal oversight over them.[15] Each student was to come from a poor family and a different county or district.[16]

The first Haitian students enrolled at Tuskegee in the 1903–1904 school year, a few years after the first Cuban and Puerto Rican students arrived but more than a decade before the U.S. occupation of Haiti. In this way, the Tuskegee–Haiti connection was initially engineered by Haitians and African Americans, although empire would later enable it also (as shown in chapter 4). Washington worked with Haitian and African American diplomats to establish scholarships for Haitian students. William F. Powell, U.S. consul to Haiti and a "regular contributor" to Tuskegee, helped to broker the partnership and recommended that it be funded.[17] A letter from Powell to a Haitian government official was translated and published in *Le nouvelliste*, a leading Haitian periodical based in Port-au-Prince. Powell shared that Washington had offered to admit two or three Haitian students free of charge as long as the government agreed to pay their travel expenses.[18] *Le nouvelliste* also published French translations of excerpts from the Tuskegee catalog on the front page, outlining the expectations for male and female students and the schools' discipline system, perhaps to ensure parents that their children would be well cared for in the United States.[19] Like the Tuskegee–Puerto Rico connection, the school's partnership with Haiti was initially facilitated by the Haitian government, which budgeted incrementally to cover expenses for twenty male students.[20] Through this partnership with Tuskegee, observed the *Indianapolis Freeman*, "Hayti [*sic*] is waking up to her necessities.... [instead of] spending its energies and genius, whatever they may be, in the art of government snatching." Perpetuating the frequent criticism that Haitians focused too much on the liberal arts, the writer extolled a partnership with Tuskegee that "promises better things for the future by absorbing the too tall talent in other fields" and applying it toward Haiti's progress.[21]

Likely after learning about the scholarships and curriculum in local newspapers, Haitian youth appealed directly to the government to fund their admission to Tuskegee, while one Haitian father himself sent his two sons along with "a check for two thousand francs to cover their expenses."[22] In the fall of 1903, the *Tuskegee Student* announced the arrival of "quite a little colony" of Haitian students on campus. Twelve male students enrolled that year, the largest number for that decade.[23] Most enrolled in the postgraduate program, using Tuskegee to complement educations they had received in Haiti. They hailed from Port-au-Prince, Gonaives, and Jérémie, all urban centers, and were most likely members of the elite. When Jean Price-Mars visited Tuskegee in the fall of 1904, however, only two Haitian students were enrolled. It seems the Haitian government cut funds to support scholarships in just a year's time.[24] While a few Haitian students continued to enroll annually, the numbers were nowhere as robust as those from Cuba and Puerto Rico.

Jamaicans had been interested in Tuskegee since the turn of the twentieth century, and, as with Afro-Cubans and Haitians, both individuals and colonial government officials forged ties with the institution. In "Booker T. Washington for Jamaica," an article published in Jamaica's leading newspaper, the *Daily Gleaner*, in 1902, an anonymous commentator noted that for years there had been talk of inviting Washington "down to the colony" because whereas "the old idea was to impart to children a purely literary education: the new idea is to train them on natural lines so that they will worthily fill the positions they are to occupy in life." They would still receive "essential elements" of education, but the new concept "implies the elimination of what is useless" to their lives "and the substitution of knowledge bearing directly on their future activities."[25] By 1912, when the Jamaican government sent a delegation of education officials to attend Tuskegee's ICON, twenty-three students and faculty from the

British West Indies, most of them from Jamaica, were enrolled and employed at Tuskegee. They had formed an affinity group on campus called the Britisher's Union, which promoted sending more British West Indian students to Tuskegee, establishing industrial schools on their respective islands to help "our boys and girls prepare themselves for the business of life," and appealing to their local governments to invite Washington to visit their respective islands.[26] Although, for some, Tuskegee had developed a reputation for being a backward institution, for others, like the Jamaican commentator, it represented "the new idea" and thus a viable approach to educating Black youth across the diaspora.

THE ROUTES OF HEMISPHERIC MIGRATION: LITERATURE, LANGUAGE, AND TRANSLATION

Print culture, translation, and the politics of English-language acquisition were essential to facilitating Afro-Caribbean student migration to Tuskegee. Writing from Key West en route to Havana, the recruitment agent Thomas Austin informed Washington: "I can get a great many, who are well acquainted with the English language, but I thought probaly [sic] you would prefer beginners. . . . I am sure if I went to Havana I could get any number as I am told that there are number of them in Cuba who are yet starving."[27] It is unclear why Austin assumed Washington desired students who were not well acquainted with English. Perhaps he considered that uplifting students from the worst conditions would further prove the legitimacy of the Tuskegee model. Whatever the case, the archive of Afro-Caribbean student and parent correspondence and institutional publications detail how students navigated the vagaries of international travel and learning the English language alongside their respective educational and career aspirations.

In Cuba especially, Washington amassed a considerable following through the translation and circulation of *Up from Slavery* under the title *De esclavo á catedratico* (From slave to professor) in 1902 (see chapter 3). Grace Minns, the Boston-based reformer who helped to facilitate its translation and dissemination, informed Washington in 1903, "One thousand copies of your book are now spread all through Cuba, and it will be read by the children in the public schools, in the orphan asylums, by patients in the hospitals, by old men and women in the almshouses, by employees in the cigar factories, and by a large number of persons who are interested in the administration of the schools, the charitable institutions, and in public affairs."[28] Like much of Tuskegee's institutional literature, *De esclavo á catedrático* included photographs of campus buildings and students engaged in learning various trades, thereby circulating the school's visual aesthetics (chapter 2) throughout Cuba as well.

De esclavo á catedratico played a significant role in recruiting Afro-Cuban students to Tuskegee, facilitating a Black hemispheric network between the Caribbean and the U.S. South. Frank Guridy writes that people of African descent on the island were inspired by the autobiography: "From the time of the book's publication until Washington's death, hundreds of letters of admiration from Cuba poured into Tuskegee."[29] These letters provide a deeper understanding of how Afro-Caribbean students and their parents engaged the Tuskegee project through linguistic and ideological translation. This archive indicates that there were many more competing goals for forging connections with Tuskegee than those espoused by Washington, government officials, reformers, or race leaders. Letters were often written in beautiful and ornate cursive script, expressing a range of desires, fears, and expectations related to education at Tuskegee and the challenges of upward mobility. For instance, Hermanno Laroche, a prospective student from Guantánamo, Cuba, wanted to enter the school but admitted being "afraid of winter," and Absalom Boco's parent sent money from Port-au-Prince for a "good winter overcoat and all that is necessary for that season."[30] Much of the correspondence relates to the financial logistics of international recruitment: receipts, account statements and balances, school fees and supplies, and international transportation. Much like Wesley Warren Jefferson, the Montserrat-based industrial school principal turned Howard-educated dentist, many students treated Tuskegee as a springboard to more elite schools. They wrote to Washington to request recommendations for art schools and architecture programs, desires that were seemingly discordant with his public advocacy for training students in industry and agriculture alone.[31] Letters also included updates on students' general welfare, disciplinary problems, and courses of study.

Most letters requested copies of the school's catalog or a similar circular delineating its course offerings and admission requirements. As the primary institutional document that circulated outside of the United States, the school catalog, like *Up from Slavery*, was central to its transnationalism. The appendix routinely included a list of current students and their respective hometowns, making Tuskegee legible as a global institution. In the first section, which listed students by year and program of study, international students were commingled with students from the United States, suggesting that apart from English-language courses, the school did not treat "foreign" students differently from their African American counterparts.[32] "Here Maine and California, far-away Washington and Central America, meet on common ground," wrote Margaret

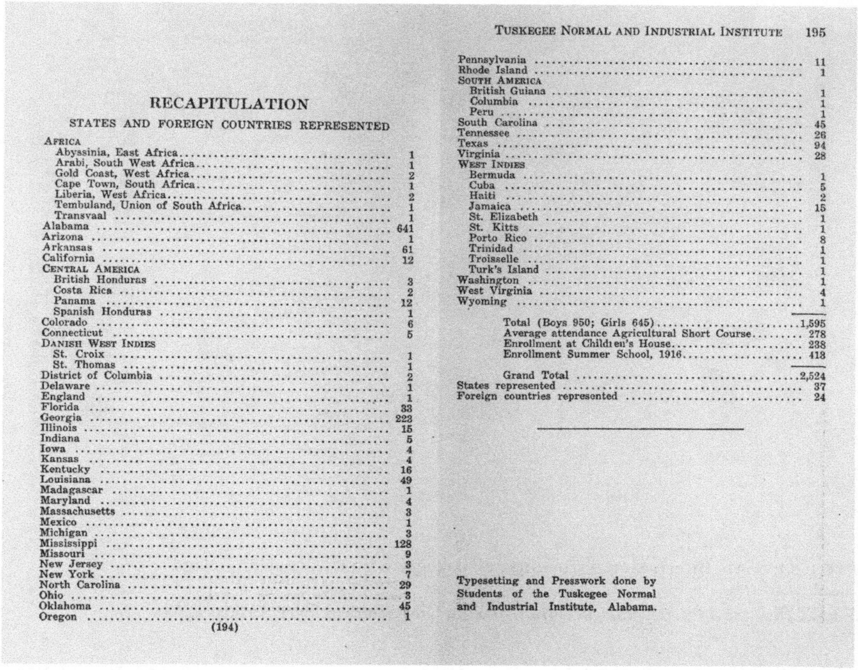

TUSKEGEE NORMAL AND INDUSTRIAL INSTITUTE 195

RECAPITULATION
STATES AND FOREIGN COUNTRIES REPRESENTED

AFRICA
Abyssinia, East Africa 1
Arabi, South West Africa 1
Gold Coast, West Africa 2
Cape Town, South Africa 1
Liberia, West Africa 2
Tembuland, Union of South Africa 1
Transvaal 1
Alabama 641
Arizona 1
Arkansas 61
California 12
CENTRAL AMERICA
British Honduras 3
Costa Rica 2
Panama 12
Spanish Honduras 1
Colorado 6
Connecticut 5
DANISH WEST INDIES
St. Croix 1
St. Thomas 1
District of Columbia 2
Delaware 1
England 1
Florida 33
Georgia 223
Illinois 15
Indiana 5
Iowa 1
Kansas 4
Kentucky 16
Louisiana 49
Madagascar 1
Maryland 4
Massachusetts 3
Mexico 1
Michigan 3
Mississippi 128
Missouri 9
New Jersey 3
New York 7
North Carolina 29
Ohio 3
Oklahoma 45
Oregon 1

(194)

Pennsylvania 11
Rhode Island 1
SOUTH AMERICA
British Guiana 1
Columbia 1
Peru 1
South Carolina 45
Tennessee 26
Texas 24
Virginia 28
WEST INDIES
Bermuda 1
Cuba 1
Haiti 2
Jamaica 15
St. Elizabeth 1
St. Kitts 1
Porto Rico 8
Trinidad 1
Troisselle 1
Turk's Island 1
Washington 1
West Virginia 4
Wyoming 1

Total (Boys 950; Girls 645) 1,595
Average attendance Agricultural Short Course 278
Enrollment at Children's House 238
Enrollment Summer School, 1916 413

Grand Total 2,524
States represented 37
Foreign countries represented 24

Typesetting and Presswork done by
Students of the Tuskegee Normal
and Industrial Institute, Alabama.

FIGURE 5.2. A page from *Tuskegee Annual Catalogue*, 1916, showing the aggregation of students' home states, countries, and territories.

Source: *Tuskegee Annual Catalogue*, 1916, Tuskegee University Archives, Tuskegee, AL.

Murray Washington in 1906. "Alabama and Georgia alone feel kinship from geographical propinquity."[33] The final section of the appendix collated and listed students geographically by state, territory, or "foreign" country of origin, and the 1916–1917 catalog included a photograph of "foreign" students holding up their respective country flags (figures 5.2 and 5.3). Together, the photograph and appendix emphasize Tuskegee's international reach and document its status as a locus of diasporic education and uplift. That year, students hailed from thirty-seven states and twenty-four foreign countries, the largest cohorts from Alabama (641), Georgia (223), Panama (12), and Jamaica (15).

Despite Washington's belief that African Americans should remain in the U.S. South, this archive of correspondence reveals how Tuskegee facilitated a dynamic transnational student migration network that intersected with the hemispheric flows of capital, labor, commerce, and empire. Students from the Caribbean and Latin America often traveled aboard United Fruit Company (UFCO)

The cosmopolitan character of the Tuskegee student body is shown by the fact that during the past year students have come from the foreign countries or colonies of foreign countries indicated by the various flags shown in this picture

FIGURE 5.3. International students at Tuskegee with their nations' flags.

Source: *Tuskegee Annual Catalogue*, 1916, Tuskegee University Archives, Tuskegee, AL.

steamships to Mobile, Alabama, and other port cities along the Gulf and East Coasts, where they were met by a Tuskegee faculty or staff member, who then accompanied them to the campus. In one letter, twenty-seven-year-old Juan Santos y Torres of Santiago, Cuba, inquired "what route is the shortest to Tuskegee," and in another letter J. Alex McKenzie, a Jamaican parent employed as the superintendent of works for UFCO, admitted being "thoroughly unacouainted [*sic*]" with the best route to bring his two sons to Tuskegee and wondered if he should travel from Port Antonio to Charleston by fruit steamer and then to Tuskegee by rail (the same route by which Claude McKay would migrate to Tuskegee just one year later).[34] After conferring with an UFCO agent in New Orleans, Washington informed the guardians of Geddes Cole, who wished to return home to Siquirres, Costa Rica, that she could travel to either New Orleans or Mobile by rail and then by steamer to Port Limón, Costa Rica, and finally to Siquirres by train. To ensure her safe passage, her guardians also had to cover expenses for a "protector" from the school to accompany her as far as Mobile, which "is not a great distance from" New Orleans, he informed them.[35] Absalom Boco of Haiti traveled to Tuskegee aboard a "sailing vessel" from Port-au-Prince to Mobile, and in another letter a Haitian parent informed Washington that they were delayed in sending their son because the steamer that traveled from Port-au-Prince to Mobile came only once every three months.[36] Washington received similar correspondence from students and parents from Trinidad, Puerto Rico, Suriname, British Guiana (now Guyana), and elsewhere in the hemisphere, indicating the ways that Tuskegee's student migration network relied on the very corporate plantation shipping, trade, and labor migration networks that circulated global commodities such as cotton, sugar, and bananas. This proximity between global commodities and the very people who, not long before, would have been forced to cultivate them for the world market and were themselves regarded as commodities brings the exigencies of the Tuskegee project into sharp relief. These students were heading toward a different future than many of their parents and grandparents: a repurposed plantation in the Jim Crow South that would equip them with the knowledge and tools to regenerate themselves and navigate the plantation's myriad afterlives.

Though Washington attempted to fold Tuskegee students into his vision of agrarian futures, enrollment in the Agricultural Department was quite modest, suggesting that few students were interested in returning to the farm to disseminate their newly acquired knowledge among the rural Black masses. Even some of Tuskegee's faculty were biased against farming, "sentencing" students to work on the campus farm as punishment for misbehavior.[37] Around 1900, the most popular trades were tailoring (enrolling thirty young men and ten young women), wheelwrighting, machine-shop work, and blacksmithing.[38]

Many Afro-Caribbean students were especially prone to specialize in industrial trades. Cuban students often studied architecture, and "hardly any" Jamaican students took up agriculture, opting instead for electrical engineering, where a number of them had enjoyed "recent success."[39] In an article in the *Technical World* in 1904, Charles W. Pierce, instructor of electrical engineering at Tuskegee, painted an inspiring portrait of the school's program, indicating how it attracted students from across the Global Black South. "The Electrical Engineering Department has proved quite attractive to students from foreign countries as well as from other states of the United States," he wrote. Pierce quoted at length from an unnamed Haitian student enrolled in the program, who explained: "Electrical Engineering is one of the branches of scientific knowledge least in vogue in Haiti.... While in school, I desired to come to America to study practical science and learn a trade. After finishing I heard that Tuskegee was a place which afforded excellent opportunities to the negro for acquiring practical knowledge."[40] This student, who planned to continue his studies at another school and then return home to Port-au-Prince, was part of the first cohort supported by the Haitian government. The fact that he studied electrical engineering and intended to return to Haiti illustrates Washington's belief that industrial and agricultural education was not only a path to individual uplift but could be scaled up to develop the Haitian nation-state as well (see chapter 4). It was a fundamentally Black nationalist (as in nation-building) project, albeit practical and conservative.

Correspondence regarding Cuban and Puerto Rican students vividly illuminates the messy intersection of racial uplift, the civilizing mission, and American imperialism. In a letter to Miss Elizabeth E. Lane, assistant to the director of housekeeping, regarding the Cuban and Puerto Rican girls, Washington wrote: "The Porto Rican [sic] and Cuban girls in respect to bodily cleanliness and the care of their clothes will need especial attention all through the summer; I do not want them neglected in this respect as the Porto Rican government expects us to give especial attention to them."[41] It seems to have been a popular sentiment among Tuskegee faculty and staff that Cuban and Puerto Rican students, in particular the girls, presented a unique challenge. Leonora Love Chapman, a grammar instructor, wrote to Washington: "What on earth, Mr. Washington, will I do [with] Cuban girls? Do you suppose I can ever manage them. It has been very easy to stand off and give Major Ramsey sympathy in his management of Pedro [Salina, Tuskegee's first Puerto Rican student], but my heart puts in an extra 'beat' at the prospect of having some of the girls to take care of. . . . However, I will do my best with them, and for them."[42]

It is unclear why Cuban and Puerto Rican girls were considered particularly challenging. Mrs. Margaret Murray Washington suggested that girls' education in general was viewed as a "problem we have been trying to solve at Tuskegee for over twenty years: What handiwork can we give our girls with their academic training that will better fit them to meet the demand for skilled teachers in the various avenues of the industrial and academic world now opening so rapidly to women?"[43] Perhaps the Cuban and Puerto Rican girls' linguistic and cultural differences from African American girls added an additional layer of difficulty in a racial-sexual landscape that viewed girls' and women's education and labor as a "problem." Or perhaps Cuban and Puerto Rican students were seen this way because they were not shy about expressing their grievances with the institution. In a letter to Washington in November 1901, for instance, Celestina Ramírez, pictured in figure 5.1, complained that she did not have enough clothing compared to other girls who had arrived more recently and despite working much harder than the Cuban boys the previous summer.[44] Indeed, Cuban and Puerto Rican students occasionally resisted what they regarded as their mistreatment, a lack of appropriate food and clothing, and the school's rigid curriculum. In a letter to Washington in 1899, they reminded him that Tuskegee's recruitment agents "told our parents we would be treated all right up here." They had considered writing to "the N.Y. Herald about how the Cubans were treated at Tuskegee," they veiledly threatened, but ultimately thought better of it because it would cause "trouble" for Washington.[45] In 1906, Manuel Gutierez, a self-proclaimed "Cuban boy," also complained of being "barefooted" and having "nothing to wear" and warned Washington that although he wanted "to carry good tidings to the people of my community, and those of the whole island, and also bring more to be educated [at Tuskegee] . . . if the treatment that the Cubans as a whole are getting here goes on this way, I will have to write . . . to my people."[46] Although some of the Cuban students sent to Tuskegee came from the working classes, most hailed from the island's Afro-Cuban elite, which may explain why they rightly felt emboldened to assert themselves this way when they felt mistreated.[47]

In a report to Samuel McCune Lindsay, U.S. commissioner of education in Puerto Rico, in 1902, Washington offered a mixed review of the progress of the first cohort of fifteen students sent to Tuskegee. They displayed more "earnestness" in their "academic studies" than in the "industrial departments," he criticized, and "[g]enerally speaking they do not like to work and it is a hard matter to get them to see the advantage of learning a trade." With an air of condescension, Washington surmised that "the conditions of life under which they have been reared in Porto Rico doubtless, in a certain measure, are responsible for the characteristics they exhibit. Here as there they like to dress gaudily and extravagantly, to spend much time in powdering their faces and in congregating for idle gossip." Nevertheless, he concluded that it was too soon to answer Lindsay's queries: " 'Of what sort of stuff are they made?' and 'Will the results pay for the outlay?' " He proposed that, like their Cuban counterparts, they may need at least two years to "really acquire the American spirit," and thus he agreed to continue educating them.[48]

In turn, Puerto Rican students also wrote to the commissioner about their grievances with Tuskegee. Rafael Ramos, the son of Federico Ramos, regarded as "one of the most distinguished musical composers and teachers of Porto Rico," and fellow student Luis Lafaye expressed dissatisfaction "with what they are doing" and wished to return home. Once their academic work was completed, they complained, there was nothing more for them.[49] In response, Washington dismissed their concerns, noting, "It is not always safe to take these Porto Rican students seriously. They have all kinds of flighty ideas and one has to be very patient and very firm with them."[50] Puerto Rican educational officials, to their credit, advocated on behalf of the students, inquiring whether there was enough free time in the schedule for "recreation" and "mental relaxation."[51] In response, Washington conceded that while the schedule "may seem a little full" to the students, the school believed that keeping them "thus busy" was not "exacting too much" and that it was best that their schedule was on par with that of other students.[52] What Washington read as Puerto Rican students' "flighty ideas" and incompatibility with the Tuskegee idea was in fact their act of resistance to the imperial project. Puerto Ricans students were supposed to learn trades to return to Puerto Rico and contribute to its industrial development. Although many of them did so, they were not docile subjects who uncritically embraced Washington's "dignity of labor" mantra—they preferred leisure, dressed themselves in the latest fashions, and sometimes chose a professional career over a strictly agricultural or industrial one.

Alfredo Pérez Encinosa and Juan Eusebio Gómez, son of the Spanish-American War veteran Juan Gualberto Gómez, would later become two of Tuskegee's most enterprising Afro-Cuban students. However, they were initially quite defiant during their time on campus, often challenging the faculty and administration. Gómez, along with the Puerto Rican student Pedro Salina, refused to eat the student meals and insisted on getting the teachers' meals instead. In a letter to Warren Logan, Tuskegee's treasurer, in January 1899, Washington noted, "They seem to regard that they are conferring a great favor upon the institution by being here."[53] Julio Despaigne, a student from Guantánamo, Cuba, who often reported the activities of his Cuban and Puerto Rican peers to Washington, relayed his frustrations with them, especially Encinosa, who was also from Guantánamo: "At the beginning of the last term the Porto Rican Eugene Lecompte was teaching us and he was angry and le[f]t the class because he knew that Alfredo P. Encinosa was trying to take the class." Consequently, the students "did not learn anything."[54]

Washington, however, was soon quite impressed by Encinosa's ingenuity and ambition. In a letter to Washington in June 1904, John S. Durham, who was then still employed by the Spanish Treaty Commission, noted that he had encountered "one of your boys"—the enterprising Encinosa—while he was home on the island for summer vacation.[55] In response, Washington praised Alfredo: "He is really a remarkable boy and one that you can thoroughly trust. He came to Tuskegee several years ago a seemingly green, unpromising fellow, but he has gradually grown from month to month until we consider him one of our best students. He has a remarkable talent for business, and there is where he is going to make his mark, and I shall not be surprised if he turns out to be a rich man soon after he gets out in life."[56]

Many of the criticisms Cuban and Puerto Rican students leveraged against the institution were shared by the broader student body. In 1897, 259 students signed a petition stating that although they "believe heartily in the spirit of work that characterizes Tuskegee," they desired "more time for recreation." Tuskegee "ought to hold her own, even in the field of athletics," they reasoned and requested one hour on Saturday afternoons for "base ball [*sic*] and other games."[57] In 1911, twenty-eight girls in the Laundry Division submitted a petition for higher pay, reasoning that "laundry *is* the hardest work done by female hands on the grounds" because they were responsible for the laundry of "both students and teachers" alike. Washington assembled a faculty committee to consider the students' request, and though the committee recommended a 20 percent pay increase, apparently "nothing ever came of it."[58] The most prolonged act of student resistance during Washington's lifetime occurred in 1903, when students staged a three-day "rebellion," including locking themselves in the campus chapel, to protest a recent change in the schedule that "required [them] to devote too much time to both indus[t]rial work and [academic] studies with too little time for preparation." Tensions were so high during the strike that forty-seven students left the school and one faculty member was stabbed by a student. Washington, who was traveling in Europe at the time and was not present to help quell the "disturbance," ultimately agreed that the students' concerns were valid and worked to develop a more reasonable schedule.[59] Perhaps in response to such criticisms that students' schedules were too restrictive, by 1901–1902 Tuskegee's annual catalogs began to state that the institution "required" "regular habits of rest and recreation."[60] By 1911, there were several literary societies, debate clubs, and sports, including football, baseball, basketball, and cricket, the latter most likely introduced by the British West Indian students and faculty.[61] Despite these changes, Tuskegee developed a reputation for over-regulating students' schedules, so much so that when Claude McKay arrived from Jamaica in 1912, he departed the institution after only a few months, describing it as too "semi-military" and "machine-like" for his taste (see chapter 6).[62]

In one of the most compelling accounts of how students shaped the culture of Tuskegee, Washington recalled that during a geography class students encountered a passage describing the South African Bushmen tribe as "the lowest type of human being" on the continent, leaving them feeling that "the Bushmen were about as low, degraded and hopeless a type of human nature as could well be imagined." A South African student, whose mother was a Bushwoman and father a Hottentot, raised his hand to contest the textbook's racist account. He stood before the class and educated them on the various tribes of South Africa and how the Bushmen had for more than one hundred years been hunted by the stronger tribes. He then went to his room to gather personal photographs to further illustrate his point. Following his presentation, the faculty and students were "convinced" that, contrary to what the textbook said, the Bushmen were not inherently inferior but rather "victims of circumstances," and Washington, too, began to "doubt the wisdom" of racial determinism.[63] In this way, despite the tensions and misunderstandings that sometimes arose between Tuskegee administrators and non-U.S.-born students, these students also helped to dispel intra-racial myths and biases and to create greater understanding between diasporic communities on campus.

Many Afro-Caribbean students and parents viewed Tuskegee as an opportunity to learn or refine their English-language skills in addition to learning a trade. The archive of correspondence is surprisingly multilingual. Students and parents from the Hispanophone Caribbean and Latin America often wrote to Washington in Spanish. As one characteristic example, throughout the fall of 1911 Adriano Medina of Campamento de Colombia, Cuba, wrote several letters expressing his desire to attend the institute. In one letter, Medina informed Washington that since he did not speak English, he could not understand the annual catalog and therefore had asked a friend to translate it into Spanish for him, perhaps assuming that since *Up from Slavery* was available in Spanish (which he had read), other institutional literature was as well.[64] There is no evidence, however, that this was the case, save perhaps Spanish translations of the school's course offerings published in Cuban newspapers, such as Serra's *Nuevo Criollo*. Even if some students and parents could not read English—or Spanish, for that matter, given Cuba's low literacy rate—Tuskegee's photographic archive may have helped them visualize the school grounds, classrooms, and type of education they would receive there. Medina requested that Washington reply to him in Spanish because his main goal in attending the institute was to learn English and graduate.[65] In another letter, a parent who spoke and wrote only Spanish admitted to having an English-speaking friend write to Washington on their behalf. Juan Cancio Guimbarda of Santa Clara, Cuba, inquired if it was necessary to know English to be admitted or if he could learn it there, and Juan Santos y Torres of Santiago, Cuba, informed the school that his reference letter would be in Spanish.[66] On both sides of the Gulf of Mexico, in Cuba, Puerto Rico, and Tuskegee alike, translation was a communal effort, whereby Afro-Cubans, Afro–Puerto Ricans, and African Americans reached across linguistic differences with varying degrees of proficiency to make themselves legible to each other for the purposes of educating the race.

African Americans, Afro-Cubans, and Afro–Puerto Ricans also viewed learning English at Tuskegee as a civilizational and sometimes imperial project. Martin Grove Brumbaugh, the first U.S. commissioner of education who helped recruit Puerto Rican students to the institute, contended "that in order to break up their Spanish language we might scatter some of them into other similar institutions." Brumbaugh viewed his educational policy in Puerto Rico as crucial to "the Americanization of the island" and mandated English as the language of instruction there.[67] In addition to Tuskegee, Brumbaugh sent Puerto Rican students to Hampton and at least three students to Tougaloo University (now Tougaloo College) in Mississippi. The dispersal of students to "break up their Spanish language" no doubt proved challenging for Pedro Salina from San Juan, the first Puerto Rican student to attend Tuskegee, and Celestina Ramírez, the first Cuban girl student. Susan Helen Porter, who taught history, English, and pedagogy, wrote to Washington about the difficulty of teaching Pedro. "Miss Cropper and myself are thoroughly convinced that we cannot help Pedro Salina... as he needs to be helped" without neglecting other students, she wrote. "It must be very discouraging to Pedro to be among children whose work he cannot keep up with; nor even understand. I do *not* consider him a hopeless case by any means," she qualified. The ever-savvy Celestina, however, navigated the language barrier by communicating her needs and concerns to the Cuban boys in Spanish, who then translated her message into English and conveyed it to faculty and administration on her behalf.[68]

Writing in 1900, the journalist Max Bennett Thrasher observed that in the newly arrived cohort of ten Cuban students, "only one of them could speak any English, but they had learned rapidly." By enrolling in industrial classes, they gained "an English education and a trade at the same time."[69] Soon thereafter, the school appears to have accommodated non-English-speaking students' unique needs by developing English classes, perhaps at the request of the students themselves. In a letter rife with complaints on behalf of the Puerto Rican students, Alfonso Reverón requested a morning English class for Spanish-speaking students, and in separate correspondence Saturnino Sierra, also Puerto Rican, asked the school's executive council to reinstate summer classes open to all students who wished to learn or improve their English (because the Puerto Rican government had changed its policy to limit student access to these summer classes). Cuban student Julio Despaigne advised Washington not to allow Cuban students to room together because it is "impossible" for them to learn their "instruction" and thus assimilate into "American costoms [*sic*]." Do not "pay any Cuban to teach" Cubans either, he recommended, for "an American is always best." Finally, Despaigne relayed that some Cuban students used their lack of English as an excuse to circumvent Tuskegee's strict disciplinary practices.[70]

Students from other parts of the Spanish-speaking Americas expressed a desire to learn English at Tuskegee as well. Two male students from Cartagena, Colombia, "both under 20 years old," came for the express purpose "of obtaining knowledge of the English language" and to study "some science or profession." José D. Rumler, a parent from Panama, wanted his son "to learn a very good trade" as a blacksmith or mechanical engineer and to get "a complete education in English which he is very backward in that language." When his son was detained by the U.S. Quarantine Department and not permitted to land in New Orleans, Rumler apologized for not informing the school sooner, but "I cannot write English only Spanish so I always have to wait for opportunity of a friend to do so."[71] Despite such language barriers, many Spanish-speaking students excelled at Tuskegee. For instance, Primitivo Leocadio Miranda of Sagua la Grande, Cuba, was awarded the Funk and Wagnalls Prize for an essay competition, no doubt written in English, and the R. C. Owens Prize for "the best design, including plans, specifications, etc., for a four-room house, to cost no more than $600."[72]

Tuskegee's non-U.S.-born students also navigated their linguistic and cultural differences by establishing their own reading publics and hosting social gatherings. In 1911, the *Tuskegee Student* announced *El ideal latino*, "a little paper in Spanish" published monthly "in the interest of the twenty or more Porto Rican students in attendance."[73] The *Foreign Leaf*, another student paper, began publication in August 1916 "in the interest of the foreign colony at Tuskegee." Claiming to be "the smallest newspaper in the world," it was published monthly and edited by Sotero Quevedo, a "colored linotype operator" in the school's Printing Division. Given the paper's title and description ("in the interest of the foreign colony"), it was likely published in English for students from across the Caribbean, Latin America, and Africa.[74] In 1905, Fermin Domenech of Laguala Grande, Cuba, requested permission to host a reception to celebrate "the 3rd anniversary of the instalation [*sic*] of the Cuban Republic" and that the "Puerto Rican young ladies" be permitted to attend also.[75] In another instance, Tomás Monte Rivera, writing on behalf of Puerto Rican students, requested permission to stage a "little comedy" "as farewell to our American classmates" and a "testimonial of friendship," suggesting that students forged affinities for each other across diasporic and linguistic backgrounds.[76]

As was the case with Cuban and Puerto Rican students, the politics of language and translation influenced the Haiti–Tuskegee connection and may have been one of the reasons for lower Haitian student enrollment. In *The Negro in the New World* (1910), Sir Harry Johnston recounted that he had suggested Tuskegee to a Haitian leader as a place for young men to get a "practical education in tropical agriculture" unavailable in Haiti. Though the leader "agreed as to the value of Tuskegee training," he maintained that the language barrier proved difficult. And yet Tuskegee must have quickly figured out how to accommodate

French-speaking students in one way or another. In 1904, Charles Pierce's essay on Tuskegee's Electrical Engineering Department noted that a young Haitian student "could speak only French last September [when he arrived], but now he can speak English quite fluently." Interestingly, the *Tuskegee Student* announced that J. Em. Martinez, "one of the young men" in the first cohort of Haitian students, "is quite proficient in French and will instruct any who are anxious to take lessons in that fascinating language."[77] The image of a Haitian student teaching French on campus is quite a contrast to the infamous scene in *Up from Slavery* where Washington ridicules an African American youth in the Alabama country districts for studying a French grammar instead of farming or engaging in some other practical labor. This tension demonstrates the disjuncture between Washington and Tuskegee: that is, the school's official narrative, or what it said it was doing, versus what its students, faculty, and in some cases even Washington himself were doing on the ground or behind the scenes. Through its students, Tuskegee campus life was far more multilingual, cosmopolitan, and ultimately dynamic than has been previously imagined.

Correspondence from Haitians in the Tuskegee archives is almost exclusively from parents instead of students, and there is rarely any mention of *Up from Slavery* or its French translation, *L'autobiographie d'un nègre* (1905), suggesting the French text did not have the same influence or broad circulation as the "Cuban-Spanish" translation. However, one Haitian youth, Athanse M. Auguste, noted that he had read Washington's first autobiography, *The Story of My Life and Work*.[78] There is no evidence that it was ever translated into French, so Auguste almost certainly read it in English (though he wrote to Washington in French), indicating that he was bilingual and likely a member of Haiti's middle- and upper-class elite.

Though the voices of Haitian students are not as amplified in the archive as those of their Cuban and Puerto Rican contemporaries, the letters from Haiti provide some insight into the Haitian students' experiences. Haitian parents wrote to Tuskegee in both French and English. In the archive, English translations of letters originally written in French suggest there was someone on staff at Tuskegee who could read French and translate it into English. In a letter dated July 19, 1911, Chrysostome Rosemond, mother of student Maurice Rosemond, wrote to the school about her son's passage from Haiti to Tuskegee. Chrysostome was a lawyer and notary public in Port-au-Prince and part of the country's professional class. She was also an activist who in the 1920s interfaced with the NAACP and Garveyites in the United States and Haiti. She informed Washington that many families "here" desired to learn more about Tuskegee and requested copies of the annual catalog. Rosemond's letter has a typed English translation in the archive and a note that it was "Translated by Mr. Chestnut," perhaps someone on staff at Tuskegee or one of Rosemond's colleagues or acquaintances in Port-au-Prince. An earlier letter from Rosemond noted that her son, Maurice, did not speak English and would need to "fill that gap as soon as possible."[79] Given the grammatical errors, the letter was seemingly translated by someone on staff at Tuskegee, perhaps a Haitian student who had a rudimentary knowledge of English or one of Tuskegee's numerous faculty members who had received a classical education. Their rough translation practice was purely utilitarian, uninvested in artfulness or grammatical correctness: it simply intended to communicate basic ideas and requests between diasporic communities.

Another Haitian parent, Madame Louis-Margron from Jérémie, Haiti, known as the city of poets, wrote to Washington entirely in English. Her son, Gastón, received recommendation letters from the Wesleyan ministries of Jérémie and Port-au-Prince. He traveled from Jérémie to Port-au-Prince, where he was supposed to sojourn on to Tuskegee by way of New York but fell ill and had to delay his travel until he regained his health. Though his mother knew English, Gastón had been educated entirely in French:

> There is only one drawback which I trust will not prevent his coming and that is his education has been entirely in French and except he has taken English as an extra language in his school and is therefore not conversant with that language, but having already a little knowledge of English, he will doubtless soon pick it up being surrounded as he must be by those who only speak English.
>
> As to his preliminary examination I am afraid he will not be able to take it except it be given in French, but as soon as he becomes conversant with that language [English] he will be able to compete satisfactorily with boys of his own age.[80]

Elite Haitians already educated in French and with English-speaking parents or parents with access to English translators would surely have had access to more elite (Black) institutions in the United States than Tuskegee and certainly in France. One wonders, then, what value they placed on a Tuskegee education. Did it come to have a similar meaning that study in France once held? Did the United States—and the rural Jim Crow South, of all places—come to replace France as an educational hub in the Haitian imagination, especially as the United States was becoming an imperial power? Perhaps they were influenced by Jean Price-Mars's promotion of the Tuskegee and Hampton models for Haiti's education system (chapter 4). Or perhaps the students and their parents reasoned that since the students had already received a classical education in Haiti, they should also learn a vocation to help build up the Haitian nation-state. According to the historian Chantalle Verna, "Since the colonial period, class and social status on the island were linked to the connections one had to the outside world. Those privileged to travel abroad or to work with educators who came from abroad gained access to education and skills celebrated for having origins off the island."[81] Thus, some elite Haitians may have also viewed attending Tuskegee and being educated in the United States as a means to buttress or maintain their social status.

Students from the British West Indies, especially Jamaica, often thrived at Tuskegee. Correspondence shows that they traveled from both their respective islands and the Panama Canal Zone, which had drawn a steady flow of British West Indian migrants since the late nineteenth century. In a letter to the editor of the *Gleaner* in April 1913, the Tuskegee student R. Samuel Stennett celebrated the "successes achieved by Jamaicans at Tuskegee." He praised James Lindo, a native of Montserrat, British West Indies, who won more than $40 in essay prizes; Hugh B. Simpson of Black River, Jamaica, who won many prizes, including a gold medal for his oratory; and the valedictorians from Jamaica in 1912 and 1913, George Sharpe and Ethelred E. Campbell, respectively.[82] Though British West Indian students did not have the same language barriers as their Cuban and Haitian counterparts, they still would have had to adjust to the cultural differences of living and learning in the Jim Crow South. Equipped with British colonial educations, Jamaican students tended to be academically well prepared and sought out Tuskegee, among many other reasons, because of a lack of "educational avenues" on the island.[83] As Stennett explained, "The avenues that should be given to the trained Jamaican at home are given to 'imported educators,' and because of this fact they are afraid to advance in the educational field at home, realizing that their efforts will not be repaid."[84]

"SPREADING THE TUSKEGEE SPIRIT"

Upon completing their studies, Tuskegee's southern African American and Caribbean students followed a variety of paths that both accorded with and defied the conception of the southern, Tuskegee New Negro that Washington projected to donors and the outside world. Institutional publications such as *Tuskegee and Its People* and the *Southern Letter*, a monthly newsletter often sent to donors, captured how graduates "spread the Tuskegee spirit." Hailing from southwestern

Alabama, Mary L. Dotson studied domestic science at Tuskegee. After graduating in 1900, she took additional courses in physiology, bacteriology, and cooking demonstration in New York and Boston before returning to Tuskegee as an instructor in the Cooking Division.[85] Born in Macon County, Alabama, Janey Leonard attended Tuskegee in 1895. Although she was unable to complete her education because of an illness, she still attributed her success as a farmer and landowner to Washington and Tuskegee. When her husband was lynched after being accused of murder, she determined not to let his violent death "coward me down." Instead, she took to heart Washington's lectures on how to stay out of debt and "raise plenty food stuff" and the teachings of the county extension agents and "profited by it." Despite an abusive second husband and a divorce in which she lost her land, Janey eventually acquired 180 acres by the late 1930s. Her lawn was "a thing of beauty," noted one observer, and her home "as modern and attractively furnished as any city home," including a "beautiful mahogany living room suite" and a victrola.[86] Indeed, she exemplified how Black women also subscribed to the notion of the bourgeois farmer as the epitome of the southern, Tuskegee New Negro. Charles H. Stevens, a 1902 graduate and native of Heflin, Alabama, became a truck farmer in Herrradura, Cuba, where he grew vegetables and watermelons and sold them locally and to the U.S. market. By 1907, Stevens owned ten acres of land, a three-room house, an orange grove, and one mule; he was clear of debt and even had "a small bank account."[87]

Several of Tuskegee's graduates participated in the school's missionary zeal for establishing "little Tuskegees" "planted in Alabama and other parts" of the Global Black South. In "A Woman's Work," Cornelia Bowen, an 1885 graduate, detailed her journey from a child born on the very "plot of ground upon which the Tuskegee Institute now stands" to director of the Mt. Meigs Institute in Alabama, which was modeled on Tuskegee. Her mother had been enslaved by Colonel William Bowen, who sold to Washington the property where Tuskegee was built. By 1905, Mt. Meigs had educated thousands of students, erected an impressive physical plant, and helped many farmers get "out of debt," teaching them that "a mortgage upon a man's crop . . . [is] as disreputable as a saloon." Graduates proved successful in many of the same industries taught at Tuskegee, and one alumna, in particular, was "a large cotton-planter and general farmer."[88] Bowen later served as president of the Alabama Federation of Colored Women's Clubs and worked alongside Mrs. Washington to establish the Mt. Meigs Reformatory for Juvenile Negro Law-Breakers and later the Mt. Meigs Rescue Home for Girls.

In 1901, Alice Mary Robertson, school supervisor for the Creek Nation in Muskogee, Indian Territory, appealed to Washington for assistance in recruiting teachers from Tuskegee. "You know Tuskegee is a Creek name," she reminded him, signifying the entangled histories of settler colonialism and plantation slavery.[89] Tuskegee had enrolled students from Indian Territory since the 1890s at least, and Washington often touted the success of William Johnson Shoals, an 1899 graduate from Clear Creek, Indian Territory, who owned and operated one of the largest "stock farm[s]" in the territory. He was a "conspicuous example of a Tuskegee graduate who is using his knowledge of stock-raising in a practical way," Washington maintained.[90] By 1906, four Tuskegee graduates and one "ex-student" had helped establish the Hallochee Industrial School in Taft, Indian Territory, and two additional students were "engaged for [the] next term."[91] In 1912, John Wesley Fentress served as "head teacher and disciplinarian at the Tullahassee, Oklahoma School for Creek freedmen," where J. E. Whitfield was "superintendent and special agent."[92] Tuskegee's faculty and students also helped organize agriculture programs at other historically Black colleges and universities, such as when Mr. P. C. Parks, Tuskegee's former farm superintendent, along with several graduates and former students, helped establish the Agricultural Department at present-day Clark Atlanta University in 1908.[93]

Not all efforts at "spreading the Tuskegee spirit" were so successful, however. Recall that Wesley Warren Jefferson abandoned his attempt to transplant the Tuskegee model to Montserrat, determining it was not conducive to the racial-labor conditions there. Stephen Taylor Powell, a 1903 graduate, supervised a land-purchase program for tenants on Hilton Head Island, South Carolina, where "they worked on long terms at low interest." Though Washington supported the scheme, it ultimately failed because of "economic crises, human failings, and natural disasters."[94] Perhaps the most notorious of these efforts, of course, was the school's cotton-growing experiment in Togo, West Africa, where at least one student perished (chapter 1).

Though Washington expected Afro-Caribbean students to return to their home islands and become agents of agricultural and industrial education, a Jamaican education official attending the ICON lamented that "hardly any" of Tuskegee's Jamaican students, "although the expressions of their patriotism are almost pathetic, spoke with confidence of returning home. The attractions of the fuller life that is possible for them in cities and elsewhere in the United States inevitably attract them, and the opportunities of industrial work."[95] The Jamaican students Sharpe and Lindo, for instance, planned to continue their education at Howard University; Campbell would pursue chemical engineering at the University of Illinois, and Simpson decided to pursue further training in electrical engineering. The same was true of African American, Puerto Rican, Cuban, and Haitian students, such as Robert Bonhomme of Port-au-Prince, who went on to earn a certificate in "machine construction" from the School of Science and Technology at the Pratt Institute.[96]

Some Afro-Caribbean students did in fact return to their home islands and pursued employment at their chosen trades. Stennett returned to Jamaica and worked as the "instructor of the compositors and pressmen apprentices at the Government Printing Office."[97] Alberta E. Allwood, a graduate of the Nurse Training Division, returned home to Kingston, where she worked as a "private duty nurse" to "surgical patients."[98] Correspondence from Puerto Rican students suggests that many returned to their island as well. Some wrote of difficulties getting their diplomas and certificates to count for employment and asked Washington and Tuskegee for assistance, while others successfully gained employment as teachers of agriculture, domestic work, English, and Spanish and as general public-school teachers. Writing from Mayaguez, Puerto Rico, Victoria Maria Altiery informed Washington that several Tuskegee graduates were appointed as "special teachers" of agriculture and home economics at the University of Puerto Rico and that their work was "remarked as splendid," a "credit to the Dear Old School."[99]

The *Southern Letter* often published updates from alumni and former students particularly about their experiences in plotting agrarian futures on their home islands. Writing from Fajardo, Puerto Rico, Pedro Concepcion taught agriculture "to the country people," emphasizing "the preparation of the soil, rotation of crops, etc.," because "the people here seem anxious for such instruction . . . [to help them] get the most out of the soil." Louis Lafaye wrote of "rais[ing] potatoes, radish, lettuce, beans, etc." with his students in Barros, Puerto Rico. Recall that Lafaye had previously complained about his studies at Tuskegee in August 1911 and wished to return home, but by May 1913 he was asking Washington to share his successes with fellow Puerto Ricans on campus to encourage them in their studies. Lafaye later led the School of Agriculture of the Disciples of Christ before teaching agriculture at the University of Puerto Rico. Cleveland H. Reeves of Nassau, Bahamas, was employed in the civil service as an "Acting Commissioner, in charge of a district," where he "us[ed] every effort to foster the development of agriculture." Because "the mainstay of my race here is the farm," Reeves reasoned, he committed himself to "preaching to the people the importance of remaining on the soil."[100] Through students like Concepcion, Lafaye, and Reeves who remained faithful to the agricultural aims of the school's racial uplift project, Tuskegee's strategies of eco-ontological regeneration spread throughout the Caribbean, helping poor, rural Black people become intellectuals of the land and circumvent the plantation's ongoing assault on Black life.

BECOMING NEW NEGROES   249

Other Afro-Caribbean students who returned to their home islands pursued altogether alternative paths. Antonio Trujillo Guil of San Juan, Puerto Rico, whom Washington praised as "a worthy young man" with "a good record," returned to the island and pursued a career in law and helped to establish a San Juan cinema company in 1916. Jose D. Miranda, a graduate of the Printing Division, was initially employed in the government printing office in his hometown of Bayamon, Puerto Rico, but eventually pursued a political career and was elected mayor of Bayamon, a city with a population of 75,000. Miranda was the youngest mayor in the city's history.[101]

On November 20, 1915, an item in the *Cuba News*, a Havana-based periodical, reported that "many Cubans have been educated at the Booker T. Washington school, and they have every one made good citizens on their return to their native land."[102] Juan Eusebio Gómez and Alfredo Pérez Encinosa in particular leveraged their Tuskegee educations to enter the island's Black professional class. In 1905, Gómez, who, we should recall, had refused to eat the student meals in 1899, published a feature article on Booker T. Washington and the Tuskegee Negro Conference in *La lucha*. The intrepid Encinosa wrote a social column for *La lucha* that covered Afro-Cuban social clubs, the theater, and musical performances.[103] Gómez and Encinosa had been friends and classmates at Tuskegee, likely bonding over their similar trajectories and experiences migrating between Cuba and Alabama. Back in Cuba, Gómez was lauded for taking the transnational journey to study at Tuskegee and would eventually follow in his father's footsteps, becoming a Cuban diplomat and serving as vice consul to Liverpool.[104]

Encinosa worked at several Cuban periodicals in this period. In addition to writing for *La lucha*, he translated the Tuskegee catalog for Serra's periodical *Nuevo Criollo* and, prior to that, worked as a "messenger boy" for the *Havana Post* during summer vacation. He was an avid recruiter for the school, writing to Emmett J. Scott in August 1901 to request an annual catalog to "show . . . to some of my friends."[105] Encinosa's columns on art, theater, and music suggest that the Afro-Cuban students who attended Tuskegee conceived of themselves as New Negroes, or Nuevo Criollos, much like the members of the Booker T. Washington Society in Havana (chapter 3). By 1912, at twenty-nine years old, Encinosa was living and working as a professional interpreter in Milan, Italy.[106] Hailing from Havana, he was perhaps already urban, but it was his education in rural Alabama, where he worked as a "laundryman," that enabled his transnational mobility and cosmopolitan career. Such were the affordances of a Tuskegee education.

FROM TUSKEGEE TO HARLEM AND BEYOND

The archive of student and parent correspondence and the school's institutional publications illuminate how literary production, translation, and circulation facilitated Tuskegee's influence throughout the Global Black South in the first two decades of the twentieth century. In the years following Washington's death in 1915, the demographic, cultural, and political shifts brought on by the Great Migration and World War I transplanted the locus of Black diasporic relation in the United States to the urban industrial North, enabling the emergence of an even more dynamic articulation of the New Negro. To be sure, labor and education were still important battlegrounds, but literature and art were the new domains for cultivating and giving expression to Black modern subjectivity. As James Weldon Johnson observed in the preface to *The Book of American Negro Poetry* (1922), "No people that has produced great literature and art has ever been looked upon by the world as distinctly inferior."[107] Though Tuskegee was no longer an epicenter of Black diasporic activity, many of Tuskegee's students and faculty would go on to become members of the Black intellectual and cultural elite of the Harlem Renaissance and the broader New Negro Movement. Furthermore, contributors to several of the era's most important publications and ur-texts of Black literary modernism and diasporic practice—*The New Negro* anthology (1925), *Opportunity* magazine, *Negro: An Anthology* (1934), and *La revue du monde noir*—acknowledged Washington and Tuskegee's indelible influence on the movement as well as their continued relevance to the goals and desires of the new generation.

In 1925, the publication of Alain Locke's *The New Negro* anthology announced the arrival of the Harlem Renaissance and the New Negro Movement. Strikingly, it acknowledged Washington's contribution to the movement at the very outset. In "Negro Art and America," the second essay in the volume, the contributor Albert C. Barnes dated the commencement of the "Negro renascence" to 1895, when the poet Paul Laurence Dunbar and Washington, "an educator in the practical business of life," "began to attract the world's attention." Barnes continued: "Washington showed that by a new kind of education the Negro could attain to an economic condition that enables him to preserve his identity, free his soul and make himself an important factor in American life."[108] Tuskegee's president, Robert Moton, also contributed an essay to the anthology, "Hampton–Tuskegee: Missioners of the Masses," describing how these schools shaped Black progress. After the Civil War, with limited opportunities for African Americans, Washington showed the "Negro race" how to create a "life for themselves," Moton argued, and as industrial opportunities opened up in the

North after World War I, men and women educated at southern historically Black institutions such as "Hampton, Tuskegee, Howard, Fisk, Atlanta, More-house, and Wiley" made up many of the skilled Black industrial laborers as well as professionals and businesspeople who migrated to the region, following their clients. Most importantly, Moton demonstrated how these southern-educated men and women were the race leaders who fueled the northern arm of the New Negro Movement by "helping their people to take advantage of new opportunities and adjust themselves to new and sometimes hostile conditions."[109] Multiple references to Washington, Tuskegee, and the U.S. South throughout *The New Negro* suggest that the architects of the movement understood and readily acknowledged their significance to Black modernity, even as later generations have tended to de-emphasize or explicitly overlook them.

In 1928, Charles S. Johnson, editor of the National Urban League's monthly magazine *Opportunity*, defended Washington's legacy in his essay "The Social Philosophy of Booker T. Washington." The National Urban League was integral to the literary phase of the Harlem Renaissance. In 1924, the organization hosted a literary contest and awards banquet that helped to bring some of the era's most prominent Black writers, including Zora Neale Hurston and Countee Cullen, to national prominence. In his essay on Washington's social philosophy, Johnson argued that many of Washington's ideals were congruent with the artistic aims of the New Negro Movement. "The most effective interest of the present is art, and even of this it may be said that it is an elaboration of Washington's principles of stressing work rather than the rewards of work." Johnson conceded that many Black people viewed Washington's promotion of work as "a kind of treachery" because they associated work with slavery. "This, however, was a prop for the broad economic platform which Washington attempted to lay," he explained in an effort to redeem Washington's increasingly beleaguered legacy. Johnson further argued that Washington's efforts to create parity between Black people and other races and cultures were "no different from the present course of the Negro writers and artists who, in their new representations of Negro life are doing the very thing for which he found a phrase": "You can beat me being a white man but I can beat you being a Negro," precisely the sentiment Washington attempted to impress upon Tuskegee's music faculty (chapter 2).[110] Rev. Arthur E. Massey contributed a similarly complimentary account of Washington and his work in *Negro: An Anthology*, Nancy Cunard's monumental attempt "to document the discourses of black internationalism" by assembling a hodgepodge of works on Black diasporic art and politics.[111] In capturing the global dimensions of the New Negro, Cunard's anthology conceived of Washington and Tuskegee as integral to its framing of Black resilience in slavery's aftermath.

Tuskegee's presence in *La revue du monde noir*, a foundational text of the Negritude Movement, has largely been underexamined as well. Clara W. Shepard, "instructress" of French in Tuskegee's high school program from 1930 to 1936, was among the journal's primary translators. She published two essays on Washington's work and the importance of teaching French to Tuskegee's African American students, indicating the school's ongoing significance within Black internationalist discourse in the 1930s. Shepard received her BS from the University of Pennsylvania and earned a "Teacher's Diploma" from the Sorbonne at the University of Paris, where she studied French language and literature while on leave from Tuskegee in 1931.[112] This is likely when she met Paulette and Jane Nardal, the Martinican writers and sisters who cofounded *La revue*. Shepard and Paulette were the primary translators of the journal's articles and short stories. Shepard also wrote "responses to certain articles by other contributors," including brief commentary on Black women's fashion in Harlem. Brent Hayes Edwards thus characterizes the journal as "a remarkable collaboration between a francophone Caribbean woman and an African American woman."[113]

In her first essay for the journal, published in its second issue, Shepard maintained that Tuskegee had "exerted a distinctive influence upon the educational development of the United States," so much so that even "white America has at last realized the futility of an Academic education for the masses" and has "eagerly accepted industrial education," as evinced by its introduction at schools such as Columbia University. Though white philanthropists in the nineteenth century once viewed industrial education as inferior and thus the only form of education fit for Black people, she wrote, Washington's "broader view saw in the closely correlated training of the mind and hand the economic salvation of the Negro." Shepard detailed Tuskegee's physical and educational growth and transformation, including the addition of a "college department," and noted that in a survey conducted in 1929 students expressed "an overwhelming preference for educational courses leading not only to the instruction of elementary pupils but to vocational agriculture and home economics." Tuskegee had so honed its method of "educating the rural public" that the extension program, "now controlled by the government," boasted a diversified program that included the Moveable School, "an annual farmer's conference, a farm demonstration agency, and a bureau of information." Shepard further championed Tuskegee for its contributions to Black commercial and economic development by introducing "skilled Negro labour" into predominately white industries and noting how the National Negro Business League facilitated Black "economic independence."[114]

Shepard's first essay in *La revue* presented Tuskegee to francophone intellectuals as a vector of Black educational innovation and economic uplift, and her second essay promoted bilingualism as the key to Black agrarian futures and diasporic affiliation, particularly for southern African Americans. In "The Utility of foreign Languages for american Negroes [*sic*]," Shepard drew on her experiences teaching at Tuskegee, which by then offered French in both its high school and college curricula. Learning French, she argued, kindled students' curiosity to learn more about the French language and culture and "the vast world of French-speaking Negroes." Through this work, she hoped to empower African American students with examples of autonomous farmers in other parts of the Black world. Shepard reflected:

> One of the most animated discussions of the entire year in my class room was a debate concerning the advantages of small property owners, which include the majority of the French peasants, as compared to the situation of the tenant share croppers who form the Negro peasantry of the United States. How much more informative my talk would have been if I had been able to bring to my students facts about the situation of Negroes plantations owners [*sic*] and farmers in the French West Indies or in Africa. For many years, the Negro farmers of the southern states have been complaining that the whites have systematically deprived them of all profit in the cotton trade. Perhaps the example of Negro farms in Dahomey and Cameroun organized especially to export raw products, and thus eliminate the middle man, will inspire the younger generation to leap over the obstacle created by the fear and the lack of solidarity which characterized their fathers.

Knowledge of the "remedies which other groups of Negroes have employed in order to demand their rights," Shepard continued, would expand African Americans' sense of the possible and awaken them to the "shortcomings of the American system." Ultimately, Shepard posited the foreign-language classroom as a space for cultivating Black autonomy through diasporic solidarity. "The American Negro student, no matter what his future occupation may be, needs to be interested in the world progress of Negroes."[115]

Though much of Tuskegee's internationalism emphasized a unidirectional flow of information from the United States to the Caribbean, Latin America, and Africa, Shepard reversed the direction and argued that African American students could benefit from learning about Black agriculturalists in the French-speaking Black world. Significantly, she imagined this bilingual, Black transnational network unfolding among farmers and through agriculture. Contrary to Washington's now-infamous criticism of a poor African American boy studying a French grammar in rural Alabama, Tuskegee was not only teaching French by the 1930s but also, through Shepard, envisioning French and the foreign-language classroom more broadly as a modality and space for cultivating Black agrarian futures and solidarities throughout the Black world.

Moton's and Shepard's contributions to two of the most influential New Negro publications as well as the profiles on Washington in *Opportunity* and *Negro: An Anthology* indicate how a southern African American institution continued to contribute culturally and intellectually to the next generation of Black diasporic artists and political leaders. Nevertheless, Tuskegee's influence throughout the Global Black South was largely felt through its students. Several of the schemes to facilitate economic cooperation between African Americans and Haitians, for instance, were led by either Tuskegee's African American graduates or African American businesspeople who were directly influenced by Washington's economic self-help philosophy through the National Negro Business League.[116]

In the early 1930s, the Negro Progress Convention of British Guiana embarked on one of the most explicit efforts to transplant the Tuskegee model to another Global Black South locale, thus demonstrating the school's continued influence during the New Negro Movement. Founded in 1922, the convention promoted "the virtue of self-help and thrift and the great benefits to be derived from fields of economic and industrial endeavour." In 1931, the convention sent two elementary teachers, Mr. James L. Kidney and Ms. Vesta Lowe, to Tuskegee to receive training in agriculture, animal husbandry, home economics, "and kindred subjects." In 1932, the convention acquired five hundred acres of land on "an old coffee, cocoa and fruit plantation" to establish an industrial school "on the lines of Tuskegee as far as practicable" and "to form a centenary memorial of negro emancipation." The convention's organizers sought advice from the colony's Department of Science and Agriculture and eventually purchased an estate located at Land of Canaan on the East Bank of the Demerara River, sixteen miles from Georgetown, British Guiana. The convention petitioned the British imperial government for a "free grant" to fund the scheme, arguing that its good influence would be "far reaching" for both the district and "the colony as a whole." As at Tuskegee, students would be expected to work on the farm to help defray costs. Despite the "charge" that "the young people despise the soil and aspire only to avenues of clerical service," the convention was "convinced" that "large numbers of boys and girls fresh from the elementary and secondary schools... are ready and willing to undergo training for life in agricultural and industrial pursuits, and this number will increase with the years." Although the imperial government denied the request, it commended the convention for showing how much it could "accomplish unaided." After returning to British Guiana, Kidney and Lowe, the two elementary teachers the convention had sent to Tuskegee, defected from their agreement to help establish "a Local Tuskegee" and instead sought employment with the government, one as "superintendent of meals at the public hospital" and "one on the Agricultural Bias Scheme of the Education Department."[117] They were pursuing the otherwise affordances of their Tuskegee educations. Despite their defection, it is important to remember that it was still their affiliation with Tuskegee that enabled their social mobility in the first place. Finally, the convention's proposed transformation of an old cocoa, coffee, and fruit plantation into an agricultural and industrial school as a strategy for Black modernity and uplift was directly inspired by Tuskegee's vision and shows how repurposing the plantation remained an important strategy for Black diasporic communities throughout the Global Black South.

As we proceed through plot III, we will explore the lives and work of three of Tuskegee's most prominent students—Claude McKay, Zora Neale Hurston, and Marcus Garvey. Through these figures, I examine how the Tuskegee project became a springboard for Black social mobility in dynamic and often unpredictable ways that enabled these figures, like the Cuban, Puerto Rican, Haitian, Jamaican, and Guianese students described here, to exceed Washington's vision of the bourgeois New Negro farmer even as they often retained select aspects of Tuskegee's political and ideological commitments. Crucially, each of them wrestled with and expressed ambivalence toward Washington and Tuskegee at some point. In McKay's and Hurston's cases, Tuskegee's focus on uplifting the masses through agriculture and industry under Washington's leadership was translated into a preoccupation with the folk. Whereas Washington was invested in uplift as a social class project that emphasized the politics of respectability and the civilizing mission, McKay's and Hurston's respective theories of Black modernity and diasporic affiliation explicitly rejected this component of the Tuskegee project. They instead embraced Black working-class people as progenitors of culture, organic intellectuals, and agents of "peasant cosmopolitanism" who had a right to self-determination (even as they also ensnared these people in primitivist logics). Similarly, Garvey translated Washington's promotion of economic self-help and Tuskegee's symbolic value as an all-Black institution into a pan-Africanist philosophy at the intersection of Black economic internationalism and empire.

If Tuskegee represented the repurposed antebellum plantation as a strategy for Black modernity, then this cohort of students grappled with yet another of the plantation's afterlives: how the rise of corporate plantation agriculture and industrial capitalism—for example, UFCO, the Everglades Cypress Lumber Company, and the Panama Canal—facilitated the mobility of Black rural and working-class peoples throughout the Global Black South. The Black rural and working classes who migrated to these frontier geographies for better economic opportunities were both the subjects of the Harlem literati's cultural and political projects and their contemporaries. They, too, were New Negroes, working in the bowels of global capitalism as the plantation took on new forms and expanded to new geographies. Through fiction and poetry, anthropology and performance, grassroots organizing and institution building, McKay, Hurston, and Garvey depict the cultural and intellectual dynamism of the Global Black South and Tuskegee's ongoing impact on Black aesthetic and political modernity.

6

At the Crossroads of Diaspora and Empire

Harvesting a Plot Logic in Claude McKay's Jamaica

In the summer of 1912, a twenty-two-year-old Claude McKay migrated from his rural village in the "green hills" of Sunny Ville, Jamaica, to rural Tuskegee, Alabama. For the first leg of his journey, he traveled aboard a United Fruit Company steamship from Port Antonio, Jamaica, one of the island's leading banana ports and commercial centers. He disembarked in Charleston, South Carolina—a city whose ties to Jamaica and the British West Indies dates back to the colonial era—and boarded a train bound for Tuskegee.[1] There, McKay was to study agronomy and eventually return to Jamaica to educate the peasantry in improved agricultural methods. Whereas most Afro-Caribbean migrants to the United States in the early twentieth century settled in northern, urban industrial centers, McKay's initial migration was to the U.S. South, a region that, much like his native Jamaica, was still in the grips of the plantation.

McKay's decision to attend Tuskegee proceeded from the publication of his debut poetry collection, *Songs of Jamaica*, in January 1912. The collection was favorably reviewed across the British Empire, earning McKay the "medal of the Institute of Arts and Sciences."[2] Despite his literary success, however, the young McKay still needed to find a steady income to support himself. After an unsatisfactory experience in the Jamaican constabulary—the focus of his second poetry collection, *Constab Ballads*, published in the late fall of 1912—and an unsuccessful attempt at finding a trade, McKay determined to migrate to "America."[3] His mentor, Walter Jekyll, initially abhorred his decision to go to America, given the rampant anti-Blackness there, especially in the South. Yet Jekyll also knew that with McKay's newfound success, he "could not just remain on the island as a poet or a peasant proprietor."[4] McKay recalls in *My Green Hills of Jamaica*, his memoir of his Jamaican boyhood and adolescence: "At that time the British Imperial Government was taking stock of the needs of the West India peasantry. They had sent out agricultural instructors from England to teach the peasants how they could cultivate the land much better. Mr. Jekyll thought that if I went to America and received a good education in agriculture I could also be an instructor. That would keep me close to the peasantry and their aspirations and ways of thinking."[5] In this way, both British colonialism and agriculture facilitated McKay's initial diasporic migration to the U.S. South. His life and work call our attention to the entanglements of movement and stasis, migration and agricultural cultivation, diaspora and empire at the heart of the Black modern condition. Indeed, the Global Black South is a geography of just such contradictions.

McKay received considerable encouragement to attend Tuskegee. Lady Henrietta Vinton Davis, an African American actress and elocutionist who was performing "selections from Shakespeare" at a local Jamaican theater at the time, supported his decision. Davis was a good friend of Booker T. Washington and would later become "one of the leading personages and one of the most brilliant speakers of the Marcus Garvey Black Star Line and Back-to-Africa-movement." She assured McKay that he would be "well protected" at Tuskegee, despite the penchant for anti-Black violence in the United States.[6] McKay also met with Mr. W. H. Plant, headmaster of the Titchfield School in Port Antonio, Jamaica, who had visited Tuskegee earlier that year as a delegate to the ICON and had reported on his impressions of the school in the Jamaican press. Mr. Plant "felt that America was a great, big, wonderfully industrialized country where I could receive a very liberal education," McKay recalls, "and that at Tuskegee I would be protected from prejudice because the student body was so large; and with the prestige of Dr. Washington, the white people themselves depending on Tuskegee for a living."[7] So in the summer of 1912, McKay departed from Port Antonio aboard a UFCO steamship bound for Charleston, South Carolina.

Scholars generally mention McKay's south-to-south migration from Jamaica to Tuskegee but typically reduce it to a biographical note, a strange detour amid his larger and more significant transnational migrations to Europe, North Africa, and Russia.[8] McKay himself did not write much about the experience, either. Consequently, there has been very little attention to how his hemispheric migration may have contributed to conceptions of Black transnationalism and diaspora within his oeuvre.[9] I argue in this chapter that the conditions surrounding his initial transnational migration yield important insights into how the plantation and agricultural labor continued to animate Black diasporic

AT THE CROSSROADS OF DIASPORA AND EMPIRE   259

movement in the aftermath of slavery. Indeed, McKay traveled at the intersection of several hemispheric networks, all of which emerged in the afterlife of the plantation: the migration of Caribbean students and intellectuals to Tuskegee; Caribbean labor migration to UFCO's corporate plantations in Central America and the Panama Canal; the burgeoning Caribbean tourist industry; and the hemispheric trade in bananas and other fruits. By reading McKay's Jamaican writings within the context of these various networks of hemispheric movement and exchange, I illuminate the Global Black South as an important geography wherein Black rural and working-class peoples—the very subjects of Tuskegee's uplift discourse—were in fact agents of modern cultural and intellectual production whose south–south migrations enabled them to cultivate a "peasant cosmopolitanism," or worldliness from below.

In what follows, I explore McKay's hemispheric migration to Tuskegee against the backdrop of the ICON and the rise of UFCO and the banana trade. Through the ICON, I examine the ideological affinities and dissonances between Jamaica's and Tuskegee's education officials that facilitated McKay's initial migration to the U.S. South. I then turn to McKay's Jamaican poetry and fiction to explore how his background as the son of prosperous peasants during the age of UFCO and the banana trade shaped his conception of agrarian futures and decision to pursue agronomy at Tuskegee. I argue that McKay possessed a plot logic that moved within and against Tuskegee's conception of the southern New Negro. Much like Washington and Carver, McKay championed rural, agricultural peoples and viewed farming as a distinctly intellectual enterprise; however, he rejected uplift and class paternalism and was fundamentally committed to Jamaican peasants' right to determine their own futures. Also, whereas Washington emphasized rootedness and discouraged migration, McKay's plot logic embraced both rootedness and labor migration as equally legitimate strategies for navigating the plantation's precarious afterlife.

McKay's ultimate ideological break with Tuskegee is perhaps best captured by his decision to leave the institute after only a few months, disapproving of the "semi-military, machine-like existence" there.[10] His attempted transplantation to the soils of the U.S. South did not take, and he lived a rather peripatetic lifestyle thereafter. However, by the mid-1930s and into the 1940s, McKay came to appreciate and defend Tuskegee as a model of Black self-determination, the possibilities of group aggregation, and the importance of race pride. In concluding this chapter, I argue that an older McKay was convinced that despite Washington's political limitations, there was something both commendable and salvageable about Tuskegee as an "exclusive Negro college" (or all-Black institution) that could be reworked and repurposed to meet the political and socioeconomic challenges that lay ahead. In this way, this chapter demonstrates how the plot logic undergirding McKay's advocacy for the peasantry—his fundamental commitment to Black self-determination—ties his Jamaican writings to his later reassessment of Tuskegee and, ultimately, how the conditions surrounding his initial migration from Jamaica to the U.S. South remained central to his conceptions of Black modernity and diasporic relation.

"THE PEASANT'S PASSION FOR THE SOIL POSSESSES ME": MCKAY'S PLOT LOGIC

Claude McKay enrolled at Tuskegee on the heels of the International Conference on the Negro in 1912, a three-day meeting held on campus that convened 125 missionary, educational, and government officials from twenty-one foreign countries who shared an interest in the development of Afro-descended peoples in the United States, Africa, the Caribbean, and South America. Jamaica, which already had a strong presence in Tuskegee's student body and faculty, sent a delegation of educational experts (the largest in fact) to ascertain the extent to which agricultural and industrial education could supplement the island colony's education system.[11] Like McKay, many attendees would have traveled to Tuskegee along the routes of hemispheric labor migration, commerce, and trade that conveyed Afro-Caribbean migrants to the Panama Canal Zone. The United States had taken over construction of the Panama Canal in 1904, importing thousands of Afro-Caribbean migrants to perform the grueling and often life-threatening labor of clearing jungles and digging a massive hole in the earth for the passage of international commerce and spread of global capitalism. Afro-Caribbean labor migrants also pursued employment on neoplantations established by agribusinesses such as the U.S.-based multinational, the United Fruit Company. By the early twentieth century, UFCO had a virtual monopoly on the hemispheric trade in bananas among the Caribbean, Central America, and the United States. It also owned a luxury steamship service known as the Great White Fleet that transported white, North American tourists to tropical vacations. McKay traveled aboard one of these steamers for his first transnational journey—signaling how the Black educational, intellectual, and political network between Tuskegee and Jamaica was deeply entangled with U.S. imperial expansion and corporate colonialism.

Recent scholarship on McKay's transnationalism has focused largely on vagabondage, communism, and horticulture, linking him to international movements and cosmopolitan circles in Harlem, Europe, Russia, and Africa. By situating his Jamaican writings within this broader sociopolitical context, I propose that hemispheric mobility is another important aspect of Black transnationalism in his life and work—namely, how Afro-Caribbean students and labor migrants actively participated in and conceived of the "practice of diaspora" on their own terms.[12] Scholars have also recently emphasized the ecology of McKay's transnational poetics. Josh Gosciak, for instance, examines how the popularity of horticulture in turn-of-the century England influenced McKay's poetry, thereby resituating him within the British pastoral tradition. Through horticulture, Gosciak maintains, McKay "rework[ed] the pastoral on an international scale to suit his colonial temperament."[13] Sonya Posmentier establishes agricultural "cultivation as literally at the root of McKay's poetic production, and as a key poetic process through which he transformed his Jamaican identity into a diasporic one."[14] By foregrounding the afterlife of the plantation in McKay's Jamaican poetry and fiction—especially UFCO and the rise of the banana trade—I contribute to this discussion of how Black diasporic mobility was inextricably tied to agricultural practices and spaces.

As a peasant-poet turned migrant, McKay defied the very conceptual biases of Black transnational and diaspora studies, which tends to regard agriculture and mobility as discreet and unrelated practices. The *roots* of planting and farming literally facilitated McKay's ability to travel along the *routes* of the Global Black South. As he awaited his departure to the United States to study agronomy at Tuskegee, for instance, McKay planted and cultivated crops: "We wrote to the Tuskegee Institute, and the reply came back that I could enter," McKay recalls in *My Green Hills of Jamaica*. "Meanwhile I did a lot of planting. With the help of the peasants I planted yams and conga peas, black-eyed peas and red peas as well as sweet potatoes, yams and like things."[15] Whereas Paul Gilroy's Black Atlantic paradigm focuses on migratory routes and genealogical roots, McKay's depiction of the relationship between farming and migration directs our attention to agricultural roots and the politics of land and soil in the Global Black South.

At the same time that growing and selling crops facilitated McKay's migration to Tuskegee economically, the global market demand for cash crops also animated Jamaican peasants' labor migration to the United States and Central America. At Tuskegee, Washington and Carver used agriculture to promote rootedness, domesticity, and placemaking, but in McKay's work the relationship between Black life and plant life is also tied to movement and migration. McKay came of age during the rise of tourism and the fruit trade in the Caribbean, so his work often depicts trans-plantation—that is, how corporate colonialism and the neoplantation facilitated the simultaneous movement of people and plants throughout the hemisphere. His Jamaican writings, set in the early 1900s as U.S. imperialism surged, depict the exigencies of rural life on the island, from the day-to-day strivings of peasant proprietors to accumulate land, cultivate their fields, and sell their harvests to the dire economic conditions that pushed them to migrate to the United States and its imperial outposts. By representing the experiences of Jamaican peasants in motion, McKay's writings illuminate peasant cosmopolitanism, by which rural labor migrants cultivated a worldliness and sophistication typically associated with urban elites in the Global North.

Ultimately, the vision of Black agrarian futures that emerges from McKay's work celebrates both stasis and movement: the ambitious peasant farmer who aims to make their way on the land and the labor migrant who chooses to immigrate to Costa Rican banana plantations and the Panama Canal. McKay's insistence on peasants' right to self-determination is the defining feature of his plot logic that unifies these ostensibly disparate visions. If Tuskegee's experiment plot emphasized sustenance, domesticity, self-help, and eco-ontological regeneration, McKay also emphasized the plot's historical role as "a source of cultural guerilla resistance to the plantation system" that afforded enslaved Africans and their descendants a sense of "pleasure," a "measure of autonomy," and a "measure of control over time and space." Ultimately, McKay's plot logic captures how provision grounds functioned as "symbolic fields for the production of individual selves by way of the production of material goods."[16]

As the son of Jamaican peasants, McKay would have been intimately familiar with the plot's material, physical benefits as well as with its eco-ontological and individualizing potential. Guided by his contention that "the peasant's passion for the soil possesses me," I approach the plot as an important analytic for interrogating his dynamic and sophisticated depictions of rurality and agriculture in his Jamaican writings.[17] McKay's plot logic was not simply a romantic pastoralism but rather harvested from this eco-ontological space a peasant sensibility that insisted on the *right* to self-determination and individualism, even if it meant migrating away from home and navigating the precarious waters of U.S. imperialism and corporate colonialism.[18] In short, McKay redefined Black rural and agricultural life as at once intellectually sophisticated (rather than backward) and transnational (rather than exclusively local and rooted), and he articulated an important class critique of Tuskegee's racial uplift project by taking the peasant masses seriously as agents of their own futures. Unlike the cultural and intellectual elite of Washington's generation, McKay and his New Negro contemporaries critiqued and departed from uplift's class paternalism in hopes of capturing Black modern subjectivity from below. By centering the language, worldviews, and values of the peasantry in his Jamaican poetry and fiction, McKay unsettled the divide between rural and urban, local and global, folk and modern. He used his artistic authority to represent the complexity of peasants' lived experiences, however crude, unrespectable, or irreverent. In contradistinction to the racial paternalism of the colonial plantation and the class paternalism of uplift, McKay's plot logic was fundamentally antielitist and egalitarian, and it unapologetically promoted the peasantry's freedom of thought and movement.

DIASPORA IN THE MIDST OF EMPIRE: JAMAICA AND THE INTERNATIONAL CONFERENCE ON THE NEGRO

Between 1911 and 1913, the years immediately leading up to and following McKay's departure to the United States, Tuskegee was featured prominently in the Jamaican press. The school's announcement for the ICON circulated frequently in at least two Jamaican periodicals—the *Daily Gleaner* and the *Jamaica Times*, a literary newspaper—to recruit a delegation from the island. By 1912, Tuskegee already had a small cohort of Jamaicans, approximately twenty-three students and seven staff, who, as noted in chapter 5, established an affinity group called the Britisher's Union. In November 1911, the group published an article in the *Gleaner* encouraging government officials to send delegates to the ICON. The article was published on the same page as—and just two columns over from—a notice announcing McKay's resignation from the Jamaican constabulary. Furthermore, in February 1912 the group published an article in the *Jamaica Times* titled "All About Tuskegee: When and How to Enter," encouraging more students from the British West Indies to attend the institute.[19] McKay, who enrolled at Tuskegee a few months after the conference, would almost certainly have witnessed the excitement over Tuskegee in the Jamaican press because he was friends with Tom Redcam, editor of the *Jamaica Times*, and his earliest poems and essays were published in the *Daily Gleaner* during these years.

While the Britisher's Union was advertising and recruiting in the island's newspapers, Jamaican intellectuals on the island were also reading publications from Tuskegee and Hampton. By February 1912, it was decided that the Jamaican government would send a delegation to the ICON to ascertain whether Washington's agricultural and industrial education model was conducive to the island colony's education system. In "A Word to Our Tuskegee Delegates," published in the *Jamaica Times* a few months before the conference, the author implored delegates to represent Jamaica proudly and to show that "we too, in the British West Indies, have not been lagging behind." The author's admonishment was prompted by and written in response to an article in a publication either "from Tuskegee or Hampton" that disparaged "the West Indian Negro, using *Negro of course as the American does for all colored persons*," for not producing "eminent men such as the Southern States could show," despite having more "freedom" and less "persecution." To underscore the point, the author cited a Mr. Lehmann, an American visitor to Jamaica, who claimed that Mr. W. H. Plant—one of the delegates to the ICON and regarded by some as "the Booker. T. Washington of Jamaica"—was in fact "a man of higher culture and Education than Booker T. Washington." Ultimately, the author impressed upon the delegates to "make it clear and sure that, whatever we are aspiring after and working to get [by going to the United States], we are loyal to our Empire and King and value substantial benefits within it."[20] The author's declaration of fealty to the British Empire illuminates how the Tuskegee–Jamaica connection operated at the complex intersection of diaspora and empire.

The literary critic Faith Smith underscores this tension between diaspora and empire as well, but from Tuskegee's perspective. In soliciting Jamaican delegates for the conference who demonstrated a commitment to racial uplift, Smith argues, Washington sought out "patriarchal authorization" from colonial administrators.[21] But this argument overlooks an important nuance in his request. When Washington asked the colonial secretary to put him in contact with "natives," or Afro-Jamaicans, who were engaged in "helping uplift their people, so we can write them directly," he sought to forge diasporic ties *through* colonial officials, not necessarily *with* them.[22] As in his vision for Tuskegee within the segregated United States, Washington aimed to promote Black self-determination in Jamaica *within* the system of British colonialism—just as Afro-Jamaican commentators in the *Jamaican Times* expressed fealty to the British Empire. Well before the anticolonial struggles of the 1930s and 1940s, Washington, like many of his Afro-Jamaican contemporaries, accepted that British colonial authority was the law of the land. Both Washington and the Jamaican commentator reflect Frank Guridy's contention that "diaspora-making was a complex process embedded in, but not reducible to, the dynamics of imperial power relations."[23]

The conference proceedings were quite attentive to nuances of Black diasporic identity, particularly how delegates from different parts of the world thought about agricultural and industrial education. As the *Tuskegee Student* noted in its report on the conference, whereas delegates representing Africa were interested primarily in mission work, West Indian delegates were recently interested in industrial education, but even within this group there were differences. "The representatives from Barbadoes [*sic*] were all Negroes," who "came apparently as representatives of the colored people, rather than the government, and were concerned not merely with the education, but with the industrial development of the colored people." However, "the Jamaica delegation"—composed of "a white man," a "brown-skinned man," and "a plain black," distinctions "only worth noting," the *Tuskegee Student* maintained, "because in all the English colonies, the colored or mulatto population is distinct from the Negro"—"was interested in the subject of education, not from the view point of race, but of method."[24] Calling to mind the *Jamaica Times* article, the reporter made clear that conceptions of race and Blackness in Jamaica were fundamentally different from those in the United States.

In his conference address on the status of the "Negro" in Jamaica, Mr. W. H. Plant reinforced this distinction. "In Jamaica the negro as such has no separate existence—no distinct race line is drawn. In short there is no *colour line*." Though he acknowledged that class prejudice existed "very strongly," particularly among the "upper coloured classes," he insisted that the "white and coloured" in Jamaica have equal access to education, religion, business, trade, travel, and justice: "The commonest negro peasant in Jamaica has the same treatment in our law courts as the largest landed proprietor or shipping magnate." Thus, Plant found it difficult to report on the "'progress of the negro race'" in Jamaica, for it "has been contributed to by both races . . . [and] benefitted all classes of the community and not one race." According to Plant, "the Jamaica delegation" was less interested in industrial education as a strategy for Black self-determination and racial uplift than in learning techniques and methods for improving the colony's educational system more generally.[25] In contrast to Plant, however, the Britisher's Union's presentation at the ICON's final session "emphasiz[ed] the importance of industrial education for the masses of the colored people on the island." In doing so, its representatives explicitly foregrounded racial uplift as their primary motivation for transplanting Tuskegee's methods to the British West Indies, implying that racial inequality was indeed a problem in the empire, even if it manifested itself less brutally than in the United States.[26]

Nevertheless, later that year Washington strategically translated Plant's claims to address racial injustice in the United States, further indicating the ICON's political significance for the Black diaspora. In "Is the Negro Having a Fair Chance?" Washington juxtaposed the conditions of African Americans with those of West Indians, Jamaicans in particular. Though he ultimately determined that African Americans enjoyed better opportunities because they did not immigrate to other countries, he conceded, "In the matter of political and civil rights, including protection of life and property and even-handed justice in the courts, negroes in the West Indies have the advantage of negroes in the United States." While "there is much agitation" regarding the "'race problem'" in the United States, "one hears almost nothing" of it in Jamaica. "Jamaica has neither mobs, race riots, lynchings, nor burnings, such as disgrace our civilization. In that country there is likewise no bitterness between white men and black men. . . . [T]he laws are conceived and executed with exact and absolute justice, without regard to race or color."[27] Washington almost certainly used the information he acquired from Plant and other Jamaican delegates at the ICON to shed light on the appalling U.S. record on African American political and civil rights. Though he did not criticize the United States outright, the stark contrast he painted between conditions there and conditions in Jamaica was an indictment in itself.

Throughout 1912 and 1913, "the Jamaica delegation" gave numerous lectures and reports on their visit to Tuskegee for the ICON as well as on their visits to Hampton Institute, Howard University, and schools in Canada. Many of their lectures were published in the *Gleaner*, and their official report to the government was published in a supplement to the *Jamaica Gazette*, suggesting that there was a broader conversation on the island about agricultural and industrial education. In one of his lectures, Plant noted that Jamaica's academic education exceeded that of Black U.S. institutions, but its industrial education program lagged behind and could benefit from techniques employed at Tuskegee. He defended his conference position on the absence of color prejudice in Jamaica, insisting "there is no country that treats its people like good old England, the home of freedom, virtue and goodness." Following his address, Plant exhibited and commented on pictures of Washington, Tuskegee students and teachers, and campus buildings—suggesting that the institute's visual archive circulated in Jamaica as in Cuba.[28] In her report, Margaret R. Geddes, "appointed Woman delegate to the Conference," observed that "the school [Tuskegee] stands on what was one of the great slave markets of the South" and praised the "singing by the Tuskegee Choir of the weird sounding plantation melodies."[29] Apparently, the institute's status as a repurposed plantation and its accompanying visual and sonic aesthetics were not lost on its Jamaican visitors (see chapters 1 and 2).

In contrast to Plant's persistent declarations of a color-blind Jamaica, the reports of at least two delegates indicate that they clearly viewed Tuskegee as a model for racial uplift on the island. The report of S. C. Thompson, Jamaica's "plain black" delegate, recommended establishing scholarships for Jamaican students to attend Tuskegee on condition that they return to the island to help maintain an industrial school modeled after Tuskegee and Hampton.[30] And while Geddes's racial background is unknown, her reflections and recommendations suggest a keen interest in Black self-determination and uplift. The "important difference" between Tuskegee and Hampton, she observed, is that while "at Hampton the work is done by the white race for the Negro race, at Tuskegee you have the Negro working for the uplift of his own race." She also proposed a scholarship for female students to attend Hampton or Tuskegee, but "preferably Tuskegee, because there a girl would be impressed by what her own race has accomplished."[31]

The Tuskegee conference was featured so frequently in the *Gleaner* that it engendered lively debate among readers about the applicability of the Tuskegee model in Jamaica and even led one reader, Mrs. A. I. Bailey, to question, with "so much talk of 'Tuskegee,'" whether the Jamaican government had sent a delegation there "to give them a holiday trip and subject matter for lectures, or must we hope to see more tangible results?"[32] The young Claude McKay's trans-plantation to Tuskegee essentially answered her question in the affirmative. The interest in and excitement about agricultural and industrial education in the Jamaican public sphere surely animated his desire to study agronomy at the institute, bring that knowledge back to the island, and disseminate it among the peasantry. In fact, after the ICON, Plant directly encouraged McKay's enrollment. As the son of proud and prosperous peasants and as a peasant-poet himself, McKay unwittingly embodied Washington's conviction that "there is just as much dignity in tilling a field as in writing a poem."[33] Although he ultimately chose the path of poet and writer, his Jamaican writings evince his profound respect for farming, agriculture, and peasant life and thus why Tuskegee would have been a viable option for him and other Afro-Jamaicans contending with the precarity of the plantation's afterlives on the island.

OF BANANAS AND MEN: UFCO AND THE RISE OF THE CORPORATE PLANTATION IN JAMAICA

As noted earlier, McKay's Jamaican writings depict the exigencies of rural life on the island in the early twentieth century, from the everyday strivings of peasant proprietors to accumulate land, cultivate their fields, and sell their harvests to the dire economic conditions that animated their decisions to migrate to the United States and its imperial outposts for work and education. In *My Green*

Hills of Jamaica, he celebrates his native parish, the Clarendon hills, as a "great agricultural parish" of "poor" but "proud peasants." "The Clarendon hills are renowned in Jamaica as one of the most fertile regions," where "there grow in abundance—as if spilled straight out of the Hand of God—bananas, oranges, coco, coffee, pimento, breadfruit, ackee, mangoes, sugar cane and all the lesser varieties of edibles such as various kinds of beans and peas, okra, cashews, cabbages, sweet potatoes, cassava and arrow-root." The beauty and fecundity of Clarendon hills are matched by the noble, hardworking peasant, who dried coffee, coco, and pimento in the "plot of ground around the house" and "readied [them] for the market." In this "rural idyll," McKay fondly recalls sugarcane production as a communal and pleasurable practice, where the men "cut the canes with machetes—singing as they work," and as "a picnic" and "great fun" for the kids, who "always had a piece of juicy cane in our mouths" and "romped together among the long ribbon-like cane leaves."[34]

McKay's sympathetic attitude toward the Jamaican peasantry was shaped by his father, Thomas, and eldest brother, U. Theo. By the time McKay migrated to the United States, Thomas McKay had accumulated more than one hundred acres of land and owned an iron sugar mill from Chattanooga, Tennessee. One of McKay's biographers, Wayne F. Cooper, observes that Thomas McKay had risen above subsistence farming to become a "small-scale commercial farmer who produced such staples as coffee, bananas, and sugar both for local markets and external trade. Claude McKay was thus born into an atypical, well-established black farm family."[35] Under the tutelage of his oldest brother, U. Theo, McKay received his early education in a school building that was once "an old slave house, plain, substantial and comfortable."[36] Like Tuskegee, the school was founded upon the ruins of an old plantation, indicating how repurposing the plantation was a common practice throughout the Global Black South. U. Theo had a tremendous impact on his younger brother's intellectual development.[37] In fact, he likely influenced McKay's decision to become an agricultural instructor for the British government because he had served in a similar capacity during McKay's boyhood. After leaving his post as a "schoolmaster," U. Theo leased land on a large sugar plantation, where he visited local farm lots to lecture tenant farmers about tropical agriculture as part of the British imperial government's scheme of "sending out instructors to show the natives how to farm scientifically."[38]

Though McKay deeply respected his brother, his writings suggest his ambivalence about the role of agricultural instructors in Jamaica. In *My Green Hills*, he suggests that the "peasants' ways" of cultivation were in some instances superior to those of the putatively more learned instructors. He recounts:

AT THE CROSSROADS OF DIASPORA AND EMPIRE 269

When the British started to send us agricultural instructors to show the peasants how to till the soil, these men protested against the burning of the debris. They said that the debris would enrich the soil and should be plowed under. Well, some of the peasants followed their [the instructors'] advice and when they did their planting, the leaves of what they had planted were consumed by worms as soon as they had grown a few inches. Those who insisted on burning this debris found that their planting had developed very healthily. The agricultural instructors make their mistakes.[39]

McKay consistently touted the peasantry's methods of agricultural cultivation throughout his oeuvre, demonstrating his steadfast commitment to a plot logic that takes rural, working-class peoples seriously as intellectuals of the land and self-determining agents. Indeed, McKay took great issue with the bias toward rural peoples as necessarily backward and Luddite in general. "People who are born and grow up in large towns and cities have a tendency to imagine that people from small towns and villages are naturally stupid and unintelligent," he writes in *My Green Hills*. "There is no greater fallacy. Personally I believe that the masses of the cities are woefully less intelligent than people who make up the population of a country town or village. The country and small town man may not be as slickly dressed but somehow he does use his brains to think. I have known so many city people from truck driver to professor who just cannot think at all."[40] Like Carver and Washington, McKay insisted that farm life was necessarily intellectual and a worthy path for the Afro-Jamaican peasantry.

One of McKay's earliest articulations of this plot logic appears in his poem "King Banana." Published in *Songs of Jamaica* in 1912, "King Banana" is essentially an ode to the banana plant, which, by McKay's coming of age at the turn of the twentieth century, had replaced sugar as Jamaica's chief export crop. The poem is composed in Jamaican patois and celebrates the process of banana cultivation by Jamaican peasant farmers:

> Green mancha mek fe naygur man;
> > Wha' sweet so when it roas'?
> Some boil it in a big black pan,
> > It sweeter in a toas'.

> A buccra fancy when it ripe,
> > Dem use it ebery day;
> It scarcely give dem belly-gripe,
> > Dem eat it diffran' way.[41]

Whereas the peasants prefer to roast or bake their bananas or eat them green or unripe, the "buccra," or white master class, prefer ripe bananas and thus eat them differently. By juxtaposing the peasants' and buccras' distinct methods of banana preparation and consumption, McKay highlights the peasantry's role as banana cultivators, who have access to the plant before it ripens and is sold on the market. Furthermore, McKay depicts the debris-burning process—"De fire bu'n and it take care / Fe mek de wo'm dem wake"—as a subtle jab at the agricultural instructors who advised peasants to plow under the debris, which ultimately ruined their crops. Further establishing the legitimacy of peasant cultivation methods, he inquires:

> Wha' lef' fe buccra teach again
> > Dis time about plantation?
> Dere's not' in dat can beat de plain
> > Good ole-time cultibation.

> Banana dem fat all de same
> > From bunches big an' 'trong;
> Pure nine-han' bunch a car' de fame,—
> > Ole met'od all along.

> De cuttin' done same ole-time way,
> > We wrap dem in a trash,
> An' pack dem neatly in a dray
> > So tight dat dem can't mash.

Afro-Jamaicans had been cultivating bananas on their plots since slavery; thus, the idea that they needed instruction was an affront to their sensibilities as stewards of the land and descendants of enslaved people. By praising the "Ole met'od" and "de cuttin' done same ole-time way," McKay explicitly opposes the newer methods introduced by the "buccra" instructors. Indeed, with the poem's narration of the peasantry's cultivation methods, we might think of "King Banana" as a peasant farmer's instruction manual.

In his short story "The Agricultural Show" (1932), McKay similarly celebrates an "old Negro" who had been enslaved but now "possessed one of the finest little patches of banana land in the village. Year after year, without fertilizers and without diminishing fertility, it had yielded the same succulent banana suckers which expanded into the same fat bunches of banana." As farmers exhibited their agricultural harvests, "many a peasant's precious exhibit

AT THE CROSSROADS OF DIASPORA AND EMPIRE   271

snatched the first prize away from a big planter's goodly rival."[42] Again, McKay insisted that the peasantry's stewardship was superior to that of the planter elite's. At the same time, his celebration of their ability to retain soil fertility without using fertilizers recalls the work and possible influence of George Washington Carver, McKay's "beloved teacher" at Tuskegee, who regularly instructed Black farmers to use organic matter to regenerate and maintain their soils (chapter 1).

McKay revisits this ambivalence toward agricultural instructors in his novel *Banana Bottom* (1933). "For the culture of the soil was like the culture of humanity, varying according to country and climate," he writes, suggesting that the instructors' knowledge about England's soil was not necessarily applicable to conditions in Jamaica. McKay somewhat tempers his critique of "academic advice," however, conceding that agricultural instructors had taught the peasantry how to "rotate and diversify their crops" and how to combat "various plant disease."[43] Perhaps McKay offers this more generous account of the Agricultural Society's work among the peasantry out of respect for U. Theo, whom he consulted while writing *Banana Bottom*, or even for Carver, whom he greatly admired. Whatever his motivation, in the novel McKay attempts to resolve the tension between peasants and agricultural instructors by putting the peasants on a level playing field as students of the soil, that "great common instructor imparting general knowledge to all alike—the scientific investigator as well as the ignorant soil-taught cultivator."[44] Ultimately, as reflected across much of his Jamaican poetry and fiction, he appears to have developed a mutual respect for both traditional and scientific farming alike.

McKay casually mentions in *Banana Bottom* that "the boom in bananas had turned the heads of many . . . to planting that fruit only," which is important for understanding the intertextuality of "King Banana" and *Banana Bottom* not only in relation to McKay's views on agricultural education but also to how agriculture facilitates labor migration and transnational commodity exchange.[45] In "King Banana," for instance, by delineating the process of carefully wrapping and packing the bunches of bananas so that "dem can't mash," McKay depicts peasants' method of transporting the fruit long distances for sale at the native market and especially to the banana ports where they were transported to the United States and Europe:

> We re'ch: banana finish sell;
>   Den we 'tart back fe home:
> Some hab money in t'read-bag well;
>   Some spen' all in a rum.

In this way, "King Banana" shows how Black agricultural labor still fueled global capitalism well after emancipation. Indeed, the mancha variety of banana is a staple not only of the peasants' diet but also of their homeland's economy. Until the late nineteenth century, Jamaica had largely been a sugar-producing colony. Bananas were "cultivated primarily by slaves on their provision grounds and by their descendants, the black peasantry," for their everyday consumption and sustenance. When the sugar industry collapsed because of competition from Cuba and Brazil and "beet sugar in Europe," the banana trade almost instantly surpassed sugar.[46] By the turn of the twentieth century, bananas had become a billion-dollar industry and a global commodity.[47] Through his ode to banana cultivation, McKay shows the inseparability of the local and the global within the Global Black South. He alludes to the hegemony of the banana in the poem's final stanza:

> Green mancha mek fe naygur man,
>   It mek fe him all way;
> Our islan' is banana lan',
>   Banana car' de sway.

By the early twentieth century, many Black people of McKay's generation increasingly viewed farming as a vestige of slavery. However, "King Banana" reclaims banana cultivation and agricultural labor more broadly as a mode of virtuosity, vitality, and socioeconomic autonomy for the Jamaican peasantry. The poem's declaration that "Dere's not' in dat can beat de plain / Good ole-time cultibation" resignifies agricultural labor as a mode of pleasure and communalism that subverts the binary of production and consumption. In *My Green Hills*, McKay notes that the time of "clearing the land and planting" was "a kind of community work," often accompanied by singing "jamma songs" or "field songs." "Today one peasant was helped by the other peasants and the next day it was another peasant. So it went round and round until every peasant had had his land cleared and planted."[48] Like Washington, McKay viewed agricultural labor as an aesthetic and potentially pleasurable practice. As the literary scholar Simon Gikandi observes, during slavery "there was an aesthetic dimension to the provision ground," wherein the enslaved transformed "the landscape of death and suffering into a space of pleasure, of aesthetic value."[49] This emphasis on pleasure and beauty is crucial to McKay's plot logic. His decision to portray agricultural labor in this light was an explicit, if counterintuitive, attempt to reclaim the banana's historic role in sustaining and propagating Black life and acknowledge that farming is not reducible to the violent history of plantation slavery alone. And yet as the colonial plantation gave way to its offspring, the corporate plantation, and the banana became a global commodity, Afro-Jamaicans' relationship to this provision ground crop would shift radically.

Much like the enslaved Africans who worked Jamaica's sugarcane plantations, bananas are not indigenous to the island and were introduced to the colony in the sixteenth century.[50] Both Black people and the banana were similarly uprooted and transplanted to the New World and transformed into global commodities. "For McKay," Gosciak argues, "produce and person are interchangeable parts of a world economy."[51] Thus, despite McKay's effort at reclamation, it is difficult to separate the poem's refrain, "Green mancha mek fe naygur man," from the sordid histories of slavery, colonialism, and the banana trade. If the banana is "King," then by the late nineteenth century the "naygur man" became his royal subject, especially following the rise of UFCO and corporate plantation colonialism. Much like Jamaica's status as a site of British and American colonialism and imperialism, respectively, the relationship between the "naygur man" and the banana trade became one of extraction and exploitation for the global market.

"King Banana" celebrates banana cultivation as an important mode of self-determination among Jamaican peasant farmers, but the poem fails to interrogate the peasantry's paradoxical relationship to the fruit both during slavery and after emancipation. As a staple of enslaved people's diet, the banana fueled their bodies, which in turn increased their capacity to labor and prolonged their exchange value. Following emancipation, banana cultivation continued to be a source of sustenance and eventually became a means of economic autonomy for the small segment of the peasantry, like McKay's father, fortunate enough to own land. As independent growers on their own plots, Jamaican peasants initially controlled their labor, but by the late 1870s, as the industry was corporatized by big business from the United States, banana cultivation became yet another site for the exploitation of Black peasant labor. UFCO secured a virtual monopoly on the industry and wrested autonomy from individual growers, a process that the historian Thomas Holt argues ultimately led to the fall of the Jamaican peasantry: "The small growers had to take whatever price the current supply-demand situation dictated, which, in absence of buyer competition, was always the bare minimum. . . . Under these conditions, deprived of autonomy in the production process and of the ability to bargain over prices, peasant producers were more like wage workers paid at a piece rate than independent contractors."[52] U.S. northern capital exploited Black labor in the Caribbean, just as it had done in the U.S. South under slavery and continued to do to Black sharecroppers and tenant farmers there following emancipation. From the colonial plantation to its corporate offspring, the laboring Black body was successively reduced to fodder for global capitalism across the Global Black South.

Despite his ambivalence toward agricultural instruction, McKay's vision of an agrarian future in "King Banana" ultimately reflected his belief in agriculture as a viable future for Afro-Jamaicans and thus why Tuskegee would have resonated with him. According to the school's 1912–1913 annual catalog, "Festus Claudius McKay" hailed from "Crooked River, Jamaica, B.W.I.," and was enrolled in the "A Middle Class," where he would have taken courses such as reading, grammar, algebra, bookkeeping, chemistry, ancient history, American history, or even "The Negro in Africa." His agricultural courses would have included "breeds and breeding," "feeds and feeding," and "veterinary science."[53] In light of the peasant autonomy he celebrates in "King Banana," one can imagine that McKay would have eventually been a culturally sensitive instructor who valued the traditional methods alongside the new, scientific ones. However, he abandoned his agricultural pursuits a few years after arriving in the United States.

Although McKay revered Washington and regarded Carver as his "beloved teacher," he ultimately disliked what he described as "the semi-military, machine-like existence" at Tuskegee.[54] He probably also found Tuskegee's curriculum too remedial. Colonial education in Jamaica was primarily literary and thus more advanced than education at Tuskegee.[55] To be sure, Tuskegee's curriculum was far more complex than Washington revealed in his publications, and more advanced students especially would have received a solid literary education that included William Shakespeare's *Julius Caesar* and works by Samuel Taylor Coleridge, Nathaniel Hawthorne, and Edgar Allen Poe, among other canonical writers. However, in the "A Middle Class" where McKay was enrolled, students were assigned works such as "Stepping Stones to Literature" and Charles and Mary Lamb's "Tales from Shakespeare," a British children's book.[56] As a published poet who had already been exposed to leading English, German, and French writers and philosophers, McKay would have likely found Tuskegee's academic curriculum underwhelming. Washington himself acknowledged the differences between these two education systems in a somewhat backhanded way, noting, "In the matter of opportunity to secure the old-fashioned, abstract book education several of the West Indian Islands give negroes a better chance than is afforded them in most of our Southern States, but for industrial and technical education they are compelled to come to the United States."[57]

On October 28, 1912, just a few months after his arrival in the United States, McKay transferred to Kansas State College (now Kansas State University), where he continued his studies in agronomy for two years before abandoning altogether his plan to become an agricultural instructor.[58] Despite the brevity of his Tuskegee matriculation, his migration there reveals an important yet often overlooked diasporic network between the U.S. South and Jamaica in the early twentieth century. As in Cuba, Haiti, and the U.S. South, Black life in postemancipation Jamaica was largely rural, making agricultural and industrial education a practical and viable response to a landscape where the plantation continued to have an outsize influence on Black futures. McKay's life and work illuminate how this educational network was part of a regional migratory trend.

While McKay and other Caribbean student migrants boarded UFCO steamships to pursue new educational opportunities, many more of his fellow passengers traveled toward very different futures as labor migrants to U.S. imperial outposts across the hemisphere, such as the Panama Canal and UFCO's Costa Rican banana plantations. Though McKay was no labor migrant, his Jamaican writings suggest that he was both privy and sympathetic to the plight of his fellow passengers who were pushed and pulled into this different future. Through his portrayal of "peasant cosmopolitanism," McKay depicts labor migration to these U.S. imperial outposts as a viable alternative to the limited economic opportunities available in Jamaica at the time. In doing so, he captures the paradox of American imperialism for Jamaica's Black peasantry as at once exploitative and yet sometimes economically viable as well.

"WE HEA' A CALLIN' FROM COLON, WE HEA' A CALLIN' FROM LIMON": PEASANT COSMOPOLITANISM IN THE "BLACK BELT OF THE CARIBBEAN"

If "King Banana" represents McKay's idealistic vision of the plot as an autonomous future for the Jamaican peasantry, then poems such as "Peasants' Ways o' Thinkin'" and "Quashie to Buccra," written contemporaneously in 1912, sound a note of resistance to the conditions of poverty that plagued Jamaican peasant life and culture. His later fiction, in particular his third and final novel (published during his lifetime), *Banana Bottom*, tempers the unbridled optimism of "King Banana" as well. Instead of benign depictions of banana cultivation as a modality of peasant autonomy, McKay wrestles with the realities of poverty in a region already ravaged by the legacy of the plantation and colonialism, elucidating the push-and-pull factors that set Jamaican peasants flowing toward sites of American imperialism. In contrast to the Black intellectual elite who often sought to uplift the peasantry by co-opting them into their normative visions of capitalist progress, McKay captures the full range of peasant voices and experiences as they negotiated the afterlife of the plantation on their own terms.

The coterminous rise of the corporate plantation and U.S. imperialism helped to facilitate Black mobility throughout the Western Hemisphere. In "The Black Belt of the Caribbean," an essay published in the *American Mercury* in 1931, the American journalist Carleton Beals traced the expansion of U.S. imperialism to the Caribbean and Central America as the impetus for "Negro dissemination" throughout the hemisphere: "The insatiable need of the United States for raw materials has flung its traders, its business men, its capital south over the Caribbean. . . . Negro emigration has gone hand in hand with expansion and mastery over new products and new regions. America provides the capital and the methods; Africa provides the labour."[59] Beals appropriated a georacial designation almost exclusively associated with the cotton-producing regions of the U.S. South, "the Black Belt," to describe the movement of Black laborers throughout the Caribbean and Central America. Delineating the process by which the United States created neoplantations in the Caribbean, Beals maintained, "The entire pattern of American economic invasion has been set by the plantation system" to produce "sugar, coffee, tobacco, or bananas on a large scale." This reinstatement of "the earlier colonial plantation by American entrepreneurs along modern lines with modern machinery," he continued, "has necessitated a new, cheap mobile labour supply. The Negro has filled the bill."[60] In the remainder of the essay, Beals traced the connection between American imperialism—by way of the plantation and the construction of the Panama Canal—and Black labor migration throughout the hemisphere.

In Jamaica, UFCO was at the forefront of developing corporate neoplantations. By buying up old sugar estates and transforming them into large banana plantations, UFCO developed a virtual monopoly on the banana trade and eventually extended its services to the tourist industry, establishing the Great White Fleet steamship line. To promote its products and services, UFCO produced a large body of literature, such as pamphlets and short films on banana production as well as brochures advertising Great White Fleet steamship tours from New Orleans, New York, and Philadelphia to Jamaica, Havana, and the Panama Canal. UFCO's promotional literature attempted to represent the U.S. imperial influence in the region as benign—promoting efficiency, cleanliness, and industrial development. The literature also went to great lengths to sanitize narratives of disease and sickness that had been associated with the region since the colonization of the Americas in the fifteenth century and that had gained renewed force with the construction of the Panama Canal in the late nineteenth century: "Disease has been driven out," a pamphlet reassured readers in 1913. "Colon [*sic*] and Panama are models of healthfulness."[61] Ultimately, UFCO's literature fueled fantasies of the Caribbean as a tropical paradise for white,

North American vacationers, obscuring the violence of U.S. imperialism. In *Jamaica Via the Great White Fleet* (1913), a forty-seven-page brochure with images of the country's top tourist sites, for instance, Afro-Jamaicans are largely absent, a glaring omission given that the colony was 90 percent Black.[62] McKay's Jamaican writings, however, which were either published contemporaneously or set during that period, restore Jamaica's Black peasantry to center stage and expose the hidden, exploitative labor that undergirded the luxury and consumption of Caribbean tourism and tropical fruit.

McKay was sympathetic to the plight of laborers wedged between poverty under the British colonial government in Jamaica and the dangers of migrating and becoming fodder for U.S. imperialism and corporate colonialism. His poem "Peasants' Ways o' Thinkin'" originally appeared in the *Daily Gleaner* in January 1912. Just above a headline announcing a special story on "the very enterprising town of Port Antonio" is a smaller headline encouraging readers to "read Claude McKay's poem appearing on page 18," the next page over. The cover story establishes Port Antonio as one of Jamaica's most important commercial centers for its role "in the building up of the banana trade on the island." It houses "the main offices" of UFCO and "the various other fruit organizations," and "it is to that port that particularly every vessel engaged in transporting bananas from Jamaica to the various distributing centres on the eastern United States seaboard goes for orders."[63] Indeed, later that year McKay himself would depart from Port Antonio en route to Charleston and Tuskegee.

The editorial continued on the next page, positioned just below McKay's poem. In contrast to the editorial's praise for U.S. commercial interests on the island, "Peasants' Ways o' Thinkin'" is arguably one of McKay's most glaring critiques of poverty among Afro-Jamaican agricultural laborers. Unlike "King Banana," this poem is not a romantic portrayal of the Jamaican peasantry's unity with the land and plant life but a protest against the injustices plaguing the poor. It opens with the speaker addressing a group of peasants who have gathered to air their collective grievances:

> Well, boys, I'm not a gwin' to preach,
> Nor neider mekin' a long speech;
> But only few short wuds fe say
> 'Bout pressin' queshtons o' de day.
>
> I sort a be'n dah wan' fe try
> To put i' in prose cut an' dry,

278   PLOT III

> But a'ter all a caan' do worse
> Dan dish i' up in rhymin' verse:
>
> . . . .
>
> A t'ink buccra ha' jawed enuff,
> 'Bout tekin' duty off foodstuff;
> An as 'tis said de good's fe we,
> Time's come for *our* talk 'bouten i'.[64]

Instead of addressing the "pressin' queshtons o' de day" in "prose cut an' dry,"
the speaker opts for the "rhymin' verse" of Jamaican patois, the dialect of the
peasantry. Unlike "King Banana," "Peasants' " tells the story of labor exploitation and heavy taxes on "foodstuff," and it promotes migration to Central
America as a viable alternative to impoverished conditions on the island. We
might think of "Peasants' " as a continuation of the sentiments expressed in
"Quashie to Buccra," the opening poem in *Songs of Jamaica*, where the peasant
speaker gives "buccra a piece of his mind."[65] In "Peasants'," the narrator
declares that "buccra ha' jawed enuff" about what is good "fe we" and that it is
now time for them to articulate their own concerns in their own voice. This is
the crux of McKay's plot logic: he depicts an autonomous, self-determining
peasantry unencumbered either by the exploitative designs of colonial officials
and the planter class or the paternalism of the Black cultural and intellectual
elite.

The very structure of McKay's poem unsettles the dichotomy between the
local and the global. In part one, the narrator outlines the myriad problems facing the Black peasantry at home in Jamaica. They are disgruntled and frustrated
by high taxes on food imports and clothing, low wages, and the "soul-grindin'
debt" that these conditions both engender and perpetuate. In part two, the narrator suggests labor migration to Central America as a potential solution to this
cycle of poverty. Although learning about "wha' foreigners think of our ways /
Is in some fashion reder nice," he states—perhaps referring to colonial officials or
British transplants such as McKay's mentor, Walter Jekyll, who studied and
often fetishized peasant life and culture—ultimately, the speaker determines
that "wha's said o' we" in "newspapers" and "in pen an' ink / Don't show de sort
o' way we think."[66] He continues:

> For hardly can de buccra find
> What pasin' in de black man's mind;

He tellin' us we ought to stay,
But dis is what' we got to say:

"We hea' a callin' from Colon,
We hea' a callin' from Limon,
Let's quit de t'ankless toil an' fret
Fe where a better pay we'll get."

The calls from Colón and Limón represent the allure of U.S. imperialist outposts for Afro-Caribbean peasants as well as their right to determine their own futures through migration. Ironically, in threatening the buccra with labor migration to Central America, the narrator also points to how neoplantation agriculture followed the same trade routes and diasporic movement as the trade in flesh less than a century earlier. Whereas some migrants even referred to this intrahemispheric labor migration as the new slave trade, UFCO's promotional literature often included detailed maps of these routes to advertise the Great White Fleet and tout its conquest of the hemisphere (figure 6.1).

The decision to "exchange" the comforts and "freedom[s]" of home, however small, "for t'ings dat will seem bad an' strange" is by no means an easy one. The speaker has doubtless heard many stories about the dangers of working in Central America and about the Afro-Jamaicans who either returned home with physical and mental ailments or simply never returned at all:

Though ober deh de law is bad,
An' dey no know de name o' God,
Yet dere is nuff work fe we han's,
Reward in gol' fe beat de ban's.

. . . .

We'll have de beastly 'panish beer,
De never-ceasin' wear an' tear,
All Sundays wuk in cocoa-walk,
An' tryin' fe larn de country's talk;

. . . .

A-meetin' mountain cow an' cat,
An' Goffs wi' plunder awful fat,

While, choppin' do'n de ru'nate wood,
Malaria suck' out we blood.

Indeed, the condition of the migrant laborer is at once "strange" and precarious for rural peasants accustomed to being rooted in the soil. The literary scholar Rhonda Frederick observes that "manual laborers" in the Panama Canal Zone

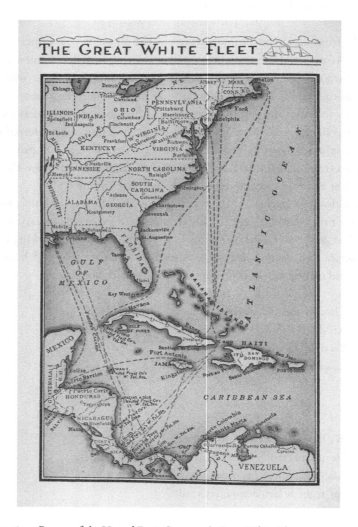

FIGURE 6.1. Routes of the United Fruit Company's Great White Fleet.

Source: *Jamaica Panama Canal Central and South America* (New York: Great White Fleet, United Fruit Company Steamship Service, 1912).

"experienced the highest risk of disease and death" as they came in contact with deadly reptiles and insects, such as mosquitos that carried yellow fever and malaria.[67] McKay's depiction of migrants navigating such life-threatening work conditions provides a sobering counternarrative to the false portrait of Colón and Panama as "sanitary" "models of healthfulness" in UFCO's promotional literature.

Though often at the bottom of the labor chain, these workers cultivated through travel a knowledge of the world that might be described as cosmopolitan. Cosmopolitanism is typically associated with the elite and has classist connotations, but I want to consider the possibility of what Ifeoma Nwankwo calls "a cosmopolitanism from below," redefined by the unique experiences of West Indian migrant laborers.[68] Peasant cosmopolitanism is not defined by luxury, leisure, or tourism but by migration for labor and survival. As the speaker in "Peasants'" observes, the migrants will be immersed in a completely new culture where they will have to "larn" to eat new foods and speak "de country's talk." Whereas the traditional Western cosmopolite's mobility is enabled by wealth and a passport, the Jamaican migrant worker's mobility is prompted by the *allure* of wealth (or at least of a basic standard of living) and a work visa. To be sure, as Nwankwo maintains, "Black people's relationship to travel is inherently fraught because of the way in which they were brought to the Americas."[69] Unlike their enslaved ancestors who were forcibly relocated under the most horrific conditions, however, Jamaican migrant laborers often traveled of their own volition, even as they were pushed and pulled by precarious living conditions at home and imperial capitalism abroad.

Rethinking cosmopolitanism along these lines demands a simultaneous reconsideration of modern subjectivity. Although I have challenged the reductive association between mobility and modernity by arguing that those who remained rooted were modern, too, I also want to dispel the class bias associated with Black cosmopolitan modernity. Cosmopolitanism was not reserved for the Black intellectual and cultural elite alone; as McKay and his generation of New Negro artists showed time and time again, migrant laborers, sailors, sharecroppers, and other working-class Black folk also cultivated a cosmopolitan sensibility, and many of them traveled to perform the agricultural labor that undergirded the global economy.

In "Peasants' Ways o' Thinkin'," the economic advantages of labor migration are a more powerful draw than the potential dangers and discomforts of living in a foreign country, especially in the face of Jamaica's "persistent poverty."[70] As such, the speaker reasons:

> But poo'ness deh could neber come,
> And dere'll be case fe sen' back home
> Fe de old heads, de bastard babe,
> An' somet'ing ober still fe sabe.

The migrant laborer's relationship to home is a distinguishing feature of peasant cosmopolitanism. Ironically, uprooting his life to work in a foreign country will provide more economic stability back home. The speaker views labor migration as a means to an end, hoping to send money home for his family's well-being and to save for the future. Whereas the Western cosmopolite is reputedly at home in the world, McKay's peasant turned migrant remains deeply connected to a traditional sense of home, rooted in the land. Hence, peasant cosmopolitanism further elasticizes the category of the cosmopolite by redefining its relationship to the local.

The narrator contends that peasants do not desire to "be rich like buccra folk" but rather want to be able to lead simple lives:

> Havin' we owna mancha-root,
> Havin' we dandy Sunday suit,
> We'll happy wi' our modest lot
> An' won't grudge buccra wha' dem got.
>
> A piece o' lan' fe raise two goat,
> A little rum fe ease we t'roat,
> A little cot fe res' we head—
> An' we're contented tell we dead.

Despite proposing migration as a viable alternative to "de t'ankless toil an' fret" of peasant life in Jamaica, the narrator ultimately desires to be a small settler with his "owna mancha-root" (banana tree) and "a piece o' lan'" in Jamaica. Here, McKay upholds the autonomous peasant as the epitome of an agrarian future in Jamaica even as he recognizes labor migration as a viable and necessary alternative. Thus, peasant cosmopolitanism is less about being at home in the world than about the sense of worldliness that comes from being cast adrift in the currents of labor and commercial exchange under capitalism.

McKay's interest in how U.S. imperialism pushed and pulled Jamaican peasants to Central America is also an important theme in *Banana Bottom*. Though published in 1933, the novel is set in early twentieth-century Jamaica— the same period as McKay's trans-plantation to Tuskegee—and portrays the aftermath of the island's transition from a sugar-producing colony to a primarily

AT THE CROSSROADS OF DIASPORA AND EMPIRE   283

banana-producing one.[71] Although *Banana Bottom* is typically read as a peasant novel about the struggle between European high culture and Jamaican folk culture, it also represents the fullest expression of McKay's plot logic.

In the novel, McKay portrays early twentieth-century Jamaica as a colony wedged between the plot and the plantation socioeconomically, culturally, and politically. In the 1820s, a "strange Scotchman" immigrated to the island and purchased the Banana Bottom estate. Unlike most plantation owners, he carved up this newly acquired property and sold individual plots to the Black peasants who wanted to buy, many of whom had been "squatting" on the land for some time. It became one of "the first of independent expatriate–Negro villages."[72] Much like Haiti and Zora Neale Hurston's Eatonville, Florida (chapter 7), the Banana Bottom community represents the importance of Black self-government after emancipation, and, like Tuskegee, it was established on the ruins of a plantation and funded by white benevolence and patronage.

Banana Bottom opens with Tabitha "Bita" Plant's return to Jamaica after seven years of study in England. As a child, Bita was raped by Crazy Bow, a mentally disabled man, and subsequently adopted by Malcolm and Priscilla Craig, local white missionaries. The Craigs sent Bita away to be educated in England in hopes that she would return to Jamaica to lead the mission. That McKay made a peasant woman and survivor of sexual assault the protagonist of his novel indicates his mother's influence on his values. Also a peasant woman, his mother was "especially nice to the young girls who had produced babies out of wedlock" and "wanted to help those who were outcast, poor and miserable."[73] This anti-elitist and egalitarian attitude toward those deemed social outcasts was McKay's ethical conviction as well and a defining feature of his plot logic.

Banana Bottom revolves around Bita's trans-plantation back into Jamaican soil. The Craigs "were happy in a praise-Godly humble way over their handiwork. The transplanted African peasant girl that they had transformed from a brown wildling into a decorous cultivated young lady" (11). The novel's central tension involves Bita's struggle between her elite British education and her peasant sensibilities. When she returns from abroad, she is confronted with the reality that though she has an elite education, the island's class politics are such that her dark skin color precludes her from "breaking into the intimate social circles of the smart light-brown or yellow groups" (101).

> For the island colony was divided into three main groups in a political and social way. The descendants of the slaves were about three-fourths of the population and classified as black or dark brown. The descendants of Europeans and slaves were about one-fifth of the population and classified as coloured or

light-brown. The rest were a few thousand East Indians and Chinese and perhaps the same number of pure European descent.... [T]he social life of the colony was finely balanced by the divisions. The coloured group stood between the mass and the wealthy and governing classes and all the white-collar jobs of business and government were reserved for it. (4–5)

McKay's commentary on color prejudice in Jamaica contrasts sharply with W. H. Plant's claim at the ICON (which took place during the same period as the novel's setting) that there was no "colour line" in Jamaica. The rigid labor and class divisions that McKay outlines limited work opportunities for the literate peasant masses to farming, teaching, mission work, and the civil service.

Throughout *Banana Bottom*, McKay uses the colors, textures, and sizes of fruits, plants, and other botanical organisms to describe characters' skin complexion and other physical features. He consistently uses metaphors that link Bita to the land, agriculture, and nature. For instance, when Bita rejects the unwanted advances of Marse Arthur, the "bastard near-white son of a wealthy country gentleman," he retorts, "You ought to feel proud a gen'man like me want fer kiss you when youse only a black gal" (262). When Bita returns to her room later that evening, she reflects on the infuriating and demeaning encounter: "'Only a nigger gal!' She undressed and looked at her body in the long mirror of the old-fashioned wardrobe. She caressed her breasts like maturing pomegranates, her skin firm and smooth like the sheath of a blossoming banana, her luxuriant hair, close-curling like thick fibrous roots, gazed at her own warm-brown eyes, the infallible indicators of real human beauty" (267). On one hand, this association between Black people and plants is largely a gendered practice in the novel. With the exception of the Plant family, McKay uses botanical similes and metaphors mainly to describe women characters, seemingly trafficking in age-old tropes linking dominion over land and nature to patriarchal authority over women's bodies.

On the other hand, McKay also uses this practice to elucidate the fraught entanglements of labor, class, and color in the colony. When a light-brown local government official seeks Bita's hand in marriage, his two sisters vehemently object to "a brown man marrying a black woman": "What did it matter that the sisters were ladies of slender education and no accomplishment or self-improvement? Their complexion was the colour of a ripe banana peel—not a fine ripe one like those that mature and yellow upon a tree in Jamaica, but rather the kind that is harvested green three-quarters fit so it can reach the far foreign market without rotting, and therefrom becomes a little bruised and blotchy" (253–54). Though the sisters possess a lighter complexion and a higher-class background, the blemishes on their skin suggest their lack of cultivation and refinement. Bita, in contrast, has skin that is "firm and smooth like the sheath of a blossoming banana." By comparing the sisters' complexion to a ripe banana, "bruised and blotchy" from transport to "the far foreign market," McKay uses the process of harvesting bananas for the fruit trade to critique both the color and class politics of Jamaica's colonial caste system and UFCO's extraction of the colony's resources. The best bananas are grown for local consumption, McKay seems to suggest, where they can "mature and yellow upon a tree in Jamaica."

Since white-collar jobs are "considered the special plums of the light-brown natives," McKay establishes the "prosperous peasant" (254) as a viable model for the "black or dark brown" Jamaican masses, epitomized through his character-ization of Jordan Plant, Bita's father. Jordan remained "rooted in the soil," culti-vating his mother's lot of land until he became "the one thriving Plant," while his older brothers went "Panamaway" in search of better work and pay (27). Jordan owns "fat acres of banana and cocoa, coffee and sugar-cane and his sugar-mill and dray-and-five-mules and a saddle horse" (74–75), and through his successful cul-tivation of the plot he has established some socioeconomic autonomy from the plantation system also.

However, Jordan cannot completely divorce himself from the logics of the plantation and the global market. Whereas enslaved peoples traded their provi-sion ground crops at the native market, creating what some scholars have termed a "slave's economy" that existed outside of the logics of global capitalism, the "prosperous peasant[s]" sell their goods both on the native and global markets through the banana and fruit trades. Moreover, Jordan has a strong "hunger for land." "He had added by purchase and other means to his mother's lot until now he possessed over a hundred acres in separate lots of the best land in the Banana Bottom region" (54–55). Though landownership represents peasant autonomy, the biographer Winston James rightly contends that it is "hardly anti-capitalist."[74] Rather, like Tuskegee's conception of the southern New Negro, the prosperous peasant is an agrarian capitalist who is still invested in capital accumulation through property ownership.

It is instructive to juxtapose McKay's vision of agrarian capitalism in *Banana Bottom* with his most explicit critique of racial capitalism in his second novel, *Banjo* (1929).[75] Now a key text for theorizing Black transnationalism and dias-pora in the interwar years, *Banjo* features a motley crew of mostly Black male vagabonds from the United States, the Caribbean, and Africa who, as Brent Hayes Edwards argues, "would rather beg for food from sympathetic black crews on Mediterranean coal freighters than work under the racist capitalism that is the only available mode of labor relations." They are self-proclaimed vagabonds who work only at their discretion and prioritize leisure, play, and indulgence. Yet vagabonding is not some "irresponsible evasion," explains Edwards, but represents Banjo and his companions' choice to "reject what they consider to be the hypocrisy and cynicism of modernity"—wage labor—and thus to "challenge the very logic of civilization itself."[76] *Banana Bottom*'s characterization of the prosperous peasant as an agrarian capitalist who deems working with the hands and being rooted in the soil as the highest of virtues is the antithesis of *Banjo*'s vagabond, who resists labor and property ownership altogether. And yet, despite its emphasis on rootedness, *Banana Bottom* still explores the possibility of transnational migration as a viable alternative for Jamaica's peasant masses. Whereas "vagabond internationalism" is the vehicle of Black transnational mobility in *Banjo*— Black drifters roaming aimlessly throughout the Mediterranean region, refusing to be pigeonholed "at the margins of the transnational wage labor system"—*Banana Bottom* illuminates Jamaican peasants navigating the hemispheric circuits of the Global Black South.[77]

Jamaican labor migration to Central America is a source of contention and ambivalence throughout *Banana Bottom*. It provides a better source of income and economic stability for peasants languishing in postemancipation, neoplantation Jamaica. Yet it is also believed to corrupt young men by introducing them to American materialism. In a conversation with Bita at the mission, Mrs. Craig laments this alleged devolution:

> "It's the Panama Canal," said Priscilla. "Our Negroes are not the same after contact with the Americans. They come back ruder."
>
> Bita replied, "But they make more money there, though. The least two dollars a day, they say. And here they get only a shilling. Eight times more gain over there." . . .
>
> "I don't like it," continued Priscilla. "Times may be hard here and our black folk terribly poor. But I like them better so than when they come back peacocks from Panama."
>
> "Money makes a difference, though," said Bita.
>
> "There was quite a stir about a blade from Banana Bottom called Tacky or some such name. He got in wrong with the police here drinking hard. They say he respects nothing and nobody. He talks Yankee, the nasal accent with the Negro dialect. And they say it's as funny as it's awful. He has been to Panama three times, and each time comes back with more money. . . . Your father says all the up-country lads want to imitate him. They all want to go to Panama."

"They say the construction is a mighty work and the black labour the best down there," Bita remarked pridefully, "especially the Jamaicans and Haitians." (35–36)

This discussion between Bita and Mrs. Craig is indicative of the tensions the novel stages between the local and the global, mobility and stasis, and the competing desires of British missionaries and self-determined Black Jamaicans. For Bita, the Panama Canal is a source of economic stability and pride, especially given the preference for Jamaican and Haitian laborers. Yet for Mrs. Craig, a British missionary, it is a source of moral corruption, diminishing the peasants' "native worth." Her romantic ideal of noble peasants content in their poverty is precisely the kind of "buccra" mentality that the speaker of McKay's "Peasants' Ways o' Thinkin'" contests. In contrast, Bita implies that their poverty or lack of formal education does not preclude their right to self-determination. Though bound up with American imperialism, the canal represents an alternative future for Afro-Jamaicans.

Banana Bottom's most explicit depiction of the debate over labor migration is presented through its characterization of Tack Tally. Shortly following her discussion with Mrs. Craig, Bita departs from the mission in Jubilee for her hometown, Banana Bottom, to participate in Emancipation Day festivities. Here she first encounters Tack Tally, whom Mrs. Craig derogatorily referred to as "Tacky." During the "big picnic at Tabletop," he is "proudly wearing his decorations from Panama: gold watch and chain of three strands, and a foreign gold coin attached to it as large as a florin, a gold stick-pin with a huge blue stone with five gold rings flashing from his fingers. He had on a fine bottle-green tweed suit with the well-creased and deep-turned pantaloons called peg-top, the coat of long points and lapels known as American style. And wherever he went he was accompanied by an admiring gang" (65–66). Tack Tally's ostentatious sartorial display represents his peasant cosmopolitanism. Unlike *Banjo*'s vagabonds, who refuse transnational wage labor, Tack Tally pursues it head-on as an alternative to poverty. He "had not only gone to Panama like many, but he had come back with the gold" (65–66). Yet his ostentation also represents the "tackiness" and "tactlessness" of American culture and its negative influence on Jamaica's rural peasantry. His gang "admired his success" but "secretly resented his Panama ways which were equivalent to bad manners" (67). Though he "had come back with the gold," he was now out of step with the "peasant ways of thinking and speaking" (71).

Nevertheless, Yoni, a teacher at the mission school, Bita's friend, and Tack's love interest, appreciates his new air and style. "And if Tack was too raw-mannered for the village circle," Yoni decides, "she would go back to Panama with him" (68). Panama represents an alternative path to upward mobility that is not circumscribed by "the rigid respectability and the moral strain" (54) that becoming a teacher requires, and it pays better wages. However, when Tack and Yoni are discovered in a tryst at the mission school, the novel exposes the limits of his success. Furious that Yoni has lost her job, Pap Legge, her stepfather, sets out to confront Tack and finds him living in a "dirt hut" with his mother. "In spite of all the cash he was reputed to have and his many fine Panama suits and jewellery [sic], Tack had never thought of building a decent home. . . . [H]is main pride was to show himself dandy in the street, the rum shop and tea-meeting booth. He was no home-loving lad" (146).

In a novel that touts rootedness, thrift, and middle-class domesticity as virtues, Tack's frivolous ostentation and disregard for home life are the ultimate affront to peasant values. During their confrontation, Tack "collared" Pap Legge, threatening to "shoot you' heart out" (147). When Pap Legge suddenly falls dead, Tack is horrified, for "surely he hadn't collared Pap hard enough to choke him to death" (147). As word of Pap Legge's murder spreads, the villagers are reminded of "that time when a poor fellow returned from Colon a little off his head, and one day murdered an old cripple in his cabin" (148). Panama is thus a site of moral corruption and outright lawlessness, harboring murderers who return to wreak havoc on poor rural Jamaican peasants. When the doctor arrives to examine Pap's body, "he announced that Pap Legge had succumbed to long-standing heart disease" and that Tack was not responsible for his death after all (149). However, Tack is nowhere to be found, and it is presumed that "he was already on his way back to Panama" (149). Two days later, however, his body is found hanging from a cashew tree. Fearing that he had indeed murdered Pap Legge, Tack died by suicide. The novel continues its portrayal of Panama as a site of moral corruption and lawlessness when Herald Newton Day, Bita's self-righteous suitor, "suddenly turned crazy and defiled himself with a nanny goat" (175) just hours before he was supposed to deliver a sermon to the Banana Bottom congregation, and so he is promptly exiled to Panama.

Through Tack's and Herald's tragic fates, the novel establishes Panama as both cause *and* effect of the peasantry's deteriorating morality. Yet the novel's stance on U.S. imperialism and Jamaican labor migration to Central America remains ambiguous. As Bita explains to Mrs. Craig, Panama and the banana trade are important alternative means of socioeconomic mobility and a source of pride. Moreover, even the prosperous peasant is not protected from the threat of natural disasters in Jamaica and may also be forced to pursue labor migration. Following a devastating drought, "one of the most catastrophic in the annals of the island" (229),

AT THE CROSSROADS OF DIASPORA AND EMPIRE   289

food and water become scarce, exacerbating the problem of labor. With economic conditions worsening, Banana Bottom peasants debate "Indian coolie and Chinese immigration" and the problem of labor competition:

> The question of the hour then was Indian coolie and Chinese immigration. After the emancipation of the Negroes the big planters instituted a campaign to import indentured coolies who were able to convince the Government that that was necessary for them to carry on. The Negro labourers, intoxicated with their new freedom, had demanded the extravagant sum of minimum wage of one shilling a day on the plantations. The planters raised their hands and their voices in horror. The plantations would all go to ruin if such large wages were paid. And so the coolies were substituted for Negroes. . . . [T]he coolie contingents arrived every year and every year larger numbers of young Negroes emigrated to [sic] the Panama Canal Zone and the banana and cocoa and coffee plantations of Central America. (236–37)

Even after the close of the transatlantic slave trade and the abolition of slavery, the plantation continued to facilitate transnational labor migration, pulling East Indian laborers toward former Jamaican slave plantations and pushing Afro-Jamaican laborers toward Panama and Costa Rica and the neoplantations of U.S.-based multinationals.

The essential difference between these two systems, of course, was wages. Afro-Jamaicans "in general would not work for the coolie wages," equating such cheapening of their labor with "chattel slavery." Instead, writes McKay in *Banana Bottom*, they migrated steadily "to the Central American jungles where their labour was indispensable" (238–39). This competition between Indian and Black peasant labor intensifies the struggle between the plot and the plantation that organizes so much of the novel, for even those peasants who do not migrate to Central America refuse to work on the old estates, opting for the socioeconomic autonomy afforded by the plot.

> And those who stayed at home worked miracles with the axe and the pick, the fork and the hoe, tilling the most difficult pieces of mountain land, bringing green growths out of stony forbidding hillside patches, eking out funds to buy the crown lands that were cutup for small proprietorship—striving and struggling against descending to the coolie level of the plantations, which to them was like a return to chattel slavery. In this they were aided by relatives, returning emigrants from Central American countries, many of whom invested their savings in small parcels of land. (238–39)

Ironically, labor migration to U.S.-owned plantations in Central America allowed many Black workers to save money to buy plots of land back in Jamaica. The novel critiques the wastefulness of migrants such as Tack Tally, who doesn't take advantage of this opportunity, but also elucidates the paradoxical reality that transnational mobilities made possible by U.S. imperial interests created opportunities for Jamaican laborers to become landowners back home. Whereas vagabondage in *Banjo* is about the deliberate evasion of the transnational wage-labor system, *Banana Bottom*'s peasants seek to operate within the plantation empire of the United States to accumulate capital and property and, ultimately, the right to a self-determined future.

This tension between farming and labor migration in *Banana Bottom* reaches its climax with a "destroying hurricane," in which both Jordan Plant and Mr. Craig perish. "The hurricane had finished the work of the drought" (292), McKay writes, wiping out life, property, and food reserves. Because of the banana trade, many peasants had begun to cultivate bananas exclusively, yet "of all plants [it] was the most susceptible to natural accidents such as hurricanes," (295), and families are now faced with starvation. Conditions deteriorate so much that "proud young peasants of the hill lands who had always prided themselves on being able to live by the careful cultivation of their patches without descending to coolie labor in the lowlands, were now compelled to go begging for work at the gates of the plantation" (293). By contrast, Jordan Plant "had been a shrewd cultivator, never planting all of his best land with banana. He reared hogs and had planted a lot of corn and sweet potatoes for them" (292). His family is able to sell the harvest "at moderate prices" to the peasants whose crops are destroyed. Ultimately, Jordan epitomizes McKay's conception of a peasant agrarian future. Nevertheless, McKay also continues to depict labor migration as a viable alternative after the hurricane, noting, "The Panama Canal was the big hope of the poor disinherited youths of Jamaica and all those islands of the Caribbean Belt that were set in the latitude of hurricanes and earthquakes—all those who did not like to sport the uniform of the army and police force" (293).

In his analysis of McKay's early poetry, the historian and McKay biographer Winston James observes that McKay's political stance was often "ambivalent" and "contradictory" ("here was one of Jamaica's first nationalists declaring love for the 'Mother Country,' Britain; here was the proud African espousing Social Darwinism").[78] This ambivalence seemingly characterizes *Banana Bottom* as well. McKay simultaneously extols the prosperous peasant while critiquing the peasant's myriad moral shortcomings and illuminating the difficulties of peasant life; he upholds labor migration to Panama as a viable economic option, while criticizing U.S. imperialism and materialism. Yet I also want to suggest that instead of supporting a specific ideological stance or political project, McKay was ultimately invested in peasants' right to self-determination, whether it led to rootedness in the soil or to migration abroad. McKay's social egalitarian vision sees value in both the rural and the urban, the local and the global. Indeed, at the novel's conclusion, Bita ultimately leaves the mission, marries Jubban, her father's drayman, and pursues a future as a peasant farmer on her family's plot. Bita and Jubban's partnership provides a reconciliation of folk and modern values that calls to mind Washington's conception of the Tuskegee-trained New Negro: "Her music, her reading, her thinking were the flowers of her intelligence and he the root in the earth upon which she was grafted, both nourished by the same soil" (313).

"FOR GROUP SURVIVAL": MCKAY'S IDEOLOGICAL RETURN

Ironically, despite abandoning his agricultural pursuits, McKay's commitment to a plot logic in his Jamaican writings underlay his ongoing appreciation for Washington and his philosophical attunement to the Tuskegee idea in his late thought. Well after his departure from Tuskegee in 1912, McKay continued to revere Washington and uphold Tuskegee as a model of Black self-determination and the importance of "group values." After Washington's death in 1915, the young McKay penned the sonnet "In Memoriam: Booker T. Washington," although it was never published in his lifetime:

> I vividly recall the noonday hour
>> You walked into the wide and well-filled hall:
>> We rose and sang, at the conductor's call,
> Dunbar's Tuskegee hymn. A splendid tower
> Of strength, as would a gardener on the flower
>> Nursed tenderly, you gazed upon us all
>> Assembled there, a serried, sable wall
> Fast mortared by your subtle tact and power.
>
> O how I loved, adored your furrowed face!
>> And fondly hoped before your days were done,
> You would look in mine too with paternal grace.
>> But vain are hopes and dreams!—gone: you are gone;

Death's hand has torn you from your trusting race,
And O! we feel so utterly alone.[79]

"In Memoriam" is one of few instances where McKay reflects on his brief tenure at Tuskegee, and it is considered "his first serious sonnet."[80] The poem suggests that McKay regarded Washington as a father figure and felt a deep sense of loss at his passing. Washington is a "gardener" who "nursed tenderly" the "flower[s]" of Tuskegee's student body, a beautiful mélange from across the Global Black South. The image of McKay standing to sing "The Tuskegee Song," written by Paul Laurence Dunbar, recalls the importance of aesthetics and musical training at Tuskegee (chapter 2). Composed in 1906 for the school's twenty-fifth anniversary, the "Tuskegee Song" celebrates the dignity of agricultural and industrial labor and is consistent with McKay's own sympathies for the peasantry and rural life in Jamaica. Dunbar extols:

The fields smile to greet us, the forests are glad,
The ring of the anvil and hoe
Have a music as thrilling and sweet as a harp
Which thou taught us to hear and to know.[81]

Since McKay composed his early poetry in Jamaican dialect and depicted Black folk life and culture, he was often compared to Dunbar and even praised Dunbar himself for showing "that the negro dialect can be used with literary effect."[82] "In Memoriam," then, firmly places McKay within a Global Black South intellectual and cultural tradition and reflects how his time at Tuskegee may have shaped his worldview.

McKay's opinion of Washington vacillated over the years, especially during his radical phase in the 1920s.[83] Ultimately, he would reject Washington's political philosophy while maintaining profound respect for his capacity as an institution builder and especially for Tuskegee's significance as an all-Black institution. Upon returning to the United States from Morocco in 1934, McKay became a staunch proponent of Tuskegee's significance as an all-Black institution that demonstrated the possibilities of "group aggregation." According to Wayne F. Cooper, "If McKay had an obsession after 1934, it was his belief that since the days of Booker T. Washington, blacks in the United States had effectively abandoned any serious effort toward community self-improvement."[84] In "For Group Survival," written in 1937 as part of a debate with fellow Harlem Renaissance writer George Schuyler on the politics of integration in the United States, McKay upheld Tuskegee as an example of what Black people could accomplish even under the stifling conditions of segregation. "When Booker T. Washington founded the great institution of Tuskegee as a practical demonstration of what Negroes might accomplish for themselves, culturally and economically, as a people, he was opposed by leading Negro intellectuals of the North," McKay wrote. "Yet although Mr. Washington may have followed a mistaken lead in national politics, his social basis was sound. He did not fold his arms and whine and wait for integration. He accomplished something different. He attracted national attention because he had something different to offer. Tuskegee Institute stands [as] a fine monument to him and is perhaps the greatest all-Negro institution in the world."[85] McKay did not support segregation or "separate but equal" but maintained that even out of such egregiously unequal conditions as Jim Crow, Black people were able to create outstanding institutions of their own. In his first autobiography, *A Long Way from Home* (1937), he elaborates that "negroes do not understand the difference between group segregation and group aggregation. . . . Negro institutions and unique Negro efforts have never had a chance for full development; they are haunted by the fear of segregation."[86] Tuskegee's success, however, represented the possibilities inherent in racial self-help through economic cooperation.

McKay's position contrasts starkly with Richard Wright's more pessimistic view in "Blueprint for Negro Writing," also published in 1937, that many Black institutions represent "the few crumbs of American civilization which the Negro has got from the tables of capitalism." Because they "have been through these segregated channels," Wright argued, they "are cowardly and incompetent." "The social institutions of the Negro are imprisoned in the Jim Crow political system of the South, and this Jim Crow political system is in turn built upon a plantation-feudal economy." He elaborated that the "group feeling" among Negroes that whites found puzzling was, therefore, a relic of segregation.[87]

Whereas McKay admired institutions such as Tuskegee as examples of Black self-determination in the face of inequality, for Wright the Black social and cultural world that emerged out of the South's "plantation-feudal economy" was essentially a carceral space. Their disagreement is most likely attributable to their vastly different experiences growing up in colonial Jamaica and Jim Crow Mississippi, respectively. McKay routinely noted that while many Black people in Jamaica suffered poverty, they did not experience the crudeness and inhumanity of racism in the United States. And although he certainly had to navigate the vagaries of Jim Crow, the relative privileges he was afforded as a British colonial subject may have prevented him from feeling the sting of segregation and resulting outrage against it as Wright and other southern African Americans did.

In his later years, McKay was in constant tension with the Black intellectual, cultural, and political elite in the United States, many of whom, like Wright, did not share his distinction between segregation and "group aggregation." McKay's position was more Washingtonian in its emphasis on economics and the "dignity and democracy of labor" at a time when Black America was increasingly focusing on civil rights and integration.[88] To be clear, McKay was in no way aligned with the accommodationist component of Washington's political philosophy; however, he still failed to appreciate the weight of segregation for African Americans. This rift between McKay and his intellectual contemporaries is evident in his promotion of Tuskegee in his late poetry. In the early to mid-1940s, less than a decade before his death, he composed a cycle of poems "distilled from my experience" that sought to "tell my feelings of today."[89] One sonnet shares his views on education for Black people in the United States:

> Tuskegee is disliked by Negro Snobs,
> Because it is an exclusive Negro college.
> And in their eyes this situation robs
> The place of quality in dispensing knowledge.
> But there are Negro schools where white folks teach,
> Who by the outraged South are ostracized,
> And are considered by the snobs to reach
> Those heights of scholarship that should be prized.
>
> And there are others where some whites attend,
> With colored students and the snobs declare:
> That is the perfect system to defend,
> As a symbol that EQUALITY is here!
> Oh for a Mencken upright on his feet,
> To blast the smugness of the black elite.[90]

Just as McKay castigates the Jamaican middle class in *Banana Bottom* for their color prejudice, in "The Cycle" he takes the African American middle class to task for their devaluation of all-Black institutions. In many respects, this defense of Tuskegee is the poetic counterpart to his position in the segregation-versus-integration debate with George Schuyler. McKay perceived integration for the sake of being proximate to whiteness as a kind of self-hatred, like Zora Neale Hurston's controversial position on the *Brown v. Board of Education* (1954) decision, published a little more than a decade later. "The whole matter revolves around the self-respect of my people," Hurston contended in

August 1955. "How much satisfaction can I get from a court order for somebody to associate with me who does not wish me near them?" Like McKay, Hurston was proud of her Blackness and thus deeply critical and suspicious of the claim that segregation necessarily produced inadequate Black institutions—hence, her ideological and creative differences with Richard Wright and many others. "If there are adequate Negro schools and prepared instructors and instructions," she reasoned, "then there is nothing different except the presence of white people. For this reason, I regard the ruling of the U.S. Supreme Court as insulting rather than honoring my race."[91] Hurston and McKay were thus somewhat ideologically aligned regarding the value of all-Black institutions as evidence of Black self-determination and sources of race pride.

The life and work of Claude McKay elucidates the afterlife of the plantation in the Global Black South as an entanglement of several transnational and diasporic networks and practices. The migration of students and intellectuals between Tuskegee and Jamaica that facilitated McKay's initial journey to the U.S. South was both temporally and materially intertwined with Afro-Caribbean labor migration to UFCO's corporate fruit plantations and the Panama Canal Zone. Although he initially rejected both Tuskegee and his aspiration to become an agricultural instructor, he retained the logics and ethics of the plot at the heart of his Jamaican peasant roots. His Jamaican writings in particular validate both the agrarian futures of the prosperous peasant determined to remain rooted in the soil and the labor migrant's right to pursue a more economically viable, if precarious, future by migrating to the outposts of U.S. imperialism.

McKay's steadfast commitment to a plot logic enabled his continued reverence for Washington and Carver and his philosophical return to Tuskegee in his late thought. Engaged in his own praxis of strategic translation, McKay rejected Washington's political philosophy and the class biases of uplift, while upholding Tuskegee as a model of Black socioeconomic autonomy and the value of "group aggregation" at a time when the intellectual and cultural elite in the United States primarily (and understandably so) promoted integration. In doing so, he exploited Tuskegee's otherwise affordances to meet the new political challenges of the 1930s and 1940s.

7

Aestheticizing Labor, Performing Diaspora

Zora Neale Hurston and the Scene of the Work Camp

Between 1927 and 1929, Zora Neale Hurston embarked on her first anthropological recording expeditions in the U.S. South and the Bahamas. Already one of the Harlem Black literati's award-winning writers, she had developed an interest in anthropology as an undergraduate at Barnard College and earned a Rosenwald fellowship to pursue a PhD at Columbia University under Franz Boas, a "father" of American anthropology. Traveling throughout Central and South Florida, Hurston visited a host of phosphate mines and sawmill, turpentine, and railroad camps, collecting work songs and blues, vernacular dances, children's games, religious rituals, and other modes of folk expression. The dynamic cast of characters she encountered and the rich cultural forms she documented in these work camps would become the basis of her larger aesthetic and anthropological projects. Hurston's folk informants and interlocutors were primarily unskilled wage laborers who had migrated to South Florida from other parts of the U.S. South and the Caribbean. Hurston recognized, as Tiffany Ruby Patterson observes, that "in the South black culture emanated from the workers—debt peons, sharecroppers, and small-town dwellers."[1] From Hurston's folk concerts and novels to her ethnographies and sound recordings, the southern work camp was the crucible for her theories of Black vernacular cultural expression.

During those early years in the field, Hurston corresponded frequently with her then dear friend and darling of the Harlem Renaissance Langston Hughes, discussing everything from her fieldwork to the most recent Harlem gossip to plans for future projects and collaborations. In a letter written in 1928, Hurston invited Hughes to visit her in the South during summer vacation, promising to take him to a phosphate mine and sawmill camp "as special added attractions."

"I have come to 5 general laws," she informed him, including drama, lack of reverence, angularity, redundance, and "restrained ferocity in everything"—which are remarkably similar to and no doubt laid the groundwork for her now canonical essay "Characteristics of Negro Expression" (1934). In another letter to Hughes in 1929 regarding a future collaboration, Hurston inquired, "Do you want to look over what I have on our show? Lets [*sic*] call it 'JOOK' that is the word for baudy [*sic*] house in its general sense. It is the club house on these sawmills and terpentine [*sic*] stills."[2] Hurston's evocation of the jook here also portends her discussion of it in "Characteristics of Negro Expression," where she establishes it as a vernacular performance venue and one of the most important places in America for music, dance, and the "real Negro theatre."

Originally published in Nancy Cunard's edited volume *Negro: An Anthology* (1934), "Characteristics of Negro Expression" is essentially a taxonomy of Black folk practices based on Hurston's anthropological fieldwork. It has recently been deemed one of her most important works and regarded by some contemporary scholars as the first Black performance studies essay.[3] From the blues to the Black bottom and the Charleston, she writes, Black popular culture is "conceived" in and "make[s] the round of Jooks and public works before going into the outside world."[4] Through her correspondence with Hughes, it becomes clear that "Characteristics" is in part an effort to theorize the cultural practices Hurston observed in southern labor camps and to cultivate a grammar of Black performance that would challenge the devaluation of Black cultural expression within European aesthetic norms and the then prevailing minstrel tradition in American popular culture.

That Hurston derived her theories of Black performance from sites of labor perhaps recalls Washington's "aesthetics of work" explored in chapter 2. However, they were not necessarily compatible philosophies because Hurston fundamentally rejected the elitism associated with uplift and was expressly critical of the "Race Man and Race Woman" discourse advanced by the "post-war generation," including at Tuskegee.[5] Receiving her early education at the Robert C. Hungerford Normal and Industrial School, established by Tuskegee graduates in Eatonville, Florida, in 1899, Hurston was a Tuskegee student once removed. As Carla Kaplan, the editor of Hurston's letters, points out, she admired Washington "for making a place for 'Negro 'untouchables'' " at Tuskegee and throughout her work often celebrated him as a Black folk hero of sorts (much preferring him to W. E. B. Du Bois).[6] She was expressly critical of those who criticized Washington's promotion of industrial education without "analysis" or "seeking for merits," and her autobiography, *Dust Tracks on a Road* (1942), signifies on *Up from Slavery*'s themes of hard work, rugged American individualism, and refusal to be bitter about racial oppression and inequality.[7] In the summer of 1927, Hurston visited Tuskegee with Hughes and Jessie Redmon Fauset, where she lectured to the student body on the short-story genre. The group of young writers posed for a photograph standing before the Booker T. Washington Monument, paying homage to the departed leader (figure 7.1).[8]

Though Hurston shared Washington's and Tuskegee's political commitment to those whom she called "the man in the gutter" (and whom Washington called "the man farthest down"), their approaches to and goals for Black rural and working-class peoples were quite distinct. Hurston viewed labor less as a mode of eco-ontological regeneration or training of bourgeois subjects than a quotidian fact of life. Her political commitments to Black rural and working-class peoples engaged them as arbiters of culture who exemplified African cultural retentions in the "New World," not as the backward beneficiaries of the civilizing mission. Yet in rejecting uplift and earlier generations' class paternalism, Hurston and many of her contemporaries often overcorrected, trafficking in the language and logics of racial primitivism that fetishized the very people they sought to celebrate and legitimize. Ultimately, much like McKay, Hurston moved within and against Tuskegee's articulated mission, at once celebrating what it enabled for Black modernity while rejecting its class and gender politics as well as its aesthetic conventions (chapters 1 and 2).[9]

As Hurston traveled throughout the U.S. South and the Caribbean, developing her theories of Black performance, she also documented how the plantation continued to shape Black life in the early twentieth century. Her folk interlocutors were often former sharecroppers and tenant farmers from the cotton plantations of the post-Reconstruction U.S. South as well as from the sugar, tobacco, and banana plantations of the Bahamas, Cuba, Jamaica, and Haiti, all of whom migrated to Florida in search of better labor opportunities. Some migrants landed in the all-Black town of Eatonville in Central Florida, while others pursued employment on public-works projects or with corporate agricultural and industrial enterprises in the state's southernmost region. By tending to the nuances of inter- and intraregional migration, Hurston acted as a Black geographer, establishing Florida as a new frontier, a domestic and international migration destination, and node of diasporic relations. She was among the first writers to capture southern Florida's transformation and development from wilderness and wetlands into a major agricultural and industrial center made possible by the work of African American and Afro-Caribbean migrant laborers. Her own family had migrated from Notasulga, Macon County, Alabama—about ten miles from Tuskegee—to Eatonville in the 1890s, when she was about three years old; thus, she was intimately familiar with how Florida drew workers

FIGURE 7.1. *Left to right*: Jessie Redmon Fauset, Langston Hughes, and Zora Neale Hurston standing before the Booker T. Washington monument at Tuskegee in 1927.

Source: Beinecke Library, Yale University, New Haven, CT.

from across the Global Black South to labor in its various industries, forming a working-class New Negro frontier and diasporic contact zone.

In Hazel Carby's now-canonical essay critiquing what she views as a nostalgic turn toward the rural U.S. South in Black studies in response to the urban blight affecting northern Black communities in the 1990s, she argues, "Hurston's work during this period [the 1930s] ... involves an intellectual's search for the appropriate forms in which to represent the folk and a decision to rewrite the geographical boundaries of representation by situating the southern, rural folk and patterns of migration in relation to the Caribbean rather than the northern states."[10] I agree with Carby that Hurston was searching for the appropriate forms for representing the folk, and in this chapter I demonstrate how performance became the chief mode for doing so. However, I also agree with Martyn Bone that Carby's critique of Hurston's alleged erasure of the Great Migration to the U.S. North in turn erases Afro-Caribbean labor migration to South Florida and with Riché Richardson that this critique "renders invisible and insignificant blacks who *do* continue to live in the rural South."[11] Carby's critique is especially ironic given her ongoing dissatisfaction with African American studies for its putative exclusion of the broader diaspora. Why is it, then, that Carby criticizes Hurston's efforts to link southern folk culture with the Caribbean and can only view those efforts as Hurston's neglect of northward migration? Carby's view illustrates the northern bias that this chapter and book aim to challenge by illuminating the south-to-south contours of Hurston's geographic imagination.

Hurston grapples with the afterlife of the plantation in two primary ways: she depicts Black laborers as arbiters and progenitors of culture to disrupt the minstrel tradition and Western aesthetic hegemony in American theater and performance, and she captures an undertheorized diasporic labor migration network to Central and South Florida that revises northern-centric narratives of the Great Migration and the New Negro Movement. She portrays the Great Migration as a south-to-south journey, following African American migrants from the cotton plantations of post-Reconstruction Alabama, Mississippi, and Georgia to the new frontiers of Central and South Florida. She then travels farther south to the Bahamas, Haiti, and Jamaica to continue her investigation of Black folk life and diasporic cultural retentions. While Hurston's characters and interlocutors work in agricultural and industrial jobs, where they are subjected to plantation styles of management, she uses performance as a mechanism to disrupt the plantation's attempted geographic, cultural, and ontological stronghold on Black life and being. As Sylvia Wynter argues, enslaved Africans "created on the plot a folk culture—the basis of a social order" that "became a source of cultural guerilla resistance to the plantation system."[12] Thus, Hurston's efforts to document, preserve, and theorize Black folk culture are evidence of her commitment to the logics and ethics of the plot. Furthermore, long before Joseph Roach's notion of "circum-Atlantic performance," Hurston was using her own theories of Black performance, conceived in southern Florida's work camps, to exemplify the dynamism and complexity of Black diasporic folk expression in the hemisphere.[13] If Tuskegee transformed the plantation into a site of Black eco-ontological regeneration, then Hurston transformed the work camp, another afterlife of the plantation, into a scene of Black performance and diasporic relationality.

In this chapter, I establish Hurston as a Black geographer as well as a performance and diaspora theorist. In documenting Black labor migration to Central and South Florida, she depicted the state as a cosmopolitan geography teeming with Black modern life and culture and recovered how its eco-ontological history is irreducible to the plantation past. Building on recent scholarship on Hurston and performance, I then resituate "Characteristics of Negro Expression" within the southern labor camp, its original milieu, to examine how Hurston reconfigured a "site of labor" into a "scene of performance" and, ultimately, to gesture toward the southern roots of Black performance studies. By attending to the inextricability of labor and performance in Hurston's archive, what I have termed the "scene of the work camp," I show how she captured the spectacle of exploited Black labor characteristic of the afterlife of the plantation in the Global Black South, on one hand, while also rendering the region as a scene of vitality and diasporic affiliation, brimming with laughter, gambling, dancing, and music, on the other.

This chapter also considers how Hurston mobilized her theories of Black performance as outlined in "Characteristics" to depict diasporic relationality in her folk concerts, fiction, plays, ethnographies, and lectures. She took seriously her mentor Franz Boas's observation in the foreword to her first ethnography (published during her lifetime), *Mules and Men* (1935), that "American Negro life" has a "strong African background in the West Indies, the importance of which diminishes with increasing distance from the south," and thus focused much of her career on documenting and theorizing southern African American and Afro-Caribbean cultural linkages. Although her second ethnography, *Tell My Horse* (1938), has been roundly criticized for its blatant American chauvinism and confounding political commentary, recent attention to her folk concerts, set in South Florida's work camps, yields a more nuanced account of how she negotiated cultural differences between diasporic communities.

The chapter concludes by recovering relatively unknown newspaper accounts of Hurston's visit to Jamaica in 1936, where she repurposed "Characteristics" yet again to draw connections between African American and Jamaican folk cultures and to forge ties with the island's cultural and political elite by supporting the development of Jamaican art and literature. Over the course of several lectures, Hurston mobilized "Characteristics" to champion an already burgeoning Jamaican cultural nationalism in a way that was far more nuanced and respectful of diasporic difference than *Tell My Horse*. Through her theories of Black performance and the call-and-response structure of the lecture form, Hurston reworked "Characteristics" into a set of protocols for validating Black diasporic folk culture against the hegemony of European aesthetic norms and articulated a more egalitarian diasporic politics overall.

HURSTON'S GEOGRAPHIC IMAGINATION:
LABOR MIGRATION AND ECO-ONTOLOGY
ON FLORIDA'S FRONTIER

Throughout her oeuvre, Zora Neale Hurston depicts the U.S. South as a dynamic region and pays careful attention to its interstate and *intra*state differences, especially within Florida.[14] For instance, in "Proposed Recording Expedition Into the Floridas" (c. 1939), composed for the Federal Writers' Project, she partitioned the state into four distinct culture areas with their own characteristics, industries, ecologies, and folk forms. She tracked how Black labor migration transformed Florida into a somewhat exceptional geography within the region and how "the unsettled country of South Florida" in particular became a new frontier and cultural contact zone that disrupted the spatiotemporal and eco-ontological legacies of the plantation in the U.S. South. Beginning in the late nineteenth century, she contended, South Florida's rapid settlement and development attracted African American migrants from Georgia, West Florida, and other parts of the U.S. South. "No more back-bending over rows of cotton; no more fear of the fury of the Reconstruction," she wrote in her memoir, *Dust Tracks on a Road* (1942). "Good pay, sympathetic White folks and cheap land, soft to the touch of the plow. Relatives and friends were sent for."[15]

Hurston first depicted this south-to-south migration stream in her debut novel *Jonah's Gourde Vine* (1934), loosely based on her family's migration from Macon County, Alabama, to Eatonville, Florida. The novel details plantation life in late nineteenth-century Alabama and the limited labor opportunities available to the formerly enslaved. The protagonist, John Pearson, works his way from being a field hand to working as a foreman on the Pearson cotton plantation, where his family had also been enslaved. Through John and his many labor migrations, the novel delineates the ambitions of the immediate postslavery generation as they sought to distance themselves from agriculture by pursuing industrial labor opportunities instead. This transition from cotton farming to industrial labor is a hallmark of Hurston's conception of Black southern modernity.

John migrates throughout Alabama, working as a sharecropper and plow hand and in a tie camp cutting timber for railroad construction. Though he eventually becomes a foreman on the Pearson plantation and "moved up into the house-servants' quarters just back of the big house," he assaults his wife's brother in a domestic dispute and must flee Alabama for Florida. Florida represents new industrial opportunities for John. "Tuh Florida, man. Dat's de new country openin' up. Now git me straight, Ah don't mean West Florida, Ah means de real place. Good times, good money, and no mules and cotton." Hurston acts as a Black geographer here, noting not only interstate but also intrastate differences between West Florida, tied like Alabama to the cotton economy, and Central Florida, a place "in the making." John finds work in a railroad camp and then migrates to Eatonville, a "little Negro village" with a "mayor and corporation," where he becomes a property owner, preacher, carpenter, and eventually town mayor. Ultimately, Florida and Eatonville in particular enable John to disrupt the plantation's attempted stranglehold on his life: "Uh man kin be sumpin' heah 'thout folks tramplin' all over yuh."[16]

Hurston extols Eatonville as an exceptional Black community throughout much of her oeuvre. It is "a pure Negro town—charter, mayor, council, town marshal and all. It was not the first Negro community in America, but it was the first to be incorporated, the first attempt at organized self-government on the part of Negroes in America."[17] Eatonville's political self-determination exemplifies a key feature of Hurston's conception of Black modernity because Black life could thrive there without the constant threat of racial terrorism. As "the city of five lakes, three croquet courts, three hundred brown skins, three hundred good swimmers, plenty guavas, two schools, and no jailhouse," Eatonville was a place where Black people were not reduced to their labor. Rather, they had the freedom to pursue leisure and education and, with no jailhouse, to defy racist pseudoscientific myths that Black people were intrinsically criminal and pathological.[18]

From 1899 to 1904, when Hurston was between nine and thirteen years old, she attended Eatonville's Robert Hungerford School, founded by Tuskegee alumni Mary Calhoun and Russell C. Calhoun.[19] Russell was considered one of Tuskegee's most accomplished graduates. He kept in close contact with Washington about his work in Eatonville and was even featured in *Tuskegee and Its People* (1906). Hungerford's curriculum was modeled on Tuskegee's, and by 1907 three of the school's six teachers were Tuskegee graduates.[20] As at Tuskegee, students at Hungerford worked to pay for their education, and the school hosted an annual farmer's conference, modeled after the Tuskegee Negro Conference. Washington touted Eatonville as a model of a Black agrarian future, featuring the town in his publication *The Negro in Business* (1907), and even visited in 1912 (well after Hurston's departure, however). At its founding, "the people of the little town began to set out groves of orange trees, which paid well for ten years," Washington wrote.[21] Residents soon learned the dangers of monocropping, however, and pursued agricultural diversification instead. The town's decision to sustain itself by farming fit squarely within Washington's conception of Black agrarian futures. Through its municipal and agricultural proficiencies, Eatonville represented Black people's capacity for self-government, a value that Hurston shared with Washington (figures 7.2 and 7.3).

At the same time, Hurston's reflections on her education at Hungerford somewhat depart from Tuskegee's articulated mission. In "A Negro Community Builder," a feature essay in *Tuskegee and Its People*, Russell Calhoun described a balanced industrial and academic curriculum, where girl students "receive[d] instruction in dressmaking, plain sewing, cooking, laundering, millinery, basketry, and housekeeping." He also assured readers that the school gave "no industry at the expense of the literary work. The academic

FIGURE 7.2. "J. E. Clark's pineapple farm, Eatonville, Fla."

Source: Booker T. Washington, *The Negro in Business* (Boston: Hertel, Jenkins, 1907), between pp. 78 and 79.

FIGURE 7.3. "City Council and jail, Eatonville, Fla."

Source: Washington, *The Negro in Business*, between pp. 78 and 79.

department covers a useful course of the English branches."[22] In *Dust Tracks*, however, Hurston only recalls her affinity for the school's academic offerings. Once, when asked to read an excerpt from the story of Pluto and Persephone from the fifth-grade reader for two northern white women visitors, she so impressed them with her superior reading skills that they took a special interest in her and supplied her with clothing and books on Greco-Roman mythology and fairy tales that spurred her already precocious imagination. Tellingly, however, Hurston omits the agricultural and industrial arms of the curriculum and never indicates what trade she studied there. Whereas Washington and the Calhouns viewed Eatonville and Hungerford as compatible with agrarian futures, Hurston, like McKay, represents how Tuskegee's students customized their educations to develop their own cultural and political projects.

To be clear, Hurston's conception of Black modernity, forged at the intersection of diasporic labor and performance, includes the possibility of an agrarian future but is not reducible to it. In her girlhood days in Eatonville, for instance, her family had a five-acre garden, and as an adult she was an avid gardener of fruits, vegetables, and flowers. Furthermore, in *Their Eyes Were Watching God* (1937), she famously draws on geography and ecology to explore the myriad dimensions of southern New Negro womanhood. Though Janie, the novel's protagonist, is born in West Florida, the state's "cotton-corn-tobacco region," where "people live under the patriarchal agrarian system" and where the "old rules of life [still] hold," as described in "Proposed Recording Expedition," Hurston depicts Janie's sexual awakening as a "blossoming pear tree": "Oh to be a pear tree—any tree in bloom! With kissing bees singing of the beginning of the world!"[23] Instead of analogizing Janie's maturation to cotton and thus the plantation, the pear tree represents an eco-ontological reorientation of the relationship between Black life and plant life, redefined by beauty, sweetness, sustenance, and sexual bliss. Janie's innocent indulgence in her sexual pleasure conveys the potential disruption of the legacy of sexual violence and trauma within her family's history. This glimpse of eco-ontological liberation is short-lived, however. Janie is coerced into a loveless marriage with Logan Killicks, where she labors on his farm and questions the value placed on land and property ownership, a significant departure from the Tuskegee New Negro ideal (though Janie respects Booker T. Washington, as we see in her conversation with Mrs. Turner later in the novel) (290–91). This begins a series of marriages and migrations throughout the state in search of greater love and freedom. Janie travels from West to Central to South Florida, where she finally achieves a semblance of freedom from the suffocating gender norms in other parts of the state that tie her to agriculture and domesticity. In a surprising reversal of the Great Migration and even the Underground Railroad, migration southward, in Hurston's hands, enables greater freedom.

When Janie moves to Eatonville, Hurston further critiques the hegemony of the plantation regime, in particular the insidious ways it came to shape Black freedom dreams. Eatonville, as an incorporated, self-governing Black town, is a symbol of Black modernity, but the novel quickly subverts this narrative of exceptionalism by showing how even all-Black communities can perpetuate forms of unfreedom and oppression through patriarchy, paternalism, and classism. The absence of criminality and racial violence in Eatonville does not equate to wholesale social equality, especially for Black women. When Janie marries Eatonville's founder and mayor, Jody Starks, she finds herself living in a "big white house" modeled on a plantation mansion both aesthetically and symbolically (284). "It had two stories with porches, with bannisters and such things. The rest of the town looked like servant's quarters surrounding the 'big house'" (212). Jody's material success, while significant for a Black man battling the structural violence and inequities of the Jim Crow South, reinscribes other forms of violence, especially misogyny and class disparities, symbolized by his preference for a "big house" painted, Hurston elaborates, in a "promenading white." Janie's departure from Eatonville's suffocating orderliness and bourgeois domesticity—essentially a rejection of Tuskegee's conception of New Negro womanhood (chapters 1 and 2)—for the wilds of the Everglades and the muck takes readers on yet another geographic and eco-ontological journey farther southward toward a seemingly greater freedom.

When Janie marries her third husband, Tea Cake, and migrates to the Everglades, Hurston demonstrates South Florida's distinctiveness within the afterlife of the plantation by capturing how African American workers from other parts of the U.S. South relocated to the region to pursue better labor opportunities in corporate agriculture and industry: "Day by day now, the hordes of workers poured in. . . . They came in wagons from way up in Georgia and they came in truck loads from east, west, north, and south. Permanent transients with no attachments and tired looking men with their families and dogs in flivvers. All night, all day, hurrying in to pick beans. . . . hopeful humanity, herded and hovered . . . chugged on to the muck. People ugly from ignorance and broken from being poor" (281-82).

The Everglades is another eco-ontological intervention within Hurston's geographic imagination. Historically, the Everglades' ecological makeup and agricultural economy distinguished it from much of the rest of the state, where the plantation had already taken root. Until the late nineteenth century, the Everglades were largely wilderness and wetlands, where Maroons had once escaped to freedom. "As late as the 1840's," write Frank Peterman and Audrey Peterman, "the entire peninsula of South Florida was considered 'too sickly and too sterile' to merit serious consideration for settlement. It was said that the Territory was uninhabitable for whites and should be left to runaway Africans and Indian 'savages.' "[24] Indeed, in *Their Eyes Were Watching God* Hurston portrays South Florida as a "wild" and untamed geography: "To Janie's strange eyes, everything in the Everglades was big and new. . . . Ground so rich that everything went wild. . . . Wild cane on either side of the road hiding the rest of the world. People wild too" (280).

The wildness of the Everglades suggests it was undegraded by the plantation's extractive agricultural practices, and as a largely uncultivated space the region portended an alternative future where the racial-sexual violence of the plantation and Jim Crow had not taken root (though it was not completely absent, as the workers learn when they are conscripted into labor following the hurricane and as Janie herself learns when Tea Cake resorts to domestic violence). Here, Tea

Cake and his fellow migrants plant and pick beans, which, unlike cotton and sugar cane, were not part of the state's slave economy. As beans are a less labor-intensive crop, their cultivation indexes differently in the racial-agricultural economy of the Global Black South, allowing Black life to flourish. On the muck, there is also ample time for leisure: gambling, singing, playing music, and dancing. When they first arrive, "Tea Cake picked his box a great deal for Janie, but he still didn't have enough to do" (281). That Tea Cake's time was not completely co-opted by work suggests that Black life exceeds and is valuable beyond its capacity to labor there. Unlike the case of the Tuskegee New Negro, work is not treated as a moral or ethical imperative in Hurston's oeuvre; it is simply a mundane fact of life. The Everglades seemingly enables a form of freedom that is unavailable on the plantations of the Upper South or even the orderly, bourgeois domesticity of Eatonville.

However, despite Hurston's efforts to establish South Florida, especially the Everglades, as an exceptional cosmopolitan geography within the Global Black South, corporate agriculture and industry were still the primary draws for workers, reinscribing them in racial-capitalist labor schemes and social arrangements. By the early twentieth century, the Everglades was regarded as a new frontier that, much like the Panama Canal Zone and the Mississippi Delta, was ripe for new labor and business opportunities. "Florida's ambitious attempt to make farm land out of swamp captured the imaginations of thousands of people . . . [who] flocked from throughout the United States and from around the globe to try their hands at Everglades farming."[25] Indeed, like UFCO, corporate agriculture and industry in Florida, such as the Everglades Cypress Lumber Company— one of Hurston's primary field sites in *Mules and Men*—represents a veritable afterlife of the plantation. Although these companies provided relative freedom and movement for Black people, the labor arrangements were often modeled on the very racial distribution of labor that helped to define the modern world order: the plantation.

Both Eatonville and the Everglades were ultimately paradoxical geographies that, despite Hurston's attempts to establish them as alternative eco-ontological spaces, remained vulnerable to the plantation and its insidious logics. By transforming sites of labor into scenes of performance, however, Hurston intimates that if she could not fully dislodge Black life from the plantation's vise grip, she could surely show that Black people were not reducible to the plantation by illuminating how they actively constructed their own cultural values that moved within and against oppressive structures. This philosophical approach to Black life and culture reflects Hurston's commitment to the logics and ethics of the plot.

SETTING THE SCENE OF THE WORK CAMP: LABOR, PERFORMANCE, AND INDUSTRIAL MODERNITY

Although Hurston's geographic imagination includes an appreciation for agrarian futures, her documentation of Black folk performance tends to prioritize sites of industrial labor. Her conception of the scene of the work camp is a composite of the phosphate mines and the railroad, sawmill, and turpentine camps she visited on her various fieldwork expeditions throughout Central and South Florida. She thus offers an alternative depiction of the U.S. South as an industrializing space rather than what Sonnet Retman describes as the popular "pastoral, preindustrial portrait of the folk."[26] Video footage from Hurston's expeditions depicts Black workers operating large industrial machinery in railroad and lumber camps, and in *Dust Tracks on a Road* she depicts Polk County, Florida, as a bustling industrial center where "the wheels of industry must move":

> Polk County. Black men from tree to tree among the lordly pines, a swift, slanting stroke to bleed the trees for gum. Paint, explosives, marine stores, flavors, perfumes, tone for a violin bow, and many other things which the black men who bleed the trees never heard about.
> Polk County. The clang of nine-pound hammers on railroad steel. The world must ride.
> Hah! A rhythmic swing of the body, hammer falls, and another spike driven to the head in the tie. . . .
> Another offering to the soul of civilization whose other name is travel.[27]

Hurston's poetic portrayal of Black laborers renders the work camp as a scene of performance, wherein the "rhythmic swing of the body" is choreographed labor. Yet she also situates the folk firmly within industrial capitalism, revealing the work camp as a paradoxical space derived from the plantation but distinct from it. The turpentine workers produce the raw materials for commodities that they have never seen or heard about, and the railroad workers lay the foundation for modern travel. Just as their enslaved ancestors' labor financed Europe's Industrial Revolution in the eighteenth century, these workers—though technically free laborers—are what Hurston refers to in another context as the "mules of the world." They are removed from the higher modes of production, so their status as modern subjects remains entangled with the violence, unfreedom, and precarity of racial-capitalist modernity.

Central and South Florida's work camps often reproduced the structural conditions of the plantation. Historical accounts of workers' living conditions are reminiscent of antebellum slave cabins or even the squalor of the barracoons aboard slave ships: migrants "slept, according to one observer, 'packed together in sordid rooms, hallways, tar-paper shacks, filthy barracks with one central faucet and toilet, sheds, lean-tos, old garages, condemned and shaky buildings.'"[28] In 1939, Hurston conducted an interview with Seaboard, a worker in the citrus industry, who observed: "The workers sing in the groves, mostly blues songs about women and likker.... [T]he field foreman ... counts the number of boxes. Sometimes we get mad at him, but we are careful not to *call* him anything."[29] Like the overseer of the antebellum plantation, the foreman enforces the workers' productivity, urging them to work longer and harder while intimidating them into silence.

Similarly, in *Mules and Men*, when the quarters boss visits the jook, Hurston notices that Box-Car, one of her worker-interlocutors, has suddenly disappeared and inquires about his whereabouts. He had been put on a chain gang after getting arrested for "vacancy" (vagrancy), but when the judge learned that he was in fact employed, he was charged for carrying "concealed cards, and attempt to gamble" and another trumped-up (unnamed) charge as well. "And dis very quarters boss was Cap'n on de gang where Ah wuz," Box-Car informs Hurston. "Me and him ain't never gointer set hawses."[30] That the quarters boss was also the chain-gang captain suggests that conditions in the work camp not only share genealogical roots with the plantation but are deeply enmeshed with the carceral logics of the prison as well.

In contrast to these other carceral spaces, Hurston depicts the work camp as a zone of a highly circumscribed and precarious freedom for Black laborers: "The law is lax on these big saw-mill, turpentine, and railroad 'jobs,'" she explains in *Dust Tracks*. "All of these places have plenty of men and women who are fugitives from justice. The management asks no questions.... In some places, the 'law' is forbidden to come on the premises to hunt for malefactors who did their malefacting elsewhere. The wheels of industry must move, and if these men don't do the work, who is there to do it?"[31] Like their enslaved ancestors, these workers occupy an extralegal status under which Black life is valuable strictly for its labor power. Yet whereas their ancestors had no *recourse to the law*, the work camp affords *protection from the law* and was often considered a viable alternative to the comparatively more oppressive conditions of sharecropping and tenant farming. At once carceral and precariously liberating, the work camp is a fugitive geography, symbolizing the problem of free labor for New World

Black subjects and the condition of Blackness as an ongoing struggle between mobility and confinement.

Despite the work camp's plantation-like living and labor conditions, Hurston sought to transform and repurpose the site of labor into a scene of performance. As "fugitives from justice," Hurston's "folk" were not the dignified laborers pictured in Tuskegee's institutional literature or Washington's periodical publications, performing a southern New Negro aesthetic. And unlike many of her male contemporaries in the 1930s, such as Sterling Brown, Richard Wright, and even Hughes, who embraced the Communist Party's agitprop philosophy, Hurston resisted the politicization of the worker and the political economy of labor altogether. She remained committed to the "cultural politics" and "aesthetic ideologies" of the Harlem Renaissance—that is, art for art's sake, unencumbered by racial uplift, antilynching, or socialist propaganda.[32] Instead, Hurston depicts the work camp as an economy of labor and leisure organized by Black performance. Waxing poetic about Polk County, she writes:

> Polk County. Black men scrambling up ladders into orange trees. Singing, laughing, cursing, boasting of last night's love, and looking forward to the darkness again. . . .
>
> Polk County. After dark, the jooks. Songs are born out of feelings with an old beat-up piano, or a guitar for a mid-wife. . . .
>
> Polk County in the jooks. Dancing the square dance. Dancing the scroush. Dancing the belly-rub. Knocking the right hat off the wrong head, and backing it up with a switchblade.[33]

Just as her contemporaries depict Harlem's underworld via the nightclub and cabaret scene, Hurston portrays the jook as a zone of vice and pleasure unique to the U.S. South. The jook is integral to Hurston's dramatic repertoire, featured prominently throughout her folk concerts, plays, and musical revues. "To those who want to institute the Negro theatre," she writes in "Characteristics," "let me say it is already established. . . . The real Negro theatre is in the Jooks and the cabarets."[34]

In his study *The Scene of Harlem Cabaret*, the performance studies scholar Shane Vogel describes Harlem's nightlife in the 1920s as consisting of two parts—"segregated cabarets" and "black cabarets"—and as organized by a dialectic of labor and leisure. In segregated cabarets, Black performers entertained white patrons and were "underpaid and overworked in the most miserable conditions." At the Cotton Club, for instance, owners reprised the plantation, staging "an entire mise-en-scène of antebellum nostalgia and modernist primitivism, setting jungle designs alongside plantation motifs."[35] The Plantation Club, established to compete with the Cotton Club, had a similar mission and in its name explicitly tied Harlem's Black performance scene to the political economy of slavery, the plantation, and their afterlives. Though Harlem's nightclubs are typically imagined as spaces of Black fun and pleasure, segregated cabarets were scenes of subjection that provided white leisure at the expense of Black labor.

The Black cabaret, in contrast, "was a scene of black vernacular world making," Vogel writes. These performances "had genealogical traces in the brief allowances of dance and sociality by slave owners, antebellum practices of 'stealing away,' church dances, and the development of the jook joint." Black performers labored nightly as spectacles in segregated cabarets to entertain white patrons before heading to "black cabarets," where they engaged in practices of "criminal intimacy" and "fugitive sociality."[36] Following Vogel, I suggest that Hurston configures the work camp as a "scene" of performance organized by the interplay of labor and leisure: the workday and the jook. Central and South Florida's work camps were organized around the logics of the antebellum plantation, just as the Cotton Club staged "antebellum nostalgia." And much like the Harlem cabaret, the "scene of the work camp" comprised performances of leisure and pleasure vis-à-vis the jook, which Hurston, "musically speaking," calls "the most important place in America." "For in its smelly, shoddy confines has been born the secular music known as blues, and on blues has been founded jazz."[37] Like the Black cabaret, then, the jook is "a hot spot, a sphere of activity, a place where *things happen*," as Vogel describes it—a fugitive soundscape.[38]

Although Vogel's dichotomy is useful, it is important to point out that "the scene of the work camp" is less tidy and thus departs from his formulation of the Harlem cabaret. Since the jook is located in the camp's living quarters, it is not entirely free of white oversight, and the spectatorial practices of the workday sometimes spill over into the jook and vice versa. "The quarters boss had a way of standing around in the dark and listening," Hurston writes, policing the consumption of "likker" and acts of violence.[39] Hurston also captures moments during the workday when the workers are not under the watchful eye of the jobs boss and instead of singing work songs engage in storytelling as a form of pleasure and resistance. In the work camp, then, labor and leisure are perhaps more deeply entangled than in the Harlem cabaret, much like the plot and the plantation.

"I WANT TO COLLECT LIKE A NEW BROOM":
ANTHROPOLOGY, LITERATURE, AND PERFORMANCE

Just as Hurston experimented across a range of media, aesthetic forms, and diasporic geographies, the scene of the work camp is equally dynamic, organized by the interplay of sound and writing, music and literature, and embodied performance and text. As she traveled throughout the Gulf South, she often used Langston Hughes's blues poetry to ingratiate herself with her folk informants. She "became something of a publicity agent for Hughes," writes her biographer Valerie Boyd, reading from and selling his early collections of poetry to the workers she encountered on "the jobs."[40] In a letter to Hughes in 1928, she delineated how her strategy for collecting folklore relied on the interplay of text and performance:

> In every town I hold 1 or 2 story-telling contests, and at each I begin by telling them who you are and all, then I read poems from "Fine Clothes." Boy! they eat it up.... You are quoted in R.R. camps, phosphate mines, Turpentine stills etc. I went into a house Saturday night (last) and the men were skinning... and when the dealer saw his opponent was on the turn (and losing consequently) He chanted
>
> > "When hard luck overtakes you
> > Nothin for you to do
> > Grab up yo' fine clothes
> > An' sell em to-ooo-de Jew Hah!!"
>
> (slaps the card down on the table)
> The other fellow was visibly cast down when the dealer picked up his money. Dealer gloating continued: "If you wuz a mule
>
> > I'd get you a waggin to haul
> > But youse *so* low down-hown [?]
> > you aint even got uh stall."
>
> So you see they are making it so much a part of themselves they go to improvising on it.
> For some reason they call it "De Party Book." They come specially to be read to.... [T]wo men came over with guitars and sang the whole book. Everybody joined in.... One man was giving the words out-lining them out as the preacher does a hymn and the others would take it up and sing. It was glorious![41]

Whereas many Harlem Renaissance writers—Hurston and Hughes included—used the raw material of Black folk culture as the basis of their art, in this scene Hurston reverses direction by reintroducing the blues to its source: the folk. To be sure, her methodology is unorthodox, especially for a social scientist with her elite training. By introducing Hughes's poetry to the workers, Hurston essentially contaminates her "data" and contradicts her later observation that "the best source" for collecting folklore "is where there are the least outside influences."[42] Yet she also demonstrates how performance can collapse the gap between literacy and orality in Black culture. Unlike the highly stylized Broadway arrangements of Black vernacular music and dance that she vehemently detested, Hughes's blues poetry was immediately recognizable to his fellow folk composers, functioning as a vernacular hymnbook for their secular temple: the jook. Hardly able to contain her flattery and adoration for Hughes, Hurston enthused in a letter: "Know what, you ought to make a loafing tour oft [sic] the South like the blind Homer, singing your songs. Not in auditoriums, but in camps, on water-fronts and the like. You are the poet of the people and your subjects are crazy about you. Why not? There never has been a poet who has been acceptable to His Majesty, the man in the gutter before, and laugh if you will, but that man in the gutter is the god-maker, the creator of everything that lasts."[43] Here, through poetry and performance, she incorporates the southern work camp into the literary geography of the New Negro movement, further attenuating the north–south and rural–urban binaries.

Hurston's ethnography *Mules and Men* is the culmination of her recording expeditions throughout the Gulf South. *Mules* is divided into two sections: a collection of folktales, gambling songs, and children's games gathered from various Florida work camps and a more straightforward ethnographic account of hoodoo practices in New Orleans. By the time Hurston published *Mules*, she was already a celebrated novelist and seasoned playwright, director, and, some would even say, choreographer.[44] Instead of straightforward ethnographic prose, *Mules* uses literature and performance to push the limits of the ethnographic form. Hurston especially draws on her theatrical background to experiment with literary and ethnographic formal and generic conventions.

In *Mules*, at the close of the workday the workers head to the jook, where they sing, dance, and gamble the night away. In one scene, Hurston's writing style shifts abruptly from prose to scriptwriting: the card players are transformed into "players" in the theatrical sense, and the jook becomes a (musical) theater, similar to what she described in her letter to Hughes:

AESTHETICIZING LABOR, PERFORMING DIASPORA   315

Dealer: "Put down! You all owe de bet a dime. Damn sitters rob St. Peter, rob St. Paul."

Larkins: "Dat nigger is gointer top somebody. He's got a cub. Ah ain't goin' in dat damn steel trap." . . .

The dealer starts down the deck, and the singing goes with it. Christopher Jenkins' deep baritone is something to remember.

. . . [lyrics to "Let de Deal Go Down"]

Each line punctuated by "hah!" and a falling card.[45]

In this scene, Hurston toggles between anthropologist and playwright. Her "script" includes not only music and dialogue but also stage directions delineating the players' sounds and movements and how they are expected to deliver their "lines." The dealer's lines include parentheticals to designate to whom he is speaking—"(To Hardy)." Then Hurston notes the breathy "hah!" that "adorns" "Let de Deal Go Down," a popular gambling song, and uses another parenthetical to indicate how Big Sweet's line should be delivered. "Big Sweet (arrogantly): 'You full of dat ole ism blood. Fat covered yo' heart. Youse skeered to bet. Gamblin' wid yo' stuff out de window'" (143). By presenting the Florida-flip game as a dramatic script, Hurston uses literary form to underscore the southern jook as a site of Black vernacular drama and theater and to establish the workers as actors and performers, enacting what the literary scholar and performance theorist Daphne Brooks calls "performative ethnography."[46]

Through the scene of the work camp, Hurston especially challenges traditional representations of Black workers in the South as culturally and politically unsophisticated. While at the camps, in addition to using Hughes's poetry to ingratiate herself with the workers, she staged "lying contests" to capture the performance of storytelling and playing the dozens, an African American vernacular art form based on verbal agility and word play. Constitutive to this ostensible performance of leisure, however, was an important social critique of the problems of race and labor, what the literary scholar David Nicholls calls "a living language of dissent."[47] In *Mules*, while visiting the Everglades Cypress Lumber Company in Loughman, Florida, Hurston accompanies the swamp gang to work. The foreman is later than usual, leading the workers to conjecture that it "must be something terrible when white folks get slow about putting us to work" (70). When the foreman finally arrives and informs them that there is "no loggin' today, boys," Joe Willard feigns disappointment at getting a day off; however, the foreman quickly dashes their hopes, instructing the men to go to the sawmill to check if it needs extra hands there. "Ain't dat a mean man?"

Jim Allen asked. "No work in the swamp and still he won't let us knock off" (71). As the workers make their way to the sawmill, they strike up a storytelling session critiquing mean bosses and the unequal racial and gender dynamics of industrial capitalism.

Jim Allen relates a folktale that draws on the biblical origin myth and plantation hierarchies about how Black people came to be relegated to the domain of hard labor. After creating animals and people, God created a "great big bundle" and placed it in the middle of the road. It remained there for "thousands of years" until "Ole Missus" instructed "Ole Massa" to pick it up because she was curious about its contents. Realizing that the box looked heavy, "Ole Massa" told "de nigger" to "fetch" it, and "de nigger" passed along the mandate to his wife. Eager to learn what was inside, "de nigger 'oman" ran and "grabbed hold of de box and opened it up and it was full of hard work. Dats the reason de sister in black works harder than anybody else in de world," Jim Allen reasons. "De white man tells de nigger to work and he takes and tells his wife" (76–77). Curiously, "Ole Missus" and "Ole Massa" are already superior to Black people when Jim Allen's origin myth begins—suggesting that white supremacy preceded racial capitalism and thus his inability to imagine an alternative social order without racial hierarchies. Jim Allen's analysis of gender oppression within the southern economy of labor, however, is spot on and consistent with Hurston's own belief that Black women, who experience both racial and sexual discrimination, are "the mules of the world," a recurrent theme throughout her oeuvre.

Jim Presley objects to Jim Allen's tale and offers another origin myth, where the white man and the Black man begin on equal footing. When God puts two bundles in the middle of the road, both men race toward them. The Black man outruns his white competitor and claims the largest bundle for himself, and the white man, resigned to his defeat, picks up "de li'l tee-ninchy bundle." However, "when de nigger opened up his bundle he found a pick and shovel and a hoe and a plow and chop-axe and then de white man opened up his bundle and found a writin'-pen and ink. So ever since then de nigger been out in de hot sun, usin' his tools and de white man been sittin' up figgerin', ought's a ought, figger's a figger; all for de white man, none for de nigger" (77). Whereas Jim Allen's account of "the order of things" begins with white supremacy firmly established, Jim Presley intimates that the racialized economy of labor is the accidental result of luck or chance. Although the Black man earns the right to the larger bundle through sheer speed and physical prowess, his "prize" is hand tools and a life consigned to manual labor. The white man loses the footrace but is given the less physically demanding gifts of literacy and writing. Such is the paradox of the modern world order, Hurston seems to intimate.

As in these origin myths, Florida's migrant workers were routinely excluded from literacy and consigned to physical labor. Through oral performance, however, especially storytelling, they destabilized the arbitrary dichotomy between literacy and embodied practice—what the performance studies scholar Diana Taylor calls "the archive and the repertoire."[48] In *Mules*, as the workers swap tales, they reinterpret literature as an oral mode. "Ah got to say a piece of *litery* (literary) fust to get my wind on," says John French (50). "Hurry up so somebody else kin plough up some *literary* and lay-by some *alphabets*," exclaims James Presley (88). These references to storytelling as "literary," "alphabets," and, in another example, "grammar" (87) resituate literature from the graphological to the soundscape of oral performance and acknowledge the workers' verbal dexterity as virtuosic in its own right.

Hurston further highlights this interplay among literature, language, and performance through modes of corporeal expression. In her letter to Hughes in 1928 where she shares the "5 general laws," she also contended, "The Negro's outstanding characteristic is drama. That is why he appears so imitative. Drama is mimicry. note [*sic*] gesture is place of words."[49] This analogy between movement and language suggests that the body in motion is a signing system—a corporeal and kinetic semiotics. In *Mules*, for instance, when Hurston accompanies the "swamp-gang" on the job to record their storytelling sessions and observe their facility with their axes, she remarks, "Not only do they chop rhythmically, but they do a beautiful double twirl above their heads with the ascending axe before it begins that accurate and bird-like descent. They can hurl their axes great distances and behead moccasins or sink the blade into an alligator's skull. . . . It is a magnificent sight to watch the marvelous coordination between the handsome black torsos and the twirling axes" (68).

Hurston interprets the laboring Black body as a work of art and virtuosity and the men's facility with their instrument as a choreography of embodied labor. Similarly, in *Dust Tracks* Hurston analogizes the laboring Black body with literature and dance: "These *poets of the swinging blade*! The brief, but infinitely graceful *dance of body* and axe-head as it lifts over the head in a fluid arc. . . . Sweating black bodies, muscled like gods, working to feed the hunger of the great tooth."[50] Like Washington, Hurston suggests that the laboring Black body approximates poetry. Yet whereas Washington uses simile to equate embodied labor with literary production—"there is just as much dignity in tilling a field as in writing a poem"—Hurston reconfigures poetry as a kinetic mode, where "gesture is place of words."[51]

During her early fieldwork expeditions, Hurston made several amateur film recordings of Black life in the U.S. South and the Bahamas, where she also

FIGURE 7.4A. Black laborer expertly wielding his axe in Zora Neale Hurston's documentary film footage.

Source: Copyright © Hurston Trust.

captured the poetics and choreography of embodied labor. In the surviving footage, Black workers can be seen operating heavy machinery and shipping lumber on the railroad, evidence of Central and South Florida as bustling sites of industrialization. In another scene, a young man expertly wields an axe (figure 7.4).

He is the sole figure in the frame and stands in an open field with only a small shack and trees in the background. After demonstrating his facility with the axe, he poses before the camera with his instrument in hand, sporting a bowtie and long-sleeved shirt tucked neatly into his pants. In the next shot, the bowtie has been removed, and he has donned a fashionable hat. He poses with arms extended, holding the axe as if about to swing and smiling into the camera. In the final shot, he stands still before the camera. His hat is slightly tilted to the right, his left leg is propped on a stone or piece of wood, and his left hand rests gently on his thigh. Rather than showing an exploited Black southern laborer, his is the highly stylized performance of an artist or craftsman.[52]

At the same time, the young man's dandified performance also calls attention to an arguably more questionable aspect of Hurston's efforts to transform

FIGURE 7.4B. Black laborer posing as a dandy in Zora Neale Hurston's documentary film footage.

Source: Copyright © Hurston Trust.

the worker into a performer. She is especially infatuated with the spectacle of "handsome black torsos" and "sweating black bodies, muscled like gods."[53] In other words, her depictions of the laboring Black male body in text and film alike are erotic. In "Characteristics," Hurston describes the erotic as integral to Black cultural production, where Black courtship rituals are "little plays by strolling players ... acted out daily," and "love-making," she maintains, is "an art among Negroes."[54] Perhaps, then, the young man wielding the axe is not smiling into the camera but flirting with Zora behind the camera, especially considering that she portrays herself in *Mules* as the object of male workers' affections and has to flee Polk County when she finds herself at the center of a lovers' quarrel. Thus, in her efforts to render the work camp and the laboring Black body aesthetically, Hurston treads precariously among fetishization, desire, and cultural validation.[55]

ESTABLISHING "THE NEW, THE *REAL* NEGRO ART THEATRE"; OR, "THE CONCERT IN THE RAW"

Thus far, I have emphasized Hurston's published fiction, ethnography, memoir, and correspondence, but she first experimented with the scene of the work camp in her dramatic repertoire. Though she is most often hailed as a novelist, she began her literary career as a playwright. At the *Opportunity* Awards Banquet in 1925, widely acknowledged as the genesis of the Harlem Renaissance, she received awards for two plays: second prize for *Color Struck* and honorable mention for *Spears*, marking her arrival on the literary scene. As early as 1928, Hurston expressed interest in developing "the new, the *real* Negro art theatre," where she planned to "act out" the "angularity and naïveté of the primitive 'bama Nigger," language that signals her trafficking in primitivist tropes that fetishized her mostly rural, working-class interlocutors as much as it celebrated them.[56] At the same time, she was studying to be an anthropologist and publishing her findings in professional journals. Shortly after returning from the field in the late 1920s, however, she became disillusioned with the stilted and restrictive form of the scientific journal article and determined that the dynamism of Black vernacular culture demanded a more elastic medium. It demanded to be performed. As she wrote to Thomas E. Jones, president of Fisk University, in 1934, "Returned to New York and began to re-write and arrange the material for Scientific publications, and while doing so, began to see the pity of all the flaming glory of being buried in scientific Journals. Took the music to Hall Johnson. . . . [He] held the music six months and returned it to me with the statement that the world was not ready for Negro music unless it were highly arranged. The barbaric melodies and harmonies were simply unfit for musical ears. I knew better."[57]

In the 1920s and 1930s, Hall Johnson was one of the foremost African American arrangers and composers who traded on making Black music more palatable for white audiences. Whereas ragtime, blues, and jazz were on their way to becoming staples of American popular music, in theater and especially on Broadway Black vernacular sound, Hurston noted in her letter, had to be highly arranged, almost to the point of unrecognizability, and aesthetic value and virtuosity were contingent on the mastery of traditional European forms. Disabused of "the colonizing influence of Western European culture" and convinced that she "knew better," Hurston broke ideologically and aesthetically with Johnson and his peers.[58] This was an important turning point in her career, spurring her quest for a new medium to present "genuine" folk material, which she ultimately realized in the "folk concert" genre.

In January 1932, Hurston produced and directed a folk concert entitled *The Great Day*, where she sought to present Black folk culture in its most "authentic" form. Staged at the John Golden Theatre in New York, it was largely a showcase of vernacular music and dance loosely connected by dialogue. Hurston produced several versions of the concert throughout the 1930s and 1940s and performed them in different cities. Variously titled *From Sun to Sun*, *Swinging Steel*, and *All de Live Long Day*, the concerts were largely consistent. Their scenes depicted a typical day in a Florida railroad or sawmill camp, following a group of migrant workers as they laid tracks and sang work songs and indulged in the pleasures of the jook and "jumped" the Bahaman fire dance at night. According to a review of *Singing Steel* in 1934, "The vehicle, packed with folklore, drama, and dancing, brings to the public not only the song and drama of the working day, but all the pathos, joy and innate feeling of freedom so characteristic of and inherent in the worker[;] . . . it is a remarkable revelation of the laborer's heart and mind."[59]

On one hand, Hurston's aestheticization of the worker is consistent with what Michael Denning calls the "laboring of American culture" that emerged in the 1930s, in particular the "pervasive use of 'labor' and its synonyms in the rhetoric of the period" and "the increased influence on and participation of working-class Americans in the world of culture and the arts."[60] On the other hand, Hurston did not have an explicitly political agenda. Instead of promoting the proletarianization of the worker, her concerts "aimed to show what beauty and appeal there was in genuine Negro material, as against the Broadway concept."[61] Her "concert in the raw" challenged the sanitization of Black culture in American theater but not necessarily the exploitation of Black workers in South Florida.[62] Rather, this was her initial effort to establish a "Negro theatre for her own people," where she could "write her own plays, direct Negro casts in Negro dramas, and present them to a Negro audience"—a project that preoccupied her throughout much of the 1930s.[63] At Mary McCleod Bethune's invitation, she even attempted to establish a school of dramatic arts "based on pure Negro expression" at Bethune-Cookman College in Daytona, Florida, and taught in the Drama Department at North Carolina College for Negroes in 1939–1940.[64]

Despite Hurston's antipathy for the "Broadway concept," her concerts still drew on the form of the Black musical established by *Shuffle Along*'s breakout success on Broadway in the early 1920s. According to the music historian Eileen Southern, "A [Black] musical's scenes would include a Harlem rent party, plantation scene, jungle scene, [and] religious scene (camp meeting or church service), if it were at all possible to slip them into the action."[65] Hurston's concerts included many of the same elements, with some notable differences—in particular the exclusion of the plantation scene. The plantation scene had been a hallmark of American theater since the nineteenth century and, with it, aestheticized depictions of the enslaved Black body. Hurston's setting of a modern-day Florida labor camp supplanted the imbecilic plantation "happy darkie" stereotype with the modern, migrant worker from the U.S. South and the Bahamas. Instead of minstrel ditties extolling the virtues of the old plantation home, the scene of the work camp in her folk concerts featured spirituals, blues, work songs, and gambling tunes that would become the foundation of modern (African) American music and performance. Significantly, the folk concerts also included Caribbean dance and spiritual practices she had observed in her fieldwork, portraying the U.S. South as a site not only of African American cultural production but of Afro-diasporic affiliation as well.

The form of Hurston's folk concerts bore a striking resemblance to the Tuskegee Singers' concerts, which consisted of a variety of folk songs, dialect readings, and, by the mid-1920s, performances of choreographed labor (chapter 2).[66] Despite similar content, however, they also differed in important ways. Whereas Washington viewed the spirituals as remnants of a slave past that should be preserved, calling them "plantation melodies," Hurston insisted they were not static vestiges of bygone days but rather dynamic, ephemeral creations that were being "made and forgotten every day."[67] Even more importantly, whereas Tuskegee played a key role in advancing and codifying the concert spiritual tradition, Hurston was interested in the raw materials coming from the sanctified churches of the day. Though she respected Washington, she detested the "trick style of delivery ... originated by the Fisk Singers; [with] Tuskegee and Hampton follow[ing] suit ... [in] spread[ing] this misconception of Negro spirituals," as she writes in "Characteristics."[68] They are "the works of Negro composers and adaptors *based* on the spirituals. . . . All good work and beautiful, but *not* the spirituals," she clarifies in "Spirituals and Neo-spirituals."[69]

Though the plots of Hurston's folk concerts are relatively thin, they provide important insights into how she staged the scene of the work camp to explore the entanglements of performance, labor, and diaspora in the Global Black South. [70] Part one typically follows workers from the start of the workday to their return to the quarters in the evening. Music is the primary vehicle that moves the story along, from blues and work songs on the job to children's games and a sermon by an itinerant preacher and his followers in the living quarters in the evening. The concert opens in the quarters with the shack rouser, "alternately singing and rapping on th[e] porches of the shacks," hurrying the workers to get to the job to begin the workday.[71] After waking, the workers sing "Joe Brown" as they depart for the job. Part two demonstrates how the power

AESTHETICIZING LABOR, PERFORMING DIASPORA   323

dynamics that organize the workday resemble the system of labor used on large plantations. The captain regulates the tempo of the workday, telling the men when to begin work and when to "knock off" and even directs their movement.[72] As the workers begin to lay the rails, they sing and "go thru all the gestures of the work songs."[73]

> CAP'N: Hey, Rousters, come on, shake that rail.
> MEN MOVE INTO POSITION:
> WATER BOY: Mr. Dugan—(Grunt)—On de L. & N.—(Grunt)—Got do [sic]
>   No. 10—(Grunt)—Got de pay care—(Grunt)—On de rear end—(Grunt)—
> CAP'N: Whoops—send her back.
> WATER BOY: Raises up tune "Can't you line it" (Four Verses)
> CAP'N: Whoops!!—Bring up the hammer gang——[74]

The work songs are a call-and-response among Cap'n, Water Boy (the song leader), and the laborers. When Cap'n instructs the workers to "shake that rail" or "send her back," Water Boy "raises up tune[s]" to help provide a rhythm for the task at hand. As the workers' grunts punctuate the rhythm of the performance, Hurston shows how labor is inextricably linked to Black cultural production in the scene of the work camp.

Whereas in *Mules and Men* the workers' commentary on their condition is limited almost exclusively to their storytelling sessions, in the folk concerts the workers express their grievances more explicitly on the job:

> CAP'N: Say, git to hittin down there—you ain't gittin paid to talk—git busy
>   and whip me some steel.
> MELVA: It's knocking off time, ain't it? I'M gointa to [sic] buy me a keg of lard
>   for dat guy.
> CLIFF ULMER: What are you gointa do with it?
> MELVA: I'm gointa grease him and swallow him.
> JOE WILLARD: I been fixin to make him eat dat pistol he totes myself.[75]

The Cap'n and his constant badgering are reminiscent of the driver or overseer on antebellum plantations. Though not addressed to Cap'n directly, the workers express their grievances among each other and even threaten him with violence. The folk concerts depict some of the bitterness that Sterling Brown, Hurston's contemporary whose poetry also focused on southern Black vernacular culture, complained was absent in *Mules and Men*.[76] This is especially evident in *From Sun to Sun*, when Too Sweet expresses her exhaustion and despair:

TOO SWEET

Lawd, I sho am tired of workin so hard. Wisht I was back home. I wouldnt have
to be chokin' no hammers and smellin' de white folks' mules.

JOE WILLARD

Why dont you put some steel in yo' pocket. De man at de depot swears he's
sellin' tickets each and every whichaways.

TOO SWEET

He's sellin 'em for money aint he? I aint even got money essence.[77]

Hurston's depiction of Too Sweet working on the "hammer gang" is one of few
instances in which we see women laborers in the scene of the work camp. Typically, the work day is dominated by men, and women appear only in the living
quarters (the domestic space), the jook (the space of leisure), and the conjure or
voodoo scene (the space of Black diasporic spirituality). Too Sweet's presence
laying rails alongside men is another example of Hurston's efforts to create Black
women characters who defy traditional gender norms, such as Janie in *Their
Eyes Were Watching God* and "Big Sweet" in her play *Polk County* (1944), who is
described as "a handsome Negro woman around thirty. Physically very strong.
She has a quick temper and great courage, but is generous and kind, and loyal to
her friends. Sings well. Has the quality of leadership."[78]

As Cap'n continues to press the workers to "whip me some steel!," Too Sweet
raises up "Mule on the Mount," one of the most widely distributed lining
rhythms in the United States:

> Every pay day pay day I gits a letter
> Every pay day, pay day I gits a letter
> Son come home, Lawd Lawd, son come home
> But I aint got, got no ready made money
> I aint got, got no ready made money
> I cant go home, Lawd, Lawd, I cant go home
> If I kin just make June July and August
> If I kin just make June July and August
> I'm going home, Lawd, Lawd, I'm going home[79]

Like the storytelling sessions in *Mules*, the work songs demonstrate both the
inseparability of labor and performance and the workers' inner lives. In "Mule
on the Mount," workers lament the hardships of migrant labor, particularly
being forced to leave their homes because of a lack of economic opportunity.
Their intense desire for home rebuts the notion that mobility is a precondition

for Black modern subjectivity. Though mobile, these workers ultimately desire rootedness and stability, much like McKay's narrator in "Peasants' Ways o' Thinkin.'" Despite the abjection and despair expressed in "Mule on the Mount," however, the workers do not dwell on their precarious condition. They sing work songs to help pass time during the workday in anticipation of the pleasures of the jook and the Afro-Bahaman fire dance at night.

CHOREOGRAPHING DIASPORIC RELATION

Significantly, Hurston's folk concerts depict the scene of the work camp as a diasporic contact zone between African American and Afro-Bahaman migrant workers, a veritable Global Black South geography. In "Go Gator and Muddy the Water" (1938), Hurston observes that Florida is "lush in [folklore] material because the state attracts such a variety of workers to its industries," indicating how labor continued to facilitate Black diasporic movement and affiliation in the Global Black South well into the twentieth century.[80] According to the historian Howard Johnson, "In the early years of the twentieth century, the Bahamas provided the mainly black labor force which built the city of Miami and was responsible for the expansion of agrarian capitalism in South Florida."[81] One-fifth of the Bahaman population worked in Florida between 1900 and 1920 in a variety of industries, including agriculture, turpentine, and railroads. By the 1920s and 1930s, however, Bahamans were joined and eventually outnumbered by African American sharecroppers and tenant farmers migrating from Georgia and other parts of the U.S. South as cotton prices plummeted and the boll weevil problem grew.[82] This influx of migrant workers from the Caribbean and the U.S. South transformed South Florida into what Hurston proudly called a Black "culture delta," with "the most highly flavored Negro plate around the American platter."[83]

Hurston initially encountered this phenomenon during her early fieldwork expeditions in the late 1920s. She became intrigued by how the influx of Caribbean migrants enriched South Florida's folklore after she witnessed the fire dance, a folk dance brought to Florida by Afro-Bahaman migrant workers. "I had heard some Bahaman music and seen a Jumping Dance in Liberty City and I was entranced," she recalls in *Dust Tracks*.[84] The fire dance, she noted in an unpublished manuscript, "originated in Africa" in honor of the "arrival of spring." It has three parts: the jumping dance, the ring play, and the crow dance.[85] Utterly enthralled, Hurston "sailed for Nassau," Bahamas, to collect more material. "I . . . ran to every Jumping Dance that I heard of, learned to 'jump,' collected more than a hundred tunes and resolved to make them known to the world."[86] The following year she published "Dance Songs and Tales from the Bahamas" (1930) in the *Journal of American Folklore,* where she explicitly links the fire dance to an economy of labor and leisure: "Every dry night the drums can be heard throbbing, no matter how hard the dancers have worked that day, or must work the next."[87] Like the music and dance in the jook, the fire dance is a mode of Black sociality that reclaims the body from the clutches of industrial capitalism. Hurston would continue to experiment with Afro-Bahaman music and dance throughout the 1930s, especially in her folk concerts, where she mobilized dance to articulate an "embodied theory" of diaspora.[88]

Writing to Hughes in 1929, Hurston noted, "I wanted the Nassau [Bahamas] material for: (1) There are so many of them in America that their folk lore definitely influences ours in South Fla. (2) For contrast with ours."[89] Her use of terms such as *them, their,* and *ours* makes clear that Hurston viewed Afro-Bahaman culture as different and distinct from African American culture. She elaborates on this differentiation in her early anthropological essays: "The Bahaman music is more dynamic and compelling than that of the American Negro, and the dance movements are more arresting; perhaps because the Bahaman offerings are more savage. The Bahaman, and the West Indian Negro generally, has had much less contact with the white man than the American Negro. As a result, speech, music, dancing and other modes of expression are infinitely nearer the African."[90] In contrast to contemporaneous diasporic movements such as pan-Africanism and Négritude that often minimized ethnic difference to promote transnational racial solidarity, as an anthropologist Hurston was acutely attuned to the importance of acknowledging differences between diasporic communities as well. She incorporated this logic into her folk concerts by staging friction between African American and Afro-Bahaman workers over their respective song and dance practices.

In *The Passing of a Day,* when Jig Wiley, an African American worker, criticizes fellow Afro-Bahaman workers for not singing the work songs, an argument ensues:

> JIG WILEY: Hey you two saws, why don't yo-all sing, whistle or dance? Taint nothing to you at all.
> STEW BEEF: Don't you call me no saw—I'll mash you like a cockroach
> JIG WILEY: You from Nassau, ain't you?
> STEW BEEF: Yeah, but don't you call us no saws—and another thing, we don't dance on no railroad—we got a time and a place.
> JOE WILLARD: Where is it and when—we ain't never seen it.[91]

Both the African Americans, Jig Wiley and Joe Willard, and the Afro-Bahaman, Stew Beef, are laborers, but they understand the relationship between labor and performance differently. Whereas African Americans sing blues and work songs to help pass the time during the workday, for Afro-Bahamans music and dance are exclusively practices of leisure and pleasure. They do not participate in the aestheticization of labor. Instead of dancing on the railroad, they hold fire dances in the palm grove late at night as a form of release from the workday.

In a similar scene in *From Sun to Sun*, Motor Boat, an Afro-Bahaman worker, tells Wiley, "We don't like yo' songs and we don't like your dance neither." And Bill, also Afro-Bahaman, adds, "We got our own songs and dance. . . . We dont sing on no railroad. We go in de woods and make a fire."[92] In this exchange, the workers' different preferred performance spaces—the railroad versus "de woods"—intensifies diasporic difference. The railroad, a symbol of modern travel and technology, suggests that African American performance is modern, whereas "de woods" links Afro-Bahaman performance to its putatively "savage" or "primitive" African background (Hurston used both terms to describe Afro-Bahaman cultural practices in her anthropological writings and in the playbill for the folk concerts). Crucially, the two ethnic groups also respond differently to white authority. African American workers respond to Cap'n's persistent badgering by singing "John Henry"—a folk ballad about a man who worked himself to death trying to outperform a machine—while the Afro-Bahamans insist on a break to indulge in the fire dance:

CAP'N

Say! Get to hittin down there! You aint gittin paid to talk yo' dance.

BILL

We homesick for our dance. We got to have one, do we dont work no more.[93]

Hurston uses the workers' ethnic and cultural differences as a foil for their disparate political statuses in the work camp. As U.S. "citizens," African Americans would have been subjected to Jim Crow with little state protection; therefore, they express their resistance to labor exploitation by masking and embedding it in the folk ballad "John Henry." Afro-Bahaman workers, however, would have had the protection of the British government.[94] They therefore wield greater agency over their labor and articulate their resistance more explicitly by threatening to strike unless their demands are met.

Indeed, the cultural differences and asymmetrical power relations between Afro-Bahamans and African Americans depicted in Hurston's concerts reflect the sociopolitical and economic conditions in South Florida's work camps. According to the historian Cindy Hahamovitch, authorities created economic competition between African American and Caribbean workers to drive down the price of labor. For instance, when African American migrants in Jacksonville learned that Bahamans were earning "25 cents a hamper for picking beans," they traveled to South Florida; however, when they arrived, "growers told the 'Naussauians that these Jacksonville folks were willing to work at 15 cents a hamper, thereby bringing the price down in direct proportion to labor surplus.'"[95] By World War II, state-sanctioned labor policies created and intensified strife between Afro-Bahaman and African American workers.

These intradiasporic tensions emerged during the production of the concerts as well. Insistent on presenting folk material "in a natural way," Hurston "assemble[d] a troup [sic] of sixteen Bahamans who could dance." Then, as she describes in "Concert," a chapter that was excised from *Dust Tracks*, she approached Hall Johnson about combining "his [African American] singers" with her Afro-Bahaman "dancers for a dramatic concert." The collaboration never came to fruition, however, because some of Johnson's singers had "the unfortunate habit of speaking of West Indians as 'monkey-chasers,' pretending to believe that the West Indians catch monkeys and stew them with rice," Hurston writes in "Concert." To protect her dancers from such "foolish prejudice," Hurston broke ties with Johnson and his singers and proceeded to produce the concert independently. When the show opened at the John Golden Theatre, it was a major success largely because of the performance of the Bahaman fire dance. Hurston's dance troupe was invited to perform at various venues around New York City, but "backstage arguments [and] eternal demands for money" soon wore her out. Some of the Bahaman dancers "preached that I was an American exploiting them," she recalls in "Concert," projecting onto Hurston, an African American, the sins of U.S. imperialism in the Caribbean. Most of the dancers defended her, however, pointing out "that they had never dreamed of dancing in public until I had picked them up. I had rehearsed them for months, fed them and routined them into something. . . . So they meant to stick with me, American or no American." Hurston eventually disbanded the group, and many of the dancers went on to join other troupes.[96] By referring to her as "American," Hurston's West Indian dancers clearly viewed her as the imperial "other," a counterpoint to the diasporic solidarity she staged in the concerts yet consistent with her own view of Afro-Bahaman cultural difference, which she articulated in her anthropological writings. In Florida's labor camps and Hurston's concerts alike, Black diasporic relationality required the negotiation of difference.

Through the scene of the work camp, however, Hurston used performance to resolve these intra-racial tensions. In *The Passing of a Day*, for example, when Cap'n gives the workers permission to "knock off," they head to the jook. After performing several gambling games, jook songs, and blues, John and Strawn, presumably both Afro-Bahaman workers, "put on their hats" and "prepare to exit," when Georgia Burke asks where they're going. John tells her they're going to the "Palm grove, to the Fire Dance," and Joe and Miss Anderson accompany them to see it.[97] At the palm grove, the workers sing a range of Bahaman folk songs and perform the fire dance. Tensions between the workers during the workday are largely resolved in the jook and palm grove at night, both spaces of leisure and performance. So although Hurston stages these cultural differences, she ultimately imagines performance as a modality that can bridge the fissures of diaspora.[98]

Likewise, in *Their Eyes were Watching God*, when Janie and Tea Cake leave Eatonville for the Everglades, they soon befriend a group of Bahaman workers who had migrated from Nassau in search of better labor conditions and higher pay. Just as in the folk concerts, it is only through dance that the workers overcome diasporic difference. The Afro-Bahaman migrants "quit hiding out to hold their dances when they found out that their American friends didn't laugh at them as they feared. Many of the Americans learned to jump and liked it as much as the 'Saws.' So they began to hold dances night after night in the quarters, usually behind Tea Cake's house. Often now, Tea Cake and Janie stayed up so late at the fire dances that Tea Cake would not let her go with him to the field. He wanted her to get her rest" (300). As a wild, uncultivated geography, the Everglades is thought to enable new and different social relations, where Hurston can ease the tensions between southern African Americans and Afro-Bahamans. The fire dance is figured as a corporeal mode of translation between these Afro-diasporic communities, and because the dance is an African survival, Hurston intimates that ultimately what connects the workers is their common African ancestry.[99]

CHARACTERISTICS OF *DIASPORIC* NEGRO EXPRESSION: JAMAICAN CULTURAL NATIONALISM AND THE LECTURE FORM

Reflecting on her folk concert experience in *Dust Tracks*, Hurston maintains that by introducing Caribbean dance to the American stage, she indelibly influenced Black musical theater and dance, including the work of Hall Johnson and Katherine Dunham. Though she "made no real money," she was "satisfied in knowing" the folk concerts "established a trend and pointed Negro expression back towards the saner ground of our own unbelievable originality."[100] In "Characteristics," typically interpreted as a "taxonomy of African American performativity" in the United States, Hurston identifies "originality" as one of "the Negro's" distinct qualities.[101] What does it mean, then, that in *Dust Tracks* she ascribes *originality* to Afro-Bahaman folk culture as well? A closer examination of Hurston's Caribbean writings and lectures demonstrates how she mobilized her theories of Black expression, initially conceived in South Florida's work camps, to document and assess Afro-Caribbean folk cultural expression as well. In other words, "Characteristics" was always-already conceived with the broader diaspora in mind.

In 1936, Hurston was awarded a Guggenheim fellowship to study the "magic practices" of the West Indies. She traveled throughout the Caribbean region but spent most of her time—almost two years—in Jamaica (six months) and Haiti and published her findings in her ethnography *Tell My Horse* in 1938. Contemporary scholars have roundly criticized this work for its offensive depictions of Afro-Caribbean peoples and cultures (especially Haitians) and its curious American chauvinism. According to Ifeoma Nkwankwo, Hurston criticizes Afro-Caribbean peoples in order to lift up African Americans and thus enacts "binaristic blackness," and for John Carlos Rowe her commentary on the U.S. occupation of Haiti demonstrates support for U.S. imperialism.[102] Hurston's primary achievement in this work is her respectful treatment of Haitian Vodou as a complex and dynamic religious system and mode of knowledge production that holds important lessons for Western science and medicine. As Daphne Lamothe argues, "Hurston's evocation of the Caribbean through Vodou . . . allows her to grapple with many of the issues being debated in cosmopolitan, intellectual circles during the Harlem Renaissance."[103] Nevertheless, Hurston biographer Robert E. Hemenway maintains that *Tell My Horse* is "Hurston's poorest book, chiefly because of its form. She was a novelist and folklorist, not a political analyst or traveloguist. Yet *Tell My Horse* is filled with political analysis, often of a naïve sort, with superficial descriptions of West Indian curiosities."[104]

Despite its shortcomings as political analysis, *Tell My Horse* demonstrates Hurston's efforts to apply her theories of Black expression to Caribbean folk culture. For example, in delineating the Nine Night ceremony in Jamaica, an elaborate ritual that seeks to release the "duppy," or spirit, of a recently deceased person, she observes: "It was *asymmetric* dancing that yet had balance and beauty. . . . There was a big movement and a little movement. The big movement was like a sunset in its scope and color. The little movement had the almost imperceptible ripple of a serpent's back. It was a cameo in dancing."[105] Asymmetry is one of the distinguishing features of Black expression Hurston identifies in the original "Characteristics" essay. "It is the lack of symmetry which makes Negro dancing so difficult for white dancers to learn," she contends. "The presence of rhythm and absence of symmetry are paradoxical, but there they are. Both present to a marked degree."[106] For Hurston, Black dance, whether in the United States or in Jamaica, is organized by paradox: it is at one and the same time asymmetric, balanced, rhythmic, and beautiful. Similarly, regarding Haiti in *Tell My Horse*, she draws on concepts first developed in "Characteristics" to acknowledge similarities between African American and Haitian speech practices. When an unnamed "upper class Haitian" points out that "the peasants of Haiti were a poetical group" who "loved the metaphor and the simile," Hurston replies, "We Negroes of America also employed the figures of speech continuously."[107] In "Characteristics," she describes this quality as the "will to adorn" and suggests that "the use of metaphor and simile" is one of the American "Negro's greatest contribution[s] to the [English] language."[108] Reading *Tell My Horse* alongside "Characteristics" demonstrates, like her incorporation of the fire dance in the folk concerts, how Hurston used Black performance to articulate a theory of diasporic relation in the Global Black South based on shared African cultural retentions.

During her research expedition in Jamaica in 1936, Hurston was invited to give several lectures that elucidate not only how she conceived of Black performance as a mode of diasporic relationality but also, and perhaps most importantly, how she attempted to forge more horizontal and egalitarian diasporic ties. Contrary to the somewhat aloof tone of *Tell My Horse* and its curious mix of ethnography and travel writing, newspaper accounts of her Jamaican lectures suggest the utility of the lecture form for a more even diasporic exchange. Whereas Hurston's folk concerts, ethnographies, fiction, and plays were her own re-presentations of Black diasporic cultural exchange, the Jamaican lectures and their newspaper coverage reveal how she negotiated her relationship to Jamaica's cultural, political, and intellectual elite as well as their reception of her. Ultimately, they enable us to see how a southern African American woman and her Jamaican contemporaries related to each other within and against disparate yet overlapping colonial and imperial histories as well as outside of global northern centers such as New York and Paris.

Feature stories in the *Daily Gleaner*, Jamaica's leading newspaper, embraced Hurston's authority as a trained anthropologist. With headlines such as "U.S. Woman Anthropologist on Hoodoo Hunt in Jamaica," she was presented to the island's reading public as a "talented writer-musician-actress" who came to "probe into our magic stories." In a photograph accompanying this article, she is depicted sporting "riding garb" with a hat, long-sleeved shirt, a tie loosely tied about her neck with the shirt collar open, and long pants with her hands pushed into her pockets. She appears to be smiling and looking confidently into the camera. The article provided an overview of her oeuvre to date: quoting extensively from *Mules and Men*, observing that the *New York Times* book review of *Jonah's Gourde Vine* called it "the most vital and original novel about the American Negro that has yet been written by a member of the Negro race," and noting that "with her troupe of Bahamian dancers she created a sensation in America. Her exposition of the 'Fire Dance' was the talk of the theatrical world."[109]

In her first documented lecture in Jamaica, given before the Shortwood Old Students Association (the alumnae organization for Shortwood College, an all-girls school), Amy Bailey, a now-celebrated Jamaican educator and Garveyite who was a champion of women's rights, toasted Hurston as a "woman Negro scholar" who aimed to "put Jamaica on the literary map of the world" and who proved that women were "soaring into the realms of literature."[110] Afro-Jamaicans were interested in Hurston's work because they, too, were grappling with questions of racial identity in the afterlife of the plantation. We see in their responses to Hurston's work a burgeoning Black and specifically Jamaican cultural nationalism. This is especially evident in Hurston's lecture titled "Negro Characteristics and Qualities," given before the Quill and Ink Club in Port Maria, Jamaica. Founded by the Jamaican nationalist Rupert Meikle, the Quill and Ink Club was dedicated to "the building up of a cultural background purely Jamaican." In his opening remarks, Meikle noted, "The negroes of Jamaica had the feeling that they were inferior to other people." As an anthropologist and scholar of Black folklore, Hurston was invited to help dismantle myths of racial inferiority and "get Jamaicans to realise that they were negroes."[111]

In another lecture held at the YMCA, Hurston presented before a "discussion group in which the American and Jamaican Negroes were compared." Audience members discussed what they described as the island's "superiority mental complex," and "the colour problem which is whispered in sitting rooms was unmasked in public and discussed too in an intelligent manner." Audience members used the space of Hurston's lecture to grapple with what they perceived as problems of racial and cultural identity in Jamaica. As one attendee lamented, "They had not even a Jamaican national song that was distinctly Jamaican. It showed that they had not that national pride and it was because of this mixed blood[,] he was quite sure," as the "greatest distinction in the island was not between black and white but coloured and coloured."[112] Such discussions of race pride and nationalism among Afro-Jamaicans were prominent themes in each of Hurston's three documented lectures.

Hurston visited Jamaica amid the labor strikes that occurred throughout the British West Indies in the mid-1930s, spurred by the Great Depression. In Jamaica, especially, the strikes began with agricultural workers and spread to urban centers.[113] Hurston herself had inquired into "banana production and wages" in Jamaica but was met with misogynistic disregard because it was not a woman's place to ask about such matters, she was informed.[114] The labor strikes turned into a call for political and cultural nationalism. Both were influenced by global cultural and political changes from the previous decade, such as World War I, Garveyism, and "the newly positive ethnological appraisal of African culture and history within European intellectual circles."[115] Afro-Jamaicans, much like their contemporaries throughout the Global Black South—Jean Price-Mars and Jacques Roumain in Haiti; Fernando Ortiz and Nicolas Guillén in Cuba; and Hurston in the United States—were in the process of reclaiming their folklore as an act of cultural nationalism, which set the groundwork for anticolonialism and, ultimately, independence. Afro-Jamaicans had begun to realize, Amy Bailey noted at Hurston's Shortwood lecture, "that as Jamaicans they had to go back to their beginning[s]," which "were to be found in many of the things which they affected to despise today. Their Anancy stories, their Digging-match songs, their bush tales that were peculiarly Jamaican, had a fund of humour, a fund of wit, a fund of commonsense which is hard to beat. They ought to be proud of their folk lore, and as teachers they ought to encourage those things in their schools." Bailey thus praised Hurston for "what you are doing for Negroes in the West Indies . . . and particularly for women Negroes." Yet she also insisted that Hurston could not do for Jamaicans what they must do for themselves. "No country merited the word great unless they themselves wrote their history as from the beginning. . . . 'We ourselves must not only feel it; we ourselves must not only see it; we ourselves have got to write it.' "[116]

The accounts of Hurston's lectures in the Jamaican press provide a more nuanced understanding of her diasporic politics in the Caribbean. The American-chauvinistic perspective in *Tell My Horse* was altogether absent in her lectures, and she explicitly rejected any notion of an intra-racial hierarchy between African Americans and Afro-Jamaicans:

> I am continually being asked about what we are doing in America . . . as if we have some special something in America that you have not got here. Well, I believe we have had more struggles than you have had. We have had less beauty

about us, much less natural stimulation than you have had. And with all God has given you . . . it is hard for me to determine why you have not got more Jamaica literature in print. I am looking for it and I hope you don't let me down (Hear, hear).[117]

In place of the condescension that permeates *Tell My Horse*'s political commentary, Hurston's Jamaican lectures expressed a desire for diasporic solidarity and mutual support, especially in literature. " 'Slavery is one hundred years behind you,' she declared. 'You have a new heritage; you have everything before you and you need not apologise. Call Jamaica the most glorious and beautiful country the world has ever seen. I have found a burning ingeniousness here and it is a wonder that it does not go outside' " to the rest of the world.[118]

As an anthropologist who often (problematically) championed notions of cultural authenticity, Hurston viewed place, the local, and rootedness as crucial to artistic production, an attitude that ultimately translated into a proto-decolonial and "cultural populist" sensibility.[119] She therefore celebrated Jamaica's natural beauty, upholding it as an inspiration for national literature. In a particularly striking moment, she followed up this association among nature, land, and literature with a more pointed decolonial critique:

It may not even be good English that one would write, but that was inconsequential. One could DISCARD ENGLISH any time one found a better tool, for language to the writer was but a tool. For herself, she was prepared to break it up and step on it, and if it didn't suit her purpose she would twist it into any form she wanted. A woman once asked her why she did not talk about Shakespeare and leave out talking about Negroes. She told her that if she was not ready to hear about Negroes, she was not ready to hear about Shakespeare. In his day Shakespeare was not considered the greatest poet of England. Ben Johnson was because he wrote the language of the Court. But Shakespeare spoke the language of the people and took the folk lore of his time and turned it into gold.[120]

Hurston's Jamaican lectures were thus steeped in a proto-decolonial logic that eschewed both white-supremacist and classist notions of culture. "She advised [audiences] not to ape the style of England," for English was simply a tool to be broken, stepped on, and twisted until it suited their purposes. By deriving "our" own aesthetic values and principles, she contended, "we would be able to do something so beautiful and glorious that we need never feel that our heritage had been against us."[121] This irreverent attitude toward high culture was common among the New Negro literati (and modernists generally). McKay, we recall, also rejected the uplift generation's classism and respectability politics. Hurston shared McKay's class critique and was likewise invested in decolonizing and liberating Black diasporic cultural expression from European aesthetic supremacy. In her lecture before the Quill and Ink Club titled "Negro Characteristics and Qualities," for instance, she asserted that while it was commonly accepted that "the negroes were not very successful people... those making such statements ought to be called upon to define what was success." The Negro had in fact made significant contributions to civilization, but "because the Western world was rushing[,] everybody who did not rush was regarded as being sort of feeble-minded," she reasoned. Clearly influenced by the cultural relativist thought of her mentor, Franz Boas, and convinced of art's political potential, Hurston urged her audience to "begin to know the difference between superiority and difference. Make up your mind and live what you are" because "nobody could respect a people who did not respect themselves."[122] Thus, the insights from "Characteristics" became the building blocks for a Black diasporic cultural-nationalist sensibility similar to her more nuanced and sympathetic treatment of African-derived religious and spiritual practices in *Tell My Horse*.

Hurston's Jamaican lectures drew heavily on the original "Characteristics" essay. Although there are some minor discrepancies between them, drama is the single characteristic consistent across both (con)texts.[123] In the original essay, she maintains that drama "permeates his [the Negro's] entire self.... Every phase of Negro life is highly dramatised," and in one of the Jamaican lectures she contended that "the negro's [*sic*] greatest contribution to Art would be drama."[124] Like her observations about Black laborers in Florida's work camps, she insisted in another lecture that Jamaica's "working men should be appreciated just for their animal significence [*sic*] with their supple muscles and fine sinews."[125] Notwithstanding the objectifying association between Black men and animality, Hurston essentially exported her theory of the Black worker as an arbiter of culture to Jamaica as well. Furthermore, she highlighted similarities between the "digging songs" on the island to work songs in the United States as well as differences between the two cultures, such as the absence of poet-preachers in Jamaica and Jamaica's superior beauty. By repurposing "Characteristics" for her Jamaican lectures and exploring Caribbean equivalents to Black cultural practices in south Florida's work camps, Hurston theorized what might be called "characteristics of *diasporic* Negro expression," organized by folk performance and African cultural retentions.

Across her lectures, Hurston expressed solidarity with Afro-Jamaicans based in part on their geographic proximity, effectively plotting a Global Black South geography. She promised to introduce audience members to publishers and ensure that "they got publication providing the work was good; because...'your future is mine and the little bit of salt water between us is nothing.'"[126] She proposed literature especially as a potential site of diasporic affiliation: "I am hoping we can stretch hands across the water and match each other, book for book (hear, hear)."[127] Moreover, she "was closer to her birth place in Jamaica than in New York," she informed audiences, "and hoped the feeling of oneness of all of them was also felt by those in Jamaica and that they would co-operate and... gain spiritually."[128]

True to her word about promoting Afro-Jamaican literature, Hurston wrote a glowing review of the Afro-Jamaican novelist Victor Stafford Reid's debut novel, *New Day* (1949), in the *New York Herald Tribune*. *New Day* establishes the Morant Bay Rebellion of 1865 as the impetus of a Jamaican cultural and political nationalism that culminates in the labor strikes of 1938 and the new constitution of 1944. It captures the growing anticolonial sentiment that would have been brewing on the island in response to the labor strikes across the region during Hurston's visit in 1936, and it is celebrated as the first novel written in Jamaican dialect. We cannot know if Reid was present at Hurston's lectures, but he did write for the *Daily Gleaner*, so it is certainly possible that they might have met during her six-month visit to the island. Hurston lauded *New Day* as a "liquid, lyrical thing of wondrous beauty.... So conscious is the author of being a Jamaican instead of an imitation Englishman that he boldly flavors the narrative with the colorful idiom of the island," the very sense of Jamaican pride she encouraged in her lectures.[129] Excerpts from Hurston's review were printed in the *Daily Gleaner* (though not attributed to her), helping to build anticipation for the novel on the island.[130] *New Day* was indeed a literary success, inspiring generations of Jamaican writers and scholars and shaping the development of the Caribbean novel.[131] Ultimately, Hurston's encouragement of Afro-Jamaican literary and cultural nationalism in her lectures and subsequent review of *New Day* suggest that her writing and thinking about the Caribbean were more nuanced and respectful of diasporic difference than what she published in *Tell My Horse*. It is thus crucial to read these texts together to gain a fuller sense of the dynamism of her diasporic politics.

Zora Neale Hurston was a cultural and intellectual maverick who firmly believed that Global Black South folk cultures were not only sophisticated and worthy of study but also constitutive to Black modernity. A Tuskegee student once removed, she respected Booker T. Washington and shared some of his values around hard work and commitment to southern working-class Black people. However, like other Tuskegee students in her generation of New Negroes, she vehemently rejected uplift and developed her own theories of Black performance and attitudes toward gender, labor, and diaspora that explicitly departed from Washington's and Tuskegee's aesthetic and political ideologies. In Hurston's experiment plot, the regeneration of Black being was tied less to agricultural labor than to the dynamic cultural practices Black people developed both in response to and in spite of the plantation's persistent hegemony.

By resituating her performance studies essay "Characteristics of Negro Expression" within the work camp and demonstrating how the site of labor shaped her engagement with Caribbean folk culture, I have shown how Hurston used performance to refigure the Black worker as an arbiter of culture and to articulate a theory of diasporic relation in the Global Black South. Hurston's depictions of South Florida as an exceptional geography, a cosmopolitan frontier zone, and agro-industrial center that attracted Black migrant workers from across the U.S. South and the Caribbean captured an alternative geography of Black transnational movement: a south-to-south migration stream that at once preceded and was coterminous with the Great Migration to the U.S. North. This geographic repositioning was tied to a cultural and epistemological project by which Hurston defied and attenuated the putative binary between high and low culture as a register of artistic and ontological value. Through "Characteristics," she insisted that Black diasporic artistic production has its own internal logic that is not inferior to Western aesthetic norms, and when relocated to the Caribbean, especially Jamaica, it could become the basis of a proto-decolonial cultural politics rooted in Black performance and folklore. Indeed, as she insisted in her Jamaican lectures, one must "know the difference between superiority and difference," for, in the words of the African American minister Rev. Jeremiah Wright, "differen[ce] is not synonymous with deficient."[132] It is simply difference, pure and simple.

8

Of Ships and Plantations

Marcus Garvey and the UNIA's Vision of a Pan-African Agro-industrial Empire

In 1922, the Jamaican-born pan-Africanist leader Marcus Garvey and his organization, the Universal Negro Improvement Association (UNIA), announced their plan to launch the Black Cross Navigation & Trading Company, a successor to the Black Star Line, "to trade with the West Indies in bananas and citrus fruit."[1] Undaunted by the Black Star Line's infamous failure earlier that year owing to poor business practices, the UNIA remained steadfast in its belief that owning and operating a steamship line was the most effective way to link up the industrial and commercial interests of the Black world and ultimately attain economic independence. Following an unsuccessful attempt at purchasing a ship from the U.S. Shipping Board, the UNIA eventually purchased the *General G. W. Goethals* from the Panama Rail Road Company—but, ominously, without a "warranty to seaworthiness."[2] General George W. Goethals, in Garvey's words, was "the genius who constructed the Panama Canal with the aid and assistance of negro labor and skill."[3] In November 1924, Garvey unofficially rechristened the ship the S.S. *Booker T. Washington*, and in January 1925 it made its first and only voyage from New York to "Central America, the West Indies, and parts of the South of the United States."[4]

Advertisements for the voyage that circulated in the *Negro World*, the official organ of the UNIA, charted a distinctly hemispheric cartography and intimated how Garvey and the UNIA adapted Booker T. Washington and the Caribbean tourism and fruit-trade industries to construct their own vision of a pan-African, agro-industrial future (figure 8.1). In Garvey's weekly addresses printed on the cover page of the *Negro World*, he promoted this "Big Negro Excursion" as an opportunity to forge diasporic linkages along "commercial and industrial" lines. "New associations can be formed with your own people," he assured readers,

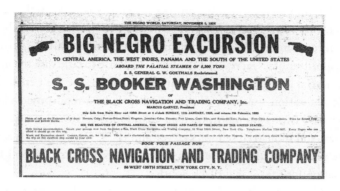

FIGURE 8.1. Ad for the SS *Booker T. Washington* in the *Negro World*.

Source: *Negro World*, November 1, 1924.

"new contacts created such as the white travelers have done" for their own benefit.[5]

Strikingly, Garvey enticed readers to support the steamship line and to purchase tickets for its initial voyage using facile, exoticized depictions of the Caribbean. He implored "American Negroes" to "see the West Indian at home," "to see the countries where the bananas, oranges, grapefruit, cocoanuts, lemons, cane, coffee and cocoa grow and at the same time enjoy seeing the beauties of the tropical climes."[6] In another weekly address, he urged, "Go and see the natives in their happy, cheerful mood, singing their songs of tropical bliss and extending to the stranger the hand of welcome and cheer. Millions of white American tourists go to the tropics yearly. This is a chance for Negroes to do likewise. Go and see the Panama Canal, the great engineering feat completed through the energy of Negroes under the direction of General G. W. Goethals, after whom the Booker T. Washington was originally named."[7] By citing imagery of corporate plantation agriculture and depicting "the natives" cheerfully singing in "tropical bliss," Garvey bafflingly trafficked in the scripts and marketing tactics of the white U.S. tourism industry and the imperialist fruit trade in the Caribbean. His vision for linking up Black commercial and agro-industrial enterprises for diasporic uplift and autonomy was thus deeply entangled with the political-economic forms and logics of U.S. hemispheric imperialism.

On January 18, 1925, the *Booker T. Washington* set sail for the port cities of the Caribbean, Latin America, and the U.S. South (figures 8.2 and 8.3). Though Washington himself never traveled elsewhere in the hemisphere, despite numerous invitations to do so, the *Booker T. Washington*'s itinerary for its first (and only) voyage figuratively plots his and Tuskegee's hemispheric influence and circulation. Garvey's affinity for Washington has been well established. But this chapter retraces specifically how he adapted the literary, symbolic, and ideological economies of Washington and Tuskegee to articulate his own project of diasporic uplift. Garvey and the UNIA's desire to cultivate the industrial and commercial interests of the race through tourism, the fruit trade, and the corporate plantation was steeped, like Tuskegee, in a repurposed plantation logic. Just as Washington repurposed an abandoned cotton plantation into an agricultural and industrial school, Garvey and the UNIA aimed to transform corporate plantation agriculture into a mode of economic and political self-determination for the Global Black South.

Indeed, Garvey, too, was a "conscript of modernity." His project was akin to Toussaint L'Ouverture's and Washington's efforts to repurpose modern political-economic forms toward a different future, which is precisely why Garvey has been variously regarded as a Black nationalist and pan-Africanist hero, on one hand, and a pro-capitalist, imperialist fascist, on the other.[8] Like his predecessors, Garvey wrestled with—and often got mired in—the logics and forms of racial-capitalist modernity while trying to create an infrastructure that did not depend on the oppression and exploitation of the Black masses. As Michelle Anne Stephens argues, Garvey and his contemporaries "attempted to chart a course for the race somewhere in the interstices between empire, nation, and state," at once "resisting empire and carrying its tropes along in their wake."[9]

In what follows, I establish Marcus Garvey as a self-taught and self-proclaimed student of Washington and Tuskegee who used print culture to school himself in the institute's curriculum and Washington's social and political philosophies. Of all the Tuskegee students studied here, Garvey and the UNIA developed the most influential and transnational project to counter the plantation's ongoing assault on Black life. Indeed, it was the largest mass movement of Black people in the twentieth century. By attending to Garvey and the UNIA's strategic translation and mobilization of Washington and Tuskegee, this chapter recovers the agricultural component of their economic agenda, specifically how they envisioned farming as well as agricultural and industrial education as essential to facilitating Black economic (inter)nationalism (chapter 4) and establishing an agro-industrial empire.

It is well known that the UNIA promoted establishing Black-owned businesses, but scholars have paid less attention to its agricultural aspirations and pursuits. One of the UNIA's earliest goals was to establish a farm and institute in Jamaica modeled on Tuskegee, and even when Garvey expanded the organization's program and moved its headquarters to New York City, he continued to promote agricultural production, consumption, and trade as integral to its

FIGURE 8.2. S.S. *Booker T. Washington*.

Source: Marcus Garvey, *The Philosophy and Opinions of Marcus Garvey, or Africa for the Africans*, vols. 1 and 2 (in one book), comp. Amy Jacques Garvey (Dover, MA: Majority Press, 1986), vol. 2, between pp. 264 and 265.

mission. Furthermore, though the UNIA is often regarded as a primarily urban movement, a significant proportion of Garveyites worked in agriculture, especially in the rural U.S. South and throughout the Caribbean and Central America. Some members were independent farmers and property owners, but most were sharecroppers, tenant farmers, and day laborers employed by white landowners and corporate plantation enterprises such as the United Fruit Company, which owned hundreds of thousands of acres of land throughout the Caribbean and Central America. In the United States, writes the historian Mary Rolinson, "the archetypal American Garveyite lived in a majority-Black community, farmed cotton on someone else's land, and struggled to maintain a stable and safe family."[10] In the Caribbean and Central America, UNIA members were often the labor migrants and peasant cosmopolitans whom McKay and Hurston portrayed in their respective works (see chapters 6 and 7).

Garvey "valued his rural constituency and saw his ideology as applicable to an agrarian setting," as did the numerous agricultural workers throughout the hemisphere who joined the movement.[11] In fact, Garvey was initially radicalized by the mistreatment of West Indian migrants laboring on UFCO's plantations and, in the case of southern African Americans, wrote to the U.S. secretary of

View of S. S. GENERAL G. W. GOETHALS, rechristened the BOOKER T. WASHINGTON January 18, alongside Pier 75, New York.

FIGURE 8.3. S.S. *Booker T. Washington* in the *Negro World*.

Source: *Negro World*, January 24, 1925.

agriculture, Henry Wallace, to "explain[ ] his program, its benefits for farmers, and its compatibility with southern rural ideology."[12] To be sure, Garveyism was not a primarily agricultural movement. The UNIA was equally, if not more so, invested in the industrial development of the race. However, the organization viewed agriculture and industry as inseparable from the development of Black commercial enterprises, imagining a distinctly *agro-industrial* future. Throughout *Afterlives of the Plantation*, I have emphasized agrarian futures in part because of Washington's and Carver's partiality to scientific agriculture as the centerpiece of Tuskegee's contribution to Black modernity. But Tuskegee's early curriculum always emphasized both agriculture and industry alike. So the UNIA's promotion of an agro-industrial future still carried the imprint of Tuskegee's strategy for Black world making. As the UNIA aspired to redirect Black labor power to achieve diasporic uplift and establish a Black "transnation," the farm and the plantation were from the very outset entangled with the ship and the factory.

OF SHIPS AND PLANTATIONS

In both the *Negro World* newspaper and the published UNIA Convention proceedings, Garveyites criticized the abuses of Black agricultural workers on the hemisphere's corporate fruit and cotton plantations and encouraged self-reliance through control of the means of production and consumption and thereby the creation of a closed economic system to protect Black people from further exploitation. Like Hurston's Jamaican lectures (chapter 7), the UNIA Convention proceedings represent an important forum where Garveyites strategized and debated the possibilities of economic cooperation and theorized "African diaspora citizenship" beyond the nation-state. They forged an agro-industrial vision that encompassed acquiring land and establishing factories; encouraging Black farmers to grow both healthy foods and cash crops and to avoid the credit system; and owning ships to ensure the effective transport, sale, and disposal of agricultural and manufactured goods between diasporic communities.

Finally, this chapter also grapples with the conundrum that, although the UNIA's agro-industrial vision was rooted in logics and ethics typically associated with the plot, such as economic cooperation and Black self-determination, it was also partially modeled on UFCO's corporate plantations and ultimately aspired to empire. Despite this ideological pitfall, however, the UNIA plotted one of the most radical and ambitious models of agro-industrial futures in the early twentieth century by attempting to create a closed economic system that could sustain, protect, and propagate Black life on a global scale.

TOWARD A "TUSKEGEE IN JAMAICA" AND "A STEAMSHIP OF THEIR OWN"

Born in 1887 in rural Jamaica, Marcus Garvey came of age during the rise of the fruit trade and "the romantic peak of the great maritime age, of hulking steamships of enormous tonnage and passenger ships of comfort and splendor."[13] Garvey's vision of commercial and industrial progress was thus influenced by UFCO's hemispheric ubiquity and especially its presence in his native Jamaica, where it owned and operated numerous banana plantations and a passenger service (the Great White Fleet) for North American tourists (chapter 6). In 1910, he left Jamaica for Port Limón, Costa Rica, where he was briefly employed as a timekeeper on a UFCO banana plantation. In this "privileged position," writes the Garvey biographer Colin Grant, he was "spared the indignities and more unpleasant aspects of plantation life" experienced by many of his fellow West

Indian migrant laborers. Along with the overseers and foremen, Garvey was "charged with ensuring that maximum efficiency did not come with the cost of bruised or scarred bananas" and with "oversee[ing] the smooth running of the 'factory in the field' (as banana plantations were commonly known) that left workers with the conviction that United Fruit were more concerned about the welfare of the bananas than [of] the people who harvested them."[14] In this way, Garvey at once facilitated the plantation's regimentation of the laboring Black body and was subjected to its anti-Black disciplinary and temporal logics.

Garvey's employment as an UFCO timekeeper was short-lived, however. Disillusioned with the mistreatment of his fellow West Indian migrant laborers, he returned to his training as a printer and journalist and established *La nacionale*, or the *Nation*, a propagandist newspaper that contested the deplorable conditions he witnessed. Yet "many for whom the paper was written could not read[, and] [t]hose who could, didn't bother."[15] Both the West Indian elite and UFCO opposed the newspaper, and Garvey, now unemployed and ostracized, was forced to leave Costa Rica.[16] He traveled to Bocas del Toro and Colón, Panama, and founded yet another paper, *La prensa* (the *Press*), but it also "failed to catch on."[17] Garvey lodged complaints with the British consul regarding the mistreatment of the workers, but to no avail. He then embarked on a tour of Central America, including visits to Nicaragua, Honduras, Colombia, Ecuador, and Venezuela, where he witnessed "the same exploitation, segregation, and hostility towards people of African descent."[18]

Garvey would have first learned about Booker T. Washington and his agro-industrial program as a youth in Jamaica. As early as 1902, we recall, there had been considerable interest in the Jamaican press about implementing a similar model of education on the island. Garvey's mentor, Dr. Robert Love, a Bahamian physician, journalist, and activist who had immigrated to Jamaica, also wrote about Washington in his newspaper, the *Jamaican Advocate*, acknowledging him as "the negro apostle of industrial education for the African race, in the United States" and a "greater man than [Theodore Roosevelt]" (after the uproar following Washington's visit to the White House). But Love also rejected "Washington's apparent acquiescence to the racism of the American South." Regarding the Atlanta Exposition Address, Love maintained, "We do not say that Mr. Washington was wrong in what he said. We would neither have said it, nor thought it, for the favour of all the whites in the United States, or blacks either."[19] Yet it was in Europe and most likely in the *African Times and Orient Review* (*ATOR*) that Garvey would have encountered Washington as a diasporic race leader and his program as broadly applicable to the Black world.

Following his travels throughout Central America and a brief return to Jamaica, Garvey set sail for England in 1912 and traveled extensively throughout Europe, where he received a broad education in pan-African and anticolonial politics as well as in Washington's work. He came under the mentorship and influence of Dusé Mohamed Ali, the Egyptian-born pan-Africanist actor and editor of the *ATOR*, an anticolonial periodical established to forge solidarities between African and Asian peoples worldwide. The *ATOR*'s inaugural issue prominently featured Tuskegee's ICON, and the following issue included a lengthy article on Tuskegee, penned by Washington. Notably, Washington explained to readers why he had made Tuskegee an industrial school. After Reconstruction, when it became clear that "members of the race could no longer look to political agitation and the opportunity of holding office as a means of gaining a reputation or winning success . . . [several African American leaders realized] there was practically no line drawn, and little discrimination in the world of commerce, banking, storekeeping, manufacturing, and skilled trades, and in agriculture; and in this lay his [the Negro's] great opportunity."[20]

In 1913, Garvey worked as an editorial assistant for the *ATOR*, and it was during this period that he first read Washington's autobiography, recalling, "I read 'Up from Slavery,' by Booker T. Washington, and then my doom—if I may so call it—of being a race leader dawned upon me in London after I had traveled through almost half of Europe. I asked: 'Where is the black man's Government?' 'Where is his King and his kingdom?' 'Where is his President, his country, and his ambassador, his army, his navy, his men of big affairs?' I could not find them, and then I declared, 'I will help to make them.'"[21] Garvey's coming into consciousness as a race leader and his desire for the accoutrements of empire for Black people illustrate his strategic translation of Washington and Tuskegee and how the literary economy of this southern African American institution inaugurated a diasporic circuit that radiated outward from the rural U.S. South.

Following his European journey, Garvey returned to Jamaica ready to transform his newfound global racial and political consciousness into an uplift project for Afro-Jamaicans. On August 1, 1914, the eightieth anniversary of British West Indian emancipation, he established the Universal Negro Improvement and Conservation Association and African Communities (Imperial) League in Kingston, Jamaica. (The organization's name was later shortened to just "Universal Negro Improvement Association," or UNIA). On October 16, the association held a public debate on whether "rural or city life" was more beneficial "in the development of the State." Garvey, who argued in favor of the rural, "submitted that in every country of the world where there is a system of industry, the rural parts are regarded as the main sources of the nation's upkeep. . . . Manufacturing cities like Manchester [England] with their cotton mills did not grow cotton or rear sheep, neither did London, Liverpool or the cities of Yorkshire grow cane, beet, or produce ore. . . . 'Let us suspend our banana cultivations and cocoa, coffee, and sugar industries for one year,' " he insisted, " 'and the whole country will go into bankruptcy.' "[22] We see here Garvey's nascent conviction that states relied on agriculture, although his determination to establish a separate Black nation-state was still in the future. Garvey's support for rural life was doubtless informed by his own rural origins in the Jamaican countryside. Although those in support of city life narrowly won the debate by two, members unanimously expressed their desire to visit the colony's Hope Farm School to gain practical knowledge and did so shortly thereafter.[23] They aimed to establish in Jamaica "a large industrial farm and institution on the same plan as" Tuskegee, "of which Dr. Booker T. Washington is head." Their proposed school was commonly referred to as a "Tuskegee in Jamaica."[24]

The Hope Farm School sat on 1,700 acres of a former sugar plantation, the Hope Estate, and provided a three-year agricultural science training program for young men. It was formerly the Hope Industrial School, established for "destitute, neglected, and orphaned children" in 1891. The school was closed in 1910 but reopened that same year as the Hope Farm School, "the premier agricultural school in the island."[25] After the association's visit to Hope, the members intended to send several students there and embarked on an extensive campaign to raise funds to establish their own "Tuskegee in Jamaica." "The object of the farm and institute will be to provide work for the unemployed and to provide the opportunity of training young coloured men and women for a better place in the moral, social, industrial and educational life of the country," the association maintained in its correspondence and literature. "Young men and women are to have the opportunity of learning a vocation and to gain a sound moral, literary and industrial training so that when they leave the institution they may by example and leadership help to change and improve the moral and industrial condition of the country."[26] To be sure, the early UNIA was influenced by the Hope School and Jamaica's own history of industrial and agricultural education, but its rhetoric could have been taken directly from a Tuskegee publication as well: members hoped to train "our men to a better knowledge and appreciation of agriculture and the soil," to train "our women to be good and efficient domestics," and to teach and illustrate "the dignity, beauty, and civilizing power of intelligent labour." One key difference from Tuskegee, however, is that the association also proposed a department for "discharged prisoners . . . to keep them from returning to crime" (figure 8.4).[27] Although Mrs. Washington and

Tuskegee graduate Cornelia Bowen had been instrumental in establishing reform schools for wayward Black youth, Booker T. Washington did not conceive of prison reform as a formal part of the Tuskegee project. Besides this distinction, though, Garvey and the UNIA's initial vision was all but a carbon copy of Tuskegee's agro-industrial aims and mission.

As Garvey traveled throughout the island fundraising for the UNIA's proposed farm and institute, he often lectured on Washington and even quoted him on the UNIA's letterhead.[28] This model of Black modernity from the U.S. South resonated with Afro-Jamaicans because, as the Jamaican ICON delegate W. H. Plant described, Jamaica "is entirely agricultural."[29] Garvey also began corresponding with Washington directly, and the two exchanged copies of the *Negro World* and the *Tuskegee Student* newspapers. In 1915, Garvey planned to travel to the United States, where he hoped to visit Tuskegee and meet Washington in person, but his trip was postponed after Washington's sudden death in November. When Garvey finally traveled to the United States in 1916, he initially continued his fundraising efforts for the association's "Tuskegee in Jamaica" but would eventually abandon the scheme, move the UNIA's headquarters to New York City, and cultivate a more global racial uplift program.

During those early years in the United States, Garvey would also develop a more critical stance toward Washington, selectively mobilizing and rejecting various aspects of his uplift philosophy. In an interview in 1921, he asserted that Washington "was not a leader of the Negro race" because he taught them "to beg rather than to make demands. We do not look to Tuskegee. The world has recognized him as a leader, but we do not. We are going to make demands."[30] Yet in some instances he repurposed lines or anecdotes taken directly from Washington's speeches, such as "cast down your bucket" from the Atlanta Exposition Address, and in an address before the Tuskegee student body in 1923 Garvey declared Washington "the greatest man of America—yea, the greatest man in the Western world."[31] And in other instances, Garvey acknowledged that his own vision for the Black world "does not mean to exclude anything that Dr. Booker Washington did or said, but we have taken in all that and have even gone further."[32] "If Washington had lived he would have had to change his program," Garvey insisted. The "Negro problem" "must be solved, not by the industrial leader only, but by the political and military leaders as well."[33]

Garvey extended his literary and ideological appropriation of Washington by recasting him as a cultural symbol. In 1922, the UNIA established the Booker T. Washington University, housed in the Phyllis Wheatley Hotel in Harlem (figure 8.5). Located at 136th Street, the university was conceived as a

FIGURE 8.4. Ad for the UNIA's Industrial Farm and Institute in Jamaica.

Source: Copyright © Robert M. Moton Papers at Hollis Burke Frissell Library, Tuskegee University, Tuskegee, AL.

FIGURE 8.5. Booker T. Washington University in Harlem, NY.

Source: Copyright © The Metropolitan Museum of Art. Art Resource, NY.

training institute for all UNIA officers, doubtless a successor to the association's by then defunct aim to establish a "Tuskegee in Jamaica." Garvey insisted that "everybody in the future who represented the association must pass through the University and prepare themselves for the work."[34] The university was advertised widely in the *Negro World* leading up to the UNIA Convention of 1922 and was set to open on September 1 of that year. At the convention, Garvey paid homage to Washington during the women's industrial exhibition because "he was a doer of things and not an imitator." He reiterated his position that "the U.N.I.A ... had the idea of fostering the industrial program set by Booker T. Washington, and in addition had the idea of nationhood—a government of our own so that our industries could be protected."[35] At this convention, the UNIA also announced its plan to relaunch its steamship line (with what became the S.S. *Booker T. Washington*), despite the failures and setbacks of the Black Star Line.

Although Garvey drew on Washington's agro-industrial and commercial philosophies, his vision of a steamship line was in many respects a distinctly Caribbean expression of global Black modernity. For most African Americans, railroad travel was a more immediate concern than ship travel because African

American migration patterns were largely domestic and intracontinental, which is why railroad cars were such a significant battlefront in the long civil rights struggle against Jim Crow. For Afro-Caribbean peoples, however, ships were the primary mode of inter-island travel and international labor migration to Central America, Europe, and the United States. Furthermore, Garvey's commitment to a steamship line derived from a deeply held conviction that Black people should have the right to free movement and travel, influenced by his knowledge of Black maritime history and his global travels. Establishing a steamship company would counter Black passengers' and seamen's routine "subjection to racist practices on existing shipping lines."[36]

African American Garveyites understood the UNIA's steamship program within the legacies of slavery, the Middle Passage, and the founding of the United States. In "The Free Ship and the Slave Ship and Our Ship," published in the *Negro World* in February 1925, a contributor juxtaposed the launching of the *Booker T. Washington* with an earlier and darker moment in maritime history: "Early in the seventeenth century, within a year, two ships set sail for America. One was the Mayflower; it carried a band of Puritans who were leaving their beloved England for the sake of liberty. The other was a slave ship; it carried a cargo of black men who were torn from their native Africa for the sake of slavery. These two ships" represented "opposite principles," the writer continued. "None of those who came over here on the free ship and the slave ship, some three hundred and five years ago, could have dreamed . . . that the descendants of those who came over on the slave ship would own and operate a steamship of their own, and call her name the S. S. Booker T. Washington. . . . Surely the old order passeth and the new order is at hand."[37] This symbolic appropriation of Washington as well as of Frederick Douglass and Phyllis Wheatley, for whom other UNIA ships were named, takes on more meaning when we consider that all three were formerly enslaved. The UNIA's steamship program was thus envisioned as a corrective to the violence of the transatlantic slave trade—it was not only a show of power and force but an effort to repurpose the meaning of ships from the countless abuses that transpired in the hold and on the deck during the Middle Passage.

Many African American intellectuals, especially the urban northern elite, were skeptical of Garvey's gilded symbolic gestures, however. In an essay published in the *Messenger* in 1923, the African American labor and civil rights activist A. Phillip Randolph blasted Garvey's politics as little more than trickery and grandiosity to dupe the gullible masses:

> In order to inveigle the enthusiastic but uncritical, the Brother proceeds from one pipe-dream to another. . . . Note the Booker T. Washington University, if

you please, the Negro Daily *Times*, The Phyllis Wheatley Hotel, the Universal Publishing House. These gestures are intended to impress the Garvey fanatics with the idea that they are owned by the U.N.I.A., that they represent great business strides of the organization, so that they will not be unwilling to dig down into their jeans again for more cash to drop into the Garvey bottomless money pits.... And, of course, the Booker T. Washington University is mere moonshine. It will neither have students nor teachers. *Students will not trust it to give out knowledge; nor will teachers trust it to give out pay.*[38]

As Randolph suspected, the Booker T. Washington University was indeed short-lived. Though "more than 100 students (from around the world) were expected in its first intake," it does not appear to have ever officially opened.[39] Fellow Tuskegee student Zora Neale Hurston also scathingly parodied this scheme with characteristic wit: "He [Garvey] wanted to be a patron of Letters so he founded or rather created Booker T. Washington University out of a twenty-foot board and nailed it up where all might see," she quipped. "Of course, the alumnae of this university might be only splinters, but even so, it shows the lofty ambition of the man."[40] Though Hurston had published in the *Negro World* and was thus one of its many literary "graduates," as Tony Martin argues, she, like many of her Harlem contemporaries, ultimately came to view Garvey's appropriation of Washington as little more than the stunt of a confidence man.[41]

As the UNIA prepared to launch the *Booker T. Washington* in 1924, Garvey began to align himself once again with Washington's public stance on industry over politics. "We are going to raise and pile up millions of dollars in resources so that when the day strikes for Africa's opportunity we will be prepared to take advantage of it."[42] On one hand, this rhetoric shares ideological affinities with Washington's Atlanta Exposition Address of 1895. Like Washington, Garvey believed "the root of prejudice . . . was merely an economic question" and that "prejudice against the Negro was due to condition."[43] On the other hand, whereas Washington believed that interracial commercial relations would eventually lead to political enfranchisement for Black Americans and was vehemently opposed to African immigration (and domestic migration, for that matter), Garvey refashioned Washington's strategic economic nationalism into a distinctly racial and cultural-nationalist enterprise that selectively jettisoned domestic politics and promoted Black agro-industrial and commercial development and trade relations as the foundation of a pan-African politics.

The historian Mark D. Matthews asserts that Garvey misunderstood Washington and that their projects were "markedly different."[44] To be sure, Garvey's reading of *Up from Slavery* radically misinterpreted Washington's program.

Nowhere did Washington promote establishing a Black king or country for Black people, as Garvey did. In fact, as noted, Washington was staunchly opposed to African immigration altogether. In the 1920s, Thomas M. Campbell, the Tuskegee graduate turned U.S. agricultural extension agent (chapter 1), blamed Garvey's back-to-Africa movement for "hinder[ing] the progress of black farmers" and dissolving community farmers' clubs in the Gulf South, further evidence of Garvey's ideological incompatibility with the Tuskegee Idea.[45] And yet Garvey's strategic translation—or even mistranslation—is constitutive of diasporic practice. In other words, I am less interested in how accurately Garvey understood Washington's program than in how he adapted and instrumentalized Washington as a "symbol of Black self-determination," as Matthews rightly observes, and inventively expanded on the Tuskegee Idea.[46] Garvey cross-bred Washington's philosophies of rugged individualism, economic independence, racial self-help, and agro-industrial education in *Up from Slavery* with contemporaneous models of pan-Africanism and corporate plantation commercialism to imagine a "black empire" all his own. These symbolic gestures reveal a diasporic intellectual genealogy whereby the political and ideological production of Washington, Tuskegee, and the U.S. South influenced pan-African politics well into the twentieth century, even if they were misunderstood or mistranslated.

Ultimately, both of Garvey's symbolic ventures—the Booker T. Washington University and the *Booker T. Washington*—failed. The university does not appear to have ever officially opened, and in 1925 James A. O'Meally, a Jamaican Garveyite living in Harlem, sued the UNIA for failure to remunerate him for designing the university's curriculum.[47] News of O'Meally's lawsuit circulated around the same time that the *Booker T. Washington* was preparing to set sail for its first and only voyage. Just before the ship's departure, Garvey was jailed in Atlanta on charges of mail fraud for the Black Star Line. In fact, he had to give his deposition for O'Meally's lawsuit from prison. And according to an exposé in the *Daily Workman*, an organ of the Communist Party, UNIA officers aboard the *Booker T. Washington* collected large sums of money and lived lavishly, while crew members practically starved. The ship was repeatedly libeled and held in the ports of Kingston and Colón for failure to pay its crewmembers, and the crew threatened to abandon ship. To make matters worse, while in Panama a UNIA officer was poisoned and other officers, Lady Henrietta Vinton Davis and George E. Carter, reportedly inquired into the "private purchase" of a banana plantation. When the ship finally returned to the United States, its officers could not afford to pay the $25 dock fee in Miami, though they had allegedly collected large sums of money in each port, which led the crew to wonder "if

OF SHIPS AND PLANTATIONS

Mr. Carter and Lady Davis had bought that banana plantation after all." While the ship was docked in Jacksonville, Florida, the Ku Klux Klan came aboard, attacked the crew, and attempted to blow up the ship.[48] Astoundingly, Carter and Davis were also accused of murdering a crew member. The beleaguered *Booker T. Washington* finally made its way back to New York City months later than its scheduled return. The ship was later confiscated and sold at auction for $25,000, about one-fourth of its original value. Though the UNIA would continue to discuss launching another steamship line, the immense failure of the *Booker T. Washington* effectively ended the association's maritime activities.[49]

FORGING AN AGRO-INDUSTRIAL EMPIRE

Although Garvey's activities may appear to be those of a charlatan, recent scholarship in Garveyism studies focuses not only on Garvey the man but also on what the infrastructure of the UNIA enabled for its lesser-known foot soldiers: the working-class Black farmers, sailors, and industrial and migrant laborers who made up the bulk of its membership. As the Jamaican social scientist and novelist Erna Brodber writes in her novel *Louisiana* (1994), Garvey's "UNIA gave them a framework within which to do concrete work," which, as the historian Adam Ewing observes, afforded "the articulation and negotiation of local knowledge and strategies of defiance."[50] Just as I have distinguished between Washington and Tuskegee throughout this book (wherever possible), I take a similar approach to Garvey and the UNIA, detailing not only what Garvey envisioned but also how UNIA members mobilized the affordances of the organization to plot an agro-industrial future that figured farmers and other agricultural laborers as essential players in facilitating Black economic (inter) nationalism.

Though the Booker T. Washington University and the S.S. *Booker T. Washington* were largely unsuccessful ventures, Garvey and the UNIA's literal and figural mobilization of Washington reveals how their ongoing confrontation with the plantation, especially corporate agriculture and shipping, animated their vision of an agro-industrial future. At the Third International UNIA Convention in 1922, the Committee on Ways and Means of Improving the Industrial Output of the Negro Peoples of the World still had Tuskegee in mind when it recommended "that a course in agriculture and commerce be provided at the Booker T. Washington University of the U.N.I.A., and men be trained as experts and sent throughout the world to train our people in the art and science of fruit raising, agriculture and business administration and efficiency."[51] Taking this scheme a step further, Hon. W. Thorpe of "Spanish Honduras" proposed establishing schools and laboratories in "agricultural and industrial science" that mirrored Jean Price-Mars's educational strategy for the Haitian peasantry (chapter 4).[52] Through the Booker T. Washington University, then, the UNIA used Washington's symbolic likeness to promote the training and dispatching of ambassadors to educate Garveyites in modern agricultural and commercial methods. The organization thus conceived of Black farmers and agricultural workers as integral to its vision for an agro-industrial empire.

The UNIA's agro-industrial program also drew on Garvey's intimate knowledge of U.S. hemispheric imperialism: corporate plantations, steamships, the fruit trade, and tourism. Alongside plans for the steamship line, the organization aimed to acquire farms and plantations in Central America, the Caribbean, and Africa to compete with U.S. multinationals such as UFCO—hence, the alleged efforts of UNIA officers aboard the *Booker T. Washington* to purchase a banana plantation in Panama. Garvey's complicated and embattled relationship with UFCO throughout his career vividly reveals how he navigated corporate plantation hegemony—moving simultaneously within, against, and alongside it. On one hand, UFCO represented the systemic exploitation, dispossession, and displacement of Afro-Caribbean migrant workers. Indeed, as we have seen, Garvey's firsthand experiences with this exploitation inspired his early understanding of race-based oppression as a systemic problem and of the need for political activism. In a speech to prospective Garveyites in Panama in 1921, he reasoned:

> Those who have labored in Costa Rica on the banana farm or the cocoa plantations of the United Fruit Company . . . as soon as you cleared the lands, dam the swamps and the lagoons[,] make the place sanitary[,] make the bananas grow, make the coffee and cocoa produce, the owners of the land for whom you worked, cut your pay, made your economic conditions harder, and ultimately drove you off the land and you had to leave Costa Rica for Guatamala [*sic*] to do what? To do the same thing in Guatamala [*sic*] as you did in Cost Rica . . . same condition develops and . . . you went to Honduras . . . they again press you, and you move into Nicaragua. . . . Where next are you going? Into Cuba.[53]

Garvey accurately captured the precarity and fungibility of exploited Afro-Caribbean migrant laborers as they traveled from one Global Black South plantation to another. They performed the back-breaking labor yet owned nothing and persisted in a state of perpetual economic insecurity, poverty, and migration.

At the same time, however, Garvey routinely looked to UFCO as a business model. Instead of deeming the corporate plantation as an inherently corrupt institution and calling for its categorical dismantlement, he sought to replicate it, but with Black people at the helm. In short, he scaled up Washington's economic self-help philosophy globally and combined it with nineteenth-century pan-Africanism and UFCO's model of agro-industrial commerce and tourism. Throughout his speeches and writings, he often used UFCO as an object lesson to justify the UNIA's steamship program, noting how in just thirty years Captain Lorenzo Dow Baker, UFCO's founder, went from a "single schooner" that traded between Boston and Jamaica to a multinational company with "a surplus of six hundred million dollars and a capital of one billion dollars, and two hundred ships."[54]

By owning ships, Garvey sought to accomplish for the Black world what Baker and other shipping magnates had accomplished for American industry. Furthermore, a Garveyite at the 1922 UNIA Convention suggested that the organization "should take a leaf out of the book of the United Fruit Company and acquire lands in countries between which they traded . . . [and] in all Negro communities and develop it [the land], have warehouses in all those sections and so help to make the steamship company a success."[55] Whereas Paul Gilroy has theorized the ship as the primary technology of diasporic formation, Garvey and the UNIA offer a theory of diaspora that links the ship to the land through corporate plantation agriculture and industry to facilitate Black economic (inter)nationalism. The Black Star Line, the Black Cross Navigation & Trading Company, and the Negro Factories Corporation were all established, in part, to facilitate the production, mass transport, and trade of fruit, cotton, sugarcane, and other "articles and commodities" produced by Black agricultural and industrial workers "for the consumption of the Negro peoples of the world."[56] If his detractors had not thwarted these efforts, Garvey maintained,

> We would have been removing raw materials from plantations of far-off Africa, from South and Central America, and the West Indies, to our factories in the United States, thus giving employment to millions of Negroes in America in the factories and clearing houses and giving employment to millions more in tropical Africa and South and Central America, and the West Indies. Today the Negro would not still be dependent upon the white man for a pittance of existence but would be his own employer . . . [and] holding his head high . . . everywhere.[57]

Garvey's imagined agro-industrial future sought to reroute the "raw materials" produced on Global Black South farms and plantations to Black-owned steamships and factories in the United States, effectively repurposing the insidious legacies of the ship and the plantation. "The very bananas that made the United Fruit Company so rich have been planted and reared by black men," he reminded *Negro World* readers in 1929.[58] What Black farmers had done for American industry, Garvey believed, they could do for themselves. By acquiring "millions of undeveloped acres of land in the West Indies and Central America," controlling sugar plantations and fruit farms therein, and distributing their products by steamship, the UNIA could effectively create a closed economic system.[59]

Each ethnic group within the diaspora—that is, African Americans, Afro-Caribbeans, Central Americans, and Africans—had a unique role to play in Garvey's scheme. Afro-Caribbean peoples, for instance, were "peculiarly talented" and suited for the task of "the establishment of independent African communities and colonies" precisely because of their labor with UFCO and on the Panama Canal. Their "brain" and "brawn" had "converted the howling wilderness and dismal swamps into thriving towns, central factories and fertile fields of sugar cane, oranges and bananas," Garvey reasoned. "What he [the Afro-Caribbean migrant] has done for others he can do for himself, and we look forward to the time when public buildings, theatres, churches, institutions of learning, docks, bridges, tunnels and railroads will be erected by him in our own African communities and colonies."[60]

African American Garveyites were to provide the industrial and economic contributions. "There are possibilities for the Negroes in the West Indies and South and Central America that the American Negroes should know about," Garvey maintained. "Unfortunately, the American Negro has not travelled; he has not been trained to invest his capital in foreign countries as white Americans have done, with great success." The "Negroes of America" can "become the industrial purveyors of the commodities needed by the African, West Indian, and Central American Negroes."[61] And in turn, the broader diaspora could provide African Americans with "raw materials produced" on their "plantations and farms."[62] Garvey felt that African Americans, perhaps because of their proximity to U.S. industrialization, philanthropy, and wealth, had access to more resources than did their Caribbean, Central American, and African counterparts. He thus came to align African Americans with the factory and industry and the rest of the diaspora with agriculture and the plantation. "In Africa, in the West Indies, in Central America," he wrote, "Negroes tilled the soil exclusively, and the harvest was reaped by the white man exclusively. It was the duty of Negroes of America to help members of the race domiciled in other parts."[63] In doing so, "we would be feeding the mills of industry in America and finding employment in the agricultural regions for millions of our people all over the world."[64]

Garvey seemed to forget that many of his members and sympathizers, especially in the U.S. South, already worked in agriculture and were still quite impoverished. These African American Garveyites sought a more mutual exchange along agricultural lines. At the UNIA Convention in 1924, for instance, Hon. Mills of Newark, New Jersey, suggested that by establishing trade relations among the United States, the West Indies, and Africa, the association could make "a splendid profit, not only on produce brought here, *but on produce shipped away.*" Similarly, Hon. I. Chambers of New Orleans proposed trade agencies, "especially in the South, through which cotton and other produce of the Negro could be bought" to prevent "white capitalists from obtaining this produce at a ridiculously low figure . . . to the undoing of the farmer."[65] Nevertheless, even if Garvey downplayed African American Garveyites in agriculture, he ultimately—though naïvely—imagined an afterlife of the plantation that did not lead to the chain gang or prison as well as a relationship between the plantation and the factory that potentially would not reproduce the plantation's history of discipline, violence, and domination.

One of the most paradoxical and frankly troubling aspects of Garvey's already complicated relationship with UFCO is that the company helped to finance the UNIA both directly and indirectly. Although UFCO's administration initially banned the *Negro World* and surveilled Garveyites' activities in the company's Caribbean and Central American enclaves, the company eventually determined that Garvey and his organization did not threaten its bottom line. Despite the radicalism that characterized his early speeches and writings, Garvey soon modified his tone when significant backlash threatened to dismantle his organization wholesale.[66] During a fundraising tour to Costa Rica (circa 1921), he "met amicably" with UFCO's president, Julio Acosta, and told workers that "they should not fight the United Fruit Company, that the work given them by the United Fruit Company meant their bread and butter."[67] Furthermore, because he understood "the importance of timing in banana cultivation," he assured UFCO that his visit would not "disrupt production."[68] He thus delayed his trip to Port Limón, where the bulk of Garveyites resided, by "a full three days . . . because the company needed to load two banana boats," and, in turn, UFCO "arranged for a 'special pay-day' [for the workers] to coincide" with his visit, enabling them to make financial contributions to the UNIA. "Clearly, Garvey and the fruit company understood each other's position with respect to the plantation workers," writes Ronald Harpelle. "The company needed a reliable workforce to ensure the timely processing of the banana crop and Marcus

Garvey needed the financial support of his followers in order to press forward with the aims of the UNIA." Garvey also reportedly received $2,000 a month from Minor Cooper Keith, one of UFCO'S founders, perhaps as a financial kickback for his cooperation.[69]

Ewing, however, understands Garvey's cooperation with UFCO and what Robert A. Hill describes as Garvey's "'retreat from radicalism'" more generally in this period as pragmatic and strategic. In the face of "mounting economic and political pressures" as well as "the likely destruction of his movement, Garvey chose survival," Ewing argues, "couch[ing] his program of African redemption in carefully crafted declarations of noninterference with constituted authority." Because Garveyites were "eager to sustain their long-term, unambiguously anti-colonial vision," Ewing continues, they "prevented their political evaporation by conceding the short-term advantages of white supremacy."[70] In this way, Garvey proved himself to be quite the astute student of Washington's political strategy of accommodating white philanthropic power brokers, at least publicly, to ensure institutional funding and survival. Consequently, his actions were similarly shrouded in contradiction and have been met with suspicion and ambivalence.

THE SEDUCTIONS AND HOPES OF EMPIRE

Garvey's relationship with UFCO represents a central paradox within his vision for Black liberation: it mimicked European and American national and corporate empires, on one hand, while critiquing and seeking to dismantle their racist underpinnings, on the other. Like the plantation and capitalism, empire was so ubiquitous as a world system that its logics appealed to many Black intellectuals and political organizers seeking resolution to the global "Negro problem." Even as the Black liberation struggle sought to contest these structures, Black political and intellectual leaders often became entangled with them along the way because Black leaders had also been forged in the very crucible of empire and modernity. As a labor migrant, Garvey had experienced firsthand the cost of statelessness for Black people; therefore, empire was a seductive mode of power and relation for him, in particular the promise of protection afforded by a sovereign Black state.[71] He modeled his African redemption scheme on acquiring ships and plantations and establishing commercial and trade relations between Black communities because these political-economic forms represented the accoutrements of power and civilization touted by modern European empires and nation-states as justification for their global supremacy.[72]

Even W. E. B. Du Bois, one of the twentieth century's foremost critics of racial capitalism and Garvey's nemesis, once supported and helped to facilitate the Firestone Rubber Company's establishment of rubber plantations in Liberia. Du Bois believed that white industrial capitalism was necessary for Liberia's development and, as Gregg Mitman argues, "posed the least threat to the country's sovereignty and self-determination."[73] For Garvey, a similar belief in the potential of industrial capitalism and empire meant redirecting the corporate plantation's agricultural and industrial aims toward racial unity to counter the exploitation and extraction perpetrated by European and U.S. empires and corporations, such as UFCO and Firestone. "Everybody is looking towards Empire to insure [sic] protection—a protection for their own," he reasoned. "'African Fundamentalism' points to Imperialism. Imperialism means that whether we are in Africa or abroad, we are united with one tie of life blood, with one tie of race, and as Four Hundred Million we must stand together, willing to fall together or die together."[74] Ultimately, Garvey, Du Bois, and numerous other Black political and intellectual leaders believed that with Black people's guidance, these political-economic forms could be adapted toward more liberatory ends without reproducing racial-capitalist exploitation.

The problems with this line of reasoning, of course, are that both empire and the plantation are fundamentally violent systems rooted in interlocking modes of oppression and that Black people are not inherently immune to being corrupted by them. The examples of African American and Caribbean "overlords" in Liberia and Sierra Leone, respectively, in the nineteenth century demonstrate how class and ethnicity could easily supersede aspirations for racial unity. Yet, as Ewing astutely points out, Garvey was rightly suspicious of whether "a world system constructed by slavery, racism, and capitalism is adaptable enough to fulfill its universalist rhetoric" and suggested that "a new center—an Afrocenter—be devised as a countervailing force." Ultimately, according to Ewing, Garvey resolved that "black women and men could never achieve freedom working *within* the labyrinth of the Eurocentric world-system, but must establish a competing center of power and authority as a *precondition* to true relations of equality."[75]

Garvey's pragmatic attitude toward capitalism as necessary and inevitable further illuminates how he reconciled his vision for Black liberation with UFCO and empire as viable forms of power and relation. He believed that "capitalism is necessary to the progress of the world, and those who unreasonably and wantonly oppose or fight against it are enemies to human advancement."[76] He struggled to conceive of any way to obtain money for racial progress outside of a capitalist system or without employment by white entrepreneurs and therefore rejected the Communist Party's directive to "smash up governments and destroy capital—the big fools! If you destroy capital, where are you going to get bread and butter? . . . [I]f you have not got it you must get it from some one [*sic*] who has it."[77] Hence, his cooperation with UFCO: as an employer, its dollars could help Black people accrue wealth, which would in turn provide the economic foundation for establishing a Black nation. "Employment" and "money" from the "capitalistic white man," Garvey insisted, is necessary for "break[ing] up the prejudice that surrounds him [the Negro]."[78]

Finally, Garvey urged Black people to resist being co-opted by the class struggle because they would be subjected to white supremacy either way. At the 1922 UNIA Convention, he acknowledged that many "working class people were being crushed by the capitalists," but Black people were often treated worse than other racial and ethnic groups. Hon. W. Wallace of Chicago reminded the audience of an instance when Black waiters went on strike with their white counterparts, but when the matter was settled, the Black workers were "left on the streets, while the whites went back to work without giving any aid to the former." He thus concluded that the white "worker of today becomes the capitalist of tomorrow."[79] That Black people seemed to always get the proverbial short end of the stick led Garvey to conclude "there is no difference between capitalistic white men and communist white men in the determination of racial interest," for they both treat "the Negro" as a "convenience." "His inferiority is eternal" to them.[80] Garvey instead encouraged "Negroes" to "pick out the good in each [economic system] and reject the bad," for their "strength lies in the happy medium between the communist and the capitalist."[81] Even if Garvey and UNIA leaders were naive or held a less sophisticated understanding of capitalism, as C. Boyd James argues, they were most sophisticated in their suspicion of the anti-Blackness that often infects interracial organizing and in their understanding of white supremacy's insistence on reproducing itself at the expense of Black people.[82]

To be sure, the UNIA's business activities reflect many of the accumulative logics and expansionist principles of global capitalism and imperialism. But in reading for its plot logics and ethics, we would be remiss to lose sight of how its vision of an agro-industrial empire was also a strategy for political and economic liberation and protection from the abuses of second-class citizenship and colonial subjecthood.[83] Garvey naively believed that he could impose ethical restraints on capitalism, such as caps on individual and corporate wealth, and a

OF SHIPS AND PLANTATIONS   361

system where "use and investment of money" were the "prerogative of the State with the concurrent authority of the people. With such a method," he reasoned "we would prevent the ill-will, hatred and conflicts that now exist between races, peoples and nations."[84]

Garveyites similarly believed that by combining capitalism with forms of economic cooperation and race pride, this exploitative economic system could be repurposed to sustain Black life rather than extinguish it. For Black farmers in the U.S. South, for instance, "the UNIA's appeal was nationalistic and racial, not capitalistic," Rolinson argues. They "did not attribute greed to human nature, but to competing races of people," and thus assumed "a black community would treat fairly and justly all of its members."[85] Viewing the world through a primarily racial lens, Garvey and UNIA members understood themselves to be reinvesting these modern political-economic forms toward more just ends. They did not attribute Black people's oppression to the capitalist mode of development but to racism and white supremacy and thus reasoned that capitalism could be salvaged and reworked to support African redemption.[86] Thus, although the UNIA's agro-industrial program was modeled on corporate plantation empire, its aims and values—to promote and sustain Black life through cooperative ventures— directly contradicted UFCO's racial-capitalist exploitation of Black life and being.

ECONOMIC COOPERATION AND THE PRACTICE OF AFRICAN DIASPORA CITIZENSHIP

The UNIA's agro-industrial program encompassed educating members in scientific farming and commerce; owning and controlling the means of production and consumption; and cultivating shipping and trade relations among communities throughout the Black world. Many of these strategies were already long-held practices across the diaspora, wherein local Black communities worked collectively and pooled resources. However, through Garvey's travels in the Americas and Europe, he developed an understanding of white supremacy and anti-Blackness as worldwide systems of oppression, which inspired him to expand and link up these local practices of mutual aid and cooperation into a distinctly diasporic and pan-Africanist liberation project.

The UNIA's agro-industrial program regarded food production by Black farmers as an especially critical component of racial survival. As Garvey warned in a speech at the 1922 UNIA Convention, "In another hundred years there will not be enough in mineral and vegetable supplies to feed the whole world and the race and nation that is strong enough to corner the output is the race that will survive; while the race of consumers is bound to die out."[87] The UNIA therefore established its Department of Labor and Industry, headed by Ulysses S. Poston of Detroit, Michigan. Poston proposed not only establishing "sound industries in every city where there is a [UNIA] division" but also "carrying its program into the rural districts[,] organizing every farmer and assisting him in controlling the commodity that he produces." The New York division, for example, announced in February 1922 the opening of the Universal Restaurant and Grocery Store. "[The UNIA's] membership, in order to subsist must eat," Poston reasoned, "and the grocery store and restaurant offer the outlet." The Universal Restaurant No. 1 was managed by Mrs. Jennie Jenkins, "a dietitian of no mean ability," and Mrs. Mary Lawrence, a "food chemist" and former "hospital dietitian," presided over the Culinary Department. Mrs. Jenkins aimed to provide "wholesome food at a nominal cost" and assured *Negro World* readers that the "menu consists of everything in season, and is served in liberal portions," thus providing an alternative to the "food gougers in Harlem" and "conserving to the race the immense profits for cheap and unsanitary lunch stands, which have sprung up like mushrooms."[88]

Through its "chain grocery and commission merchant system," the UNIA sought to "co-operate" with farmers by acting as an agent and distributor for their commodities, enabling the farmer to "raise and sell his produce without sharing his profits with the unscrupulous agents." The organization had already "received a car of nice sweet potatoes from Georgia and a shipment" of oranges, grapefruits, lettuce, and beans from Florida and had "disposed" of them in New York, "netting the producers and the association neat profits." When the UNIA told its rural membership about this opportunity, it was "flooded with correspondence, samples of produce, etc." from farmers looking to partner with the organization. The UNIA hoped to secure "produce raised by Negro farmers" in South and Central America and the West Indies. "By getting our produce direct from the producers we will be in a position to sell [to] our stores and restaurants at a cheap rate, which will enable them to sell to the consumer at a cheaper rate than other concerns," Poston reasoned. He understood this business exchange between UNIA members and divisions as a distinctly cooperative practice and encouraged "any farmer who would like to co-operate with us" to contact the minister of the association's Department of Labor and Industry.[89]

Jessica Gordon Nembhard, a scholar of community justice and social-economic development, argues that notwithstanding Garvey's interest in pooling resources and philosophical commitment to cooperative economics and the

OF SHIPS AND PLANTATIONS 363

like, the UNIA's business ventures were "joint-stock companies . . . not cooperative business enterprises" in accordance with the Rochdale Principles.[90] Garveyites seemingly used the rhetoric of economic cooperation loosely, Nembhard argues, while their approach was somewhere between Black capitalism and cooperative economics. Nevertheless, the organization did articulate the logics and ethics of its cooperative vision, and according to Monica White, a sociologist of environmental justice, their efforts prefigured many of the strategies used by the Black cooperative movement of the mid- to late twentieth century.[91]

In the *Negro World*, Poston posited that cooperative enterprises would undercut private enterprises' exploitative practices.[92] In response, one W. J. Hyatt of Tacoma, Washington, offered a series of "practical business suggestions" to aid the organization's cooperative schemes. Hyatt blamed "individualism" as the primary culprit "for our present condition of affairs" and "community effort cooperation" as the "remedy." Hyatt outlined a set of ethical principles for successful cooperation commensurate with the logics and ethics of the plot: "It means concert for the diffusion of wealth. It leaves nobody out who helps to produce it. It touches no man's fortune[.] It seeks no plunder. It causes no disturbance in society. It gives no trouble to our government[.] It enters into no secret associations. It contemplates no violence[.] It subverts no order[.] It loses no dignity[.] . . . It means self-help, self-dependence and such share of the common competence as labor shall earn or thought can win[,] by means which shall leave every other an equal chance of the same good."[93] It is unclear how much attention UNIA officials gave to Hyatt's cooperative "business suggestions"; however, the fact that they were published in the *Negro World* means they were taken seriously enough to distribute in the organization's primary organ.

Later in 1922 at the Third International Convention of Negroes of the World, Garveyites continued to work out the contours of their agro-industrial program. In addition to education in agriculture and business, they proposed creating "agricultural loan banks" and farmers' associations in rural farming communities and debated strategies for controlling agricultural and industrial production, manufacturing, trade, and consumption. The Committee on Ways and Means of Improving the Industrial Output of the Negro Peoples of the World made a most ambitious set of recommendations that included encouraging sugarcane and cotton cultivation by "Negroes in the Southland and West Indies"; acting as buyers for that cotton; entering the textile industry to process the cotton" and "distribut[ing] its finished products among Negro peoples needing same"; importing and exporting cotton as well as many other agricultural commodities and foodstuff; and "encourag[ing] their growth in all countries productive of same where Negroes live."[94]

Ultimately, Garveyites' agricultural philosophy upheld producerism as paramount to self-determination and racial survival.[95] "The world is interested in those nations and peoples that produce wheat, sugar, rice, gold, oil, rubber and such like produce, but nobody cares anything about the Negro, who does not produce anything of his own," Garvey told listeners at the 1922 UNIA Convention.[96] Citing efforts by "the late Booker T. Washington" to encourage "the black man" to "stay on the farms and produce those things that he must consume," Garveyites understood their project as a direct outgrowth of and improvement on Tuskegee's agro-industrial self-help philosophy. Simply owning the means of production was not sufficient, however. Hon J. W. McHurse of Chicago proposed that the UNIA "organize and purchase land for the purpose of securing production and establishing manufactures or exchanges where they would be able to dispose of their produce" as well. Whereas Garvey promoted steamships for conveying produce, Hon. W. Thorpe of Spanish Honduras recommended that "a line of schooners would be cheaper and more easily handled than big steamers." Instead of "agricultural development," Hon. Leroy Bundy of Ohio proposed entering the textile industry by establishing factories that could transform "raw material" into "articles which were easily salable [sic]." Such an enterprise would be mutually beneficial to producers and consumers alike. Hon. Dr. Eason's solution included both agricultural and industrial development, suggesting that the organization "produce cotton," "erect gins," and establish "factories to manufacture the cotton into necessary articles."[97]

Owning land and controlling the means of production and manufacturing were ultimately regarded as strategies for combating the vast dispossession and exploitation of Black agricultural workers throughout the hemisphere. At the 1924 convention, Hon. R. A. H. Batchelor of Oriente, Cuba, noted "the amazing fertility of the Haitian and Dominican soil, which, tilled and tended exclusively by Negroes who were adept . . . only enriched the white foreigner." By immigrating to Haiti and the Dominican Republic, he continued, Garveyites "could not only enrich themselves . . . but help their brothers, the farmers, who were practically slaves in the hands of the white man." Hon. J. B. Eaton, of Berkeley, Virginia, "emphasized that it was practically useless for Negroes to start manufacturing establishments in the face of the keen competition to be found everywhere in the United States unless they owned steamships to permit them marketing their products abroad." Garvey agreed with Eaton, "stressing that it was their [the UNIA's] aim to build up industrially and commercially by getting the raw materials from Negro communities all over the world and bring[ing] them to factories here and returning the finished article."[98] Throughout the convention proceedings, then, Garveyites actively cultivated a theory

OF SHIPS AND PLANTATIONS

and practice of diaspora based on agriculture, the corporate plantation, and various systems of "linking up" the Black world under a collective future—from establishing a steamship line to purchasing farms and plantations; colonizing Africa, Haiti, or the Dominican Republic; developing cotton and sugar mills; and establishing a global food cooperative.

In *The Practice of Citizenship* (2019), Derrick Spires argues that the nineteenth-century Black press—including proceedings from Black state conventions, which were often reprinted in newspapers—have much to teach us about how Black people theorized citizenship both within and beyond "the nation-state form."[99] The UNIA Convention proceedings have a similar function. They depict Garveyites working out the terms of transnational citizenship, or what Carol Boyce Davies and Babacar M'Bow have termed "African diaspora citizenship," "an international relationship of belonging to a larger polity."[100] Proceedings were printed in the *Negro World* so that members who were unable to attend could read and engage in the debates and resolutions. As such, the proceedings elucidate how "Garvey's black empire was a vision of the race as a transnation . . . [,] a way of imagining racial empowerment and representation in statehood that cut across the power of other geopolitical formations."[101] Like Hurston's Jamaican lectures and the subsequent press coverage, the proceedings represent the call-and-response of diasporic practice. They depict Garveyites mining the forms of empire, the nation-state, and the corporate plantation for their alternative affordances, to discover otherwise pathways to the rights, privileges, and protections of citizenship at a time when much of the Black world was subjected to colonial and imperial domination.

In the weeks following the 1922 convention, Garveyites continued to propose ways to harness agriculture to establish economic autonomy and an agro-industrial empire. In an op-ed in the *Negro World*, one writer proposed cotton as a potential area of development "for the colored manufacturer." "Though hampered in his political aspirations in America," the writer maintained, "the Negro can create his own opportunity in industry and commerce."[102] Writing to the *Negro World* from Denver, Colorado, Mrs. Kate Fenner, was confident that "Garveyism will find other places outside of the South to grow cotton. . . . To be free of America's cotton monopoly, Europe would be glad to share her claims in Africa with the cotton experts from the Southern States."[103] Fenner's description of southern Black sharecroppers and tenant farmers as "cotton experts" construes them as intellectuals of the land, whose longtime cultivation of cotton endowed them with a superior and invaluable knowledge. Yet she also illustrated one of the risks of repurposing the corporate plantation: the potential reinforcement of colonial and imperial logics. Her assurance that Europe would "share her claims in Africa" did not interrogate European colonialism and failed to engage Africans as equal partners in the organization's cooperative scheme, demonstrating an instance of "binaristic blackness" that, in part, foreclosed the UNIA's dealings with Liberia and its dream of African redemption.[104]

The shortsightedness of Mrs. Fenner's proposal aside, some UNIA members did in fact view farming and agriculture as crucial to dismantling European empire. In "Our Farmers Should Raise Their Home Supplies," published in the *Negro World* in January 1926, the writer observed that England's colonial system had become "a drain on the production and taxpayers of the colonies," and, consequently, "several of the dominions have broken away" from the "home country" and "have begun to manufacture these raw materials at home." Drawing on this anticolonial critique of extraction and dependency, the writer encouraged independence and self-determination among the *Negro World*'s "very large number of readers who are farmers . . . in the United States, in the West Indies and in Africa." Despite UNIA officers' alleged efforts to purchase a banana plantation in Panama and proposals at the conventions to grow sugar and cotton on an industrial scale, this writer understood all too well how corporate monocrop agriculture had "well nigh ruined the farms of the Southern States and impoverished the workers. Cotton and tobacco as the money crops have driven out very largely the raising of home supplies," creating "dependence on the credit system for necessary supplies." To combat this cycle of dependence and exploitation, the editorialist advised farmers and tenants alike "to own land wherever they can and to raise their own home supplies, and thus become independent of the country storekeeper and the credit system. . . . The money crops should be considered only after the home supplies crops have been provided for." The writer's acknowledgment of the UNIA's diasporic community of farmer-readers underscores agricultural workers' crucial role in the organization's political aspirations, and the article's shift from a critique of colonial extraction of resources to the local conditions of Black farmers throughout the diaspora suggests that the UNIA viewed agriculture as the connective tissue within its own world system of trade and commerce between and among Black communities. "We believe in the farmer and in ownership in the soil as the most independent life," the editorial declared. "The man who owns the land will own the man who works the land."[105]

Garveyites remained committed to plotting agro-industrial futures through education, farming, shipping, and trade as late as the mid-1930s. The 1929 UNIA Convention, for instance, aimed to discuss creating a "thorough educational system" through the "founding of three Negro universities of a purely technical character—one in America, one in the West Indies and one in Africa."

The convention attendees also hoped to launch a new steamship line, create "general economic opportunities in [scientific] agriculture, industry, and commerce" to facilitate "proper trade relationships" between Black communities, and acquire and control land.[106] They reprised these kinds of goals yet again at the 1934 convention in Kingston, Jamaica, as part of the "five-year plan," which included establishing "farms and plantations" throughout the diaspora and a "training College" for the UNIA leaders who would "supervise" the venture.[107] Ultimately, for Garvey and the UNIA, agriculture was an essential component of their goal to facilitate economic (inter)nationalism between "independent African communities and colonies" living in existing nation-states. This closed economic circuit would afford them the rights, privileges, and protections of African diaspora citizenship within a Black transnation.

Like Tuskegee, land acquisition, farming, and agricultural and industrial education were central to the UNIA's economic internationalist agenda. If Washington and Carver promoted agriculture to sustain individual Black farm families—ensuring they could both feed themselves and sell their surplus food and cash crops on the global market—Garveyites scaled the project by envisioning Black farmers and industrial laborers as part of a transnational economic network. The UNIA's efforts to establish a closed economic system through cooperative business enterprises and thus to circumvent white European and U.S. empire and disrupt racial-capitalist exploitation of Black laborers were in many ways radical and ambitious. Yet its strategy was also contingent on co-opting and replicating such inherently corrosive political-economic forms as the corporate plantation and European empire. Moreover, there does not seem to have been much discussion among Garveyites about how to produce agricultural commodities at scale without replicating labor exploitation—the plantation's most deleterious yet abundant crop—or about the ecological implications of modeling the organization's agro-industrial liberation project on such an extractive enterprise as UFCO.

Yet we cannot lose sight of the fact that in mining the corporate plantation and empire for their otherwise affordances, the UNIA attempted to imbue these modern forms with new possibilities that were not reducible to a naive mimicry of the titans of industrial capitalism. On their experiment plot, Garveyites imagined Black economic internationalism as a way to sustain and propagate Black life globally. Through agro-industrial cooperation and the linking of Black producers directly to Black consumers, Garvey and the UNIA hoped to counter the continuation of centuries of racial exploitation and labor extraction by ensuring employment opportunities, access to quality foods, and the protections of transnational citizenship for those who remained stateless and dispossessed. In these ways, Garveyites were ultimately committed to the logics and ethics of the plot, even as they, like so many others before and after them, struggled to fully extricate themselves from the plantation's vise grip. Such were the quandaries and contradictions of Black world making in the plantation's precarious afterlives.

Epilogue

Gathering and Assessing Our Harvests; or, Lessons from Our Experiment Plots

In *Afterlives of the Plantation*, I have plotted an alternative diasporic geography to illuminate how Black people in the rural, agricultural regions of the Western Hemisphere crafted visions of progress, self-determination, and world making as the abolition of slavery gave way to new forms of unfreedom, anti-Blackness, and underdevelopment. As these global Black southerners strategized about the precarious conditions confronting them in the plantation's immediate aftermath, they wrestled over the meaning of the slave past; innovated literary, sonic, and visual aesthetic and performance practices; and debated how to address the myriad political, economic, and educational challenges that shaped their present in hopes of forging a better future. They were anything but backward or antimodern. They were New Negroes in every way. "How *does* one plot a new world for Black people in the aftermath of such apocalyptic violence?" they must have asked themselves. My goal here has been to trace how they went about answering such a colossal question and interrogating the problems they both solved and created in conducting their respective experiments in Black world making.

In redrawing the map and reorienting us toward the South, I have assembled an archive of both canonical and lesser-known texts, figures, and networks to illuminate theories and practices of Black world making often overlooked by our tendency to privilege hegemonic geographic frameworks. In doing so, I have plotted an alternative Black intellectual and cultural genealogy that foregrounds south–south cultural and intellectual exchange and highlights the centrality of farming and agriculture to Black modernity and Black transnational and diaspora studies. Critically, what also emerges from this cartographic shift is a more nuanced lens through which to evaluate the contributions of Tuskegee, a

370   EPILOGUE

historically Black educational institution and eco-ontological project in the rural U.S. South, that, in both scholarship and the popular imagination alike, is more often reduced to its limitations than what it afforded for Black modernity. I demonstrate how to engage Tuskegee and Booker T. Washington both generously and critically—thinking with, through, and against them. In doing so, I at once grapple with the future they envisioned and what it enabled for Black modernity, while acknowledging their imaginative constraints as well.

Like Black people, Black studies has always had to do more with less and to "hit a straight lick with a crooked stick," as Hurston might put it. Long before Black people could attend predominantly white institutions or Black studies became an institutionalized discipline, historically Black colleges and universities were early crucibles for educating Black people and promoting research about Black life. Tuskegee, in particular, was a locus and model of Black study and Black studies: documenting, archiving, innovating, and experimenting with ways to sustain Black life and culture with and among those who had survived the most brutal forms of exploitation and dispossession. Many of the strategies promoted at Tuskegee—repurposing the plantation, agricultural and industrial education, food sovereignty, and eco-ontological regeneration—remained central aims of twentieth-century Black freedom struggles. Recovering Tuskegee's plot logics and ethics, then, allows us to resituate it within a genealogy of Black liberatory agriculture, including Martin Delany's conceptions of Black agro-economic internationalism in the nineteenth century; the Communist Party's Black Belt Nation Thesis; Eric Williams's desire to prioritize agriculture within British West Indian primary, secondary, and university education systems; Fannie Lou Hamer's cooperative farm in Mississippi; the agronomist Amilcar Cabral's agro-decolonial efforts in Cape Verde and Guinea Bissau; and the Black Panther Party's free-breakfast program, among many others. These figures understood agriculture as essential to Black progress and survival. It was at once a mode of nourishment, self-determination, communal subsistence, political-economic development, and ultimately freedom and sovereignty. This is not to suggest that all subsequent visions of agrarian futures were directly influenced by Tuskegee, per se, but rather to elucidate how the strategies Tuskegee's faculty and staff attempted are a part of a rich legacy of Black liberatory agriculture and environmentalism that gives us a new or at least a more nuanced way to consider the contributions of an institution—and region—we think we know and sometimes dismiss as a result.

It is perhaps easy from our postemancipation, allegedly postcolonial, and firmly neoimperial place in modern history to criticize and enumerate the shortcomings of past freedom dreams. Today, we tend to think of missionary work and empire as antithetical to the struggle for Black liberation. The ties among, say, industrial capitalism, imperialism, and anti-Blackness are self-evident to us, but they were by no means a foregone conclusion for past generations. Our understanding of systemic oppression is possible largely because of their past successes, failures, and missteps. As such, in our dealings with the past we must acknowledge that we have the benefit of history on our side and thus give proper consideration to what past generations were up against: appreciating the constraints under which they labored while also holding them accountable for the limits of their political and aesthetic imaginations. This has been one of my chief aims in *Afterlives of the Plantation*.

Historically, Black people have always had to use their ingenuity and creativity to salvage and adapt the debris of modernity to sustain and propagate Black life. For instance, Tuskegee's faculty and students made the bricks and built the campus by hand. They supplied their own electricity, grew their own food, and regenerated the soil while regenerating themselves. But this matter of repurposing the political-economic forms of plantation modernity and negotiating with power under oppressive and seemingly impossible conditions is tricky business rife with potential pitfalls. On one hand, such repurposing was a practical and necessary strategy, requiring considerable genius and vision. What Washington and Tuskegee's faculty, staff, and students accomplished on the former Bowen Plantation was nothing short of astonishing, especially in the post-Reconstruction, Jim Crow South. They plotted a course for Black rural modernity that resignified farming and agriculture for Black people as scientific, intellectual, beautiful, pleasurable, and self-proprietorial. It was an experiment in Black world making that viewed the regeneration of Black being as inextricably tied to being good stewards of the earth and as enacting care for the most vulnerable. No wonder it inspired a host of similar efforts throughout the diaspora. Rafael Serra y Montalvo, Jean Price-Mars, and a host of other Afro-Caribbean intellectuals and political leaders saw in Tuskegee the tools and methods for addressing their respective postslavery turned colonial and imperial dilemmas. Hundreds of students and parents from Cuba, Puerto Rico, Jamaica, British Guiana, Haiti, Central and South America, and Africa as well as thousands from the U.S. South selectively embraced and strategically translated agricultural and industrial education into myriad pathways to becoming New Negroes now that they were less constrained by the slave past.

On the other hand, one of the most important lessons we have learned in our journey through the Global Black South is that transforming the plantation landscape and regenerating its soils, although crucial first steps, are ultimately insufficient alone. We must recall that "to repurpose" means "to convert or adapt for a *different* purpose or for use in a *different* way." So a thorough repurposing of the plantation would have meant uprooting its *ideological* stronghold as well. Washington and his fellow Black elites' adherence to the civilizing mission, bourgeois gender ideals, and class paternalism toward the Black masses, as explored in plots I and II, fell short of the wholesale transformation and ideological decolonization needed to plot a thoroughly different future. Though unquestionably committed to regenerating Black being and creating a better world for Black people, they often adhered too closely to the racial, class, and gender hierarchies that plantation modernity set in motion. The thing about experiments, though, is that they often fail the first time around and must be tweaked and repeated continuously before they reach their desired end. Given the magnitude of the obstacles these figures confronted—the plantation's material, ontological, moral, ideological, and ecological stronghold on the modern world order—it is no wonder aspects of their experiments failed and had to be adjusted and revised by successive generations.

In plot III, then, we witnessed how Tuskegee's students exploited the positive affordances of the uplift generation, even while critiquing and jettisoning the limits of that generation's political and aesthetic imaginations. Claude McKay's celebration of Jamaican peasants as intellectuals of the land who reserved the right to self-determination and Zora Neale Hurston's depictions of African American and Afro-Caribbean migrant workers as arbiters of modern Black art and performance are crucial correctives to the previous generation's class biases. Marcus Garvey, too, took working-class Black people seriously as architects of Black economic (inter)nationalism. Yet this generation had its shortcomings, too: Hurston and McKay engaged in primitivism and were often shortsighted in their depictions of other diasporic communities (McKay's southern African American characters in *Banjo*, for instance), and Garvey was obsessed with power and empire.[1] Yet we would be hard-pressed to find a perfect Black social movement or political project. Just as uplift was undermined by the civilizing mission and class paternalism, male chauvinism and heterosexism were the Achilles' heels of the Civil Rights Movement, and racism undercut the communist and feminist movements. My point is not to excuse their limitations but to remind us that all experiments in Black freedom have their unique problems, contradictions, blind spots, and unforeseen consequences.

The project of Black freedom is unfinished, of course, and I am convinced that these past experiments in plotting agrarian futures have much to teach us still about how to forge a new and more just world. Tuskegee's experiment plot and extension program, for instance, are important models for how to share and redistribute institutional knowledges and resources to ensure the health and

EPILOGUE

well-being of the most vulnerable. In our current moment of impending climate catastrophe, where the extractive practices of plantation colonialism and industrialization have reached a proverbial boiling point, Tuskegee's legacy of liberatory agriculture holds invaluable lessons for how to restore ourselves by becoming better stewards of the world around us. Yet we can also learn from Tuskegeeans' failure to jettison paternalism and their tendency to moralize and condescend to the very people they aimed to help. As we mount our own experiments in forging new worlds, we must continuously refine our methods and values to ensure that the freedoms we are pursuing are supple, capacious, and, ultimately, loving enough to encompass us all.

A chief aim of this book is to demonstrate what thinking with and through the Global Black South enables for Black studies. My focus on agrarian futures recovers how liberatory agriculture was constitutive to conceptions of Black modernity and practices of transnational and diasporic relation. Yet it also presents a challenge to the field because most of the agrarian futures explored here relied on notions of property ownership and practices of territoriality that emerged from the history of colonial conquest. In her plot–plantation schema, Sylvia Wynter argues that "while the official plantation ideology would develop as an idea of property and the individual's rights to property, i.e., as the right to own the property of Black labor-power, the provision ground ideology would remain based on man's relation to the earth, the base of his social being."[2] Though Wynter establishes the plot as the rejection of property ownership in favor of a more communal and ethical relation between Black people and the earth, in practice and especially in the British Caribbean it introduced enslaved peoples and their descendants to the scripts and logics of land possession.[3] As a site of quasi-property ownership that in some cases could be inherited, the plot was also the source of property disputes "among the enslaved and free black labor[ers]," as Kaneesha Parsard reminds us.[4] The plot, then, was not immune to liberal attitudes toward land, including notions and practices of individual possession, capital accumulation, resource extraction, and dominion.

In slavery studies and the fields of Black geographies and Black ecologies, scholars have rightly critiqued notions and practices of property and possession, for in the Western juridical-ontological order of things the very notion of private property in land as the basis of the rights-bearing subject and legal personhood was inextricably tied to arguments and beliefs about the possession of Black people and their labor. In the case of racial-sexual violence specifically, "geographic conquest and expansion [were] extended to the reproductive and sexually available body" (hence McKay's exclusive use of botanical metaphors to refer to Black women in *Banana Bottom*, for instance).[5] Yet despite the ideological ties among the possession and exploitation of land and people, geno-cide and ecocide, and white-supremacist dominion, we must not lose sight of the ways property ownership remained a crucial strategy of Black self-determination and resistance to and protection from legal and extralegal forms of labor exploi-tation as well as from conditions of debt, hunger, and poverty. I agree that we should "envision . . . personhood and autonomy separate from the sanctity of property and proprietorial notions of the self" and that "the claim to place should not be naturally followed by material ownership and black repossession but rather by a grammar of liberation, through which ethical *human*-geographies can be recognized and expressed."[6] Yet historically throughout the Global Black South, land possession also *enabled* just such grammars of liberation and ethical "human-geographies." Though land ownership may not represent the most rad-ical approach to uprooting plantation logics and ideologies, it is no less legiti-mate, as indicated by many of the figures and projects explored here. For enslaved peoples and their descendants navigating the precarious entanglements of prop-erty and personhood, acquiring land was a necessary pathway to personal and often communal protection and liberation, and we mustn't lose sight of this cru-cial fact, even if we determine that such a strategy is no longer useful for our present-day freedom struggles.

Black liberatory agriculture through land ownership is further complicated when we consider the history of settler colonialism and the expropriation of lands from Indigenous peoples. Scholars working at the intersection of Black and Native studies have long wrestled with the dilemma of Black people's claims to lands and territories originally inhabited by Native peoples. This dilemma has been especially pertinent within debates about the alleged Black "exoduster, ambiguous settler, arrivant, or exiled settler" in Indian Territory in the nine-teenth century, as the historian Tiya Miles points out.[7] Although this question is important and necessary, especially as we consider the possibility of reparations and justice for the past harms of slavery and settler colonialism, the practice of repurposing plantation lands, as I have described here, is a slightly different issue than that of the alleged "Black settler." Tuskegee, Tougaloo College, the Univer-sity of the West Indies at Mona, and other Black institutions that were estab-lished on former plantation ruins had no role whatsoever in Native removal and plotted futures on these lands *after* Native removal had already transpired.

Furthermore, and perhaps most importantly, formerly enslaved peoples and their descendants were not in positions of power to cede land back to Native peoples. They could no more reverse Native removal than they could the Middle Passage. Regarding them as "settlers" flattens and reduces the brutalities exacted against them and, as Miles argues of the Black refugees in Indian Territory, fails

EPILOGUE

to acknowledge the limited options available to them.[8] Like Jovan Scott Lewis's position on Black settlement in Indian territory, my attention to the ways Black people repurposed plantation geographies to plot agrarian futures rejects the notion that "Native dispossession facilitated Black freedom. Such an argument would be disingenuous because of the many racial entanglements and exchanges of dispossession and exclusion between the groups."[9] For instance, among the Creeks who inhabited the Indian town of Tuskegee at the time of removal, four Creek slave owners owned a total of thirty-five people. Given the complexity of Creek slaveholding practices, it is impossible to know how many of these nameless enslaved people were Black or if they were engaged in plantation labor.[10] However, we know for certain that Creeks enslaved Black people and owned and operated cotton plantations. In fact, many Creeks took the Black people they enslaved with them to Indian Territory during removal and only manumitted them following the Civil War. As Tiffany Lethabo King soberingly reminds us, "Under relations of conquest, Black and Indigenous people made difficult and agonizing choices when it came to negotiating and fighting for their existence," including repurposing the plantation and being seduced by other modern political-economic forms such as capitalism and empire. "The endeavor of surviving under conditions of conquest is never clean," indeed.[11]

As the inheritors of the precarious future set in motion by the plantation, and as we attempt to sustain life in its social, political, and ecological ruins, we must continue asking ourselves the crucial question: *What are justice and repair in the wake of the apocalyptic violence of the transatlantic slave trade, Native genocide and removal, and persistent colonial and imperial exploitation?* The stakes of grappling with such a colossal question could not be more urgent. In the United States, for instance, race—one of the plantation's most deleterious affordances—continues to play an outsized role in determining health outcomes, access to education and the rights and privileges of citizenship, and nearly every other indicator of a good life. Furthermore, in both secondary and higher education, efforts to confront and take accountability for the country's sordid past are being strategically dismantled at every turn. The plantation also remains with us in ways that perpetuate its originary use as a technology of racial-sexual violence, ecological degradation, and capital accumulation. At Louisiana's Angola Prison, established on a complex of former cotton plantations, inmates are still forced to perform farm labor in extreme, life-threatening heat, as prison guards riding on horseback surveil their every move. Throughout the United States, tourists can visit former plantation estates that whitewash the history of brutality that occurred on their grounds by referring to enslaved peoples as "workers" (as if they had any agency or choice in being incarcerated there) and depicting slave owners as benevolent paternalists. Incredibly, some sites ignore the history of slavery altogether, focusing on the beautiful architecture and botanical gardens or historical reenactments that extol the beauty and simplicity of the old pastoral South before the putative "War of Northern Aggression." In Brazil, as recently as 2016, tourists visiting the former coffee plantation Santa Eufrásia could be served and entertained by Afro-Brazilians dressed up as enslaved people while one of the great-granddaughters of the plantation's original owner cosplayed as a plantation mistress. Furthermore, in both the United States and the Caribbean alike, former plantations often serve as ostentatious wedding venues and quaint bed-and-breakfasts, where newlyweds consummate their marriages on the blood-soaked soils of genocide and ecocide.[12]

These are the literal and figural plantation ruins that pollute our present-day social, cultural, and political landscape. Although there are no easy resolutions, perhaps some of the hard-won lessons, values, and strategies cultivated on the experiment plots of the Global Black South can point us in the right direction. After all, repurposing the plantation through soil regeneration is nothing short of a proto-conservationist ethic akin to contemporary practices of recycling, composting, reusing, and engaging in other sustainable techniques and methods. So as we teeter on the precipice of our own apocalypse—climate change, food insecurity, and the ongoing social and ecological carnage wrought by the plantationocene—recovering the eco-ontological knowledges and strategies of the Global Black South and foregrounding a Black studies praxis rooted in the logics and ethics of the plot are imperative if we are to uproot the plantation's stronghold on how we narrate the past and, most importantly, how we forge a more just and sustainable present and future in its wake.

Notes

ABBREVIATIONS

BTWP   *The Booker T. Washington Papers*, 14 vols., ed. Louis R. Harlan and Raymond W. Smock

MG and UNIA Papers   *Marcus Garvey and Universal Negro Improvement Association Papers*, 10 vols., ed. Robert A. Hill

INTRODUCTION: REGENERATING BLACK LIFE IN PLANTATION RUINS

1. My use of "otherwise" is drawn from Ashon T. Crawley's conception of "otherwise possibilities" in *Blackpentecostal Breath: The Aesthetics of Possibility* (New York: Fordham University Press, 2017), 2–3.
2. Robin D. G. Kelley, *Freedom Dreams: The Black Radical Imagination* (Boston: Beacon, 2002).
3. Booker T. Washington, *Up from Slavery* (1901), ed. Louis R. Harlan (New York: Penguin, 1986), 128–29.
4. Anna Lowenhaupt Tsing, *The Mushroom at the End of the World: On the Possibility of Life in Capitalist Ruins* (Princeton, NJ: Princeton University Press, 2015).
5. Booker T. Washington, "Signs of Progress Among the Negroes," *Century Magazine*, January 1900.
6. Booker T. Washington, "Some Results of the International Conference on the Negro," n.d., box 96, folder 5, Papers of Booker T. Washington: The Tuskegee Collection, Tuskegee University Archives, Tuskegee, AL.
7. Washington, "Some Results."
8. Two important exceptions that situate the ICON within this genealogy include Michael O. West, "The Tuskegee Model of Development in Africa: Another Dimension of the African/African-American Connection," *Diplomatic History* 16, no. 3 (1992): 371–87; Jeanette Eileen Jones, "'Brightest Africa' in the New Negro Imagination," in *Escape from New York: The New Negro*

Renaissance Beyond Harlem, ed. Davarian L. Baldwin and Minkah Makalani (Minneapolis: University of Minnesota Press, 2013), 31–51.

9. My notion of the "Global Black South" elaborates on the work of the literary critic Gay Wilentz, who was arguably the first scholar to articulate a notion of "the Black South" as a hemispheric geography. See Farah Jasmine Griffin, "The Daughter's Geography: The Poetics of Diaspora," in *The African Presence and Influence on the Cultures of the Americas*, ed. Brenda M. Greene (Newcastle, U.K.: Cambridge Scholars, 2010), 78–79.

10. For "Black aliveness," see Kevin Quashie, *Black Aliveness, or A Poetics of Being* (Durham, NC: Duke University Press, 2021).

11. Saidiya Hartman, *Lose Your Mother: A Journey Along the Atlantic Slave Route* (New York: Farrar, Straus, and Giroux, 2007), 6. On "plantation modernity," see Amy Clukey and Jeremy Wells, "Introduction: Plantation Modernity," in "The Global South and/in the Global North: Interdisciplinary Investigations," ed. Amy Clukey and Jeremy Wells, special issue, *Global South* 10, no. 2 (2016): 1–10.

12. Hartman, *Lose Your Mother*, 6.

13. My use of "affordances" draws on Caroline Levine's conception of the "affordances of form." "Affordances," she writes, are "the potential uses or actions latent in materials and designs" that "point us both to what all forms are capable of—to the range of uses each could be put to . . . and also to their limits, the restrictions intrinsic to particular materials and organizing principles." See Levine, *Forms: Whole, Rhythm Hierarchy, Network* (Princeton, NJ: Princeton University Press, 2015), 6, 3.

14. Katherine McKittrick, "Plantation Futures," *Small Axe* 17, no. 3 (2013): 10.

15. On "social death," see Orlando Patterson, *Slavery and Social Death: A Comparative Study* (Cambridge, MA: Harvard University Press, 1982).

16. C. L. R. James, *The Black Jacobins: Toussaint L'Ouverture and the San Domingo Revolution*, 2nd ed. (New York: Vintage, 1989), appendix; Antonio Benítez-Rojo, *The Repeating Island: The Caribbean and the Postmodern Perspective*, 2nd ed. (Durham, NC: Duke University Press, 1996).

17. Scholarship on W. E. B. Du Bois's early sociological studies at Atlanta University is an important exception to the tendency to ignore how historically Black colleges and universities were forerunners to Black studies.

18. The term *New Negro* as I use it here draws on recent scholarship that extends the New Negro era back into the nineteenth century and expands its geography beyond New York and the broader Global North to encompass the U.S. South, the Caribbean, and other parts of the Black world. See Davarian Baldwin, *Chicago's New Negroes: Modernity, the Great Migration, and Black Urban Life* (Chapel Hill: University of North Carolina Press, 2007); Jacqueline Goldsby, *A Spectacular Secret: Lynching in American Life and Literature* (Chicago: University of Chicago Press, 2006); Jennifer Brittan, "The Terminal: Eric Walrond, the City of Colón, and the Caribbean of the Panama Canal," *American Literary History* 25, no. 2 (2013): 294–316; Brent Hayes Edwards, *The Practice of Diaspora: Literature, Translation, and the Rise of Black Internationalism* (Cambridge, MA: Harvard University Press, 2003); Michelle Ann Stephens, *Black Empire: The Masculine Global Imaginary of Caribbean Intellectuals in the United States, 1914–1962* (Durham, NC: Duke University Press, 2005); Claudrena N. Harold, *The Rise and Fall of the Garvey Movement in the Urban South, 1918–1942* (New York: Routledge, 2007); Harold, *New Negro Politics in the Jim Crow South* (Athens: University of Georgia Press, 2013); Gabriela A. Briggs, *The New Negro in the Old South* (New Brunswick, NJ: Rutgers University Press, 2015); Baldwin and Makalani, *Escape from New York*.

19. Édouard Glissant, "Closed Place, Open Word," in *Poetics of Relation*, trans. Betsy Wing (Ann Arbor: University of Michigan Press, 1997), 75.

20. For my analysis of how Black corporate plantation workers employed by UFCO and the Delta and Pine Land Company forged hemispheric literary and political ties, see Jarvis C. McInnis, "A

INTRODUCTION

Corporate Plantation Reading Public: Labor, Literacy, and Diaspora in the Global Black South," *American Literature* 91, no. 3 (September 2019): 523–55.

21. Thadious Davis, *Southscapes: Geographies of Race, Region, and Literature* (Chapel Hill: University of North Carolina Press, 2011); John Wharton Lowe, *Calypso Magnolias: The Crosscurrents of Caribbean and Southern Literature* (Chapel Hill: University of North Carolina Press, 2016).

22. Jon Smith and Deborah Cohn, "Introduction: Uncanny Hybridities," in *Look Away! The U.S. South in New World Studies*, ed. Jon Smith and Deborah Cohn (Durham, NC: Duke University Press, 2004), 6.

23. See also Edgar T. Thompson, preface to *The Plantation: An International Bibliography* (Boston: G. K. Hall, 1983), ix–xi.

24. Shalini Puri, ed., *Marginal Migrations: The Circulation of Cultures Within the Caribbean* (London: Macmillan Caribbean, 2003).

25. Matthew Pratt Guterl, *American Mediterranean: Southern Slaveholders in the Age of Emancipation* (Cambridge, MA: Harvard University Press, 2008).

26. Paul Gilroy, *The Black Atlantic: Modernity and Double Consciousness* (Cambridge, MA: Harvard University Press, 1993); Caroline Levander and Walter Mignolo, "The Global South and World Dis/Order," *Global South* 5, no. 1 (2011): 8.

27. Houston A. Baker and Dana D. Nelson, "Preface: Violence, the Body, and 'The South,'" in "Violence, the Body, and 'the South,'" ed. Houston A. Baker Jr., special issue, *American Literature* 73, no. 2 (June 2001): 234, 235.

28. Marlon Ross, "Callaloo, Everyone?," *Callaloo* 30, no. 1 (2007): 92.

29. Zandria Robinson, *This Ain't Chicago: Race, Class, and Regional Identity in the Post-soul South* (Chapel Hill: University of North Carolina Press, 2014); Regina Bradley, *Chronicling Stankonia: OutKast and the Rise of the Hip Hop South* (Chapel Hill: University of North Carolina Press, 2021); Brittney C. Cooper, Susana M. Morris, and Robin M. Boylorn, eds., *The Crunk Feminist Collection* (New York: Feminist Press, 2017); L. H. Stallings, *A Dirty South Manifesto: Sexual Resistance and Imagination in the New South* (Oakland: University of California Press, 2020); Riché Richardson, *Black Masculinity and the U.S. South: From Uncle Tom to Gangsta* (Athens: University of Georgia Press, 2007).

30. Davis, *Southscapes*, 2. Although Davis also interrogates the region's ties to the Global South, her primary focus is on writers in Louisiana and Mississippi.

31. Melvin Dixon, "South of the South," *Callaloo*, no. 8/10 (February–October 1980): 16. *Callaloo's* subtitle has undergone several revisions over the years. It was first changed to *A Tri-annual Journal of Afro-American and African Arts and Letters* in 1985, presumably to reflect the diasporic scope of its content. It was given its current subtitle, *A Journal of African Diaspora Arts and Letters*, in 2002.

32. Magalí Amrillas-Tiseyra and Anne Garland Mahler, "Introduction: New Critical Directions in Global South Studies," in "New Critical Directions in Global South Studies," ed. Magalí Amrillas-Tiseyra and Anne Garland Mahler, special issue, *Comparative Literature Studies* 58, no. 3 (2021): 465–84; Magalí Amrillas-Tiseyra and Anne Garland Mahler, "Introduction: New Critical Directions in Global South Studies, Continuing the Conversation," in "New Critical Directions in Global South Studies, Continuing the Conversation," ed. Magalí Amrillas-Tiseyra and Anne Garland Mahler, special issue, *Comparative Literature Studies* 59, no. 1 (2021): 1–10.

33. Glissant, "Closed Place, Open Word," 63.

34. George Beckford, *Persistent Poverty: Underdevelopment in Plantation Economies of the Third World* (New York: Oxford University Press, 1972), xxv–xxvi.

35. Harry Haywood, *Negro Liberation* (New York: International, 1948), 146.

36. *Investigation of Panama Canal Matters: Hearings Before the Committee on Interoceanic Canals*, vol. 1 (Washington, DC: U.S. Government Printing Office, 1907), 52, 485–86, 680.

INTRODUCTION

37. Quoted in Velma Newton, *The Silver Men: West Indian Labour Migration to Panama, 1850–1914* (Mona, Jamaica: Institute of Social and Economic Research, University of West Indies, 1984), 131.

38. Stephens, *Black Empire*, 5.

39. Manning Marable, "Black Skin, Bourgeois Masks," in *Profiles of Self-Determination: African Responses to European Colonialism in Southern Africa 1652–Present*, ed. David Chanaiwa (Northridge: California State University Foundation, 1976), 320, 321–22, 327.

40. Saidiya Hartman, *Scenes of Subjection: Terror, Slavery, and Self-Making in Nineteenth-Century America* (New York: Oxford University Press, 1997).

41. Walter Rodney, *The Groundings with My Brothers* (1969; reprint, Chicago: Research Associates School Times Publications, 1990), 25.

42. Two important exceptions can be found in the work of Thadious Davis and Houston Baker. Davis refers to "southern modernity" as a postemancipation phenomenon, whereas Baker dates the onset of "Afro-modernity" to the Civil Rights Movement. For both, modernity is tied to notions of freedom, citizenship, and progress for southern African Americans especially. Davis, *Southscapes*, 12; Houston A. Baker Jr., *Turning South Again: Re-thinking Modernism/Re-reading Booker T.* (Durham, NC: Duke University Press, 2001), 33–34.

43. Sylvia Wynter, "Novel and History, Plot and Plantation," *Savacou* 5 (1971): 95–102.

44. Edgar T. Thompson, *The Plantation*, ed. Sidney M. Mintz and George Baca (Columbia: University of South Carolina Press, 2010), 4.

45. Sylvia Wynter, "Black Metamorphosis: New Natives in a New World," unpublished manuscript, n.d. (c. 1970s), 20, Institute of the Black World Papers, Schomburg Center for Research in Black Culture, New York Public Library.

46. James, *Black Jacobins*, 392.

47. David Scott, *Conscripts of Modernity: The Tragedy of Colonial Enlightenment* (Durham, NC: Duke University Press, 2004), 127–28, emphasis added. Throughout the notes, where I have not given "emphasis added," emphasis should be assumed to be in the original.

48. Glissant, "Closed Place, Open Word," 65.

49. Glissant, "Closed Place, Open Word," 65.

50. Davarian L. Baldwin, "Introduction: New Negroes Forging a New World," in *Escape from New York*, ed. Baldwin and Makalani, 2, 19.

51. Derrick R. Spires, *The Practice of Citizenship: Black Politics and Print Culture in the Early United States* (Philadelphia: University of Pennsylvania Press, 2019), 6–7; Britt Rusert, *Fugitive Science: Empiricism and Freedom in Early African American Literature* (New York: New York University Press, 2017), 22; Elizabeth McHenry, *To Make Negro Literature: Writing, Literary Practice, and African American Authorship* (Durham, NC: Duke University Press, 2021), 6.

52. C. Vann Woodward, *Origins of the New South, 1877–1913* (Baton Rouge: Louisiana State University Press, 1971); Donald Spivey, *Schooling for the New Slavery: Black Industrial Education, 1868–1915* (Westport, CT: Greenwood Press, 1978); James D. Anderson, *The Education of Blacks in the South, 1860–1935* (Chapel Hill: University of North Carolina Press, 1988).

53. For an excellent one-hundred-year overview of historical scholarship on Booker. T. Washington, see Pero Gaglo Dagbovie, "Exploring a Century of Historical Scholarship on Booker T. Washington," *Journal of African American History* 92, no. 2 (2007): 239–64.

54. Houston A. Baker Jr., *Modernism and the Harlem Renaissance* (Chicago: University of Chicago Press, 1987), 15, 37.

55. Baker, *Turning South Again*, 81.

56. Robert J. Norrell, *Up from History: The Life of Booker T. Washington* (Cambridge, MA: Belknap Press of Harvard University Press, 2009), 436, 437, 15. On how Baker reconsidered his position after reading Harlan's biography, see Desmond Jagmohan, "Booker T. Washington and the

Politics of Deception," in *African American Political Thought: A Collected History*, ed. Melvin L. Rogers and Jack Turner (Chicago: University of Chicago Press, 2021), 170 n. 15.

57. Kelley, *Freedom Dreams*, ix.

58. Gary Wilder, *Freedom Time: Negritude, Decolonization, and the Future of the World* (Durham, NC: Duke University Press, 2015), 13.

59. Monica White, *Freedom Farmers: Agricultural Resistance and the Black Freedom Movement* (Chapel Hill: University of North Carolina Press, 2018), 6.

60. Booker T. Washington to Oswald Garrison Villard, January 10, 1911, in *The Booker T. Washington Papers*, 14 vols., ed. Louis R. Harlan and Raymond W. Smock (Urbana: University of Illinois Press, 1972–1989), 10:541, hereafter *BTWP*.

61. On "the white architects of black education," see William H. Watkins, *The White Architects of Black Education: Ideology and Power in America, 1865–1954* (New York: Teachers College Press, 2001).

62. For an excellent history of how a later generation of Tuskegee students challenged Washington and his successors' political and educational philosophies during the Civil Rights Movement, see Brian Jones, *The Tuskegee Student Uprising: A History* (New York: New York University Press, 2022).

63. Philip J. Kowalski, "No Excuses for Our Dirt: Booker T. Washington and a 'New Negro' Middle Class," in *Post-bellum, Pre-Harlem: African American Literature and Culture, 1877–1919*, ed. Barbara McCaskill and Caroline Gebhard (New York: New York University Press, 2006), 182.

64. Katherine McKittrick, *Demonic Grounds: Black Women and the Cartographies of Struggle* (Minneapolis: University of Minnesota Press, 2006), xiv, xix.

65. Steven Hahn, *A Nation Under Our Feet: Black Political Struggles in the Rural South from Slavery to the Great Migration* (Cambridge, MA: Belknap Press of Harvard University Press, 2003), 475.

66. James, *Black Jacobins*, 242.

67. James, *Black Jacobins*, 248.

68. Laurent Dubois, *Haiti: The Aftershocks of History* (New York: Holt, 2012), 33.

69. Jean Casimir, *The Caribbean: One and Divisible* (Santiago, Chile: United Nations, 1992), 112–13.

70. James, *Black Jacobins*, 393.

71. James, *Black Jacobins*, 288. See also Scott, *Conscripts of Modernity*, 168.

72. Scott, *Conscripts of Modernity*, 129, 168.

73. Booker T. Washington, "A Sunday Evening Talk," in *BTWP*, 9:381.

74. Wynter, "Black Metamorphosis," 16 (quoting Jean Price-Mars), 52.

75. Wynter, "Black Metamorphosis," 54, 63.

76. Casimir, *The Caribbean*, 117.

77. Wynter, "Novel and History," 95.

78. J. T. Roane, "Plotting the Black Commons," *Souls: A Critical Journal of Black Politics, Culture, and Society* 20, no. 3 (2018): 239–66; Janae Davis, Alex A. Moulton, Levi Van Sant, and Brian Williams, "Anthropocene, Capitalocene, . . . Plantationocene? A Manifesto for Ecological Justice in an Age of Global Crises," *Geography Compass* 13, no. 5 (2019): art. e12438, https://doi.org/10.1111/gec3.12438; Kaneesha Cherelle Parsard, "Siphon, or What Was the Plot? Revisiting Sylvia Wynter's 'Novel and History, Plot and Plantation,'" *Representations* 162 (2023): 56–64.

79. Farah Jasmine Griffin, *Read Until You Understand: The Profound Wisdom of Black Life and Literature* (New York: Norton, 2021), 223 n. 10.

80. For another analysis of agricultural and ecological agency in Washington's writings, see John Claborn, "Up from Nature: Racial Uplift and Ecological Agencies in Booker T. Washington's Autobiographies," in *Civil Rights and the Environment in African-American Literature, 1895–1941* (London: Bloomsbury Academic, 2017), 19–44.

81. Washington to George Washington Carver, April 1896, quoted in White, *Freedom Farmers*, 40.

82. Washington quoted in White, *Freedom Farmers*, 40–41. For a different take on the concept of "eco-ontology," particularly in relation to Martin Heidegger's *Being in Time* (1927) and the broader field of ecocriticism, see John Claborn, "Toward an Eco-ontology: A Response to Greg Garrard's 'Heidegger Nazism Ecocriticism,'" *ISLE: Interdisciplinary Studies in Literature and Environment* 19, no. 2 (Spring 2012): 375–79.

83. Washington, *Up from Slavery*, 113.

84. Booker T. Washington, *Working with the Hands: Being a Sequel to "Up from Slavery" Covering the Author's Experiences in Industrial Training at Tuskegee*, special subscription ed. (New York: Doubleday, Page, c. July 1904), 164.

85. For a comprehensive overview of Tuskegee's extension programs, see Virginia Lantz Denton, "Social Change Through Extension: Taking Adult Education to the Masses," in *Booker T. Washington and the Adult Education Movement* (Gainesville: University Press of Florida, 1993), 106–53.

86. "A Circular of the Tuskegee Negro Conference," in *BTWP*, 5:23–24. For "beautifying their home," see *Tuskegee Student*, February 14, 1903; issues of the *Tuskegee Student* are archived in the Tuskegee University Archives, Tuskegee, AL, and the Schomburg Center for Research in Black Culture, New York Public Library.

87. Washington, *Up from Slavery*, 127; Washington, *Working with the Hands* (subscription ed.), 29.

88. Stephens, *Black Empire*, 99.

89. Zora Neale Hurston, *Their Eyes Were Watching God* (1937), in *Zora Neale Hurston: Novels and Stories*, comp. Cheryl A. Wall (New York: Library of America, 1995), 187.

90. "Wife of a Negro farmer" quoted in Emmett J. Scott and Lyman Beecher Stowe, *Booker T. Washington: Builder of a Civilization* (Garden City, NY: Doubleday, Page, 1916), 169.

91. Rhussus L. Perry, "Janey Gets Her Desires," in *Up Before Daylight: Life Histories from the Alabama Writers' Project, 1938–1939*, ed. James Seay Brown Jr. (Tuscaloosa: University of Alabama Press, 1982), 175.

92. Mrs. R. R. Moton, "Mrs. Booker T. Washington," *Tuskegee Messenger*, August 1925; issues of the *Tuskegee Messenger* are archived in the Tuskegee University Archives, Tuskegee, AL, and the Schomburg Center for Research in Black Culture, New York Public Library.

93. British Guiana changed its name to Guyana in 1966, but I continue to use "British Guiana" for historical accuracy within the period discussed in this book and to distinguish it from French Guiana.

94. Frank Andre Guridy, *Forging Diaspora: Afro-Cubans and African Americans in a World of Empire and Jim Crow* (Chapel Hill: University of North Carolina Press, 2010), 22–23.

95. Glissant, "Poetics," in *Poetics of Relation*, 23; Gilroy, *The Black Atlantic*; Sonya Posmentier, *Cultivation and Catastrophe: The Lyric Ecology of Modern Black Literature* (Baltimore, MD: Johns Hopkins University Press, 2017).

96. Gilroy, *The Black Atlantic*, 16.

97. Elizabeth DeLoughrey, Renée K. Gosson, and George B. Handley, introduction to *Caribbean Literature and the Environment: Between Nature and Culture*, ed. Elizabeth DeLoughrey, Renée K. Gosson, and George B. Handley (Charlottesville: University of Virginia Press, 2005), 18.

98. See Edwards, *The Practice of Diaspora*.

99. Watkins, *White Architects*, 1.

100. Michael O. West, "The Tuskegee Model of Development in Africa: Another Dimension of the African/African-American Connection," *Diplomatic History* 16, no. 3 (1992): 371–87; Angela Zimmerman, *Alabama in Africa: Booker T. Washington, the German Empire, and the Globalization of the New South* (Princeton, NJ: Princeton University Press, 2010); Sven Beckert, "From Tuskegee to Togo: The Problem of Freedom in the Empire of Cotton," *Journal of American History* 92, no. 2 (September 2005): 498–526; Andrew E. Barnes, *Global Christianity and the Black Atlantic: Tuskegee, Colonialism, and the Shaping of African Industrial Education* (Waco, TX: Baylor University Press, 2017).

I. AN EXPERIMENT IN BLACK WORLD MAKING   383

101. Brandon Byrd, *The Black Republic: African Americans and the Fate of Haiti* (Philadelphia: University of Pennsylvania Press, 2019), 9.

102. Kevin K. Gaines, *Uplifting the Race: Black Leadership, Politics, and Culture in the Twentieth Century* (Chapel Hill: University of North Carolina Press, 1996), 21.

103. Jeremy Wells, "Up from Savagery: Booker T. Washington and the Civilizing Mission," *Southern Quarterly* 42, no. 1 (Fall 2003): 53–74; David Sehat, "The Civilizing Mission of Booker T. Washington," *Journal of Southern History* 73, no. 2 (2007): 323–62; Brian Kelly, "Sentinels for New South Industry: Booker T. Washington, Industrial Accommodation, and Black Workers in the Jim Crow South," *Labor History* 44, no. 3 (2003): 337–57.

104. Washington, "Signs of Progress."

105. Julius B. Fleming Jr., *Black Patience: Performance, Civil Rights, and the Unfinished Project of Emancipation* (New York: New York University Press, 2022), 12.

106. Washington to Charles Chesnutt, in *BTWP*, 7:196–98; Booker T. Washington, *The Story of the Negro: The Rise of the Race from Slavery*, 2 vols. (1909; reprint, Gloucester, MA: Peter Smith, 1969); Washington and Robert E. Park, *The Man Farthest Down* (Garden City, NY: Doubleday, Page, 1913).

107. Washington, *Story of the Negro*, 1:33, 25.

108. Booker T. Washington, "How the Negro Will Be Judged," *Tuskegee Student*, October 15, 1904; Washington, *Story of the Negro*, 1:17; *Tuskegee Annual Catalogue*, 1909–1910, 33, Tuskegee University Archives.

109. Gaines, *Uplifting the Race*, 39.

110. Washington, *Working with the Hands* (subscription ed.), 226–27.

111. Beckert, "From Tuskegee to Togo," 507.

112. West, "The Tuskegee Model of Development in Africa," 386.

113. Washington, *Story of the Negro*, 1:34.

114. Booker T. Washington, "The Future of Congo Reform," in *The Congo News Letter*, ed. Congo Reform Association (Boston: n.p., 1906), 9–10.

115. Booker T. Washington, "Fair Play for Negro Aliens," in *BTWP*, 13:209–10.

116. Booker T. Washington, "Dr. Booker T. Washington on the American Occupation of Haiti," *New York Age*, October 21, 1915.

117. Marable, "Black Skin, Bourgeois Masks," 325, 333; W. Manning Marable, "Booker T. Washington and African Nationalism," *Phylon* 35, no. 4 (1974): 398, 404.

118. See Guridy, *Forging Diaspora*.

1. AN EXPERIMENT IN BLACK WORLD MAKING: CULTIVATING INTELLECTUALS OF THE LAND IN THE ALABAMA COUNTRYSIDE

1. Mark Hersey, *My Work Is That of Conservation: An Environmental Biography of George Washington Carver* (Athens: University of Georgia Press, 2011), 55.

2. Hersey, *My Work*, 55.

3. Hersey, *My Work*, 59.

4. Booker T. Washington, "The Rural Negro Community," *Annals of the American Academy of Political and Social Science* 40 (March 1912): 84.

5. Allen Tullos, "The Black Belt," *Southern Cultures*, April 19, 2004, https://southernspaces.org/2004/black-belt/.

6. Washington, *Up from Slavery*, 108.

I. AN EXPERIMENT IN BLACK WORLD MAKING

7. Kenrick Ian Grandison, "Negotiated Space: The Black College Campus as a Cultural Record of Postbellum America," *American Quarterly* 51, no. 3 (September 1999): 540–50.
8. Washington to James F. B. Marshall, July 16, 1881, in *BTWP*, 2:142.
9. Grandison, "Negotiated Space," 544.
10. Booker T. Washington, *The Story of My Life and Work* (Cincinnati: W. H. Ferguson, 1900), 93.
11. Leah Penniman, "After a Century in Decline, Black Farmers Are Back and on the Rise," *yes!*, May 5, 2016, posted at the Positive Futures Network, April 19, 2024, https://www.yesmagazine .org/democracy/2016/05/05/after-a-century-in-decline-black-farmers-are-back-and-on-the-rise; Claude McKay, *My Green Hills of Jamaica: And Five Jamaican Short Stories*, ed. Mervyn Morris (Kingston, Jamaica: Heineman Educational Book (Caribbean), 1979), 29.
12. Washington quoted in White, *Freedom Farmers*, 40–41.
13. Carver quoted in B. D. Mayberry, *The Role of Tuskegee University in the Origin, Growth, and Development of the Negro Cooperative Extension System, 1881–1990* (Tuskegee: Tuskegee University, 1989), 110.
14. Carver quoted in Gary Kremer, *George Washington Carver in His Own Words* (Columbia: University of Missouri Press, 2017), 116–17, 119.
15. Booker T. Washington, *The Future of the American Negro* (Boston: Small, Maynard, 1899), 46–47.
16. William L. Andrews, "The Representation of Slavery and the Rise of Afro-American Literary Realism, 1865–1920," in *Slavery and the Literary Imagination*, ed. Deborah McDowell and Arnold Rampersad (Baltimore, MD: Johns Hopkins University Press, 1989), 66.
17. Washington, *Future of the American Negro*, 52.
18. James, *The Black Jacobins*, 392.
19. Scott, *Conscripts of Modernity*, 128.
20. Washington, "Signs of Progress Among the Negroes."
21. Booker T. Washington, "Tuskegee Institute," *African Times and Orient Review*, August 1912, 52.
22. Washington, "The Rural Negro Community," 84. See also Hersey, *My Work*, 150.
23. Washington, "Tuskegee Institute," 52.
24. Washington, *Working with the Hands* (subscription ed.), 135.
25. Kenrick Ian Grandison, "From Plantation to Campus: Progress, Community, and the Lay of the Land in Shaping the Early Tuskegee," *Landscape Journal* 15, no. 1 (1996): 15, 19.
26. Gaines, *Uplifting the Race*, 21.
27. Washington, "Tuskegee Institute," 52; Louis R. Harlan, introduction to Washington, *Up from Slavery*, xxxvii.
28. Jones, *The Tuskegee Student Uprising*, 11, 14–15; Norrell, foreword to *Reaping the Whirlwind*, ix–xi.
29. Sherman's Field Order No. 15 was conceived by a group of twenty Black leaders in Savannah, Georgia. Henry Louis Gates Jr., "The Truth Behind Forty Acres and a Mule," n.d., https://www .pbs.org/wnet/african-americans-many-rivers-to-cross/history/the-truth-behind-40-acres-and-a -mule/, accessed August 28, 2023.
30. Eleanor Marie Brown, "On the Evolution of Property Ownership Among Former Slaves, Newly Freedmen," George Washington University Legal Studies Research Paper No. 2016-22, June 23, 2016.
31. Fortune quoted in McHenry, *To Make Negro Literature*, 135.
32. McHenry, *To Make Negro Literature*, 151.
33. McHenry, *To Make Negro Literature*, 137, 138, 148. Other Washington publications ghostwritten by Fortune include *The Future of the American Negro*, *The Story of My Life and Work*, and *Sowing and Reaping* (Boston: L. C. Page, 1900).
34. Norrell, *Up from History*, 305.
35. T. Thomas Fortune, *Black and White: Land, Labor, and Politics in the South* (1884; reprint, New York: Atria, 2022), 149–50.

1. AN EXPERIMENT IN BLACK WORLD MAKING

36. Fortune, *Black and White*, 136; T. Thomas Fortune, "Who Will Own the Soil of the South in the Future?" (1883), in *T. Thomas Fortune, the Afro-American Agitator: A Collection of Writings, 1880–1928* (Gainesville: University Press of Florida, 2010), 5.

37. Fortune, *Black and White*, author's preface, 136, 151.

38. Fortune, "Who Will Own the Soil?," 5.

39. Anna Julia Cooper, *A Voice from the South, by a Black Woman of the South* (1892), in *The Portable Anna Julia Cooper*, ed. Shirley Moody-Turner (New York: Penguin, 2022), 133, 148.

40. Fortune, *Black and White*, 47.

41. Brittney C. Cooper, *Beyond Respectability: The Intellectual Thought of Race Women* (Urbana: University of Illinois Press, 2017), 25–26.

42. Veronica G. Thomas and Janine A. Jackson, "The Education of African American Girls and Women: Past to Present," *Journal of Negro Education* 76, no. 3 (Summer 2007): 360–61.

43. For Du Bois's praise of the Atlanta Exposition Address, see W. E. B. Du Bois to Washington, September 24, 1895, in *BTWP*, 4:26; for his criticism of Washington, see W. E. B. Du Bois, "Of Mr. Booker T. Washington and Others," in *The Souls of Black Folk* (1903) (New York: Barnes & Noble Classics, 2003), 41.

44. Washington to the editor of the *Indianapolis Star*, April 15, 1912, in *BTWP*, 11:517.

45. Ida B. Wells, "Booker T. Washington and His Critics" (1904), in *The Light of Truth: Writings of an Anti-lynching Crusader*, ed. Mia Bay (New York: Penguin Classics, 2014), 418, 420.

46. Chalmers Archer Jr., *Growing Up Black in Rural Mississippi: Memories of a Family, Heritage of a Place* (New York: Walker, 1992), 26–27.

47. Charles S. Johnson, *Shadow of the Plantation* (Chicago: University of Chicago Press, 1934), 144.

48. Simpson quoted in Thomas Monroe Campbell, *The Movable School Goes to the Negro Farmer* (Tuskegee, AL: Tuskegee Institute Press, 1936), 139.

49. Johnson, *Shadow of the Plantation*, 144, 148 (quoting resident).

50. Cobb quoted in Theodore Rosengarten, *All God's Dangers: The Life of Nate Shaw* (New York: Vintage Books, 1974), 542–43.

51. Hahn, *A Nation Under Our Feet*, 441.

52. Hahn, *A Nation Under Our Feet*, 417, 419, 421.

53. Omar H. Ali, *In the Lion's Mouth: Black Populism in the New South, 1886–1900* (Jackson: University of Mississippi Press, 2010), 165.

54. Hahn, *A Nation Under Our Feet*, 423; Charles Postel, *The Populist Vision* (Oxford: Oxford University Press, 2007), 41.

55. Ali, *In the Lion's Mouth*, 54, 157; Postel, *The Populist Vision*, 61–62; Hahn, *A Nation Under Our Feet*, 417; R. M. Humphrey, "History of the Colored Farmers' National Alliance and Cooperative Union," in *The Farmers' Alliance History and Agricultural Digest*, ed. N. A. Dunning (Washington, DC: Alliance Publishing, 1891), 288–92.

56. Ali, *In the Lion's Mouth*, 54.

57. Humphrey quoted in Hahn, *A Nation Under Our Feet*, 433.

58. Postel, *The Populist Vision*, 48, 26, 49, 66–67.

59. "The Principal's Sunday Evening Talk in the Chapel, February 8, 1903," *Tuskegee Student*, February 14, 1903.

60. Hersey, *My Work*, 114.

61. Allen Jones, "Improving Rural Life for Blacks: The Tuskegee Negro Farmers' Conference, 1892–1915," *Agricultural History* 65, no. 2 (Spring 1991): 109; Booker T. Washington, "How I Came to Call the First Negro Conference," in *BTWP*, 5:99.

62. "The Tuskegee Negro Conference," in *BTWP*, 5:23–24; *Tuskegee Student*, February 14, 1903.

63. Scott and Stowe, *Booker T. Washington*, 167–68.

64. Washington, *Working with the Hands* (subscription ed.), 139.

65. Scott and Stowe, *Booker T. Washington*, 168.

66. Hersey, *My Work*, 113.

67. *Tuskegee Student*, December 10, 1904.

68. Hersey, *My Work*, 149.

69. Mayberry, *Role of Tuskegee University*, 97, 102.

70. Scott and Stowe, *Booker T. Washington*, 74–76.

71. Mayberry, *Role of Tuskegee University*, 69.

72. Mayberry, *Role of Tuskegee University*, 71.

73. T. M. Campbell quoted in Mayberry, *Role of Tuskegee University*, 73.

74. Washington quoted in Mayberry, *Role of Tuskegee University*, 103.

75. Hersey, *My Work*, 114.

76. Mayberry, *Role of Tuskegee University*, 74, 75 (quoting Allen Jones); *Negro Farmer*, February 14, 1914.

77. Alice M. Dunbar-Nelson, "To the Negro Farmers of the United States," *Negro Farmer*, April 11, 1914.

78. Archer, *Growing Up Black*, 26–27.

79. Mayberry, *Role of Tuskegee University*, 72; Jones, "Improving Rural Life for Blacks," 113.

80. *Tuskegee Student*, November 6 and 10, 1909; "The Tenth Annual Chrysanthemum Show," *Southern Letter*, November 1917 (issues of the *Southern Letter* are archived in the Tuskegee University Archives).

81. Mayberry, *Role of Tuskegee University*, 99.

82. Thomas Campbell quoted in Mayberry, *Role of Tuskegee University*, 105.

83. Hersey, *My Work*, 148.

84. "To the Editor of the Montgomery *Journal*," in *BTWP*, 13:219.

85. Scott and Stowe, *Booker T. Washington*, 80–81.

86. Carver quoted in Hersey, *My Work*, 105.

87. G. W. Carver, *Fertilizer Experiments on Cotton*, Agricultural Experiment Station Bulletin No. 3 (Tuskegee, AL: Tuskegee Institute, 1899), 3; all of the bulletins are given at https://www.nal.usda .gov/exhibits/ipd/carver/exhibits/show/bulletins/carver.

88. Washington to Thomas Jesse Jones, December 2, 1910, in *BTWP*, 10:497–98.

89. George Washington Carver to James Wilson, July 23, 1904, roll 2, George Washington Carver Papers, Tuskegee University Archives.

90. Washington, *Working with the Hands* (subscription ed.), 163.

91. Carver quoted in Hersey, *My Work*, 194.

92. Judith A. Carney, *Black Rice: The African Origins of Rice Cultivation in the Americas* (Cambridge, MA: Harvard University Press, 2001), 156.

93. Rusert, *Fugitive Science*, 18, 220; Britt Rusert, "Plantation Ecologies: The Experimental Plantation in and Against James Grainger's *The Sugar-Cane*," *Early American Studies* 13, no. 2 (Spring 2015): 343–44 ("experimental plantation"), 367 n. 52, citing Britt Rusert, "'A Study in Nature': The Tuskegee Experiments and the New South Laboratory," *Journal of Medical Humanities* 30, no. 3 (September 2009): 155–71.

94. Scott and Stowe, *Booker T. Washington*, 72–74.

95. "The Annual Chrysanthemum Show," *Southern Letter*, November 1919.

96. G. W. Carver, *How to Build Up Worn Out Soils*, Agricultural Experiment Station Bulletin No. 6 (Tuskegee, AL: Tuskegee Institute Steam Print, 1905), 5.

97. G. W. Carver, *How to Build Up and Maintain the Virgin Fertility of Our Soils*, Agricultural Experiment Station Bulletin No. 42 (Tuskegee, AL: Tuskegee Institute, October 1936), 3–4.

98. Hersey, *My Work*, 103; G. W. Carver, *The Need of Scientific Agriculture in the South*, Farmer's Leaflet No. 7 (Tuskegee, AL: Extension Department, Tuskegee Institute, April 1902).

I. AN EXPERIMENT IN BLACK WORLD MAKING

99. Carver, *How to Build Up Worn Out Soils*, 4, 5, 7.

100. G. W. Carver, *Cotton Growing on Sandy Upland Soils*, Agricultural Experiment Station Bulletin No. 7 (Tuskegee, AL: Tuskegee Institute, 1905), 3.

101. Hersey, *My Work*, 134–42.

102. G. W. Carver, *What Shall We Do for Fertilizers Next Year?* (Tuskegee, AL: Agricultural Experiment Station, Tuskegee Institute, 1916), 1, 2.

103. G. W. Carver, *Cow Peas*, Agricultural Experiment Station Bulletin No. 5 (Tuskegee, AL: Tuskegee Institute, 1903), 5 n. B.

104. Carver quoted in Hersey, *My Work*, 131, 132.

105. G. W. Carver, *A New and Prolific Variety of Cotton*, Agricultural Experiment Station Bulletin No. 26 (Tuskegee, AL: Tuskegee Institute, printed by the Tuskegee Students from funds supplied by the Ash Fund established in memory of Mrs. Ellen L. Ash, 1915), 3.

106. Carver, *A New and Prolific Variety of Cotton*.

107. Washington quoted in Mayberry, *Role of Tuskegee University*, 102.

108. Farmer's wife and Washington quoted in Scott and Stowe, *Booker T. Washington*, 169.

109. Washington to David Franklin Houston, August 4, 1914, included in Mayberry, *Role of Tuskegee University*, 80–81, and in *BTWP*, 13:109.

110. Washington quoted in Mayberry, *Role of Tuskegee University*, 84.

111. Thomas Campbell quoted in Mayberry, *Role of Tuskegee University*, 103.

112. Jones, "Improving Rural Life for Blacks," 111; Washington, "How I Came to Call the First Negro Conference," in *BTWP*, 5:95–101.

113. Campbell quoted in Mayberry, *Role of Tuskegee University*, 105; Karen J. Ferguson, "Caught in 'No Man's Land': The Negro Cooperative Demonstration Service and the Ideology of Booker T. Washington, 1900–1918," *Agricultural History* 72, no. 1 (Winter 1998): 35.

114. Ferguson, "Caught in 'No Man's Land,'" 35.

115. Washington, *Up from Slavery*, 213.

116. Hersey, *My Work*, 84.

117. Kenrick Ian Grandison, "Landscapes of Terror: A Reading of Tuskegee's Historic Campus," in *The Geography of Identity*, ed. Patricia Yaeger (Ann Arbor: University of Michigan Press, 1996), 356, 360–62.

118. Washington, *Working with the Hands* (subscription ed.), 228.

119. Marable, "Booker T. Washington and African Nationalism," 399, 398.

120. Beckert, "From Tuskegee to Togo."

121. Washington, *Story of the Negro*, 1:34

122. Washington quoted in Beckert, "From Tuskegee to Togo," 507.

123. W. E. B. Du Bois made a similar miscalculation when he helped to facilitate the Firestone Rubber Company's encroachment into Liberia. See Greg Mitman, *Empire of Rubber: Firestone's Scramble for Land and Power in Liberia* (New York: New Press, 2021), 26–61.

124. Beckert, "From Tuskegee to Togo," 517.

125. Louis R. Harlan, *Booker T. Washington: Making of a Black Leader, 1856–1901* (New York: Oxford University Press, 1972), 198.

126. Ferguson, "Caught in 'No Man's Land,'" 47, 48.

127. Washington, "The Rural Negro Community," 85; Hersey, *My Work*, 151.

128. Washington, "The Rural Negro Community," 87.

129. Mayberry, *Role of Tuskegee University*, 83.

130. G. W. Carver, *Three Delicous [sic] Meals Every Day for the Farmer*, Agricultural Experiment Station Bulletin No. 32 (Tuskegee, AL: Tuskegee Institute, 1916), 4.

131. Washington quoted in Mayberry, *Role of Tuskegee University*, 102.

2. PERFORMING THE TUSKEGEE NEW NEGRO: THE RACIAL AND GENDERED AESTHETICS OF THE REPURPOSED PLANTATION

1. Booker T. Washington, "The Atlanta Exposition Address," in *Up from Slavery*, 220.

2. Louis R. Harlan, *Booker T. Washington: The Wizard of Tuskegee, 1900–1915* (New York: Oxford University Press, 1983), 262.

3. Ellen Weiss, *Robert R. Taylor and Tuskegee: An African American Architect Designs for Booker T. Washington* (Montgomery, AL: New South Books, 2012), 86–87.

4. Zimmerman, *Alabama in Africa*, 54.

5. "What the Carnegie Library Does for Tuskegee Students/What Negro Students Read," typescript, [1905?], reel 64, Booker T. Washington Papers, Library of Congress; Booker T. Washington, "What the Carnegie Library Does for Tuskegee Students," *Appleton's Booklovers Magazine* 6, no. 2 (August 1905): 253–54.

6. Carney, *Black Rice*, 156; Wynter, "Novel and History," 99.

7. *Online Etymology Dictionary*, s.v. "repurpose," https://www.etymonline.com/word/repurpose #etymonline_v_40536.

8. Henry Louis Gates Jr., "The Trope of the New Negro and the Reconstruction of the Image of the Black," *Representations* 24 (1988): 129–55.

9. The phrase "criteria of black art" references W. E. B. Du Bois's essay "Criteria of Negro Art" (1926), where he outlined his proscriptions for the utility of Black art during the Harlem Renaissance, (in)famously declaring, "I do not care a damn for any art that is not used for propaganda." Du Bois, "Criteria for Negro Art," *Crisis* 32, no. 6 (October 1926): 290–297, para. 29.

10. Kowalski, "No Excuses for Our Dirt," 181.

11. Washington, *Up from Slavery*, 67, 154.

12. Andrews, "The Representation of Slavery," 72–73.

13. "A real man or a real thing" from Washington, *Up from Slavery*, 263.

14. Washington to Walter Hines Page, April 20, 1899, MS Am 1090, box 23: 1098, Walter Hines Page Papers, Houghton Library, Harvard University, Cambridge, MA.

15. In *Uplift Cinema*, Allyson Nadia Field identifies "raw material" as one of three main themes that characterize Washington's rhetorical strategy for garnering support for Tuskegee. Across "word, image, and live performance" alike, Field maintains, "students are shaped and molded to become effective agents of uplift just as the materials with which they work are transformed by their labor." Field, *Uplift Cinema: The Emergence of African American Film and the Possibility of Black Modernity* (Durham, NC: Duke University Press, 2015), 38.

16. Baker, *Modernism and the Harlem Renaissance*, 37.

17. Daphne A. Brooks, *Bodies in Dissent: Spectacular Performances of Race and Freedom, 1850–1910* (Durham, NC: Duke University Press, 2006), 214–15; Koritha Mitchell, *Living with Lynching: African American Lynching Plays, Performance, and Citizenship, 1890–1930* (Urbana: University of Illinois Press, 2012), 44.

18. Harlan, *Wizard of Tuskegee*, 262.

19. Baker, *Modernism and the Harlem Renaissance*, 15.

20. Baker, *Modernism and the Harlem Renaissance*, 17, 24. In addition to Baker's claim regarding the primacy of minstrelsy for Black discursive modernism, the historical musicologist Matthew D. Morrison brilliantly argues that American popular music and the rise of the recording industry are likewise rooted in blackface minstrelsy. See Morrison, *Blacksound: Making Race and Popular Music in the United States* (Oakland: University of California Press, 2024).

21. Washington, *Up from Slavery*, 130.

2. PERFORMING THE TUSKEGEE NEW NEGRO

22. Baker, *Modernism and the Harlem Renaissance*, 22.

23. Wells, "Booker T. Washington and His Critics," 416.

24. Gaines, *Uplifting the Race*, 74.

25. Interestingly, James Smethurst argues that although such racial caricaturing is commonplace in *Up from Slavery*, Washington's most successful autobiography, it is absent in *The Story of My Life and Work*, his first autobiography, which was written for and primarily marketed to African Americans and was the bestseller in its day. Smethurst, *The Afro-American Roots of Modernism* (Chapel Hill: University of North Carolina Press, 2011), 45–46.

26. Washington, *Story of the Negro*, 2:290.

27. Washington, *Up from Slavery*, 67, 244.

28. James Creelman, *New York World*, quoted in Washington, *Up from Slavery*, 239–40.

29. W. D. Howells, "An Exemplary Citizen," *North American Review*, August 1901, 288, 280–81.

30. Washington, *Story of the Negro*, 1:v–vi. The *Story of the Negro* was largely ghostwritten by A. O. Stafford and Robert E. Park. However, following the debacle of his first autobiography, *The Story of My Life and Work*, Washington vowed to read and approve everything published under his name. Thus, it is likely that he at least read *The Story of the Negro* before publication. Harlan, *Wizard of Tuskegee*, 291.

31. Booker T. Washington, "Why I Wrote My Latest Book: My Aim in 'The Story of the Negro,'" *World's Work* 20 (May–October 1910): 13568–69.

32. Fortune quoted in McHenry, *To Make Negro Literature*, 158.

33. Washington, "Why I Wrote My Latest Book," 13569.

34. Washington, *Working with the Hands* (subscription ed.), 86–87.

35. Harlan, *Wizard of Tuskegee*, 149.

36. Errol Hill and James Vernon Hatch, *A History of African American Theatre* (Cambridge: Cambridge University Press, 2003); *BTWP*, 5:269 n. 1.

37 "An Item in the Tuskegee Student," in *BTWP*, 5:500.

38. Garfield McCaster to Washington, January 30, 1914, in *BTWP*, 12:427–32.

39. Booker T. Washington, "Samuel Coleridge-Taylor," preface to *Twenty-Four Negro Melodies Transcribed for Piano by S. Coleridge Taylor* (Boston: Oliver Ditson, 1905), viii, ix; Washington, *Story of the Negro*, 1:165, 167.

40. Booker T. Washington, "Plantation Melodies, Their Value," *Musical Courier* 71 (December 13, 1915): 47; Washington, "Samuel Coleridge-Taylor."

41. Washington, "Samuel Coleridge-Taylor," viii, ix.

42. Tim Brooks, *Lost Sounds: Blacks and the Birth of the Recording Industry, 1890–1919* (Urbana: University of Illinois Press, 2004), 476; Washington to Harry T. Burleigh, October 17, 1904, and Harry T. Burleigh to Washington, October 22, 1904, Booker T. Washington Papers, Manuscript Division, Library of Congress, Washington, DC.

43. Washington, "Samuel Coleridge-Taylor," viii.

44. Washington to W. C. Buckner, April 19, 1909, in *BTWP*, 10:90.

45. Washington to Charles G. Harris, April 22, 1899, in *BTWP*, 5:89–90.

46. Helen W. Ludlow, *Tuskegee Normal and Industrial School, for Training Colored Teachers: Its Story and Its Song* (Hampton, VA: Normal School Steam Press, 1884), 18.

47. Washington to Robert Hannibal Hamilton, September 23, 1894, in *BTWP*, 3:472.

48. Eloise Bibb Thompson, "Quintet Sings to Aid Tuskegee; Wins Much Praise," *Chicago Defender*, January 16, 1915.

49. R. H. Hamilton, arr., *Cabin and Plantation Songs as Sung by the Tuskegee Singers*, in Ludlow, *Tuskegee Normal and Industrial School*, 1–21 (separate pagination); N. Clark Smith, *Favorite Folk Melodies as Sung by Tuskegee Students* (Wichita: n.p., 1913).

50. Washington to Robert H. Hamilton, September 23, 1894, in *BTWP*, 3:471–72.

51. Washington to Charles G. Harris, May 22, 1897, and April 22, 1899, in *BTWP*, 4:281–82, 5:89–90.

52. Frederick Douglass, *My Bondage and My Freedom* (New York: Miller, Orton & Mulligan, 1855), 462.

53. On the history of this song, see Alex Lubet and Steven Lubet, "The Complicated Legacy of 'My Old Kentucky Home,'" *Smithsonian Magazine*, September 30, 2020, https://www.smithsonianmag .com/arts-culture/complicated-legacy-my-old-kentucky-home-180975719/.

54. Kelly Miller to Washington, December 27, 1909, in *BTWP*, 10:255–56.

55. Washington to William Henry Baldwin Jr., May 19, 1904, in *BTWP*, 7:506.

56. Washington to N. Clark Smith, May 26, 1913, in *BTWP*, 12:183–84.

57. N. Clark Smith to Washington, June 13, 1913, *BTWP* 12:198–99.

58. Will Marion Cook to Washington, March 29, 1901, in *BTWP*, 6:67–68.

59. Isaac Fisher to Washington, August 25 and October 23, 1899, in *BTWP* 5:183–84, 242.

60. Isaac Fisher to Washington, October 23, 1899, and August 7, 1900, in *BTWP*, 5:242–43, 5:592–93.

61. Isaac Fisher to Washington, August 25, 1899, in *BTWP*, 5:183–84.

62. Fisher to Washington, August 7, 1900, in *BTWP* 5:592–93.

63. Review quoted in Thompson, "Quintet Sings to Aid Tuskegee."

64. "Tuskegee Octette to Sing on West Side," *Chicago Defender*, July 3, 1915.

65. "Tuskegee Quintette Passes Through Chicago," *Chicago Defender*, May 15, 1915.

66. Brooks, *Lost Sounds*, 320.

67. Tuskegee Institute Singers, Recorded Sound Section, Library of Congress, recording included in the National Jukebox, courtesy of Sony Music Entertainment, https://www.loc.gov/collections /national-jukebox/?fa=contributor:tuskegee+institute+singers, accessed January 21, 2025. I am grateful to Dr. Malcolm J. Merriweather for his invaluable insights into the Singers' vocal techniques and the songs' arrangements.

68. Frank Morton Todd, *The Story of the Exposition: Being the Official History of the International Celebration Held at San Francisco in 1915 to Commemorate the Discovery of the Pacific Ocean and the Construction of the Panama Canal*, vol. 4 (New York: Knickerbocker Press, 1921), 96; "Tuskegee Octette to Sing on West Side."

69. Washington to Charles Winter Wood, March 13, 1915, in *BTWP*, 13:254–55.

70. Thompson, "Quintet Sings to Aid Tuskegee."

71. "Radio Broadcasts Bricklaying," *Baltimore Afro-American*, March 28, 1925.

72. A blurry image of *Songs and Scenes from Dixie* can be found on the front page of the *Carbondale Free Press*, April 16, 1925.

73. Wakenfield quoted in "Institute Quartette Thrills Radio Fans," *Tuskegee Student*, March 1–15, 1923.

74. Washington, *Up from Slavery*, 154.

75. Shawn Michelle Smith, *Photography on the Color Line: W. E. B. Du Bois, Race, and Visual Culture* (Durham, NC: Duke University Press, 2004).

76. Morris Lewis, "Paris and the International Exposition," *Colored American Magazine* 1, no. 5 (1900): 291–95.

77. Washington, *Working with the Hands* (subscription ed.), 16–17.

78. Gates, "The Trope of the New Negro."

79. Michael Bieze, "Ruskin in the Black Belt: Booker T. Washington, Arts and Crafts, and the New Negro," *Source: Notes in the History of Art* 24, no. 4 (Summer 2005): 24.

80. Michael Bieze, *Booker T. Washington and the Art of Self-Representation* (New York: Peter Lang, 2008), 69.

81. Washington to George Eastman, November 28, 1905, in *BTWP*, 8:451–52.

2. PERFORMING THE TUSKEGEE NEW NEGRO

82. Booker T. Washington, *"The Negro in the New World"* (review), *Journal of the African Society* 10 (1911): 174.

83. Du Bois, for instance, grappled with a similar logic, titling his photo album for the Paris Exposition *Types of American Negroes, Georgia, U.S.A.* in response to Francis Galton's pseudoscientific attempts to use photography to codify "criminal types." Smith, *Photography on the Color Line*, 61–62.

84. Field, *Uplift Cinema*.

85. "Isaac Fisher Not Resting on His Oars," *Tuskegee Student*, October 2, 1915.

86. Washington to Florence E. Sewell Bond, June 30, 1915, in *BTWP*, 13:335.

87. *BTWP*, 6:502 n. 1.

88. Shawn Michelle Smith, "Booker T. Washington's Photographic Messages," *English Language Notes* 51, no. 1 (Spring–Summer 2013): 138.

89. Laura Wexler, *Tender Violence: Domestic Visions in an Age of U.S. Imperialism* (Chapel Hill: University of North Carolina Press, 2000), 132; Shawn Michelle Smith, "Photographing the 'American Negro': Nation, Race, and Photography at the Paris Exposition in 1900," in *With Other Eyes: Looking at Race and Gender in Visual Culture*, ed. Lisa Bloom (Minneapolis: University of Minnesota Press, 1999), 65, 66.

90. Smith, "Photographing the 'American Negro,' " 66, 78, quoting bell hooks, "In Our Glory: Photography and Black Life" in *Picturing Us: African American Identity in Photography*, ed. Deborah Willis (New York: New Press, 1994), 50.

91. Wexler, *Tender Violence*, 130, 147–48.

92. Smith, "Booker T. Washington's Photographic Messages," 137–39.

93. Imani Perry, *May We Forever Stand: A History of the Black National Anthem* (Chapel Hill: University of North Carolina Press, 2018), 8.

94. Wexler, *Tender Violence*, 299.

95. Autumn Womack, *The Matter of Black Living* (Chicago: University of Chicago Press, 2022), 16.

96. Field, *Uplift Cinema*, 58, 80, quoting "antiracist propaganda" from Smith, *Photography on the Color Line*, 147.

97. Washington, *Future of the American Negro*, 52.

98. Booker T. Washington, "Twenty-Five Years of Tuskegee," *World's Work* 11, no. 6 (1906): 7436–37.

99. Woodward, *Origins of the New South*, 365.

100. Charles Pierce, "How Electricity Is Taught at Tuskegee," *Technical World* 1, no. 4 (June 1904): 425, 428, 430.

101. Wells, "Booker T. Washington and His Critics," 418.

102. Washington, *Working with the Hands* (subscription ed.), from the section titled "Introduction to the Special Subscription Edition," n.p.; "gospel of Work and Money" from Du Bois, "Of Mr. Booker T. Washington and Others," 41.

103. Emmett J. Scott, preface to *Tuskegee and Its People: Their Ideals and Achievements*, ed. Booker T. Washington [and Emmett J. Scott] (New York: D. Appleton, 1905), vii; Booker T. Washington, "General Introduction," in *Tuskegee and Its People*, ed. Washington, 8, 9. Though Washington is listed as the editor of the volume, in his general introduction he acknowledges Scott as the official editor. The press likely attributed the editing of the book to Washington because of this prominence.

104. For the first edition, see Booker T. Washington, *Working with the Hands: Being a Sequel to "Up from Slavery" Covering the Author's Experiences in Industrial Training at Tuskegee* (Toronto: William Briggs, May 1904).

105. Smith, "Booker T. Washington's Photographic Messages," 139.

106. *Tuskegee Student*, May 14, 1904.

107. Smith, "Booker T. Washington's Photographic Messages," 140.

108. Bieze, *Booker T. Washington and the Art of Self-Representation*, 31.

109. Washington to Emmett J. Scott, July 8, 1904, in *BTWP*, 8:10.

110. Bieze, *Booker T. Washington and the Art of Self-Representation*, 213.

111. Washington, *Working with the Hands* (subscription ed.), 14.

112. Washington, *Working with the Hands* (subscription ed.), 162.

113. On the "real man" of "action," see Andrews, "The Representation of Slavery," 70–76.

114. Washington, *Working with the Hands* (subscription ed.), 153.

115. Washington, *Working with the Hands* (subscription ed.), 28, 32.

116. Washington, "General Introduction," in *Tuskegee and Its People*, ed. Washington, 9.

117. Bieze, *Booker T. Washington and the Art of Self-Representation*, 46.

118. Washington, *Working with the Hands* (subscription ed.), 118, 166.

119. Washington, *Working with the Hands* (subscription ed.), 164.

120. Henry McNeal Turner to Washington, March 3, 1899, in *BTWP*, 5:50.

121. "Of any size, even down to a garden patch" from Washington, *Working with the Hands* (subscription ed.), 167–68.

122. Hersey, *My Work*, 104.

123. On Booker T. Washington and manhood, see Marlon B. Ross, *Manning the Race: Reforming Black Men in the Jim Crow Era* (New York: New York University Press, 2004), passim; Ross, *Sissy Insurgencies: A Racial Anatomy of Unfit Manliness* (Durham, NC: Duke University Press, 2021).

124. On Margaret Murray Washington and the Black women's club movement, see Jacqueline Anne Rouse, "Out of the Shadow of Tuskegee: Margaret Murray Washington, Social Activism, and Race Vindication," *Journal of Negro History* 81, nos. 1–4 (Winter–Autumn 1996): 31–46; Sheena Harris, *Margaret Murray Washington: The Life and Times of a Career Club Woman* (Knoxville: University of Tennessee Press, 2021); Linda Rochell Lane, *A Documentary of Mrs. Booker T. Washington* (Lewiston, NY: Edwin Mellen Press, 2001).

125. Mrs. Booker T. Washington, "The New Negro Woman," *Lend a Hand: A Record of Progress* 15, no. 4 (October 1895): 255.

126. Gaines, *Uplifting the Race*, 79–80.

127. Max Bennett Thrasher, *Tuskegee: Its Story and Its Work* (Boston: Small, Maynard, 1900), 93.

128. *Tuskegee Annual Catalogue*, 1899–1900, 1901–1902, and 1911–1912; Thrasher, *Tuskegee*, 93.

129. *Tuskegee Annual Catalogue*, 1901–1902, 19–20; Mrs. Washington, "What Girls Are Taught, and How," in *Tuskegee and Its People*, ed. Washington, 84–85.

130. *Tuskegee Annual Catalogue*, 1901–1902, 16.

131. African Americans have long regarded military service as proof of their patriotism and fitness for citizenship. Tuskegee likely used young men's military training to convey a similar message. Washington, *Story of the Negro*, 1:332.

132. Thrasher, *Tuskegee*, 85, 86.

133. Grandison, "Landscapes of Terror," 356, 360–62.

134. *Tuskegee Annual Catalogue*, 1901–1902, 20.

135. Ross, *Sissy Insurgencies*, 65, 64, 68, 71.

136. "Incidents of Indian Life at Hampton," in *BTWP*, 2:78–85; Lisa Lowe, *The Intimacies of Four Continents* (Durham, NC: Duke University Press, 2015), 63.

137. Scott and Stowe, *Booker T. Washington*, 168.

138. Ross, *Sissy Insurgencies*, 11, 103.

139. Thrasher, *Tuskegee*, 93.

140. Mary L. Dotson, "The Story of a Teacher of Cooking," in *Tuskegee and Its People*, ed. Washington, 207.

3. STRATEGIC TRANSLATIONS   393

141. Mrs. Washington, "What Girls Are Taught," 72, 81, 78, 83, 84–85; *Tuskegee Annual Catalogue,* 1901–1902, 58–59 ("capable workers" and "equal aptitude").

142. Washington, *Working with the Hands* (subscription ed.), 107–8.

143. Hortense Spillers, "Mama's Baby, Papa's Maybe: An American Grammar Book," *Diacritics* 17, no. 2 (1987): 72.

144. Mrs. Washington, "The New Negro Woman," 257.

145. Washington, *Working with the Hands* (subscription ed.), 110.

146. *Tuskegee Annual Catalogue,* 1902–1903, 88.

147. Mrs. Washington, "What Girls Are Taught," 74–75.

148. Washington, *Working with the Hands* (subscription ed.), 94.

149. Mrs. Washington, "What Girls Are Taught," 76–77, 80.

150. Griffin, *Read Until You Understand,* 185–208.

151. Mrs. Washington, "What Girls Are Taught," 74–75.

152. Mrs. Washington quoted in Washington, *Working with the Hands* (subscription ed.), 120.

153. Washington, *Working with the Hands* (subscription ed.), 125, 126, 122, 127.

154. Harris, *Margaret Murray Washington,* 112–17; Deborah Gray White, *Too Heavy a Load: Black Women in Defense of Themselves, 1894–1994* (New York: Norton, 1999), 32.

155. Washington, *Working with the Hands* (subscription ed.), 139.

156. Booker T. Washington, "Negro Homes," *Century Magazine,* May 1908.

157. Washington, *Working with the Hands* (subscription ed.), 98.

158. Tina Campt, "The Sounds of Stillness: Dwelling in the Visual Archive of Diaspora," lecture, Center for Black Diaspora, DePaul University, Chicago, April 14, 2013, http://www.wbez.org /series/chicago-amplified/sounds-stillness-dwelling-visual-archive-diaspora-107051. In *Embodying Black Experience,* Harvey Young also theorizes "stillness" as an alternative to the emphasis placed on movement and mobility as the organizing principles of diaspora. See Young, *Embodying Black Experience: Stillness, Critical Memory, and the Black Body* (Ann Arbor: University of Michigan Press, 2010), 39–44.

3. STRATEGIC TRANSLATIONS: RACE, NATION, AND THE AFFORDANCES OF BOOKER T. WASHINGTON AND TUSKEGEE IN CUBA

1. "Three News Items on the 1875 Graduation Exercises at Hampton Institute," in *BTWP,* 2:50, 57–58, 63.

2. Booker T. Washington, "Industrial Education for Cuban Negroes," *Christian Register,* August 18, 1898.

3. Washington to John Davis Long, March 15, 1898, in *BTWP,* 4:389; Washington, *Working with the Hands* (subscription ed.), 106.

4. W. A. Johnson to Washington, November 16, 1904, in *BTWP,* 8:134.

5. Edwards, *The Practice of Diaspora,* 7.

6. Booker T. Washington, "Cuban Education" (1898), in *Story of My Life and Work,* 264–65.

7. Washington, "Cuban Education," in *Story of My Life and Work,* 266.

8. Washington, "Cuban Education," in *Story of My Life and Work,* 269.

9. Washington, *Story of My Life and Work,* 275.

10. "Extracts from Address at Peace Jubilee Exercises," October 18, 1898, 2–3, box 114, folder 9, Papers of Booker T. Washington (1887–1915): The Tuskegee Collection, Tuskegee University Archives. It is unclear if this passage was part of the Chicago address "Cuban Education." According to a note

in the Tuskegee Collection of Washington's papers, it is an "extract" from the Chicago speech. However, the "extract" is not included in published versions of the speech and is almost identical to a speech Washington gave in Nashville, Tennessee, in July 1898 (see "The Mutual Dependence of the Races," July 7, 1898, in *BTWP*, 4:438–41). Either way, the passage reveals how Washington instrumentalized Cuba and the Spanish-American War to "educate" white Americans about continued injustice toward African Americans.

11. Washington to E. B. Webster, August 15, 1913, in *BTWP*, 12:256–57.

12. Washington, "Industrial Education for Cuban Negroes."

13. Hartman, *Scenes of Subjection*, 130.

14. T. Edward Owens, "The Negro Here and in Cuba," *Outlook*, September 24, 1898.

15. Aline Helg, "Black Men, Racial Stereotyping, and Violence in the U.S. South and Cuba at the Turn of the Century," *Comparative Studies in Society and History* 42, no. 3 (July 2000): 585.

16. Washington, "Signs of Progress."

17. Washington, "Signs of Progress."

18. Alejandro de la Fuente, *A Nation for All: Race, Inequality, and Politics in Twentieth-Century Cuba* (Chapel Hill: University of North Carolina Press, 2001), 111.

19. Melina Pappademos, *Black Political Activism and the Cuban Republic* (Chapel Hill: University of North Carolina Press, 2011), 254 n. 5.

20. For "style of life," see Glissant, "Closed Place, Open Word," 63.

21. Guridy, *Forging Diaspora*, 37, 38.

22. *The Freeman*, May 23, 1896.

23. John S. Durham to Washington, February 2, 1906, reel 9, and Durham to Washington, May 13, 1901, June 14, 1901, and October 7, 1909, reel 44, Booker T. Washington Papers, Manuscript Division, Library of Congress.

24. Washington, "Signs of Progress," emphasis added.

25. Wells, "Up from Savagery," 68.

26. Washington, "Signs of Progress."

27. Washington, "Signs of Progress."

28. Washington, "Signs of Progress."

29. José I. Fusté, "Translating Negroes Into Negros: Rafael Serra's Transamerican Entanglements Between Black Cuban Racial and Imperial Subalternity, 1895–1909," in *Afro-Latin@s in Movement: Critical Approaches to Blackness and Transnationalism in the Americas*, ed. Petra R. Rivera-Rideau, Jennifer A. Jones, and Tianna S. Paschel (New York: Palgrave Macmillan, 2016), 222.

30. Michael Hanchard, "Afro-Modernity: Temporality, Politics, and the African Diaspora," *Public Culture* 11, no. 1 (1999): 257–58.

31. Jossianna Arroyo, *Writing Secrecy in Caribbean Freemasonry* (New York: Palgrave Macmillan, 2013); Fusté, "Translating Negroes into Negros"; Raúl C. Galván, "Rafael Serra y Montalvo: The Man and His Work," *Caribe: Revista de cultura y literatura* 15, no. 2 (2012–2013): 67–82; Nancy Racquel Mirabal, *Suspect Freedoms: The Racial and Sexual Politics of Cubanidad in New York, 1823–1957* (New York: New York University Press, 2017).

32. Joy Elizondo, "Rafael Serra y Montalvo," Oxford African American Studies Center, December 1, 2006, https://doi-org.proxy.lib.duke.edu/10.1093/acref/9780195301731.013.43326.

33. Arthur A. Schomburg, "General Evaristo Estenoz," *Crisis* 4, no. 3 (July 1912): 143–44.

34. Martí quoted in Galván, "Rafael Serra y Montalvo," 74.

35. Galván, "Rafael Serra y Montalvo," 69. Rafael Serra, "Promesa cumplida: Booker T. Washington, interpretado por la preocupación cubana," in *Para blancos y negros: Ensayos políticos, sociales y económicos* (Havana, Cuba: El Printa "El Score" Aguila 117, 1907), 144, 143, English translations of "Promesa" by Kathryn Litherland.

36. Serra, "Promesa cumplida.

3. STRATEGIC TRANSLATIONS

395

37. Rafael Serra, "De relieve," in Serra, *Para blancos y negros*, 39, English translation of "De relieve" by Kathryn Litherland.

38. Serra, "Promesa cumplida," 143.

39. Washington quoted in Serra, "Promesa cumplida," 143.

40. Washington, "Signs of Progress."

41. "Most pretentious building" from Warren Logan, "Resources and Material Equipment," in *Tuskegee and Its People*, ed. Washington, 51.

42. Serra, "Promesa cumplida," 144.

43. Fusté, "Translating Negroes Into Negros," 225.

44. "La escuela de Tuskegee," Tuskegee promotional article, trans. Alfredo Pérez y Encinosa, in Serra, *Para blancos y negros*, 147, 149, English translations of "La escuela" by Kathryn Litherland. It seems Pérez both wrote and translated this promotional article; however, there is a discrepancy between the bylines in the original article and the reprint. The reprint in *Para blancos* includes "(Traductor)," "translator," behind Pérez's name, suggesting he only translated the article, whereas the byline in the original article published in *Nuevo Criollo* does not include "Traductor" behind his name, suggesting that he in fact wrote it.

45. Guridy, *Forging Diaspora*, 56–60.

46. "La escuela," 149.

47. Fusté, "Translating Negroes Into Negros," 225.

48. Rafael Serra, editorial commentary on Dr. R. O. C. Benjamin, "Los negros americanos," trans. Rafael Serra, in *Para blancos y negros*, 177, English translations of Serra's commentary by Kathryn Litherland.

49. Serra, editorial commentary on Benjamin, "Los negros americanos," 178, 177.

50. Mirabal, *Suspect Freedoms*, 151.

51. Patrice C. Brown, "The Panama Canal: The African American Experience," *Prologue* 29, no. 2 (Summer 1997), https://www.archives.gov/publications/prologue/1997/summer/panama-canal.

52. Rafael Serra, "La anexión," in *Para blancos y negros*, 189, English translations of "La anexión" by Kathryn Litherland.

53. César J. Ayala, *American Sugar Kingdom: The Plantation Economy of the Spanish Caribbean, 1898–1934* (Chapel Hill: University of North Carolina Press, 1999).

54. Serra, "La anexión," 188.

55. Serra, "La anexión," 191, citing "Do We Want to Annex Cuba?," *The World To-Day*, November 1906; Fusté, "Translating Negroes Into Negros," 232; Mirabal, *Suspect Freedoms*, 152.

56. Serra, "La anexión," 188, 189.

57. "Race Gleanings: Hampton Negro Conference," *Baltimore Afro-American*, August 27, 1898.

58. John S. Durham to Washington, February 2, 1906, reel 9, Booker T. Washington Papers, Manuscript Division, Library of Congress.

59. Serra, "La anexión," 189.

60. Booker T. Washington, *De esclavo a catedrático: Autobiografía de Booker T. Washington*, trans. Alfredo Elías y Pujol (New York: D. Appleton, 1902), vi, English translation by Kathryn Litherland.

61. Such as *Cuba y América* and *El Diario*.

62. *La lucha*, July 21, 1910. *Saliendo de la esclavitud* was originally published in 1905 in Barcelona, Spain. For a comparative analysis of the two Spanish translations of *Up from Slavery*, see Juan José Lanero, "Eduardo Marquina y la autobiografía de Booker T. Washington: *De esclavo a catedrático*," *Hermēneus: Revista de traducción e interpretación* 1 (1999): 1–10.

63. "Conferencia Internacional," *La lucha*, April 20, 1911.

64. Emilio Céspedes Casado to Washington, November 13 or 15, 1905, English translation by Kathryn Litherland, reel 254, Booker T. Washington Papers, Manuscript Division, Library of Congress.

3. STRATEGIC TRANSLATIONS

65. *La lucha*, February 26, 1906, my translation.

66. Pappademos, *Black Political Activism*, 144.

67. Emilio Céspedes Casado, *La cuestion social cubana*, pamphlet publication of lecture given on April 12, 1906 (Havana, Cuba: La Propagandista, Imprenta y Papelería, Monte núms 87 y 89, 1906), English translations of *La cuestion* by Kathryn Litherland.

68. Casado, *La cuestion social cubana*."

69. Alejandro de la Fuente, "Myths of Racial Democracy: Cuba, 1900–1912," *Latin American Research Review* 34, no. 3 (1999): 51.

70. de la Fuente, *A Nation for All*, 161.

71. Casado, *La cuestion social cubana*.

72. Pappademos, *Black Political Activism*, 144–47.

73. de la Fuente, *A Nation for All*, 162–63.

74. Bernardo C. Calderón to Washington, January 14, 1912, English translation by Kathryn Litherland, reel 684, Booker T. Washington Papers, Manuscript Division, Library of Congress.

75. Pappademos, *Black Political Activism*, 150.

76. La Dirección, "Nuestro programa," *Labor nueva* 1, no. 1 (February 20, 1916): 4, English translations of "Nuestro programa" by Kathryn Litherland.

77. de la Fuente, *A Nation for All*, 78.

78. La Dirección, "Nuestro programa," 4.

79. de la Fuente, *A Nation for All*, 166.

80. César Bascaro, "Booker T. Washington," *Labor nueva* 1, no. 6 (March 26, 1926): 10, English translations of "Booker T. Washington" by Kathryn Litherland; "El ilustre Labra y la Asociación Booker Washington," *Labor nueva* 1, no. 18 (June 18, 1916): 6.

81. de la Fuente, *A Nation for All*, 166 ("greatest moral and intellectual monument"); Bascaro, "Booker T. Washington," 10.

82. de la Fuente, *A Nation for All*, 165.

83. Abelardo Vasconcelos, "Clarinada," *Labor nueva* 1, no. 34 (October 22, 1916): 7, English translations by Kathryn Litherland.

84. G. Bécquer Altuna, "Semillas de discordias," *Labor nueva* 1, no. 35 (October 29, 1916): 11, English translations of "Semillas de discordias" by Kathryn Litherland.

85. George S. Schuyler, *The Reminiscences of George S. Schuyler, 1962*, ed. William T. Ingersoll (Alexandria, VA: Alexander Street Press, 2003), 120–21.

86. Altuna, "Semillas de discordias," 11.

87. Marable, "Black Skin, Bourgeois Masks," 320.

88. Booker T. Washington, "Race Friction in Cuba—and Elsewhere," *Continent*, October 3, 1912.

89. Schomburg, "General Evaristo Estenoz," 143.

90. Washington, "Race Friction in Cuba."

91. Attache [*sic*], "En el Sur," *Labor nueva* 1, no. 18 (June 18, 1916): 5–6, English translations of "En el Sur" by Kathryn Litherland.

92. Robert Moton quoted in Attache, "En el Sur," 5.

93. Attache, "En el Sur," 5–6, 5 n. 1.

94. Lino Dóu, "Velos no, murallas," *Labor nueva* 1, no. 20 (July 5, 1916): 4, English translations of "Velos" by Kathryn Litherland.

95. Dóu, "Velos no, murallas," 4.

4. JOINING HANDS ACROSS THE SEA: AGRICULTURAL EDUCATION, BLACK ECONOMIC (INTER)NATIONALISM, AND HAITIAN–AFRICAN AMERICAN RELATIONS

1. Sven Beckert, *Empire of Cotton: A Global History* (New York: Vintage, 2014), 90, 96–97.

2. Booker T. Washington, "On the Paris Boulevards," *New York Age*, June 8, 1899.

3. Jacques C. Antoine, *Jean Price-Mars and Haiti* (Washington, DC: Three Continents Press, 1981), 29, 41.

4. Washington, "On the Paris Boulevards."

5. Jean Price-Mars, Massillon Coicou, and A. Cambuy to Washington, n.d., quoted in *Tuskegee Student*, October 24, 1903. Massillon Coicou's name was misspelled as "Massion Coicon" in the *Tuskegee Student*; I have corrected the misspelling in the reference here.

6. Jean Price-Mars to Washington, August 19, 1904; Emmett J. Scott to Price-Mars, August 22, 1904; and Price-Mars to Scott, August 31, 1904, all in container 243, reel 246, Booker T. Washington Papers, Manuscript Division, Library of Congress.

7. Jean Price-Mars, "Le préjugé des races," in *La vocation de l'élite* (Port-au-Prince, Haiti: Impremerie Edmond Chenet, 1919), 179, English translations of "Le préjugé des races" by Barbara Crockett Dease.

8. In *Silhouettes de nègres et de nègrophiles* (Paris: Présence africain, 1960), Price-Mars dedicated an entire chapter to George Washington Carver and his work at Tuskegee.

9. *Tuskegee Student*, October 17 and September 26, 1903; Washington, *Working with the Hands* (subscription ed.), 20, 226.

10. Chantalle Verna, *Haiti and the Uses of America: Post-U.S. Occupation Promises* (New Brunswick, NJ: Rutgers University Press, 2017), 30, 32.

11. James, *Black Jacobins*, 242.

12. Julia Gaffield traces the significance of agriculture for the formation of the Haitian nation-state. Toussaint's Constitution of 1801 left the plantation economy intact and maintained too much continuity with the economic policies of colonial Saint Domingue. Dessaline's Constitution of 1805 and the Constitution of 1807 enshrined agriculture as central to Haitian identity. The Constitution of 1806, however, favored commerce over agriculture. See Gaffield, "Complexities of Imagining Haiti: A Study of National Constitutions, 1801–1807," *Journal of Social History* 41, no. 1 (Fall 2007): 81–103.

13. Verna, *Haiti and the Uses of America*, 34, quoting the Haitian Constitution.

14. Verna, *Haiti and the Uses of America*, 34; Michel-Rolph Trouillot, *Haiti: State Against Nation* (New York: Monthly Review Press, 1990), 44.

15. Trouillot, *State Against Nation*, 16.

16. Trouillot, *State Against Nation*, 44.

17. James, *Black Jacobins*, 393.

18. Booker T. Washington, *Frederick Douglass: A Biography* (Philadelphia: George W. Jacobs, 1906), 144.

19. W. F. Powell, "Hayti as a Refuge," *Cleveland Gazette*, April 6, 1901.

20. *The Freeman*, April 25, 1903.

21. "The Voice of the Negro for April," *Voice of the Negro* 1, no. 3 (March 1904): n.p., advertisements section.

22. "Two Views," *New York Times*, November 27, 1906.

23. John Stephens Durham to Washington, May 13, 1901, reel 44, Booker T. Washington Papers, Manuscript Division, Library of Congress.

24. John Stephens Durham, "Hidden Wealth of Hayti," *Voice of the Negro* 1, no. 4 (April 1904): 143, 145.

25. Durham, "Hidden Wealth of Hayti," 145–46.

26. Byrd, *The Black Republic*, 186.

27. Arthur A. Schomburg, "Is Hayti Decadent?," *Unique Advertiser*, August 1904, archived in Manuscripts, Archives, and Rare Books Division, Schomburg Center for Research in Black Culture, New York Public Library.

28. Schomburg, "Is Hayti Decadent?," quoting James Franklin in "every plantation."

29. Schomburg, "Is Hayti Decadent?"

30. Raphael Dalleo, *American Imperialisms Undead: The Occupation of Haiti and the Rise of Caribbean Anticolonialism* (Charlottesville: University of Virginia Press, 2016), viii.

31. Throughout the first half of the nineteenth century at least, Haitian leaders continued to wrestle with the role of the plantation. Touissant and Jean-Pierre Boyer reinstated it, whereas Jean Jacques Dessalines and Henri Christophe instituted land reforms that redistributed plantation lands to the peasantry. Michael Largey, *Voudou Nation: Haitian Art, Music, and Cultural Nationalism* (Chicago: University of Chicago Press, 2006), 33, 37, 68.

32. Casimir, *The Caribbean*, 117.

33. Lorgia García Peña, *Translating Blackness: Latinx Colonialities in Global Perspective* (Durham, NC: Duke University Press, 2022), 95, 100–101, 102.

34. Washington, *Working with the Hands* (subscription ed.), 17, 18, 20, 17, 19.

35. Washington, *Working with the Hands* (subscription ed.), 19, 22, 20.

36. Rev. Owen Meredith Waller, M.D., "Booker T. Washington's Unsound Doctrine Riddled Too [*sic*] Pieces," *Chicago Broad Ax*, May 7, 1904.

37. Jacques Nicolas Léger, *Haiti, Her History and Her Detractors* (New York: Neale, 1907), 292. One such negative depiction of Haiti was also published in the *North American Review*: Archibald R. Colquhoun claimed that "with the removal of white control [in Haiti], the negroes have reverted to a condition almost of savagery." Colquhoun, "The Future of the Negro," *North American Review*, May 1903, 665.

38. Léger, *Haiti, Her History*, 293, 294, 321.

39. Dr. H. W. Furniss, "Notes of Haiti: Dr. Henry W. Furniss Gives Information of Country, Its People, and Their Customs," *Indianapolis Freeman*, June 12, 1909, and "Black Republic Lovely Haiti!," *Cleveland Gazette*, July 17, 1909.

40. Price-Mars quoted in Antoine, *Jean Price-Mars and Haiti*, 49–50.

41. Antoine, *Jean Price-Mars and Haiti*, 50.

42. Magdaline W. Shannon, introduction to Jean Price-Mars, *So Spoke the Uncle*, trans. Magdaline W. Shannon (Washington, DC: Three Continents Press, 1983), xi.

43. Jean Price-Mars, "La vocation de l'élite," trans. Claire Payton, in *The Haiti Reader: History, Culture, Politics*, ed. Laurent Dubois, Kaiama L. Glover, Nadève Ménard, Millery Polyné, and Chantalle F. Verna (Durham, NC: Duke University Press, 2020), 208.

44. Jean Price-Mars, "L'education technique," *Haiti littéraire et scientifique*, October 20, 1912, 522.

45. Mercer Cook, "Booker T. Washington and the French," *Journal of Negro History* 40, no. 4 (1955): 318–40.

46. Fleury Féquière, *L'education haitienne* (Port-au-Prince, Haiti: Imprimerie de L'Abeille, 1906), 490.

47. Antoine, *Jean Price-Mars and Haiti*, 51.

48. Washington to Walter Hines Page, March 19, 1902, in *BTWP*, 6:419–20 n. 1.

49. Dr. Jean Jacques quoted in "Haitiens Need Tuskegee Ideas," *Cleveland Gazette*, July 1, 1911.

50. R. W. Thompson, "Haitian Minister to Go to Tuskegee," *The Freeman*, January 14, 1911; "News from Foreign Shores," *The Freeman*, January 14, 1911. Sannon and Hurst had to "indefinitely postpone" their visit to contend with a boundary dispute with the Dominican Republic. Washington never visited Haiti, either. See *Tuskegee Student*, January 28, 1911.

4. JOINING HANDS ACROSS THE SEA 399

51. Matthew Casey, *Empire's Guestworkers: Haitian Migrants in Cuba During the Age of US Occupation* (Cambridge: Cambridge University Press, 2017).

52. García Peña, *Translating Blackness*, 96.

53. Mary A. Renda, *Taking Haiti: Military Occupation and the Culture of U.S. Imperialism, 1915–1940* (Chapel Hill: University of North Carolina Press, 2001), 51–52; Marvin Chochotte, "The Twilight of Popular Revolutions: The Suppression of Peasant Armed Struggles and Freedom in Rural Haiti During the US Occupation, 1915–1934," *Journal of African American History* 103, no. 3 (Summer 2018): 277.

54. Scott and Stowe, *Booker T. Washington*, 309.

55. Washington, "Dr. Booker T. Washington on American Occupation of Haiti."

56. Washington, "Dr. Booker T. Washington on American Occupation of Haiti."

57. Washington, "Dr. Booker T. Washington on American Occupation of Haiti."

58. Washington, "Dr. Booker T. Washington on American Occupation of Haiti."

59. Edwards, *Practice of Diaspora*; Guridy, *Forging Diaspora*.

60. Dubois, *Haiti*, 220.

61. Brenda Gayle Plummer, "The Afro-American Response to the Occupation of Haiti," *Phylon* 43, no. 2 (1982): 125–43; Matthew J. Smith, "Capture Land: Jamaica, Haiti, and the United States Occupation," *Journal of Haitian Studies* 21, no. 2 (2015): 181–206; Verna, *Haiti and the Uses of America*, 45–46.

62. Washington, "Dr. Booker T. Washington on American Occupation of Haiti." Washington quoted another "American" writer here but didn't name that person in the article.

63. Brenda Gayle Plummer, *Haiti and the Great Powers, 1901–1915* (Baton Rouge: Louisiana State University Press, 1988), 229.

64. Casey, *Empire's Guestworkers*.

65. Chochotte, "Twilight of Popular Revolutions," 280–81.

66. Dalleo, *American Imperialisms Undead*, 12.

67. Chochotte, "Twilight of Popular Revolutions," 278.

68. *Le moniteur*, November 22, 1916; Plummer, "The Afro-American Response," 130–31.

69. "More Light on the Haitian Situation," *Crisis* 25, no. 1 (November 1922): 39.

70. "Making Educational Survey of Haiti," *Baltimore Afro-American*, December 29, 1922.

71. Leon D. Pamphile, *Clash of Cultures: America's Educational Strategies in Occupied Haiti, 1915–1934* (Lanham, MD: University Press of America, 2008), 70, 71.

72. "Two Invited to Haiti," *Baltimore Afro-American*, November 10, 1922.

73. Millery Polyné, *From Douglass to Duvalier: U.S. African Americans, Haiti, and Pan Americanism, 1870–1964* (Gainesville: University Press of Florida, 2010), 63; Pamphile, *Clash of Cultures*, 72, 73.

74. "Students and Teachers Hear Address on Haiti," *Tuskegee Student*, March 1–15, 1923.

75. "Haitian President's Message to the United States," *Baltimore Afro-American*, June 26, 1926.

76. "Haitian President's Message."

77. Pamphile, *Clash of Cultures*, 86.

78. Polyné, *From Douglass to Duvalier*, 77–79.

79. Verna, *Haiti and the Uses of America*, 34, 56.

80. Polyné, *From Douglass to Duvalier*, 87.

81. Verna, *Haiti and the Uses of America*, 55–56.

82. Pamphile, *Clash of Cultures*, 124.

83. Pamphile, *Clash of Cultures*, 125.

84. Jean Price-Mars, "Qu'est-ce que le pays peut-il attendre du Service Technique de l'agriculture?," *La relève: Politique, littéraire* 2, no. 6 (December 1933): 25, 27, English translations of "Qu'est-ce que le pays" by Barbara Crockett Dease. The address at the agricultural school was published in two installments in 1933 and 1934.

400   4. JOINING HANDS ACROSS THE SEA

85. Price-Mars, "Qu'est-ce que le pays," 27, 28.

86. Price-Mars, "Qu'est-ce que le pays," 28, 29.

87. Jean Price-Mars, "Que peut attendre le pays du Service technique d'agriculture," *La relève: Politique, littéraire* 2, no. 7 (January 1934): 52, 54, English translations of "Que peut attendre" by Barbara Crockett Dease.

88. Price-Mars, "Que peut attendre," 52, 53, 54.

89. Pamphile, *Clash of Cultures*, 150.

90. Brenda Gayle Plummer, *Haiti and the United States: The Psychological Moment* (Athens: University of Georgia Press, 1992), 119.

91. Magdaline W. Shannon, *Jean Price-Mars, the Haitian Elite, and the American Occupation 1915–1935* (New York: St. Martin's Press, 1996), 94.

92. Plummer, *Haiti and the United States*, 119.

93. Robert Moton, *Report of the United States Commission on Education in Haiti* (Washington, DC: U.S. Government Printing Office, 1931), 57–59, 58.

94. Moton, *Report of the United States Commission on Education in Haiti*, 41, 55.

95. Shannon, *Jean Price-Mars*, 94.

96. Pamphile, *Clash of Cultures*, 150.

97. "Haitian Masses Tell U.S. Get Out," *New York Liberator*, March 8, 1930.

98. James, *Black Jacobins*, 394.

99. Shannon, *Jean Price-Mars*, 66; Kevin Meehan and Marie Léticée, "A Folio of Writing from 'La Revue Indigène' (1927–28): Translation and Commentary," *Callaloo* 23, no. 4 (2000): 1377–80.

100. Imani D. Owens, "Beyond Authenticity: The US Occupation of Haiti and the Politics of Folk Culture," *Journal of Haitian Studies* 21, no. 2 (2015): 350–70.

101. This essay was published across three issues under three slightly different names: "A propos de la 'Renaissance Negre' aux Etats-Unis" [part 1], *La relève: Politique, littéraire* 1, no. 1 (1932): 14–20; "A propos de 'la Renaissance Nègre aux Etats-Unis'" [part 2], *La relève: Politique, littéraire* 1, no. 2 (1932): 9–15; "A propos de la 'Renaissance Nègre aux Etats-Unis'" [part 3], *La relève: Politique, littéraire* 1, no. 3 (1932): 8–14; all quotes are from part 3.

102. Price-Mars, "A propos de la 'Renaissance Nègre aux Etats-Unis,'" [part 3], 13–14, my translation.

103. Price-Mars, "A propos de la 'Renaissance Nègre'" [part 3], 14, my translation.

104. Washington, "The Atlanta Exposition Address," in *Up from Slavery*, 219.

105. Price-Mars, "A propos de la 'Renaissance Nègre'" [part 3], 14.

106. Jean Price-Mars, "The Problem of Work in Haiti" (in English), *La revue du monde noir* 1, no. 1 (1931): 13–14, 20.

107. Price-Mars, "The Problem of Work in Haiti," 18, 19.

108. Polyné, *From Douglass to Duvalier*, 92.

109. "Mr. Vincent's Gesture," *New York Amsterdam News*, April 21, 1934.

110. "Mr. Vincent's Gesture"; "Solidarity of Races Lauded: President of Haitian Republic Speaks at Harlem Luncheon," *New York Amsterdam News*, April 14, 1934.

111. "Solidarity of Races Lauded." Interestingly, the *New York Amsterdam News* article "Mr. Vincent's Gesture," published in 1934, claimed that President Borno did not welcome African Americans to Haiti and "ignored" them when he visited the United States. However, in the *Baltimore Afro-American* article "Haitian President's Message to the United States," published in 1926, Borno at least paid lip service to Haitian–African American solidarity.

112. "Mr. Vincent's Gesture"; "Solidarity of Races Lauded."

113. The title of the magazine was alternately printed as *Good Will* and *Goodwill*. It seems the earliest issues used the former, but at some point during 1935 editors switched to the latter. Since most issues use *Goodwill*, I have done the same.

4. JOINING HANDS ACROSS THE SEA

114. Polyné, *From Douglass to Duvalier*, 22.
115. Polyné, *From Douglass to Duvalier*, 90–91. Coincidentally, Barnett enrolled in Tuskegee in 1904, the same year that Jean Price-Mars visited and one year after the first cohort of Haitian students enrolled.
116. E. L. Dimitry, *Official Report of the Haitian Afro-American Chamber of Commerce's Commission to Study the Commercial, Agricultural, and Industrial Possibilities of the Haitian Republic, August 17 to September 4, 1934* (N.p.: n.p., [1935?]), 1, 7, 2.
117. Dimitry, *Official Report*, 6, 24, 25, 6.
118. Dimitry, *Official Report*, 18, 9.
119. Dimitry, *Official Report*, 29, 28.
120. Dimitry, *Official Report*, 32, 33, 46.
121. Dimitry, *Official Report*, 29–30 (sympathy for peasants' poverty), 41.
122. Polyné, *From Douglass to Duvalier*, 93.
123. "Won't You Cooperate with Us?," *Goodwill*, June 1937. Though *Goodwill* was bilingual, some articles were exclusively published in either French or English, while others were printed in both languages. The primary contributors appear to have been Haitians, not African Americans. I am grateful to Felix Jean Louis III for bringing *Goodwill* to my attention. See Felix Jean Louis III, "Harlemites, Haitians, and the Black International, 1915–1934," MA thesis, Florida International University, 2014.
124. "Greetings" and "Editorial," *Goodwill*, December 1934.
125. *Goodwill*, January 1935.
126. "Visit the Republic of Haiti, Eden of the Western World," *Goodwill*, March 1936.
127. D. Charles Govan, "A Report of the Existing Commercial and Industrial Conditions of the Republic of Haiti," *Goodwill*, January 1936.
128. "His Excellency Franklin D. Roosevelt President of the United States," in "Actualites haitiennes: Haiti of 1936," special issue, *Goodwill*, December 1936.
129. Ludovic J. Rosemond, "Pour une heureuse campagne de propagande haitienne," *Goodwill*, May 1937, English translations by Barbara Crockett Dease.
130. Franck R. Dale, "Visit the Republic of Haiti, Eden of the Western World," *Goodwill*, February 1936; *Goodwill*, April 1937.
131. Theophile Salnave, "Let Us Go to Haiti," in "Actualites haitiennes: Haiti of 1936," special issue, *Goodwill*, December 1936.
132. Govan, "A Report of the Existing Commercial and Industrial Conditions."
133. Jean Price-Mars, "Haiti's Exportable Articles," *Goodwill*, January 1935, an excerpt from Price-Mars, "The Problem of Work in Haiti."
134. "Haiti Is on the Road to Progress," *Goodwill*, December 1936.
135. Moton, *Report of the United States Commission on Education in Haiti*, 42.
136. "Port-au-Prince et la structure économique d'Haiti," *Goodwill*, May 1937 and June 1937, capitalization as given in the original, English translations by Barbara Crockett Dease. The series' author is unnamed, but it was likely Rosemond, the journal's editor.
137. Kate Ramsey, *The Spirits and the Law: Vodou and Power in Haiti* (Chicago: University of Chicago Press, 2011), 177–247; Casey, *Empire's Guestworkers*, 20.
138. *Goodwill*, February 1936, cover.
139. R. R. Wright Sr., "Is There a Negro Problem and Is It Being Solved?," *Pittsburgh Courier*, February 16, 1935.
140. "Give Haitian Coffee to Family and Friends," *Crisis* 47, no. 1 (January 1940): 31.
141. George S. Schuyler, "Views and Reviews," *Pittsburgh Courier*, December 17, 1932, and July 20, 1935; quotes from "Quelques considérations de Mr. Schuyler: Haïti et l'Amérique Noir," *La relève: Politique, littéraire* 5, no. 7 (January 1937): 2–6, English translations by Barbara Crockett Dease.

142. Plummer, *Haiti and the Great Powers*, 22.
143. Plummer, *Haiti and the United States*, 54.
144. Trouillot, *Haiti*, 36; Plummer, *Haiti and the Great Powers*, 22.
145. Plummer, *Haiti and the United States*, 21; Plummer, *Haiti and the Great Powers*, 22.
146. Moton, *Report of the United States Commission on Education in Haiti*, 40.
147. Brandon R. Byrd, "C. C. Spaulding and Major R.R. Wright—Companions on the Road Less Traveled? A Reconsideration of African American International Relations in the Early Twentieth Century," MA thesis, College of William and Mary, 2011, 28.
148. Plummer, *Haiti and the Great Powers*, 23.
149. Trouillot, *Haiti*, 61.
150. Plummer, *Haiti and the Great Powers*, 23; Price-Mars, "The Problem of Work in Haiti," 19–20.
151. Trouillot, *Haiti*, 61.
152. Plummer, *Haiti and the Great Powers*, 35.

5. BECOMING NEW NEGROES: STUDENT ASPIRATIONS, HEMISPHERIC MIGRATION, AND THE OTHERWISE USES OF TUSKEGEE

1. Wesley Warren Jefferson to Washington, December 6, 1899, in *BTWP*, 5:286–288; *BTWP*, 5:129–130 n. 1.
2. In Booker T. Washington's general introduction to the volume, he identifies Scott as its official editor; however, Washington is the only editor listed on the book itself.
3. Scott, preface to *Tuskegee and Its People*, ed. Washington, vii, ix.
4. By "Booker T. Washington's papers" here, I mean the *BTWP*, the Booker T. Washington Papers at the Library of Congress, and the Papers of Booker T. Washington (1887–1915): The Tuskegee Collection in the Tuskegee University Archives.
5. See, for example, Baker, *Modernism and the Harlem Renaissance*; Gates, "Trope of the New Negro"; Ross, *Manning the Race*; Kowalski, "No Excuses for Our Dirt"; and Smethurst, *Afro-American Roots of Modernism*.
6. The term *New Negro*, as I use it here, draws on recent scholarship that extends the New Negro era back into the nineteenth century and expands its geography beyond New York and the broader Global North to encompass the U.S. South, the Caribbean, and other parts of the Black world. See Baldwin, *Chicago's New Negroes*; Goldsby, *A Spectacular Secret*; Brittan, "The Terminal"; Edwards, *Practice of Diaspora*; Stephens, *Black Empire*; Harold, *Rise and Fall of the Garvey Movement* and *New Negro Politics*; Briggs, *New Negro in the Old South*; Baldwin and Makalani, *Escape from New York*.
7. de la Fuente, *A Nation for All*, 138–71.
8. Washington to Allen Alexander Wesley, November 8, 1898, in *BTWP*, 4:506–7.
9. Thomas Austin to Washington, November 1, 1898, in *BTWP*, 4:501.
10. Washington to Wesley, November 8, 1898.
11. Joseph Forney Johnston to Washington, June 28, 1899, and Washington to Johnston, July 5, 1899, in *BTWP*, 5:140, 148.
12. *Report of Commissioner of Education of Porto Rico* [*sic*] (Washington, DC: U.S. Government Printing Office, 1902), 34, 74.
13. *Report of Commissioner of Education of Porto Rico* [*sic*] (Washington, DC: U.S. Government Printing Office, 1903), 246; *Report of Commissioner of Education of Porto Rico* (1902), 33–34.

5. BECOMING NEW NEGROES   403

14. Juan José Osuna, *A History of Education in Puerto Rico* (Rio Piedras: Editorial de la Universidad de Puerto Rico, 1949), 256; *Report of Commissioner of Education of Porto Rico [sic]* (Washington, DC: U.S. Government Printing Office, 1901), 75.

15. *Report of Commissioner of Education of Porto Rico* (1901), 75.

16. *Report of Commissioner of Education of Porto Rico* (1903), 246.

17. "Students for Tuskegee," *Baltimore Afro-American*, April 18, 1903.

18. "Une bonne lettre du Ministre W. F. Powell.," *Le nouvelliste*, September 16, 1903 (the letter was published in 1903 but is dated June 12, 1902); "Excellent vœu," *Le nouvelliste*, July 31, 1903.

19. "Tuskegee," *Le nouvelliste*, August 26, 1903; "Institut de Tusegkee," *Le nouvelliste*, October 29, 1903.

20. "Haiti Recognizes Tuskegee," *Colored American*, April 18, 1903.

21. *Indianapolis Freeman*, April 25, 1903.

22. *Le moniteur*, November 19, 1904; *Tuskegee Student*, September 26 and October 17, 1903.

23. Byrd, *The Black Republic*, 270 n. 28.

24. Haitian Senate proceedings published in *Le moniteur* on December 14, 1904, reported that $1,000 allotted for the Booker Washington school had been removed.

25. "Booker T. Washington for Jamaica," *Daily Gleaner*, November 13, 1902.

26. "Resolutions," International Conference on the Negro, 1912, reel 709, Booker T. Washington Papers, Manuscript Division, Library of Congress.

27. Thomas Austin to Washington, November 5, 1898, in *BTWP*, 4:503.

28. Grace Minns to Washington, January 10, 1903, quoted in the note that goes with Grace Minns to Washington, May 24, 1901, in *BTWP*, 6:124–25 n. 1.

29. Guridy, *Forging Diaspora*, 34.

30. Hermanno Laroche to Washington, June 14, 1911, and V. Jacques Boco to Washington, October 19, 1911, reel 685, Booker T. Washington Papers, Manuscript Division, Library of Congress.

31. See, for example, Armando F. Marrero to Washington, April 5, 1909, reel 684, Booker T. Washington Papers, Manuscript Division, Library of Congress.

32. Guridy, *Forging Diaspora*, 51.

33. Mrs. Washington, "What Girls Are Taught," 72–73.

34. Juan Santos y Torres to Washington, January 27, 1911, and January 14, 1912, and J. Alex McKenzie to Washington, June 16, 1911, reel 685, Booker T. Washington Papers, Manuscript Division, Library of Congress.

35. Washington to Mr. W. D. Black, May 20, 1911, reel 685, Booker T. Washington Papers, Manuscript Division, Library of Congress.

36. Mme. Boco to Washington, June 9, 1911, reel 685, and Mr. Domouch to Washington, April 22, 1911, reel 684, Booker T. Washington Papers, Manuscript Division, Library of Congress.

37. Jones, "Improving Rural Life for Blacks," 106; Hersey, *My Work*, 109.

38. Thrasher, *Tuskegee*, 75–76.

39. "Report of Delegates to the International Conference on the Negro at Tuskegee, U.S.A., 23rd November, 1912," *Supplement to the Jamaica Gazette* (Kingston), November 1, 1913, 706.

40. Pierce, "How Electricity Is Taught at Tuskegee," 426.

41. Washington to Miss Lane, June 24, 1902, box 4, folder 7, Papers of Booker T. Washington (1887–1915): The Tuskegee Collection, Tuskegee University Archives.

42. Leonora Love Chapman to Washington, November 7, 1898, in *BTWP*, 4:505.

43. Mrs. Washington, "What Girls Are Taught," 68.

44. Guridy, *Forging Diaspora*, 49–50. Interestingly, only four Afro-Cuban girls attended Tuskegee in the two decades that made up the "Tuskegee–Cuba connection." It is perhaps, as Frank Guridy suspects, that Afro-Cuban parents were less likely to send their daughters abroad at an age when they could potentially engage in sexual activity and were integral to maintaining the household

404   5. BECOMING NEW NEGROES

through their domestic labor. Afro-Cuban "boys were encouraged to get an education while girls were not." This was not the case for Puerto Rican girls, however, who attended Tuskegee in much larger numbers. Guridy, *Forging Diaspora*, 41–42.

45. "From Cuban Students at Tuskegee Institute," September 8, 1899, in *BTWP*, 5:199; Guridy, *Forging Diaspora*, 50–51.

46. Manuel Gutierez to Washington, November 7, 1906, reel 684, Booker T. Washington Papers, Manuscript Division, Library of Congress.

47. Guridy, *Forging Diaspora*, 38.

48. Washington to Samuel McCune Lindsay, May 20, 1902, in *BTWP*, 13:504–6.

49. The description of Federico Ramos is given in *Tuskegee Student*, May 17, 1913, where his first name is misspelled "Ferderico" and which quotes *Metronome* magazine, May 1913. Lafaye and Puerto Rican students' complaint from E. G. Dexter to Washington, August 23, 1911, reel 68, Booker T. Washington Papers, Manuscript Division, Library of Congress.

50. Washington to E. G. Dexter, September 15, 1911, reel 68, Booker T. Washington Papers, Manuscript Division, Library of Congress.

51. E. G. Dexter to Washington, February 16, 1912, reel 68, Booker T. Washington Papers, Manuscript Division, Library of Congress.

52. Washington to E. G. Dexter, March 12, 1912, reel 68, Booker T. Washington Papers, Manuscript Division, Library of Congress.

53. Washington to Warren Logan, January 21, 1899, in *BTWP*, 5:17.

54. Julio Despaigne to Washington, September 22, 1905, in *BTWP*, 8:366.

55. John S. Durham to Washington, June 12, 1904, reel 44, Booker T. Washington Papers, Manuscript Division, Library of Congress.

56. Washington to John S. Durham, July 9, 1904, reel 44, Booker T. Washington Papers, Manuscript Division, Library of Congress.

57. "A Petition from Tuskegee Students," October 7, 1897, in *BTWP*, 4:330.

58. "A Petition from Laundry Workers at Tuskegee Institute," July 12, 1911, in *BTWP*, 11:266; Spivey, *Schooling for the New Slavery*, 60.

59. Washington to William Henry Baldwin Jr., October 20 and October 23, 1903, in *BTWP*, 7:298–300 (especially 300 n. 1), 306–7; Harlan, *Wizard of Tuskegee*, 145–48. Although Washington agreed to adjust the schedule in his letter to Baldwin, a school trustee, the historian Donald Spivey's alternative account of the strike maintains that Washington's response to the school's executive council was "No concessions." The executive council meeting where Washington would have made this statement was about one month (September 27) before his initial letter to Baldwin (October 20). So it seems Washington was initially resistant to making concessions, but ultimately determined to do so. See Spivey, *Schooling for the New Slavery*, 62, 70 n. 71.

60. *Tuskegee Annual Catalogue*, 1901–1902.

61. *Tuskegee Annual Catalogue*, 1911–1912, 16.

62. For more on students' and faculty's dissatisfaction with Tuskegee's academic curriculum and overregulation of students' schedules, see Spivey, *Schooling for the New Slavery*, 45–70, and Harlan, *Wizard of Tuskegee*, 143–73.

63. Washington, *Story of the Negro*, 1:25–27.

64. Adriano Medina to Washington, November 1911, reel 685, Booker T. Washington Papers, Manuscript Division, Library of Congress. See also Adriano Medina to Washington, October 14, 1911, reel 685, Booker T. Washington Papers, Manuscript Division, Library of Congress.

65. Medina to Washington, November 1911.

66. Juan Cancio Guimbarda to Washington, August 29, 1911, and Juan Santos y Torres to Washington, January 14, 1912, reels 684 and 685, Booker T. Washington Papers, Manuscript Division, Library of Congress.

5. BECOMING NEW NEGROES

67. Martin Grove Brumbaugh to Washington, May 7, 1901, in *BTWP*, 6:106–7; Brumbaugh quoted in Pablo Navarro-Rivera, "Acculturation Under Duress: The Puerto Rican Experience at the Carlisle Indian Industrial School, 1898–1918," n.d., http://home.epix.net/~landis/navarro.html, accessed July 22, 2022.

68. Susan Helen Porter to Washington, November 9, 1898, in *BTWP*, 4:507. Porter also misidentified Pedro as Cuban rather than Puerto Rican. On Celestina Ramírez, see "From Cuban Students at Tuskegee Institute," September 8, 1899, in *BTWP*, 5:199.

69. Thrasher, *Tuskegee*, 82.

70. Alfonso Reverón to Washington, n.d., and Saturnino Sierra to Washington, July 14, 1907, reel 684, Booker T. Washington Papers, Manuscript Division, Library of Congress; Julio Despaigne to Washington, September 22, 1905, in *BTWP*, 8:364–66.

71. Rafael Castillo to Washington, September 16, 1911, and José D. Rumler to Washington, September 25 and September 27, 1912, reel 685, Booker T. Washington Papers, Manuscript Division, Library of Congress.

72. *Tuskegee Annual Catalogue*, 1911–1912, 43; *Tuskegee Annual Catalogue*, 1912–1913, 43. Primitivo's last name is listed as both "Miranda" and "Mirando" in the archive.

73. *Tuskegee Student*, January 7, 1911.

74. *Tuskegee Student*, September 2, 1916; "The Horizon," *Crisis* 12, no. 6 (October 1916): 298.

75. Fermin Domenech to Washington, May 19, 1905, reel 683, Booker T. Washington Papers, Manuscript Division, Library of Congress. The United States had just relinquished its occupation authority over Cuba on May 20, 1902.

76. Tomás Monte Rivera to Washington, May 4, 1909, reel 684, Booker T. Washington Papers, Manuscript Division, Library of Congress.

77. Sir Harry H. Johnston, *The Negro in the New World* (New York: Macmillan, 1910), 190; Pierce, "How Electricity Is Taught at Tuskegee," 426; *Tuskegee Student*, October 17, 1903.

78. Athanse M. Auguste to Washington, November 11, 1902, reel 191, Booker T. Washington Papers, Manuscript Division, Library of Congress.

79. Chrysostome Rosemond to Washington, July 19, July 8, and September 23, 1911, reel 685, Booker T. Washington Papers, Manuscript Division, Library of Congress.

80. Mme. Louis-Margron to Washington, March 7 and May 16, 1911, reel 685, Booker T. Washington Papers, Manuscript Division, Library of Congress.

81. Verna, *Haiti and the Uses of America*, 30.

82. R. Samuel Stennett, "Bright Youths. Successes Achieved by Jamaicans at Tuskegee. Carry Off Honours. Claim That the Educated Avenues Here Are Restricted," *Gleaner*, April 9, 1913.

83. "Report of Delegates," 706.

84. Stennett, "Bright Youths."

85. Dotson, "Story of a Teacher of Cooking," 205–7.

86. Perry, "Janey Gets Her Desires," 172, 175.

87. "A Successful Truck Farmer in Cuba," *Southern Letter*, June 1907.

88. Cornelia Bowen, "A Woman's Work," in *Tuskegee and Its People*, ed. Washington, 211, 221, 222.

89. Alice Mary Robertson to Washington, February 6, 1901, in *BTWP*, 6:27.

90. Washington, *Working with the Hands* (subscription ed.), 221.

91. W. E. Glenn, "Building an Industrial School in Indian Territory," *Southern Letter*, August 1907.

92. "Work of Tuskegee Graduates," *Southern Letter*, May 1912. Creek freedmen were the descendants of Black people enslaved by the Creek and traveled with them from Alabama and Mississippi to Indian Territory in the mid-1850s.

93. *Tuskegee Student*, July 18, 1908.

94. *BTWP*, 8:221 n. 1.

95. "Report of Delegates," 706.

96. *Le moniteur*, March 3, 1917; "Pratt Graduates Told to Be Ready," *Brooklyn Daily Eagle*, June 20, 1916.

97. "Mr. R. S. Stennett," *Gleaner*, June 4, 1930; "Annual Record of Government Printing Office," *Gleaner*, August 8, 1930.

98. *Southern Letter*, August 1915.

99. Victoria Maria Altiery to Washington, September 29, 1912, reel 68, Booker T. Washington Papers, Manuscript Division, Library of Congress.

100. *Southern Letter*, February 1911 (Concepcion), May 1913 (Lafaye), January 1916 (Reeves).

101. Washington to Lindsay, May 20, 1902, in *BTWP*, 13:504–6; J. H. Palmer, "Elect Tuskegee Graduate for Mayor of Colonial Town," *Southern Letter*, March–April 1929.

102. *Cuba News*, November 20, 1915.

103. Alfredo Pérez y Encinosa, "Juan Eusebio Gómez," *La lucha*, May 20, 1906.

104. "The Senate and House," *La lucha*, April 27, 1909.

105. Alfredo Pérez Encinosa to E. J. Scott, August 18, 1901, reels 177–78, Booker T. Washington Papers, Manuscript Division, Library of Congress.

106. *Boletin oficial de la secretaria de estado* (Havana, Cuba: Imprenta y Papeleria de Rambla, Bouza Y C, Obispo nums. 33 y 35, 1913), 97, https://archive.org/details/xivcongresointer10inte/page/n7/mode/2up.

107. James Weldon Johnson, preface to *The Book of American Negro Poetry*, ed. James Weldon Johnson (New York: Harcourt, Brace, 1922), vii.

108. Albert C. Barnes, "Negro Art and America," in *The New Negro: Voices of the Harlem Renaissance*, ed. Alain Locke (1925; reprint, New York: Touchstone, 1997), 22.

109. Robert R. Moton, "Hampton–Tuskegee: Missioners of the Masses," in *The New Negro*, ed. Locke, 325, 331.

110. Charles S. Johnson, "The Social Philosophy of Booker T. Washington," *Opportunity*, April 1928.

111. Rev. Arthur E. Massey, "Dr. Booker T. Washington: Negro Educationalist and Founder of the Tuskegee Institute" in *Negro: An Anthology*, ed. Nancy Cunard (London: Wishart, 1934), 16–20; Edwards, *Practice of Diaspora*, 309 ("to document the discourses").

112. *Tuskegee Annual Catalogue*, 1931, 11; *Tuskegee Messenger*, November 1931.

113. Clara W. Shepard, "An Indirect Reply to Our Inquiry," *La revue du monde noir*, no. 3 (1931): 53–54; Brent Hayes Edwards, "Pebbles of Consonance: A Reply to Critics," *Small Axe* 9, no. 1 (2005): 139, 140.

114. Clara W. Shepard, "Tuskegee Normal and Industrial Institute," *La revue de monde noir*, no. 2 (1931): 15, 16, 17, 18.

115. Clara W. Shepard, "Utility of foreign Languages for american Negroes [*sic*]," *La revue de monde noir*, no. 4 (1932): 30, 31.

116. Polyné, *From Douglass to Duvalier*, 89–130.

117. "Memorandum on the Need for Agricultural and Industrial Education," box RE 146, Robert A. Hill Collection, David M. Rubenstein Rare Book & Manuscript Library, Duke University, Chapel Hill, NC.

6. AT THE CROSSROADS OF DIASPORA AND EMPIRE: HARVESTING A PLOT LOGIC IN CLAUDE MCKAY'S JAMAICA

1. For example, British colonials from Barbados settled South Carolina.

2. William J. Maxwell, "Notes to the Poems," in Claude McKay, *Complete Poems*, ed. William J. Maxwell (Urbana: University of Illinois Press, 2004), 312.

6. AT THE CROSSROADS OF DIASPORA AND EMPIRE

3. In this chapter, I use "America," as McKay does, to refer to the United States.

4. McKay, *My Green Hills of Jamaica*, 79, hereafter *MGHJ*.

5. McKay, *MGHJ*, 82. *My Green Hills of Jamaica* was written around 1946 but first published posthumously in 1979.

6. McKay, *MGHJ*, 81.

7. McKay, *MGHJ*, 85.

8. Winston James's biography of McKay is an important exception and makes some brief mentions of his time at Tuskegee. James, *Claude McKay: The Making of a Black Bolshevik* (New York: Columbia University Press, 2022).

9. More recently, Sonya Posmentier has explored McKay's migration to Tuskegee as the basis of her analysis of "agricultural spaces in McKay's poetry as part of his modern, transnational identity." Posmentier, "The Provision Ground in New York: Claude McKay and the Form of Memory," *American Literature* 84, no. 2 (2012): 278.

10. Claude McKay, "Claude McKay Describes His Own Life: A Negro Poet," *Pearson's Magazine*, September 1918.

11. "International Conference of the National Negro Tuskegee Institute (509A)," box 96, folder 5, Papers of Booker T. Washington (1887–1915): The Tuskegee Collection, Tuskegee University Archives; "International Conference on the Negro, 1912," box 969, reel 709, Booker T. Washington Papers, Manuscript Division, Library of Congress.

12. Edwards, *Practice of Diaspora*.

13. Josh Gosciak, *The Shadowed Country: Claude McKay and the Romance of the Victorians* (New Brunswick, NJ: Rutgers University Press, 2006), 8.

14. Posmentier, *Cultivation and Catastrophe*, 277.

15. McKay, *MGHJ*, 82–83.

16. Wynter, "Novel and History," 99–100; Simon Gikandi, *Slavery and the Culture of Taste* (Princeton, NJ: Princeton University Press, 2011), 239, 240, 241; Michel-Rolph Trouillot, "North Atlantic Universals: Analytical Fictions, 1492–1945," *South Atlantic Quarterly* 101, no. 4 (Fall 2002): 852.

17. Claude McKay, "How Black Sees Green and Red," *Liberator* 4, no. 6 (June 1921): 20.

18. Sonya Posmentier reads McKay's sonnets, an already transnational poetic form, as provision grounds and explores agricultural "cultivation [on the provision ground] as a central trope of his poetry." Posmentier, "The Provision Ground," 274.

19. "The Tuskegee Conference," *Gleaner*, November 11, 1911; "All About Tuskegee: When and How to Enter," *Jamaica Times*, February 3, 1912.

20. "A Word to Our Tuskegee Delegates," *Jamaica Times*, April 13, 1912.

21. Faith Smith, "Good Enough for Booker T. to Kiss: Hampton, Tuskegee, and Caribbean Self-Fashioning," *Journal of Transnational American Studies* 5, no. 1 (2013): 5.

22. Washington quoted in Smith, "Good Enough for Booker T. to Kiss," 5. Tuskegee's internationalism is replete with examples of diasporic ties with colonial officials, of course.

23. Guridy, *Forging Diaspora*, 59.

24. "International Conference on the Negro," *Tuskegee Student*, April 27, 1912.

25. "Report of Delegates," 710.

26. Robert E. Park, "The International Conference on the Negro," *Southern Workman* 41 (1912): 351.

27. Booker T. Washington, "Is the Negro Having a Fair Chance?," *Century Magazine*, November 1912.

28. W. H. Plant, "An Interesting Lecture at Port Antonio on Tuskegee," *Gleaner*, July 9, 1912.

29. "Report of Delegates," 713, 714.

30. "Plain black" from "International Conference on the Negro," *Tuskegee Student*, April 27, 1912; Thompson's recommendation in "Report of Delegates," 712–13.

408   6. AT THE CROSSROADS OF DIASPORA AND EMPIRE

31. "Report of Delegates," 713, 714.

32. "Tuskegee Visit," *Gleaner*, September 24, 1912. See also "Great Conference at Tuskegee," *Gleaner*, May 1, 1912; "Big Congress: Jamaica's Participation in Tuskegee Conference," *Gleaner*, May 10, 1912; "Educational: Important Conference at Mico College Today, the Work at Tuskegee," *Gleaner*, June 1, 1912; "Work of the Teachers Here, Recent Meetings of Two Branch Associations, a Lecture on Tuskegee," *Gleaner*, September 20, 1912; "Educational," *Gleaner*, October 15, 1912; "The Opening of the Annual Conference of the Jamaica Union of Teachers," *Gleaner*, January 7, 1913; "Great Value of Training Given at Tuskegee," *Gleaner*, November 3, 1913.

33. Washington, "The Atlanta Exposition Address," in *Up from Slavery*, 220.

34. McKay, *MGHJ*, 3, 4, 23, 9, 24–25. "Rural idyll" from Winston James, *A Fierce Hatred of Injustice: Claude McKay's Jamaica and His Poetry of Rebellion* (London: Verso, 2000), 67.

35. Wayne F. Cooper, *Claude McKay: Rebel Sojourner in the Harlem Renaissance* (Baton Rouge: Louisiana State University Press, 1987), 8–9.

36. McKay, "Claude McKay Describes His Own Life."

37. James, *Fierce Hatred of Injustice*, 26–41.

38. McKay, *MGHJ*, 23.

39. McKay, *MGHJ*, 28–29.

40. McKay, *MGHJ*, 44.

41. Claude McKay, "King Banana" (1912), in *Complete Poems*, 28–29; all quotations from this edition.

42. Claude McKay, "The Agricultural Show," in *Gingertown* (New York: Harper, 1932), 187, 189.

43. Claude McKay, *Banana Bottom* (1933; reprint, San Diego: Harcourt Brace, 1961), 275.

44. McKay, *Banana Bottom*, 275.

45. McKay, *Banana Bottom*, 275.

46. James, *Fierce Hatred of Injustice*, 6.

47. Thomas C. Holt, *The Problem of Freedom: Race, Labor, and Politics in Jamaica and Britain, 1832–1938* (Baltimore, MD: Johns Hopkins University Press, 1992), 353.

48. McKay, *MGHJ*, 29.

49. Gikandi, *Slavery and the Culture of Taste*, 241, 242–43.

50. James, *Fierce Hatred of Injustice*, 3–18.

51. Gosciak, *The Shadowed Country*, 64.

52. Holt, *The Problem of Freedom*, 355.

53. *Tuskegee Annual Catalogue*, 1912–1913.

54. Claude McKay, *A Long Way from Home* (1937; reprint, New York: Harcourt Brace & World, 1970), 208; McKay, "Claude McKay Describes His Own Life."

55. "Report of Delegates," 706; Cooper, *Claude McKay*, 66.

56. *Tuskegee Annual Catalogue*, 1912–1913.

57. Washington, "Is the Negro Having a Fair Chance?"

58. Maxwell, "Notes to the Poems," in McKay, in *Complete Poems*, 313; Cooper, *Claude McKay*, 66–70.

59. Carleton Beals, "The Black Belt of the Caribbean," *American Mercury* 24, no. 94 (1931): 131.

60. Beals, "The Black Belt of the Caribbean," 131.

61. *Great White Fleet: Summer Cruises from New York Boston New Orleans to Jamaica Havana Panama Canal Central and South America* (Boston: United Fruit Company Steamship Service, 1913), 10–11.

62. *Jamaica Via the Great White Fleet* (Boston: United Fruit Company Steamship Service, 1913).

63. "The Very Enterprising Town of Port Antonio," *Daily Gleaner*, January 27, 1912.

64. Claude McKay, "Peasants' Ways o' Thinkin'" (1912), in *Complete Poems*, 9–12; all quotations from this edition.

6. AT THE CROSSROADS OF DIASPORA AND EMPIRE 409

65. James, *Fierce Hatred of Injustice*, 59.

66. Walter Jekyll, McKay's mentor, published a study on Jamaican folk culture entitled *Jamaican Songs and Story: Annancy Stories, Digging Songs, Ring Tunes, and Dancing Tunes* (1907).

67. Rhonda D. Frederick, *"Colón Man a Come": Mythographies of Panamá Canal Migration* (Lanham, MD: Lexington, 2005), 27.

68. Ifeoma Kiddoe Nwankwo, *Black Cosmopolitanism: Racial Consciousness and Transnational Identity in the Nineteenth-Century Americas* (Philadelphia: University of Pennsylvania Press, 2005), 14. Whereas Nwankwo defines "Black cosmopolitanism" as the ways in which "people of African descent decided to stake their claim to personhood by defining themselves in relation to the new notions of 'Black community'" in the nineteenth century, peasant cosmopolitanism is concerned primarily with destabilizing the elite, classist connotations associated with the cosmopolite.

69. Nwankwo, *Black Cosmopolitanism*, 13.

70. *Persistent Poverty* is also the title of a study by George Beckford that details how the plantation continues to impede economic progress throughout "Plantation America."

71. McKay, "Author's Note," in *Banana Bottom*, n.p.

72. McKay, *Banana Bottom*, 9; subsequent page citations to *Banana Bottom* are given parenthetically in the text.

73. McKay, *MGHJ*, 60, 61.

74. James, *Fierce Hatred of Injustice*, 138.

75. Claude McKay, *Banjo: A Story Without a Plot* (San Diego: Harcourt Brace, 1929). McKay published *Home to Harlem* in 1928, *Banjo* in 1929, and *Banana Bottom* 1933.

76. Edwards, *Practice of Diaspora*, 200, 204, 205.

77. Edwards, *Practice of Diaspora*, 208.

78. James, *Fierce Hatred of Injustice*, 57–58.

79. Claude McKay, "In Memoriam: Booker T. Washington," in *Complete Poems*, 130.

80. Maxwell, "Notes on the Poems," in McKay, *Complete Poems*, 302.

81. Paul Laurence Dunbar, "Tuskegee Song," in *The Collected Poetry of Paul Laurence Dunbar*, ed. Joanne M. Braxton (Charlottesville: University Press of Virginia, 1993), 333.

82 Claude McKay, "Claude McKay Defends Our Dialect Poetry," *Gleaner*, June 7, 1913.

83. Claude McKay, *The Negroes in America*, trans. Robert J. Winter, ed. Alan L. McLeod (Port Washington, NY: Kennikat Press, 1979),16–19.

84. Cooper, *Claude McKay*, 335.

85. Claude McKay, "For Group Survival" (1937), *Black Scholar* 42, no. 1 (2012): 20–21.

86. McKay, *A Long Way from Home*, 350.

87. Richard Wright, "Blueprint for Negro Writing" (1937), in *The Norton Anthology of African American Literature*, 2nd ed., ed. Henry Louis Gates Jr. and Nellie Y. McKay (New York: Norton, 2004), 1406.

88. McKay quoted in Cooper, *Claude McKay*, 337.

89. Claude McKay, "The Cycle" (c. 1943), in *Collected Poems*, 241.

90. Claude McKay, "The Cycle," No. 7 (1943), in *Collected Poems*, 244–45.

91. Zora Neale Hurston, "Court Order Can't Make Races Mix," letter to the editor, *Orlando Sentinel*, August 11, 1955, reprinted in *Zora Neale Hurston: Folklore, Memoirs, and Other Writings*, comp. Cheryl A. Wall (New York: Library of America, 1995), 956.

7. AESTHETICIZING LABOR, PERFORMING DIASPORA: ZORA NEALE HURSTON AND THE SCENE OF THE WORK CAMP

1. Tiffany Ruby Patterson, *Zora Neale Hurston and a History of Southern Life* (Philadelphia: Temple University Press, 2005), 10.

2. Zora Neale Hurston to Langston Hughes, April 12, 1928, and spring–summer 1929, in *Zora Neale Hurston: A Life in Letters*, ed. Carla Kaplan (New York: Doubleday, 2002), 115, 143.

3. See, for example, Daphne A. Brooks, "'Sister, Can You Line Out?' Zora Neale Hurston and the Sound of Angular Black Womanhood," *Amerikastudien* 55, no. 4 (2010): 618.

4. Zora Neale Hurston, "Characteristics of Negro Expression" (1934), in *Hurston: Folklore, Memoirs, and Other Writings*, 841–42.

5. Zora Neale Hurston, "Art and Such" (1938), in *Hurston: Folklore, Memoirs, and Other Writings*, 906.

6. In 1947, Hurston was invited to write an entry for *The Encyclopedia Americana* on the "Negro in the US." She relished the opportunity to "replace the 'Negro in America' essay written by W. E. B. Du Bois which had run in the [volume] . . . since 1904. Hurston was not shy about using the occasion to celebrate Booker T. Washington for making a place for 'Negro 'untouchables'" (Carla Kaplan, editorial commentary in *Hurston: A Life in Letters*, 442).

7. Zora Neale Hurston, *Dust Tracks on a Road* (1942), in *Hurston: Folklore, Memoirs, and Other Writings*, 730.

8. "Diplomas Awarded to Forty-Three Summer School Graduates," *Tuskegee Messenger*, June 25, 1927.

9. Hurston makes numerous celebratory and mostly sympathetic references to Washington and Tuskegee throughout her work (e.g., *Meet the Mamma, Their Eyes Were Watching God, Dust Tracks on a Road, Polk County*, and "The Rise of the Begging Joints"). Yet both Hurston and her characters sometimes question and debate the limits and possibilities of Washington's political views and Tuskegee's influence on Black aesthetics. For more on Hurston's affinity for and ideological compatibility with Washington, see Deborah G. Plant, *Every Tub Must Sit on Its Own Bottom: The Philosophy and Politics of Zora Neale Hurston* (Urbana: University of Illinois Press, 1995), 36–41.

10. Hazel V. Carby, "The Politics of Fiction, Anthropology, and the Folk: Zora Neale Hurston," in *Cultures in Babylon: Feminism from Black Britain to African America* (London: Verso, 1999), 176.

11. Martyn Bone, "The (Extended) South of Black Folk: Intraregional and Transnational Migrant Labor in *Jonah's Gourde Vine* and *Their Eyes Were Watching God*," *American Literature* 79, no. 4 (December 2007): 753–79; Riché Richardson, "'A House Set Off from the Rest': Ralph Ellison's Rural Geography," *Forum for Modern Language Studies* 40 (April 2004): 127.

12. Wynter, "Novel and History," 99–100.

13. Joseph Roach, *Cities of the Dead: Circum-Atlantic Performance* (New York: Columbia University Press, 1996).

14. Bone, "The (Extended) South of Black Folk," 761.

15. Hurston, *Dust Tracks*, 564.

16. Zora Neale Hurston, *Jonah's Gourd Vine* (1934), in *Hurston: Novels and Stories*, 69, 88, 94, 92.

17. Hurston, *Dust Tracks*, 561.

18. Zora Neale Hurston, *Mules and Men* (1935), in *Hurston: Folklore, Memoirs, and Other Writings*, 12. Interestingly, in Hurston's account of Eatonville, the town has no jail.

19. Nathalie Lord, "Washington at the Hungerford School," *Southern Workman* 41 (1912): 387–88.

20. Booker T. Washington, *The Negro in Business* (Boston: Hertel, Jenkins, 1907), 79, 80.

21. Washington, *The Negro in Business*, 78.

7. AESTHETICIZING LABOR, PERFORMING DIASPORA   411

22. Russell C. Calhoun, "A Negro Community Builder," in *Tuskegee and Its People*, ed. Washington, 336.

23. Zora Neale Hurston, "Proposed Recording Expedition Into the Floridas," in *Go Gator and Muddy the Water: Writings by Zora Neale Hurston from the Federal Writers' Project*, ed. Pamela Bordelon (New York: Norton, 1999), 63; Hurston, *Their Eyes Were Watching God*, in *Hurston: Novels and Stories*, 183 (subsequent page citations to *Their Eyes Were Watching God* are given parenthetically in the text).

24. Frank Peterman and Audrey Peterman, *African Americans and the Saw Mills of Big Cypress: A Brief History* (Washington, DC: National Park Service, U.S. Department of the Interior, n.d.), 8, https://www.nps.gov/bicy/learn/historyculture/upload/African-Americans-and-the-Sawmills -of-Big-Cypress.pdf.

25. Joe Knetsch, "The Broward Rice Plantation: Dream or Merely Speculation?," *Broward Legacy: A Journal of South Florida History* 12, nos. 1–2 (Winter–Spring 1990): 2, https://journals.flvc.org /browardlegacy/article/view/77103/74619.

26. Sonnet Retman, *Real Folks: Race and Genre in the Great Depression* (Durham, NC: Duke University Press, 2011), 157.

27. Hurston, *Dust Tracks*, 691.

28. Cindy Hahamovitch, *The Fruits of Their Labor: Atlantic Coast Farmworkers and the Making of Migrant Poverty, 1870–1945* (Chapel Hill: University of North Carolina Press, 1997), 126.

29. Zora Neale Hurston, "The Citrus Industry" (c. 1930s), in *Go Gator and Muddy the Water*, 135.

30. Hurston, *Mules*, 150.

31. Hurston, *Dust Tracks*, 690.

32. Michael Denning, *The Cultural Front: The Laboring of American Culture in the Twentieth Century* (London: Verso, 1997), xix–xx.

33. Hurston, *Dust Tracks,* 692–93.

34. Hurston, "Characteristics of Negro Expression," 845.

35. Shane Vogel, *The Scene of Harlem Cabaret: Race, Sexuality, Performance* (Chicago: University of Chicago Press, 2009), 91 (quoting Lena Horne), 81.

36. Vogel, *Scene of Harlem Cabaret*, 83, 94, 24, 28.

37. Hurston, "Characteristics of Negro Expression," 841.

38. Vogel, *Scene of Harlem Cabaret*, 83.

39. Hurston, *Mules*, 141.

40. Valerie Boyd, *Wrapped in Rainbows: The Life of Zora Neale Hurston* (New York: Scribner, 2003), 166.

41. Hurston to Langston Hughes, July 10, 1928, in *Hurston: A Life in Letters*, 121–23.

42. Hurston, *Mules*, 10.

43. Hurston to Langston Hughes, November 22, 1928, in *Hurston: A Life in Letters*, 131–32.

44. Anthea Kraut, *Choreographing the Folk: The Dance Stagings of Zora Neale Hurston* (Minneapolis: University of Minnesota Press, 2008).

45. Hurston, *Mules*, 142–43; subsequent page citations to *Mules* are given parenthetically in the text.

46. Brooks, " 'Sister, Can You Line Out?,' " 620 n. 9.

47. David G. Nicholls, *Conjuring the Folk: Forms of Modernity in African America* (Ann Arbor: University of Michigan Press, 2000), 44.

48. Diana Taylor, *The Archive and the Repertoire: Performing Cultural Memory in the Americas* (Durham, NC: Duke University Press, 2003).

49. Hurston to Hughes, April 12, 1928, in *Hurston: A Life in Letters*, 115.

50. Hurston, *Dust Tracks*, 690, emphasis added.

51. For "there is just as much dignity," see Washington, "The Atlanta Exposition Address," in *Up from Slavery*, 220.

7. AESTHETICIZING LABOR, PERFORMING DIASPORA

52. This footage can be seen in Sam Pollard, dir., *Zora Neale Hurston: Jump at the Sun* (2008), written by Kristy Andersen, DVD, home edition, dual-layer format (San Francisco: California Newsreel, 2009).

53. "Handsome black torsos" from Hurston, *Mules*, 68; "sweating black bodies" from Hurston, *Dust Tracks*, 690.

54. Hurston, "Characteristics of Negro Expression," 831, 840.

55. Ifeoma Nwankwo provides a similar reading of this scene in "Insider and Outsider, Black and American: Rethinking Zora Neale Hurston's Caribbean Ethnography," *Radical History Review* 87 (2003): 56.

56. Hurston to Hughes, April 12, 1928, in *Hurston: A Life in Letters*, 116.

57. Hurston to Thomas E. Jones, October 12, 1934, in *Hurston: A Life in Letters*, 314–15.

58. Robert Hemenway, *Zora Neale Hurston: A Literary Biography* (Urbana: University of Illinois Press, 1980), 102.

59. "Zora Hurston's 'Singing Steel' for Chicago," *Baltimore Afro-American*, November 10, 1934.

60. Denning, *Cultural Front*, xvi–xvii.

61. Hurston, *Dust Tracks*, 701.

62. Hurston to Charlotte Osgood Mason, October 15, 1931, in *Hurston: A Life in Letters*, 231.

63. See program notes for the performance of *From Sun to Sun* at Rollins College, February 11, 1933, box 13, folder 2, Zora Neale Hurston Papers, George A. Smathers Libraries, University of Florida, Gainesville.

64. Cheryl Wall, editorial note, in *Hurston: Folklore, Memoirs, and Other Writings*, 969.

65. Eileen Southern, *The Music of Black Americans: A History*, 2nd ed. (New York: Norton, 1983), 433.

66. *From Sun to Sun* program, February 11, 1933, Zora Neale Hurston Papers.

67. Zora Neale Hurston, "Spirituals and Neo-spirituals" (1934), in *Hurston: Folklore, Memoirs, and Other Writings*, 869.

68. Hurston, "Characteristics of Negro Expression," 845.

69. Hurston, "Spirituals and Neo-spirituals," 870.

70. No complete scripts of Hurston's folk concerts have survived. Therefore, my analysis is based primarily on partial drafts of scripts found in the Moorland-Spingarn Research Center at Howard University and the Smathers Library at the University of Florida, playbills (also at the Smathers Library), contemporaneous reviews published in newspapers, and Hurston's autobiographical writings.

71. Zora Neale Hurston, *The Passing of a Day*, typescript, Alain Locke Papers, Manuscript Division, Moorland-Spingarn Research Center, Howard University, Washington, DC.

72. Zora Neale Hurston, *From Sun to Sun*, typescript, 3, Alain Locke Papers.

73. Hurston to Edwin Osgood Grover, June 15, 1932, in *Hurston: A Life in Letters*, 260.

74. Hurston, *Passing of a Day*, 2–3.

75. Hurston, *Passing of a Day*, 4–5.

76. Sterling Brown, "Old Time Tales," *New Masses*, February 25, 1936.

77. Hurston, *From Sun to Sun*, 5.

78. Zora Neale Hurston, *Polk County* (1944), in *Zora Neale Hurston: Collected Plays*, ed. Jean Lee Cole and Charles Mitchell (New Brunswick, NJ: Rutgers University Press, 2008), 271.

79. Hurston, *From Sun to Sun*, 5.

80. Zora Neale Hurston, "Go Gator and Muddy the Water" (1938), in *Go Gator and Muddy the Water*, 70.

81. Howard Johnson, "Bahamian Labor Migration to Florida in the Late Nineteenth and Early Twentieth Centuries," *International Migration Review* 22, no. 1 (1988): 85.

82. Hahamovitch, *Fruits of Their Labor*, 123.

83. Zora Neale Hurston, "Other Negro Folklore Influences" (1938), in *Go Gator and Muddy the Water*, 93.

7. AESTHETICIZING LABOR, PERFORMING DIASPORA   413

84. Hurston, *Dust Tracks*, 700.
85. "THE FIRE DANCE, January 25, 1939 — 8 P. M." typescript, box 13, folder 6, Zora Neale Hurston Papers.
86. Hurston, *Dust Tracks*, 701.
87. Zora Neale Hurston, "Dance Songs and Tales from the Bahamas," *Journal of American Folklore* 43, no. 169 (1930): 295.
88. Kraut, *Choreographing the Folk*, 119–44.
89. Hurston to Langston Hughes, October 15, 1929, in *Hurston: A Life in Letters*, 149.
90. Hurston, "Other Negro Folklore Influences," in *Go Gator and Muddy the Water*, 90.
91. Hurston, *The Passing of a Day*, 4
92. Hurston, *From Sun to Sun*, 7–8.
93. Hurston, *From Sun to Sun*, 7–8.
94. Hahamovitch, *Fruits of Their Labor*, 113–37.
95. Hahamovitch, *Fruits of Their Labor*, 128.
96. Zora Neale Hurston, "Concert" (c. 1942?), in *Hurston: Folklore, Memoirs, and Other Writings*, 805–8.
97. Huston, *The Passing of a Day*, 8.
98. Kraut, *Choreographing the Folk*, 144.
99. The fire dance performed for the Federal Writers' Project in Florida in 1939, for instance, was described as "a folk dance that originated in Africa . . . brought to Florida by immigrant Negro workers from the Bahama Islands." "THE FIRE DANCE, January 25, 1939 — 8 P. M," typescript.
100. Hurston, "Concert," 808.
101. Thomas F. DeFrantz and Anita Gonzalez, *Black Performance Theory* (Durham, NC: Duke University Press, 2014), 2.
102. Nwankwo, "Insider and Outsider," 68–69; John Carlos Rowe, "Opening the Gate to the Other America: The Afro-Caribbean Politics of Hurston's *Mules and Men* and *Tell My Horse*," in *Literary Culture and U.S. Imperialism: From the Revolution to World War II* (Oxford: Oxford University Press, 2000), 253–92.
103. Daphne Lamothe, "Vodou Imagery, African-American Tradition, and Cultural Transformation in Zora Neale Hurston's 'Their Eyes Were Watching God,'" *Callaloo* 22, no. 1 (1999): 171.
104. Hemenway, *Zora Neale Hurston*, 249.
105. Zora Neale Hurston, *Tell My Horse* (1938), in *Hurston: Folklore, Memoirs, and Other Writings*, 323.
106. Hurston, "Characteristics of Negro Expression," 835.
107. Hurston, *Tell My Horse*, 479.
108. Hurston, "Characteristics of Negro Expression," 832.
109. "U.S. Woman Anthropologist on Hoodoo Hunt in Jamaica," *Daily Gleaner*, April 24, 1936.
110. "Shortwood Old Students Sponsor Brilliant Function at South Camp Rd. Hotel," *Daily Gleaner*, May 28, 1936.
111. "American Lady Writer Gives Lecture at Quill and Ink Club," *Daily Gleaner*, July 25, 1936.
112. "Greatest Distinction in Island Is Between Colour and Colour," *Daily Gleaner*, July 23, 1936.
113. O. Nigel Bolland, "Labor Protests, Rebellions, and the Rise of Nationalism During Depression and War," in *The Caribbean: A History of the Region and Its People*, ed. Stephan Palmié and Francisco A. Scarano (Chicago: University of Chicago Press, 2001), 471.
114. Hurston, *Tell My Horse*, 326.
115. Winston James, "Culture, Labor, and Race in the Shadow of US Capital," in *The Caribbean*, ed. Palmié and Scarano, 455.
116. "Shortwood Old Students."

117. "Shortwood Old Students."

118. "Greatest Distinction in Island Is Between Colour and Colour."

119. Leigh Anne Duck refers to Hurston as a "cultural populist," distinct from a "cultural nationalist." Cultural populism is "a belief system similarly hostile to cultural hierarchies but not necessarily interested in stabilizing the meaning of 'race' or prioritizing it as a political category." Duck, "'Rebirth of a Nation': Hurston in Haiti," *Journal of American Folklore* 117, no. 464 (Spring 2004): 130.

120. What Hurston said is reported in "Shortwood Old Students," capitalization in the original.

121. "Greatest Distinction in Island Is Between Colour and Colour." My reference to English as "a tool to be broken" and so on refers back to the previous long quote from "Shortwood Old Students."

122. Hurston quoted in "American Lady Writer."

123. For instance, whereas the *Gleaner* article "American Lady Writer" lists "symmetry" as a dominant characteristic of Black folk practices, in the "Characteristics of Negro Expression" essay Hurston identifies *a*symmetry as a primary characteristic. The former may have been a typo or mishearing on the part of the journalist, however, since it is inconsistent with Hurston's original "Characteristics" essay.

124. Hurston, "Characteristics of Negro Expression," 830, as reported in "American Lady Writer."

125. As reported in "Greatest Distinction in Island Is Between Colour and Colour."

126. "American Lady Writer."

127. "Shortwood Old Students."

128. "American Lady Writer."

129. Zora Neale Hurston, "At the Sound of the Conch Shell," review of *New Day* by Victor Stafford Reid, *New York Herald Tribune*, weekly book review, March 20, 1949.

130. Unattributed excerpts of Hurston, "At the Sound of the Conch Shell," *Daily Gleaner*, March 21, 1949.

131. M. Keith Booker and Dubravka Juraga, "V. S. Reid: *New Day*," in *The Caribbean Novel in English: An Introduction* (Portsmouth, NH: Heinemann, 2001), 131–35; Victor L. Chang, "'So Differently from What the Heart Arranged': *Voices Under the Window, New Day*, and *A Quality of Violence*," in *The Routledge Companion to Anglophone Caribbean Literature*, ed. Michael A. Bucknor and Alison Donnell (London: Routledge, 2011), 165–72.

132. Rev. Jeremiah Wright, "Different, Not Deficient," *The Guardian*, April 28, 2008, https://www.theguardian.com/commentisfree/2008/apr/28/differentnotdeficient.

8. OF SHIPS AND PLANTATIONS: MARCUS GARVEY AND THE UNIA'S VISION OF A PAN-AFRICAN AGRO-INDUSTRIAL EMPIRE

1. "Speech by Marcus Garvey," December 18, 1927, in *Marcus Garvey and Universal Negro Improvement Association Papers*, 10 vols., ed. Robert A. Hill (Berkeley: University of California Press, 1983–2006), 7:59, hereafter *MG and UNIA Papers*.

2. *MG and UNIA Papers*, 6:11–12 n. 2.

3. "Enclosure: Application for Executive Clemency by Marcus Garvey," June 13, 1925, in *MG and UNIA Papers*, ed. Hill, 6:189.

4. See the ad from *Negro World*, November 1, 1924, shown in figure 8.1. Notably, the voyage itinerary listed only ports of call in the Caribbean and Central America, and as the departure date neared, the U.S. South was removed from the list of locales. The voyage was eventually advertised as a trip to the Caribbean and Central America exclusively, though, in fact, it made several stops in the U.S. South.

8. OF SHIPS AND PLANTATIONS

5. Marcus Garvey, "American Negro Tourists Going to the West Indies Aboard Ship of Negro Race," *Negro World*, December 6, 1924.

6. Garvey, "American Negro Tourists."

7. Marcus Garvey, "Getting Ready for Cruise of the West Indies and Central America," *Negro World*, November 29, 1924.

8. Paul Gilroy, *Against Race: Imagining Political Culture Beyond the Color Line* (Cambridge, MA: Belknap Press of Harvard University Press, 2000), 231–34.

9. Stephens, *Black Empire*, 2, 31.

10. Mary G. Rolinson, *Grassroots Garveyism: The Universal Negro Improvement Association in the Rural South, 1920–1927* (Chapel Hill: University of North Carolina Press, 2007), 103.

11. Rolinson, *Grassroots Garveyism*, 88.

12. Rolinson, *Grassroots Garveyism*, 88.

13. Colin Grant, *Negro with a Hat: The Rise and Fall of Marcus Garvey* (Oxford: Oxford University Press, 2008), 185.

14. Grant, *Negro with a Hat*, 25, 29.

15. Elton C. Fax, *Garvey: The Story of a Pioneer Black Nationalist* (New York: Dodd, Mead, 1972), 30.

16. Ronald Harpelle, "Cross Currents in the Western Caribbean: Marcus Garvey and the UNIA in Central America," *Caribbean Studies* 31, no. 1 (2003): 49.

17. Fax, *Garvey*, 33.

18. Harpelle, "Cross Currents," 49.

19. Rupert Lewis, "Garvey's Forerunners: Love and Bedward," *Race and Class* 28, no. 3 (1987): 35–36; Robert J. Love, "The Affair of Booker T. Washington," *Jamaica Advocate*, November 2, 1901. In 1901, President Theodore Roosevelt invited Washington, who served as his African American adviser, to dine at the White House and discuss public affairs. It was the first time an African American was entertained there. The visit elicited considerable criticism and backlash in the white press, especially in the U.S. South.

20. "The Negro in Conference at Tuskegee Institute," *African Times and Orient Review*, July 1912; Washington, "Tuskegee Institute."

21. Marcus Garvey, "The Negro's Greatest Enemy," in *The Philosophy and Opinions of Marcus Garvey, or Africa for the Africans*, vols. 1 and 2 (in one book), comp. Amy Jacques Garvey (1923, 1925, reprint, Dover, MA: Majority Press, 1986), 2:126.

22. "Newspaper Report: Improvement Association, City Life, and the Development of the State Debate in Kingston," October 16, 1914, in *MG and UNIA Papers*, ed. Hill, 1:79–80.

23. "Newspaper Reports: Location Association," November 5, 1914, and "Visit to Hope Farm School by Members of the Negro Improvement Association of Kingston, Interesting Outing, Proposal Is to Send a Few Students to Study Agriculture," November 14, 1914, in *MG and UNIA Papers*, ed. Hill, 1:89, 90–91.

24. "Newspaper Report: Improvement Association Proposal to Establish Industrial Farm in Jamaica," August 3, 1915, and "Address by Marcus Garvey," August 26, 1915, in *MG and UNIA Papers*, ed. Hill, 1:128, 1:135.

25. *MG and UNIA Papers*, ed. Hill, 1:80–81 n. 4; Shani Roper, "Creating Good Colonial Citizens: Industrial Schools and Reformatories in Victorian Jamaica," in *Victorian Jamaica*, ed. Tim Barringer and Wayne Modest (Durham, NC: Duke University Press, 2018), 204, 207 n. 46.

26. "Newspaper Report: Improvement Association Proposal to Establish Industrial Farm in Jamaica," August 3, 1915, in *MG and UNIA Papers*, ed. Hill, 1:128.

27. "Appeal by Marcus Garvey: The Proposed Industrial Farm," September 9, 1915, in *MG and UNIA Papers*, ed. Hill, 1:139.

28. "Marcus Garvey to Emmett J. Scott, Secretary of Tuskegee Institute," February 4, 1916, and editorial note to "Letter of Recommendation," February 18, 1916, in *MG and UNIA Papers*, ed. Hill, 1:173, 175.

29. "Report of Delegates," 710.

30. "Garveyism: An Interview with Marcus Garvey, A. U. N. I. Head," *Baltimore Afro-American*, August 12, 1921.

31. "Address by Marcus Garvey," November 1, 1923, in *MG and UNIA Papers*, ed. Hill, 5:490. For Garvey's appropriation of Washington's "cast down your buckets" phrase, see "Speech by Marcus Garvey," September 7, 1921, in *MG and UNIA Papers*, ed. Hill, 4:35, and editorial notes 10 and 12 on 4:43.

32. "Speech by Marcus Garvey," October 16, 1921, in *MG and UNIA Papers*, ed. Hill, 4:120.

33. Marcus Garvey, "Booker T. Washington's Program," in *Philosophy and Opinions*, 1:56.

34. "Convention Report," August 21, 1922, in *MG and UNIA Papers*, 4:939–40.

35. "Convention Report," August 21, 1922, in *MG and UNIA Papers*, 4:938, 940.

36. Stephens, *Black Empire*, 22, 109–10; Tony Martin, *Race First: The Ideological and Organizational Struggles of Marcus Garvey and the Universal Improvement Association* (Dover, MA: Majority Press, 1976), 152.

37. "The Free Ship and the Slave Ship and Our Ship," *Negro World*, February 7, 1925.

38. A. Phillip Randolph, "The Only Way to Redeem Africa," *Messenger* 5, no. 1 (January 1923): 570.

39. Grant, *Negro with a Hat*, 352.

40. Zora Neale Hurston, "The Emperor Effaces Himself" (c. 1924–1925), in *You Don't Know Us Negroes and Other Essays*, ed. Genevieve West and Henry Louis Gates Jr. (New York: Amistad 35, 2022), 180.

41. Tony Martin, *Literary Garveyism: Garvey, Black Arts, and the Harlem Renaissance* (Dover, MA: Majority Press, 1983), x.

42. "Speech by Marcus Garvey," December 14, 1924, in *MG and UNIA Papers*, ed. Hill, 6:70.

43. "Convention Report," August 14, 1924, in *MG and UNIA Papers*, ed. Hill, 5:737.

44. Mark D. Matthews, "Booker T. Washington and His Relationship to Garveyism: An Assessment," *Western Journal of Black Studies* 7, no. 2 (1983): 110.

45. Rolinson, *Grassroots Garveyism*, 88.

46. Matthews, "Booker T. Washington and His Relationship to Garveyism," 106.

47. *New York Times*, February 1, 1925; *New York Amsterdam News*, February 4, 1925.

48. "Articles in the Daily Worker," October 28–November 10, 1930, in *MG and UNIA Papers*, ed. Hill, 7:422–40.

49. There was a steamship committee at the UNIA Convention of 1929, for instance. Martin, *Race First*, 164.

50. Erna Brodber, *Louisiana* (Jackson: University Press of Mississippi, 1994), 153; Adam Ewing, "Challenge of Garveyism Studies," *Modern American History* 1, no. 3 (November 2018): 417.

51. "Convention Reports," August 30, 1922, in *MG and UNIA Papers*, ed. Hill, 4:1036.

52. "Convention Reports," August 14, 1922, in *MG and UNIA Papers*, ed. Hill, 4:860.

53. Garvey's speech is included in Laurence Bro[g] (?), "Hon. Marcus Garvey Electrifies Audience at Panama Prospective Chapter of U.N.I.A.," *Negro World*, June 4, 1921.

54. "Convention Report," August 14, 1924, in *MG and UNIA Papers*, ed. Hill, 5:737.

55. "Convention Reports," August 14, 1922, in *MG and UNIA Papers*, ed. Hill, 4:872.

56. "Autobiography: Articles from the *Pittsburgh Courier*" (articles published between March 1 and May 31, 1930), in Marcus Garvey, *Marcus Garvey: Life and Lessons*, ed. Robert A. Hill (Berkeley: University of California Press, 1987), 92.

57. "Autobiography: Articles from the *Pittsburgh Courier*," in *Life and Lessons*, 91.

58. Marcus Garvey, "Travel as Aid to Race Advancement Urged by Garvey on Negroes of U.S.," *Negro World*, January 5, 1929.

59. "Sink Petty Differences and Unite for Promotion of Common Cause," *Negro World*, April 14, 1928.

8. OF SHIPS AND PLANTATIONS

417

60. "Report on the UNIA Convention Opening," August 1, 1914, in *MG and UNIA Papers*, ed. Hill, 5:622.

61. Garvey, "Travel as Aid to Race."

62. "Autobiography: Articles from the *Pittsburgh Courier*," in *Life and Lessons*, 92–93.

63. "Convention Report," August 15, 1924, in *MG and UNIA Papers*, ed. Hill, 5:742.

64. "Autobiography: Articles from the *Pittsburgh Courier*," in *Life and Lessons*, 92–93.

65. "Convention Report," August 15, 1924, in *MG and UNIA Papers*, ed. Hill, 5:742–45.

66. Adam Ewing, "An Ethiopian Tent: Garveyism and the Roots of Caribbean Labor Radicalism," *Africology: The Journal of Pan African Studies* 10, no. 9 (October 2017): 199–200.

67. Ewing, "An Ethiopian Tent," 199 ("met amicably" is from Ewing; "they should not fight" is from Garvey quoted in Ewing).

68. Ronald N. Harpelle, "Radicalism and Accommodation: Garveyism in a United Fruit Company Enclave," *Journal of Iberian and Latin American Research* 6, no. 1 (July 2000): 10.

69. Harpelle, "Radicalism and Accommodation," 11; Harpelle, "Cross Currents," 58.

70. Ewing, "An Ethiopian Tent," 198, 200; "retreat from radicalism" quoted from Robert A. Hill, "General Introduction," in *MG and UNIA Papers*, 1:lxxviii.

71. Stephens, *Black Empire*, 100.

72. Stephens, *Black Empire*, 19.

73. Mitman, *Empire of Rubber*, 61.

74. Marcus Garvey, "African Fundamentalism," in *Life and Lessons*, 23.

75. Ewing, "Challenge of Garveyism Studies," 416.

76. Marcus Garvey, "Capitalism and the State," in *Philosophy and Opinions*, 2:72.

77. Marcus Garvey, "Speech by Marcus Garvey," September 4, 1921, in *MG and UNIA Papers*, ed. Hill, 4:24.

78. Marcus Garvey, "Communism and the Negro," in *MG and UNIA Papers*, ed. Hill, 7:682.

79. "Convention Report," August 18, 1924, in *MG and UNIA Papers*, ed. Hill, 5:749.

80. Garvey, "Communism and the Negro," in *MG and UNIA Papers*, ed. Hill, 7:681.

81. Garvey, "Communism and the Negro," in *MG and UNIA Papers*, ed. Hill, 7:682; Marcus Garvey, "International Convention Enters Vigorous Protest Against Recruiting of War Veterans by Spanish to Fight Moors in Morocco," *Negro World*, August 27, 1921.

82. C. Boyd James, *Garvey, Garveyism, and the Antinomies in Black Redemption* (Trenton, NJ: Africa World Press, 2009), 10–13.

83. Stephens, *Black Empire*, 100.

84. Garvey, "Capitalism and the State," in *Philosophy and Opinions*, 72.

85. Rolinson, *Grassroots Garveyism*, 130.

86. Daniel Hanglberger, "Marcus Garvey and His Relation to (Black) Socialism and Communism," *American Communist History* 17, no. 2 (2018): 218.

87. "Convention Reports," August 14, 1922, in *MG and UNIA Papers*, ed. Hill, 4:859.

88. "Thriving Business Enterprises of the Universal Negro Improvement Association," *Negro World*, July 8, 1922.

89. "Department of Labor and Industry," *Negro World*, February 4, 1922; "Department of Labor and Industry," *Negro World*, February 11, 1922.

90. Jessica Gordon Nembhard, *Collective Courage: A History of African American Cooperative Economic Thought* (University Park: Pennsylvania University Press, 2014), 70. The Rochdale Society of Equitable Pioneers established the first modern cooperative in England in 1844, and its principles, which were adopted by the International Cooperative Alliance in 1895, are largely regarded as the benchmark for how cooperatives should operate.

91. White, *Freedom Farmers*, 15–16.

92. "Department of Labor and Industry," February 11, 1922.

418   8. OF SHIPS AND PLANTATIONS

93. W. J. Hyatt, "Our Money: Practical Business Suggestions," *Negro World*, March 4, 1922.

94. "Convention Reports," August 30, 1922, in *MG and UNIA Papers*, ed. Hill, 4:1036, 1035.

95. Jarod Roll, "Agrarian Producerism After Populism: Socialism and Garveyism in the Rural South," in *Populism in the South Revisited: New Interpretations and New Departures*, ed. James M. Beeby (Jackson: University Press of Mississippi, 2012), 199–226.

96. "Review of Third Week of International Convention of Negroes of the World," *Negro World*, August 26, 1922.

97. "Convention Reports," August 14, 1922, in *MG and UNIA Papers*, ed. Hill, 4:860–62; "Review of Third Week."

98. "Convention Report," August 15, 1924, in *MG and UNIA Papers*, ed. Hill, 5:742–43.

99. Spires, *Practice of Citizenship*, 8.

100. Carole Boyce Davies and Babacar M'Bow, "Towards African Diaspora Citizenship: Politicizing an Existing Global Geography," in *Black Geographies and the Politics of Place*, ed. Katherine McKittrick and Clyde Woods (Cambridge, MA: South End Press, 2007), 27.

101. Stephens, *Black Empire*, 99–100.

102. "The Negro as a Manufacturer," *Negro World*, September 16, 1922.

103. "Mrs. Kate Fenner of 1385 Osceola St., Denver, Col.," *Negro World*, September 30, 1922.

104. Martin, *Race First*, 122–37; Mitman, *Empire of Rubber*, 52–57.

105. "Our Farmers Should Raise Their Home Supplies," *Negro World*, January 23, 1926.

106. "International Convention of the Negro Peoples of the World," *Negro World*, March 2, 1929.

107. "Revived Programme of the Universal Negro Improvement Association: Five-Year Plan to Be Executed," *Black Man* 1, no. 9 (August–September 1935): 5–6.

EPILOGUE: GATHERING AND ASSESSING OUR HARVESTS; OR, LESSONS FROM OUR EXPERIMENT PLOTS

1. For more on Claude McKay's unfavorable depictions of southern African Americans throughout his work, see Julius B. Fleming Jr., " '[Not Altogether One of Them': Blackness, Diaspora, and the Limits of Transnationalism in Claude McKay's Fiction," as yet unpublished.

2. Wynter, "Black Metamorphosis," 63.

3. Eleanor Marie Brown and Ian Ayres, "The Nature of the Farm: Explaining Different Methods of Feeding Enslaved People in the Antebellum South and British West Indies," Penn State Law Research Paper No. 08-2021, April 29, 2021.

4. Parsard, "Siphon," 57–58.

5. McKittrick, *Demonic Grounds,* 45.

6. Hartman, *Scenes of Subjection*, 115; McKittrick, *Demonic Grounds*, xxiii.

7. Tiya Miles, "Beyond a Boundary: Black Lives and the Settler–Native Divide," *William and Mary Quarterly* 76, no. 3 (July 2019): 426.

8. Miles, "Beyond a Boundary."

9. Jovan Scott Lewis, *Violent Utopia: Dispossession and Black Restoration in Tulsa* (Durham, NC: Duke University Press, 2022), 189. Lewis is explicitly interested in Black people's relationship to land beyond the plantation regions of the U. S. South, such as in Indian Territory; however, his assessment rings true of the plantation South, too.

10. Unraveling these relations is made even more complex by the fact that at least one "free negro" named Mary lived among the Creeks in Indian Tuskegee, suggesting that Blackness was not necessarily the precondition for bondage. Kathryn E. Holland Braund, "The Creek Indians, Blacks,

and Slavery," *Journal of Southern History* 57, no. 4 (November 1991): 601–36; Braund, "The African American Experience and the Creek War, 1813–14: An Annotated Bibliography," 2017, http://npshistory.com/publications/hobe/braund-2017.pdf; "1832 Creek Nation Census," https://freepages.rootsweb.com/~texlance/genealogy/1832census/tuskeega.htm.

11. Tiffany Lethabo King, *Black Shoals: Offshore Formations of Black and Native Studies* (Durham, NC: Duke University Press, 2019), xi.

12. Cecília Olliveira, "Tourists Visit Plantation in Brazil and Are Served by Black 'Slaves,'" *Intercept*, December 6, 2016, https://theintercept.com/2016/12/06/tourists-visit-plantation-in-brazil-and-are-served-by-black-slaves/.

Bibliography

ARCHIVAL COLLECTIONS

Alain Locke Papers. Manuscript Division, Moorland-Spingarn Research Center, Howard University, Washington, DC.

Booker T. Washington Papers. Manuscript Division, Library of Congress, Washington, DC.

"1832 Creek Nation Census." N.d. https://freepages.rootsweb.com/~texlance/genealogy/1832census/tuskeega.htm. Accessed March 3, 2024.

George Washington Carver Papers. Tuskegee University Archives, Tuskegee, AL.

Institute of the Black World Papers. Schomburg Center for Research in Black Culture, New York Public Library.

Manuscripts, Archives, and Rare Books Division. Schomburg Center for Research in Black Culture, New York Public Library.

National Library of Jamaica. Kingston, Jamaica.

Papers of Booker T. Washington (1887–1915): The Tuskegee Collection. Tuskegee University Archives, Tuskegee, AL.

Recorded Sound Section. Library of Congress, Washington, DC.

Robert A. Hill Collection. David M. Rubenstein Rare Book and Manuscript Library, Duke University, Durham, NC.

Tuskegee Annual Catalogue. Tuskegee University Archives, Tuskegee, AL. Also available online via HathiTrust and Archives.org.

Walter Hines Page Papers. Houghton Library, Harvard University, Cambridge, MA.

Zora Neale Hurston Papers. George A. Smathers Libraries, University of Florida, Gainesville.

PERIODICALS

Baltimore Afro-American
Brooklyn Daily Eagle
Carbondale Free Press
Century Magazine

Chicago Broad Ax
Chicago Defender
Christian Register
Cleveland Gazette
Colored American
Continent
Cuba News
Daily Gleaner
The Freeman
Gleaner
Goodwill
Indianapolis Freeman
Jamaica Advocate
Jamaica Times
Labor nueva
La lucha
Le moniteur
Negro Farmer
Negro World
New York Age
New York Amsterdam News
New York Liberator
New York Times
Le nouvelliste
Opportunity
Outlook
Pittsburgh Courier
Southern Letter. Tuskegee University Archives, Tuskegee, AL.
Tuskegee Messenger. Tuskegee University Archives, Tuskegee, AL, and Schomburg Center for Research in Black Culture, New York Public Library.
Tuskegee Student. Tuskegee University Archives, Tuskegee, AL, and Schomburg Center for Research in Black Culture, New York Public Library.

PUBLICATIONS

Ali, Omar H. *In the Lion's Mouth: Black Populism in the New South, 1886–1900.* Jackson: University of Mississippi Press, 2010.

Amrillas-Tiseyra, Magalí, and Anne Garland Mahler. "Introduction: New Critical Directions in Global South Studies." In "New Critical Directions in Global South Studies," ed. Magalí Amrillas-Tiseyra and Anne Garland Mahler. Special issue, *Comparative Literature Studies* 58, no. 3 (2021): 465–84.

——. "Introduction: New Critical Directions in Global South Studies, Continuing the Conversation." In "New Critical Directions in Global South Studies, Continuing the Conversation," ed. Magalí Amrillas-Tiseyra and Anne Garland Mahler. Special issue, *Comparative Literature Studies* 59, no. 1 (2021): 1–10.

Anderson, James D. *The Education of Blacks in the South, 1860–1935.* Chapel Hill: University of North Carolina Press, 1988.

BIBLIOGRAPHY

Andrews, William L. "The Representation of Slavery and the Rise of Afro-American Literary Realism, 1865–1920." In *Slavery and the Literary Imagination*, ed. Deborah McDowell and Arnold Rampersad, 62–80. Baltimore, MD: Johns Hopkins University Press, 1989.

Antoine, Jacques C. *Jean Price-Mars and Haiti*. Washington, DC: Three Continents Press, 1981.

Archer, Chalmers, Jr. *Growing Up Black in Rural Mississippi: Memories of a Family, Heritage of a Place*. New York: Walker, 1992.

Arroyo, Jossianna. *Writing Secrecy in Caribbean Freemasonry*. New York: Palgrave Macmillan, 2013.

Attache [*sic*]. "En el Sur." *Labor nueva* 1, no. 18 (June 18, 1916): 5–6.

Ayala, César J. *American Sugar Kingdom: The Plantation Economy of the Spanish Caribbean, 1898–1934*. Chapel Hill: University of North Carolina Press, 1999.

Baker, Houston A., Jr. *Modernism and the Harlem Renaissance*. Chicago: University of Chicago Press, 1987.

——. *Turning South Again: Re-thinking Modernism/Re-reading Booker T.* Durham, NC: Duke University Press, 2001.

Baker, Houston A., Jr., and Dana D. Nelson. "Preface: Violence, the Body, and 'the South.' " In "Violence, the Body, and 'the South,' " ed. Houston A. Baker Jr. Special issue, *American Literature* 73, no. 2 (June 2001): 231–44.

Baldwin, Davarian. *Chicago's New Negroes: Modernity, the Great Migration, and Black Urban Life*. Chapel Hill: University of North Carolina Press, 2007.

——. "Introduction: New Negroes Forging a New World." In *Escape from New York: The New Negro Renaissance Beyond Harlem*, ed. Davarian Baldwin and Minkah Makalani, 1–28. Minneapolis: University of Minnesota Press, 2013.

Baldwin, Davarian, and Minkah Makalani. *Escape from New York: The New Negro Renaissance Beyond Harlem*. Minneapolis: University of Minnesota Press, 2013.

Barnes, Albert C. "Negro Art and America." In *The New Negro: Voices of the Harlem Renaissance*, ed. Alain Locke, 19–25. 1925. Reprint. New York: Touchstone, 1997.

Barnes, Andrew E. *Global Christianity and the Black Atlantic: Tuskegee, Colonialism, and the Shaping of African Industrial Education*. Waco, TX: Baylor University Press, 2017.

Beals, Carleton. "The Black Belt of the Caribbean." *American Mercury* 24, no. 94 (1931): 129–38.

Beckert, Sven. *Empire of Cotton: A Global History*. New York: Vintage, 2014.

——. "From Tuskegee to Togo: The Problem of Freedom in the Empire of Cotton." *Journal of American History* 92, no. 2 (September 2005): 498–526.

Beckford, George. *Persistent Poverty: Underdevelopment in Plantation Economies of the Third World*. New York: Oxford University Press, 1972.

Benítez-Rojo, Antonio. *The Repeating Island: The Caribbean and the Postmodern Perspective*. 2nd ed. Durham, NC: Duke University Press, 1996.

Bieze, Michael. *Booker T. Washington and the Art of Self-Representation*. New York: Peter Lang, 2008.

——. "Ruskin in the Black Belt: Booker T. Washington, Arts and Crafts, and the New Negro." *Source: Notes in the History of Art* 24, no. 4 (Summer 2005): 24–34.

Bieze, Michael, and Marybeth Gasman, eds. *Booker T. Washington Rediscovered*. Baltimore, MD: Johns Hopkins University Press, 2012.

Boletin oficial de la secretaria de estado. Havana, Cuba: Imprenta y Papeleria de Rambla, Bouza Y C, Obispo nums. 33 y 35, 1913. https://archive.org/details/xivcongresointer10inte/page/n7/mode/2up.

Bolland, O. Nigel. "Labor Protests, Rebellions, and the Rise of Nationalism During Depression and War." In *The Caribbean: A History of the Region and Its People*, ed. Stephan Palmié and Francisco A. Scarano, 459–74. Chicago: University of Chicago Press, 2001.

Bone, Martyn. "The (Extended) South of Black Folk: Intraregional and Transnational Migrant Labor in *Jonah's Gourde Vine* and *Their Eyes Were Watching God*." *American Literature* 79, no. 4 (December 2007): 753–79.

Booker, M. Keith, and Dubravka Juraga. "V. S. Reid: *New Day*." In *The Caribbean Novel in English: An Introduction*, 131–35. Portsmouth, NH: Heinemann, 2001.

Bowen, Cornelia. "A Woman's Work." In *Tuskegee and Its People: Their Ideals and Achievements*, ed. Booker T. Washington [and Emmett J. Scott], 211–23. New York: D. Appleton, 1905.

Boyd, Valerie. *Wrapped in Rainbows: The Life of Zora Neale Hurston*. New York: Scribner, 2003.

Bradley, Regina. *Chronicling Stankonia: OutKast and the Rise of the Hip Hop South*. Chapel Hill: University of North Carolina Press, 2021.

Braund, Kathryn E. Holland. "The African American Experience and the Creek War, 1813–14: An Annotated Bibliography." 2017. http://npshistory.com/publications/hobe/braund-2017.pdf.

——. "The Creek Indians, Blacks, and Slavery" *Journal of Southern History* 57, no. 4 (November 1991): 601–36.

Briggs, Gabriela A. *The New Negro in the Old South*. New Brunswick, NJ: Rutgers University Press, 2015.

Brittan, Jennifer. "The Terminal: Eric Walrond, the City of Colón, and the Caribbean of the Panama Canal." *American Literary History* 25, no. 2 (2013): 294–316.

Brodber, Erna. *Louisiana*. Jackson: University Press of Mississippi, 1994.

Brooks, Daphne A. *Bodies in Dissent: Spectacular Performances of Race and Freedom, 1850–1910*. Durham, NC: Duke University Press, 2006.

——. "'Sister, Can You Line Out?' Zora Neale Hurston and the Sound of Angular Black Womanhood." *Amerikastudien* 55, no. 4 (2010): 617–27.

Brooks, Tim. *Lost Sounds: Blacks and the Birth of the Recording Industry, 1890–1919*. Urbana: University of Illinois Press, 2004.

Brown, Eleanor Marie. "On the Evolution of Property Ownership Among Former Slaves, Newly Freedmen." George Washington University Legal Studies Research Paper No. 2016-22. June 23, 2016.

Brown, Eleanor Marie, and Ian Ayres. "The Nature of the Farm: Explaining Different Methods of Feeding Enslaved People in the Antebellum South and British West Indies." Penn State Law Research Paper No. 08-2021. April 29, 2021.

Brown, Patrice C. "The Panama Canal: The African American Experience." *Prologue* 29, no. 2 (Summer 1997). https://www.archives.gov/publications/prologue/1997/summer/panama-canal.

Brown, Sterling. "Old Time Tales." *New Masses*, February 25, 1936.

Byrd, Brandon R. *The Black Republic: African Americans and the Fate of Haiti*. Philadelphia: University of Pennsylvania Press, 2019.

——. "C. C. Spaulding and Major R. R. Wright—Companions on the Road Less Traveled? A Reconsideration of African American International Relations in the Early Twentieth Century." MA thesis, College of William and Mary, 2011.

Calhoun, Russell C. "A Negro Community Builder." In *Tuskegee and Its People: Their Ideals and Achievements*, ed. Booker T. Washington [and Emmett J. Scott], 317–37. New York: D. Appleton, 1905.

Campbell, Thomas Monroe. *The Movable School Goes to the Negro Farmer*. Tuskegee, AL: Tuskegee Institute Press, 1936.

Campt, Tina. "The Sounds of Stillness: Dwelling in the Visual Archive of Diaspora." Lecture, Center for Black Diaspora, DePaul University, Chicago, April 14, 2013. https://www.wbez.org/2013/04/14/the-sounds-of-stillness-dwelling-in-the-visual-archive-of-diaspora.

Carby, Hazel V. "The Politics of Fiction, Anthropology, and the Folk: Zora Neale Hurston." In *Cultures in Babylon: Feminism from Black Britain to African America*, 168–85. London: Verso, 1999.

Carney, Judith A. *Black Rice: The African Origins of Rice Cultivation in the Americas*. Cambridge, MA: Harvard University Press, 2001.

Carver, G. W. *Cotton Growing on Sandy Upland Soils*. Tuskegee Agricultural Experiment Station Bulletin No. 7. Tuskegee, AL: Tuskegee Institute Steam Print, 1905. https://www.nal.usda.gov/exhibits/ipd/carver/exhibits/show/bulletins/carver.

BIBLIOGRAPHY

——. *Cow Peas*. Tuskegee Agricultural Experiment Station Bulletin No. 5. Tuskegee, AL: Tuskegee Institute, 1903. https://www.nal.usda.gov/exhibits/ipd/carver/exhibits/show/bulletins/carver.

——. *Fertilizer Experiments on Cotton*. Tuskegee Agricultural Experiment Station Bulletin No. 3. Tuskegee, AL: Tuskegee Institute Steam Print, 1899. https://www.nal.usda.gov/exhibits/ipd/carver/exhibits/show/bulletins/carver.

——. *How to Build Up and Maintain the Virgin Fertility of Our Soils*. Tuskegee Agricultural Experiment Station Bulletin No. 42. Tuskegee, AL: Tuskegee Institute Press, October 1936. https://www.nal.usda.gov/exhibits/ipd/carver/exhibits/show/bulletins/carver.https://www.nal.usda.gov/exhibits/ipd/carver/exhibits/show/bulletins/carver.

——. *How to Build Up Worn Out Soils*. Tuskegee Agricultural Experiment Station Bulletin No. 6. Tuskegee, AL: Tuskegee Institute Steam Print, 1905. https://www.nal.usda.gov/exhibits/ipd/carver/exhibits/show/bulletins/carver.

——. *How To Make Cotton Growing Pay*. Tuskegee Agricultural Experiment Station Bulletin No. 14. Tuskegee, AL: Tuskegee Institute Steam Print, 1908. https://www.nal.usda.gov/exhibits/ipd/carver/exhibits/show/bulletins/carver.

——. *The Need of Scientific Agriculture in the South*. Farmer's Leaflet No. 7. Tuskegee, AL: Extension Department, Tuskegee Institute, April 1902.

——. *A New and Prolific Variety of Cotton*. Tuskegee Agricultural Experiment Station Bulletin No. 26. Tuskegee, AL: Tuskegee Institute, printed by the Tuskegee Students from funds supplied by the Ash Fund established in memory of Mrs. Ellen L. Ash, 1915. https://www.nal.usda.gov/exhibits/ipd/carver/exhibits/show/bulletins/carver.

——. *Three Delicous [sic] Meals Every Day for the Farmer*. Tuskegee Agricultural Experiment Station Bulletin No. 32. Tuskegee, AL: Tuskegee Institute, 1916.

——. *What Shall We Do for Fertilizers Next Year?* Tuskegee, AL: Agricultural Experiment Station, Tuskegee Institute, 1916.

Casado, Emilio Céspedes. *La cuestion social cubana*. Pamphlet publication of a lecture given on April 12, 1906. Havana, Cuba: La Propagandista, Imprenta y Papelería, Monte núms 87 y 89, 1906.

Casey, Matthew. *Empire's Guestworkers: Haitian Migrants in Cuba During the Age of US Occupation*. Cambridge: Cambridge University Press, 2017.

Casimir, Jean. *The Caribbean: One and Divisible*. Santiago, Chile: United Nations, 1992.

Chang, Victor L. "'So Differently from What the Heart Arranged': *Voices Under the Window, New Day*, and *A Quality of Violence*." In *The Routledge Companion to Anglophone Caribbean Literature*, ed. Michael A. Bucknor and Alison Donnell, 165–72. London: Routledge, 2011.

Chochotte, Marvin. "The Twilight of Popular Revolutions: The Suppression of Peasant Armed Struggles and Freedom in Rural Haiti During the US Occupation, 1915–1934." *Journal of African American History* 103, no. 3 (Summer 2018): 277–308.

Claborn, John. "Toward an Eco-ontology: A Response to Greg Garrard's 'Heidegger Nazism Ecocriticism.'" *ISLE: Interdisciplinary Studies in Literature and Environment* 19, no. 2 (Spring 2012): 375–79.

——. "Up from Nature: Racial Uplift and Ecological Agencies in Booker T. Washington's Autobiographies." In *Civil Rights and the Environment in African-American Literature, 1895–1941* (London: Bloomsbury Academic, 2017), 19–44.

Clukey, Amy, and Jeremy Wells. "Introduction: Plantation Modernity." In "The Global South and/in the Global North: Interdisciplinary Investigations," ed. Amy Clukey and Jeremy Wells. Special issue, *Global South* 10, no. 2 (2016): 1–10.

Colquhoun, Archibald R. "The Future of the Negro." *North American Review*, May 1903, 657–74.

Cook, Mercer. "Booker T. Washington and the French." *Journal of Negro History* 40, no. 4 (1955): 318–40.

Cooper, Anna Julia. *A Voice from the South, by a Black Woman of the South.* In *The Portable Anna Julia Cooper*, ed. Shirley Moody-Turner, 3–160. New York: Penguin, 2022.

Cooper, Brittney C. *Beyond Respectability: The Intellectual Thought of Race Women.* Urbana: University of Illinois Press, 2017.

Cooper, Brittney C., Susana M. Morris, and Robin M. Boylorn, eds. *The Crunk Feminist Collection.* New York: Feminist Press, 2017.

Cooper, Wayne F. *Claude McKay: Rebel Sojourner in the Harlem Renaissance.* Baton Rouge: Louisiana State University Press, 1987.

Crawley, Ashon T. *Blackpentecostal Breath: The Aesthetics of Possibility.* New York: Fordham University Press, 2017.

Cunard, Nancy, ed. *Negro: An Anthology.* London: Wishart, 1934.

Dagbovie, Pero Gaglo. "Exploring a Century of Historical Scholarship on Booker T. Washington." *Journal of African American History* 92, no. 2 (2007): 239–64.

Dalleo, Raphael. *American Imperialisms Undead: The Occupation of Haiti and the Rise of Caribbean Anticolonialism.* Charlottesville: University of Virginia Press, 2016.

Davies, Carole Boyce, and Babacar M'Bow. "Towards African Diaspora Citizenship: Politicizing an Existing Global Geography." In *Black Geographies and the Politics of Place*, ed. Katherine McKittrick and Clyde Woods, 14–45. Cambridge, MA: South End Press, 2007.

Davis, Janae, Alex A. Moulton, Levi Van Sant, and Brian Williams. "Anthropocene, Capitalocene, . . . Plantationocene? A Manifesto for Ecological Justice in an Age of Global Crises." *Geography Compass* 13, no. 5 (2019): art. e12438. https://doi.org/10.1111/gec3.12438.

Davis, Thadious. *Southscapes: Geographies of Race, Region, and Literature.* Chapel Hill: University of North Carolina Press, 2011.

DeFrantz, Thomas F., and Anita Gonzalez. *Black Performance Theory.* Durham, NC: Duke University Press, 2014.

de la Fuente, Alejandro. "Myths of Racial Democracy: Cuba, 1900–1912," *Latin American Research Review* 34, no. 3 (1999): 39–73.

——. *A Nation for All: Race, Inequality, and Politics in Twentieth-Century Cuba.* Chapel Hill: University of North Carolina Press, 2001.

DeLoughrey, Elizabeth, Renée K. Gosson, and George B. Handley. Introduction to *Caribbean Literature and the Environment: Between Nature and Culture*, ed. Elizabeth DeLoughrey, Renée K. Gosson, and George B. Handley, 1–30. Charlottesville: University of Virginia Press, 2005.

Denning, Michael. *The Cultural Front: The Laboring of American Culture in the Twentieth Century.* London: Verso, 1997.

Denton, Virginia Lantz. "Social Change Through Extension: Taking Adult Education to the Masses." In *Booker T. Washington and the Adult Education Movement*, 106–53. Gainesville: University Press of Florida, 1993.

Dimitry, E. L., ed. *Official Report of the Haitian Afro-American Chamber of Commerce's Commission to Study the Commercial, Agricultural, and Industrial Possibilities of the Haitian Republic, August 17 to September 4, 1934.* N.p.: n.p., [1935?].

Dixon, Melvin. "South of the South." *Callaloo*, no. 8/10 (February–October 1980): 16–17.

Dotson, Mary L. "The Story of a Teacher of Cooking." In *Tuskegee and Its People: Their Ideals and Achievements*, ed. Booker T. Washington [and Emmett J. Scott], 200–210. New York: D. Appleton, 1905.

Douglass, Frederick. *My Bondage and My Freedom.* New York: Miller, Orton & Mulligan, 1855.

Du Bois, W. E. B. "Criteria for Negro Art." *Crisis* 32, no. 6 (October 1926): 290–97.

——. "Of Mr. Booker T. Washington and Others." In *The Souls of Black Folk* (1903), 35–47. New York: Barnes & Noble Classics, 2003.

Dubois, Laurent. *Haiti: The Aftershocks of History.* New York: Holt, 2012.

BIBLIOGRAPHY

Dubois, Laurent, Kaiama L. Glover, Nadève Ménard, Millery Polyné, and Chantalle F. Verna, eds. *The Haiti Reader: History, Culture, Politics*. Durham, NC: Duke University Press, 2020.

Duck, Leigh Anne. "'Rebirth of a Nation': Hurston in Haiti." *Journal of American Folklore* 117, no. 464 (Spring 2004): 127–46.

Dunbar, Paul Laurence. "Tuskegee Song." In *The Collected Poetry of Paul Laurence Dunbar*, ed. Joanne M. Braxton, 332–33. Charlottesville: University Press of Virginia, 1993.

Durham, John Stephens. "The Hidden Wealth of Hayti." *Voice of the Negro* 1, no. 4 (April 1904): 142–46.

Edwards, Brent Hayes. "Pebbles of Consonance: A Reply to Critics." *Small Axe* 9, no. 1 (2005): 134–49.

——. *The Practice of Diaspora: Literature, Translation, and the Rise of Black Internationalism*. Cambridge, MA: Harvard University Press, 2003.

Elizondo, Joy. "Rafael Serra y Montalvo." Oxford African American Studies Center, December 1, 2006. https://doi-org.proxy.lib.duke.edu/10.1093/acref/9780195301731.013.43326.

Ewing, Adam. "Challenge of Garveyism Studies." *Modern American History* 1, no. 3 (November 2018): 399–418.

——. "An Ethiopian Tent: Garveyism and the Roots of Caribbean Labor Radicalism." *Africology: The Journal of Pan African Studies* 10, no. 9 (October 2017): 188–216.

Fax, Elton C. *Garvey: The Story of a Pioneer Black Nationalist*. New York: Dodd, Mead, 1972.

Féquière, Fleury. *L'education haitienne*. Port-au-Prince, Haiti: Imprimerie de L'Abeille, 1906.

Ferguson, Karen J. "Caught in 'No Man's Land': The Negro Cooperative Demonstration Service and the Ideology of Booker T. Washington, 1900–1918." *Agricultural History* 72, no. 1 (Winter 1998): 33–54.

Field, Allyson Nadia. *Uplift Cinema: The Emergence of African American Film and the Possibility of Black Modernity*. Durham, NC: Duke University Press, 2015.

Fleming, Julius B., Jr. *Black Patience: Performance, Civil Rights, and the Unfinished Project of Emancipation*. New York: New York University Press, 2022.

Fortune, T. Thomas. *Black and White: Land, Labor, and Politics in the South*. 1884. Reprint. New York: Atria, 2022.

——. "Who Will Own the Soil of the South in the Future?" (April 28, 1883). In *T. Thomas Fortune, the Afro-American Agitator: A Collection of Writings, 1880–1928*, ed. Shawn Leigh Alexander, 3–5. Gainesville: University Press of Florida, 2010.

Frederick, Rhonda D. *"Colón Man a Come": Mythographies of Panamá Canal Migration*. Lanham, MD: Lexington, 2005.

Furniss, Dr. H. W. "Black Republic Lovely Haiti!," *Cleveland Gazette*, July 17, 1909.

——. "Notes of Haiti: Dr. Henry W. Furniss Gives Information of Country, Its People, and Their Customs." *Indianapolis Freeman*, June 12, 1909.

Fusté, José I. "Translating Negroes Into Negros: Rafael Serra's Transamerican Entanglements Between Black Cuban Racial and Imperial Subalternity, 1895–1909." In *Afro-Latin@s in Movement: Critical Approaches to Blackness and Transnationalism in the Americas*, ed. Petra R. Rivera-Rideau, Jennifer A. Jones, and Tianna S. Paschel, 221–45. New York: Palgrave Macmillan, 2016.

Gaffield, Julia. "Complexities of Imagining Haiti: A Study of National Constitutions, 1801–1807." *Journal of Social History* 41, no. 1 (Fall 2007): 81–103.

Gaines, Kevin K. *Uplifting the Race: Black Leadership, Politics, and Culture in the Twentieth Century*. Chapel Hill: University of North Carolina Press, 1996.

Galván, Raúl C. "Rafael Serra y Montalvo: The Man and His Work." *Caribe: Revista de cultura y literatura* 15, no. 2 (2012–2013): 67–82.

García Peña, Lorgia. *Translating Blackness: Latinx Colonialities in Global Perspective*. Durham, NC: Duke University Press, 2022.

Garvey, Marcus. "American Negro Tourists Going to the West Indies Aboard Ship of Negro Race." *Negro World*, December 6, 1924.

——. "Booker T. Washington's Program." In *The Philosophy and Opinions of Marcus Garvey, or Africa for the Africans*, vols. 1 and 2 (in one book), comp. Amy Jacques Garvey, 1:56. Dover, MA: Majority Press, 1986.

——. "Capitalism and the State." In *The Philosophy and Opinions of Marcus Garvey, or Africa for the Africans*, vols. 1 and 2 (in one book), comp. Amy Jacques Garvey, 2:72–73. Dover, MA: Majority Press, 1986.

——. "Getting Ready for Cruise of the West Indies and Central America." *Negro World*, November 29, 1924.

——. "International Convention Enters Vigorous Protest Against Recruiting of War Veterans by Spanish to Fight Moors in Morocco." *Negro World*, August 27, 1921.

——. *Marcus Garvey: Life and Lessons*. Ed. Robert A. Hill. Berkeley: University of California Press, 1987.

——. "The Negro's Greatest Enemy." In *The Philosophy and Opinions of Marcus Garvey, or Africa for the Africans*, vols. 1 and 2 (in one book), comp. Amy Jacques Garvey, 2:124–34. Dover, MA: Majority Press, 1986.

——. *The Philosophy and Opinions of Marcus Garvey, or Africa for the Africans*. Vols. 1 and 2 (in one book). Comp. Amy Jacques Garvey. Dover, MA: Majority Press, 1986.

——. "Travel as Aid to Race Advancement Urged by Garvey on Negroes of U.S." *Negro World*, January 5, 1929.

Gates, Henry Louis, Jr. "The Trope of the New Negro and the Reconstruction of the Image of the Black." *Representations* 24 (1988): 129–55.

——. "The Truth Behind Forty Acres and a Mule." N.d. https://www.pbs.org/wnet/african-americans-many-rivers-to-cross/history/the-truth-behind-40-acres-and-a-mule/. Accessed August 28, 2023.

Gates, Henry Louis, Jr., and Gene Andrew Jarrett, eds. *The New Negro: Readings on Race, Representation, and African American Culture, 1892–1938*. Princeton, NJ: Princeton University Press, 2007.

Gikandi, Simon. *Slavery and the Culture of Taste*. Princeton, NJ: Princeton University Press, 2011.

Gilroy, Paul. *Against Race: Imagining Political Culture Beyond the Color Line*. Cambridge, MA: Belknap Press of Harvard University Press, 2000.

——. *The Black Atlantic: Modernity and Double Consciousness*. Cambridge, MA: Harvard University Press, 1993.

Glenn, W. E. "Building an Industrial School in Indian Territory." *Southern Letter*, August 1907.

Glissant, Édouard. "Closed Place, Open Word." In *Poetics of Relation*, trans. Betsy Wing, 63–75. Ann Arbor: University of Michigan Press, 1997.

——. "Poetics." In *Poetics of Relation*, trans. Betsy Wing, 23–36. Ann Arbor: University of Michigan Press, 1997.

Goldsby, Jacqueline. *A Spectacular Secret: Lynching in American Life and Literature*. Chicago: University of Chicago Press, 2006.

Gosciak, Josh. *The Shadowed Country: Claude McKay and the Romance of the Victorians*. New Brunswick, NJ: Rutgers University Press, 2006.

Goyal, Yogita. *Romance, Diaspora, and Black Atlantic Literature*. Cambridge: Cambridge University Press, 2010.

Grandison, Kenrick Ian. "From Plantation to Campus: Progress, Community, and the Lay of the Land in Shaping the Early Tuskegee." *Landscape Journal* 15, no. 1 (1996): 6–32.

——. "Landscapes of Terror: A Reading of Tuskegee's Historic Campus." In *The Geography of Identity*, ed. Patricia Yaeger, 334–67. Ann Arbor: University of Michigan Press, 1996.

——. "Negotiated Space: The Black College Campus as a Cultural Record of Postbellum America." *American Quarterly* 51, no. 3 (September 1999): 529–79.

Grant, Colin. *Negro with a Hat: The Rise and Fall of Marcus Garvey*. Oxford: Oxford University Press, 2008.

Great White Fleet: Summer Cruises from New York Boston New Orleans to Jamaica Havana Panama Canal Central and South America. Boston: United Fruit Company Steamship Service, 1913.

Griffin, Farah Jasmine. "The Daughter's Geography: The Poetics of Diaspora." In *The African Presence and Influence on the Cultures of the Americas*, ed. Brenda M. Greene, 71–90. Newcastle, U.K.: Cambridge Scholars, 2010.

——. *Read Until You Understand: The Profound Wisdom of Black Life and Literature.* New York: Norton, 2021.

Guridy, Frank Andre. *Forging Diaspora: Afro-Cubans and African Americans in a World of Empire and Jim Crow.* Chapel Hill: University of North Carolina Press, 2010.

Guterl, Matthew Pratt. *American Mediterranean: Southern Slaveholders in the Age of Emancipation.* Cambridge, MA: Harvard University Press, 2008.

Hahamovitch, Cindy. *The Fruits of Their Labor: Atlantic Coast Farmworkers and the Making of Migrant Poverty, 1870–1945.* Chapel Hill: University of North Carolina Press, 1997.

Hahn, Steven. *A Nation Under Our Feet: Black Political Struggles in the Rural South from Slavery to the Great Migration.* Cambridge, MA: Belknap Press of Harvard University Press, 2003.

Hamilton, R. H., arr. *Cabin and Plantation Songs as Sung by the Tuskegee Singers.* In Helen W. Ludlow, *Tuskegee Normal and Industrial School, for Training Colored Teachers: Its Story and Its Song,* 1–21 (separate pagination). Hampton, VA: Normal School Steam Press, 1884.

Hanchard, Michael. "Afro-Modernity: Temporality, Politics, and the African Diaspora." *Public Culture* 11, no. 1 (1999): 245–68.

Hanglberger, Daniel. "Marcus Garvey and His Relation to (Black) Socialism and Communism." *American Communist History* 17, no. 2 (2018): 200–219.

Harlan, Louis R. *Booker T. Washington: The Making of a Black Leader, 1856–1901.* New York: Oxford University Press, 1972.

——. *Booker T. Washington: The Wizard of Tuskegee, 1901–1915.* New York: Oxford University Press, 1983.

——. Introduction to Booker T. Washington, *Up from Slavery* (1901), vii–xlviii. New York: Penguin, 1986.

Harold, Claudrena N. *New Negro Politics in the Jim Crow South.* Athens: University of Georgia Press, 2013.

——. *The Rise and Fall of the Garvey Movement in the Urban South, 1918–1942.* New York: Routledge, 2007.

Harpelle, Ronald. "Cross Currents in the Western Caribbean: Marcus Garvey and the UNIA in Central America." *Caribbean Studies* 31, no. 1 (2003): 35–73.

——. "Radicalism and Accommodation: Garveyism in a United Fruit Company Enclave." *Journal of Iberian and Latin American Research* 6, no. 1 (July 2000): 1–28.

Harris, Sheena. *Margaret Murray Washington: The Life and Times of a Career Club Woman.* Knoxville: University of Tennessee Press, 2021.

Hartman, Saidiya. *Lose Your Mother: A Journey Along the Atlantic Slave Route.* New York: Farrar, Straus, and Giroux, 2007.

——. *Scenes of Subjection: Terror, Slavery, and Self-Making in Nineteenth-Century America.* New York: Oxford University Press, 1997.

Haywood, Harry. *Negro Liberation.* New York: International, 1948.

Helg, Aline. "Black Men, Racial Stereotyping, and Violence in the U.S. South and Cuba at the Turn of the Century." *Comparative Studies in Society and History* 42, no. 3 (July 2000): 576–604.

Hemenway, Robert. *Zora Neale Hurston: A Literary Biography.* Urbana: University of Illinois Press, 1980.

Hersey, Mark. *My Work Is That of Conservation: An Environmental Biography of George Washington Carver.* Athens: University of Georgia Press, 2011.

Hill, Errol, and James Vernon Hatch. *A History of African American Theatre.* Cambridge: Cambridge University Press, 2003.

Hill, Robert A. "General Introduction." In *Marcus Garvey and Universal Negro Improvement Association Papers,* 10 vols., ed. Robert A. Hill, 1:lxxviii–lxxx. Berkeley: University of California Press, 1983–2006.

Hill, Robert A., ed., *Marcus Garvey and Universal Negro Improvement Association Papers.* 10 vols. Berkeley: University of California Press, 1983–2006.

Holt, Thomas C. *The Problem of Freedom: Race, Labor, and Politics in Jamaica and Britain, 1832–1938.* Baltimore, MD: Johns Hopkins University Press, 1992.

hooks, bell. "In Our Glory: Photography and Black Life." In *Picturing Us: African American Identity in Photography*, ed. Deborah Willis, 43–54. New York: New Press, 1994.

Howells, W. D. "An Exemplary Citizen." *North American Review*, August 1901, 280–88.

Humphrey, R. M. "History of the Colored Farmers' National Alliance and Cooperative Union." In *The Farmers' Alliance History and Agricultural Digest*, ed. N. A. Dunning, 288–92. Washington, DC: Alliance Publishing, 1891.

Hurston, Zora Neale. "At the Sound of the Conch Shell." *New York Herald Tribune*, weekly book review, March 20, 1949.

——. "Dance Songs and Tales from the Bahamas." *Journal of American Folklore* 43, no. 169 (1930): 294–312.

——. "The Emperor Effaces Himself" (c. 1924–1925). In *You Don't Know Us Negroes and Other Essays*, ed. Genevieve West and Henry Louis Gates Jr., 173–81. New York: Amistad 35, 2022.

——. *Go Gator and Muddy the Water: Writings by Zora Neale Hurston from the Federal Writers' Project.* Ed. Pamela Bordelon. New York: Norton, 1999.

——. *Zora Neale Hurston: Collected Plays.* Ed. Jean Lee Cole and Charles Mitchell. New Brunswick, NJ: Rutgers University Press, 2008.

——. *Zora Neale Hurston: Folklore, Memoirs, and Other Writings.* Comp. Cheryl A. Wall. New York: Library of America, 1995.

——. *Zora Neale Hurston: A Life in Letters.* Ed. Carla Kaplan. New York: Doubleday, 2002.

——. *Zora Neale Hurston: Novels and Stories.* Comp. Cheryl A. Wall. New York: Library of America, 1995.

Hyatt, W. J. "Our Money: Practical Business Suggestions." *Negro World*, March 4, 1922.

Investigation of Panama Canal Matters: Hearings Before the Committee on Interoceanic Canals. Vol. 1. Washington, DC: U.S. Government Printing Office, 1907.

Jagmohan, Desmond. "Booker T. Washington and the Politics of Deception." In *African American Political Thought: A Collected History*, ed. Melvin L. Rogers and Jack Turner, 167–91. Chicago: University of Chicago Press, 2021.

Jaji, Tsitsi Ella. *Africa in Stereo: Modernism, Music, and Pan-African Solidarity.* Oxford: Oxford University Press, 2014.

Jamaica Panama Canal Central and South America. New York: Great White Fleet, United Fruit Company Steamship Service, 1912.

Jamaica Via the Great White Fleet. Boston: United Fruit Company Steamship Service, 1913.

James, C. Boyd. *Garvey, Garveyism, and the Antinomies in Black Redemption.* Trenton, NJ: Africa World Press, 2009.

James, C. L. R. *The Black Jacobins: Toussaint L'Ouverture and the San Domingo Revolution.* 2nd ed. With the appendix "From Toussaint L'Ouverture to Fidel Castro." New York: Vintage, 1989.

James, Winston. *Claude McKay: The Making of a Black Bolshevik.* New York: Columbia University Press, 2022.

——. "Culture, Labor, and Race in the Shadow of US Capital." In *The Caribbean: A History of the Region and Its People*, ed. Stephan Palmié and Francisco A. Scarano, 445–58. Chicago: University of Chicago Press, 2001.

——. *A Fierce Hatred of Injustice: Claude McKay's Jamaica and His Poetry of Rebellion.* London: Verso, 2000.

Johnson, Charles S. *Shadow of the Plantation.* Chicago: University of Chicago Press, 1934.

——. "The Social Philosophy of Booker T. Washington." *Opportunity*, April 1928.

Johnson, Howard. "Bahamian Labor Migration to Florida in the Late Nineteenth and Early Twentieth Centuries." *International Migration Review* 22, no. 1 (1988): 84–103.

Johnson, James Weldon. Preface to *The Book of American Negro Poetry*, ed. James Weldon Johnson, vii–xlviii. New York: Harcourt, Brace, 1922.

Johnston, Sir Harry H. *The Negro in the New World*. New York: Macmillan, 1910.

Jones, Allen. "Improving Rural Life for Blacks: The Tuskegee Negro Farmers' Conference, 1892–1915." *Agricultural History* 65, no. 2 (Spring 1991): 105–14.

Jones, Brian. *The Tuskegee Student Uprising: A History*. New York: New York University Press, 2022.

Jones, Jeanette Eileen Jones. "'Brightest Africa' in the New Negro Imagination." In *Escape from New York: The New Negro Renaissance Beyond Harlem*, ed. Davarian L. Baldwin and Minkah Makalani, 31–51. Minneapolis: University of Minnesota Press, 2013.

Kelley, Robin D. G. *Freedom Dreams: The Black Radical Imagination*. Boston: Beacon, 2002.

Kelly, Brian. "Sentinels for New South Industry: Booker T. Washington, Industrial Accommodation, and Black Workers in the Jim Crow South." *Labor History* 44, no. 3 (2003): 337–57.

King, Tiffany Lethabo. *The Black Shoals: Offshore Formations of Black and Native Studies*. Durham, NC: Duke University Press, 2019.

Knetsch, Joe. "The Broward Rice Plantation: Dream or Merely Speculation?" *Broward Legacy: A Journal of South Florida History* 12, nos. 1–2 (Winter–Spring 1990): 2–10. https://journals.flvc.org/browardlegacy/article/view/77103/74619.

Kowalski, Philip J. "No Excuses for Our Dirt: Booker T. Washington and a 'New Negro' Middle Class." In *Post-bellum, Pre-Harlem: African American Literature and Culture, 1877–1919*, ed. Barbara McCaskill and Caroline Gebhard, 181–96. New York: New York University Press, 2006.

Kraut, Anthea. *Choreographing the Folk: The Dance Stagings of Zora Neale Hurston*. Minneapolis: University of Minnesota Press, 2008.

Kremer, Gary R. *George Washington Carver in His Own Words*. Columbia: University of Missouri Press, 2017.

Lamothe, Daphne. "Vodou Imagery, African-American Tradition, and Cultural Transformation in Zora Neale Hurston's 'Their Eyes Were Watching God.'" *Callaloo* 22, no. 1 (1999): 157–75.

Lane, Linda Rochell. *A Documentary of Mrs. Booker T. Washington*. Lewiston, NY: Edwin Mellen Press, 2001.

Lanero, Juan José. "Eduardo Marquina y la autobiografía de Booker T. Washington: *De esclavo a catedrático*." *Hermēneus: Revista de traducción e interpretación* 1 (1999): 1–10.

Largey, Michael. *Voudou Nation: Haitian Art, Music, and Cultural Nationalism*. Chicago: University of Chicago Press, 2006.

Léger, Jacques Nicolas. *Haiti, Her History and Her Detractors*. New York: Neale, 1907.

Levander, Caroline, and Walter Mignolo. "The Global South and World Dis/Order." *Global South* 5, no. 1 (2011): 1–11.

Levine, Caroline. *Forms: Whole, Rhythm, Hierarchy, Network*. Princeton, NJ: Princeton University Press, 2015.

Lewis, Jovan Scott. *Violent Utopia: Dispossession and Black Restoration in Tulsa*. Durham, NC: Duke University Press, 2022.

Lewis, Morris. "Paris and the International Exposition." *Colored American Magazine* 1, no. 5 (1900): 291–95.

Lewis, Rupert. "Garvey's Forerunners: Love and Bedward." *Race and Class* 28, no. 3 (1987): 29–40.

Locke, Alain, ed. *The New Negro: Voices of the Harlem Renaissance*. 1925. Reprint. New York: Touchstone, 1997.

Logan, Warren. "Resources and Material Equipment." In *Tuskegee and Its People: Their Ideals and Achievements*, ed. Booker T. Washington [and Emmett J. Scott], 35–55. New York: D. Appleton, 1905.

Lord, Nathalie. "Washington at the Hungerford School." *Southern Workman* 41 (1912): 387–88.

Louis, Felix Jean, III. "Harlemites, Haitians, and the Black International, 1915–1934." MA thesis, Florida International University, 2014.

Love, Robert J. "The Affair of Booker T. Washington." *Jamaica Advocate*, November 2, 1901.

Lowe, John Wharton. *Calypso Magnolias: The Crosscurrents of Caribbean and Southern Literature*. Chapel Hill: University of North Carolina Press, 2016.

Lowe, Lisa. *The Intimacies of Four Continents.* Durham, NC: Duke University Press, 2015.

Lubet, Alex, and Steven Lubet. "The Complicated Legacy of 'My Old Kentucky Home.'" *Smithsonian Magazine,* September 30, 2020. https://www.smithsonianmag.com/arts-culture/complicated-legacy-my-old-kentucky-home-180975719/.

Ludlow, Helen W. *Tuskegee Normal and Industrial School, for Training Colored Teachers: Its Story and Its Song.* Hampton, VA: Normal School Steam Press, 1884.

Marable, Manning. "Black Skin, Bourgeois Masks." In *Profiles of Self-Determination: African Responses to European Colonialism in Southern Africa 1652–Present,* ed. David Chanaiwa, 320–45. Northridge: California State University Foundation, 1976.

——. "Booker T. Washington and African Nationalism." *Phylon* 35, no. 4 (1974): 398–406.

Massey, Rev. Arthur E.. "Dr. Booker T. Washington: Negro Educationalist and Founder of the Tuskegee Institute." In *Negro: An Anthology,* ed. Nancy Cunard, 16–20. London: Wishart, 1934.

Martin, Tony. *Literary Garveyism: Garvey, Black Arts, and the Harlem Renaissance.* Dover, MA: Majority Press, 1983.

——. *Race First: The Ideological and Organizational Struggles of Marcus Garvey and the Universal Improvement Association.* Dover, MA: Majority Press, 1976.

Matthews, Mark D. "Booker T. Washington and His Relationship to Garveyism: An Assessment." *Western Journal of Black Studies* 7, no. 2 (1983): 103–12.

Mayberry, B. D. *The Role of Tuskegee University in the Origin, Growth, and Development of the Negro Cooperative Extension System, 1881–1990.* Tuskegee: Tuskegee University, 1989.

McHenry, Elizabeth. *To Make Negro Literature: Writing, Literary Practice, and African American Authorship.* Durham, NC: Duke University Press, 2021.

McInnis, Jarvis C. "A Corporate Plantation Reading Public: Labor, Literacy, and Diaspora in the Global Black South." *American Literature* 91, no. 3 (September 2019): 523–55.

McKay, Claude. "The Agricultural Show." In *Gingertown,* 163–91. New York: Harper, 1932.

——. *Banana Bottom.* 1933. Reprint. San Diego: Harcourt Brace, 1961.

——. *Banjo: A Story Without a Plot.* San Diego: Harcourt Brace, 1929.

——. "Claude McKay Defends Our Dialect Poetry. *Gleaner,* June 7, 1913.

——. "Claude McKay Describes His Own Life: A Negro Poet." *Pearson's Magazine,* September 1918.

——. *Complete Poems.* Ed. William J. Maxwell. Urbana: University of Illinois Press, 2004.

——. "For Group Survival" (1937). *Black Scholar* 42, no. 1 (2012): 20–21.

——. "How Black Sees Green and Red." *Liberator* 4, no. 6 (June 1921): 17, 20–21.

——. *A Long Way from Home.* 1937. Reprint. New York: Harcourt Brace & World, 1970.

——. *My Green Hills of Jamaica: And Five Jamaican Short Stories.* Edited by Mervyn Morris. Kingston, Jamaica: Heineman Educational Book (Caribbean), 1979.

——. *The Negroes in America.* Trans. Robert J. Winter. Ed. Alan L. McLeod. Port Washington, NY: Kennikat Press, 1979.

McKittrick, Katherine. *Demonic Grounds: Black Women and the Cartographies of Struggle.* Minneapolis: University of Minnesota Press, 2006.

——. "Plantation Futures." *Small Axe* 17, no. 3 (2013): 1–15.

McKittrick, Katherine, and Clyde Woods, eds. *Black Geographies and the Politics of Place.* Cambridge: South End Press, 2007.

Meehan, Kevin, and Marie Léticée. "A Folio of Writing from 'La Revue Indigène' (1927–28): Translation and Commentary." *Callaloo* 23, no. 4 (2000): 1377–80.

Miles, Tiya. "Beyond a Boundary: Black Lives and the Settler–Native Divide." *William and Mary Quarterly* 76, no. 3 (July 2019): 417–26.

Mirabal, Nancy Racquel. *Suspect Freedoms: The Racial and Sexual Politics of Cubanidad in New York, 1823–1957.* New York: New York University Press, 2017.

BIBLIOGRAPHY

Mitchell, Koritha. *Living with Lynching: African American Lynching Plays, Performance, and Citizenship, 1890–1930*. Urbana: University of Illinois Press, 2012.

Mitman, Gregg. *Empire of Rubber: Firestone's Scramble for Land and Power in Liberia*. New York: New Press, 2021.

Morrison, Matthew D. *Blacksound: Making Race and Popular Music in the United States*. Oakland: University of California Press, 2024.

Moton, Mrs. R. R. "Mrs. Booker T. Washington." *Tuskegee Messenger*, August 1925.

Moton, Robert. "Hampton–Tuskegee: Missioners of the Masses." In *The New Negro: Voices of the Harlem Renaissance*, ed. Alain Locke, 323–32. 1925. Reprint. New York: Touchstone, 1997.

——. *Report of the United States Commission on Education in Haiti*. Washington, DC: U.S. Government Printing Office, 1931.

Navarro-Rivera, Pablo. "Acculturation Under Duress: The Puerto Rican Experience at the Carlisle Indian Industrial School, 1898–1918." N.d. http://home.epix.net/~landis/navarro.html. Accessed July 22, 2022.

Nembhard, Jessica Gordon. *Collective Courage: A History of African American Cooperative Economic Thought*. University Park: Pennsylvania University Press, 2014.

Newton, Velma. *The Silver Men: West Indian Labour Migration to Panama, 1850–1914*. Mona, Jamaica: Institute of Social and Economic Research, University of West Indies, 1984.

Nicholls, David G. *Conjuring the Folk: Forms of Modernity in African America*. Ann Arbor: University of Michigan Press, 2000.

Norrell, Robert J. *Reaping the Whirlwind: The Civil Rights Movement in Tuskegee*. New York: Knopf, Random House, 1985.

——. *Up from History: The Life of Booker T. Washington*. Cambridge, MA: Belknap Press of Harvard University Press, 2009.

Nwankwo, Ifeoma Kiddoe. *Black Cosmopolitanism: Racial Consciousness and Transnational Identity in the Nineteenth-Century Americas*. Philadelphia: University of Pennsylvania Press, 2005.

——. "Insider and Outsider, Black and American: Rethinking Zora Neale Hurston's Caribbean Ethnography." *Radical History Review* 87 (2003): 49–77.

Olliveira, Cecília. "Tourists Visit Plantation in Brazil and Are Served by Black 'Slaves.' " *Intercept*, December 6, 2016. https://theintercept.com/2016/12/06/tourists-visit-plantation-in-brazil-and-are-served-by-black-slaves/.

Osuna, Juan José. *A History of Education in Puerto Rico*. Río Piedras: Editorial de la Universidad de Puerto Rico, 1949.

Owens, Imani D. "Beyond Authenticity: The US Occupation of Haiti and the Politics of Folk Culture." *Journal of Haitian Studies* 21, no. 2 (2015): 350–70.

Owens, T. Edward. "The Negro Here and in Cuba." *Outlook*, September 24, 1898.

Palmer, J. H. "Elect Tuskegee Graduate for Mayor of Colonial Town." *Southern Letter*, March–April 1929.

Pamphile, Leon D. *Clash of Cultures: America's Educational Strategies in Occupied Haiti, 1915–1934*. Lanham, MD: University Press of America, 2008.

Pappademos, Melina. *Black Political Activism and the Cuban Republic*. Chapel Hill: University of North Carolina Press, 2011.

Park, Robert E. "The International Conference on the Negro." *Southern Workman* 41 (1912): 347–52.

Parsard, Kaneesha Cherelle. "Siphon, or What Was the Plot? Revisiting Sylvia Wynter's 'Novel and History, Plot and Plantation.' " *Representations* 162 (2023): 56–64.

Patterson, Orlando. *Slavery and Social Death: A Comparative Study*. Cambridge, MA: Harvard University Press, 1982.

Patterson, Tiffany Ruby. *Zora Neale Hurston and a History of Southern Life*. Philadelphia: Temple University Press, 2005.

Penniman, Leah. "After a Century in Decline, Black Farmers Are Back and on the Rise." *yes!* magazine, May 5, 2016. Posted at the Positive Futures Network, April 19, 2024. https://www.yesmagazine.org /democracy/2016/05/05/after-a-century-in-decline-black-farmers-are-back-and-on-the-rise.

Pérez y Encinosa, Alfredo. "La escuela de Tuskegee." In Rafael Serra, *Para blancos y negros: Ensayos políticos, sociales y económicos*, 147–50. Havana, Cuba: El Printa "El Score" Aguila 117, 1907.

——. "Juan Eusebio Gomez." *La lucha*, May 20, 1906.

Perry, Imani. *May We Forever Stand: A History of the Black National Anthem*. Chapel Hill: University of North Carolina Press, 2018.

Perry, Rhussus L. "Janey Gets Her Desires." In *Up Before Daylight: Life Histories from the Alabama Writers' Project, 1938–1939*, ed. James Seay Brown Jr., 169–75. Tuscaloosa: University of Alabama Press, 1982.

Peterman, Frank, and Audrey Peterman. *African Americans and the Saw Mills of Big Cypress: A Brief History*. Washington, DC: National Park Service, U.S. Department of the Interior, n.d. https://www.nps .gov/bicy/learn/historyculture/upload/African-Americans-and-the-Sawmills-of-Big-Cypress.pdf.

Pierce, Charles. "How Electricity Is Taught at Tuskegee." *Technical World* 1, no. 4 (June 1904): 425–31.

Plant, Deborah G. *Every Tub Must Sit on Its Own Bottom: The Philosophy and Politics of Zora Neale Hurston*. Urbana: University of Illinois Press, 1995.

Plant, W. H. "An Interesting Lecture at Port Antonio on Tuskegee." *Gleaner*, July 9, 1912.

Plummer, Brenda Gayle. "The Afro-American Response to the Occupation of Haiti." *Phylon* 43, no. 2 (1982): 125–43.

——. *Haiti and the Great Powers, 1901–1915*. Baton Rouge: Louisiana State University Press, 1988.

——. *Haiti and the United States: The Psychological Moment*. Athens: University of Georgia Press, 1992.

Pollard, Sam, dir. *Zora Neale Hurston: Jump at the Sun* (2008). Written by Kristy Andersen. DVD, home edition, dual-layer format. San Francisco: California Newsreel, 2009.

Polyné, Millery. *From Douglass to Duvalier: U.S. African Americans, Haiti, and Pan Americanism, 1870–1964*. Gainesville: University Press of Florida, 2010.

Posmentier, Sonya. *Cultivation and Catastrophe: The Lyric Ecology of Modern Black Literature*. Baltimore, MD: Johns Hopkins University Press, 2017.

——. "The Provision Ground in New York: Claude McKay and the Form of Memory." *American Literature* 84, no. 2 (2012): 273–300.

Postel, Charles. *The Populist Vision*. Oxford: Oxford University Press, 2007.

Powell, W. F. "Hayti as a Refuge." *Cleveland Gazette*, April 6, 1901.

Price-Mars, Jean. "A propos de la 'Renaissance Negre' aux Etats-Unis" [part 1]. *La relève: Politique, littéraire* 1, no. 1 (1932): 14–20.

——. "A propos de 'la Renaissance Nègre aux Etats-Unis' " [part 2]. *La relève: Politique, littéraire* 1, no. 2 (August 1932): 9–15.

——. "A propos de la 'Renaissance Nègre aux Etats-Unis' " [part 3]. *La relève: Politique, littéraire* 1, no. 3 (1932): 8–14.

——. "L'education technique." *Haiti littéraire et scientifique*, October 20, 1912, 520–24.

——. "Le préjugé de races." In *La vocation de l'élite*, 167–87. Port-au-Prince, Haiti: Impremerie Edmond Chenet, 1919.

——. "The Problem of Work in Haiti" (in English). *La revue du monde noir* 1, no. 1 (1931): 12–20.

——. "Que peut attendre le pays du Service Technique d'agriculture." *La relève: Politique, littéraire* 2, no. 7 (January 1934): 52–54.

——. "Qu'est-ce que le pays peut-il attendre du Service Technique de l'agriculture?" *La relève: Politique, littéraire* 2, no. 6 (December 1933): 24–29.

——. *Silhouettes de Nègres et de Nègrophiles*. Paris: Présence africain, 1960.

——. *So Spoke the Uncle*. Trans. Magdaline W. Shannon. Washington, DC: Three Continents Press, 1983.

BIBLIOGRAPHY

——. "La vocation de l'élite." Trans. Claire Payton. In *The Haiti Reader: History, Culture, Politics*, ed. Laurent Dubois, Kaiama L. Glover, Nadève Ménard, Millery Polyné, and Chantalle F. Verna, 202–10. Durham, NC: Duke University Press, 2020.

Puri, Shalini, ed. *Marginal Migrations: The Circulation of Cultures Within the Caribbean*. London: Macmillan Caribbean, 2003.

Putnam, Lara. *Radical Moves: Caribbean Migrants and the Politics of Race in the Jazz Age*. Chapel Hill: University of North Carolina Press, 2013.

Quashie, Kevin. *Black Aliveness, or A Poetics of Being*. Durham, NC: Duke University Press, 2021.

Ramsey, Kate. *The Spirits and the Law: Vodou and Power in Haiti*. Chicago: University of Chicago Press, 2011.

Randolph, A. Phillip. "The Only Way to Redeem Africa." *Messenger* 5, no. 1 (January 1923): 568–70.

Renda, Mary A. *Taking Haiti: Military Occupation and the Culture of U.S. Imperialism, 1915–1940*. Chapel Hill: University of North Carolina Press, 2001.

Report of Commissioner of Education of Porto Rico [sic]. Washington, DC: U.S. Government Printing Office, 1901.

Report of Commissioner of Education of Porto Rico [sic]. Washington, DC: U.S. Government Printing Office, 1902.

Report of Commissioner of Education of Porto Rico [sic]. Washington, DC: U.S. Government Printing Office, 1903.

"Report of Delegates to the International Conference on the Negro at Tuskegee, U.S.A., 23rd November, 1912." *Supplement to the Jamaica Gazette* (Kingston, Jamaica), November 1, 1913, 704–14. Archived in the National Library of Jamaica, Kingston, Jamaica.

Retman, Sonnet. *Real Folks: Race and Genre in the Great Depression*. Durham, NC: Duke University Press, 2011.

"Revived Programme of the Universal Negro Improvement Association: Five-Year Plan to Be Executed." *Black Man* 1, no. 9 (August–September 1935): 5–8.

Richardson, Riché. *Black Masculinity and the U.S. South: From Uncle Tom to Gangsta*. Athens: University of Georgia Press, 2007.

——. "'A House Set Off from the Rest': Ralph Ellison's Rural Geography." *Forum for Modern Language Studies* 40 (April 2004): 126–44.

Roach, Joseph. *Cities of the Dead: Circum-Atlantic Performance*. New York: Columbia University Press, 1996.

Roane, J. T. "Plotting the Black Commons." *Souls: A Critical Journal of Black Politics, Culture, and Society* 20, no. 3 (2018): 239–66.

Robinson, Zandria. *This Ain't Chicago: Race, Class, and Regional Identity in the Post-soul South*. Chapel Hill: University of North Carolina Press, 2014.

Rodney, Walter. *The Groundings with My Brothers*. 1969. Reprint. Chicago: Research Associates School Times Publications, 1990.

Rolinson, Mary G. *Grassroots Garveyism: The Universal Negro Improvement Association in the Rural South, 1920–1927*. Chapel Hill: University of North Carolina Press, 2007.

Roll, Jarod. "Agrarian Producerism After Populism: Socialism and Garveyism in the Rural South." In *Populism in the South Revisited: New Interpretations and New Departures*, ed. James M. Beeby, 199–226. Jackson: University Press of Mississippi, 2012.

Roper, Shani. "Creating Good Colonial Citizens: Industrial Schools and Reformatories in Victorian Jamaica." In *Victorian Jamaica*, ed. Tim Barringer and Wayne Modest, 190–208. Durham, NC: Duke University Press, 2018.

Rosengarten, Theodore. *All God's Dangers: The Life of Nate Shaw*. New York: Vintage Books, 1974.

Ross, Marlon B. "Callaloo, Everyone?" *Callaloo* 30, no. 1 (2007): 87–94.

——. *Manning the Race: Reforming Black Men in the Jim Crow Era*. New York: New York University Press, 2004.

——. *Sissy Insurgencies: A Racial Anatomy of Unfit Manliness*. Durham, NC: Duke University Press, 2021.

Rouse, Jacqueline Anne. "Out of the Shadow of Tuskegee: Margaret Murray Washington, Social Activism, and Race Vindication." *Journal of Negro History* 81, nos. 1–4 (Winter–Autumn 1996): 31–46.

Rowe, John Carlos. "Opening the Gate to the Other America: The Afro-Caribbean Politics of Hurston's *Mules and Men* and *Tell My Horse*." In *Literary Culture and U.S. Imperialism: From the Revolution to World War II*, 253–92. Oxford: Oxford University Press, 2000.

Rusert, Britt. *Fugitive Science: Empiricism and Freedom in Early African American Literature*. New York: New York University Press, 2017.

——. "Plantation Ecologies: The Experimental Plantation in and Against James Grainger's *The Sugar-Cane*." *Early American Studies* 13, no. 2 (Spring 2015): 341–73.

——. "'A Study in Nature': The Tuskegee Experiments and the New South Laboratory." *Journal of Medical Humanities* 30, no. 3 (September 2009): 155–71.

Schomburg, Arthur A. "General Evaristo Estenoz." *Crisis* 4, no. 3 (July 1912): 143–44.

——. "Is Hayti Decadent?" *Unique Advertiser*, August 1904. Archived in Manuscripts, Archives, and Rare Books Division, Schomburg Center for Research in Black Culture, New York Public Library.

Schuyler, George S. *The Reminiscences of George S. Schuyler, 1962*. Ed. William T. Ingersoll. Alexandria, VA: Alexander Street Press, 2003.

——. "Views and Reviews." *Pittsburgh Courier*, December 17, 1932.

——. "Views and Reviews." *Pittsburgh Courier*, July 20, 1935.

Scott, David. *Conscripts of Modernity: The Tragedy of Colonial Enlightenment*. Durham, NC: Duke University Press, 2004.

Scott, Emmett J. Preface to *Tuskegee and Its People: Their Ideals and Achievements*, ed. Booker T. Washington [and Emmett J. Scott], v–ix. New York: D. Appleton, 1905.

Scott, Emmett J., and Lyman Beecher Stowe. *Booker T. Washington: Builder of a Civilization*. Garden City, NY: Doubleday, Page, 1916.

Sehat, David. "The Civilizing Mission of Booker T. Washington." *Journal of Southern History* 73, no. 2 (2007): 323–62.

Serra, Rafael. *Para blancos y negros: Ensayos políticos, sociales y económicos*. Havana, Cuba: El Printa "El Score" Aguila 117, 1907.

Shannon, Magdaline W. Introduction to Jean Price-Mars, *So Spoke the Uncle*, trans. Magdaline W. Shannon, vii–xxviii. Washington, DC: Three Continents Press, 1983.

——. *Jean Price-Mars, the Haitian Elite, and the American Occupation 1915–1935*. New York: St. Martin's Press, 1996.

Shepard, Clara W. "An Indirect Reply to Our Inquiry." *La revue du monde noir*, no. 3 (1931): 53–54.

——. "Tuskegee Normal and Industrial Institute." *La revue de monde noir*, no. 2 (1931): 15–18.

——. "The Utility of foreign Languages for american Negroes [*sic*]." *La revue de monde noir*, no. 4 (1932): 28–31.

Smethurst, James. *The Afro-American Roots of Modernism*. Chapel Hill: University of North Carolina Press, 2011.

Smith, Faith. "Good Enough for Booker T. to Kiss: Hampton, Tuskegee, and Caribbean Self-Fashioning." *Journal of Transnational American Studies* 5, no. 1 (2013): 1–15.

Smith, Jon, and Deborah Cohn. "Introduction: Uncanny Hybridities." In *Look Away! The U.S. South in New World Studies*, ed. Jon Smith and Deborah Cohn, 1–19. Durham, NC: Duke University Press, 2004.

Smith, Matthew J. "Capture Land: Jamaica, Haiti, and the United States Occupation." *Journal of Haitian Studies* 21, no. 2 (2015): 181–206.

Smith, N. Clark. *Favorite Folk Melodies as Sung by Tuskegee Students*. Wichita, KS: n.p., 1913.

BIBLIOGRAPHY

Smith, Shawn Michelle. "Booker T. Washington's Photographic Messages." *English Language Notes* 51, no. 1 (Spring–Summer 2013): 137–46.

——. "Photographing the 'American Negro': Nation, Race, and Photography at the Paris Exposition in 1900." In *With Other Eyes: Looking at Race and Gender in Visual Culture*, ed. Lisa Bloom, 58–87. Minneapolis: University of Minnesota Press, 1999.

——. *Photography on the Color Line: W. E. B. Du Bois, Race, and Visual Culture*. Durham, NC: Duke University Press, 2004.

Southern, Eileen. *The Music of Black Americans: A History*. 2nd ed. New York: Norton, 1983.

Spillers, Hortense. "Mama's Baby, Papa's Maybe: An American Grammar Book." *Diacritics* 17, no. 2 (1987): 64–81.

Spires, Derrick R. *The Practice of Citizenship: Black Politics and Print Culture in the Early United States*. Philadelphia: University of Pennsylvania Press, 2019.

Spivey, Donald. *Schooling for the New Slavery: Black Industrial Education, 1868–1915*. Westport, CT: Greenwood Press, 1978.

Stallings, L. H. *A Dirty South Manifesto: Sexual Resistance and Imagination in the New South*. Oakland: University of California Press, 2020.

Stennett, R. Samuel. "Bright Youths. Successes Achieved by Jamaicans at Tuskegee. Carry Off Honours. Claim That the Educated Avenues Here Are Restricted." *Gleaner*, April 9, 1913.

Stephens, Michelle Ann. *Black Empire: The Masculine Global Imaginary of Caribbean Intellectuals in the United States, 1914–1962*. Durham, NC: Duke University Press, 2005.

Taylor, Diana. *The Archive and the Repertoire: Performing Cultural Memory in the Americas*. Durham, NC: Duke University Press, 2003.

Thomas, Veronica G., and Janine A. Jackson. "The Education of African American Girls and Women: Past to Present." *Journal of Negro Education* 76, no. 3 (Summer 2007): 357–72.

Thompson, Edgar T. *The Plantation* (1983). Ed. Sidney M. Mintz and George Baca. Columbia: University of South Carolina Press, 2010.

——. *The Plantation: An International Bibliography*. Boston: G. K. Hall, 1983.

Thompson, Eloise Bibb. "Quintet Sings to Aid Tuskegee; Wins Much Praise." *Chicago Defender*, January 16, 1915.

Thompson, R. W. "Haitian Minister to Go to Tuskegee." *The Freeman*, January 14, 1911.

Thrasher, Max Bennett. *Tuskegee: Its Story and Its Work*. Boston: Small, Maynard, 1900.

Todd, Frank Morton. *The Story of the Exposition: Being the Official History of the International Celebration Held at San Francisco in 1915 to Commemorate the Discovery of the Pacific Ocean and the Construction of the Panama Canal*. Vol. 4. New York: Knickerbocker Press, 1921.

Trouillot, Michel-Rolph. *Haiti: State Against Nation*. New York: Monthly Review Press, 1990.

——. "North Atlantic Universals: Analytical Fictions, 1492–1945." *South Atlantic Quarterly* 101, no. 4 (Fall 2002): 839–58.

Tsing, Anna Lowenhaupt. *The Mushroom at the End of the World: On the Possibility of Life in Capitalist Ruins*. Princeton, NJ: Princeton University Press, 2015.

Tullos, Allen. "The Black Belt." *Southern Cultures*, April 19, 2004. https://southernspaces.org/2004/black-belt/.

Verna, Chantalle. *Haiti and the Uses of America: Post–U.S. Occupation Promises*. New Brunswick, NJ: Rutgers University Press, 2017.

Vogel, Shane. *The Scene of Harlem Cabaret: Race, Sexuality, Performance*. Chicago: University of Chicago Press, 2009.

Waller, Rev. Owen Meredith, M.D. "Booker T. Washington's Unsound Doctrine Riddled Too [*sic*] Pieces." *Chicago Broad Ax*, May 7, 1904.

Washington, Booker T. *The Booker T. Washington Papers*. 14 vols. Ed. Louis R. Harlan and Raymond W. Smock. Urbana: University of Illinois Press, 1972–1989.

——. *De esclavo a catedrático: Autobiografía de Booker T. Washington*. Trans. Alfredo Elías y Pujol. New York: D. Appleton, 1902.

——. "Dr. Booker T. Washington on the American Occupation of Haiti." *New York Age*, October 21, 1915.

——. *Frederick Douglass: A Biography*. Philadelphia: George W. Jacobs, 1906.

——. "The Future of Congo Reform." In *The Congo News Letter*, ed. Congo Reform Association, 9–10. Boston: n.p., 1906.

——. *The Future of the American Negro*. Boston: Small, Maynard, 1899.

——. "General Introduction." In *Tuskegee and Its People: Their Ideals and Achievements*, ed. Booker T. Washington [and Emmett J. Scott], 1–16. New York: D. Appleton, 1905.

——. "How the Negro Will Be Judged." *Tuskegee Student*, October 15, 1904.

——. "Industrial Education for Cuban Negroes." *Christian Register*, August 18, 1898.

——. "Is the Negro Having a Fair Chance?" *Century Magazine*, November 1912.

——. "Negro Homes." *Century Magazine*, May 1908.

——. *The Negro in Business*. Boston: Hertel, Jenkins, 1907.

——. "*The Negro in the New World*" (review). *Journal of the African Society* 10 (1911): 173–78.

——. "On the Paris Boulevards." *New York Age*, June 8, 1899.

——. "Plantation Melodies, Their Value." *Musical Courier* 71 (December 13, 1915): 47.

——. "Race Friction in Cuba—and Elsewhere." *Continent*, October 3, 1912.

——. "The Rural Negro Community." *Annals of the American Academy of Political and Social Science* 40 (March 1912): 81–89.

——. "Samuel Coleridge-Taylor." Preface to *Twenty-Four Negro Melodies Transcribed for Piano by S. Coleridge Taylor*, vii–ix. Boston: Oliver Ditson, 1905.

——. "Signs of Progress Among the Negroes." *Century Magazine*, January 1900.

——. *Sowing and Reaping*. Boston: L. C. Page, 1900.

——. *The Story of My Life and Work*. Cincinnati: W. H. Ferguson, 1900.

——. *The Story of the Negro: The Rise of the Race from Slavery*. 2 vols. 1909. Reprint. Gloucester, MA: Peter Smith, 1969.

——, ed. *Tuskegee and Its People: Their Ideals and Achievements*. New York: D. Appleton, 1905. [Also edited by Emmett J. Scott.]

——. "Tuskegee Institute." *African Times and Orient Review*, August 1912, 52.

——. "Twenty-Five Years of Tuskegee." *World's Work* 11 (1906): 7436–37.

——. *Up from Slavery* (1901). Ed. Louis R. Harlan. New York: Penguin, 1986.

——. "What the Carnegie Library Does for Tuskegee Students." *Appleton's Booklovers Magazine* 6, no. 2 (August 1905): 253–54.

——. "Why I Wrote My Latest Book: My Aim in 'The Story of the Negro.'" *World's Work* 20 (1910): 13568–69.

——. *Working with the Hands: Being a Sequel to "Up from Slavery" Covering the Author's Experiences in Industrial Training at Tuskegee*. Toronto: William Briggs, May 1904.

——. *Working with the Hands: Being a Sequel to "Up from Slavery" Covering the Author's Experiences in Industrial Training at Tuskegee*. Special subscription ed. New York: Doubleday, Page, c. July 1904.

Washington, Booker T., and Robert E. Park. *The Man Farthest Down*. Garden City, NY: Doubleday, Page, 1913.

Washington, Mrs. Booker T. "The New Negro Woman." *Lend a Hand: A Record of Progress* 15, no. 4 (October 1895): 254–60.

——. "What Girls Are Taught, and How." In *Tuskegee and Its People: Their Ideals and Achievements*, ed. Booker T. Washington [and Emmett J. Scott], 68–86. New York: D. Appleton, 1905.

Watkins, William H. *The White Architects of Black Education: Ideology and Power in America, 1865–1954*. New York: Teachers College Press, 2001.

Weiss, Ellen. *Robert R. Taylor and Tuskegee: An African American Architect Designs for Booker T. Washington*. Montgomery, AL: New South, 2012.

Wells, Ida B. "Booker T. Washington and His Critics" (1904). In *The Light of Truth: Writings of an Antilynching Crusader*, ed. Mia Bay, 415–20. New York: Penguin Classics, 2014.

Wells, Jeremy. "Up from Savagery: Booker T. Washington and the Civilizing Mission." *Southern Quarterly* 42, no. 1 (Fall 2003): 53–74.

West, Michael O. "The Tuskegee Model of Development in Africa: Another Dimension of the African/African-American Connection." *Diplomatic History* 16, no. 3 (1992): 371–87.

Wexler, Laura. *Tender Violence: Domestic Visions in an Age of U.S. Imperialism*. Chapel Hill: University of North Carolina Press, 2000.

White, Deborah Gray. *Too Heavy a Load: Black Women in Defense of Themselves, 1894–1994*. New York: Norton, 1999.

White, Monica. *Freedom Farmers: Agricultural Resistance and the Black Freedom Movement*. Chapel Hill: University of North Carolina Press, 2018.

Wilder, Gary. *Freedom Time: Negritude, Decolonization, and the Future of the World*. Durham, NC: Duke University Press, 2015.

Womack, Autumn. *The Matter of Black Living*. Chicago: University of Chicago Press, 2022.

Woodward, C. Vann. *Origins of the New South, 1877–1913*. Baton Rouge: Louisiana State University Press, 1971.

Wright, Rev. Jeremiah. "Different, Not Deficient." *The Guardian*, April 28, 2008. https://www.theguardian.com/commentisfree/2008/apr/28/differentnotdeficient.

Wright, Richard. "Blueprint for Negro Writing" (1937). In *The Norton Anthology of African American Literature*, 2nd ed., ed. Henry Louis Gates Jr. and Nellie Y. McKay, 1403–8. New York: Norton, 2004.

Wright, R. R., Sr. "Is There a Negro Problem and Is It Being Solved?" *Pittsburgh Courier*, February 16, 1935.

Wynter, Sylvia. "Black Metamorphosis: New Natives in a New World." Unpublished manuscript, n.d. (c. 1970s). Institute of the Black World Papers, Schomburg Center for Research in Black Culture, New York Public Library.

——. "Novel and History, Plot and Plantation." *Savacou* 5 (1971): 95–102.

Young, Harvey. *Embodying Black Experience: Stillness, Critical Memory, and the Black Body*. Ann Arbor: University of Michigan Press, 2010.

Zimmerman, Angela. *Alabama in Africa: Booker T. Washington, the German Empire, and the Globalization of the New South*. Princeton, NJ: Princeton University Press, 2010.

Index

Acosta, Julio, 357

aesthetics: aestheticizing labor, 296–302, *299*; aesthetic philosophy, 83–84, 100–101; of Black farmers, 90; of Black modernity, 38; BTW on, 297–98; of eco-ontology, 84–85; gendered, 81–85; Hurston and, 313–19, *318–19*, 410n9; of New Negro Movement, 85–90, 311; racial, 81–85; sonic, 87–88; of uplift, 104–5; Victorian, 89–90; of visual culture, 114–18, *115–20*, 120–24, *122–24*; of work, 101–6, 130–31

affordances: of BTW, 141–44; imperial, 195–201, 365–68; literary, 152–61, *155*, *158–59*; on plantations, 31–35, 51, 57, 181, 365–68, 406; of racial uplift, 372; scholarship on, 375–76, 378n13; at Tuskegee Institute, 152–61, *155*, *158–59*, 176, 249, 255, 295

Africa: agriculture in, 76–77; BTW on, 77–78; Caribbean and, 147; colonialism in, 31, 34; ethnicity in, 356; Germany in, 32–33; Indigenous peoples of, 8, 239–40; Liberia, 59; Pan-African Congress, 3; pan-Africanism, 27, 35, 121; West, 76–77, 137, 225

African Americans: agriculture for, 183–85; anti-Black violence against, 59; Black Panther Party for, 370; BTW for, 12; in business, 37; Caribbean for, 356–57; Carver for, 68–69; citizenship for, 146, 292n131, 327–28; after Civil War, 100, 250–51, 375; culture of, 52–53; economics of, 216–18; education of, 36, 61, 239–45; elitism and, 190, 194–95, 218–19;

ethnicity of, 356; genres for, 95; Global Black South for, 253; in Great Migration, 300; Haitian-African American Chamber of Commerce, 210–13, 216; Haiti for, 183–92, 400n111; Harlem Renaissance for, 86, 206–7; Historically Black Colleges and Universities for, 247, 370–71, 378n17; at ICON, 6; Jamaica for, 333–34; Jim Crow South for, 103–4, 207; in labor migration, 300–301; leadership for, 86, 337, 358–61, 384n29; in Macon County, 51–52, 58–59; marginalization of, 46–47; Native Americans and, 150–51; ontological violence against, 4–5; performance and, 320–25; politics and, 51–52, 59–60, 121, 211–12, 415n19; progress for, 99; rural, 74, 76–77, 116–18, 120–24, 137, 149–50; scholarship on, 389n25; slavery and, 49–50, 79–80; as students, 231–39, *233–34*; studies, 5, 15, 79–80; Tuskegee Institute Singers for, 95–99, *97*; unskilled labor for, 48; U.S. imperialism for, 209–18, 226–31, *228*; in U.S. South, 11, 39, 418n1

African diaspora. *See* diaspora

African diaspora citizenship, 361–67

African Exclusion Bill, 34

Afro-Bahamans. *See* Bahamas

Afro-Cubans. *See* Cuba

Afro-Latine/Afro-Latinidad, 148, 167

Afro–Puerto Ricans. *See* Puerto Rico

afterlife, of slavery, 4–5

"Agricultural Show, The" (C. McKay), 270–71

INDEX

agriculture: in Africa, 76–77; for African Americans, 183–85; agrarian futures, 23–30, 52–61, 114–18, 120–24, 205–9, 309–12, 342; agrarian reform, 55–56; agricultural experimental plot, 67–73, *70–72*, *120–21*; agricultural extension program, 61–67; Black economic (inter)nationalism and, 367–68; for Black farmers, 340–41; Black liberatory, 374; BTW and, 6, 25–26, 52, 130–31, *132*; Carver for, 37–38, 63, 261–62; Colored State Agricultural Wheel, 60; domesticity and, 124–34, *135–36*; education, 47–48, 177–82, 192–95, 205–9, 218–19; empiricism and, 114–18, *115–20*, 120–24, *122–24*; ethics of, 33–34; Garvey for, 353–58; in Global Black South, 180–81; in Haiti, 179–82, 397n12; ideology of, 41–42; Jesup Agricultural Wagon, 64–65; in Jim Crow South, 25; labor migration and, 250–54; in Macon County, 74; for C. McKay, 260–63; in New Negro Movement, 17–18; plantations and, 7–12, 79–80, 187–88; Port Royal experiment, 20–21; Price-Mars on, 399n84; in Puerto Rico/Afro–Puerto Ricans, 68; scholarship on, *115–20*, *122–24*, 130–31, *132*; soil analysis, 122, *124*, 124–25; soil regeneration, 176; in South America, 121; State Agricultural and Mechanical College for Negroes, 74–75; steamships and, 343–47, *348–49*, 349–53; sustainable farming, 69–70, *70–72*; in Togo, 137; at Tuskegee Institute, 26, 61–67, 73–79; in U.S. South, 1–2, 63–64. *See also specific topics*

Ainsi parla l'oncle (Price-Mars), 206

Ali, Dusé Mohamed, 3, 345

"All About Tuskegee" (ICON), 263

Allwood, Alberta E., 248

Altiery, Victoria Maria, 148

Altuna, G. Bécquer, 171

"American Blacks, The" (Benjamin, R. O. C.), 161–62

American Negro Exhibit, 99–101

Anderson, James D., 16

"anexión, La" (Serra), 162–64

Angola Prison, 375–76

anthropology, 13, 313–19, *318–19*

anti-Black propaganda, 100–101, 200–201, 291–95, 397n37

anti-Black racism, 151–52, 172–75

anti-Black violence, 59, 76, 78–79, 147, 196, 258

Antoine, Jacques C., 192

Archer, Chalmers, Jr., 58

assimilation, 103

Atlanta Exposition Address, 2–3, 16, 57, 81, 86, 126

Attaché. *See* Muñoz, Victor

Bahamas/Afro-Bahamans: Black life in, 12, 317–19, *318–19*; Caribbean and, 12, 296–301, 317–18, *318*, 321–22, 325–30; fire dances in, 321, 325–29, 331–32, 413n99; in literature, 296–301, 317–18, *318*, 321–22, 325–30; U.S. South and, 296–97, 325–29

Bailey, A. I., 267

Bailey, Amy, 332–33

Baker, Houston A., Jr., 16–17, 86–87, 380n42, 380n56, 388n20

Baker, Lorenzo Dow, 355

Baldwin, Davarian L., 14

Baldwin, William Henry, Jr., 94, 404n59

Banana Bottom (C. McKay), 271, 275, 282–91

Banjo (C. McKay), 285–87, 290

Barnett, Claude, 211, 401n115

Batchelor, R. A. H., 364

Battey, C. M., 101

Beals, Carleton, 276

Beckert, Sven, 33n111, 77, 122, 124, 387n120, 397n1

Beckford, George, 10–11, 409n70

Bedou, A. P., 101

Benjamin, R. O. C., 161–62

Bethune, Mary McLeod, 56–57, 321

Bieze, Michael, 100–101, 113, *114*

Birth of a Nation, The (film), 102

Black agrarian futures, 114–18, *115–20*, 120–24, *122–24*

Black aliveness (Kevin Quashie), 4

Black and White (Fortune), 55, 61

Black Atlantic, 9, 29–30, 261

Black being, 1, 22, 25, 84, 134, 371, 373–74

Black Belt: of Caribbean, 276–79; Global Black South and, 147, 152; history of, 3, 6, 11, 185; Macon County and, 51–52; nationalism, 370; reputation of, 46–47, 48, 87, 179

Black bodies, 14, 25, 85–90, 100, 105, 317

Black civil rights, in Cuba: in U.S., 145–46, 174; in West Indies, 266

Black cosmopolitanism, 409n68

INDEX 443

Black diaspora. *See* diaspora

Black economic (inter)nationalism: agriculture and, 367–68; Black nationalism and, 34–35, 151; Black self-determination and, 192–95; Black women for, 252–53; Delany on, 370; in Global Black South, 181; Haiti and, 209–18; politics of, 201–5, 218–19; scholarship on, 3, 177–82; at Tuskegee Institute, 372; U.S. imperialism and, 183–92, 195–201, 205–9

Black entertainers, 85–86, 95–96

Black farmers, 26; aesthetics of, 90; agriculture for, 340–41; Black landowners and, 78–79; Black periodicals for, 65, 69, 355–56; Black women and, 28; in British West Indies, 362; in Caribbean, 75; CFA for, 60–62, 79; Dubar-Nelson on, 65–66; education of, 75–76, 80, 116–18, *117–20*, 120–21, *122*; Hope Farm School, 346–47; in Macon County, 65–67, 78–79; New Negro Movement and, 203; periodicals for, 96; on plantations, 72–73; after slavery, 48–49; State Agricultural and Mechanical College for Negroes for, 74–75; in sugarcane farming, 114–16, *115*, 115–16; at Tuskegee Negro Farmers' Conference, 58–59, 63; in U.S. South, 26, 317–19, *318–19*, 361, 365–66; women and, 28

Black folk culture: in Global Black South, 336–37; for Hurston, 313–24; performance of, 297–98, 300–301, 309–12, 320–24; scholarship on, 57–58, 92–94, 98–99

Black Jacobins, The (James), 21, 50–51

Black liberatory agriculture, 374

Black life: anti-Black racism in, 172–75; in Bahamas/Afro-Bahamans, 12, 317–19, *318–19*; Black self-determination and, 5, 7; Black social life, 13–14; in British West Indies, 245; in Caribbean, 249–50, 344; Committee on Ways and Means of Improving the Industrial Output of the Negro Peoples of the World, 353–54, 363; on corporate plantations, 267–75; education about, 15–20; in Global Black South, 7–12, 41–42, 142, 307–8; in Global North, 10, 293; in Hemisphere/Hemispheric, 275–79, *280*, 301, 339–40, 364, 369; history of, 37–41; in Industrial Revolution, 24; in Jamaica, 27–28, 275–82, 332–33, 367; in Jim Crow South, 2–3, 67, 128, 350; in literature, 310–11; in Panama Canal Zone, 262, 280–81; in plantation ruins, 1–7; plantations

modernities and, 12–15; racial progress in, 31–35; on repurposed plantations, 20–23; scholarship on, 35–37, 148, 163, 177; in U.S. imperialism, 141–44; in U.S. South, 20–21. *See also specific topics*

Black masculinity, 125–29. *See also* New Negro manhood

Black modernity: aesthetics of, 38; agrarian futures and, 53–61; in Atlanta Exposition Address, 16; H. Baker on, 388n20; Black discursive modernism, 388n20; Black self-determination and, 257–60; in Black world making, 369–70; BTW for, 27, 51, 105; diaspora and, 17; in Global Black South, 1, 3–4, 7, 190, 224, 373; in Global North, 27–28; in Harlem Renaissance, 15; industrial modernity and, 309–12; James on, 50–51; in Jim Crow South, 38; in literature, 305–6; for L'Ouverture, 181; in New Negro Movement, 262–63; on plantations, 49–50, 255–56; politics of, 86–87; scholarship on, 13–14; Scott on, 22; slavery in, 49–53; on steamships, 349–50; subjectivity in, 134; at Tuskegee Institute, 61–62, 192–93, 336–37; in U.S. South, 5–6, 81–85, 347

Black nationalism, 34–35, 151, 329–36. *See also* Black economic (inter)nationalism

Blackness: in Black freedom, 418n10; Black identity formation, 23; in Cuba, 167; in Jamaica, 265; in music, 96–97; New World, 5–6, 23–24; stereotypes of, 86; in U.S. South, 9–10. *See also specific topics*

Black Panther Party, 370

Black periodicals: for Black farmers, 65, 69, 355–56; Haiti and, 183–92, 401n136; by NAACP, 66; from Négritude Movement, 252; scholarship on, 64, 344–45, 400n113; strategic translations of, 401n123; in U.S. South, 54. *See also specific periodicals*

Black professionals, 133–34, *135–36*

Black radicalism, 6–7

Black self-determination: Black economic (inter)nationalism and, 192–95; Black life and, 5, 7; Black modernity and, 257–60; in education, 104; in Haiti, 39; C. McKay on, 257–95; Panama Canal Zone and, 40; philosophy of, 352; Tuskegee Institute for, 259–60; in U.S. South, 78

Black Star Line, 212, 258, 338, 349, 352, 355

444   INDEX

Black vernacular culture, 88. *See also* Black folk culture

Black women: activism by, 56; Bethune for, 56–57; for Black economic (inter)nationalism, 252–53; Black farmers and, 28; Black women's club movement, 29, 125–26, 133, 246; in British West Indies, 235–37; BTW on, 130; Carver's support for, 73, 124; in education, 28–29; education of, 241, 252; at ICON, 266–67; International Council of Women of the Darker Races of the World, 29, 125–26; in Jamaica, 331–32; in Jim Crow South, 127; in Macon County, 69; National Association of Colored Women, 29, 125–26; National Training School for Women and Girls, 57; in New Negro Movement, 124–34, *135–36*, 307; rural, 73; scholarship on, 414n123; at Tuskegee Institute, 28–29, 69, 125–34, *131–32*; Tuskegee Women's Club, 125–26; M. M. Washington for, 29, 125–26, 132–33

Black world making: in agrarian futures, 53–61; in agricultural extension program, 61–67; Black modernity in, 369–70; paternalism in, 73–79; in photographs, 113; racial uplift and, 63, 67–69, 72–73; in repurposed plantations, 49–53; scholarship on, 23; soil regeneration and, 67–73, *70–72*; at Tuskegee Institute, 24, 45–49, 79–80

"Blueprint for Negro Writing" (R. Wright), 293

Boas, Franz, 296

Boco, Absalom, 232, 234–35

Bone, Martyn, 300

Bonhomme, Robert, 247–48

Booker T. Washington (steamship), 338–40, *339, 341–42*, 349–54

Booker T. Washington Society, 35, 170–74

Booker T. Washington University, 347, *349*, 349–54

Book of American Negro Poetry (Johnson, J. W.), 250

Borno, Louis, 197–200, 400n111

Bowen, Cornelia, 246, 347

Bowen, William Banks, 46, 246

Boyer, Jean-Pierre, 398n31

Brazil, 376

Bridgeforth, George, 64

British West Indies: Black farmers in, 362; Black life in, 245; Black women in, 235–37; Caribbean and, 373; in colonialism, 54;

culture of, 328–29; diaspora in, 34; education in, 21, 230–31, 239, 366–67; Great Depression in, 333; history of, 12–13; labor migration in, 344; scholarship on, 265–66, 370; UNIA in, 338–43, *339, 341–42*, 345–46; University of the West Indies at Mona, 374. *See also specific countries*

Brodber, Erna, 353

Brooks, Daphne A., 315

Brown, Sterling, 311, 323

Brown v. Board of Education, 294–95

Brumbaugh, Martin Grove, 229, 240–41

BTW. *See* Washington, Booker T.

Buckner, W. C., 92

Bunyan, John, 82

Burleigh, Harry T., 91–92, 95

Burroughs, Nannie Helen, 57

Byrd, Brandon, 186, 217–18

Cabral, Amilcar, 370

Caco rebellion, 198

Calhoun, Mary, 303–5

Calhoun, Russell C., 303–5

Callaloo journal, 9–10

Campbell, Ethelred E., 245

Campbell, George W., 46, 64–66, 75

Campbell, Thomas M., 64, 66, 75, 352

Campt, Tina, 134

Cape Verde, 370

Carby, Hazel, 299–300

care, ethic of, 25–26, 38, 53, 64–69, 79–82, 103–4

Caribbean: Africa and, 147; for African Americans, 356–57; archipelago, 8–9; Bahamas/Afro-Bahamians and, 12, 296–301, 317–18, *318*, 321–22, 325–30; Black Belt of, 276–79; Black farmers in, 75; Black life in, 249–50, 344; British West Indies and, 373; culture, 336–37; Global Black South and, 402n6; Global North and, 12–13; Hurston on, 37, 372; Jamaica and, 19; labor migration in, 14, 354; Latin America and, 2, 32–33, 240; scholarship on, 4, 414n4; travel in, 350; UFCO plantations in, 8; U.S. South and, 37–38, 223–24, 298–300, 322, 329–30, 371, 376; Wynter on, 24. *See also specific Caribbean countries*

Carnegie, Andrew, 159–60

Carney, Judith, 68

INDEX

Carter, George E., 352–53

Carver, George Washington: for agriculture, 37–38, 63, 67–73, 261–62; Black masculinity/New Negro manhood and, 128–29; BTW and, 47–49, 63–64, 68, 295, 342, 367; colleagues of, 38; eco-ontological regeneration by, 25–27, 47–48, 67–73, 121–24, 202–3; education of, 18–19; influence of, 271, 274; innovation by, 65; reputation of, 25, 66, 179–80; research from, 67, 79–80; scholarship from, 26, 69–72, *70–72*, *120*, 120–24, *122–24*, 176; support for Black girls and women, 73, 124; at Tuskegee Institute, 25–27, 47–48, 67–73

Casado, Emilio Céspedes, 165–69

Casimir, Jean, 21–22, 23–24, 182, 188

Central America. *See specific Central American countries*

CFA. *See* Colored Farmers' Alliance

Chambers, I., 357

"Characteristics of Negro Expression" (Hurston), 297–98, 311, 330–31, 337

Chesnutt, Charles, 82

Chicago Broad Ax (Waller), 190

Christophe, Henri, 398n31

citizenship, 146, 292n131, 327–28, 361–67

civilization, scale of, 32–33

civilizing mission, 31–35, 146, 150–51

Civil Rights Movement, 9–10, 372, 381n62

Civil War, 46, 100, 145–46, 250–51, 375, 376

"Clarion Call" (Vasconcelos), 170–71

Clark, J. E., *304*

class paternalism, 372; Dunbar-Nelson and, 65; Hatian elite and, 201, 203, 209; Hurston's rejection of, 298; C. Mckay's rejection of, 259, 262–63; racial uplift and, 31, 75; Tuskegee Institute and, 75

"Closed Place, Open World" (Glissant), 10

Cobb, Ned, 59

Cockburn, Joshua, 212

coffee plantations, 10

Cohn, Deborah, 8–9

Coicou, Massillon, 397n5

Cole, Geddes, 234

Coleridge-Taylor, Samuel, 91–92, 95

Colombia, 241–42

colonialism: in Africa, 31, 34; for BTW, 32–33; economics of, 217; by Europe, 11, 320; by France, 194–96, 199–200; Germany in, 77;

Jim Crow South and, 18; legacy of, 21; Marable on, 77; self-determination in, 156; Spain in, 152–53; U.S. imperialism and, 146; West Indies in, 54

Colored Farmers' Alliance (CFA), 60–62, 79

Colored State Agricultural Wheel, 60

Color Struck (Hurston), 320

Colquhoun, Archibald R., 397n37

Columbia Tennessean Jubilee Singers, 92

Committee on Ways and Means of Improving the Industrial Output of the Negro Peoples of the World, 353–54, 363

Communist Party, 311, 360

Concepcion, Pedro, 248

Constab Ballads (C. McKay), 257

Cook, Will Marion, 95–96

Cooper, Anna Julia, 56–57, 66–67, 125–26

Cooper, Brittney C., 57

Cooper, Wayne F., 268, 292–93

cooperatives/cooperation (economic): UNIA and, 361–67, 417n90; in U.S. South, 60; R. R. Wright and, 216–17. *See also* Black economic (inter)nationalism

corporate plantations: Black life on, 267–75; diaspora on, 276–82, *280*; in Liberia, 387n123; scholarship on, 197, 260–62. *See also* neoplantations; United Fruit Company plantations

the counter-plantation, 21, 23–24, 54, 182, 188, 215; logics/ethics of, 73, 186, 216–17

Creek Nation, 45–46, 246–47, 375, 418n10

Creelman, James, 88–89

Cuba/Afro-Cubans: BTW and, 227–28, 231–32, 393n10; Cuban education, 144–51, 164–72, *166*, 173; culture of, 121; diasporic fractures in, 161–64; Dominican Republic and, 198, 209; education of, *228*, 228–29; elitism in, 237; family and, 403n44; Haiti and, 12, 18–19, 137, 364–65; imperialism in, 184; Jamaica and, 37–38; Jim Crow South and, 148; Morúa Amendment in, 170; Partido Independiente de Color and, 154, 170, 172–73; Puerto Rico and, 38, 148–52, 229–30, 236, 238–42; racial uplift for, 156–64, 167–72, 175; slavery and, 141–42, 152–53; after Spanish-American War, 227; trans-plantations and, 154, 176; Tuskegee Institute and, 35, 141–44, 152–61, *155*, *158–59*, 176; U.S. imperialism in, 405n75; U.S. South and, 172–75

"Cuban Education" (BTW), 144–51, 173–74, 393n10
"cuestion social Cubana, La" (Casado), 166–67
cultural populism, 414n119
Cunard, Nancy, 226, 251, 297
"Cycle, The" (C. McKay), 294–95

Dalleo, Raphael, 188, 198
dance: the cakewalk, 89; Hurston and, 311–12, 314, 317, 325–32; minstrelsy and, 96
"Dance Songs and Tales from the Bahamas" (Hurston), 326
Dartigue, Maurice, 200–201
Dartiguenave, Philippe Sudré, 197
David Copperfield (Dickens), 82
Davies, Carol Boyce, 365
Davis, Henrietta Vinton, 258, 352–53
Davis, Thadious, 9, 380n42
Daytona Normal and Industrial School for Negro Girls, 56–57
Delany, Martin, 163, 370
De l'égalité des races humaines (Féquière), 193
DeLoughrey, Elizabeth, 30
Denning, Michael, 321
Despaigne, Julio, 238, 241
Dessalines, Jacques, 398n31
diaspora: African diaspora citizenship, 361–67; anti-Black propaganda against, 200–201, 291–95; Black modernity and, 17; choreographing diasporic relation, 325–29; on corporate plantations, 276–82, *280*; diasporic fractures, 161–64; diasporic Negro expression, 329–36; education and, 7; Gilroy on, 9–10, 29–30; in Global Black South, 35–36, 149–50, 364–65; in Haiti, 30; Hurston on, 296–302, *299*, 336–37; in imperialism, 18; in Jamaica, 263–67; leadership and, 344–45; ontology and, 16; philosophy of, 355; scholarship on, 4, 9, 196–97, 282–91; after slavery, 251; at Tuskegee Institute, 226–31, *228*, 257–60, 407n22; in U.S. South, 9–10; in West Indies, 34
Dickens, Charles, 82
diplomacy, 177–84, 190–91, 194, 196–97, 229–30
Dixon, Melvin, 9–10
Domenech, Fermin, 242

domesticity (bourgeois/middle class): Hurston's rejection of, 306–8; at Tuskegee Institute, 118, 124–34, *135–36*
Dominican Republic, 198, 209, 398n50
Dotson, Mary L., 246
Dóu, Lino, 175
Douglass, Frederick: autobiography of, 93; BTW and, 56; death of, 154; influence of, 150; Jacobs and, 50–51; reputation of, 86, 179, 185; Wheatley and, 350
Dube, John Langalibalele, 34–35
Dubois, Laurent, 21–22
Du Bois, W. E. B.: on Atlanta Exposition Address, 57; BTW and, 57–58; elitism for, 197; against eugenics, 99–100, 105; Galton and, 391n83; Garvey and, 359; on Harlem Renaissance, 388n9; Hurston and, 410n6; politics of, 387n123; scholarship on, 6, 378n17; Wells-Barnett and, 16, 110
Duck, Leigh Anne, 414n119
Dunbar, Paul Laurence, 97, 250–51, 292
Dunbar-Nelson, Alice M., 65–66
Dunham, Katherine, 330
Durham, John Stephens, 150, 163–64, 185–87, 190–91, 193, 238
Dust Tracks on a Road (Hurston), 297–98, 302, 305, 309–11, 317, 325–30

Eastman, George, 101
Eatonville, Florida, 283, 297–99, *299*, 302–8, *304–5*, 329. *See also* Hurston, Zora Neale
economics: of African Americans, 216–18; Black economic (inter)nationalism, 209–18; of colonialism, 217; economic cooperation, 361–67
eco-ontology: aesthetics of, 84–85; eco-ontological regeneration, 133–34; education, 23–30, 122–24, *123–24*; ideology of, 373–74; labor migration and, 302–8, *304–5*; Price-Mars' philosophy of, 202–3; regeneration, 206; scholarship on, 23–30, 40–41, 382n82; at Tuskegee Institute, 137
education: of African Americans, 36, 61, 239–45; agriculture, 47–48, 177–82, 192–95, 205–9, 218–19; of Black farmers, 75–76, 80, 116–18, *117–20*, 120–21, *122*; about Black life, 15–20; Black politics and, 16; Black self-determination in, 104; Black women in,

INDEX

28–29, 241, 252; Booker T. Washington University, 347, *349*, 349–54; in British West Indies, 21, 230–31, 239, 366–67; *Brown v. Board of Education*, 294–95; BTW on, 39, 62–63; of Carver, 18–19; of Cuba/Afro-Cubans, *228*, 228–29; Cuban, 144–51, 164–72, *166*, 173; diaspora and, 7; eco-ontology, 23–30, 122–24, *123–24*; English language lessons, 225–26, 231–33, 240–45; French language lessons, 252–54; in Global Black South, 16–19, 24–30, 57–58, 85; in Haiti, 205–9, 235–36, 243–44; hegemony in, 9–10; higher, 194, 206–7, 247, 370–71, 374–76, 378n17; Historically Black Colleges and Universities, 194, 206–7, 247, 370–71, 378n17; of Hurston, 226; in Jamaica, 230–31; of Native Americans, 229; peasant cosmopolitanism and, 276–79; performance and, 91–99, *97*; philosophy of, 18–19, 41–42; Price-Mars on, 354; in Puerto Rico/Afro–Puerto Ricans, 237–38; racial uplift and, 48–49, 58–60, 233, 248, 255, 259, 262–67; reform in, 61–62; in South Africa, 34–35; at Tuskegee Institute, 11–12, 31–35, 231–39, *233–34*, 254–55, 381n62; in U.S. South, 48–49, 53–54; M. M. Washington for, 38, 83, 236–37; in West Indies, 21. *See also* Tuskegee Institute

Edwards, Brent Hayes, 30, 143, 285–86

electoral politics, 53–54, 59–60, 79

elitism: African Americans and, 190, 194–95, 218–19; BTW and, 372; in Cuba/Afro-Cubans, 237; for Du Bois, 197; in Global Black South, 219; in Haiti, 244–45; politics of, 31

empiricism, 114–18, *115–20*, 120–24, *122–24*

English language acquisition, 225–26, 231–33, 240–45

esclavo á catedrático, De (BTW), 164–65

"escuela de Tuskegee, La" (Pérez), 160–61

Estenoz, Evaristo, 154

eugenics, 69, 99–100, 105

Europe, 11, 145, 195–96, 320

Ewing, Adam, 353, 358–59

experiment plots, 23–30, 67–73, *120*, 120–21

faculty, at Tuskegee Institute, 93–95, 108–9, *109*

Farmers' Alliance, 62

Fauset, Jessie Redmon, *299*

Federal Writers' Project, 302

Fenner, Kate, 365–66

Fentress, John Wesley, 247

Féquière, Fleury, 181–82, 193

Ferguson, Karen J., 75–76

Field, Allyson Nadia, 102, 388n15

fire dances, 321, 325–29, 331–32, 413n99. *See also* Bahamas; Hurston, Zora Neale

Firestone Rubber Company, 359, 387n123

Firmin, Antenor, 181–82, 193

Fisher, Isaac, 65, 95–97, 102

Fisk Jubilee Singers, 92–93, 97

Fleming, Julius B., Jr., 32

"For Group Survival" (C. McKay), 292–93

Fortune, T. Thomas, 18–19, 54–56, 61, 90

Foster, W. F., 46

France, 194–96, 199–200, 244–45

Franck, Harry, 11

Frederick, Rhonda, 280

French language acquisition, 243, 252–54

From Sun to Sun (Hurston), 323–24, 327

Fuente, Alejandro de la, 168, 170

Furniss, Henry W., 191–94

Fusté, José I., 158–59, 394n29

Future of the American Negro, The (BTW), 49–50

Gaffield, Julia, 397n12

Gaines, Kevin, 32, 87

Galton, Francis, 391n83

García Peña, Lorgia, 188–89

Garvey, Marcus: activism by, 210; for agriculture, 353–58; Ali and, 3; for Black liberation, 358–61; for Black Star Line, 212, 258, 338, 349, 352, 355; BTW and, 339–40; Hurston and, 226, 351; leadership of, 361–67; legacy of, 258, 367–68, 372; pan-Africanism for, 121, 338–43, *339*, *341–42*; Price-Mars and, 28; reputation of, 19, 212, 255–56; sholarship from, 345–46; strategic translations and, 340, 345, 352; UFCO and, 343–47, *348–49*, 349–53; for UNIA, 41

Gates, Henry Louis, Jr., 100–101

Geddes, Margaret R., 266–67

gendered aesthetics, 81–85, 124–33

General G. W. Goethals (steamship), 338–39

Germany, 32–33, 77

Gikandi, Simon, 272–73

Gilded Age, 61–62

Gilroy, Paul, 9–10, 29–30, 261, 355

Glissant, Édouard, 10, 13–14, 30

INDEX

Global Black South: for African Americans, 253; agriculture in, 180–81; Black Belt and, 147, 152; Black economic (inter)nationalism in, 181; Black folk culture in, 336–37; Black life in, 7–12, 41–42, 142, 307–8; Black modernity in, 1, 3–4, 7, 190, 224, 373; BTW on, 149–51; Caribbean and, 402n6; collaboration in, 196–97; culture of, 322–23; diaspora in, 35–36, 149–50, 364–65; education in, 16–19, 24–30, 57–58, 85; elitism in, 219; English language lessons in, 225–26, 231–33, 240–45; Haiti and, 47; Harlem Renaissance for, 39–40; Hemisphere/Hemispheric and, 148, 163, 177, 369; history of, 37–41, 374; Hurston for, 325–29; identity in, 144; Jamaica and, 335–36; labor migration in, 254–56, 301; pan-Africanism in, 27, 356–57; perspectives, 176; plantations in, 7–12; racial uplift in, 147–51, 345–47, 372; relations, 36–37; repurposed plantations in, 371–72; scholarship on, 35–37, 376; solidarity, 184; strategic translations for, 142–43, 157–59, 164–72, *166*, 181–82, 193; Tuskegee Institute in, 30; UFCO plantations in, 256, 267–73, 295, 357–61; UNIA for, 347, *348–49*, 349–58; U.S. South and, 5; M. M. Washington on, 232–33; Wilentz on, 378n9

Global North: Black life in, 10, 293; Black modernity in, 27–28; Caribbean and, 12–13; Great Migration to, 337; hegemony of, 10–11; Jamaica and, 331; urban, 219; U.S. South and, 36, 402n6

Global South. *See specific topics*

"Go Down Moses" (song), 97–98

Goethals, G. W., 339

Gómez, Juan Eusebio, 238, 249

Gómez, Juan Gualberto, 142–43, 168–69, 173, 227

Good Neighbor Policy, 210–11, 213–14

Gosciak, Josh, 261, 273

Gosson, Renée, 30

Grandison, Kenrick Ian, 46–47, 52–53

Great Day, The (folk concert), 321

Great Depression, 209, 333

Great Migration: African Americans in, 300; Black business in, 134; to Global North, 337; Liberia and, 59; New Negro Movement and, 6, 40–41; after World War I, 208

Great White Fleet, 261, 276–77, 279–80, *280*, 343

Griffin, Farah Jasmine, 25, 132–33

Griffith, D. W., 102

Guil, Antonio Trujillo, 249

Guillaume-Sam, Jean Vilbrun, 194–95

Guillén, Nicolas, 333

Guinea Bissau, 370

Guridy, Frank, 35, 142–43, 232, 264, 403n44

Gutierez, Manuel, 237

Hahn, Steven, 60

Haiti: for African Americans, 183–92, 400n111; agricultural education for, 186–95, 198–205; agriculture in, 179–82, 397n12; anti-Black propaganda about, 397n37; Black economic (inter)nationalism and, 209–18; Black periodicals and, 183–92, 401n136; Black self-determination in, 39; BTW on, 189–91, 195–97, 201–3; Casimir on, 23–24, 188; coffee plantations in, 10; counter-plantation and, 21, 23–24, 54, 182, 188, 212, 215; Cuba/Afro-Cubans and, 12, 18–19, 137, 364–65; diaspora in, 30; eco-ontology in, 201–5; education in, 205–9, 235–36, 243–44; elitism in, 244–45; Global Black South and, 47; Haitian-African American Chamber of Commerce, 210–13, 216; Haitian American Sugar Company, 195, 197, 215; Haitian Coffee and Products Trading Company, 37, 210–12; Haitian Indigenist Movement, 185–86, 216; Haitian Revolution, 4–5, 51, 172–73, 188–89, 194, 196, 218; Hemisphere/Hemispheric and, 194–95; Jamaica and, 34; James on, 22; L'Ouverture for, 4, 21; plantations in, 398n31; plot/plotting in, 182, 198; Price-Mars in, 39, 192–93, 230; Puerto Rico/Afro–Puerto Ricans and, 32–33; racial uplift in, 196–97, 200–203, 207–10, 217–19; Tuskegee Institute for, 184–92; U.S. imperialism in, 177–82, 192–95, 201–5, 218–19, 229–30, 330

Haiti, Her History and Her Detractors (Léger), 191

"Haitian President's Message to the United States" (Borno), 199–200

Hamer, Fannie Lou, 370

Hamilton, Robert H., 93

Hampton Institute Glee Club, 98

Hampton Institute Photographs for the American Negro Exhibit, 102–5, 120–21

Hampton Negro Conference, 164

Handley, George, 30

Harlan, Louis R., 16–17, 380n56

INDEX

Harlem Renaissance: for African Americans, 86, 206–7; H. Baker on, 16–17; Black modernity in, 15; BTW and, 250–51; Du Bois on, 388n9; for Global Black South, 39–40; history of, 36; Hughes in, 296–97; Négritude Movement and, 206; New Negro Movement and, 14; performance in, 311–12; Washington and, 250–51

Harpelle, Ronald, 357–58

Harris, Charles G., 92–93

Hartman, Saidiya, 4–5, 147

"Hayti as a Refuge" (Powell, W. F.), 183–84

Haywood, Harry, 11

hegemony: of Global North, 10–11; Lorde on, 18; of racial stereotypes, 82–83; of Tuskegee model, 57–58

Helg, Aline, 148

Hemenway, Robert E., 330

Hemisphere/Hemispheric: Black life in, 275–79, *280*, 301, 339–40, 364, 369; Global Black South and, 148, 163, 177, 369; Haiti and, 194–95; labor migration and, 231–39, *233–34*; New Negro Movement and, 254–56; scholarship on, 1, 4–6, 9–13, 22, 41, 213–14, 239–45; Tuskegee Institute and, 223–26, 245–49; UFCO plantations, 343–44

Hersey, Mark, 70

"Hidden Wealth of Hayti, The" (Durham), 185–87

higher education, 194, 206–7, 247, 370–71, 374–76, 378n17

Hill, Robert A., 358

Historically Black Colleges and Universities, 194, 206–7, 247, 370–71, 378n17

History and Culture of the Chrysanthemum, The, 66

Holt, Thomas, 273

Homer, 82

Hope Farm School, 346–47

House Behind the Cedars, The (Chesnutt), 82

Houston, David Franklin, 74–75

Howard University, 194, 266

"How Electricity Is Taught at Tuskegee" (Pierce), 106, *108–9*, 108–10

Howells, William Dean, 89

How to Build Up Worn Out Soils (Carver), 71–72

Hughes, Langston: Fauset and, *299*; in Harlem Renaissance, 296–97; Hurston and, 313–19, *318–19*, 326; politics of, 311

Humphrey, R. M., 61

Hurst, John, 193

Hurston, Zora Neale: aesthetics and, 313–19, *318–19*, 410n9; on agrarian futures, 309–12; Black folk culture for, 320–24; BTW and, 303–4, *304–5*, 410n9; on Caribbean, 37, 298–302, 325–26, 372; dance and, 311–12, 314, 317, 325–32; on diaspora, 296–302, *299*, 336–37; Du Bois and, 410n6; Eatonville, Florida and, 283, 297–99, *299*, 302–8, *304–5*, 329; education of, 226; Garvey and, 226, 351; for Global Black South, 325–29; Hughes and, 313–19, *318–19*, 326; in lectures, 329–36; legacy of, 14, 19–20, 37, 40–41, 251; C. McKay and, 19, 27–28, 208; minstrelsy and, 297, 300, 321–22; New Negro womanhood and, 305–7; performance and, 296–302, 309–37; plot/plotting and, 300, 308; racial uplift for, 337; reputation of, 255–56, 294–96; scholarship on, 341, 412n70, 414n119; on U.S. South, 302–8, *304–5*

Hyatt, W. J., 363

ICON. *See* International Conference on the Negro

ideology: of agriculture, 41–42; of BTW, 347, 349; of eco-ontology, 373–74; of C. McKay, 257–59, 291–95; Old Negro, 171; of plantations, 373; racial uplift, 53, 87–90, 99, 102–6, 125–28, 182, 295

Iliad (Homer), 82

imperial affordances, 195–201, 365–68

imperialism. *See* U.S. imperialism

Indian Territory, 246–47

Indigenous/Native peoples: of Africa (Togolese), 33, 77–78, 137, 239–40; of the Americas, 8, 45–46, 91, 128, 150–51, 162, 229, 246–47, 374–75. *See also* Native Americans

industrial modernity, 309–12

Industrial Revolution, 24

"In Memoriam" (C. McKay), 291–92

Instituto Booker T. Washington, 35, 144, 165–69, *166*, 172

International Conference on the Negro (ICON): African Americans at, 6; BTW and, 165; on Jamaica, 247–48; Plant at, 284; plantations at, 259; politics of, 172; scholarship on, 3, 377n8; Tuskegee Institute and, 263–67; U.S. South in, 40

International Cooperative Alliance, 417n90
International Council of Women of the Darker
    Races of the World, 29, 125–26
Ivanhoe (Scott, W.), 82

Jacobs, Harriet, 50–51
Jacques, Jean, 193
Jamaica: for African Americans, 333–34; Black life
    in, 27–28, 275–82, 332–33, 367; Blackness in,
    265; Black women in, 331–32; Caribbean and,
    19; Cuba/Afro-Cubans and, 37–38; culture of,
    301–2; diaspora in, 263–67; education in,
    230–31; Global Black South and, 335–36;
    Global North and, 331; Haiti and, 34; ICON
    on, 247–48; Jamaican cultural nationalism,
    329–36; C. McKay and, 14, 36, 40, 257–60,
    291–95; New Negro Movement in, 334–35;
    plantations in, 234–35, 267–75; scholarship
    on, 260–63; sugarcane plantations in, 10;
    Tuskegee Institute and, 343–47, *348–49*,
    349–53; Tuskegee Institute photographic
    archive of, 266; U.S. imperialism in, 282–91;
    U.S. South and, 275. *See also* United Fruit
    Company plantations
Jamaica Via the Great White Fleet (pamphlet),
    277. *See also* United Fruit Company
James, C. Boyd, 360
James, C. L. R., 13, 21, 22, 50–51, 182
James, Winston, 285, 290–91
Japan, 32
Jefferson, Wesley Warren, 223–24, 232, 247
Jekyll, Walter, 257–58, 278–79
Jenkins, Jennie, 362
Jesup Agricultural Wagon, 64–65
Jim Crow South: for African Americans, 103–4,
    207; Afro-Cubans and, 148; agriculture in, 25;
    anti-Black violence in, 78–79; as
    antimodernity, 17; Black life in, 2–3, 67, 128,
    350; Black modernity in, 38; Black women in,
    127; BTW and, 33, 225–26; citizenship in,
    327–28; colonialism and, 18; legacy of, 151–52;
    in literature, 306–8; Panama Canal Zone and,
    11; philosophy of, 38; plantations and, 293, 371;
    Price-Mars in, 179; repurposed plantations in,
    235; rural African Americans in, 137; slavery
    and, 134; for Tuskegee Institute, 66; violence
    in, 6, 179
Johnson, Charles S., 58–59, 251
Johnson, Hall, 320, 328–30

Johnson, Howard, 325
Johnson, James Weldon, 91, 197, 250
Johnston, Frances Benjamin, 76, 101–5, 110–11,
    116, 120–21, 133. *See also specific photographs*
Johnston, Joseph Forney, 227–28
Johnston, Sir Harry, 101–2, 242–43
Jonah's Gourde Vine (Hurston), 302–3, 332
Jones, Peter, 101
Jones, Thomas E., 320
Juan Gualberto Gómez Center, 168–69
Julius Caesar (Shakespeare), 274

Kaplan, Carla, 297–98
Keith, Minor Cooper, 358
Kelley, Robin D. G., 17
Kidney, James L., 254–55
King, Tiffany Lethabo, 375
"King Banana" (C. McKay), 269–75, 277–78
Knights of Labor, 60
Ku Klux Klan, 353

labor, performance of, 98, 309–12
labor migration: African Americans in, 300–301;
    agriculture and, 250–54; in British West
    Indies, 344; in Caribbean, 14, 354; eco-
    ontology and, 302–8, *304–5*; in Global Black
    South, 254–56, 301; Haitian peasants and, 194,
    198, 209, 215–16; Hemisphere/Hemispheric
    and, 231–39, *233–34*; in New Negro
    Movement, 223–26; in Panama Canal Zone,
    275–91, 356; scholarship on, 14; Tuskegee
    Institute and, 239–45; UFCO plantations
    and, 341–42
Lafaye, Luis, 237–38, 248
La Lucha (periodical), 165–66, 170, 172, 174, 249
Lamothe, Daphne, 330
Laroche, Hermanno, 232
Latin America, 2, 8–9, 32–33, 233–34, 240. *See also
    specific Latin American countries*
Lawrence, Mary, 361
Lecompte, Eugene, 238
L'éducation haitienne (Féquière), 193
Lee, Jennie C., 93
Léger, Jacques Nicolas, 191–93, 397n37
Leonard, Janey, 246
"Let Us Go to Haiti" (Salnave), 214–15
Levander, Caroline, 9
Levine, Caroline, 378n13
Lewis, Jovan Scott, 418n9

INDEX 451

Liberia, 59, 366, 387n123
Lindo, James, 245, 247–48
Lindsay, Samuel McCune, 229, 237
literary affordances, 152–61, *155, 158–59*
Locke, Alain, 14, 226, 250–51
Logan, Warren, 238
Long Way from Home, A (C. McKay), 293
Look Away! (Smith, J., and Cohn), 8–9
Lord, Churchstone, 198
Lorde, Audre, 18
Louis, Felix Jean, III, 401n123
Louisiana (Brodber), 353
Louis-Margron, Gastón, 244
L'Ouverture, Toussaint: Black modernity for, 181;
   Boyer and, 398n31; BTW and, 22–23, 53;
   leadership of, 4, 21, 180; repurposed
   plantation and, 21–23; reputation of, 178, 190,
   340; scholarship on, 397n12
Lowe, Vesta, 254–55

Macon County: African Americans in, 51–52,
   58–59; agriculture in, 74; Black Belt and,
   51–52; Black farmers in, 65–67, 78–79; Black
   women in, 69; culture of, 45–46; scholarship
   on, 2, 40
Marable, Manning, 11, 35, 77, 172
Marrow of Tradition, The (Chesnutt), 82
Marshall, James F. B., 46–47
Martí, José, 153–54, 168
Martin, Tony, 351
Martinez, J. Em., 243
Matthews, Mark D., 351–52
M'Bow, Babacar, 365
McHurse, J. W., 364
McKay, Claude: agriculture for, 260–63; on Black
   self-determination, 257–95; on BTW, 291–93;
   Hurston and, 19, 27–28, 208; ideology of,
   257–59, 291–95; influence of, 226, 267–75,
   289–91, 325, 418n1; Jamaica and, 14, 36, 40,
   257–60, 291–95; legacy of, 295, 334–35; plot
   logic of, 259–63, 269, 272, 278, 283, 291, 295;
   Posmentier on, 261, 407n18; reputation of,
   255–56, 277–79, 281–87; scholarship on, 3, 341;
   Tuskegee Institute and, 257–60, 274–75,
   293–95, 407n9
McKay, Thomas, 268
McKay, U. Theo, 268
McKenzie, J. Alex, 234
McKinley, William, 99

McKittrick, Katherine, 5, 20
Medina, Adriano, 240
Meikle, Rupert, 332
Middle Passage, 350, 374–75
Mignolo, Walter, 9
Miles, Tiya, 374–75
Miller, Kelly, 94
Milton, John, 82
Minns, Grace, 231–32
minstrelsy: BTW and, 82–83, 84–90, 388n20;
   Hurston and, 297, 300, 321–22; Tuskegee
   Institute Singers and, 95–98
Miranda, Jose D., 249
Miranda, Primitivo Leocadio, 242
Modernism and the Harlem Renaissance (Baker,
   H.), 16
Monroe Doctrine, 197
Morant Bay Rebellion, 336
Morill Acts (1862 and 1890), 61
Morúa Amendment (1910), 170
Moton, Robert R., 98, 174–75, 198–99, 204–5,
   250–51, 254
Moton Commission, 204–5, 211, 215–16
Mt. Meigs Institute, 76, 246
M. Roosevelt (Firmin), 193
"Mule on the Mount" (Hurston), 324–25
Mules and Men (Hurston), 301, 308, 310, 314–19,
   323, 332
Muñoz, Victor, 174–75
music, 90–99, *97*, 292, 320–22, 325–27. *See also*
   sonic aesthetics
My Bondage and My Freedom (Douglass), 93
My Green Hills of Jamaica (C. McKay), 257–58,
   261, 267–69, 272–73

NAACP. *See* National Association for the
   Advancement of Colored People
Nardal, Jane, 226, 252
Nardal, Paulette, 226, 252
National Association for the Advancement of
   Colored People (NAACP), 66
National Association of Colored Women, 29,
   125–26
National Training School for Women and Girls,
   57
National Urban League, 251
Native Americans, 8, 45–46, 91, 128, 150–51, 162,
   229, 246–47, 374–75. *See also* Indigenous/
   Native peoples

Négritude Movement, 28, 206, 252

Negro (Cunard), 226, 251, 297

"Negro Characteristics and Qualities" (lecture, Hurston), 332, 335

"Negro Homes" (BTW), 133–34, *135–36*

Negro in Business, The (BTW), 304, *304–5*

Negro in the New World, The (Johnston, H.), 101–2, 242–43

Negro Progress Convention, 21, 254–55

Nembhard, Jessica Gordon, 362–63

neoplantations, 197, 260–62, 276–79, 286–89. *See also* corporate plantations; United Fruit Company plantations

New Day (Reid), 336

New Negro, The (Locke), 14, 226, 250–51

New Negro manhood, 125–29

New Negro Movement: aesthetics of, 85–90, 311; agriculture in, 17–18; Black farmers and, 203; Black modernity in, 262–63; Black professionals in, 133–34, *135–36*; Black subjectivity in, 99; Black women in, 124–34, *135–36*, 307; BTW for, 39–40; Great Migration and, 6, 40–41; Harlem Renaissance and, 14; Hemisphere/Hemispheric and, 254–56; history of, 300–301; in Jamaica, 334–35; labor migration in, 223–26; politics of, 19; scholarship on, 378n18, 402n6; students of, 226; Tuskegee Institute and, 38–39, 73, 81–85, 137, 250–54; in U.S. South, 6; visual culture of, 83, 99–106, *107–9*, 108–13, *111–14*. *See also* Black farmers

"New Negro Woman, The" (Washington, M. M.), 126

New Negro womanhood: Haiti and, 186; Hurston and, 305–7; M. M. Washington and, 28–29, 125–26, 130–33

"New World" Blackness, 5–6, 23–24

Nicholls, David, 315–16

Norrell, Robert J., 16–17

"Nuestra América" (Martí), 154

Nwankwo, Ifeoma Kiddoe, 330, 409n68

Odyssey (Homer), 82

"Old Kentucky Home" (song), 93

Old Negro ideology, 171

O'Meally, James A., 352–53

"On the Paris Boulevards" (BTW), 178

ontology. *See* eco-ontology

oratory, 81, 85–91. *See also* sonic aesthetics

Original Dixie Jubilee Concert Company, 92

Ortiz, Fernando, 333

Othello (Shakespeare), 82, 91

"Our Farmers Should Raise Their Home Supplies" (*Negro World*), 366

Owens, T. Edward, 148–49, 151–52

Page, Walter Hines, 84

Pamphile, Leon D., 199–201

pan-Africanism: for Garvey, 121, 338–43, *339, 341–42*; in Global Black South, 27, 356–57; Pan-African Congress, 3; philosophy of, 35; U.S. imperialism and, 358–61

Panama Canal Zone: Black life in, 262, 280–81; Black self-determination and, 40; Jim Crow South and, 11; labor migration in, 356; scholarship on, 162, 245; tourism at, 339; UFCO plantations in, 5, 259, 260–61, 275, 295

Para blancos y negros (Serra), 143, 153–54, *155, 157–61, 158–59*, 165

Paradise Lost (Milton), 82

Parks, P. C., 247

Parsard, Kaneesha, 373

Partido Independiente de Color, 154, 170, 172–73

Passing of a Day, The (Hurston), 326–27, 329

paternalism, 28, 34, 53, 73–79, 126, 169–70, 201, 203, 218

Patterson, Tiffany Ruby, 296

peasant cosmopolitanism, 262, 276–82, 287, 409n68

"Peasants' Ways o' Thinkin'" (C. McKay), 277–82, 325

Pérez (y) Encinosa, Alfredo, 160–61, 238, 249, 395n44

performance: African Americans and, 320–25; anthropology and, 313–19, *318–19*; of Black folk culture, 297–98, 300–301, 309–12, 320–24; BTW and, 85–90, 111, 116–18; choreographing diasporic relation, 325–29; gender and, 127–29, 131–33; in Harlem Renaissance, 311–12; Hurston and, 296–302, 309–37; labor, 309–12; scholarship on, 12, 91–99, *97*; at Tuskegee Institute, 82–83, 90–99, 103–4, 109, 115, 120, 137

Perry, Imani, 104

Peterman, Audrey, 307

Peterman, Frank, 307

photographic archive, of Tuskegee Institute, 99–106, *107–9*, 108–13, *111–14*; in *De esclavo á*

catedrático, 231–32, 240; in Jamaica, 266; in *Para blancos y negros*, 157–59
Photography on the Color Line (S. M. Smith), 99
Pickens, William, 191
Pierce, Charles, 106, 108–11, *109*, 235–36
Pilgrim's Progress (Bunyan), 82
Plant, W. H., 3, 258, 264–67, 284, 347
the plantation: history and theories of, 7–14; legacies of, 41–42, 375–76; the plot/provision grounds and, 23–30. *See also* corporate plantations; neoplantations; repurposed plantations; United Fruit Company plantations
plantations. *See specific topics*
plot/plotting: Garvey/UNIA and, 360, 363, 368; in Haiti, 182, 198; history and definition of, 23–26; Hurston and, 300, 308; of C. McKay, 259–63, 269, 272, 278, 283, 291, 295; scholarship on, 381n78; Tuskegee Institute and, 61–73; Tuskegee plot logics/ethics of, 23–27, 61–79, 370. *See also* counter-plantation
Plummer, Brenda Gayle, 217–18
politics: African Americans and, 51–52, 59–60, 121, 211–12, 415n19; Black, 16; of Black economic (inter)nationalism, 201–5, 218–19; of Black modernity, 86–87; Caco rebellion, 198; of CFA, 60–61; of Communist Party, 360; of Du Bois, 387n123; in elections, 53–54; of elitism, 31; of Hughes, 311; of ICON, 172; James on, 182; of marginalization, 14; of New Negro Movement, 19; philosophy and, 362–63; race and, 63, 67–69, 72–73; of racial uplift, 133–34, 141–42, 236, 275, 297–98, 311; of segregation, 293–95; with UFCO plantations, 354, 358–61; of UNIA, 19–20, 35
Polk County (Hurston), 324–25
Polyné, Millery, 210–11
populism/populists, 53–54, 59, 334–35
Porter, Susan Helen, 241
Porter Hall, 112–13, *113*
Port Royal experiment, 20–21
Posmentier, Sonya, 261, 407n9, 407n18
Postel, Charles, 61–62
Poston, Ulysses S., 362–63
Powell, Stephen Taylor, 247
Powell, William F., 180, 183–84, 190–91, 194, 229–30
Practice of Citizenship, The (Spires), 365

Price-Mars, Jean: on agriculture, 399n84; Barnett and, 401n115; diplomacy by, 177–83, 196–97; on education, 354; Garvey and, 28; in Haiti, 39, 192–93, 230; on identity, 23; influence of, 12, 18–19, 333, 371; reputation of, 211, 215, 218–19, 244–45; scholarship from, 200–209
prison reform, 347
"Problem of Work in Haiti, The" (Price-Mars), 208–9, 215
"Promesa cumplida" (Serra), 154, *155*, 157, 160
provision grounds. *See* plot/plotting
Puerto Rico/Afro–Puerto Ricans: agriculture in, 68; BTW and, 148–52; Cuba/Afro-Cubans and, 38, 148–52, 229–30, 236, 238–42; education in, 237–38; family and, 403n44; Haiti and, 32–33; after Spanish-American War, 229; students from, 142; Tuskegee Institute and, 229, 236–38, 240–42, 404n49; Washington and, 148–52

"Race Friction in Cuba" (BTW), 172–73
racial aesthetics, 81–85
racial-capitalism, 12–13, 17–18, 19–20
racial progress, 31–35
racial uplift: affordances of, 372; antinomies of, 31–35; Black world making and, 63, 67–69, 72–73; class paternalism and, 31, 75; for Cuba/Afro-Cubans, 156–64, 167–72, 175; education and, 48–49, 58–60, 233, 248, 255, 259, 262–67; in Global Black South, 147–51, 345–47, 372; in Haiti, 196–97, 200–203, 207–10, 217–19; for Hurston, 337; ideology, 53, 87–90, 99, 102–6, 125–28, 182, 295; philosophy of, 16–19, 24–30; politics of, 133–34, 141–42, 236, 275, 297–98, 311; scholarship on, 6, 12, 178–82, 184–87, 335–37, 339–40, 342–43; solidarity and, 39; in Togo, 225; underside of, 73–79
Ramírez, Celestina, 228, *228*, 241
Ramos, Federico, 404n49
Ramos, Rafael, 237–38
Randolph, A. Phillip, 350–51
Reconstruction, 59–60, 345
Redcam, Tom, 263
Reeves, Cleveland H., 248
regendering, 124–34, *135–36*
regeneration. *See* agriculture; eco-ontology
rehumanization, 26–27
Reid, Victor Stafford, 336

repurposed plantations, 20–23, 49–53, 81–85, 235, 371–72

Reverón, Alfonso, 241

rice plantations, 10

Rochdale Society of Equitable Pioneers, 363, 417n90

Rockefeller, John, 159–60

Rodney, Walter, 12

Roosevelt, Franklin Delano, 210–11, 213–14

Roosevelt, Theodore, 193, 415n19

Rosemond, Chrysostome, 243–44

Rosemond, Ludovic J., 214

Rosemond, Maurice, 243–44

Ross, Marlon, 9, 128–29

Roumain, Jacques, 333

Rowe, John Carlos, 330

Rumler, José D., 242

rural African Americans, 74, 76–77, 116–18, 120–24, 137, 149–50

rural Black women: in Haiti, 186, 208–9; in U.S., 73, 74, 130–33, 246

Rusert, Britt, 68–69

Ruskin, John, 101

Salina, Pedro, 238, 241

Salnave, Theophile, 214–15

Sannon, H. Pauleus, 193

Santos y Torres, Juan, 240

Scene of Harlem Cabaret, The (Vogel), 311–12

Schomburg, Arturo, 153–54, 173, 186–93

Schuyler, George, 171, 216–17, 292–94

Scott, David, 13, 22, 51

Scott, Emmet J., 110, 112, 178–79, 224–25, 249, 391n103

Scott, Walter, 82

Scurlock, Addison, 101

segregation, 2–3, 293–95

Serra y Montalvo, Rafael: influence of, 12, 18–19, 240, 371; leadership of, 38, 207–8; philosophy of, 161–64; reputation of, 143–44, 159–61, 165, 214; scholarship from, 152–64, 155, 158–59

Service Technique, 200–202, 204

settler/settler colonialism, 7, 30, 45, 162, 212, 246–47, 374–75

Shakespeare, William, 82, 274, 334

Shannon, Magdaline W., 204

Sharpe, George, 245, 247–48

Shepard, Clara, 28, 252–54

Shoals, William Johnson, 247

Shuffle Along (musical), 321–22

"Signs of Progress Among the Negroes" (BTW), 150–51, 157

Simon, François C. Antoine, 191–92

Simpson, Hugh B., 245

Simpson, Mary, 58–59

slavery: African Americans and, 49–50, 79–80; afterlife of, 4–5; in anthropology, 13; Black bodies and, 85; Black farmers after, 48–49; in Black modernity, 49–53; for BTW, 46–47, 322; Cuba/Afro-Cubans and, 141–42, 152–53; diaspora after, 251; emancipation from, 1; institutions of, 187; Jim Crow South and, 134; legacy of, 22–23; Middle Passage, 350, 374–75; in music, 91–99, 97; plantations after, 67–68; scholarship on, 51, 130; slave gardens, 24, 26–27, 37–38; slave trade, 45–46; studies, 373–74; Tuskegee Institute after, 190; in U.S. South, 55, 405n92; violence of, 375–76

Smethurst, James, 389n25

Smith, Faith, 264

Smith, Jon, 8–9

Smith, Nathaniel Clark, 93–95

Smith, Robert Lloyd, 60

Smith, Shawn Michelle, 99, 102–3

Smith-Lever Fund, 75

social Darwinism, 101–2

social death, 5

Sociedad la Armonía, 155

soil analysis, 122, 124, 124–25

soil regeneration, 67–73, 70–72, 176

Songs and Scenes from Dixie (music show), 98

Songs of Jamaica (C. McKay), 257, 269–70, 278–80

sonic aesthetics (oratory/music): of BTW, 85–90; at Tuskegee Institute, 90–99, 97

Souls of Black Folk, The (Du Bois), 57–58

South Africa, 34–35, 239–40

South America, 121

Spain: in colonialism, 152–53; Spanish-American War, 144–45, 149, 151, 227, 229; Spanish Treaty Claims, 163–64; Spanish Treaty Commission, 238; U.S. and, 144–46

Spears (Hurston), 320

Special Field Order No. 15, 20–21

Spires, Derrick, 365

Spivey, Donald, 16

State Agricultural and Mechanical College for Negroes, 74–75

INDEX

"Steal Away" (song), 97
steamships: agriculture and, 343–47, *348–49*, 349–53; Black modernity on, 349–50; Garvey/UNIA and, 338–43, 349–53, 355, 367; UFCO plantations, 40, 258, 338–43, *339*, *341–42*. *See also specific steamships*
Stennett, R. Samuel, 245
Stephens, Michelle Ann, 11, 340
Stevens, Charles H., 246
Story of My Life and Work (BTW), 243, 389n25
Story of the Negro, The (BTW), 89–90, 91
Stowe, Harriet Beecher, 82, 93
strategic translations: of Black periodicals, 401n123; of BTW, 142–43, 157–59, 164–72, *166*, 181–82, 193, 207–8, 243, 345–46; Garvey and, 340, 345, 352; for Global Black South, 142–43, 157–59, 164–72, *166*, 181–82, 193; scholarship on, 141–44, 172–76, 395n44, 395n62; Tuskegee students and, 225. *See also* Serra y Montalvo, Rafael
Strenuous Life, The (T. Roosevelt), 193
sugarcane farming, 114–16, *115–16*, 150
sugarcane plantations, 10
sustainable farming, 69–70, *70–72*
"Swanee River" (song), 93
"Swing Low, Sweet Chariot" (song), 97

Taskigi (chief), 45
Tell My Horse (Hurston), 37, 301–2, 330–31, 333–36
Ten Years' War, 152
Terrell, Mary Church, 57
Their Eyes Were Watching God (Hurston), 27–28, 305–8, 324, 329
Third World. *See specific topics*
Thirkield, Wilbur, 93–94
Thompson, Charles, 108
Thompson, Eloise Bibb, 98
Thompson, S. C., 266–67
Thorpe, W., 354, 364
Thrasher, Max Bennett, 241
Togo, West Africa, 76–78, 137, 225
Tougaloo College, 21, 241, 374
tourism, 11, 214–15, 339, 375–76, 414n4
translation. *See* strategic translations
transnationalism, 232–33, 261. *See also* diaspora; Hemisphere/Hemispheric; labor migration
trans-plantations: of Caribbean students to Tuskegee, 233–35, 257–61, 267; Cuba and, 154,

176; definition of, 23–30; of Tuskegee to Haiti, 205
Trotter, William Monroe, 57–58
Truth, Sojourner, 86
Turner, Henry McNeal, 121
Turner, Nat, 183
Turning South Again (Baker, H.), 16
Tuskegee and Its People (Scott. E. J.), 110, 224–25, 245–46, 303–5
Tuskegee Annual Catalogue, 232–33, *233*
Tuskegee Institute, *97*; affordances of, 152–61, *155*, *158–59*, 176, 249, 255, 295; agriculture at, 26, 61–67, 73–79; Black economic (inter)nationalism at, 372; Black freedom at, 372–73; Black modernity at, 61–62, 192–93, 336–37; for Black self-determination, 259–60; Black women at, 28–29, 69, 125–34, *131–32*; Black world making at, 24, 45–49, 79–80; BTW and, 3–4, 11, 15–20, 51–53, 58–59, 64–65, 90–99; Carver at, 27, 72–73; for CFA, 79; class paternalism and, 75; criticism of, 404n62; Cuba/Afro-Cubans and, 35, 141–44, 152–61, *155*, *158–59*, 176; culture of, 36–37; diaspora at, 226–31, *228*, 257–60, 407n22; domesticity (bourgeois/middle class) at, 118, 124–34, *135–36*; eco-ontology at, 40–41, 137; education at, 11–12, 31–35, 231–39, *233–34*, 254–55, 381n62; English language acquisition at, 225–26, 231–33, 240–45; experiment plot at, 67–73, *70–72*; Experiment Station Bulletins, 68–69, *70–72*; faculty, 108–9, *109*; Fortune on, 54–55; in Global Black South, 30; ground breaking at, 112, *112*; for Haiti, 184–92; hegemony of, 57–58; Hemisphere/Hemispheric and, 223–26, 245–49; history of, 1–2, 371; ICON and, 3, 263–67; influence of, 370–71; international students at, 232–34, *234*; Jamaica and, 343–47, *348–49*, 349–53; Jim Crow South for, 66; labor migration and, 239–45; legacy of, 291–95; C. McKay at, 257–60, 274–75, 293–95, 407n9; model, 56–57; monument at, 298, *299*; Native Americans at, 128; Négritude Movement at, 28; New Negro Movement and, 38–39, 73, 81–85, 137, 250–54; performance at, 82–83, 90–99, 103–4, 109, 115, 120, 137; photographic archive of, 83, 99–106, *107–9*, 108–13, *111–14*; plantations at, 375; plot/plotting and, 61–73; Porter Hall at, 112–13, *113*; Puerto Rico/

INDEX

Tuskegee Institute (*continued*)
Afro–Puerto Ricans and, 229, 236–38, 240–42, 404n49; Puerto Rico and, 404n49; regendering at, 124–34, *135–36*; reputation of, 172–76, 240–45; rural African Americans at, 76–77; scholarship on, 114–18, *115–20*, 120–24, *122–24*; Singers, 95–99, *97*; slave gardens at, 26–27; after slavery, 190; Smith-Lever Fund at, 75; sonic aesthetics at, 90–99, *97*; soundscape of, 90–99, *97*; Syphilis Experiments, 69; Togo and, 77–78; Tuskegee Negro Farmers' Conference, 58–59, 63; Tuskegee Normal and Industrial Institute, 113, *114*; Tuskegee Quintette, 98; Tuskegee Shoe Shop, 106, *108*; Tuskegee Women's Club, 125–26; unskilled labor at, 106, *107*; U.S. South and, 29; visits to, 177–80; Wells-Barnett on, 151; in World War II, 37–38. *See also specific topics*

"Twenty-Five Years of Tuskegee" (BTW), 106, *107*
Twenty-Four Negro Melodies (Coleridge-Taylor), 92

UFCO plantations. *See* United Fruit Company plantations
Uncle Tom's Cabin (Stowe), 82, 93
UNIA. *See* Universal Negro Improvement Association
United Fruit Company (UFCO) plantations: abroad, 234–35, 267–75; BTW on, 12; contracts with, 195; Garvey, Marcus and, 343–47, *348–49*, 349–53; in Global Black South, 256, 267–73, 295, 357–61; Hemisphere/Hemispheric for, 343–44; history of, 5; influence of, 276–77, 279–81, *280*; labor migration and, 341–42; in Latin America, 233–34; in Panama Canal Zone, 5, 259, 275, 295; politics of, 354, 358–61; reputation of, 285; scholarship on, 367–68; steamships, 40, 258, 338–43, *339, 341–42*; tourism with, 11; in U.S. South, 8. *See also* corporate plantations; Great White Fleet; Jamaica; neoplantations
Universal Negro Improvement Association (UNIA): Black Star Line, 212, 258, 338, 349, 352, 355; in British West Indies, 338–43, *339, 341–42*, 345–46; for economic cooperation, 361–67; Garvey for, 41; for Global Black South, 347, *348–49*, 349–58; Liberia and, 366; politics of, 19–20, 35; scholarship on, 358–61,

367–68; steamships and, 338–43, 349–53, 355, 367
Universal Races Congress, 3
Universal Restaurant and Grocery Store, 362
University of the West Indies at Mona, 374
unskilled labor, 48, 74–75, 106, *107*
Up from History (Norell), 17, 89
Up from Slavery (BTW): aesthetic philosophy of, 83–84; Black vernacular culture in, 88; criticism of, 128, 154–55, 297–98, 352–53; Fortune and, 54–55; French translations of, 193, 243; Garvey and, 345–46; Hurston and, 297–98; influence of, 81–82, 207–8, 224–26, 243; minstrel conventions in, 87; scholarship on, 2, 30, 38, 46, 389n25; Spanish translations of, 142–43, 157–58, 164–65, 231–32, 240; strategic translations of, 142–43, 157–59, 164–72, *166*, 181–82, 193, 207–8, 345–46; success of, 53; themes of, 50
U.S. imperialism: for African Americans, 209–18, 226–31, *228*; anti-Black racism and, 151–52; Black economic (inter)nationalism and, 183–92, 195–201, 205–9; Black life in, 141–44; colonialism and, 146; in Cuba/Afro-Cubans, 405n75; Good Neighbor Policy and, 210–11, 213–14; after Great Depression, 209; in Haiti, 177–82, 192–95, 201–5, 218–19, 229–30, 330; in Jamaica, 282–91; in Monroe Doctrine, 197; pan-Africanism and, 358–61; scholarship on, 137; trans-plantations and, 161–64; wars and, 144–45
U.S. South: African Americans in, 11, 39, 418n1; African Exclusion Bill, 34; agriculture in, 1–2, 63–64; anti-Black violence in, 76, 147, 196, 258; Bahamas/Afro-Bahamans and, 296–97, 325–29; Black farmers in, 26, 317–19, *318–19*, 361, 365–66; Black leadership in, 384n29; Black life in, 20–21; Black modernity in, 5–6, 81–85, 347; Blackness in, 9–10; Black periodicals in, 54; Black self-determination in, 78; Caribbean and, 37–38, 223–24, 298–300, 322, 329–30, 371, 376; Civil Rights Movement in, 9–10; Civil War for, 46, 146; cooperatives/cooperation (economic) in, 60; Creek Nation in, 45–46; Cuba/Afro-Cubans and, 172–75; culture of, 92–93; diaspora in, 9–10; education in, 48–49, 53–54; in Gilded Age, 61–62; Global Black South and, 5; Global North and, 36, 402n6; Hurston on, 302–8, *304–5*; in

ICON, 40; industrial modernity in, 309–12; Jamaica and, 275; Latin America and, 8–9; New Negro Movement in, 6; plantations in, 47, 418n9; racial-capitalism in, 17–18, 19–20; Reconstruction in, 59–60, 345; rural areas of, 73–74; scholarship on, 4, 414n4; slavery in, 55, 405n92; social segregation in, 2–3; Tuskegee Institute and, 29; UFCO plantations in, 8; violence in, 179; after World War I, 251

Valdés, Luis Delfín, 160–61
Vasconcelos, Abelardo, 170–71
Verna, Chantalle, 245
Vesey, Denmark, 183
Victorian aesthetics, 89–90
Victor Talking Machine Company, 97–98
Vieux, Max, 201
Vincent, Stenio, 210–16, 218
visual affordances, 152–61, *155*, *158–59*
visual culture: aesthetics of, 114–18, *115–20*, 120–24, *122–24*; of New Negro Movement, 83, 99–106, *107–9*, 108–13, *111–14*
vocation de l'élite, La (Price-Mars), 192–93
Vogel, Shane, 311–12
Voice from the South, A (Cooper, A.), 56

Wakenfield, M. E., 98
Wallace, W., 360
Waller, Owen M., 190
Washington, Booker T. (BTW), *97*; on aesthetics, 297–98; affordances of, 141–44; on Africa, 77–78; for African Americans, 12; agriculture and, 6, 25–26, 52, 130–31, *132*; in Atlanta Exposition Address, 2–3; W. H. Baldwin, Jr., and, 404n59; biographies of, 249, 389n25, 389n30; for Black modernity, 27, 51, 105; Black nationalism for, 34–35; on Black self-sufficiency, 31; on Black women, 130; Booker T. Washington Society, 35, 170–74; Booker T. Washington University, 347, *349*, 349–54; Campbell on, 75; Carver and, 47–48, 63–64, 68, 295, 342, 367; Casado and, 165–69; colleagues of, 53–61, 128–29, 137; colonialism for, 32–33; A. J. Cooper and, 57; criticism of, 264; Cuba/Afro-Cubans and, 227–28, 231–32, 393n10; Cuban education for, 144–51, 164–72, *166*; Douglass and, 56; Du Bois and, 57–58; on education, 39, 62–63; elitism and, 372; family

of, 125, 158, *159*, 160; Garvey and, 339–40; on Global Black South, 149–51; on Haiti, 189–91, 195–97, 201–3; Harlem Renaissance and, 250–51; Hurston and, 303–4, *304–5*, 410n9; ICON and, 165; ideology of, 347, 349; influence of, 2, 49–50, 274, 370–71, 395n62; Instituto Booker T. Washington, 35, 144, 165–69, *166*, 172; Jim Crow South and, 33, 225–26; leadership of, 38, 177–78, 180, 189, 192–93, 211, 223–24; legacy of, 291–95, 336–37, 410n6; L'Ouverture and, 22–23, 53; manhood for, 127–28; C. McKay on, 291–93; minstrelsy and, 82–83, 84–90, 388n20; monument, 298, *299*; Moton on, 250–51; Native Americans and, 45–46, 246–47; for New Negro Movement, 39–40; in office, 111, *111*; performance and, 85–90, 111, 116–18; philosophy of, 32, 143–44, 155–56, 207–8, 233–34; photographs for, 100–101; Puerto Rico/Afro–Puerto Ricans and, 148–52; on racial progress, 133–34, *135–36*; on racism, 102; recruitment by, 227, 230–31, 234–40; reputation of, 6–7, 30, 53–161, 344–47, 349–53; rhetorical strategies of, 105–6, 388n15; T. Roosevelt and, 415n19; on rural African Americans, 149–50; scholarship from, 106, *107*, 110–18, *111–13*, *115–20*, 120–24, *122–24*; E. J. Scott and, 391n103, 402n2; slavery for, 46–47, 322; sonic aesthetics of, 85–90; strategic translations of, 142–43, 157–59, 164–72, *166*, 181–82, 193, 207–8, 243, 345–46; with students, 141; Tuskegee Institute and, 3–4, 11, 15–20, 51–53, 58–59, 64–65, 90–99; Tuskegee Shoe Shop for, 106, *108*; on unskilled labor, 74–75; on U.S. imperialism, 151–52. *See also specific works*
Washington, Booker T., Jr., 160
Washington, Ernest, 160
Washington, John H., 89
Washington, Margaret Murray: for education, 38, 83, 236–37; family of, 158, *159*, 160; on Global Black South, 232–33; leadership of, 346–47; on New Negro womanhood, 29, 125–26, 132–33; scholarship on, 29, 38, 154; as third wife, 18–19, 89; writings from, 129–30
Washington, Portia, 160
Watkins, William H., 31
Wells-Barnett, Ida B., 16, 57–58, 87, 110, 125–26, 151

West Africa, 76–78, 137, 225
Wexler, Laura, 103–4
Wheatley, Phyllis, 350
When True Love Wins (film), 65, 102
White, Monica, 18, 363
white paternalism, 169–70
Whitfield, J. E., 247
Whiting, Robert J., 141
Wilder, Gary, 17
Wilentz, Gay, 378n9
Williams, Eric, 370
Williams, Frannie Barrier, 57
Williams, W. T. B., 199, 205
Wilson, Woodrow, 194–95, 197
Womack, Autumn, 104
"Woman's Work, A" (C. Bowen), 246

women. *See* Black women
Wood, Charles Winter, 91, 97–98
Woodward, C. Vann, 16, 17, 106
"Word to Our Tuskegee Delegates," 263–64
work camps, 296–302, *299*, 309–12
Working with the Hands (BTW): agriculture in, 130–31, *132*; first edition of, 110–13, *111–13*; Haiti in, 189; multiple editions of, 114–18, *115–20*, 120–24, *122–24*; slavery in, 130; use of photographs and diagrams in, 110–24, 130–31
World War I, 194–95, 208, 251
World War II, 37–38
Wright, Jeremiah, 337
Wright, Richard, 293, 311
Wright, R. R., 37, 210–12, 216–17
Wynter, Sylvia, 13, 23, 24, 37–38, 373

Printed and bound by CPI Group (UK) Ltd, Croydon, CR0 4YY
31/07/2025

14712034-0004